Ramus,
Method, and the Decay
of Dialogue

Terry Corsberg

Qui iacuit miseris mutilus lacer obrutus vndis
  Ramus, ab obscœna iam reuirescit humo:
Nam facit expresi rapiamur imagine vultus
  Artificis docta linea ducta manu.
At meliore sui sat erit vir parte superstes,
  Ingenij vigeant cùm monimenta sui.

                        Nic. Berg. Pic. Er. Pof.

PETER RAMUS THE YEAR OF HIS DEATH

RAMUS

Method, and the Decay of Dialogue

FROM THE ART OF DISCOURSE TO THE ART OF REASON

By

Walter J. Ong, S.J.

> Young man, listen to me: You will
> never be a great man if you think
> that Ramus was a great man.
>   —Justus Lipsius, *Misc. Letters*, 89

Harvard University Press
Cambridge, Massachusetts
London, England

10 9 8 7 6 5 4 3

Publication of this book has been aided by a grant
from the Ford Foundation

Library of Congress Cataloging in Publication Data
Ong, Walter J.
      Ramus, method, and the decay of dialogue.
      Bibliography: p.
      Includes index.
          1. Ramus, Petrus, 1515–1572   I. Title.
B785.L24O5 1983   160   83–10663
ISBN 0–674–74802–6 (pbk.)

FOR
BERNARD AND MARY
MULLER-THYM

PREFACE TO THE PAPERBACK EDITION

When this book first appeared in 1958, sensitivity to the interactions between academic practice, the technologies of writing and print, and the evolution of consciousness was not so widespread as it has since become and, in fact, in most quarters was simply nonexistent.

The book grew from a hunch in the late 1940s that the intellectual "reforms" so passionately advocated by the French Renaissance humanist and philosopher Pierre de la Ramée (Petrus Ramus, anglicized to Peter Ramus, 1515–1572), and by his thousands of followers across central and northwest Europe, somehow registered a major shift in consciousness marking the transit from the ancient and medieval world into the modern. Ramus' streamlined reorganization of the age-old Western tradition of logic and rhetoric seemed to signal a reorganization of the whole of knowledge and indeed of the whole human lifeworld. My own work here in testing out this hunch consisted in what has since been called the archaeology of thought, an excavation into intellectual history to expose the often nonabstract underpinning — social, technological, and other — of abstract thinking. The major (but not the only) underpinning of the new Ramist mindset turned out to have been print technology. Print gave to visualist organization of thought and to textuality (both initiated much earlier by writing) a force unknown before, and in doing so effectively served pedagogical expediency and at the same time dissociated knowledge from discourse and gave it a quasi-monologic setting. The fact that in Ramus' day no one was aware of the effects of print in the disestablishment of the old oral world of discourse and rhetoric in favor of a new, seemingly quiescent, visualist noetic world made the effects especially intriguing once they were noticed.

My findings here, or at least many of them, appear to have been since corroborated and extended by colleagues working across a pretty wide front, for, to judge only from those citations which have actually come to my attention, this book has been found useful by many scholars working in philosophy, literature (from Spenser and Milton on), linguistics, in the history of memory systems and the history of medicine, in anthropology, sociology, psychology, theology, education, and intellectual and cultural studies generally. More recently, developments here treated have been usefully related to work in still newer fields — for example, in semiotics, in discourse analysis, in studies of textuality and of writer-reader relationships, in structuralism and in deconstruction. Certain other developments still call for further exploration, notably the rhetorical (rather than logical) origins of the modern concern with method that leads into Descartes (pages 225–239).

Were I to do this work again — the thought leaves me aghast — I know there are many things that would need reconsideration and revised assessment. One connection that would have to be brought out would be the resemblance of Ramus' binary dichotomized charts (see pages 202 and 317, and cf. pages 200–201) to digital computer programs. Like computer programs, the Ramist dichotomies were designed to be heuristic: they belong to the part of logic known as "invention," that is, finding. The quantifying drives inherited from medieval logic were producing computer programs in Ramus' active mind some four hundred years before the computer itself came into being. Perhaps nothing shows more strikingly the subterranean connections between much that was going on in the sixteenth-century consciousness and what is going on in the modern world. When this book was written, computers were not present enough to our own consciousness to have made this now obvious comparison compelling.

With this new edition readers may perhaps tolerate a concluding bit of autobiography which may not be entirely irrelevant to my credibility. Richard Harrier, a fellow graduate student with me at Harvard University in the early 1950s, once reported later in my hearing that when word got around that a man named Ong had arrived at Harvard to try to explicate Ramism more thoroughly than had ever been done before, someone remarked that the Ramist question had apparently become so involved that the ordinary native Western mind was helpless before it, so that Harvard in entrepreneurial desperation had decided to capture the market by calling in a Chinese sage. Well, hardly a sage and hardly Chinese either. The name Ong is English and I suspect that some of my own ancestors were Ramists already in sixteenth-century and seventeenth-century England. The family name is still found where it first appears in the Middle Ages, in what was later the heart of Ramist territory, East Anglia, where Ongs were studying at Cambridge University when Ramism was rampant there. Francis Ong, the primordial American Ong from whom this native Missourian is descended, left Lavenham in Suffolk in 1630 and in 1631 arrived, on the same ship with Roger Williams, in the Ramist-oriented Massachusetts Bay Colony. What Ramus would have made of all this it is hard to say. But, since human ancestry is essentially binary, anyone's family works out in Ramist dichotomies much better than do most of the countless other subjects to which the dichotomies were indiscriminately applied.

W.J.O.

Saint Louis University

FOREWORD

THIS book is an attempt to study Ramism in its historical context. Any historical study is selective, and the selection of items one makes is inevitably determined not only by what one is studying but also by one's own position in history, which provides each of us with certain more or less fixed and familiar perspectives. Viewed in perspectives familiar to us today, Ramism is in many ways an inexplicable phenomenon, and thus an invaluable one, for to interpret it we are forced to establish new alinements in the history of thought and sensibility and to revise some of our ideas from the inside.

Ramus was not a great intellectual but a savant with wide-ranging interests whose most distinctive attitudes were superficially revolutionary but at root highly derivative. His way of attacking the genuine weaknesses of the scholastic heritage while preserving unwittingly the basic presuppositions responsible for these weaknesses (and for much strength) made his views congenial to the vast numbers of impatient but not too profound thinkers who became his followers, and it gives both him and them tremendous historical value today. Like a nerve ganglion, Ramism connects not only with readily discernible end-organs — explicit doctrines or theories of one sort or another — but also with more hidden, and at least equally important areas in Western culture, alerting us to unsuspected connections between pedagogical developments and the rise of modern physics, between rhetoric and scientific method, or between dialectic and the invention of letterpress printing.

Besides demanding some realinements in our thinking, the study of Ramism presents certain practical difficulties. The treatment of the history of ideas and sensibility in the Western world before 1750, particularly when one is dealing in terms of formal education, is becoming increasingly difficult today, when many students and even scholars passionately interested in this history have no real command of Latin. The present work has been written in frank acknowledgement of the realities of this situation. All Latin citations have been put into English (the more important ones being given also in the original in footnotes). Latin book titles in the text are ordinarily translated into English so as to preserve the reality and urgency which the concepts in play had for their authors and readers. The Latin original of such titles can always be found in the footnotes and, in fuller form, through the Bibliography, where copies of now rare books — and, in the present work, these are many — are also located. For a guide through the labyrinth of Ramus' own works and those of his literary lieutenant Omer Talon, the reader is referred to the pres-

ent author's *Ramus and Talon Inventory*, which appears simultaneously with
the present book.

Having been extended the courtesies of so many libraries, I find it difficult
to begin my thanks for fear I shall never end. To Professor W. A. Jackson and
Miss Carolyn Jakeman of Houghton Library at Harvard University I owe a
special debt of gratitude, as also to Mr. H. M. Adams of Trinity College,
Cambridge, and Mr. A. N. L. Munby of King's College, Cambridge. At Oxford, Dr. David Rogers and Mr. F. J. King of the Bodleian Library have been
both generous with their time and encouraging, as have Messrs. R. A. Wilson
and A. F. Allison of the British Museum. Mlle Thérèse d'Alverny and the
staff of the Salle de Réserve at the Bibliothèque Nationale and Mlle Yvonne
Lanhers of the Archives Nationales in Paris have been helpful and gracious,
as has also Père Paul Doncoeur, S.J., who turned up an important manuscript
for me at the Archives Nationales. To the staffs of the more than one hundred
other libraries in which I have worked and which are listed in the *Ramus and
Talon Inventory*, I am, in varying degrees, indebted, and, to all of them,
grateful.

In the conception and preparation of the present work, my greatest debt
of gratitude is to Professor Perry Miller of Harvard University, whose work
on Ramism provided the immediate stimulus for the present study and who
could always be relied on for enthusiasm and encouragement when the mass
of material in which the study is necessarily involved grew occasionally op-
pressing. Professor Myron P. Gilmore of Harvard has likewise been generous
in his enthusiasm, providing the reassurance which can come only when a
scholar whose knowledge and competence one can trust enters into and shares
one's own insights. Similar generous encouragement and stimulating exchange of ideas with others at Harvard as well as with fellow members of the
Society of Jesus *un peu partout* has been too great and too frequent to be
acknowledged in detail, but special mention should be made of the Jesuit
fathers at the *Études* residence in Paris, where I lived for three wonderful
years and where most of this book was written, just a few minutes' walk from
Place Maubert and the site of Ramus' old Collège de Presles. Professor H.
Marshall McLuhan of the University of Toronto, formerly of St. Louis University, has likewise been a constant source of intellectual stimulation, and to
him I owe my initial interest in the present subject. As is the case with a
growing number of scholars and writers, a special debt of gratitude is also
owing in my case to the John Simon Guggenheim Memorial Foundation,
which granted me a Fellowship over the extended period of two years and
thus made possible this study in its present form.

WALTER J. ONG, S.J.

St. Louis University
January 1, 1957

CONTENTS

Book One. ISSUES

Book Two. BACKGROUND

Book Three. RAMISM

Book Four. SEQUEL

LIST OF ILLUSTRATIONS

Frontispiece PETER RAMUS THE YEAR OF HIS DEATH

The elegiac verses by Ramus' contemporary Nicolas Bergeron speak of Ramus' cruel death and announce his survival less in these "lines drawn out by the skilled craftsman" than in the products of his own genius. The motto reads: "Hard work conquers everything." — From the *Testamentum Petri Rami* (Paris, 1576) in the British Museum. For the connection between the figure given here (LVIII) and the actual age of Ramus (1515–1572) at the time of his death, see the note with this edition of the *Testamentum* or *Will* in the present author's *Ramus and Talon Inventory*.

This is the "explanation" of Ramus' work, *The Ciceronian* (*Ciceronianus*), as laid out by Ramus' editor Johann Thomas Freige. Sixteenth-century works entitled *The Ciceronian* commonly set out, as Ramus' work does, to explain what a true follower of Cicero should be. Here we are shown that the true Ciceronian models not only his Latin but, so far as possible, his entire career, and especially the educational curriculum preparing and initiating his career, upon Cicero. After the initial "distribution" of Cicero's career into the somewhat ill-balanced dichotomies of (1) his life and (2) his death, the life is further dichotomized and subdichotomized to make a neat spatial display, with the educational curriculum occupying a prominent position. — From the copy of Freige's collection of some of Ramus' works entitled *The Regius Professorship* (*Professio regia*, 1576) in Houghton Library, Harvard University.

The invention of printing invited large-scale manipulation of words in space and gave new urgency to the drive toward handling logic or dialectic quantitatively, a drive long manifest in the medieval arts scholastics. Here Jacques Lefèvre d'Etaples, in his highly original work of the early post-Gutenberg era in logic, *In hoc opusculo he continentur Introductiones: in suppositiones . . .* (Paris, 1500), attempts an exposition of exceptives or "exponibles," a highly quantified section of medieval logic, by means of a quasi-geometrical or tabular arrangement, as well as by means of arithmetical figures, and of what looks like algebra. The urge to use letters misfires here, for the "a," "e," "i," and "o" here employed are related to the old mnemonic *Barbara, celarent . . .* and are less real logical variables such as will make fruitful post-Fregean logic, than they are memory devices. The tendency for quantitative or quasi-quantitative manipulation of logic to dissipate itself in memory devices will be a noteworthy feature of Ramism. The reproduction is from a copy in the Bibliothèque Nationale.

Before the invention of printing, logic manuals copied out in longhand had generally to content themselves with relatively simple spatial displays of terms, such as this old favorite, popularly known as the Porphyrian Tree, which displays species "branching out" from genera (Porphyry's *Isagoge* or *Introduction* to Aristotle's logical treatises featured much on genus and species). With the invention of printing, it became feasible to include in the new mass-produced logic manuals not only this simple diagram but the much more elaborate spatial displays (see Figures IV and V) which a manuscript culture had not been able to produce with accuracy and facility in any great quantity. The present reproduction is from a copy of Pierre Tartaret, [*Commentarii in Summulas logicales Petri Hispani* . . . (Paris, ca. 1514)], in the Bibliothèque Nationale (Rés. m. R. 68 — title page missing and conjectural as given here). The student or master who in pen and ink moved Sortes (logicians' argot for Socrates) over from branch to trunk had a different notion of the relation of individual and species than had the original draftsman. Out of conceptual formulations involving diagrams of this sort comes Ramus' insistence that man (*homo*) is not a species but a genus and that each individual man and woman — and *a fortiori* each of the two sexes — is a distinct species.

This diagram represents a fairly elaborate attempt to deal with logic geometrically, such as could be exploited on a large scale with the invention of printing. The emblems of the four Evangelists added by someone in pen and ink are irrelevant to the subject matter here and suggest that these diagrams derive not only from the quantification encouraged by the study of logic but also perhaps in part from the common human urge to construct mandalas or magic figures featuring circular and quadripartite attengements, such as C. J. Jung has studied in detail.

The present diagram deals with the problem of finding a middle term when one wants to prove a connection between a given subject and predicate. The problem is treated in terms of the various moods and figures of the syllogism, such as were otherwise worked out in the more vocal mnemonic devices *Barbara, celarent*, etc. Deriving from the schema of the sixth-century Philoponus, this particular type of diagram is known as the "asses' bridge" — not to be confused with that of Euclidean geometry — and the words *asinus cadens* (the falling ass) at bottom center have reference to this title. See I. M. Bochenski, *Formale Logik* (Freiburg, Switzerland, 1956), pp. 254–256. The irony of the expression asses' bridge is enhanced by the fact that in sample propositions set up by scholastic logicians or dialecticians, when the subject used was not Socrates (in logicians' argot, *Sortes*) or man (*homo*), it was commonly ass (*asinus*) — the "nasty little scholastic ass," as the humanist Vives styled the animal. This plate, doubtless well known to Ramus, is here reproduced from the copy of Tartaret's *Expositio* . . . *super textu Logices Aristotelis* (Paris, 1514) in the Bibliothèque Nationale.

This attempt to deal with logic geometrically is interesting not only because of its agonizing detail but also because of its subject matter; for it deals with the conjoined or compound propositions ("The sun shines and it is day") which have proved so fruitful in modern symbolic or "mathematical" logic. Here the drive toward quantification which could not yet find its proper outlet spends itself in a kind of geometrizing, the results of which are accurate but doomed to be without issue. This is the sort of diagram which is introduced by its author, Juan de Celaya, an older contemporary of Ramus' at Paris, with such remarks as, "All this which I have just said is made clear by the following diagram." The present skull-breaker is from the copy of Celaya's *Expositio* . . . *in primum tractatum Summularum Magistri Petri Hispani* . . . (Paris, 1525), in the Bibliothèque Nationale.

John Knox's teacher, the famous John Major, tries a geometrical or diagrammatic analysis of the matter of exceptives or "exponibles" to which Lefèvre d'Etaples had earlier applied a tabular quasi-arithmetical analysis (see Figure II). The geometrical analysis proved a cul-de-sac for the quantifying drive in logic. This illustration is from a copy of Major's *Libri quos in artibus . . . compilavit* (Paris, [1506]) in the Bibliothèque Nationale. The simple designs here are derived from the squares of opposition common in the manuscript tradition, but Major's works feature also designs of the elaborate type found in other post-Gutenberg logicians (see Figures IV and V).

These are the instruments for pounding Peter of Spain's *Summulae logicales* into the heads of youngsters of the post-Gutenberg era devised by the whimsical satirist Thomas Murner and here reproduced from a copy of his *Logical Card-Game*, or *Logica memorativa, Chartiludium logice* . . . (Strasbourg, 1509) in the Bibliothèque Nationale. See the explanation in the text and Figures VIII, IX, and X.

This attempt to picture logic visually serves the same sort of purpose as the Ramist dichotomies — memory, with a dash of understanding. The design here is called by the same name — *Typus logice*, outline or schema of logic — which would be repeatedly used for Ramists' dichotomized bracketed outlines. Like Ramus' dichotomies, this "outline" is an attempt to make logic simple and "natural" for little boys by resort to visual devices which at first medieval logic and now the newly invented art of printing made seem more and more attractive. Ramist dichotomies would be displays of words in purely neuter, geometrical space. But here the visual is allegorical, too, loaded with heavy symbolic or anogogic overtones which elude direct visual expression. This is from the same copy (1509) of Murner's *Logical Card-Game* as Figure VII. The allegorical approach here has, of course, medieval and earlier sources. This particular design is highly reminiscent of similar designs in Gregorius Reisch's *Margarita philosophica* (1504), especially that entitled *Typus grammatice* and reproduced in George A. Plimpton, *The Education of Shakespeare* (London, 1933), p. 4.

This picture, called the "Third Application," explained in the first half of the page which faces it and which is reproduced here, implements the retention in memory of material from Peter of Spain concerning the categorical proposition. Here the birches normally used to beat the pupil are sublimated into a mnemonic device — see the explanation in the text. This is from the same 1509 copy of Murner's *Logical Card-Game* as Figure VII.

Here a "square of opposition," one of the favorites in the simple or primitive type of spatial display current already in the manuscript logic tradition, is seen side by side with the allegorical type of visualism applied to logic by Murner. The allegorical display is related on the one hand to Ramists' dichotomized outline tables and on the other to the emblem books which printing would make so popular. This plate is from the same (1509) copy of Murner's *Logical Card-Game* as Figure VII.

This is a symbolic representation of human knowledge proposed as a summary or *argumentum* of book II of the *Theoria Analytica* (London, 1579) by the anti-Ramist Everard Digby. Ramists would produce the argument of a work by "logical analysis," not by anything like this; for the allegorical density of such designs was repugnant to the semigeometrized Ramist sensibility. The human mind, pictured as an old man who "lives by his inborn genius" (*vivitur ingenio*) and whose connection with body and earth are marked for death (*caetera mortis erunt*), here looks out through the sensible universe (*sensibilis*), through the intelligible universe (*intelligibilis*), and toward transcendent or unnamable Truth (*innominabilis*). This figure has obvious affinity with the mandalas or magic circles which have been studied by Carl J. Jung and others, and which figure in representations of the self found in the most diverse and apparently unrelated human cultures. The plate is from a copy of Digby's work in the Bodleian Library.

This is the table or chart of "things" made possible by dialectic or logic as the table first appears in Ramus' printed works, that is, as it appears in the *Training in Dialectic* (*Dialecticae institutiones*) of 1543. It is not new, for similar outlines occur in the pre-Gutenberg manuscript tradition, but in the new visualist age of which printing is perhaps more symptom than cause, and particularly in the semigeometrized Ramist mind, these outlines will proliferate further and more convincingly than ever before. This plate is from a copy of the 1543 work in Houghton Library, Harvard University.

This can be considered the definitive dichotomized bracketed outline of Ramist logic or dialectic. It appeared in the 1576 edition of Ramus' "arts" prepared by the Swiss Johann Thomas Freige and published under the title of *The Regius Professorship* (*Professio regia*), and it has recently been reproduced in Perry Miller, *The New England Mind* (New York, 1939), p. 126. Tables or "outlines" even more complex than this, some of them extending through whole folio volumes where every word and sentence is spitted on a dichotomy, will be prepared by others of Ramus' followers. The Ramist mind finds that words are best used (and best remembered) when deployed in this neuter space, congenial to the post-Copernican outlook. In this semigeometrical approach to language, Ramism is not unique in its age, but the drives in evidence elsewhere appear in it as more uninhibited and extreme. The present plate is from a copy of the *Professio regia* in Houghton Library, Harvard University.

This is the bracketed table of dichotomies in which Johann Thomas Freige summarizes in "methodized" arrangement the content of his 1576 edition of Ramus' "arts" entitled *The Regius Professorship* (*Professio regia*). Here Ramus' arts curriculum, which purportedly produced a master of arts (including all of philosophy) "in reality and not in name alone" at the age of fifteen, is analyzed and exposed to view. The program is dichotomized into days and years, the former yielding classroom procedure in almost perfect dichotomies, and the latter the various arts, in a rather less tidy arrangement, which, however, comes out in even dichotomies at the end. The traditional number seven is preserved in connection with the arts, it will be seen, but the arts listed here as those actually taught do not, of course, correspond very well with the seven liberal arts. They never had in university history. This plate is reproduced from the copy of the *Professio regia* in Houghton Library, Harvard University.

Although he was aware that words are primarily spoken phenomena, the Ramist (and the early grammatical tradition generally) made little of this fact and habitually assigned as the ultimate components of words not phones (sounds) but letters (visual reductions of sounds). Here the Ramist Freige makes a further geometrical reduction of letters themselves, deriving the whole of the Hebrew alphabet out of a ramification of dichotomies — almost, for the dichotomies do not all come out quite evenly. In an age when the study of language was centered on learned languages which were controlled by a written tradition rather than by living oral development, Hebrew was certainly the least vocal of all these more or less nonvocal languages. The present illustration is from a copy of Freige's *Paedagogus* (Basle, 1582) in the St. Louis University Library.

The present Ramist analysis of the bubonic plague is an attempt to apply engineering and geometrical order of a sort to medical problems, by dealing not with the plague itself so much as with what one knew about the plague. The plague is "distributed" into its causes and "contrary remedies," and both these in turn into further dichotomies. The dagger after the term *Therapeutica* keys in the material on the next page, which is a further bracketed analysis, showing where it is to be hooked onto the present chart. It will be noted that the prophylactic remedies here include not only a large pill or bolus and surgical instruments (*armena*), but also "flight: rapid, distant: belated return." This illustration is from the same book as is Figure XVI, by Ramus' disciple Freige, who, by some strange irony, died of the plague shortly after he had attacked the disease with these dichotomies.

This selection of pages from a 1617 edition of Ramus' *Dialectic* which its editor, Marcus Rutimeier, calls *The Methodical Idea, or General and Special Logical Analysis*, is interesting particularly for the terms which Rutimeier introduces as the headings for each of the charts here which, chapter by chapter, deploy Ramus' matter in space. These terms, *delineatio, typus, analysis*, and so on, are discussed in the text of Chapter XVIII. Rutimeier's use of these space models for "mapping" the possessions of the mind is representative of the mental habits which, inside and outside Ramism, but more inside it than outside, are bringing into prominence in the consciousness of Western man notions such as "method," "system," "bodies of knowledge," or "contents of the mind," and which are connected with the topical or "place" logics and testify to a growing disposition to conceive of mental activity itself as an operation by means of local motion on a spatial field. The present display of pages is from the copy in the Bodleian Library (greatly reduced).

Book One

ISSUES

I enunciatio

CHAPTER I

RAMISM IN INTELLECTUAL TRADITION

Not through dialectic has God
elected to save his people.
— St. Ambrose of Milan (title-page
motto in Newman's *Grammar of Assent*).

I. THE PRESENT FRONT

WITHIN the past two decades, students of literary and intellectual history have become increasingly conscious of the presence in the Renaissance of a definite set of philosophical and literary attitudes derived from the Paris arts professor Pierre de la Ramée or Peter (Petrus) Ramus. Ramism has been noticed particularly by students of English and American literature. But general awareness of the movement is spreading in the scholarly world as a whole. Ramism is now regularly mentioned in works on Renaissance philosophy and political science and on the general history of thought. Detecting its scent has become a kind of game — one which would have been encouraged by Ramus himself, who insisted that the dialectic which was his specialty supported the whole fabric of the world's consciousness.

The present wave of interest dates from 1935 and 1936, when Professor Samuel Eliot Morison published his tercentennial Harvard volumes, *The Founding of Harvard College* and *Harvard in the Seventeenth Century*. Morison did a dismaying amount of work in the original records, and his inventory traced New England's first fruits back to branches on the tree of knowledge long forgotten in the traditional accounts of America's heritage. One of the most productive branches of all turned out to be the heretofore obscure Peter Ramus.

In *The Enchanted Glass*, a slender volume less heavily documented than Morison's, Professor Hardin Craig had also in 1936 reported the presence of Ramism in the Elizabethan and Jacobean world. He labeled Ramus "the greatest master of the short-cut the world has ever known." As far as it goes, the label is consummately accurate, but, because it goes only so far, it was more tantalizing than exact. Further study was needed.

Three years later, following Morison's clues and turning up new ones of his own, Professor Perry Miller published *The New England Mind: The*

Seventeenth Century, which all those concerned with Ramism quote regularly today, and which makes it possible to talk Ramism without reading Ramus himself. Miller's detailed study of certain aspects of Ramism is part of his thoroughgoing examination of the early New England mentality, and cuts back of our earlier pious and chauvinist reconstructions to the actual literature which formed and developed the early colonial mind. During the course of the wide reading necessary for boring through the drifts of New England Latin, Miller finds Ramism on every side. He discovers that it was a connecting link between Puritanism and scholasticism, establishing in the Puritan mind its obsession for logic and distaste for symbolism, shaping its views of nature, determining its literary preferences and style, and in great part accounting for its attitudes, if any, toward epistemology. Seen as the outgrowth of a kind of simplified logic which imposed itself by implication on the external world to make this simple, too, Ramism here is correlated also with the Puritan preference for the plain style and hence with a good many Puritan virtues and vices associated with a *simpliste* view of things. Ramism is a kind of downrightness, if you will.

This news about Ramus fell on ears cocked to receive it. From the time of the medieval scholastics, the Anglo-Saxon world has been generating a good deal of thought around linguistic analysis. Since the beginning of the twentieth century, the feeling had been growing that the Renaissance, and especially the sixteenth century, was somehow or other a critical period for linguistic attitudes, that during this period something happened in the way man talked about things, that sometime after the sixteenth century a "dissociation of sensibility," to use Mr. T. S. Eliot's now well-worn phrase, had become discernible in the way man confronted the world around him.

Ramus is a man of the sixteenth century, and he is eminently a man concerned with language, with the traditional arts of expression, grammar, rhetoric, and logic. As the first and only professor of eloquence and philosophy at what was later to be called the Collège de France, he was a kind of humanist-scholastic who stood on the middle ground between linguistics and metaphysics. If he is himself no real thinker, all the more reason why the flurry his works created deserved looking into. The weird sound of some of the Harvard theses published by Morison and commented on by Miller was fascinating: "Rhetoric is the garden of the affections"; "Dialectic is the sun of the microcosm, the arguments are the radii of logic"; "A thing is in a place, and time is in the thing"; "Grammar is perfect without rhetoric, but the converse is not true"; "Languages exist for the sake of the arts"; "Method is the parent of intelligence, the mistress of memory." [1]

In addition, it was becoming apparent that in the sixteenth and seventeenth centuries Ramism had a tremendous vogue, no one knew exactly how tremendous. The *Ramus and Talon Inventory*, published simultaneously with the present work, shows how modest were the early estimates of the currency of Ramism. There are over 750 separately published editions (including some adaptations) of single or collected works by Ramus or his collaborator Omer Talon (Audomarus Talaeus, *ca.* 1510–1562) — close to 250 editions of the important *Dialectic* alone. Counting separately each of the works in these 750-odd volumes, some of which include more than one item, one gets a total of around 1100 separate printings of individual works. All but a few of these fall in the century roughly between 1550 and 1650.

Before Morison's and Miller's works, there was not much written concerning the fuller implications of Ramism in the history of the human mind. In the nineteenth century, when the historian of medieval logic, Carl von Prantl, had concluded, quite rightly, that Ramism could in no real sense be considered an advance or even a reform in logic,[2] two sizable studies of Ramus had appeared: one at Paris in 1855 by Charles Waddington, *Ramus: sa vie, ses écrits, et ses opinions;* and the other at Strasbourg in 1878 by Paul Lobstein, *Petrus Ramus als Theologe.* Lobstein's sober and discerning work is restricted chiefly to Ramus' posthumous *Commentary on the Christian Religion* (*Commentariorum de religione christiana libri quatuor*), and concludes that theologically Ramus stood for a mild Zwinglianism which is in the long run quite uneventful. Lobstein is entirely right. Ramus' significance does not lie in his own theology. This was the only theological work out of his sixty-odd separate productions, and it was never printed by any other than the Wéchel firm at Frankfort on the Main. Its chief significance lies in its curious deformation of religion. For, as Theophilus Banosius remarks in the preface which dedicates the work to Sir Philip Sidney, Ramus here attempts to reduce religion to an art similar to the arts of expression, grammar, rhetoric, and logic — an event truly momentous if we examine the long-neglected history of the scholasticism of the arts course and its connection with the sixteenth-century passion for "method," or with Calvin's *Institution de la religion chrétienne* and its patently schoolroom type of title.

Waddington's work is more ambitious than Lobstein's, and the valuable mass of facts he assembles merits more competent exegesis than he provides. His resolution of the issues is almost exclusively personal and moral, often to a passionate degree. There are good people and bad people, and Ramus was one of the good ones. The real issues are hardly exposed, for Waddington gives no evidence of having read either the people Ramus reacted against, headed by Peter of Spain, Pierre Tartaret (Tartaretus or Tataretus, d. 1522), and the like, or Ramus' chief source after Cicero, Rudolph Agricola. Characteristically, Waddington can garble the significance of a sixteenth-century term such as *hypothesis*, while making a passionate issue of it.[3] He has long remained the basis of most encyclopedia articles on Ramus, and of reports such as Abel Lefranc's lengthy account of Ramus in his *Histoire du Collège de France*,[4] which is nothing but a totally uncritical summary of Waddington.

The most pretentious study devoted entirely to Ramus since Waddington's and Lobstein's is Frank Pierrepont Graves' *Peter Ramus and the Educational Reformation of the Sixteenth Century*, which appeared in New York in 1912. This work is the best all-round brief of the positive content of Ramus' various works, and it will remain permanently useful. Unfortunately, the background in which it sets the works is immaturely, and even sophomorically, conceived, without any sense of the real movement of intellectual history and with a repetition, sometimes word for word, of Waddington's moral indignation as a substitute for historical perspective. Waddington had seen Ramus as a sixteenth-century Victor Cousin;[5] Graves brings him up to date by viewing him as a sixteenth-century John Dewey. To make this interpretation plausible he forces on the technical legal term *usuarius*, sometimes applied to Ramus by his contemporaries, the unheard-of meaning of "utilitarian" and even "pragmatist."[6] The 1922 thesis of M. Robert Barroux at the École Nationale des Chartes at Paris, *Pierre de la Ramée et son influence philosophique*, is far more intelligently provocative in its handling of the context of Ramism, for it suggests the huge perspectives in which Ramus' "method" is set, perspectives which open into the very center of the intellectual heritage of Western man.

Occasional articles, mostly German, on Ramism appeared in the past century or at the opening of this century. But each of these articles, as well as each of the longer works just mentioned, constitutes a fairly isolated phenomenon. Present-day interest in Ramism in the English-speaking world is a different kind of thing. It is communal; it tends to regard Ramism not as a mere *cause célèbre* admitting of revival from time to time, but rather as a phenomenon or symptom which, studied dispassionately, may yield helpful and even startling information concerning intellectual history and the formation of the modern mind. The articles on Ramism which multiply apace after Miller's work in 1939 and the chapters on Ramus in longer works discuss such things as Ramus and the metaphysical poets, Ramism and Shakespeare, Ramus and Milton (Milton was a Ramist of sorts, with an adaptation of Ramus' logic to his credit), Ramus and Hobbes, Ramus and Jean Bodin, Ramus and political theorists such as Johann Althusius, Ramism and how John Wesley's coterie got to be called Methodists. Interest in Ramism has reached such proportions that it has evoked a circumstantial warning against a distorted view, not of Ramus' historical importance, which has to be conceded, but of his intrinsic worth as an arbiter between the disputing claims of logic, rhetoric, and poetry.[7]

Much of the most recent interest in Ramism lodges in the area around these three arts. Rosemond Tuve's *Elizabethan and Metaphysical Imagery* sees Ramism as heightening the prestige of logic, both in poetry and elsewhere, as accelerating the development of wit at the expense of purely "decorative" poetic objectives, and thus as implementing metaphysical poetry in general. Wilbur Samuel Howell's *Logic and Rhetoric in England, 1500–1700* focuses on the rhetorical more than on the logical heritage, and provides the most thorough firsthand treatment of Ramism since Miller. It points out that in England at least Ramism is the central route over which the Ciceronian rhetorical tradition and the scholastic logical tradition move in reorienting themselves for the modern world. Ray Nadeau shows in his shorter studies how Ramism infiltrates even the books, such as Thomas Farnaby's *Index rhetoricus*, which were written to oppose it. And Paul Dibon's recent volume traces the Ramist influence in the Low Countries before Descartes. Detailed studies of the movement in other countries are as yet lacking, but all the studies so far reveal the difficulty of pinning down the movement in terms of any simple formula or formulas. Its powers of both adaptation and absorption indicate that Ramism is a state of mind arising within a complex of established intellectual and cultural traditions and exhibiting them in new aspects.

2. THE ANONYMOUS CENTER OF TRADITION

In its entire perspective, Ramism is not properly a philosophy or a theology or a type of classical humanism or a literary school, although it affects philosophy, theology, and literature, and many other things besides. Its central element is a logic or dialectic which cannot be taken very seriously by any competent logician. Yet, together with the rhetoric which complements it, this logic or dialectic is indeed the clue to Ramism. Like most logics from the Renaissance to Gottlob Frege, it can be described as a residual logic, a selection of items from an earlier, more complex and sensitive science.

Ramus was known to his contemporaries as the *usuarius,* the usufructuary, the man living off the increment of intellectual capital belonging to others. This capital had been amassed over centuries and even millennia — which indicates the necessity of approaching Ramism historically. Yet, as Ramist logic is of little interest to a serious logician from the point of view of his science, so its relevance to intellectual history rests very little on formal logical grounds. It attests not a respectable theory, but a set of mental habits. Ramus is no Aristotle or Boole or Frege, to be credited with findings which open new logical horizons. He is not even a Descartes, discovering, if not logical, at least mathematical theorems of paralogical interest. Ramus does not enter into intellectual history in terms of abstract theorems, nor do his immediate followers, for his abstract theorems are often not viable at all. His most confident assertions, as his opponent Jacques Charpentier delighted in pointing out, were likely to be reversed by their author — with unabated confidence — in the very next edition of his *Dialectic.*

Ramus is a man ostensibly at outs with much of his age, but his specific formulations of his position give only equivocal indication of what is really going on in his mind. His anti-Aristotelianism, his proposals for changing university teaching practice, his curriculum reforms (based on the three rules of method he ascribes to Aristotle!) — all these, on closer examination, do not explain his mind as much as they make one ask what really underlies his impatience. It is certainly something deeper than what he and his followers formulate, and something more pervasive than even rhetoric or dialectic. Among his "reforms," the one which is most obviously in line with subsequent developments is his stress on mathematics. Yet Ramus' position here is itself enigmatic: Why this blind faith in mathematics on the part of one whose mathematical competence was so modest and whose real excellence, in the opinion of his contemporaries, lay in oratory? Ramus' over-all program was to combine philosophy and eloquence. However, as one observes the sequel of Ramus' work, dry-as-dust "technology" and systematization, this proposed juncture becomes more and more puzzling.

Ramism formed a huge movement of some sort. The documentary evidence makes this clear. The question is, What made the movement? What does Ramism come to? We are more aware than Waddington of the subtleties of intellectual history, which, perhaps more than other kinds of history, has its "cunning passages, contrived corridors." Seen in its historical context, Ramism reveals itself as something which eludes description in Waddington's moral terms quite as much and more than in terms of abstract formulas proposed by the Ramists themselves or by their enemies. Ramism, if the results of the present study can be accepted, is at root a cluster of mental habits evolving within a centuries-old educational tradition and specializing in certain kinds of concepts, based on simple spatial models, for conceiving of the mental and communicational processes and, by implication, of the extramental world.

Even in these perspectives, Ramism has little which is *absolutely* distinctive of itself. Most things which originate in the Ramist camp — for example, the concept of "logical analysis," which seems certainly to put in its first appearance among Ramists — soon prove so congenial to other "systems" that they are quickly assimilated by them and, like logical analysis, seem always to have belonged to non-Ramists as well as to Ramists. What is really distinctive about Ramism is not one or another such item, but its special concentration of items, most of which can be discerned individually outside Ramist circles. Because of its curiously amateurish cast, it does not repress the crude conceptualizing tendencies which more astutely controlled philosophies block or disguise. A study of Ramism, therefore, makes it possible to discern the nature of subconscious drives which have been obscured elsewhere and which often call for radical revision in our ways of viewing intellectual history. For example, Ramism specialized in dichotomies, in "distribution" and "collocation" (*dispositio* rather than judgment or *judicium*), in "systems" (a philosophical "system" was a new notion generated in the Renaissance), and in other diagrammatic concepts. This hints that Ramist dialectic represented a drive toward thinking not only of the universe but of thought itself in terms of spatial models apprehended by sight. In this context, the notion of knowledge as word, and the personalist orientation of cognition and of the universe which this notion implies, is due to atrophy. Dialogue itself will drop more than ever out of dialectic. Persons, who alone speak (and in whom alone knowledge and science exist), will be eclipsed insofar as the world is thought of as an assemblage of the sort of things which vision apprehends — objects or surfaces.

It is difficult to assess the meaning of Ramism not only because its explicit formulations are so puzzlingly related to its historical import but also because it is transmitted in a curiously anonymous way. Ramus' influence is in school or university textbooks, and is perpetuated as part of that great deposit of textbook literature dealing with the most familiar of our ideas which is rewritten in every generation, while remaining so much a part of the universal heritage that no one can believe it has ever changed or even derived from a particular source.

Individual effectiveness in this tradition is actually certified by a certain anonymity. Thus, in Charles Butler's adaptations of the Talon *Rhetoric*, the very first editions drop the name of Talon from the title page. For Butler, Talon and rhetoric are synonymous — a fact flattering enough to Talon's reputation. Butler's title page at first does record that the *Rhetoric* is "Ramist" (*Ramea*), but subsequent editions liquidate even the adjectival Ramus, and he also becomes synonymous with rhetoric. Meanwhile, Butler's own name has crept from the signature of his preface onto his title page, where at first he enjoys an uncertain billing, but where, since Talon and Ramus have disappeared, he is soon promoted to author. Following this ascent to fame, Butler must have qualified for anonymity, too, becoming himself synonymous with rhetoric and thus achieving an immortal, if unpublicized, influence. This is the general fate of Ramism:[8] Ramist logics act the same way, casting off Ramus' name and becoming simply logic. The protective anonymity which Ramism thus acquires is a great handicap to its study.

This very protective anonymity, however, hints at the importance of Ramism for understanding even our present day, when we are likely to think of our sensibility as formed chiefly by the great authors of the Renaissance and other past epochs. Yet in many ways the pedagogical literature which was rewritten from generation to generation under the sponsorship of eclectic opportunism, and which was encouraged by classroom need for courses in logic or rhetoric or other "arts," is as important in the history of the human mind as the monumental Renaissance literature of Shakespeare, Milton, the Bible or perhaps Donne. This more anonymous output, at first almost entirely in Latin, largely pedagogical in orientation, often shabby

but always effective, is what was pounded into the minds of whole generations of schoolboys — as Shakespeare or Milton never were. It is a part of
the sinews and bones of civilization, growing with civilization and meeting
its living needs in a way in which the literary masterpiece, cast and preserved in an unalterable form, fails to do.

3. THE UNIVERSAL LANGUAGE

Familiarity with Renaissance educational and intellectual tradition is
difficult to achieve today for two reasons which are complementary: our stead-
ily decreasing familiarity with Latin, and the nineteenth-century campaigning for national literatures. The extinction of Latin in favor of national literatures was certainly long — perhaps far too long — in coming, but having
come, it has closed to us *most* important Renaissance books, and even books
written up to the eighteenth century in surprisingly large quantities. The
national literature campaigns have convinced us that the Latin books are
not even there. The vernacular interest today reproduces old vernacular
works in quantity, but Renaissance Latin works, far more common in their
day than vernacular works, are almost never reprinted.

Increased attention has been given recently to Latin influences on Shakespeare and his contemporaries, as in works by Douglas Bush, J. A. K. Thomson, and T. W. Baldwin. Such books alert us chiefly to the presence of the
classic authors in the Renaissance milieu. The work of Pierre Duhem, Lynn
Thorndike, Anneliese Maier, and other historians has begun to remind us
of the huge mass of Latin scientific or semiscientific works. But there exists
no general history of modern Latin literature, from the fourteenth through
the eighteenth century, for the good reason that such a history is simply too
vast to think about. It would cover all Europe and America, and weave in
and out of the history of every vernacular literature from Portuguese to
Hungarian, and from Italian to Icelandic, and be simply the history of the
Western mind.

We remain unaware, therefore, that Latin existed not only as an influence
in the way French or German literature exists in America today or as
scientist's argot, but also as the accepted frame of reference and the instrument of thought and sensibility for nearly everyone whom we should style an
"intellectual" today and for many others besides. Ascham's *Scholemaster* is
concerned about getting the schoolboy into a good linguistic environment,
but this means one where Latin, not English, is spoken well. The scattered
sixteenth- and seventeenth-century protestations, such as those of Richard
Mulcaster or John Brinsley, in favor of some English in the schools, are
decidedly a minority voice. They are concerned, moreover, almost entirely
with elementary education, and even then are hardly audible till amplified

by the nineteenth-century vernacular enthusiasms. As can be seen from the *Parnassus* plays, boys were drilled in Ramus' Latin "arguments" before they were old enough to read literary English. There are, practically speaking, simply no textbooks for teaching the vernacular in schools, although some vernacular skills were communicated haphazardly. Significantly, Ramus' Latin *Grammar* was never translated into French, but his French *Gramere* was immediately translated into Latin. The Ramist English grammar, with its Chaucer vocabulary, is in Latin, too.[9] It was foolish to have a grammar for the vernacular in the vernacular itself, for, with no vernacular in the school program, those who would want to study it would normally be foreigners who knew Latin but not the vernacular in question. Thus Richard Mulcaster's *Elementarie*, printed in 1582, appeared next in 1925, and *The English Grammar* by Ben Jonson (1640) never knew classroom use.

In the sixteenth century and well through the seventeenth, even the Latin grammars for beginners in Latin were in Latin themselves. The direct method for Latin was favored — indeed it could be said to be the only method which existed in principle in the sixteenth century — as far as the textbooks were concerned, although there is reluctant provision, as in Ascham, for construing in English for the smaller boys.

The objective in teaching Latin was what it commonly is in the teaching of any language: use of the language in speaking and reading. The scholar's entire career, elementary, secondary, and university, was to be lived through in Latin. There were practically no books other than Latin books — for Latin itself, for Greek and Hebrew, for logic, for physics or other philosophy, for mathematics, for law, medicine, or theology.

Moreover, Latin was certainly not taught to "form character" or to "train the mind." These are rationalizations which appear only with the nineteenth century when it was on its way out. In the sixteenth- or seventeenth- or even eighteenth-century context, such rationalizations were uncalled for and unreal. In Latin the boy had to learn to think, and in Latin — hence internationally — the vast evolution of thought from the fifteenth to the seventeenth centuries was subconsciously prepared and in great part finally undergone.

During the Renaissance, as during the Middle Ages (see Raymond W. Chambers' *The Continuity of English Prose*), vernacular literature tended to be regarded as literature for women, who were mostly denied formal schooling — that is, denied the Latin which would have opened the philosophy and science books to them. Hence, the importance in vernacular history of romances and of devotional books and sermons for mixed audiences. Occasionally, through the sixteenth century, the vernacular is regarded as particularly fit not only for women's literature or for the literature of love, but for light and coarse productions. Thus Ramus' works, his opponent Pierre Galland tells him, should be read for amusement, "as are the vernacular works of the ridiculous Pantagruel." [10] Rabelais' Latin medical works were in a totally different class.

The retention of Latin among learned men was no more Catholic than Protestant. To be sure, as a group, the Dissenters, many of whom espoused Ramism, had a certain predilection for the vernacular. But it was due not only to the preservation and flowering of the old Catholic devotional and preaching tradition, but also to the Dissenter's tendency to incorporate linguistic skills in an economy of practical, commercial life rather than in an intellectual economy. Still, the more the rising bourgeois class to which so many Dissenters belonged developed their schooling, the more they drifted into Latin, and, as they hoped, intellectual distinction. Dudley Fenner's 1584 adaptation of the Ramist *Dialectic* and *Rhetoric* for the Puritan exiles at Middelburg in the Low Countries was in English, but a generation or two later, the adaptation by William Ames, professor at nearby Franeker, was in Latin. At Harvard College, where, had he lived a little longer, Ames might well have been the first president, Latin was honored from the beginning as the official scholastic language, although sometimes more in the breach than in the observance.

In the Latin era, there is little positive hostility towards the use of the vernaculars in educational and intellectual circles, but simply an indifference and blindness which occasional vernacular campaigning failed to overcome. When there is hostility, it is more likely to be on the side of the vernacular against the Latin. Even this is not very marked, for champions of the vernacular did not want the extinction of Latin but rather the elevation of the vernacular to an equally high position.

It is difficult to trace the gradual abandonment of Latin, although it is certain that the language lingers longer the closer one keeps to strictly educational circles and the higher in these circles one stays. As noted, protests against Latin begin modestly among those teaching at the elementary level and move up. But they move slowly, and the occasional information we have concerning lecture-room practice at the university shows surprising viability for Latin, in the English-speaking world as elsewhere. The regius professor Louis Le Roy's experiment with lecturing in French in mid-sixteenth-century Paris proved abortive. Francis Hutcheson (1694–1746) seems to have been the first to begin effectively to teach philosophy in the vernacular in any Scottish university, and when he began this daring procedure, it was nearing the middle of the eighteenth century.[11] The eighteenth was the century when the vernaculars began to make themselves felt, and actually to be taught at the universities.[12] It was also the age when vernacular prose, removed to some extent from the haunts of real dialogue and put under the tutelage of science at the universities and by the dictionary writers,[13] established its modern "clear" tone.

Even quite late in the eighteenth century Latin is not dead. One finds such titles as *A Compendium of the Art of Logick as It Is Read in the University of Dublin, literally translated into English from the Latin edition* [*Artis logicae compendium,* 1773] (Dublin: George Bohman, 1792). Latin is not restricted to university circles, and certainly not to Ireland or Scotland. Samuel Johnson, who had only an honorary degree and abhorred all things distinctively Scottish, slipped into Latin in preference to French when Sir Joshua Reynolds presented him to a Frenchman at the Royal Academy.[14] Parallel instances can be multiplied indefinitely.

Unless this linguistic situation is kept in mind the meaning of Ramism and its connection not only with a world of Latin humanists but with all life cannot be appreciated. What passes today as Renaissance literature — vernacular literature — no matter how great its excellence, occupied the periphery of the Renaissance consciousness insofar as this consciousness thought of literature as connected with formal education. The common heritage, perpetuated in the schools and universities, was chiefly Latin, not Chaucer or Shakespeare or Spenser or any other writer in English or in the other vernaculars. Milton's diffidence about writing his first divorce tract in English,[15] his turning to English in poetry "long choosing and beginning late" and then only because he despaired of developing a Latin style above "second rank," [16] and the success of Latin epics such as the *Argenis* of the Franco-Scot John Barclay (1582–1621), which went through far more editions than the *Arcadia* of Sidney on which it was based, are significant and typical phenomena. So, too, are the preponderance of Latin Renaissance writers and the neglect of English in Thomas Pope Blount's *Evaluation of Famous Writers* (*Censura celebriorum authorum*), which was still being published in Latin as late as 1690, and in other biographical encyclopedias of the seventeenth century.

Latter-day campaigning for national literatures has distorted the relationship between Latin and the Renaissance scholarly world in which Ramism came into being. The *Dictionary of National Biography* can give the impression that writers were all working to schedule to create a national vernacular literature. Without conspiring to do so, the *Short-Title Catalogue* generates a quite false impression of the total literary activity of English-speaking peoples before 1640 by restricting the Latin works it reports to those printed in England, Scotland, and Ireland, omitting all foreign (Continental) editions of books not in English. The reason, however, is not that such editions are inconsequential but that they run into such near-astronomical figures that they could never all be included. Ironically, in ruling out such Continental editions by British authors, the *Short-Title Catalogue* fails to publicize the very works which these authors put into Latin so that they would be the most widely publicized of their works. Thus, George Downham's lengthy commentary on Ramus' *Dialectic* appears in the *Short-Title Catalogue* in one edition, that of 1669, the first and only English imprint of the work. But before that date no less than six Continental editions had been published.

In view of the undisputed monopoly of Latin in the teaching tradition, our tendency to base studies of Renaissance rhetoric on the scattered and short-lived rhetorics put out in English (almost always to teach *Latin* expression) and on similar English editions of dialectics or logics and of Latin grammars, is not entirely valid. The English-language texts provide roughly the same material as the Latin texts, but they do so in a medium which was unfamiliar to the Renaissance schoolboy, to whom these vernacular rhetorics and logics and grammars were normally quite unknown.

Ramism is at the forefront of the vernacular movement in England, France, the Netherlands, and Germany. Yet all the vernacular editions of the most translated Ramist work, the *Dialectic* — including all languages and including as vernacular editions even those which do no more than supply occasional vernacular synonyms in the Latin text — come to some thirty as against nearly 250 Latin editions. The proportion of vernacular rhetorics is far less.[17] These vernacular editions of both dialectics and rhetorics are mostly *tours de force* printed once or twice by their translators and never heard of again. In contrast to the well-thumbed copies of the Latin dialectics and rhetorics, black with manuscript annotations, their title pages often worn loose or missing, which come down to us today, the vernacular dialectics and rhetorics uniformly survive in beautifully preserved, unused copies.

"Shall we then," asks the Scottish translator of Ramus, Roland M'Kilwein, "think the Scottische or Englische tongue is not fit to wrote any art into? No in dede." [18] But this is a clear case of the lady who doth protest too much. When he wrote this, M'Kilwein had already a Latin edition of Ramus (often reprinted, and on the Continent, too) safely to his credit, and in the very English translation in which he prints this protest, he absent-mindedly leaves his good Scottish name on the title page in its outlandish Latin form, Makylmenaeus. Without a sense of the force of the Latin educational tradition which registers here, the impact of Ramism on Renaissance society as a whole can escape us.

4. RAMISM INTERNATIONAL

Supported by the Latin traditions of educators and intelligentsia, Ramism is an international cultural phenomenon. It takes form in a milieu dominated by the Italian Lorenzo Valla, the Dutchman Rudolph Agricola (Roelof Huusman, 1444–1485), who taught in Germany and Italy, the cosmopolite Erasmus, the Spaniard Juan Luis Vives teaching in England, the German Johann Sturm, who taught at Paris, the Scot John Major, who taught also at Paris when not teaching (and listening to John Knox) in Scotland, and others of similar international stamp. A German memory expert spawned in the Ramist milieu gives a list of no fewer than eighty-six places where he taught mnemonics (obviously in Latin) — among them being Antwerp, Basle, Brussels, Carcassonne, Cologne, Douay, Frankfurt-am-Main, Frankfurt-an-der-Oder, Freiburg in Switzerland, Heidelberg "by proxy" (*per alium*), London, Lyons, Marburg, Munich, Paris, Prague, Tübingen, Vienna, Wittenberg, and Rouen.[19]

Ramist works were printed indifferently in Paris, London, Frankfurt-am-Main, Cambridge, Basle, Edinburgh, La Rochelle, Amsterdam, Leyden, Strasbourg, Salamanca, Prague, Cologne, and elsewhere. Any of these Latin editions had an immediate market in a way vernacular editions could not. While local editions of course enjoyed the greatest sale in any given community, copies of any of these editions, no matter where they were published, might make their way all over Europe, and regularly did. There was no waiting for translations to be made. The German savant, Jakob Schegk, held as his chief grudge against Ramus the fact that the latter had given Schegk's *Physics* a bad press and killed off its sale in France.[20] Books not only crossed national frontiers on the Continent, but made their way back and forth across the Channel and the Irish Sea as well as the Atlantic. Continental editions of Ramist works are as well known in Aberdeen as are the British editions, and better known at Oxford,[21] while both British and Continental editions make their way to the British Colonies in America, and especially to Harvard. The important 1546 Paris edition of Ramus' *Training in Dialectic*, cited in Paris in 1555, so far as I can find is known today in only two copies, each of which came to rest hundreds of miles from where it was printed: one is in Munich, the other in Bologna.

The contours of Ramism have been lost just as we have lost a sense of the internationalism of the Renaissance intellectual milieu. But even such a phenomenon as the Cambridge Ramist activity, which involved Abraham Fraunce, Gabriel Harvey, Everard Digby, William Temple, Dudley Fenner, George Downham, William Ames, and others, is itself an international incident. This is not because of the editions of Fenner's Ramist logic and rhetoric published in Holland, for these were English-language editions and hence, even when brought back into England, attracted so little attention that until 1951 no one questioned the attribution of the rhetoric to Thomas Hobbes.[22]

Cambridge Ramism would have been international even if all the works involved had been printed at Cambridge, instead of at Frankfurt-am-Main where some of them first appeared. All except Fenner's were in Latin, and thus addressed to scholars all over Europe. It is entirely normal that the Temple-Digby round had as its third protagonist the German semi-Ramist Johannes Piscator. In 1610, Temple himself is still being cited by the German Wilhelm Ursin in his *Disputations in Philosophy* side by side with the

Italian philosopher Jacopo Zabarella, the Portuguese Jesuit Pedro da Fonseca, the German Protestant Rudolph Göckel or Goclenius (the elder), not to mention the Frenchman Ramus himself, and Aristotle.[23] George Downham was a good Ramist, Thomas Fuller tells us, and his "clunch fist of logic (good to knock down a man at a blow) can so open itself as to smooth and stroke one with the palm thereof," [24] but, like all who wrote for this audience, he clunch-fisted and stroked on an international scale.

CHAPTER II

VECTORS IN RAMUS' CAREER

Briefly explained by dialectical
summaries of the matter.
— Title page of Ramus' translation
of Plato's *Letters* (1547).

I. BIOGRAPHICAL SOURCES

R AMUS' life is meaningful in terms of the philosophy, expressed
or implied, which unfolds out of it and which it in turn helps to explain.
There are numerous contemporary sources for approaching it and Ramus'
thought.[1] Three biographies, all in Latin, were published by his associates,
Johann Thomas Freige or Freigius (1575), Théophile de Banos or Theophilus
Banosius (1576), and Nicolas de Nancel or Nancelius (1599). There are
autobiographical passages in Ramus' *Lectures on Dialectic* and in others of
his writings, such as the *Inaugural Address as Regius Professor*, the *Defense
of Aristotle against Jacob Schegk*, and in various letters and prefaces. There
is also material in *The Academy* by the closest of Ramus' associates, Omer
Talon. Freige and Banosius, who write only in part from personal acquaintance, make frequent and often verbatim use of these last four sources. Further material on Ramus' biography is to be found in the works against Ramus
by his academic opponent, Jacques Charpentier,[2] and elsewhere in similar
writings.

The best biography — Waddington's 1855 *Ramus* included — is that by
Nancel, from the points of view of immediacy of information, of objectivity,
of urbanity, and of style. It is written in the detached, whimsical, tantalizing
vein which is characteristic of the international medical tradition. With some
foreboding, Nancel had been Ramus' understudy, secretary, and coauthor
over a period of some twenty years before he turned to the study of medicine,
which he practiced from about 1568 till his death in 1610, aged seventy-one
years. His works include the huge posthumous *Analogy of the Microcosm to
the Macrocosm* (*Analogia microcosmi ad macrocosmum*), which in some
ways puts Burton's *Anatomy of Melancholy* to shame.

In his life of Ramus, written for the "old boys" of the Collège de Presles,
where Ramus had long been rector, Nancel remembers details in abundance

and often with clinical exactness — how Ramus' fine figure was marred by a slightly protruding belly, how magnificent was Ramus' beard, and how Ramus once treated his chronic eye trouble by shaving off his hair.[3] We are told of Ramus' ordinarily pleasant mien and frequent terrible fits of temper, how he washed his face and hands twice a day, or at the very least once a day, in a mixture of water and white wine, and how, regular as the stars themselves, he "took a bath once a year about the time of the summer solstice."[4] Nancel's account is really a firsthand and large-scale "character" of Ramus, touching everything except controversial religious questions, which he avoids expressly "so as not to offend either side."[5]

Compared with Nancel's gossipy and circumstantial irreverence, diagnostic rather than malicious, Freige's and Banosius' lives are earnest and stuffy attempts to make Ramus a hero.[6] Waddington uses Freige and Banosius without trepidation, but when he comes to Nancel, he makes a very circumspect selection of items to maintain in Ramus' character the outlines which he wants and which post-Waddington accounts all retail.

Later works on Ramus use the contemporary sources with varying degrees of objectivity and exactness. In this brief biographical account, except where otherwise noted, the details can be substantiated by tracing back the references in the more recent sources, Waddington, Desmaze, and Graves. Where I differ from these sources, full documentation is always supplied.

2. FROM BIRTH TO REGIUS PROFESSORSHIP

Pierre de la Ramée, who called himself in Latin Petrus Ramus and was known in the English-speaking world by the name Peter Ramus, was born almost certainly in 1515 in the tiny Picard village of Cuts (formerly written Cuth or Cut and in a half-dozen other ways including Banosius' remarkable Qwt). Cuts is about five miles southeast of Calvin's birthplace at Noyon, in the canton of Noyon and the département of the Oise. Writing dejectedly after World War I, Barnard says the village no longer exists.[7] But it certainly does exist, and in 1939 Cuts erected on the façade of its *mairie* a plaque to its most famous son, which is very much in evidence today. Over the centuries, the village has crept uphill, and local tradition has it that Ramus was born at what is now the edge of the village proper.

Ramus came of a noble family, originally from Liège, fallen into poverty. His grandfather was a charcoal burner, his father a farmer. Pierre seems never to have laid claim to any title.[8] In his early works he was to identify himself as *Veromanduus.* This assured him an enviable, if loose, pedigree out of classical antiquity, for the district around Cuts is the old *Vermandois,* land of Caesar's and Pliny's Veromandui or Viromandui. Ramism was to be at first a rather distinctively Vermandois product, for Pierre's friends in the Picard "nation" at the University of Paris, such as Nancel and Antoine Fouquelin, were often Veromandui, too, and the family seat of his patron, Charles de Guise, was in the bordering district of the Thiérache.

Pierre's early schooling was at Cuts, from which he fought his way to Paris some sixty miles distant three different times in his quest of further learning, being twice forced to return home. The headstrong aggressiveness which Parisian dialectic was to bring to fine maturity in this "branch of Mars," as Beza was to call him, was encouraged in its development by the hardships against which Pierre had to contend in early life. The third time he tried to get established at Paris, after putting up briefly with his maternal uncle Henri Charpentier and studying as a day student or *martinet*, he managed to move into the College of Navarre. Waddington's own persecution complex and his psychopathic identification of himself with Ramus prompts him to present this move — and almost all of Ramus' gestures — as a sacrifice on Ramus' part.[9] As a matter of fact, Ramus was doubtless following the general trend into the colleges and the irresistible drive of the adolescent boy to conform as exactly as possible to the crowd.

Exactly when this trying period of adjustment to the university milieu took place is hard to say, for after being accepted by one of the masters, boys were taken into the university community at various levels of instruction from the age of some seven years on. Banosius believes that the youngster first came to Paris at the age of eight, but Bayle favors twelve.[10] Waddington believes that Pierre was around twelve when he finally entered the College of Navarre.[11]

At Navarre our young Vermandois was to find such companions as Charles Bourbon (1523–1590), future cardinal and (according to the League) King of France, and Charles de Guise (1525–1574), later Cardinal of Lorraine and, still later, upon the death of his uncle, Cardinal of Guise. But besides the companionship of new-found friends, Pierre drank at Navarre the bitter dregs of resentment, for he had got into the college only by becoming the paid valet of a wealthy fellow student, the Sieur de la Brosse.[12] In later life Ramus remembers only the painfulness of his early experiences:

> I confess that my whole life has been one bitter struggle (*vitam meam totam acerbissimis fluctibus iactatam esse*). As a young boy [*iuvenis*, not *puer*, and hence, as Bayle notes, perhaps hardly so young as eight] under every possible handicap I came to Paris to study the liberal arts. Twice I was forced to return from Paris, but the more studies were denied me, the more I wanted to study.[13]

Burdened with his chores for La Brosse, Ramus had chiefly the night or early morning left for study, and Nancel tells of his homemade alarm clock, a stone which thundered to the floor when a rope wick to which it was rigged had burned its allotted distance.[14]

There are stories that young Pierre was slow in learning and found it hard to reason to the point,[15] and it is possible that he showed up poorly in disputations, which were still used, although the Agricolan dialectic which was taking hold in Paris had somewhat weakened their grip. Pierre's wild desire to learn, frustrated by the extracurricular demands on his time and given edge by the humiliation of being somewhat older than the others in his class,[16] only intensified his savage resentment against the pedagogical world which formed the setting for his frustrations and where he would quarrel with his colleagues all his life.

Pierre had certainly done some grammar and perhaps some rhetoric before leaving home. On the other hand, grammar was also taught at the university, a curious community including little boys not yet in their teens as well as teen-agers,[17] so that he may have done some of his grammar at Paris. True to the humanist tradition, Pierre will later pretend that practically the only permanent influences on his thought were the ancients (and "things themselves"). Thus it is difficult to name his actual teachers although it is certain that at the College of Navarre, one of the most important of these boarding-and-lecture houses at Paris, he came into contact with most of the intellectual currents of the time.[18] In its general organization, Pierre's course corresponded to that taught during the late Middle Ages and registered in the statutes for the university drawn up in 1453[19] for the commission of Cardinal d'Estouteville, who had died some twenty years before Ramus' birth. This arts course consisted of grammar, rhetoric, and "philosophy," the last being chiefly logic and "physics," with a certain amount of ethics, a tiny dash of metaphysics, and variable incidental items such as rudimentary geometry or other mathematics, or occasionally music.

The two extremes of the course, grammar and "physics," remained relatively unmodified in Pierre's youth. The humanists had brought in better grammars than the versified *Grecismus* of Eberhard of Béthune and *Doctrinale* of Alexander of Villedieu. But the Latin grammar, which was taught to boys not yet in their teens was pretty much Latin grammar — to be got through, as Jacques Charpentier remarks, "somehow or other."[20] Most of the changes which the humanists were able to effect in elementary instruction did not have to do with grammar reform but with style.

The "physics" which Pierre studied defies description in terms meaningful in the twentieth century.[21] It was a mixture of items approximating what we should today call physics, chemistry, alchemy, astronomy, biology, taxonomy, psychology, neuro-psychology, anatomy, physiology, and many other things besides, all sprinkled with a certain amount of metaphysics, which led a very precarious existence as a separate discipline of its own. This curious mixture is one of the most important items in medieval and Renaissance philosophy both insofar as its weight in the curriculum and its influence in forming the modern mind are concerned. Some of its implications in the formation of Ramus' outlook will be discussed later. The point to be made is that in Ramus' youth it remained substantially what it had been in the Middle Ages.

Rhetoric and dialectic or logic (the terms were, in practice, synonymous) had not remained the same. The humanists were replacing the practical medieval rhetoric with a more elaborate art designed to teach perfect Latin expression as a literary and stylistic instrument. Young Pierre was one of the outstanding products of this new stress on rhetoric, perhaps *the* outstanding product of all times. The exact circumstances of his training deserve more detailed study than is possible here, for, to believe Nancel, who is seldom given to adulation, Ramus was "by far the leader of his whole age"[22] in both writing and speaking Latin. Nancel adds that in preceding ages, no one could be compared to him in Latin eloquence except Cicero. This verdict, concurred in by the dozens of adulatory verses affixed to Ramus' works, makes Ramus surpass all the Italian humanists such as Bembo or Petrarch as well as Erasmus and his associates, and a good many fathers of the Church to whom Latin had been a native and not a learned language. Nancel's remark may be discounted a bit on the score of Gallic bias—Ramus was, after all, a Frenchman like his biographer—but it is representative of the general opinion of him held by contemporaries who were avid connoisseurs of Latinity.[23]

Pierre's education was influenced not only by the stress on rhetoric, but by a new orientation of dialectic which this stress entailed. This orientation had been due indirectly to Italians but was immediately traceable in great part to Rudolph Agricola, like his successor Erasmus a man from the Low Countries who plied back and forth between Italy and the North. When Agricola died in 1485, his *Dialectical Invention* (*De inventione dialectica*) had begun to catch on in the Rhineland and the Low Countries. But it was not until 1529, when Pierre de la Ramée was probably already a student at the university, that it was brought by Johann Sturm into the dialectical center of Christendom, Paris, to begin a new fermentation there. Pierre's dialectical training took place in this ferment, but he seems to have received his own instruction in the old pre-Agricolan dialectic or logic, and turned to the Agricolan dialectic afterwards when he started teaching as a young Master of Arts.[24] Ramus' later historical importance is defined by his reaction to—or, rather, his continuation of—Agricola's dialectic rather than by the field in which he could claim genuine excellence, that of a practicing rhetorician or orator. Even the rhetoric known as Ramist will be the product of this dialectic, not of his oratorical practice.

Pierre took his degree of Master of Arts at the age of twenty-one, an age slightly retarded but not excessively so.[25] The new full-fledged master of arts (whom we shall hereafter call by his mature Latin name Ramus) immediately began his teaching career in one of the colleges or boarding houses which for some generations had been becoming more common at the university and which had gradually evolved into centers of instruction, particularly for the smaller fry among the students.[26] He taught first at the Collège du Mans (a college in Paris itself, not, as has been sometimes thought, at Le Mans), then at the little Collège de l'Ave Maria,[27] where he was associated with Omer Talon of Beauvais and Bartholomew Alexandre of Champagne. Most of Ramus' coterie, friendly and hostile, was always a part of the "nation" of Picardy, as was normal at the university where the arts students and masters had always been organized by geographical origin into the four nations, French (including all South Europeans), Norman, Picard, and English or German (for this last nation included both of these nationalities).

During this period devoted to teaching, Ramus did what three centuries of young masters of arts had done before him — he got up the courses he was to give to younger boys. If he had done any teaching as bachelor (apprentice teacher) in the last three years or so before his admission to full status in the teachers' guild, Ramus failed later to take it seriously, for he tells us that he worked back over his former studies after his master's degree.

He talks of this procedure of getting up his courses in the most momentous terms, mentioning as his sources, in accordance with the literary fiction of the time, none but classical authors — Plato, Aristotle, Galen, Cicero[28] — a fiction he was to maintain all his life and which has strewn the train of Ramism with innumerable red herrings. But if modern commentators have been misled by Ramus' lip service to the party ideology here, his fellow masters were not. They were perfectly aware that Ramus was doing what many young masters under pressure of a teaching assignment have always done — he was not rethinking the problems so much as rethumbing the textbooks. Antonio de Gouveia names, in addition to Agricola, some half-dozen contemporaries whom Ramus had availed himself of: Johannes Caesarius (ca. 1458–1550?), Christophorus Hegendorf or Hegendorphinus (fl. early sixteenth century), the Capuchin Franciscus Titelmans or Titelmannus (1502–1537), Philip Melanchthon (1497–1560), and Gouveia himself.[29] All these are post-Agricolan dialecticians, more or less under Agricola's influence. Pierre Galland, repeating some of Gouveia's sources for Ramus' dialectic, adds three new names of his own as forerunners of Ramus in the widespread anti-Aristotelian movements of the age, saying that what Ramus says had already been said by Lorenza Valla, Juan Luis Vives, and Cornelius Agrippa, as well as by Agricola and Melanchthon, while Nancel suggests as among Ramus' predecessors three more still, Jacques Lefèvre d'Etaples, Bartholomew Latomus, and Johann Sturm.[30]

University legislation over the centuries had had to repeat injunctions against young masters' "lecturing" by dictating to their classes from notes. Masters were supposed to be individually enterprising and the legislation had occasionally even gone so far as to forbid students to use pen and ink in the classroom, so that such dictation would be impossible.[31] Ramus' inclination to recast his course was thus in the best university tradition. If such an inclination was revolutionary, then revolution was prescribed by statute. By the same token, the inclination derives not from new and fresh insights but from pedagogical exigency. This point is important, not only because pedagogical exigency, rather than intellectual integrity, is thus seen to be the real focus of Ramism, but because of the unique force which pedagogical exigency had acquired in the university milieu, and its ability to force a crisis. It is only after the pedagogical build-up of the Middle Ages that the crucial question for philosophy becomes not, Is it true? but Is it teachable?

Ramus' reworking of the course did, however, go further than most such reconstructions. By 1543 he could publish the results of his efforts. This he did in the twin works *The Structure of Dialectic (Dialecticae partitiones)* or *Training in Dialectic (Dialecticae institutiones)* and *Remarks on Aristotle (Aristotelicae animadversiones)*. Therein was established a framework which he and his followers would indefinitely extend but which he himself — and most of his followers — would never radically overhaul. Ramus' reform was one of many. And, since university control over the curriculum was rather loose, had he sought only to put it into effect in his own classrooms at the little Collège de l'Ave Maria, his reform might have been overlooked. But the two 1543 books were his attempt to extend it beyond his classrooms, and hit the university below the intellectual belt at the administrative level. Aristotle was an "authority" largely in the sense that he was the center of the accepted curriculum, so that Ramus' savage and sweeping attack on Aristotle and Aristotelians in both these 1543 works was a denunciation by a single teacher of the curriculum followed by the rest of the faculty. Appearing in print as it did, the denunciation was thus a public announcement to the whole teen-age and younger community of undergraduates, a community which habitually lived in a state of unruliness which the modern imagination can hardly steel itself to reconstruct. Little wonder that the faculty became panic-stricken and turned on Ramus.

The whole antiauthoritarian issue involved in Ramism is set in these very down-to-earth perspectives, although Waddington and others have portrayed it as a cloak-and-sword drama with Ramus as hero. The literature of the time is uniformly concerned not so much with the effect of Ramus' two works on Aristotle's reputation as with their effect on the curriculum as a social factor and on "the minds of children."[32] No doubt, there was resistance to Ramus in some quarters, which was prompted by the tendency to equate all innovators with Lutherans or other heretics. But even there, the irritation at his books was associated with their disturbance of the pedagogical rather than of the religious or theological front. The works provoked the university in its entirety, and the university was directed not by the theologians but by the masters of arts. Antonio de Gouveia, who with Joachim de Perion was among the first to reply to Ramus, insisted that, since there never was a "simple" or "pure" dialectic available for teaching little boys, as Ramus pretended, he was simply out "to upset and muddle the whole curriculum."[33]

At the instigation of Gouveia, the matter was referred to Francis I. The golden days of papal-protected university autonomy were gone, and for nearly a century, the Crown had been the effective arbiter of university squabbles. A commission was selected, significantly, from all the university faculties. Jean Quentin of the law faculty and the physician Jean de Bomont[34] were Ramus' representatives. Gouveia's party was represented by Francesco Vicomercato of the faculty of arts, a Milanese with a background of teaching at Pavia (where Aristotelianism was even more oriented toward physics than it was at Paris), and Pierre Danès of the same faculty, who had also been regius professor of Greek. The fifth and nonpartisan member of the commission alone, Jean de Salignac, was from the faculty of theology.

After two days of fruitless debate between Ramus and Gouveia, during which Ramus seems to have held against Aristotle chiefly the fact that he did not start each book of the *Organon* with a definition, Ramus' own two representatives resigned from the commission, and Ramus failed to produce any substitutes. On March 1, 1544, a royal decree[35] pronounced the decision against Ramus. It forbade his two books to be sold or republished anywhere in the realm and enjoined their author not to teach publicly or write on philosophy without permission of the king.

The grounds are clearly not Ramus' anti-Aristotelianism so much as his demonstrated incompetence. In obvious bad faith (*mauvaise voulente*), he attacks the dialectic "received by all the nations" (with reference to the teaching setup by nations at Paris) without giving evidence of understanding it. It not only contains things which are *faulses et estranges*, but also misrepresents the very meaning of what it pretends to comment on. For this latter reason especially, the *Remarks on Aristotle* should be condemned in the interest of letters and science (*le grand bien et prouffit des lettres et sciences*).

One may well quarrel here with the highhandedness of the government intervention — or, of the intervention by Ramus' fellow faculty members — but, along with Ramus' more competent contemporaries such as Adrien Turnèbe or Jacob Schegk or Gouveia himself, any serious scholar of today would own Ramus' incompetence. We shall examine his two books in detail later.

The first editions of Ramus' manifold works indicate the course of his career from now on.[36] He remained fully active at the University, even though for the time being he was inhibited in the exercise of one of his master's prerogatives. Free to teach anything in the arts course except philosophy (which included logic or dialectic), he turned to the teaching of classical authors and of mathematics. The latter was a subject which had normally been minimized in the universities, and he had to pick it up as he taught it.[37] Bartholomew Alexandre and Omer Talon, the two teachers associated with Ramus at the Collège de l'Ave Maria, had proclaimed their loyalty to him in speeches made in the Collège at the opening of the 1544 school year and published with Ramus' own *Address on the Study of Mathematics* delivered on the same occasion. Ramus began his close collaboration with Talon at this time. He even smuggled into print under Talon's name another edition of the condemned *Training in Dialectic*, the rare and important 1546 edition in which he first treats of method as such.

Ramus was evidently an effective teacher. In 1545 he was invited to teach at the more pretentious Collège de Presles.[38] Here Talon rejoined him, but Alexandre left to head a school at Reims[39] (the Reims municipal library still houses some rare Ramus and Talon editions). At Presles, Ramus bettered the teaching and soon replaced the aging Nicolas Sapiens (Le Sage?) as principal. To effect the ouster of his predecessor Ramus had resort to a parliamentary hearing, thus incidentally keeping alive his own record for litigation.

In 1547 Francis I had been succeeded by Henry II, to whom, as Dauphin, Ramus had prudently dedicated his *Brutus' Problems*. Through the intercession of Ramus' old and long cultivated[40] schoolfellow Charles of Lorraine, Cardinal of Guise, the new king lifted the ban against Ramus' teaching and writing on philosophy. It is at this period that Ramus' and Talon's works begin to be dedicated in great profusion to the Cardinal, who, in consequence, perhaps has no rival in the history of literature as a title-page dedicatee.

The cultivation of the Cardinal's friendship bore wonderful fruit. By 1551, Ramus was appointed to his regius professorship and well on the highroad to preferment. On the death of Pascal Duhamel in 1565, he would become himself dean of the whole body of regius professors, eventually styled the Collège de France. A royal writ of 1557 was to provide him perhaps the most sweeping copyright in the history of publishing, covering not only his works already written but also those not yet even thought of.[41]

Although he later fell out with the Cardinal for reasons which are not clear, the dominant note of Ramus' career from 1547 on is that of a court favorite, who worked hard at his educational task but enjoyed vast influence and privileges. His is far from the role of the persecuted intellectual which writers reading the tragedy of his death back through his whole life have made him out to be. Typically, when other Protestants were having to hide out almost anywhere, Ramus was himself to be sheltered in the royal palace at Fontainebleau, as guest of the King, or in the royal abbey of Royaumont on the other side of Paris.[42] Even at the time of his cruel death, he was still the favorite, killed against the express order of Charles IX and his mother.[43]

3. REGIUS PROFESSOR OF ELOQUENCE AND PHILOSOPHY

The central event of his rise to fame was Ramus' appointment as regius professor in 1551. The regius professorships had been created in 1530 by Francis I and at first were predominantly in the three languages of Latin, Greek, and Hebrew.[44] Francis envisioned a royal collection of humanists which would outshine the smaller collections assembled by great Italian families, such as the Medici.[45] However, Francis' professors were to give not domestic, but public courses (were not all people of France his children?). At first they addressed themselves to those preparing university degrees, and later to any and all who wanted to drop in and listen (as their successors now do in the Collège de France).

The regius professors, supported by royal grants (at least in theory — the grants were sometimes hard to collect in practice), gave Francis I one of his chief claims to the title "Père et Restaurateur des lettres." Although he had initiated the professorial chairs to encourage the humanism of which he was convinced the university took too dim a view, Francis had not envisioned his lecturers as constituting an institution pitted against the university. He had recruited his early appointees, of whom Ramus was the twenty-first, from among university personnel and had styled them "lisans du Roy en l'Université de Paris."[46]

But the university tradition proved allergic to injections of humanism, and the relations between the regius professors, soon to be known collectively as the Collège de France, and the University of Paris began to deteriorate. By 1546, five years before Ramus' nomination, the regius professors were being styled not "lecturers in the University of Paris," but, on occasion, simply "lecturers at Paris."[47] This or similar titles finally superseded those connecting the professors with the university. The process of dissociation was fairly slow; the 1587 Paris edition of Ramus' French *Grammaire* styles its author "lecteur du roy en l'université de Paris" (perhaps with intentional archaism), but by the end of the century, all illusion is gone, and the anonymous pamphlet *Pour l'Université de Paris contre les professeurs du Roy* complains that, unlike Ramus, the present incumbents style themselves "Professeurs Royaux au Collège de France" and say that they are "in the University but not of the University."[48]

The history of the regius professorships is relevant to Ramus' title, Regius Professor of Eloquence and Philosophy, certainly one of the most significant in the history of the Collège de France. Lefranc remarks that the titles of regius professors were bestowed at the King's good pleasure and that "it is not necessary to take the titles literally."[49] But Ramus took his title very literally and featured it after his name in hundreds of editions of his works, for it reinstated him as a teacher of philosophy and underwrote his particular variant of the humanist program to combine philosophy and literary elegance. His contemporaries, friend and foe, were highly sensitive to it. By virtue of your title, "regius professor of rhetoric and philosophy and dean [of the regius professors]," a pamphleteer taunts Ramus, you rove about at large through the whole curriculum, "following no particular route but merely barking at theoretical odds and ends."[50] At a higher level than that of a pamphleteer, the scholarly Turnèbe, one of the most distinguished classicists of any age, complains that Ramus is the first in the memory of man to have consecrated himself to eloquence and philosophy, and that by his own will (*tuo suffragio*).[51] For it was perfectly obvious that Ramus' title was of his own designing, effectively canonizing his 1546 *Address on Combining Philosophy and Eloquence* and giving royal sanction to his practice of using selections from oratory and poetry, rather than formally set-up logical statements, as examples in logic.

In terms of this title, Ramus' personal career mirrors the history of the whole intellectual epoch, when humanism (eloquence) and scholasticism (philosophy) were struggling with one another at Paris. For Ramus was not only the first to be regius professor of eloquence and philosophy; he was also the last. After his return to Paris during the temporary peace in 1563 between religious wars and his resumption of his chair, his enthusiasm for eloquence and philosophy began to wane, and he is identified in his 1563 *Address on the Regius Professorship of Liberal Arts* simply as "regius professor."[52] A mysterious interest in mathematics was taking hold of him — mysterious because he was so ill-educated in mathematics — and this interest would carry the day. With his death, the chair joining philosophy and eloquence went out of existence; a new chair arose, phoenix-like, the chair of mathematics founded by Ramus himself in his will. This progress from humanism and eloquence to mathematics Ramus shares with the age which follows him and which his own career and works help elucidate.

4. SUCCESS, TROUBLES, AND DEATH

At his accession to the regius professorship in 1551, Ramus was already well known as a teacher and university man. From then on, the number of his works (largely his lectures put into print) grew apace. His career after 1551 is as spotted as before with quarrels with other university people and scholars,[53] and with university business. He fought with vigor, if not always with understanding, for the cause of serious and competent teaching, goading others less ambitious to match his own tremendous industry. This industry was undeniable, for Ramus led a frugal life entirely devoted to his work as head of the Collège de Presles and as regius professor. He never married, says Nancel, simply for the reason that marriage was forbidden by university statute to heads of colleges.[54] Indeed, it was prohibited for all university teachers, whether or not in orders, except for doctors of medicine.[55] Ramus enjoyed the vague clerical status — that is, exemption from ordinary civil laws — which was attached to university students and teachers. He may even have been tonsured and thus technically a cleric, but, despite the benefices he held, he was never in orders.

His career takes its next great turn in 1562. In this year occurred the death of his best friend, fellow teacher, and literary associate, Omer Talon. Somewhere toward the end of his life, Talon was ordained priest; he died as curé of Saint Nicolas du Chardonnet at Paris,[56] just a stone's throw from the present Place Maubert, then the site of Ramus' Collège de Presles. A talented man, Nancel calls Talon, high-spirited, easygoing, urbane, learned, and a good teacher. Ramus felt his loss keenly.[57]

How far the upset of losing Talon had to do with Ramus' abandoning his Catholic religion for Protestantism in this latter period of his life, we shall never know. Nancel, who knew Ramus better than anyone save perhaps Talon, says that no one could assign a specific reason for Ramus' change of religion,[58] nor even date its occurrence. Ramus himself dates his change of heart from the 1561 Colloquy of Poissy, but he does this retrospectively in 1570 in a somewhat petulant letter to Charles of Lorraine with whom he had quarreled,[59] so that it is difficult to say how objective Ramus' recollection is here. We know from Nancel, who describes him as having been a rather devout, or at least observant, Catholic, that he received Communion at Mass on Easter Day, probably as late as 1562.[60] But, even when he was a practicing Catholic, Ramus had had a reputation for being a secret Protestant. This was attributable to the fact that some statues from his Collège de Presles chapel were broken by careless or mischievous students — apparently while Ramus was trying to save the statues from rioters.[61] Ramus' *Notes on the Reform of the University of Paris* could be given a Protestant reading, however, so that after the outbreak of the Wars of Religion in 1562, he withdrew under royal safe-conduct from Paris to Fontainebleau, where he remained until 1563. But his relationship with Protestantism remained ambiguous still when he returned to Paris in 1563.

More important than this absence at Fontainebleau was Ramus' second absence from Paris during the latter part of 1568 to 1570 when he was a kind of royal commissioner of French culture to Switzerland and Germany. This period gave him the means of establishing Ramism firmly in the Rhine Valley, from Basle, Zurich, and Berne, to Strasbourg and Heidelberg. He visited and lectured at all these places and as far east as Nuremberg and Augsburg. In 1570, while at Heidelberg, he took part for the first time in a Protestant Communion service.[62] No doubt, his posthumous *Commentary on the Christian Religion*, which proposes a mild Zwinglian theology, dates from his contact with the Rhenish Protestant theology during this period also. It did not have much lasting influence on Protestant thought. However, it was Ramus' fierce anti-Aristotelian record, rather than this mild theology, which led Beza to warn him away from Geneva for a time.[63] But Beza or no Beza, Ramus' international reputation was established. He was sought as far away as Cracow and Bologna.[64]

The close of Ramus' career was as troubled as its beginning. Returning to Paris in 1570, he found his place at the Collège de Presles and his regius professorship compromised by his Protestantism and by royal edicts which alternately disqualified Protestants for such posts and then restored their rights to them. In 1572, after a brief success at the Synod of the Ile-de-France, he found himself condemned, even in the Protestant camp, by the Synod of Nîmes for favoring lay government in the Church.[65] Late that year the tragedy struck, and he met death in his rooms at the Collège de Presles at the hand of a band of murderers on August 26, when the St. Bartholomew's Day Massacre had entered its third day of terror.[66] His body was thrown out the window, decapitated, and cast into the Seine.

Nancel, knowing that Ramus' enemy Charpentier had perished by fire, that is, by the "fever caused by jealousy such as is fatal to literary men,"[67] notes carefully that Ramus perished by the other three elements, earth (the metal of the sword), air, and water. Hardly less imaginative than this lucubration is Waddington's curious attempt to pin the murder on Ramus' enemy Charpentier. Along with most of what Waddington says, this version of Ramus' death is generally accepted today, despite the fact that its inconclusiveness was long ago pointed out in detail by Joseph Bertrand. There is little doubt that the only possible objective verdict concerning Ramus' death is murder on the occasion of the St. Bartholomew's Day Massacre by persons unknown,[68] apparently acting contrary to royal orders which excepted him personally from the effect of the horrible Edict.

At the time of his death, much of Ramus' library and many of his manuscripts were seized or destroyed. In a letter to Sir Philip Sidney dated January 15 [5?], 1576,[69] and also at the end of his life of Ramus published with Ramus' *Commentary on the Christian Religion* the same year, Banosius had noted that he had received some of Ramus' books and manuscripts and that he hoped to recover more. Among the manuscripts he had received was that of the *Commentary*. In concluding his life of Ramus, Nancel pleads for information from anyone who knows of the whereabouts of any of the missing manuscripts, but apparently nothing further was forthcoming.

The poor boy from Cuts had amassed a considerable fortune during his life, and by his will founded the chair of mathematics mentioned earlier, attached to no college and thereby analogous to the regius professorships themselves, by which eventually it was absorbed.[70] This legacy to learning was of a piece with Ramus' real generosity during his life, for he had always supported a good number of students free of charge at his Collège de Presles and had been seriously interested in bettering knowledge and instruction.

5. RAMUS AS TEACHER AND WRITER

Ramus' entire career is that of a teacher and writer. Most of his works are the direct product of his teaching, being either textbooks designed to present a curriculum subject (*ars*) in orderly, methodical fashion, or lectures (*scholae*) disposing of "adversaries" and difficulties connected with the art,[71] or finally commentaries on classical texts given as series of lectures and subsequently put into print.

If one takes the 1543 dialectical works as a kind of rhetoric (as one can, quite legitimately), Ramus' didactic-literary career will be seen to have four rather well-defined phases. The first phase is rhetorical in character; Ramus is the classical commentator, but despite his claims to be a Platonist, he specializes almost exclusively in Cicero. Nancel notes that, despite the great number of Ciceronian commentaries published by Ramus, there were at least ten more of his commentaries on Cicero's orations that never made their way into print.[72] The *Letters of Plato* (some of which we now know are spurious) is the only writing of Plato which either Ramus or Talon ever handled. Ramus attacks Cicero's rhetorical treatises together with Quintilian's *Training in Oratory* (*Institutiones oratoriae*) as savagely as he had attacked Aristotle, offering in their stead a new *Institutiones oratoriae*, which was brought out during this same period under Talon's name but written with the coöperation of Ramus, if not by him.

The second phase began within a few years after the regius professorship. It was the dialectical or methodical phase and was initiated by the 1555 and 1556 *Dialectic*, less rhetorical than the two 1543 dialectical works, even in presentation. "Method" (*methodus*), Ramus' term for orderly pedagogical presentation of any subject by reputedly scientific descent from "general principles" to "specials" by means of definition and bipartite division, will be explained at length in a later chapter, for it proves on close inspection to be as involved historically and psychologically as it is superficially simple.[73] This "method" had put in its initial appearance by name as early as 1546 in the edition of the *Training in Dialectic* published by Ramus under the pseudonym of Talon, but, with the 1555 period, Ramus begins seriously to "methodize" everything, beginning with dialectic itself. Applied to Virgil's *Bucolics* and *Georgics*, "method" produces a substitute for the art or science of physics.[74] Applied to Caesar's works, it produced on the one hand a science of ethics in *The Customs of the Ancient Gauls* (*Liber de moribus veterum Gallorum*), as can be seen most clearly in Freige's edition of Ramus' "arts" entitled *The Regius Professorship* (*Professio regia*); on the other it produced an "art" of war in *Caesar's Military Science* (*Liber de Caesaris militia*). Applied to the person of Cicero, it produced a "methodized" biography in which Cicero's life is significantly made a kind of projection of the arts curriculum, which is adapted nicely to outlining in tables of bracketed dichotomies so that, at the hands of Freige, Cicero appears in what is probably the first geometrically schematized biography in the history of belles lettres (see Figure I).

This same "methodical" or "dialectical" treatment now sweeps through the rest of the curriculum, enabling Ramus to define each art or curriculum

PETRI RAMI
CICERONIANVS.

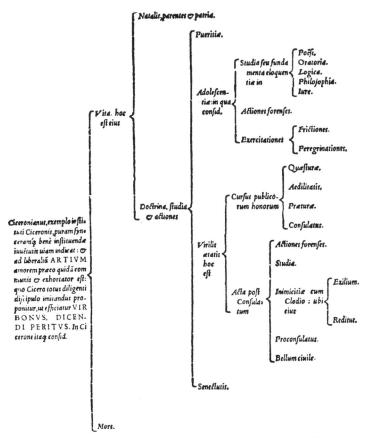

DISCE PVER VIRTVTEM EX ME,
VERVM'QVE LABOREM.

In Cicerone imitando, non Latinitatem folam, fed ornatum prudentiam, cognitionem rerum, uitæ in primis, morum'qz uirtutem: neqz folùm Ciceronis epiftolas, orationes, fcholas & difputationes· fed multó magis pædagogos, proceffus artium, labores edifcendi & uigilias meditationum, quibus orator tantus inftructus eft, Ciceronis imitator intueri, & eloquentiæ Ciceronianæ principia potius, quàm extrema contemplari: Ciceronemqz ipfum non næuo aliquo aut crepundrjs, fed tóto corpore, uel potius animo uirraqz tota complecti: gradus ætatis, magiftrorum prudentiam, difciplinarum genera, commentationum labores: continentiæ, fortitudinis, fapientiæ, iuftitiæ, omnesqz uitæ uniuerfæ tanquam fabulæ actus confiderare debet: ut appareat, quomodo efficiatur Vir ille bené dicendi peritus.1. Orator, fiue in fore ciuilium caufarum actor, quales f.. r h. recófulti: fiue religionis interpres & populi Doctor, quales funt Theologi: Hûc enim modó generaliter & communiter inquirimus, non unius artis hominem.

LABOR OMNIA VINCIT.

I. CICERO'S BIOGRAPHY IN DICHOTOMIES (ED. FREIGE)

subject with supreme assurance, to divide it into two "parts," redefine each part, subdivide the parts each into two more "parts," and so on until he reached the atomic particles which admitted no further halving. Thus Ramus produces a "true" art of grammar — Latin, Greek (Greek appearing bit by bit as Ramus learned the subject), and even French. (The latter displayed in an interesting reformed spelling, which Ramus did not originate, however, as has sometimes been thought, but adapted from Louis Meigret and soon abandoned when, despite the support of Baïf, it failed to establish itself.) [75] This period terminated with the *Lectures on Physics*, attacking Aristotle's *Physics*, and the *Lectures on Metaphysics*, calculated to annihilate the Stagirite's *Metaphysics* too, and to replace them with dialectic or logic.

In the third period, dialectic was turned on mathematics, which had claimed Ramus' attention to some extent as early as 1545, when his translation of Euclid's *Elements* made him aware how badly "methodized" even this work was. In this phase, we have textbooks in arithmetic, geometry, and algebra (the last named clogging Ramus' oversimplified defining apparatus: Was it geometry or arithmetic?), together with lectures (*scholae*) explaining difficulties and demolishing "adversaries" again. With mathematics, Ramus found himself happy if not at home. He was of no great consequence as a mathematician himself, but he spurred interest in the subject, for the quantified world was the real spiritual home of this apostle of "method."

The fourth period is represented by the posthumous work, *Commentary on the Christian Religion in Four Books*, in which, as Theophilus Banosius' preface to Sir Philip Sidney explains, Ramus reduces religion to an "art," assimilating it as "the art of living well" (*ars bene vivendi*), to grammar (*ars bene loquendi*), rhetoric (*ars bene dicendi*), dialectic (*ars bene disserendi*), and geometry (*ars bene metiendi*). His posthumous translation of Aristotle's *Politics* belongs with this art of religion; it is related to his projected art of ethics which the art of religion finally supersedes.

In the true humanist tradition, Ramus was widely read, and his commentaries on classical texts earned him a well-merited reputation for encyclopedic learning. But in his handling of abstract subjects, particularly in his school manuals or "arts," a brashness is evident which is particularly annoying today. The humanists' apotheosis of the past enforced the assumption, if it did not articulate it, that the curriculum subjects had once been perfectly organized and that all that was needed was some sort of key to restore them to their normal simplicity and order. Although at times he openly repudiates this assumption in favor of a quite advanced evolutionary view of the development of learning, Ramus most often not only encourages the assumption but suggests that his own logic or dialectic was the missing key. Confident in the power of his key, he felt no hesitation — nor did many of his contemporaries, who had keys of their own cut to the Ramist or other models — in teaching and actually reorganizing or "methodizing" curriculum subjects while he was in process of learning them and in publishing the results in textbook form.[76]

His work on the Christian religion is no exception, for until he wrote it, he had never touched theology, having had in his entire huge library not even a Bible, but only a New Testament edited by Castalio (Sébastien Castalion or Castellion) and a Roman breviary.[77] His mathematical writings are particularly interesting in this respect. When lecturing on mathematics, he would frequently (*non raro*) make mistakes with the abacus, especially with large numbers, and get into tangles he could not get out of.[78] He even took to memorizing his Euclid and practicing his regius mathematics lectures on the inmates of the Collège de Presles in advance.[79] However, unfamiliarity with mathematics had never been a real disability for masters of arts, and one can only admire Ramus' efforts to better the mathematical tradition as he worked faithfully over all of Euclid, Archimedes, and Ptolemy for a period of ten years.[80] When Jacques Charpentier, who knew even less mathematics than Ramus, sought to function as regius professor of mathematics by lecturing on the nature of mathematical abstraction and similar subjects instead of teaching real mathematics, Ramus protested in his usual energetic fashion.[81] And he pushed others on to achievements which he himself could not realize.[82]

Ramus' assurance that his logic was the key to all knowledge led him outside the arts course not only into theology but into medicine as well. He read Galen, as Nancel notes, chiefly the *Method of Healing* (*De methodo medendi*). But his objectives were somewhat limited: he wanted to exploit Galen's notions of method for his own logic.[83] He had done very little in law.[84] Ramus' other works, scattered through the four periods indicated above, are made up of occasional orations, miscellaneous controversy with savants inside and outside his own university, and various letters. The great Latin orator wrote no poetry (in Latin), Nancel informs us, because he was not sure of syllabic count.[85] His commentaries on poetry could hardly be called successful. His lectures on the *Bucolics* and *Georgics* of Virgil drew so much laughter that he seemed not to have the heart to continue with the *Aeneid*, as he had originally intended.[86]

Talon's works form a unit with Ramus', which they were intended to complement, and should be mentioned here. Except for the *Rhetoric*, the *Institutiones oratoriae* out of which the *Rhetoric* grows, and contributions to Ramus' *Dialectic*, Talon's production consists almost entirely of commentaries on Cicero, plus a brief attack on Porphyry's *Isagoge* or *Introduction* which was traditionally attached to Aristotle's *Organon*, a brief commentary on the first book of the *Nicomachean Ethics* which includes a brush with Aristotle on method, and a minuscule oration on rhetoric.

Ramus' lectures were tremendous rhetorical performances. They manifested a confident spontaneity. We have it from Nancel that he commonly lectured from very brief notes, three lines of which would at times suffice for an hour's continuous performance in Latin, and that he wrote down what he had said only afterwards in a rough draft which he turned over to Nancel to tidy up and transcribe.[87] The various "arts," such as his *Dialectic*, may not have been given as lectures, but it is from the lecture series commenting on dialectic — the *Remarks on Aristotle* and the *Training in Dialectic* in their almost annual revisions — that the *Dialectic* finally emerges, and all the arts or textbooks were normally closely associated with his oral lectures on or around the art in question. Most of Ramus' lectures in print seem to be those which he delivered as regius professor for public audiences, although some — at least those delivered before his appointment in 1551, such as the *Evaluation of Quintilian's Rhetoric* and *Brutus' Problems* — were those which he delivered simply as a master of arts, to how public an audience, it is difficult to say.

We are told that Ramus' public lectures were attended by huge crowds, at least at times, and his popularity with the teen-agers who made up his audience seems quite credible. Even the groundlings among the *bejauni* or "yellow-beaks," as the newcomers at the university were called, would have their souls torn out of them by the histrionics of this man, whose remarks, whether concerned with a literary text or with dialectic or physics, are salted with constant denunciation of the authors his fellow professors were teaching and peppered everywhere with "Holy Jupiter!" and "Good God!" and who roared all this out with the most spectacular declamation and gesture.[88] Even in the days of the quarrelsome and excitable followers of Tartaret, Cranston, the Coronels, and John Major, logic had never been like this.

Although as an administrator, Ramus bettered the teaching at his Collège de Presles and, less directly, throughout the University of Paris and among the regius professors by agitating the subject of aims and methods, the essential ambiguity of his educational "reform" can be seen in the fact that, although he followed the humanist line in calling for more training in classical Latin, Greek, and even Hebrew (to this last, he, like most of those who talked loudly about it, never got around), so as to make the ancient texts rather than scholastic aridities the focus of attention, the end result of the use of his "analysis," logical or dialectical, rhetorical, and grammatical, on a text was inevitably the recreation of aridities and of *Wissenschaft* in its most opprobrious sense, as the history of Ramism shows.

As an educational administrator, Ramus deviated in other ways from twentieth-century ideals. Although, despite his reticence in strange company, he had generally a pleasant smile and manner, he nevertheless was given to beating and kicking students unmercifully at home in his Collège de Presles, in outbursts of temper during which he became the terror of pupils and prefects alike, but during which he never swore — for which, Nancel adds, "you have to give him credit."[89] He lived, of course, in a tradition which regarded teaching as impossible without severe physical punishment, but here, as in his anti-Aristotelianism, he seems to have somewhat exceeded the norm.

6. THE METAMORPHOSIS AND SIGNIFICANCE OF RAMUS' REPUTATION

Students of intellectual history generally agree with Ramus himself that his significance is to be found in his dialectic or logic.[90] But what this dialectic or logic is remains largely an unanswered question. Although described quite accurately by Carl von Prantl, T. W. Baldwin, and others as a rhetorical dialectic or logic, Ramus himself considered it to be totally uncontaminated by rhetoric. This clash of views suggests that the relationship of Ramist dialectic and of the companion Ramist rhetoric to the complicated rhetorico-logical tradition at the center of Western thought is far from simple.

Such a conclusion is reinforced by the shifts in Ramus' own reputation among his contemporaries and near-contemporaries. Tabulation of the editions of the *Dialectic* and *Rhetoric* shows that Ramus was first accepted as a rhetorician. Thus, by 1572, only thirteen editions of the Ramist *Dialectic* had appeared as against twenty-eight of the *Rhetoric*, and his classical commentaries, which quickly went off the market after his death, were being published in quantity. But when Ramism reached its full strength, it did so as a movement specializing in logic and "method," although Ramist logic cannot be taken seriously as a logic, and although "method" of the Ramist and other sorts is radically, as detailed study will show in a later chapter, something excised from rhetoric and grafted into the logic textbooks.

The interaction of dialectic and/or logic and rhetoric has been discussed in the past from various points of view by von Prantl, Grabmann, and many others. Because closer study of Ramus' career and Ramism and recent work in the history of ideas have made possible new insights into this interaction, we shall re-examine it here.

CHAPTER III

THE STRUCTURE OF REFORM

God made the world and turned
it over to man for disputation.
— Medieval Adage.

I. THE M. A. THESIS: ITS CONTEXT

THE anti-Aristotelian thesis, *Quaecumque ab Aristotele dicta essent, commentitia esse*, with which Ramus reputedly began his career and which is the standard tag associated with his name everywhere today, is the accepted starting point for the study of Ramism. Ramus' stagey anti-Aristotelianism has always attracted lovers of partisan histrionics, and they have made the so-called thesis something that it was not. Waddington, for instance, and those who follow him still picture Ramus as defending this thesis valiantly from morn to noon, from noon to dewy eve, against the assembled arts faculty, and as finally forcing them, at the point of one of their own brittle syllogisms, to grant him his degree.[1] This is nonsense, of course. Only Waddington's determination to make Ramus a hero, implemented by what appears to be ignorance of university practice makes a view such as this possible.

Ramus, as earlier biographical notes and our present knowledge of university procedure make plain, had his degree before he defended any thesis. The objectors challenged him "in vain," certainly — but only because he could not lose. This oral presentation of a subject and its defense, known as the *inceptio*, was strictly speaking not an examination, but the first exercise of the new master of arts' freshly acquired right and duty of teaching. It was an *inceptio* or "commencement" in the literal sense, and the protagonist risked little more than a class valedictorian does today in attending his own commencement exercises (we have changed the formalities, but kept the name). All the tests having been finished well before, the *inceptio* was required as a formality because the conferring of the master's degree was the reception of a hitherto apprentice teacher or "bachelor" into the teacher's guild. Like other similar inductions into trade confraternities, this one was not complete until the former apprentice had done once what he was now qualified to do as a master — in this case teach.[2]

As the equivalent of a present-day commencement, a master's *inceptio* was routine and a generally boring affair. Instances are known where, for such performances, after every member of a faculty had been ceremoniously invited, the university had actually to dispatch a posse to force at least one of the reluctant invitees to accept the invitation and come.[3]

Not only were all M.A. *inceptiones* extremely routine, but even the most spectacular theses imaginable were routine. This was because of the tradition of dealing with "sophismata" or startling paradoxes which, until the sixteenth century, had formed a regular part of the scholastic logical tradition and which, even much later, echoed in the disputatious university atmosphere.[4] The many scholastic treatises devoted to sophismata are only now becoming known, and with them, the similarity between the medieval logic (long forgotten by those who think of themselves as neoscholastics) and modern "mathematical" logic or "logistics." In an edition in use at Paris when Ramus was studying there, Ralph Strode (Chaucer's friend, "Philosophical Strode") among dozens of others, gives us samples of sophismata — wrapped up, to make it worse, in an *obligatio* ("Let it be posited that," etc.). For example:

> Here is another sophisma. Let it be posited that the term man alone signifies nonman. If this assertion is then denied, the contrary follows, for it follows that the term man alone signifies brute or ass; therefore it signifies nonman . . . .[5]

In an intellectual climate where this sort of thing had been the fare of teenagers, even a thesis such as that of Ramus would be only one apple in a cartload. Moreover, this very anti-Aristotelian thesis, which is supposed to have established Ramus as the antischolastic par excellence, really shows him as the scholastic par excellence, reviving at least in echo the *sophisma* tradition which was dying off when he came up to the university.[6] Far from appearing as an intellectual knight-errant sent in from outside to dispatch scholasticism, Ramus appears here as part of the apparatus which is cast off while scholastic logic is committing suicide.

2. THE M. A. THESIS: ITS AUTHENTICITY

Did Ramus ever defend the famed thesis, *Quaecumque ab Aristotele dicta essent, commentitia esse?* If he did, because of the routine character of M. A. theses in general and of spectacular sophisms in particular, Ramus himself and his contemporaries, almost to a man, attached no significance whatsoever to the event — despite his subsequent anti-Aristotelian career. All references to this thesis seem to trace, directly or indirectly, to Johann Thomas Freige. A rabid follower of Ramus at Basle and a phenomenally dull pedant, he let the world know of the thesis (he calls it not *thesis* but *problema*) in his often reprinted *Life of Peter Ramus* first published in 1575, three years after Ramus' death.[7] Freige gives no source for the *problema*, but says that from his success in defending it began Ramus' interest in going further into the Aristotelian question. Freige's interpretation thus makes Ramus' whole career a trajectory whose initial momentum comes from an intellectual duel between Ramus and all comers at the University of Paris in which the issues were as clear as scholastic formalism could make them and in which Ramus won a crushing victory.

It is always possible that Freige may have had such a story from Ramus himself. He had met Ramus personally during the latter's visit to Basle in 1569 and 1570, where Freige had been studying law and teaching rhetoric.[8] But his biography of Ramus does not derive much from personal contact with his subject (although it is written with deep personal feeling for him). The sources Freige used turn out to be largely printed works available in Basle editions. He quotes them extensively, but anyone could have had access to them: Ramus' orations and controversies with Schegk, the autobiographical passages in Ramus' Lectures on Dialectic, and Talon's Academia. These sources do not discuss the thesis subject at all. Since the term commentitius occurs repeatedly in Ramus' work independently of the thesis, it is possible that Freige's persuasion that Ramus defended such a thesis may have been due to some misunderstanding and that the actual wording of the thesis arose in Freige's mind as an echo out of Ramus' later works, of which he was the doting editor.

Theophilus Banosius, another biographer, had known Ramus at Heidelberg too, if only briefly.[9] His dependence on written sources is likewise great. Printed first in 1576 and dedicated to Sir Philip Sidney, his Life of Peter Ramus freely uses Freige's newly published life, even when quoting purportedly from Ramus himself. For, in citing Ramus' autobiographical passage from the Lectures on Dialectic, Banosius repeats Freige's erroneous assignment of the passage to book V instead of to book IV. This abject dependence on Freige makes Banosius' failure to mention the anti-Aristotelian thesis all the more astonishing, and one wonders whether he considered it untrue or merely insignificant. One might perhaps suspect that a reason was that Banosius was uncertain of the philosophical stand of his dedicatee, Sir Philip Sidney, and did not want to risk antagonizing him on the Aristotelian issue. But this reason is unconvincing both because of Sidney's known Ramist sympathies, and because Banosius does not hesitate throughout to advertise Ramus' general anti-Aristotelianism.

Strangest of all is Nicolas de Nancel's omission of the thesis in his Life of Peter Ramus published in 1599. Nancel had been Ramus' close associate and understudy at the Collège de Presles for thirty years — he remarks with obvious distaste that he was often referred to as "little Ramus"[10] — and he had a devouring passion for the unusual or spectacular. Moreover, he treats of Ramus' reception of the M. A. in great detail, noting that Pierre's mother and uncle stood the expenses of the party which Pierre gave on the occasion and later collected interest from Pierre for their loan.[11] But not a word about any anti-Aristotelian subject.

To these surprising omissions must be added others equally surprising. In the face of the continual battle which rages around Ramus' anti-Aristotelianism, the thesis is curiously absent from the armory of vituperation on either side. Ramus' enemies[12] do not, so far as I can find, taunt him with the brashness of such a thesis as they constantly taunt him with the brashness of his two anti-Aristotelian books, *Training in Dialectic* and *Remarks on Aristotle*. And Ramus himself does not brag about having successfully brought off the defense of such a thesis, as we might expect him to do. Only after his death, under Freige's sponsorship, did the thesis become the *cause célèbre* which it remains to our present day.

Ramus himself assigns the beginnings of his anti-Aristotelianism to a context entirely different from such a public performance. He introduces a detailed account of his reform of logic retrospectively in one of his frequent revisions of his original *Remarks on Aristotle*.[13] The account says nothing about the commencement thesis. It does say that he began to rework the logical arts after the *inceptio* was all over with (*iam ut absolutus artium scilicit magister, philosophica laurea donatus essem*). This statement establishes a significant fact regarding the starting point of Ramism which makes its two-century trajectory the product of quite different vectors than those Freige suggests. For it means that Ramus was getting down to the business of teaching after his degree, and his anti-Aristotelianism developed as a result of a practical pedagogical situation rather than as a result of intellectual insight. His disgust with Peripateticism appears thus not when he is facing the best intellects the University of Paris could muster during the defense of his thesis but when he is faced with a prospective class of logic students in their early teens. The failure of modern scholarship to notice this fact can be traced to Waddington, who gives Ramus' account of his reworking of logic in a mutilated translation.[14] Waddington drops the section ascribing the anti-Aristotelian beginnings to the teaching period to make the translation fit his statement that Ramus' anti-Aristotelianism belongs to the period before he finished his degree work.

In replying to Ramus' 1551 attack on the University of Paris curriculum, Pierre Galland gives an account of Ramus' pre-1543 attacks on Aristotle. This account, also, makes no express mention of any anti-Aristotelian master's thesis, but does give details concerning Ramus' early stands which are worth noting. It reads as follows:

Now let us turn back to your inconsistencies. I shall recount what your first achievement was during your noviceship (*tui tyrocinii*) in your fight against Aristotle, in case you yourself cannot recall it. First you denied that the works of Aristotle which have come down to us were by Aristotle, on the grounds that you could not find in them the golden river of eloquence which Cicero so often says he found in Aristotle. You maintained that these works were the productions of some other upstart and crotchety sophist. When your friends had with great trouble won you away from this position, you began to say that the books were not Aristotle's in the sense that they were corrupted from their original grace and beauty and contaminated first by Appelicon, then by Tyrannion, and that what pass for Aristotle's works today are only schemata (*tabulae*) of his works drawn up by Andronicus. When you were warned and informed by your friends again that the authority of Plato and Strabo to which you appealed worked rather against you, you came around to saying that there were two kinds of works by Aristotle, one of them being the exoteric [the other being called acroamatic], and that in these exoteric works your richness of style was to be found. You were convinced by the testimony, you said, of all the commentators on Aristotle, and by Galen, Cicero, and Pliny, who, you said, included in their works whole pages of Aristotle, copied out word for word, for the true Aristotle was inimitable by others, and the fabric of his style could be recognized wherever it was found. Then suddenly, changing sail as sailors do in a storm, you took another tack. You no longer denied that these books were Aristotle's, but when you were passed over and another lecturer on Aristotle was appointed to our college [apparently Francesco Vicomercato, named professor of Greek and Latin philosophy in the "college" of regius professors in 1542], you opened your attack, and, openly declaring yourself his enemy and the enemy of all Aristotelians, you struck out at these distinguished persons in your *Remarks* [*on Aristotle*] and, to wipe out the name of Aristotle, you published your *Training in Dialectic*, a wonderful fabrication made up not of art alone but of nature and exercise as well. Since your little twin brother [i.e., Talon] brought out his commentaries on this work of yours, in which he praised you to the skies and compared you with Aristotle — excrement with sugar (*oletum videlicet cum saccharo*) — and then hammered Aristotle into the earth, it becomes rather difficult to see on what grounds you can manage as you actually do to read and explain Aristotle to your students today.[15]

Galland is evidently referring here to the period before 1543, when the *Remarks on Aristotle* and the *Training in Dialectic* were published. But, in place of any reference to the 1536 M. A. thesis, which would have been an event of rather less than twenty-four hours' duration, we have an account of an apparently much longer seesaw developmental process. This is presented as the *beginning* of Ramus' anti-Aristotelianism and echoes to some extent in Ramus' *Remarks on Aristotle*, where we find hints that Aristotle did not write the works attributed to him curiously interwoven with recriminations against him for writing them.[16] The evolution, or rather series of spastic postures, which Galland adverts to here, probably occurred in lectures which Ramus was giving early in his teaching career — and, we are here made aware, giving with an eye to making a loud academic noise which might result in nomination as regius professor, as it eventually did.

In view of the curious silence of all but one in Ramus' numerous entourage and of the competing accounts of Ramus' anti-Aristotelian beginnings, one can only conclude that it is quite possible that Ramus did not defend at his *inceptio* the anti-Aristotelian thesis commonly attributed to him. It is quite certain that, if he did, it attracted no particular attention and involved no great show of courage, but only quick footwork and bravado. Ramus' own account of his anti-Aristotelian beginnings itself does not include the supposed thesis in the picture. To this account, in some detail, we now turn.

3. RAMUS' OWN ACCOUNT OF HIS REFORM

In ascribing a post-1536 setting (a pedagogical rather than a debate setting) to Ramus' anti-Aristotelian beginnings, Galland actually agrees with Ramus. For Ramus traces his reform of logic (and hence of everything else) to his interest in "use." He wants to put logic to the "use" of erudition (*ad eruditionis usum*). *Usus*, with the other term *exercitatio*, is a telling term employed by Ramus in respect to practice in general, but particularly in respect to students' classroom exercise or drill. The result is that the term makes doubly evident the fact that the crisis of dialectical or logical reform came to a head for Ramus during his early teaching experience. We can let him speak for himself:

After my regular three and a half years of scholastic philosophy, mostly the *Organon* of Aristotle's logical works, terminating with the conferring of my master's degree, I began to consider how I should put the logical arts to use. But they had left me no better off in history, antiquity, rhetoric, or poetry. ["Use" evidently refers not only to teaching but particularly to teaching these "literary" subjects which the humanist trend made compulsory for young boys. Although officially qualified to teach any and all "arts," including philosophy subjects, as well as grammar and rhetoric, the new master, such as Ramus was, in practice had often to work up to philosophy through the subjects lower in the curriculum.]

Thus, I went back to my study of rhetoric, ended when I began my philosophy course four years before [there had been, roughly, a half year between the spring M. A. and this return to the study of rhetoric at the opening of classes in late autumn, which made the three and one-half years a full four]. My aim was to put the logical books of the *Organon* to the service of erudition (*ad eruditionis usum*).[17]

More plainly, Ramus proposes here to apply to *eruditio* — that is, to the material of history, antiquity, rhetoric, oratory, and poetry — the rules of logic, and thus in effect to cut short the reign of scholasticism. But he proposes to do it in a way which will extend the purlieus of logic all the way from the higher reaches of the curriculum (philosophy) to the lower (humanities). The maneuver is particularly interesting in that it is new in his day and thus reveals at least one kind of excessive logicizing as a Renaissance rather than as a medieval phenomenon.

To effect his maneuver, Ramus needs a logic which can be taught with dispatch. His account of how he arrived at such a logic by a series of transactions with textbooks can best be given, as it continues, in brief paraphrase (with numerals added to mark the stages on the trail of his thought):

> For implementing my program, I discovered (1) the distribution of dialectic [that is, a division of dialectic into two "parts," invention and judgment] in Cicero [*Topica* 1, etc.] and (2) in Quintilian. (3) I found that Rudolph Agricola was the only one who had envisioned a dialectic fitted to humanistic aims (*usum humanitatis*), but that Agricola explained only a part of the art [his work is restricted to invention, as its title indicates, *De inventione dialectica libri tres*].
>
> At this point, I finally hit on (4) Galen, whom I found commending to (5) Hippocrates not (6) Aristotle but (7) Plato, whose dialogues I then read avidly, getting from his Socratic dialogues the equation that to discourse (*disserere*) is the same as to use one's reason (*ratione uti*), and hence that the distribution of dialectic which I had come across applied to the whole mental apparatus (*logica*). (8) Thereupon, I began to think that Aristotle's authority was a deception.
>
> Nevertheless, I am grateful to Galen, more grateful to Plato, and most grateful of all to Aristotle, for from his *Posterior Analytics* I learned about the matter and form of an art.

This passage enables us to take a preliminary measure of some of the furniture of Ramus' mind. If we can believe him, Plato's dialogues are meaningful chiefly because they give sweep to a definition of dialectic found in Cicero and Quintilian. This is an important clue to the nature of Ramus' much-touted "Platonism." Aristotle is a fraud because the definition of dialectic found in Cicero and Quintilian, as explained (in Ramus' enterprising anachronism) out of Plato on the basis of a recommendation from Galen, is much simpler than what is found in Aristotle's *Organon*. Nevertheless the *Organon* has a point to recommend it — namely, its trick of breaking down the content of the mind in terms of an analogy best known to Ramus and to arts scholasticism generally from physics, that is to say, the analogy of matter and form.

The equation of dialectic and logic, which Ramus goes to such lengths here to explain, is simply what he and tens of thousands of other first-year philosophy students had soaked up, directly or indirectly, from the opening of Peter of Spain's *Summulae logicales*. This work served as the medieval and early Renaissance introduction to Aristotle, and thus Ramus is here doing no more than proposing the common, and careless, medieval interpretation of Aristotle against what Aristotle himself says. This and similar transactions in Ramus are carried on under cover, because, true to the humanist fiction, Ramus will never own, not even to himself, that his position is ultimately derivative from anything postclassical (Agricola's is a mediating role: it recovers the classical possessions). This stubborn antiquarianism interferes with the real perspectives also of Ramus' distinction between invention and judgment here, for this distinction, which he fathers only on Cicero, gains its more than Ciceronic urgency in Ramus' milieu from the live interest in *via inventionis* and *via iudicii* which peppers the discussion on "method" in late scholasticism.

This studied maneuvering of his sources enables Ramus to moor one item of his dialectic here, another item there, in classical antiquity. But neither in this passage, nor elsewhere does he explain the cavalier picking and choosing which results in his particular mix. There is certainly no insight into processes of cognition or communication or into logical structure to give his amalgam an interior consistency inviting theoretical explanation. One is left with the impression — which turns out to be the correct one — that the assemblage is made up of items whose presence in Ramus' consciousness must be explained, on infra-intellectual grounds, in terms of basic attitudes and symbols which possessed his mind. Items deriving from such sources are held together mostly from the outside under the sheer pressure of the need to provide something "practical" to teach youngsters in the classroom. Ramus' account of how he put the assemblage together immediately follows the passage last paraphrased and is itself paraphrased briefly thus:

> In Plato, I found the Socratic method, which is to withdraw from the senses and from human testimony to calm of mind and freedom of judgment (*aequitas animi et libertas iudicii*), for it is foolish for a philosopher to look to human opinion rather than to the thing known. 'Well,' I said to myself, 'what is to keep us from Socratizing a little?'

As his adversaries liked to remind him, Ramus often quoted others in order to impute to their words his own meaning; that is what he has done here. For, in the sense in which the term ordinarily applies to Socrates, Ramus does not really "Socratize" at all. The Socratic method, the maieutic method of procedure by a vocal dialectic in which the more knowing and more humble man questions and the less knowing learns by formulating his answers, has no place whatsoever in Ramist theory or practice. What he reads into "Socratic method" is clear in the light of Ramus' earlier remarks about the incompleteness of Rudolph Agricola's work. His notion, we observe, turns on the "freedom of *judgment*" which one is to cultivate by calm of mind. This fact is capital; judgment is for Ramus simply the second half of dialectic. This half, Ramus had just announced, was neglected by the Dutch humanist Agricola. A sponsor for it is needed, and Ramus hits on Socrates. Because this reputedly "Socratic method" is Ramist judgment, it seems natural to Ramus, here in retrospect, to set it against human opinion. For, in Ramist dialectic human "testimony" belongs to invention, which is precisely the other half of dialectic which judgment complements. Ramus' account runs on, again in loose translation:

> Next, I took the notion of matter and form of an art from the *Posterior Analytics*, going to the *Organon* and asking myself how much of all this really belongs to these principles and laws (*principia et leges*) [that is, matter and form — in

what sense these are "laws" Ramus does not explain here, although he treats the subject elsewhere under method].

From the Platonic rule of categorical method (*ex illa Platonica categoricae methodi regula*), that is, from the calm examination of the thing known [in this case, *logica* itself], I determined the final and general end (*summus et generalissimus finis*) of *logica*, which is expressed by its definition, *ars bene disserendi*, which in turn is just as general as *uti ratione*. My definition I could find nowhere in the *Organon*.

So much the worse for the *Organon*, concludes our author. The definition which Ramus here reproaches Aristotle for not producing, and which will be discussed later on in detail, is one which comes into his mind as part of the medieval rhetorical heritage transmitted through St. Augustine from Cicero, the ultimate verbatim source of Ramus' *ars bene disserendi*.[18] The definition exists in Ramus' mind with a companion medieval piece: the conviction that dialectic (which for Aristotle is a logic dealing with and terminating in probabilities, such as is used in debate or in discussion of hypotheses) and scientific logic (such as is used in geometrical reasoning) are quite the same thing. Ramus' account runs on, in summary:

Finding no division of logic in the *Organon*, I called to mind (*commemini*) the division of dialectic into invention and judgment. With this in mind, I went back to the *Organon* and found the chaos fall into order — a great light had dawned on me.

Aristotle's *Organon* is, of course, no self-contained unit, but a collection of his separate logical treatises (or most of them — his *Art of Rhetoric* could well have been included, or appended, but commonly it was not) put together by his followers. There is a good deal of overlapping and conflict between the treatises. The fact that, with the long-established notions of invention and judgment (discussed at length in Chapter V), Ramus could instill into this sprawling mass an order which Aristotle himself was far from attributing to it and on which his followers could never agree, suggests that these two well-worn notions have an interesting future before them. Ramus' term for his own "calling to mind," *commemini*, is a cognate of the *commentitia* which occurs in his reported anti-Aristotelian master's thesis and in many of his other charges against Aristotle, and suggests that Ramus' indictment of Aristotle is based on the idea that the Stagirite did not properly "call to mind" his logical and other works. As will be seen below, this is pretty close to what Ramus means.

Having discovered that things could be so readily clicked into place by means of his definition and division, Ramus goes on, he knew that he had been deceived by false scholastic opinions. Aristotle was really a great lover of "Socratic method" (that is, of calm judgment), he adds, and this mere thought touches off a dithyramb (here given in exact translation):

Please excuse me, I beg you, if I speak frankly with you. But would you believe how happy I was at finding this out, how moved, how carried off my feet? . . . I can only thank God in the name of Galen, Plato, and Aristotle, who gave these men to me to save me from the waves and tempests . . . .[19]

4. THE MEANING OF *Commentitia*

Galland makes Ramus' initial anti-Aristotelianism consist, as has just been seen, in the assertion that the works attributed to Aristotle were not really his. Is it possible that the thesis which Freige says Ramus presented, *Quaecumque ab Aristotele dicta essent, commentitia esse*, if it was ever presented, meant precisely this, that the works attributed to Aristotle were by another or others? It seems not, for the word *commentitius* occurs normally in Ramus' writing in quite a different sense and context. In fact, it is a key term, so that, whatever error Freige may have made in reporting the thesis, he did not err in imputing the term *commentitia* to his master's vocabulary. The wording Freige gives us, whether his own or Ramus', is representative of Ramus' mind at least from 1543 on.

Recent scholarship has become aware of the capital importance of this term and of the possibility of its having complex nuances. Many cautious writers today cite the thesis in Latin simply for what it is worth. Earlier writers were more brash. Hegel, relying on Buhle and on the common identification, particularly in Germany, of *dicta* with *docta*, makes it read, "Alles, was Aristoteles gelehrt habe, sey nicht war."[20] In the same vein, the most recent attempt to deal with the term interprets it as signifying a lie.[21] A few decades ago, Graves and others had taken the word quite simply to mean "false."[22] They have early precedent for this in Niceron, and in the *Encyclopédistes* d'Alembert and Diderot.[23] These latter two actually interpolate their own *falsa* in the Latin to make the wording come out even with eighteenth-century notions of what an attack on Aristotle should be.[24] Professor Morison is aware that, under cover of bravado, the wording may conceal some solid circumspection, and he records that at the master's commencement in 1536, Ramus defended "the thesis that everything in Aristotle was forged or false," a wording which Professor Miller slightly adapts.[25] The authors of these last two renditions are evidently casting about in Ramus' writings to account for this term more fully.

It is true that we find there the notion of forgery connected tentatively with Aristotle, when Ramus remarks that the only way to restore Aristotle's reputation is to show that the writings attributed to him (at least in the form in which we have them) are not his.[26] But the forgery notion is not directly connected with *commentitia*, and it is to this term itself in Ramus' works that we must turn for further explanation.

Reputedly the greatest Latin stylist since Cicero,[27] Ramus used terms, with some rather notable exceptions, in conformity with the strictest classical practice. *Commentitius*, with its cognate verb *comminiscor*, comes from the root MEN, from which derive the common Latin terms having to do not with truth directly but with memory (*meminisse, memoria*), as well as the word *mens*, corresponding roughly to the word "mind," (as in the human mind, the mind of this or that man). The ordinary Latin word for a lie, *mendacium*, is related to this same root, but the words in the *comminiscor* group have a distinctive orientation of their own, due probably to the *com-* suffix, which usually suggests assemblage or grouping together. *Comminiscor* does not mean strictly to lie or to falsify, therefore, so much as to invent irresponsibly, to let the imagination or storehouse of memory run riot. It covers the same situation as the child's admission in English, "I made it all up," or as the more adult notion of "fabrication." All this substantiates P. Albert Duhamel's assertion that *commentitia* is to be understood in the sense of "artificial," "fabricated," or "contrived," and only by inference therefore false.[28] Ramus thus attacks the elaborate Aristotelian logical machinery as an unnaturally complicated and ridiculous one from the practical point of view. His attack, as Professor Duhamel explains, was essentially the same as those enunciated by the humanist world for some generations, having been made earlier by Lorenzo Valla in his *Disputationes dialecticae*, by Erasmus in his *Anti-Barbari*, and less directly by the writers of the *Epistles of Obscure Men*.

Professor Duhamel's interpretation, based on the general tenor of Ramus' critique, is confirmed by examining Ramus' actual use of the term *commentitia* in a variety of contexts. Thus, in a scolding Ramus gives Cicero, the *commentitia* are "irrelevancies" which fail because they weaken the structure of his art of rhetoric as a whole.[29] Or *commentitia* are like dreams, where fancies are too loosely associated.[30] "The *commentitia* of Aristotle" are thought of by Ramus as opposed not to *true* arts or to *true* precepts of arts, but rather to "the precepts of arts *ranged in a universally consistent and methodical order*."[31] With this assertion is connected his charge that Aristotle's doctrine is full of irrelevancies, that it is not "homogeneous."[32] There are dozens of other instances of Ramus' use of *commentitia*, some of them less clear in their exact signification than the instances cited here, but insofar as they are clear, only reinforcing this signification.[33]

Capital examples of *commentitia* for Ramus are the mnemonic constructs *barbara, celarent, baralipton*, and the rest, used for classifying the moods of the syllogism, the vowel "a" in these words standing for universal affirmative propositions, "e" for universal negatives, and so on. These mnemonic schemes are *commentitia* not because they are untrue but because they are "external," or, as we should say, arbitrary.[34] Ramus made much of basing memory on what he called "natural" schemes. Freige's wording, *Quaecumque ab Aristotele dicta essent, commentitia esse*, therefore, can be finally paraphrased: *All the things that Aristotle has said are inconsistent because they are poorly sys-*

tematized and can be called to mind only by the use of arbitrary mnemonic devices. The thesis is thus worded rather more cunningly than has been commonly believed.

Ramus criticizes Aristotle's "structure" of his sciences not because it was too mechanistic a thing, but precisely because he envisioned a more solid structure of his own. Significantly, in explaining his own procedure in creating his own dialectic, he launches directly into the *commentitia* area for a serviceable term. "I called to mind . . .," he says; "I assembled out of the storeroom of memory . . . ." The word he uses is *commemini*,[35] and the echo we catch in this term is from Rudolph Agricola, as will be seen later.

5. RAMUS ON THE HISTORY OF DIALECTIC

Ramus' account of his reform of dialectic and his notion of *commentitia* is associated with a special view of the history of dialectic. This view finds expression in different forms throughout his works, but it always supposes a Golden Age of philosophy when the "true" dialectic not only existed but was all of philosophy and was joined to eloquence, followed by a long period of darkness, which was in turn followed by Rudolph Agricola (a kind of Ur-Ramus), and then by Ramus himself. Not all Ramus' contemporaries by any means accepted this simplistic picture. His adversaries such as Antonio de Gouveia, Jacques Charpentier, Adrien Turnèbe, and Jacob Schegk, taunted him with it,[36] although they, too, were happy to write off the medieval interlude, and were willingly convinced, as we can no longer be, that it had no effect on their own outlook.

In one of its typical and most complete forms, Ramus' notion of the history of dialectic can be summarized from his 1555 *Dialectique*:

> Even more than the arts of grammar, rhetoric, arithmetic, and geometry, dialectic has been a coöperative development over the centuries. Plato makes Prometheus a teacher of this art. The Pythagoreans, Heraclitus, Democritus, and Hippocrates set it down in fragments. Protagoras published many books on it. Zeno had a school of dialectic, so that Aristotle in the *Sophistics* thought him the discoverer of the art. Socrates made much of it as that by which he knew his own ignorance. His disciples, Anaxarchus, Aristippus, Euclid, Antisthenes, and Plato, treated of dialectic with care, Anaxarchus and the Pyrrhonians and the New Academicians, indeed, misusing it to overthrow certitude and science. Epicurus, after annihilating dialectic, made it the third part of his philosophy under the name of "canonic" (*Canonique*). Euclid's followers were known as "Dialecticians." Antisthenes' followers, the Cynics, and their followers, the Stoics, wrote many books on dialectic.
>
> Although he wrote no treatise on dialectic, but rather the Socratic dialogues, nevertheless Plato is the prince of dialecticians (*le prince de ceste louange*), having noted the part of dialectic so perfectly in many places.
>
> The Academicians and Peripatetics, the issue of Plato — and among the former

of these, especially Speusippus, Xenocrates, Polemon, Crates, Crantor, Arcesilaus, Dion, Lacydes, Carneades, Clitomachus, and Cicero's teacher Philo — all worked at dialectic, at least in practicing it, if not in theorizing about it.

Aristotle wrote at least 130 [*sic!*] books on dialectic. He disputed long and hard against the opinions of other philosophers, "par liberté propre à tous grandz philosophes," and exercised rhetoric with his dialectic. Aristotle's followers in dialectic were Theophrastus (the chief of his followers), Straton, Lycon, [Demetrius] Phalereus, and Galen. Galen was the last. He closed the door of dialectic, which was never after opened until our day. Adrastus, Aspasius, [Alexander] Aphrodisius, and the other Peripatetics lost the true love of wisdom and became servile followers of Aristotle.

Among the books of the ancients gathered together by Aristotle, there are thirty-five books of "arguments" and "disposition and judgment," which constitute the true dialectic (*la vrai Dialectique*): the seventeen books of the Aristotelian *Organon* (without Porphyry's *Introduction*), the four books of Aristotle's *Rhetoric*, and the fourteen books of his "philosophy" (*philosophie*) [i.e., the *Metaphysics*].[37]

Ramus makes no mention here of any individual between the last named and himself, thereby passing over the entire medieval (and most of the Roman) period without a word. Elsewhere he gives credit to Rudolph Agricola for restoring to an "incredulous" generation the "true dialectic" of the ancients, of which his own was the daughter.[38]

6. RAMUS AND ITALIAN HUMANISM

Insofar as the development of Ramist dialectic is part of the history of humanism, it has definite relationships with Italy. Nevertheless, despite the increased contact between France and Italy under Louis XII and Francis I, the connections between Ramism and Italian humanism remain curiously indirect. This is evident when we look for individual representatives of Italian culture who may have affected Ramus.

The climax of direct Italian humanist influence at Paris has been put at around 1485 in the time of Girolamo Balbi's lectures,[39] a generation before Ramus' birth. It is noteworthy that of Ramus' contemporaries only Galland mentions an Italian, Valla, among Ramus'[40] predecessors in the reconstitution of dialectic. And he brings in Valla to show that Ramus' Ciceronian and vaguely Stoic anti-Aristotelianism was unoriginal, being everywhere in the air.[41] Mario Nizzoli, the anti-Aristotelian Italian contemporary of Ramus, is not named by Galland. Among the forerunners of Ramus cited by his contemporaries, the almost total dominance of Dutch or German, and particularly Rhineland, dialecticians — Rudolph Agricola (the principal forerunner), Cornelius Agrippa, Caesarius, Hegendorf, Titelmans, Melanchthon, Latomus, Sturm — shows that the age was well aware that the Italian influence on Ramus, however real, came filtered through the Rhine valley rather than over more direct routes.

Ramus' moderate Ciceronianism alines him with North European humanism rather than with Italian, and Ramus himself, despite his enthusiasm for the classics and dislike of "barbarians," is careful not to associate any of his aims or successes too closely with Italy. When he rehearses the humanist achievements which he hopes to see emulated in Paris, he lumps the Italian contribution with the humanist successes in Germany, Britain, and other parts of France, taking care at the same time never to place Italy first in his enumeration of these countries.[42] His account of the decay and revival of learning explains that after the "Goths" destroyed learning in Italy and the Turks in Greece, it was Gaul which first recovered some knowledge of letters in the time of Charlemagne, and that when Constantinople was sacked by the Turks a further recovery was made as scholars fled to the Latins (*Latini*) of Italy *and* France (Gaul).[43] This account mentions the Greeks and Levantines Lascaris, Bessarion, Gaza, and Trapezuntius, but avoids any suggestion that the Italians acted as mediators between antiquity and Ramus' France.

Furthermore, Ramus' writings often manifest positive dislike of the Italian type of humanism. For example, he exclaims that the Parisian educational tradition has stood always for the cultivation of the mind alone, not for the cultivation of mind and body after the manner of the Italians.[44] He is referring, of course, to the regimen of humanist gymnastics to which even Rudolph Agricola was devoted in Italy. Several major incidents in Ramus' life also suggest antipathy to Italians or Italian culture. His initiative in ousting the Sicilian Dampestre Cosel from the regius chair of mathematics can perhaps be explained by the man's incompetence and Ramus' own preëminence among the regius professors.[45] But there remain the more significant facts that he refused the chair offered him at Bologna and that he never visited Italy in his travels. Even minor personal encounters with Italians proved occasionally unfortunate, for Nancel, who details Ramus' cordial relations with other foreigners, German, Swiss, and Scottish, reports how when some Italians had Ramus to dinner and he found that they could speak neither Latin nor French, he left in a huff.[46]

Ramus' anti-Italian bias is particularly noteworthy in the light of his own prowess and reputation as an orator. In a very real sense Italian humanism stood for a rhetorically centered culture opposed to the dialectically or logically centered culture of North Europe. Although in part inspired by Gallic patriotism, Ramus' violent rejection of Italy while he promotes the cause of eloquence thus suggests an uneasiness at his own rhetorical prowess and aims which amounts to something like schizophrenia. The same schizoid outlook is hinted at also in his compulsion to divorce completely the arts of rhetoric and logic and to interpret his own successes as due to true "logic" rather than to rhetoric — despite his rebellion against Northern logical culture. The story of Ramism, in fact, is largely the story of unresolved tensions between the logical and the rhetorical traditions.

Book Two

BACKGROUND

CHAPTER IV

THE DISTANT BACKGROUND: SCHOLASTICISM AND THE QUANTIFICATION OF THOUGHT

> Why do you follow the windings
> of the rivers? Lay hold of the
> source, and you have all.
> — Hugh of St. Victor,
> *Didascalicon*, III, xi.

I. RAMISM, HUMANISM, AND SCHOLASTICISM

IF Ramism arises out of opposition to scholasticism, it arises in devious ways. For the abstract formalism of Ramist rhetoric and dialectic resembles scholasticism more than it does the humanist "eloquence" that spearheaded the antischolasticism of Ramus' day. Ramism thus obliges us to re-examine certain forces at play in the humanist-scholastic quarrel, and in the first place the scholastic logic itself against which the humanists inveigh.

During the last four centuries we have lost sight of what this logic was. For to know what is commonly considered "scholasticism" today is not to know what is peculiar to medieval scholastic logic. Only within the past decade or so, with the work of Bochenski, Boehner, Moody, and others competent not so much in neoscholasticism as in modern formal logic, has the nature of medieval logic begun to be adequately understood. In its major developments this logic went far beyond Aristotle and seems never to have been known to Thomas Aquinas.

Medieval logic in its plenary form was very suggestive of modern formal or "mathematical" logic, also called "logistics," or less aptly, "symbolic logic," which is typified in the work of Boole, Russell, Whitehead, Carnap, Lukasiewicz, or Quine. An inability to develop a sufficiently abstract symbolism and a neglect of a calculus of propositions, to which the Stoics had earlier given elementary treatment, were apparently the chief things which kept medieval logic from developing further in the direction of symbolic logic than it did.[1] Nevertheless, it developed quite far, and one cannot but be struck by the fact that the charges leveled against medieval logic by the humanists — its aridity, its difficulty, its finicky attention to detail, its highly technical vocabulary, its concern with real or apparent impossibilities (*insolubilia, impossibilia, sophismata*), not to mention Ramus' celebrated charge that "ordinary people don't talk like that"[2] — are singularly like the charges often leveled against mathematical logic today.

The definition of the scholastic logic of the Renaissance and later ages is not easy. This logic is marked by a concern with epistemology and psychology rather than with purely formal logic or logical structure. Thus, it is to some extent a continuation of what has been called medieval "philosophical logic,"[3] which may perhaps better be styled theologians' philosophical logic since its chief and best exponents, such as St. Thomas Aquinas and many of his followers, were members of religious orders and hence, at least at Paris, forbidden to teach philosophy in the university; their logical interests tended to be not those of the main scholastic philosophical tradition, but projected from theology. Compared with St. Thomas' epistemological and metaphysical preoccupations, those of the medieval scholastic logicians known strictly as such — arts faculty people — are formally logical in that they are concerned with the labyrinthine complexities of logical structure. Therefore, in its main stream, medieval logic tends to be as innocent of epistemological commitments — without denying either the necessity of epistemology or the existential implication of judgments — as mathematics is, and for much the same reasons.

Its psychological and epistemological orientation makes postmedieval scholastic logic resonant and profound whereas "formal" medieval and modern logic is neither; at the same time it is amateurish and even occasionally imprecise where formal medieval and modern logic is not, or is less so. Post-Renaissance scholastic logic differs sharply from medieval logic in its failure to share the latter's all-consuming interest in the "properties" of terms, such as supposition, ampliation, and restriction. These "properties" bring into prominence the syncategorematic aspects of logical structure ("all," "every," "each," etc.). Neoscholastic logic, when it does treat of the supposition of terms, does so chiefly for commemorative purposes and is inclined to conclude its treatment with explanations detailing the limitations of this kind of thing and calling the discussion back to epistemological or metaphysical territory.[4] Such limitations, of course, are real enough, but they did not distress the medieval scholastic logicians.

Renaissance and post-Renaissance scholasticism, although it perpetuates many features of medieval logic, is also marked by a tendency to endorse the Kantian opinion (more an outlook than opinion) that "Aristotle's logic is perfect: nothing can be added to it, nor has anything been added to it during the course of centuries."[5] In such an outlook neoscholastic logic has quite obliterated its own medieval past. For a clearly discernible addition was made to Aristotle's logic in the medieval treatises on the properties of terms.[6] These theories played a significant role in preparing the way for Renaissance topical logic, and thus, ironically enough, for their own demise.

2. SCHOLASTIC LOGIC: PETER OF SPAIN

For the last decade or two the impression has been growing that Peter of Spain is probably the most important of all scholastics and his *Summulae logicales* the most widely read of all scholastic works. This impression is founded on the originality and influence of his logic but it is confirmed by examining his work in relation with Ramus and Ramus' predecessor, Rudolph Agricola, both of whom reacted against him.

There have been some doubts regarding the identity of the author of the *Summulae logicales* and also the originality of the treatise. But these have been rather definitely resolved. The treatise is a Latin work of Peter of Spain (Petrus Hispanus) a contemporary of St. Thomas Aquinas and, like St. Thomas, a pupil of St. Albert the Great, under whom he studied at Paris.[7] This Peter of Spain is the same as Petrus Juliani, born between 1210 and 1220, the onetime dean of the cathedral chapter at Lisbonne. He made his way ultimately into high ecclesiastical circles as physician to Pope Gregory X and became the latter's successor in 1276, taking the name of John XXI, but died the next year from injuries suffered when the roof in his study collapsed. His principal works are a famous medical treatise, the *Thesaurus pauperum*, and the infinitely more important *Compendium of Logic* or *Summulae logicales*, written probably before 1246. From the seventeenth to the mid-nineteenth century the latter work was commonly thought to be the translation of the Greek *Synopsis* attributed to Michael Psellus. It is now known to be an original composition, one of a small constellation of similar contemporary works such as the *Summulae* of William of Shyreswood (d. 1249) and Lambert of Auxerre (fl. *ca.* 1250). The interrelation of these works is not clear, but Peter of Spain's is historically certainly the most important.

The most interesting act of the pontificate of Peter of Spain was his bull of January 18, 1277, commissioning the bishop of Paris, Etienne Tempier, to inquire into the errors reportedly being taught in the arts and theology courses at Paris. It would be interesting to know if any of the 219 propositions condemned by Tempier, with the Pope's subsequent approval, had been occasioned by the Pope's own logical work of an earlier period. For at a slightly later date, 1340, the condemned errors of Ockhamists in the arts faculty cluster around the theories regarding the properties of terms, supposition, and the like, which seem to have received their first definitive formulation in the *Summulae logicales*[8] and later are paramount as background for Ramism.

Although he was Pope, Peter of Spain at best merely dabbled in theology. Great as it was, his posthumous reputation as a logician was second to his reputation as a physician — a practitioner both of medicine and of all sorts of physical experimentation, including black magic. This fact is of some significance in establishing the general setting and climate of medieval logic of which he is so outstanding a representative. As we shall see, this logic is an arts-course product, and accordingly is oriented more toward medicine than toward theology — as is confirmed by the trouble that the arts professors occasionally had with theologians. Medieval logic, like its modern counterpart mathematical logic, arises as a science closely allied psychologically with the natural sciences. The odor of empirical science which clings not only to Peter of Spain, but to so many other scholastic logicians such as Roger Bacon, St. Albert the Great, or Raymond Lully, is too strong and too persistent to be regarded quite as an accident. The *Summulae logicales* shows to some extent why this is.

3. THE HUMANISTS' BOGIE: *The Summulae logicales*

Histories of philosophy which are written from nineteenth- and twentieth-century theological and metaphysical points of view still describe Peter of Spain's *Summulae logicales* as a "dialectical fencing manual." [9] Such a description gives an inadequate and even false interpretation of this book. Actually, it is an introductory textbook on logic and dialectic, written to familiarize the teen-age student with notions found in or associated with the study of the logical works of Aristotle. At the same time, it added certain logical treatises of a peculiar kind which formed a new medieval non-Aristotelian development.

As any work on logic might be, the *Summulae logicales* is serviceable for those engaging in the disputations in which medieval students took part, but it gives no directions for such disputations. The work opens with what is probably, after the definition of man himself, the most repeated definition in all scholastic philosophy: "Dialectic is the art of arts and the science of sciences, possessing the way to the principles of all curriculum subjects." [10] There is no definition or mention of a logic apart from this dialectic, except in the title *Summulae logicales* itself, so that the impression is left that dialectic and logic are one and the same thing.

The *Summulae logicales* proceeds by treating in skeletal fashion material found in Porphyry's *Introduction* or *Isagoge* to the Aristotelian *Organon*, in the *Organon* treatises themselves, and in related literature such as Boethius' work *On the Different Kinds of Topics*. This it does in tracts covering successively propositions, the predicables, the predicaments, syllogisms, the topics or places, and fallacies. [11] Notably absent is any treatment of demonstration, corresponding to Aristotle's *Posterior Analytics*, the work which in great part stimulates Ramus' theories on method. To the *Organon* material, Peter of Spain adds six (possibly seven) other tracts which constitute the central development peculiar to medieval logic and which correspond to what modern mathematical logic calls quantification. The tracts are on supposition (*suppositio*), relative terms (*relata*), extension (*ampliatio*), appellation (*appellatio*), restriction (*restrictio*), distribution (*distributio*), and perhaps exponibles (*exponibilia*). This last may belong, as Bochenski holds, more properly with another work, the *Syncategoremata*, also by Peter of Spain. But it was commonly lumped with the other tracts of the *Summulae logicales*. These six or seven tracts were called collectively the *Little Logicals* (*Parva logicalia*) or the treatises *On the Properties of Terms* (*De proprietatibus terminorum*), or the *Modern Logic* (*Logica moderna* — not to be confused with the *Logica nova*, which meant the second and larger half of the Aristotelian *Organon* translated into Latin later than the *Logica vetus* or first half). Treatises by others, notably Marsilius of Inghen (d. *ca.* 1396), covering this same matter were also referred to, both in university statutes and in the works of Ramus,[12] as *Parva logicalia*, but such treatises are ultimately parallel with and mostly derivative from, or are commentaries on Peter of Spain.[13] The term *Parva logicalia* therefore means, in one way or another, the material in Peter of Spain's six or seven tracts. Of these, the key to all the others is the tract on supposition, which treats of terms as "supposing" or "standing" for individual existents. It raises a characteristic kind of question, a rough example of which is: In the proposition *All men are animals,* what happens to the term "man" when an individual man dies? or when another is conceived or born? The origins of suppositional theory, the medieval counterpart of the "quantification" of post-Boolean logic, somewhat antedate Peter of Spain, but it was he who gave the theory its first definitive formulation.[14]

The importance of the *Summulae logicales* in the Middle Ages is now beginning to be realized, the more so because the work defines negatively the aims of Renaissance humanism. When the humanists, particularly those of northern Europe, descend to particulars in their recriminations against scholastics, there is no name they cite with such regularity and cold fury as that of Peter of Spain. He represents the point to which there must be no return. The individuals with whom our present age identifies scholasticism, a St. Thomas Aquinas or a St. Bonaventure, were theologians, members of an important but relatively small higher faculty, and quite unknown to the general mass of students of scholastic philosophy in the arts course. St. Thomas, in particular, was regarded benignly by many humanists. Erasmus, who scorned scholastics, generally tended to aline St. Thomas with the patristic rather than the scholastic tradition.[15] The first edition of St. Thomas' works at Paris in the early sixteenth century actually placed him within the humanist movement, since it came in the first flood of humanist printing and curricular activity.[16] Before humanism got a serious hold at the French capital, however, Peter of Spain had gone through numerous Paris editions, sponsored by the old guard on the arts faculty which had presented the *Summulae logicales* to its thousands of students year in and year out as the rock-bottom basis of all philosophical study, the "door to all logic," as John Major says.[17]

With Porphyry and some of Aristotle, Peter of Spain was matter for the bachelor of arts' *determinatio*.[18] Indeed, the *Summulae logicales* is one of the very few works by a medieval scholastic mentioned in the statutes of the arts faculty at Paris, where the work figures side-by-side with the works of Aristotle. Together with Aristotle's logical works, this work of Peter of Spain was commented on from at least the fourteenth to the sixteenth century by nominalist and realist, Scotist and Thomist alike.[19]

Historians of philosophy note that "it is impossible to reckon the number of Peter of Spain's commentators,"[20] and, at least by the early fourteenth century, his characteristic treatises on supposition and associated subjects had entered directly or indirectly into the whole general logical tradition, and had made his influence felt among the most important scholastic logicians.[21] Ramus notes later that first-year students were referred to as *Summulistae* because they studied chiefly the *Summulae logicales* and in particular the non-Aristotelian medieval part, the *Little Logicals*.[22] But this term *Summulistae* and the unique prestige it accords to Peter of Spain far antedates Ramus[23] and runs well back into the Middle Ages. Works by Ockham (d. 1349) are already derivative from the *Summulae logicales*, and the 1340 condemnation of Ockhamism at Paris turned largely on supposition theory.[24] Indeed, in the nominalist disputes which rock through the whole fourteenth and fifteenth centuries at Paris, the Nominalists are commonly identified in university documents as Terminists — which means, in effect, specialists (to an extent not matched by Thomists or perhaps by Scotists) in Peter of Spain's treatises in the *Summulae logicales* on terms and their properties.

Since a three-and-a-half year course of philosophy was customary at Paris through most of the later scholastic period, the year devoted to Peter of Spain which Ramus reports would have taken up nearly a third of the period given philosophy. The length of time given to Peter was not surprising considering the difficulty of his subject matter and the tender age of the students. Ramus' report refers only to Paris, but all evidence indicates that the *Summulae logicales* were equally in vogue in the other universities of northern Europe.[25]

Modern scholarship has found that "the first classical success as regards systematization of logic is undoubtedly that of Peter of Spain."[26] At the university, where theologians studied their Lombard, law students their Gratian, and medical students their Galen, every one of them had previously studied the *Summulae logicales* in the arts course, where they had as fellow students the countless others who did not go on to the higher faculties but who studied Peter, too.

It is significant that the humanists' attacks center on the "Little Logicals." Sir Thomas More makes this focus clear in a letter to Martin Dorp, a friend of his and Erasmus:

A certain dialectician . . . might have said, ". . . And now children (*pueri*) are so solidly founded in the *Little Logicals* that I should believe in all truth that if Aristotle himself were to rise from his grave and argue with them, they would argue him right back down into his grave again, not only with the logic of the sophists but with his very own logic."

Now this book of the *Little Logicals* (*Parva logicalia*), which is so called, I suppose, because it has very little logic in it, is a precious piece of work to see, with its suppositions, as they are called, its ampliations, restrictions, and appellations, with its little rules, not only clumsy but even false, as when it tries to distinguish the two enunciations, "Leo animali est fortior," and "Leo est fortior animali" . . . .[27]

Other humanists agree with More. In the Cambridge play, *The Returne from Parnassus*, a student finds himself castigated as a "pagan, Tartarian, heathen man, base plebian."[28] "Tartarian" means a Tartar, synonymous with savage, but with an oblique and uncomplimentary reference to one of Peter of Spain's best known commentators, Pierre Tartaret, who is explicitly named in at least two other places in the *Parnassus* plays. Lists of "barbarians," such as that proposed by Johannes Caesarius, make Peter of Spain *the* barbarian for dialectic.[29] Ramus' adversary, Jean Riolan the elder, says that the whole trouble with prehumanist philosophy was that it was masquerading behind the *Parva logicalia*.[30] As will be explained later, Agricola has to be defended by his commentator Joannes Matthaeus Phrissemius against the charge of revising dialectic with the sole object of differing from the author of the *Summulae logicales*.[31] Writing as an avowed humanist, Ramus lists the barbarians as Jean Buridan, John Dullaert (Dullardus), Pierre Tartaret, and, underneath and behind and in them all, their predecessor Peter of Spain.[32] In its preface to "the most humane Sabellus," Talon's *Dialectical Explanations of Porphyry* attacks the "suppositions, ampliations, and restrictions" which form the core of the *Summulae logicales*. Although Peter of Spain receives little attention after 1530 or 1540, at least one later Ramist, Frederic Beurhaus, recalls that it is he whom Agricola and Ramus have supplanted, and provides in parallel columns sections from Ramus' *Dialectic* and the *Summulae logicales*.[33] This appearance side-by-side with his heir apparent is nearly the final appearance until the twentieth century of the key figure in medieval scholastic logic. It confirms rather dramatically the line of succession here indicated: Peter of Spain — Rudolph Agricola — Peter Ramus.

4. THE *Summulae logicales* AND PROBABLE LOGIC

The text of the *Summulae logicales*, including the *Little Logicals* has become available in the past few years in the Bochenski and Mullally editions, and may be examined therein. Only its relevance to Agricolan and Ramist topical logics need be discussed here; the *Summulae* shows some specifically medieval aspects of the psychological framework of these logics.

Mullally believes that "the topical analysis of dialectical argument is probably the ultimate aim of the *Summulae*."[34] This seems a strange statement to make about a logic as highly formalized as the *Summulae*. Yet it is quite certain that, in its concern with the effective exploitation of material or "topics" for debating either side of an issue rather than with formal logical structure, the *Topics* of Aristotle and Boethius represent a major preoccupation of medieval logic much more than is commonly realized. This is clear from university statutes and textbooks alike. Despite its formalized aspects which ally it with modern mathematical logic, the *Summulae* does not neglect this topical focus, which allies it not with the formal logic of scientific certainty but with the probable logics, including rhetoric.

Paralleling the *Organon* itself, the *Summulae* includes a tract on the *loci* (topics or places). But, unlike the *Topics* in the *Organon*, Peter of Spain's treatise on the topics contains no clear indication that it treats of probabilities only. It is not explicitly disengaged from the other parts of logic concerned with scientific demonstration. The treatise is presented as an integral part of Peter's "dialectic" precisely because Peter persistently blurs the question whether this dialectic is an instrument of scientific certainty, of mere probability, or of both together. The blurring is evidenced in the opening words of the *Summulae*, which introduced the medieval philosophy student to dialectic and the whole field of philosophy. An echo of Cicero, these words are themselves re-echoed everywhere in philosophical literature from the thirteenth through the sixteenth centuries and on into Ralph Waldo Emerson:

Dialectic is the art of arts and the science of sciences, possessing the way to the principles of all curriculum subjects. For dialectic alone disputes with probability concerning the principles of all other arts, and thus dialectic must be the first science to be acquired.[35]

This is apparently an explicit decision that dialectic be concerned with probable argumentation. But Peter of Spain's mind is not really so clearly made up. For, from this point on, the *Summulae logicales* actually treats dialectic as dealing with scientific certainties. The author and the audience whom he is addressing are too preoccupied with a *simpliste* formalism, controlled, as will become apparent, by rather elemental geometrical analogies, to be able to hold in focus anything so elusive as probable argumentation.

The later treatise on the loci in the *Summulae*, however, forces the question momentarily to the fore again. Peter of Spain's notion of a place involves the traditional, visual, quantified analogy, which the term locus necessarily registers, although this has not yet been clothed explicitly in the "receptacle" imagery of Agricola's later description, and is given the most summary of treatments. According to Peter (who takes after Cicero), a place is "the seat of an argument" (*sedes argumenti*) or "that (*id*) whence a convenient argument is drawn toward the question proposed." [36] An argument is a means for inferring a conclusion so as to "create conviction in a doubtful matter" (*ratio rei dubiae faciens fidem*).[37]

Peter of Spain's thought here moves along lines later to be followed by Ramus. Beginning by making arguments aim at conviction or persuasion (*fides*), he seems to be in the Aristotelian tradition of dialectical or rhetorical argumentation, which moves from a question through probable argument to a probable conclusion — as Aristotle indicates, the best that can be hoped for in most instances from practical life. Nevertheless, he immediately upgrades *fides* by treating it as though it referred to certain truth. Notable tremors develop in his explanation, but he finally blurs the whole matter successfully by pretending that uncertainty or probability came into play only in connection with the *starting* point which is the "question" itself: "before the conclusion is proved, it is doubtful, but then it is the question." [38] In like vein, he follows the mistaken reading which Boethius gives to Aristotle and which after Boethius was general all through the Middle Ages and Renaissance and into the twentieth century; he makes out an enthymeme to be a syllogism which is defective not in the sense that it proceeds from merely probable arguments to a merely probable conclusion (always Aristotle's sense), but in the cruder sense that one of its propositions is not made explicit but simply understood.[39]

Several separate notions are evidently in confused play in Peter of Spain. One is the notion of a Socratic dialectic which proceeds by interrogation through doubtful states to a state which is less doubtful (and hence a relative certainty). By being considered as the preparatory step in getting together a science, this particular kind of Socratic dialectic can be assimilated to what we call today a kind of rational or experimental induction, such as is practiced in controlled scientific experiment (the scientist thinks that the answer he is seeking is perhaps A, or perhaps B, or perhaps C, and so on, and by experimental elimination proceeds from probabilities to the finding of a real certainty). This technique of elimination is not a dialogue nor a dialectic, but a kind of induction. It is hardly attended to explicitly by premodern man. Nevertheless, sensed as a kind of rule-of-thumb (rather than scrupulously scientific) procedure, the technique may be read into Peter of Spain's text. The existential aspect of Socratic dialogue passes quite unnoticed in the *Summulae* tradition.

Also disquieting to Peter is the Aristotelian notion of dialectic which conceives of dialectic as a rational structure, more or less involved in dialogue between persons, made up of probabilities only, so that it never arrives at full certainty, but argues rather from probable premises to probable conclusions. Finally, Peter is faced with the confused actuality of the medieval two-sided scholastic dispute, or dialectic as it existed in practice. This real dialectic, underlying Abélard's *Sic et Non* and the origins of scholasticism and the universities, and reflected even in treatises designed to be strictly scientific such as St. Thomas Aquinas' *Summa theologica*,[40] was in theory concerned with two more or less balanced probabilities. But in fact, one of the sides was often certain, or at least more favored. Moreover, in the actual occurrence of a two-sided oral disputation, each side was prone to regard its own case as certain and to argue it as such. Thus, even if the *Summulae logicales* was simply a "dialectical fencing manual," the situation it set out to manualize was quite a tangle.

Why is it that our manualist, moving through all this maze, thrusts aside by a kind of sleight of hand all question of probability and regards the concern of dialectic or logic to be certainties alone? Basically, because he is a manualist, supplying the need for a handbook for the teen-age medieval student. In this he differs from Aristotle, whose *Organon* treatises are hardly to be assimilated in their entirety by teen-agers. A logic cast in terms of certainties and oriented toward scientific demonstration — such as applies in mathematics — is the perfect type of logic and hence the simplest. Because logic was an elementary subject and because grammar and rhetoric were even more elementary, the central scholastic tradition of the *arts* course as it was actually taught to young boys has little real place for the nice theoretical distinctions between logic, dialectic, and rhetoric (not to mention poetry) such as one finds in Aristotle and, perhaps slightly more developed in St. Albert the Great or St. Thomas Aquinas, or, still further developed in graduate courses today. There were no graduate faculties of philosophy, let alone of literature, in medieval or Renaissance times. After becoming a master of arts (that is, a doctor of philosophy, to use a variant form of the title) between the ages of eighteen and twenty, or sometimes rather younger, one began immediately teaching others to be masters of arts.[41] Although there were outstanding scholars and logicians on the arts faculty — Ockham, Strode, and Buridan — they can hardly be taken as the rule in a tradition where logic was learned and taught also by hordes of young M. A.'s in their adolescence. The recurrent statutes prohibiting word-for-word dictation of lectures bear eloquent testimony to the general pedagogical situation in which logic manuals grew.[42]

Under such teaching conditions, distinctions inculcated by medieval logic (whatever an individual treatise here or there may have to say) were normally not of a fine psychological or epistemological cast, but rather of a "formalistic" kind. This means (as we shall see shortly), that they were of a kind with a high mechanistic or mathematical valence, adapted to diagrammatic manipulation. Peter of Spain's successful blurring of the issue of probable logics is paralleled by the short shrift he gives to the question of universals[43] as well as by his studiously offhand description of induction; he seems thereby to make this intriguing psychological process a matter of complete enumeration, but nevertheless avoids really saying that that is what induction is.[44]

Lawyers, physicians, and theologians alike were introduced to philosophy through Peter of Spain, and his mark can be discerned everywhere in the scholastic tradition, although not always in the same way. Some of those who learned their logic from his manual were able later to supplement his perspectives from more mature experience. It is against all the evidence to suppose that most of them did. The system tended to perpetuate its own horizons. The ordinary medieval scholastic was never quite sure what the dialectic he studied really was. This state of affairs will continue into Ramus' day, when there were almost as many explanations of what dialectic was — and of how the treatises in the *Organon* were related to one another — as there were masters at Paris. The situation was wholly *commentitius*.

5. PETER'S PLACES

In contrast to his tightly organized treatises on the properties of terms, Peter of Spain's treatise V, "On Places" (*De locis*), is the usual loose agglomerate of topics or headings. No single principle for selection of "places" is discernible. Like other assortments (those of the early Greek Sophists, Aristotle, Themistius, Boethius, and later, Rudolph Agricola and Ramus), Peter's is an imaginative stimulus and recall device suggesting something to say for speakers who have to develop a subject or "topic." Thus *De locis* is not only an attempt to analyze for oratorical or literary exploitation the contents of the mind or of memory (and indirectly of reality), but also a register of the live front of ideas or notions which at a given era served as effective suggesting-apparatuses. It is significant that the general framework of argumentation into which treatise IV, "On Syllogisms," fits, is connected with the treatise on the loci, so that argumentation is thus given a dialectical or quasi-rhetorical rather than a scientific or strictly "demonstrative" status.

Peter's places are derivative, it seems, chiefly from those in book II of Boethius' work *On the Different Kinds of Topics*, which, in turn are from those of Themistius.[45] They are made up indifferently of propositions (*locus maxima* [*sic*]), substances, wholes and parts, matter and form, metaphors (*transumptiones*), ends, generation, corruption, use or employment (as of an axe), or witnesses. Nevertheless, in keeping with supposition theory, a quantitative bias is rather more discernible here than in the earlier traditions. Wholes and parts receive extremely detailed treatment. Of course, wholes and parts can be other than quantitative. But in reality they have a strong bias toward quantity, which is thoroughly exploited in Peter's detailed treatment of integral whole (*totum integrale*) and quantitative whole (*totum in quantitate*), and in his use of such wholes to provide analogical approaches to nonquantitative aspects of reality.

Ramus will reproduce the quantitative bias and other tendencies in evidence here, among them the tendencies to throw testimony last as the least satisfactory argument (not peculiar to Peter of Spain), and to dichotomies.

This latter tendency exists because topical logic is not really a logic but a recall mechanism where simplicity counts, and dichotomies have a stark simplicity to recommend them. When the *Summulae logicales* was written, the time was not ripe for the proliferation of the huge bracketed Ramist tables. Nevertheless, it is more than likely that a study of the manuscripts of the *Summulae logicales* would reveal some remarkable beginnings in the form of charts, as do the printed editions of Peter of Spain which were current when Ramus was a boy.

Compared with the places retailed later by Agricola and Ramus, the first two of Peter's places are quickly seen to be of major importance. The first of these places is the maxim (*locus maxima* [*sic* — for *maxima propositio?*] or simply *maxima*), which is defined as "a proposition which depends on no other prior or more known proposition, such as 'every whole is greater than its part.'" [46] The second is the difference between maxims (*locus differentia maximae*), that is, "that through which one maxim differs from another, as these two maxims, 'every whole is greater than its part' and 'of whatever a definition is predicated, the thing defined (*definitum*) is predicated.'" [47] Peter of Spain's maxims are really a thin residual deposit transmitted through Boethius. In part they correspond to Aristotle's treatises on scientific demonstration, the *Posterior Analytics*, which are otherwise missing from the *Summulae logicales*. The maxims are essentially the same as the *dignitates* or axioms which form the starting points of deductive sciences as discussed in the *Posterior Analytics*, from which echo the "prior" (*prior*) and "more known" (*notior*) also met in Peter's text. Maxims will not be found among Agricola's list of places nor among Ramus' arguments; they seem to have been introduced among the loci by Boethius. They will turn up in Ramus elsewhere, however — in axiomatic judgment and in the all-important Ramist "method."

Peter of Spain's insertion of this attenuated equivalent of the suppressed *Posterior Analytics* in the most nonscientific and loosely organized treatise of the *Summulae logicales* is significant. It is the effective beginning of the irresponsible use of the notion of axiom which will come to a climax in the revision of his own *Dialectic* brought out by Ramus a few months before his death. Then the *axioma* of this scholastic tradition is practically equated with enunciation (*axioma* in the Stoic sense). The curious implication is that everything one utters is a self-evident truth! — if one is a Ramist.

In Peter of Spain, the maxims or axioms remain for the most part genuinely self-evident principles, but they are freed from any close-knit scientific control by being thrown in helter-skelter among the *loci*, where they occur in such quantity that Bochenski devotes an entire special index to listing them. Situated thus among the topics, these axioms are associated not with the rigorous analyses which the *Summulae logicales* develops in its quantified treatises (on supposition and related properties of terms), nor with any other careful analysis, but rather with argumentation or "argufying" in the dialectical or even literary or rhetorical sense.

Many of the axioms in Peter of Spain have a genuinely metaphysical ring. Thus in his introductory course in philosophy, the medieval student came across these metaphysical "principles" not in connection with the metaphysics or the logical predicaments but in the more loosely controlled, semirhetorical context of the topics: "If the formal cause is removed, its effect is removed," "If the end of something is good, the thing itself is good," "Given an integral whole, one has given its various parts." [48] These and like axioms are presented not so much to provide insights into reality as to provide something to say on any given subject.

In another and related aspect, Peter of Spain's treatise on the places is significant for the future. Here, in the loosely organized economy of the topical arguments, not in the tighter economy of the predicaments and the syllogism, the concept of "reason" (*ratio*) makes its appearance. Peter distinguishes various senses in which the term *ratio* is used. It can mean the definition or description of a thing, or a power of the soul, or speech making something manifest (as in English, "the *reason* why this is done," etc.), or form as opposed to matter, or an essence. Finally, it can mean "a means for inferring a conclusion." This is the sense in which Peter takes it. It is approximately the sense which appears in Ramus' *argumentum*. Peter puts the term to use in defining an argument as a means for inferring a conclusion thereby (in Cicero's and Boethius' words, which Peter appropriates) to create conviction in a doubtful matter (*ratio rei dubiae faciens fidem*).[49] There are a few other instances where the term *ratio* occurs in the *Summulae logicales*, but this is far and away the *locus classicus*. The key word in Peter's explanation of *ratio* is thus not truth at all, but confidence or trust (*fides* — understood as the rhetorical and dialectical term, not the theological virtue). Here, already, reason appears in almost its full eighteenth-century panoply. It is a way of getting at truth which is sure, common sense, and by implication and association, thoroughly scientific; but when actually pinned down to explanation, somehow it is only instinctive. Here in the thirteenth century, when the goddess of reason makes her most definitive appearance in scholastic philosophy in the most distinctive and influential of all scholastic manuals, she is supported not on the pillars of science, but on the topics or arguments of a merely probable dialectic or rhetoric.

6. SUPPOSITION THEORY AND CORPUSCLES

Characteristic Agricolan and Ramist habits of mind are foreshadowed not only in the treatise on the places but also in the treatises on the properties of terms, the *Little Logicals*, which make up roughly the latter half of the *Summulae logicales*. In these treatises, the corpuscular psychology or outlook, which sees both the real and the mental worlds as agglomerates of discrete items and later makes the Agricolan places or "receptacles" plausible to whole corps of students, can be discerned taking form. It comes into being beneath the complications and involutions of supposition theory and related theories. To see how this occurs, these treatises must be examined briefly in some of their salient aspects.

The notion of supposition is prepared for by the notion of signification. "Signification, as it is taken here, is the representation, established by convention, of a thing by an utterance."[50] "Thing" is *res*; its ambiguity is due not only to Peter of Spain's skimping on the treatment of universals but also to the use of the term *res* in the Roman rhetorical and legal heritage; an accurate rendition is the English word "matter," as when one speaks of the "matter under discussion." This is quite clear from the tract on places in the *Summulae logicales*. Thus the "things," or "arguments," which crop up in Ramism are not bits of the physical world transferred to the intellectual realm, nor bits of the intellectual realm slipped into the physical; they are noncommittal terms with an extraphilosophical, legal and rhetorical history which admirably conditions them for spreading out indifferently into both realms.

In rhetorical and legal parlance, the "matter" or "thing" under discussion could be an individual existent, a legal "case," or simply a definition, or a word. In this tradition, the epistemological questions have not been scanted; they have never existed. However, they will now arise, for Peter's treatment has the effect of fixing the "thing," and with it the universal concept, in the external world, and that in a very definite way:

> Of significations, one is that of a substantival thing and is accomplished through a substantive noun, as "man"; another is that of an adjectival thing and is accomplished through an adjective, as "white" (*albus*), or through a verb, as "runs" (*currit*). This is not, in the strict sense, substantival or adjectival signification, but is rather the signification of something substantively or adjectivally, because to signify something substantively or adjectivally are modes of words, while adjectivity and substantivity are modes and differences of the things which are signified and which do not signify.[51]

The focus is on substantives — reductively on individual substances, such as individual men; it is shown in the following description of supposition:

> Substantive nouns are said to stand for or denote (*supponere*), but adjectives or verbs are said to couple (*copulare*). Supposition (*suppositio*) is the acceptance (*acceptatio*) of a substantive term in place of something (*pro aliquo*). Supposition and signification differ, however, because signification is accomplished through the imposition of a word to signify a thing, while supposition is the acceptance of a term, already significant, in place of something (*pro aliquo*), as when one says, "Man runs," the term "man" is taken to stand for Socrates, Plato, and the rest of men. Thus signification is prior to supposition, and they are not the same. The two differ in that signification belongs to the word (*vox*), whereas supposition

belongs to the terms (*termini*) already composed of word and signification. Furthermore, signification refers the sign (*signum*) to the thing signified (*signatum*), whereas supposition refers that which stands for something (*supponens*) to the supposit (*suppositum*). Therefore supposition is not signification. Copulation (*copulatio*) is the acceptance of an adjectival term in place of something (*pro aliquo*).[52]

It is apparent from this description that:

supposition is principally, though not exclusively concerned with the quantity of terms [and that] it deals for the most part with the extension or range of predicates in reference to individuals. On this point the theory of supposition is, to a very large extent, one with the modern theory of quantification

used in mathematical logic.[53] Supposition theory focuses medieval logic on the extension of terms, and hence on number and quantity. "Man" is viewed with reference not only to the concept it represents, but also with reference to Socrates, Plato, and "the rest of men" — or, as we should say today, *n* men (for the quantity is indeterminate here).

Even though this quantification makes possible a highly developed formal logic comparable in many ways to modern formal or "mathematical" logic, there are also differences between supposition theory and modern formal logic which are important in their psychological implications. There is first of all the fact that suppositional theory maintains some relations with predication itself. It does not develop a predicational theory, for this would be irrelevant to formal logic and lead off into epistemology and metaphysics, where Peter of Spain was unwilling to venture. Nevertheless, as has been well remarked,

the theory of supposition studies the signs or terms as predicates in relation to their subject or subjects. The universal or universalized terms are not so much considered as classes, the members of which are characterized by a predicate, but, rather, as predicates, which, by various linguistic or logical devices, have a definite relation to the subject or subjects of which they are predicated.[54]

There are some attempts to break away from this predicational framework, for medieval logicians dispute whether a term need be in a proposition before it have supposition (Peter of Spain is not explicit here) although they generally conclude that it must.[55] The quantification of this logic registers the progressive visualization of thought. At the same time concern with the vocalizing aspects of cognition remains, so that predication is explicitly retained. Still, these highly visile logicians never know quite what to do with the notion of predication itself. It is left a *donnée*, unexploited.

This residual interest in predication also differentiates suppositional logic from Agricolan and the post-Agricolan developments of Ramism. There is, however, another difference between suppositional logic and modern formal logic which reveals suppositional logic as a direct psychological preparation for Ramism. This is the tendency of suppositional logic not only to "treat terms as substances" in the way Mullally notes,[56] but also to keep at the center of the discussion terms for substances such as man or donkey, readily evocative of images of concrete, individual existents. Such a tendency (avoided in modern mathematical logic to some extent by the use of variables, "A," "B," "n," in place of concrete terms), is connected with the interest in predication which lingers in suppositional logic. It is manifest in the *Categories* of Aristotle because of the way these are concerned with predication, but it is by no means so insistent in Aristotle as in the logic developed from Peter of Spain. This latter logic goes far beyond Aristotle in its interest in the extension of terms — that is, in its greater quantification — and thus is more given to a kind of head-counting (*n* men, no more than *n* men, etc.).

To understand in a rudimentary way the psychological forces at work here, it should be noted that for much logical manipulation all terms are made over by analogy with substance. This is true even when, as in the case of terms discussed in the *Categories* of Aristotle, they are of interest primarily not as subjects of enunciations but as predicates. We take substance here in the sense in which a man, a dog, and a mouse are substances, that is, unit beings not inhering in something else (as color does, for example) and having each a unit economy of its own. Thus "white" (as in "the white dog") or "runs" (as in "The man runs") are in a way logical nuisances in that they cannot, as they stand, be the direct subjects of discourse. "White*ness*" can; we can say that whiteness is a quality (although Aristotle would not have thus expressed himself). "Run*ning*" can; it is an action. White*ness* and run*ning* are substantives, that is, they are reprocessings, in the form of nouns or quasi-substances, of concepts which in their initial condition are not nouns or substances at all. Quality (*qualitas*, from *qualis*, what kind of?) itself is a similarly contrived term: an interrogative adjective remodeled as a noun.

It is a commonplace that what the adjective "white" designates does not exist in a substantive way as white*ness*; only white things exist, just as running does not exist, only running things. Yet here whiteness is intellectually so formulated as to suggest to the unwary that it exists by itself, in the same sense as a man or a donkey exists. In short, it is made into a substan*tive* or substance-like term, a noun. It is, in scholastic language, conceptualized as "being *per se*." Only being *per se* can be talked about directly, for only such being can be made the subject of assertions — the grammarian would say only substantives can be the subjects of sentences. To be made the subject of a sentence — and anything being investigated must be expressed in a term fitted for use as the subject of a sentence — the adjective has to be converted into a substantive. The biologist, for example, cannot study "runs" as in "The rabbit runs" or "white" as in "The rabbit is white," producing treatises on "runs" and "white." His treatises are on run*ning* and white*ness* in rabbits. Of course, "white" can be made the subject of a sentence in the way it is when one says, " 'White' is an adjective." But this is only another way of transmuting it into a substantive or noun to be the "subject" this time of grammar — even while saying that it is something else.

The economy of the human mind thus bears inexorably toward substances or substance-like conceptualizations (substantives). It has been noted previously that Peter of Spain and other logicians treat terms like substances.[57] But in the sense just explained, terms *have* to be treated like substances. In some measure, everything one treats, everything one says something about, has to be treated like a substance by the fact that it is made the subject of a sentence. This is one of the ironies of the human cognitive process. A measure of hypostatization is the rule for all science. Such hypostatization can be controlled not by being avoided, but only by being recognized for what it is.

The recognition existed among the terminist logicians and is evident in their distinction between denominative terms (*termini denominativi*) and connotative terms (*termini connotativi*) — a distinction not to be confused with the now standard distinction between denotation and connotation introduced by John Stuart Mill and cutting across or even in part reversing the denominative-connotative distinction. A denominative term is one which refers directly to a substance or substantive, such as man or Peter; that which it denominates is the denominate (*denominatum*). A connotative term is one which "materially" signifies a thing (substance or substantive) while "formally" signifying something about the thing. Thus a "white" (*albus*) or a "black" (*niger*) can signify a man "materially" while formally signifying his skin color. In this case, it connotes man (not whiteness or blackness), for, although not directly mentioned, man is cosignified with white or black.[58]

This denominative-connotative system of reference is thus also tied in with substantival and predicational considerations in such a way as to focus attention again on substances, such as man or donkey, for the clearest instance of a substance was man, or, if one had to have something different from man, one of the higher animals, like man readily discernible as an individual and readily distinguishable as a member of a class from other things. This is the situation which provides Peter of Spain and medieval logicians generally with their code terms, *homo*, *Sortes* (the form commonly written, printed, and, apparently, pronounced for Socrates) and *asinus* — the "nasty little scholastic ass" which Vives complains he was never able to exorcise from his consciousness.

The terminist logicians thus tried to develop a formal, quantified logic which maintains at the same time an awareness of the elaborate structure in which a substance is modified by or "stands under" (*sub-stare*) its accidents or modifications. This way of dealing with wholes without, as it were, dismantling them, which is a part of the attempt to develop a formal logic relatively close to ordinary language (that is, without special symbols, but only with specially defined words), makes suppositional theory more cumbersome than the quantification in modern mathematical logics. At the same time, the constant traffic in the visible and tangible maintained by suppositional theory reinforced the tendency of the unwary to consider objects as somehow lifted into the mind by conceptualization and as being equipped with their accidental modifications in a fashion only too crudely analogous with processes observable in the external world — as if the mind were to predicate whiteness of a house by mentally painting it.

This tendency is reinforced by the notion of *suppositio* itself when one examines the elementary metaphor it involves. In Cicero and others, *supponere* meant to substitute, so that the unwary easily came to think of terms not as "signifying" things or reality, not as affording an insight into reality, but as surrogates or substitutes for things. Apparently, the tendency to see the semantic situation this way is perennial; it threatens in the English-language way of conceiving of words as "standing for" things. This substitution view lends itself readily to visualist conceptualization: a term is not seen in its relation to a word, a cry, but rather one imagines the thing as whisked away in space and a term as set in its place. The psychological complexities and mysteries of the actual semantic situation can never be completely reduced thus visually or spatially, since this situation involves an irreducible analogy with auditory activity, the "calling" of the names of things. The substitution theory is the worst of semantics, but one can well imagine it as the only semantics possible for the fifteen-year-old *summulistae* doing their Peter of Spain.

A good many items in medieval and Renaissance thought, from the metaphysical notion of supposit itself to Ariosto's *I Suppositi* and George Gasgoigne's *Supposes* might well be re-examined in the light of Peter of Spain's ubiquitous influence. All sorts of suppositions are distinguished in the *Summulae logicales* and in the commentaries and treatises derivative from it.[59] A term can suppose for or stand for a universal as universal, as in "man is a species," or "animal is a genus," where "man" and "animal" suppose for the concept in the mind as such, and these universal suppositions can in turn be distinguished in various ways. But the most basic of all suppositions is personal supposition, when a common or universal (*communis*) term is "accepted" for each of its inferiors, as when in, "Man runs," the "man" stands for Sortes, Plato, and all the other men. Such supposition can be confused or determinate, and each of these in various ways. In these various sorts of supposition, rules can be worked out governing the conclusions possible in reasoning processes.

This reduction in terms of discrete and often actually existing things is developed in infinite detail by means of other tracts in the *Parva logicalia* which protract this reduction in both time and place. Tract IX, on "ampliations" (*ampliationes*) explains how suppositions can be restricted by qualifiers (in "white man," "white" prevents "man" from supposing for all men), or again deployed in time by other qualifiers (in "Man can be Antichrist," the term "man" supposes or stands for not only men who exist already, but for those who will exist in the future).[60] Obviously, in this perspective, the supposition of terms referring to men's bodies or to animals will be different from that referring to men's souls. The latter, once in existence, continue in existence; whereas the restriction in time of terms referring to men's bodies or to animals must take into account the fact that those which have existed are not necessarily the same as those which do exist. Such perspectives are elaborated in tract X, "On Appellations" (*De appellationibus*), for appellation is "the acceptance of a term for an existent thing."[61] Thus we arrive at such theorems as: "'Antichrist' signifies Antichrist and supposes for Antichrist, but it has no appellation, whereas 'man' signifies man and, in itself, supposes for existing and nonexisting men, but has appellation (or 'calls for,' *appellat*) only existing men."[62]

From such developments, these treatises on the properties of terms proceed naturally to their climax in tracts XI and XII, which treat restrictions (*restrictiones*) and distributions (*distributiones*), both of which are concerned with syncategorematic terms ("all," "every," "each," "whatever," "however many," "none," "if-then," and the like). At this point the *Summulae logicales* best reveal their connection with modern logistics, which in great part develops by taking the syncategorematic terms as logical constants, and by elaborating what, in general, is styled quantification.

As explained here informally, the *Little Logicals*, developed out of and around the notion of supposition, may seem useless and ludicrously paralogical, and have so been understood by persons unfamiliar with either modern formal (symbolic) logic or the medieval tradition itself. Actually, these tracts on the properties of terms were used to obtain results comparable to those of symbolic logic today.

The results were not more elaborate, but more limited. This limitation, it has been suggested, turns on the absence of a calculus of conditional propositions, in which the medieval logical tradition failed to go as far as the Stoic logic,[63] but even more on the condition of the symbols employed. The symbols of medieval logic were not sufficiently abstract for the work they were called on to do. Rarely, if ever, do medieval logicians go even so far as to use variables, symbols such as X and Y for terms, although this practice had been introduced by Aristotle, who is reproached for it by Ramus.[64] In effect, while pursuing lines of analysis parallel to or even virtually identical with those of modern mathematical logic, instead of writing out its exceedingly complicated theorems in the special shorthand symbols which have become current since Gottlob Frege's *Begriffschrift* (1879) — such as the now familiar $\sim$ or $\supset$ or $\cdot \supset :$ or $\vdash \ulcorner \urcorner$ or $\exists$ — logicians were saying in words what such symbols would indicate.

The situation which resulted was something like that which would be created if mathematics books, instead of employing numbers and signs, had all their contents and formulas written out in longhand: two thousand three hundred and seventy-one times eighty-six divided by the product of nine minus seven . . . , and so on — without the possibility of conceptualizing in any way except in the words themselves. In this way, the astonishing precision of the old scholastic logic, which far exceeds that of the post-Renaissance pre-Fregean age, was attained only at the expense of great verbosity, in a maze of qualifications involving ampliation, appellation, and the other properties of terms, mostly derivative from supposition. Within and beneath these qualifications move the key terms "man," "ass," and "Sortes," which dominate thousands of pages of old logical tracts.

The badly needed simplification which these key terms supply is of another order, that which comes in dealing with terms which one can represent imaginatively in pictures of discrete individual existents. This is not the ideal sort of simplification for formal logic, and, outside the field of such logic, it can occasion misrepresentation of the whole epistemological field by inducing what can be called a corpuscular view of reality and of the mind, a kind of epistemological or psychological atomism, which regards reality as coming in little chunks — like tiny men or asses or troops of little Socrateses — and intellectual activity as the marshalling and maneuvering of corresponding little chunks of mind-stuff. This will be the long-term, and unintentional preparation for Ramism and the *Theses logicae* in seventeenth-century Harvard College.

A comprehensive study of the actual use of suppositional theory in scholastic philosophy (that is, in the scholasticism of the arts course), has never been made. From a cursory examination of the various works which are cited here and which were in use at Paris in Ramus' early youth, it appears that supposition was used throughout logic and sporadically through physics — for example, to establish the difference between artificial and natural objects,[65] or in treating the question of an actually infinite body.[66] Not much is done with supposition in metaphysics — but then, not much is done with metaphysics by these arts-course scholastics, or scholastic philosophers.[67] Discussions of contingent future events are often completely controlled by a suppositional approach.[68]

When, in the wake of humanism after 1530 and 1540, scholastic logic disappeared abruptly, supposition theory survives only in a truncated form, with epistemological rather than formally logical implications. Modern neo-scholastic logics, such as Maritain's, show a residual interest in supposition derivative from the Renaissance logicians and not directly connected with the old scholastic logic.

7. QUANTIFICATION AND THE *Summulae logicales*

The advance in quantification[69] which medieval logic exhibits is one of the chief differences between it and the earlier Aristotelian logic. The extraordinarily heavy emphasis on quantification in the *Summulae logicales* is shown not only in its development of suppositional theory but in its entire structure. The traditional order in the logical treatises of Aristotle's *Organon* had been one which led from simple terms through propositions or enunciations to syllogisms, or from single terms to the more terminologically complex constructs. Peter of Spain puts propositions first in order to treat syncategorematic terms ("all," "every," "each," "no," etc.) immediately, in connection with the square of opposition which is featured at the beginning of the *Summulae*. The work builds up from these quasi-arithmetical terms to the treatise on suppositions and related treatises (which include most of its second half), finishing with the treatises on restrictions and distributions (quantification again). The treatise on exceptives or "exponibles" ("everything but," "only," "after," "until," and the like) is often added to the latter; [70] these again are quasi-arithmetical terms involving limit concepts easily represented by diagrams.[71] The *Summulae logicales* thus begins and ends in quantity, which is just what modern mathematical logic is likely to do.

The *Summulae logicales*, however, lacks the treatment of the hypothetical or conditional syllogism which has been combined with quantification to bring about the great developments of modern formal logic. Ramus' later attempts to make more of conditional propositions, although he produces no true conditional calculus and probably was quite unaware of the real achievements of the Stoics along this line (he castigates as false the Stoic syllogistic, which he seems to have known chiefly through Cicero and Boethius) [72] is interesting in the light of the deficiencies of the old scholastic logic along this same line. His attempts are evidence perhaps of the high quantifying drive of his thought; for, as will be seen, the quantifying drive was in his day obviously finding new — if not always fruitful — outlets.

Any logic dealing with consequences (formal logic), is necessarily a highly quantified instrument. For instance, to draw a consequence from the enunciation "Men are dialecticians," one must advert in some way to the coverage or "extension" of the terms, noting whether "men" means, or extends to all men, or to fewer than all men (some men). Thus no formal logic can be divorced from a quantitative system, although the quantities concerned need not be numerically precise. The possibility of representing extension and consequences in geometrical fashion by means of circles is well known and is resorted to in the most elementary logics which are not at all consciously "mathematical."

The metaphysical mind of a St. Thomas Aquinas would explain the tendency to quantification, which marks all logic and which must be allowed free play if a formal logic is to develop to full maturity, by observing that reasoning, the drawing of consequences from one or more propositions, is not the same thing as understanding, and that the presence of discursive reason in the human intellectual apparatus is due to the material component in man's cognitive make-up and in the make-up of the reality he is immediately faced with.[73] Aquinas takes a rather dim view of discursive reason or ratiocination as compared to sheer understanding, which in its pure state would be intuitive. The drawing-out process or *discursus* whereby one or more enunciations can be made to yield other enunciations — which is to say, ratiocination, the "reasoning process" generally vaunted by those who vaunt "reason" — reveals a curious property of human intellectual activity: its way of proceeding by lighting up only successive little patches of understanding, as one or another conclusion is arrived at or recalled and then left behind for the next. This process is parallel with one in the material world, that whereby material things undergo change; the same matter lives out its limitless possibilities successively, now as a blade of grass or a leaf of clover, now as a rabbit, now as the man who eats the rabbit. Like the blade of grass, knowledge as it lies in the human mind has hidden possibilities, actualized by reasoning processes, which thus reflect the changeableness and potentiality of the material world man is faced with.

Seen in this context, which Aquinas and others have elaborated, reasoning, as against pure understanding (in which reasoning terminates and annihilates itself), is spiritual in its objective but in its procedure radically controlled by matter. These perspectives are offered for the light they throw upon the post-Ramist insistence that it is reasoning or ratiocination, not understanding, which differentiates men from animals, and on the insistence of Ramists such as Dudley Fenner that God prescribes "method," which is conceived of as a kind of protracted ratiocinative process.[74] The emphasis here is an old one destined to have a new history. Looking back, we can see that this emphasis on reason is related to the scholastic logic represented by Peter of Spain, and looking ahead we see that it leads into the eighteenth-century world of "reason," which proves to be a highly materialistic world. But the two worlds are in great part one; although any effective logic is a spiritual possession, it is at the same time desperately engaged in quantity and hence in the material world. Logic is a study of the reflection of this material world — the world with which man is directly confronted — in the structures of the mind.

8. LOGIC IN SPACE: LEFÈVRE D'ETAPLES, TARTARET, MAJOR, CELAYA

By the end of the fifteenth century, the age when Peter of Spain has been superseded by Agricola, scholastic logic was dying of the frustration attendant upon its failure to develop a symbolic system adequate to its ambition and the promise of its initial development. The famous "rules" of scholastic logic were one result of this failure. They could be expressed today by symbolic formulas. Moved by the cumbersome verbiage which lack of symbols necessitated, the humanists inveighed against the rules with obvious relish — they were spiny, gnarled, twisted, altogether impossible things. They still seem so today, and they must have seemed so to the medieval and early Renaissance schoolboy when, at the age of fifteen or less, he first encountered one, such as this in Peter's *Summulae logicales*:

The second rule is that a proposition concerning the infinite, taken syncategorematically, is expounded by a copulative whose first part affirms the predicate of the subject taken according to some quantity, continuous or discrete, and whose second part denies that the predicate is in such a subject according to a determined quantity: as "Infinite men run," which is expounded thus: "Some men run and not so many as to exclude two or three more," or thus: "Some men run and as many more as you please."[75]

The lack of adequate symbolism necessitated developing a language which was sufficiently remote from common parlance to serve as a highly specialized tool. The humanists thought that the scholastic logicians had gone too far here; it is evident now that they had not gone far enough, although some of their attempts to devise a formal artificial language seem unfortunate, or at least undiplomatic. The history of medieval scholasticism is sprinkled with occasional contentions over syntax — for example, whether verbs must have different forms for different persons — and Ramus reports the well-known instance from an earlier day when certain masters at Paris had maintained that *ego amat* was quite as admissible as *ego amo*.[76] This performance, which the humanists distorted in order to suggest that the scholastics were ignorant of Latin (quite false, for they were very glib in a Latin which, if technical and colloquial by turns, was grammatical and expressive enough) is obviously connected with a search for a medium of communication from which all nontechnical superfluities were pared. It is probably related to the interest, only recently awakened among modern logisticians or mathematical logicians, in the use of what is beginning to be styled the "indexical I."[77] Quite certainly, it is related to the notion of *denomination*[78] and to the suppositional theory dear to the terminists and the nominalists,[79] who maintained, with what looked like the same fine indifference to grammar, that *albus, alba,* and *album* have all the same *significatio* or meaning.[80]

These apparently antigrammatical positions caused trouble because they looked more like the product of illiteracy than attempts to control language in a special way for special technical purposes. Indeed, they were not very happy ventures in language control. Caught in the difficulties inherent in a "natural" language, the scholastic logicians hardly knew what to do; they bogged down further in the linguistic actuality and in the development of elaborate and refined rules.

Then came the age of printing, bringing new ideas about how to arrange the spoken word in space and a kind of release for the drive toward quantification which had been torturing the logicians. The release can be seen in a series of developments which, at the very time when printing and Agricola's topical logic were becoming current, manifested themselves, in the work of such persons as Lefèvre d'Etaples, Thomas Murner, and the Paris terminists such as Juan de Celaya, and finally played out in the Ramist dichotomies and in the new post-Gutenberg quest of philosophical "systems." The men who figured in these developments have long been regarded as a race of intellectual Nibelungen, but new perspectives have been provided within the past decade by the rediscovery of the old scholastic logic. When these discoveries are viewed in connection with Ramist developments, these men are seen in a position somewhere between the old logic and Ramism, where, if not entirely comprehensible, they appear as far more intelligible phenomena than they have been.

Jacqus Lefèvre d'Etaples (Iacobus Faber Stapulensis, 1455–1537), student and teacher at Paris and elsewhere, was half scholastic, half humanist, as Ramus himself was to be, and like Ramus, fired with the desire to simplify philosophy, particularly logic.[81] This is no place to attempt an exhaustive study of his performance, especially since he was a very complex character with pietistic tendencies foreshadowing those of Erasmus. Only certain trends can be pointed out. His logic certainly deserves more careful study than it has been given, for, in addition to the kind of real, but extrinsic, importance which one finds in Ramism, it perhaps contributed to the intrinsic development of logical science.

Unlike Ramus, Lefèvre does not jettison Peter of Spain, Ockham, and their confreres, but tries to rework their kind of suppositional logic in order to make it more readily understandable.[82] His means of "simplification" include the introduction of charts like multiplication tables, showing, for example, what happens when the conjunction "and" and the disjunction "or" (*vel*) are introduced into different types of propositions, and open resort to arithmetical symbolism, especially in treating the temporal implication (*implicatio*, a form of *ampliatio*) of propositions,[83] or in dealing with the schemata of mood and figure, *Barbara, Celarent*, and the rest.

Lefèvre d'Etaples' rules are certainly not "simplifications" over Peter of Spain's by any popular standards: "The subject of a proposition supposing with regard to a copula in the present tense holds for the present only," or "The subject of a proposition supposing with regard to a copula in the future tense or to a predicated participle in the future tense is amplified (*ampliatur*) so as to extend to those which are or will be."[84] Against these and his other more complicated rules, one could well urge Ramus' general indictment of Aristotelians; namely, that ordinary people certainly do not talk like that. What Lefèvre d'Etaples' simplification really comes to is greater reduction to quantitative analogies, in terms of symbols, charts, and modes of conceptualization.[85] His *Grammatography* attempts a schematization of grammar, evincing a similar preoccupation with space as a vehicle of intelligibility, and, more important, an aid to memory.[86] Here we are already dealing with a mentality matured in the Gutenberg era. But Lefèvre is only manifesting the

II. ARITHMETICAL LOGIC (LEFÈVRE D'ETAPLES)

innate quantitative bias of the logic to which he was heir. When Rudolph Agricola takes over at this point, this quantitative drive exhibited in the *Summulae logicales* does not diminish but only changes direction. Through

De predicabilibus
Fo. xv.

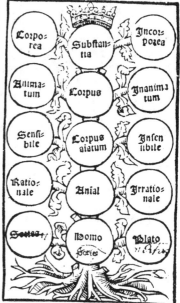

Porphyrian tree labels: Corporea · Substantia · Incorporea · Animatum · Corpus · Inanimatum · Sensibile · Corpus animatum · Insensibile · Rationale · Animal · Irrationale · Sortes · Homo · Plato

III. THE PORPHYRIAN TREE (TARTARET)

the notion of "places" and associated paraphernalia in the *Weltanschauung* of the newly ascendant topical logics, it will come into its own.

Lefèvre's tables commonly take the form of quasi-algebraic, or arithmetical displays (see Figure II); for this reason, he stands out as something of an anomaly among the scholastic logicians at Paris at the close of the fifteenth century and opening of the sixteenth. Most of these logicians favored, in the new printed editions of logical works now appearing, a diagrammatic, geometrical display. These more primitive manifestations of the quantitative drive in logic had been famous from antiquity in two well-known forms, the Porphyrian tree (see Figure III) which made possible a spatial representation of the genus-species relationship (in certain of its aspects only), and the square of opposition (cf. below, Figures VI and X) which had geometrically charted, intriguingly rather than informatively or usefully, the relation between propositions in terms of their extension.

Certain other related diagrams, which can be examined in typical form in the 1947 edition of Peter of Spain's *Summulae logicales,* had also developed in the pre-Gutenberg ages. But, when compared with what emerges after the invention of printing, these, on the whole, are very primitive. The relatively simple diagrammatics — based chiefly on variations of the circle applied in terms of logical extension — which one finds, for example, in an edition of the *Dialectic* of George of Trebizond (1395–1486) published with an evaluation by Lefèvre d'Etaples,[87] are the sort of thing which could also be perpetuated with some success in a manuscript tradition. But more elaborate diagrams or charts could not be so perpetuated, for they were too difficult to reproduce in quantity and with the necessary accuracy by hand. Therefore, even when one or another logician devised such diagrams, as certain of them assuredly did, there was no large-scale reproduction or transmission of his creation comparable to that of a written text.

All this was changed, or promised to be changed, with printing. The most elaborate sort of displays had only to be set up once in type to yield an indefinite number of reproductions, all exactly like one another. Or, if one wanted ornament or geometrical design as well as a controlled spatial display of words, the design could be cut on a wood block as in early sixteenth-century editions of Tartaret and Celaya (see Figures IV and V). Here holes could be left into which the type could be set, or the letters could actually be cut on the block, too.

Diagrams of this sort are a regular feature of the old scholastic logical works published in the early days of printing, especially up to 1530, when the Agricolan topical logic began definitively to drive out the old scholastic logic. They are especially to be met with in the logicians who were teaching or whose works were being taught at Paris when Ramus was studying there: Juan de Celaya, Antonio Coronel, Luis Nunez Coronel, Juan Dolz, John Dullaert, Pierre Tartaret, Juan Ribeyro, Juan Martinez Siliceo, Gervase Waim, Ramus' onetime defender Jean Quentin, Robert Caubraith, and David Cranston, who, with still another Scot, Gavin Douglas, has been associated with the dean of them all, the author of a famous Latin *History of Great*

Non pergunt aſini per pontem ſint niſi cauti
  Póntem vel caueant pretereundo cadent:
Impedit:hic oculos ſenſus firmat vat τ alios
  In doctis, ſaltus eſt ſibi nulla ſalus

horret equus talem validus certe titubantem.
  Dum graditur cernens ſit licet ire potens
Non igitur rurſum dico veniant ſtinorum
  Qui:ſed eos retro nunc remanere volo.

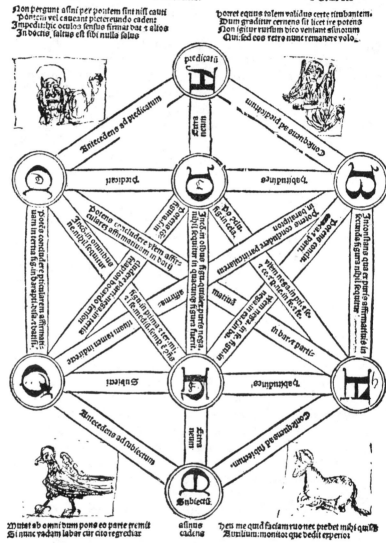

aſinus
pgens

Mutat ab omni dum pons eo parte tremit
  Si nunc vadam labar cur cito regrediar

aſinus
cadens

heu me quid faciam ruo nec prebet mihi quiſ
  Auxilium:monitor que dedit experior

IV. LOGIC IN SPACE (TARTARET)

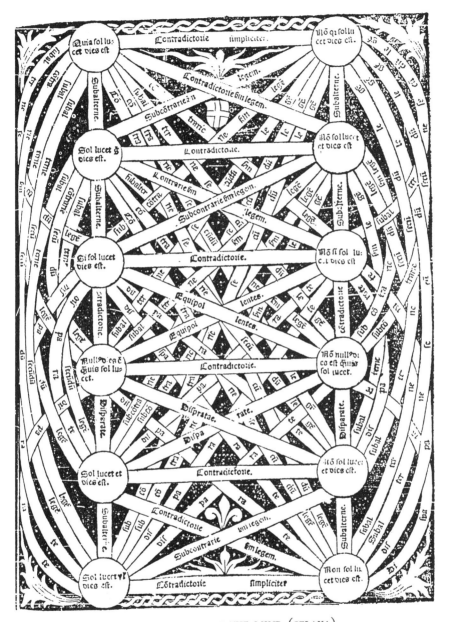

V. THE GEOMETRY OF THE MIND (CELAYA)

Britain and "storehouse of all the learning of the Middle Ages," John Major (or Mair), teacher (but not partisan) of John Knox.

The high incidence of Scottish and Spanish names here gives special point to Ramus' remark that the humanist movement took shape at Paris against the "Scots and Spaniards," [88] since Ramus' *Scoti* (not *Scotistae*) and *Hispani* refer not only to the intellectual epigoni of Duns Scotus and Petrus Hispanus but also, indirectly at least, to their fellow countrymen. As early as Petrarch, Benvenuto da Imola, and Coluccio Salutati, humanists had regarded their scholastic enemies as coming typically from the British Isles.[89] Logical treatises by the Englishmen Ockham, Richard Suiseth or Swinehead, Walter Burleigh, and Chaucer's philosophical friend Ralph Strode, together with the still more popular Peter of Spain, are indeed among those most commented on at Paris in Ramus' youth. And the commentators at this time remained largely British and Spanish, as the names just given in the preceding paragraph indicate.

The charts and diagrams with which these logicians sprinkle their works appealed to this first generation matured in the post-Gutenberg world, for whom they seemed to provide real explanation. Villoslada notes how Celaya,

treating of the various kinds of propositions in his commentary on Peter of Spain, explains himself thus: "All this is clear from the following diagram." And he draws one of the many geometrical figures which appear in the dialectical manuals . . . , a real skull-breaker with propositions at times nonsensical.[90]

Villoslada wrote this before the current studies rehabilitating the old scholastic logic and its study of nonsensical propositions had begun. Logic can, of course, profitably study apparently nonsensical propositions; all serious formal logic does, for it is interested in structure. More worthy of note than these, however, is Celaya's launching into geometrization in response to his drive to do something quantitative with logic.

This geometrization of logic, has much more to do with medieval developments in logic than with the logic of the ancient world, whatever remote origins it may have had there. Such diagrams as those in Major's works (see Figure VI) appears as attempts to deal with the quantified developments peculiar to medieval logic, such as exponibles or insolubles. Preoccupation with quantity here translated itself into geometrical arrangements of words in space. The development proved fruitless. Geometrical logic soon degenerated into mere dichotomized tables. The impulses stimulated by quantification would prove fruitful only when translated not into geometry but, centuries later, into the algebra which, with Boole and Frege, has brought about the impressive development of modern mathematical logic. The recent algebraic developments have their own roots in antiquity, of course, particularly in Aristotle's regular use of the letters of the alphabet as variables for terms in his syllogistic (he uses terms such as "man," "animal," only for nonvalid syllogisms).[91] But, neglected by medieval logicians in favor of supposition theory, the use of variables remained unexploited in logic through the Renaissance. Ramus' unavowed entanglement with the medieval developments is nowhere better illustrated than in the way in which he heaps scorn on Aristotle precisely for this use in logic of letters[92] — which, in his own view of the arts, belong really to grammar.

9. THE GEOMETRY OF PEDAGOGY: THE ALLEGORY AS DIAGRAM

The fad for a diagrammatic logic and the groping toward an algebraic logic which followed on medieval logical quantification are epiphenomena of Western man's gradual revision of his attitude toward space. Spatial constructs and models were becoming increasingly critical in intellectual develop-

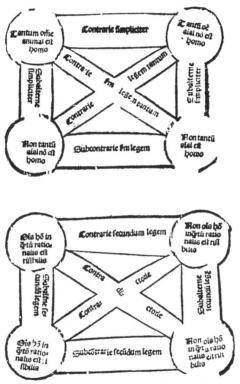

VI. GEOMETRICAL LOGIC (MAJOR)

ment. The changing attitude manifested itself in the development of printing, in the new Copernican way of thinking about space which would lead to Newtonian physics, in the evolution of the painter's vision climaxed by Jan van Eyck's use of the picture frame as a diaphragm, and in the topical logics of Rudolph Agricola and Ramus, as well as in other phenomena. Some of

7 Suppositio  8 Ampliatio

9 Restrictio 10 Appellatio

11 Distributio 12 Expositio

13 Exclusio 14 Exceptio

15 Reduplicatio 16 Defectus

Notica tractatuum

Tractatus cuiusuisumqz noticiam & ordinem: facili quadam via prehendes: nec potest id esse laboriosum: si subscripta signa: tractatibus singulis ac commodarim̄ete teneris: Numerus equidem signorum in capitibus positus: quotam prebet tractatuum: sed & quod numerorum sequitur: marcarā illius tractatus: de qua sit indicat

Signa tractatuum

1 enunciatio 2 predicabile

3 predicamentū 4 sillogismus

5 locus dialeticus 6 fallacia

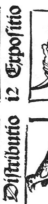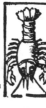

VII. LOGIC FOR LITTLE BOYS (MURNER)

the details of this pattern will be discussed later, but two other curious logical developments closely associated with the invention of printing should be mentioned here. The first is the *Mnemonic Logic* or *Logical Card-Game*[93] of the Franciscan religious satirist and anti-Lutheran writer, Thomas Murner (1475–1537). Murner, a native of the environs of Strasbourg (and thus a product of the same area as Gutenberg and his associates, Peter Schöffer and Johann Fust, and of the same general Rhineland area as Agricola and his first commentators) was a Franciscan friar who led a wandering life which took him as far as Cracow. There, according to his preface, he got up the *Mnemonic Logic*.[94]

This work is written with not a little humor, for the "soft youth" of this generation which, as the preface notes, is pretty weak in Latin (especially in Cracow?). It provides a simplified text of Peter of Spain's *Summulae logicales*, including the well-known Porphyrian tree and squares of opposition, which is set within one of the most amusing mnemonic schemes ever devised. About one-third of the book is illustrations, crudely but strongly done woodcuts, in which the various terms and rules are associated with various designs in ways calculated to beat the terms and rules into little boys' heads if not really to teach any genuinely formal logic. A table of signs (see Figure VII) is given at the beginning of the book: an enunciation (a little bell or *grelot* or hawk bell, quite like the sleigh bells more familiar today), a predicable (a lobster), a predicament (a fish), a syllogism (an acorn), a dialectical locus (a scorpion), a fallacy (a coronet), a supposition (a heart-shaped leaf), an *ampliatio* (a grasshopper or cricket, two-legged and four-toed, and obviously ready for action), a *restrictio* (a sun), an *appellatio* (a star), a *distributio* (a bird, perhaps a crow), an *expositio* (a moon), an *exclusio* (a cat, slinking somewhat), an *exceptio* (a shield), a *reduplicatio* (a crown), and a *descensus* (a serpent). These will be used in Murner's ensuing illustrations, together with a wealth of other signs. After the table, there follow the "Playing Rules" (*modus ludendi*), which explain "place" (*locus*), material, and practice for those indulging in this "game" of learning what is in Peter of Spain's *Summulae logicales*. The "place" refers to the sequence of the various diagrams, which run through the adventures of a royal household, treating first the King of the Bells (*rex nolarum*), that is, of the enunciations, then his Queen, and finally the rest of the family, who descend from the King and Queen like the rest of a suit of cards. This sequence enabled the young student using the book to remember, by association, which tract comes after which.

The text of the *Summulae logicales* follows, or at least scraps of it, for abridgment and simplification are Murner's objective. Peter's famous opening definition is knocked down to: "Dialectic is the art of arts, holding the way to the principles of all the sciences."[95] Opposite this beginning of the abridged text, in the first *locus*, is an elaborate woodcut in a style suggesting Dürer, entitled "Typus Logice" (see Figure VIII), which could perhaps be rendered

"Outline of Logic" or "Schema of Logic" — the Hellenic Latin term *typus* means the mark of a blow, and hence a stamp or footprint or print or mark, whence our printer's "type." The term is fascinating not only because of its

VIII. OUTLINE OF LOGIC (MURNER)

connection with printing, as well as with Scriptural interpretation (typology), but also because in Marcus Rutimeier's edition of Ramus' *Dialectic* entitled *Idea methodica* (1617 and 1618), and in other similar works, this same term *typus* will be used to designate the Ramist tables of bracketed dichotomies. Against Murner's highly symbolic "loci," these represent for a Ramist the outline of logic drawn from "things themselves" and hence the footprint or cast of logic as it "really" is.

The "Schema of Logic" is rather complicated and, being a general conspectus of the art, is not quite of a piece with the separate "cards" or diagrams which follow in the succeeding loci. These cards are each headed "First Application" or "First Picture" (*imago*), "Second Application," and so on, to

Primus

Applicatio tertia

Tractatus

Tertia imago quattuo: habet

significata. Suma 1 diuisio pponis cathegotice 2 triplex quesituu 3 pticipatio ppolitionu cathegoricaruin 4 ordo pticipannu. Primu significatu a Zborda p positione negatiua accipe.qui em suppleis deputadi ad choidam trabunt negant b Sed lapidib' appensis affirmant,ideo lapide ppone affirmatiua intellige, 2 triplici virga: triplex esse quesituu,nam virgie iuuerneo inquirimus. 3 a p pullos equales ppone equaliter pticipantes b p inceales inequaliter seu vno tm termino participantes c auicalis diuersax speciex ppones nullo termio pticipantes 4 a p pullos debito oidine comedentes,ppones intellige eodem oidine pticipantes b p pullos conuersos diuerso oidine participantes,

Quartus passus

Propositionu cathegoricaru;

vtroq; terio pticipantiu eode oidine qda; opponutur cotrarie: qdam subcotrarie:qdam cotradictorie:qdam sub alterne. 1 Cotrarie sunt vlis affirmatia: X vlis negatiua tis pase,p eode & p eisde supponeib':vniuoce teti:eq aple:eq stricte:i vna sic in alia.vt qlib; ho carrit:qmlibet ho no carrit, 2 Subcotrarie sunt pticularis affirmatiua & pticlaris negatiua tis pase,p eode & p eisde supponetibus:vniuoce teti:eq aple:eq stricte in vna sic in alia: vt quida ho non carrit. 3 Cotradictorie sut vlis affirmatiua & pticlaris negatiua: X vlis negaria & pticlaris affirmatiua tis pase,p eode & pro eisde supponeib':vniuoce teti:eq aple:eq stricte in vna sic in alia vt qlibet ho carrit:qda ho no carrit:& qlibet ho no carrit & qda ho carrit. 4 Subalterne sut vlis affirmatiua & pticlaris affirmatia:& vlis negatiua & pticlaris negatiua tis pase,p eode:& p eisde supponenib':vniuoce teti

IX. LOGIC APPLIED (MURNER)

correspond with and clarify the similarly numbered "steps" (*passus*) which they accompany — for one moves through the "places" in this book by "steps." The "Third Application" of tract I (see Figure IX) is a relatively simple and typical one, and shows the general economy of Murner's whole effort. The little bell signifies that we are in the realm of enunciations. (The connection of enunciations with sound, not sight, is here recalled — but by a *visual* symbol.) The weight in the man's hand is an affirmative proposition, the cord with which he can restrain it a negative proposition. The three switches in the man's hand the three questions, What? What kind? and How many? — for, we are told, it is with the aid of the switches that answers to these questions are extracted from the pupils. The little birds of different species, one with a ruff, another with a crest, another with neither ruff nor crest, are propositions which have no common term. And so through the rest of the symbolism. With such pictures in mind, the little boy — however weak his Latin — can remember what Peter of Spain is about.

Several points could be made here, but the important one is that this performance dramatically illustrates how the pedagogical crisis had shaped itself around 1500, when Peter of Spain was to recoil before Agricola and, finally, Ramus. The original *Summulae logicales* of Peter of Spain is not the sort of

Primus

rqñe ãple:eq̃ ſtricte:in vna ſic in alia:vt qlɩ́l et hõ currit: gdã hõ currit:vl' qlɩbȝ hõ nõ currit & gdã hõ nõ currit.
5   Lex & natura contrariarũ talis eſt: quod impoſſibile eſt duas cõtrarias eſſe ſiml' veras in quacũȝ materia: p̃nt tñ ſimul eſſe falſe in materia cõtingenti & in materia na turali:qñ eſt predicatio indirecta: & etiã quando eſt pre dicatio indirecta ſi ſunt exponibiles: vt omnis homo p̃ter ſortem eſt animal; nullus homo preter ſortes eſt animal.
6   Lex cõtrariarȝ talis eſt:ȝ nũcȝ p̃nt ſimul eē falſe: tñ in materia cõtingenti p̃nt ſimul eſſevere: vt quidam homo currit: quidam hõ non currit: ſed non in materia remota:ſaltem de predicatione directa.
7   Lex contradictoriaȝ talis eſt:ȝ non poſſunt ſiml'eſſe vere necȝ ſimtl falſe in q̃cunȝ materia
8   Lex ſubalternarũ talis eſt: ȝ poſſunt ſimul eſſe vere & etiã ſimul falſe: & ſi p̃ticularis erit falſa vl'is erit falſa ſi formetur:etiam ſi vniuerſalis erit vera: p̃ticularis erit vera
Figurata oppoſitio.

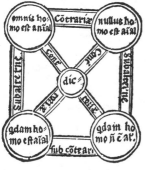

X. PRIMITIVE AND ADVANCED VISUALISM (MURNER)

thing which Murner makes it at all, as is shown by the serious, respectful, and meticulous attention being given it and related scholastic treatises today by scholars far advanced in modern mathematical logic. In providing a logic suited to little boys' needs, Murner has destroyed the very thing he is trying to teach. The older university tradition (Murner was a wandering scholar, like many early humanists, not a man with a well-defined university career) had regarded students as little other than apprentice teachers who simply had to shape themselves to the demands of the trade, which meant the demands of the "arts." Apprentices were not to be catered to.

The results of this attitude in the case of most of the youngsters who had been condemned from the thirteenth century on to the study of the technicalities of a highly quantified logic in their mid-teens can only be wondered at. Results in many cases were certainly questionable — perhaps in the majority of cases — and one can well understand the inclination of a young master of eighteen or twenty, perhaps busy studying medicine at the same time, to teach his course in dialectic or logic by dictating from his notes, despite the fulminations of university statutes against this procedure. Nevertheless, murderous as the tradition may have been for the youth of the times, logic as a science survived.

In Murner it no longer survives. There are only lists of terms and a fog of half-apprehended "rules." The manner of its demise is interesting. Murner's amusing diagrammatics is not only allegorical but also continuous with the more geometrical tradition. He mingles the geometrical type of schema with his own allegorical pictures (see Figure X), while his allegory itself is not pure allegory but a device for fixing his symbols in mnemonically serviceable space. One basic objective is perfectly discernible: simplification. This can be a quite laudable motive, since it powers all scientific thinking, but it here takes the form not of simplification-for-understanding, but of simplification-for-recall. The chief psychological implement is a sense of diagrammatic structure, strongly influenced by the mnemonic tradition which is evident from the "dialectical locus" prominent among Murner's sixteen key symbols and from his thinking of his whole book as a series of "places" moved through by "steps."

The tendency here to traffic in space was encouraged by the premium placed on spatial displays with the arrival of printing, already common at Strasbourg when Murner was a boy at Oberehnheim nearby. In the pre-Gutenberg era Murner's diagrams could never have been so satisfactorily multiplied as to become widely influential. Even though Murner's popularity is founded on diagrams, the nature of these diagrams shows that his connection with printing is not entirely of the same sort as Ramus'. Murner's use of allegorical figures relates him to the emblem books which the new inventions also popularized and thus marks a divergence from tendencies leading into Ramism. For at the heart of the Ramist enterprise is the drive to tie down words themselves, rather than other representations, in simple geometrical patterns. Words are believed to be recalcitrant insofar as they derive from a world of sound, voices, cries; the Ramist ambition is to neutralize this connection by processing what is of itself nonspatial in order to reduce it to space in the starkest way possible. The spatial processing of sound by means of the alphabet is not enough. Printed or written words themselves must be deployed in spatial relationships, and the resulting schemata thought of as a key to their meanings. Displayed in diagrams, words transmute sounds into manipulable units like "things" — such as the visually discrete man and donkey who jog through Peter of Spain's logic.

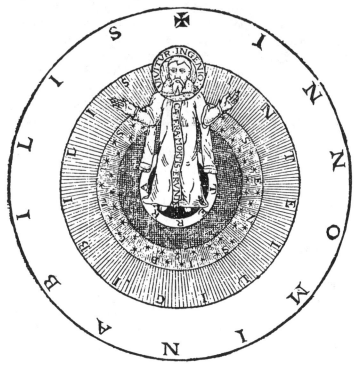

Argumentum Libri secundi.

Per metam apprehensionis sublimata mens humana, & propè summitatem lucibilis pyramidis locata, eius beneficio lucis, distinctè iam videt lumen in omnibus intelligibilibus sensibilibusq́, quod antea confusè tantùm apprehenderat, Ideas, Angelos, actus puros, simul ac naturales infra se cernens, decernens, demonstrans, haud aliter atq̄, is qui per multos gradus gressusq́ difficulter cacumen montis aduolauerit: cuius semel superata altitudine, vno conspectu omnem ad cacumen montis methodum vndiq̄, dirigentem clara luce intuetur, è præsenti vt lucet figura.

XI. AN ALLEGORY OF KNOWLEDGE (DIGBY)

Murner is compelled somewhat by this drive when he distributes through his allegorical pictures names tagged onto his figures (see Figure VIII). Like all allegorists, however, he connects the names not merely by simple spatial relationships with one another, as Ramus was to do in his dichotomized charts (see Figures XII and XIII), but by means of a story, which is, after all, something *told*. Even when pictured, this allegory of logic maintains disquieting connections with a world of sound. The Ramist would prefer quasi-geometrical inspection of words in space to such allegorical insight into a symbol.

The consistent hostility of the Ramist sensibility to allegorical pictures of mental operations is recognizable in the tensions in Murner's pedagogical approach to logic and brought into clear focus in the Digby-Temple dispute by the end of the sixteenth century.[96] In 1579, Everard Digby will publish his *Theoria analytica*, which merits comparison with Murner's earlier work, in which he subsumes some of his ideas in beautifully done woodcuts with a high allegorical charge, making explicit allowance, moreover, for what escapes not only the printed picture but utterance itself — the ineffable or unnamable in knowledge (see Figure XI). It is true that in his 1580 work, *The Twofold Method* (*De duplici methodo*), Digby resorts to the Ramist outline tables, refuting Ramus' analysis of method with whole shoals of outline analyses of his own; but he is fighting fire with fire. His radical opposition to Temple is due to something more profound than a preference for one sort of table over another: it is due to his symbolic or allegorical cast of mind. When Temple takes up the cudgels against Digby, he accuses him of employing the term method (*methodus*) in too many different senses. This practice of Digby's has obvious relationships with allegorical habits of thought, and makes difficult the treatment of words as "things" which are obviously "distinct" from one another; Temple's teeth are set on edge.

Murner's emblem-book logic, which sets out to eliminate mystery from the "art" by making it a story to be "told" in plain pictures, and Digby's emblem-book theory of knowledge, which seeks to express the ineffable by means of visual aids, reveal some of the stresses and strains which put in their appearance as the spatialized world apprehended by vision came to be more and more exploited to aid thinking. In both authors the stresses were particularly great because spatial models were being pressed into service to deal not merely with reality but with thought itself. It is in this sort of background that Ramist dialectic appears.

CHAPTER V

THE IMMEDIATE BACKGROUND: AGRICOLA'S PLACE-LOGIC

> Where is the seat of the trope?
> — The Ramist Johannes Piscator
> in his *Responsio* concerning
> the Last Supper.

I. THE DIALECTICAL REVOLUTION

WHEN Pierre de la Ramée was a youngster toddling up and down the gently sloping streets of the Picard village of Cuts, something had been happening to the logic of the schools. Change was in the air. Humanism was a factor affecting the change. But in what precise ways it made itself felt has always been difficult to ascertain, especially since the humanists' conventional protests that they should and did derive all things from the ancients has so badly fouled their own trails.

We are aware today that, since the humanists were postmedieval men, they operated in the normal, postmedieval frames of thought. Their preference for an engrafted rather than indigenous culture is the characteristic preference of the barbarian tribes vis-à-vis the Hellenic–Roman world, although it has special complications of its own. Their determination that linguistic expression was to be controlled by the *written* words of Cicero and his coevals reflects the dependence on a culture out of the past typical of the Middle Ages. Cicero himself had helped transplant an unfamiliar culture to Rome, but he had moved it through space only, not through time.

He had gone to Greece and learned by listening. Early barbarians in contact with the Graeco-Roman empire had done much the same. But the humanist, like his medieval predecessor, was conditioned to learning by reading. The scholastic, scientific passion for fixity and exactitude, associated with dependence upon written documents, was extended by the humanists even to the matter of literary style. No longer left to the vagaries of the changing world of sound (although humanist orators obviously loved this world, too), style was to be controlled by modes of speech fixed in writing and thus freed of the transiency of present time. This was not the only attitude of the humanists toward language, but it was a very real one.

Unable to escape from its past or negate the scholastic experience, humanism could only minimize scholasticism in certain areas where it obtruded spectacularly for one reason or another. The most profound effects of scholasticism, such as the outlooks mentioned above, remained a part of humanism. Humanism and scholasticism, therefore, must be studied not as movements opposed to one another, but as interacting ones. The interaction has been complex. Not only was humanism in great part the product of the scholastic mind, but it also in turn has passed on to us many of our present notions of scholasticism. Thus, ironically, what is commonly thought of as "scholastic" logic by neoscholastics today is in reality a residual, quasi-scholastic, post-humanist logic, not the scholastic logic of the central medieval tradition.[1]

Certain aspects of the scholastic-humanist interaction come into remarkable focus when one examines the immediate prehistory of Ramism. There one observes immediately a maneuver which is both critical and easy to describe: the substitution of the logic or dialectic of Rudolph Agricola for that of Peter of Spain. Ramism demands that we focus our attention here not only because Ramus' dialectic is by its author's own admission derivative from Agricola, but because Ramus' "method" is also the byproduct of Ramus' attempt to complete Agricola's *Dialectical Invention in Three Books* (*De inventione dialectica*), which had been left unfinished at its author's death.

Because these facts have not been adverted to, Agricola's importance has not been recognized. It is difficult to exaggerate this importance. Just as in the Middle Ages Peter of Spain's logic *was* logic (even more than Aristotle's was), so Agricola's reoriented logic became for generations after him, in the absolute sense, logic unqualified. We have been unaware of Agricola's importance because as his influence spreads his name actually tends to disappear. His logic achieves some of the impersonality of inevitable abstract truth. When Antonio de Gouveia taunts Ramus with a list of recent authors who he says are Ramus' unacknowledged sources, he fails to include Agricola among them,[2] so much was the Dutch humanist's work synonymous with logic. Ramus himself has to remind his own generation that the "true dialectic" which he professed had not sprung from nowhere, but was that of Rudolph Agricola.[3]

Only occasionally do authors of later generations, such as Franco Burgersdijk, remind their readers that it was Lorenzo Valla and Juan Vives, but especially the predecessor of Vives, Rudolph Agricola, who turned logic away from Aristotle to Cicero and (in this sense, via Cicero) to the "Stoic" tradition.[4] But such avowals are rare; they are seldom adverted to today, and even when they are, their implications are no longer caught. We have long forgotten the change which came over scholastic theology in the Renaissance. What helped make Melchior Cano, Francis Suarez, Robert Bellarmine, and even Francisco de Vitoria, not to mention Melanchthon, Bullinger, and Alsted, different from St. Thomas Aquinas, stemmed, in great part directly, from Agricola, who supplied the initial impetus and the very exiguous theory, taken over verbatim by Cano and others, for the theologies of "places" or "loci." Agricola's chief impact on mental habits was at the core — the dialectic which even humanism failed to dislodge as the focal point in all the curricula. Many an early humanist was a philologist, an educator, and a litterateur. Agricola was these too, but he was also the logician of the new age.

Erasmus himself knew the capabilities and the importance of Agricola and owned them; he rated himself a decided second to Agricola "in eloquence and in all regions of learning," but especially in dialectic[5] — which to him meant practically all philosophy. Later German humanists, in almost one voice, trace their inspiration to Agricola. Melanchthon seconds Erasmus' high estimate of Agricola's worth, and credits him with bringing the new light from Italy to the North. Alexander Hegius says he owes all he knows or all that people think he knows to Agricola. Wimpheling and Johann von Dalberg, Agricola's patron and a humanist in his own right, agree with Erasmus, Melanchthon, and Hegius. Without adopting it so slavishly as Ramus did, Johann Sturm gave Agricola's logic equally high marks and was largely responsible for its currency at Paris, where he taught from 1529 to 1536. (Thus he was indirectly responsible for Ramus' taking it up, although Ramus' real debt is not to Sturm's dialectic but to Agricola's work itself.) [6] In the preface to a Basle collection of Ramus' letters, Agricola's place was said to yield to no one's, for he was the very first after the "happy times" of Greece and Italy to revive "the use of the logical faculty," [7] and Ramus' task was simply to facilitate the practice of Agricola's directives, which if they were badly observed, were certainly given lip service everywhere.[8]

Agricola's fame was not restricted to the Continent. The Royal Injunctions given to Cambridge by Henry VIII in 1535 prescribe that students in arts should read him together with Aristotle, Trapezuntius, and Melanchthon instead of the "frivolous questions and obscure glosses of Scotus, Burleigh, Anthony Trombet, Bricot, Bruliferius, etc." [9]

At Paris, the introduction of Agricolan logic came about with amazing rapidity. It coincides with and, indeed, is simply the converse of the apparent extinction of the old scholastic logic at the turn of the sixteenth century. This extinction is spectacularly documented in the list of early editions of the *Summulae logicales* of Peter of Spain published in Mullally's recent edition of part of this work.[10] In the few decades between the appearance of the first printed book and 1530, Mullally finds 160 editions of the *Summulae* — and his list is not exhaustive. Between 1530 and 1639, there were six only; between 1639 and 1945, not one. For the other old scholastic logicians singled out for attack by the humanists, such as Jean Buridan, Walter Burleigh, Ralph Strode (the dedicatee of Chaucer's *Troilus and Creseyde*), and even William Ockham, the picture is the same: there seem to have been no editions between the beginning of the sixteenth century and about 1950. The table was swept clean around 1530, and Agricola's dialectic was the reagent which effected, or at least expedited, the purge.

As a result of this spectacular action of Agricola's dialectic, Ramus' adversaries at Paris, the mid-sixteenth-century "Aristotelians" or scholastics had no more studied Peter of Spain, the archscholastic, than had Ramus — as one of them, Antonio de Gouveia, is at pains to make clear.[11] In 1530, the Faculty of Theology at Paris accused the Faculty of Arts of studying Rudolph Agricola more than Aristotle, only to be told by the Arts Faculty that they themselves had better change, since there was nothing more outmoded than the sophistical sort of dialectic which they professed (the reference was to the "sophisms" which ally Peter of Spain's kind of logic with modern logistic).[12] Such dialectic stood between the theologians on the one hand and the Gospels and Fathers of the Church on the other, for, the Masters of Arts added with an oblique reference to St. Ambrose's famous remark, such dialectic was "not the means fixed on by God to save his people."[13] The Arts Faculty was soon in a position to have its way. As the Theology Faculty renewed itself out of the new generation of arts students trained in Agricola, the old bastions crumbled. It is then that the "loci theologici" sprout everywhere, in Protestant and Catholic camps, and signal the arrival, almost always via Paris, of the new Agricolan mind.

2. RUDOLPH AGRICOLA

Rudolph Agricola,[14] originally Roelof Huusman, was one of the scholarly commuters who in the late fifteenth century shuttled back and forth through the Rhine Valley and over the Alps, transplanting Italian humanism into Northern Europe. The available details of his life are sketchy. He was born in Bafloo near Groningen February 17, 1444. It is possible that one of his first teachers was Thomas à Kempis. His early education was under the Brethren of the Common Life, but when a very young boy he began his migrations in quest of culture which were to continue through his whole life (as they commonly did for first-generation humanists, who were often extra-university people and footloose hangers-on at courts). He was in Erfurt about 1456, and two years later in Louvain, where he appears to have received the degree of Master of Arts. Soon after, he was in Cologne, whence he made his way to Paris; there he formed a friendship with John Reuchlin. By 1468 or 1469, he was in Italy, studying law at Pavia and writing a biographical "oration" on Petrarch. Soon after, he abandoned law for classical literature, and in a few years moved to Ferrara, which he called "the true home of the Muses." Here he had Theodore Gaza and Battista Guarino for masters, and studied Lucan, Isocrates, Aristotle, Thucydides, Xenophon, Isidore of Seville, and Polybius. Caught up in all the currents of Italian humanism simultaneously, he devoted himself also to gymnastics, took up painting, sculpture, and music, and became a sort of minor Leonardo da Vinci; he even took time to build an organ for his Italian friends. In Italy, Agricola found himself teaching youngsters of the nobility, among them Johann von Dalberg, who in 1482, at the age of twenty-six, was to become bishop of Worms, and later Agricola's patron.

Before Agricola left Italy he had begun his most important work, the Latin *Dialectical Invention in Three Books* (*De dialectica inventione libri tres*), which he finished in Germany by 1479. This same year he visited Holland. Returning to Germany at the instigation of Dalberg, he lived chiefly at Heidelberg, but also spent some time at Worms, and finally made his way to Rome as Dalberg's emissary to congratulate the new Pope Innocent VIII on his election. On October 27, 1485, shortly after returning to Heidelberg from Rome, he died.

After his *Dialectical Invention*, Agricola's best-known work is the Latin translation of the *Progymnasmata* by the fourth-century Greek Aphthonius. This manual for elementary rhetorical exercises went through scores of Latin editions during the sixteenth and seventeenth centuries.[15] A short tract in the form of a letter *On the Curriculum* (*De formando studio*) is Agricola's next best-known work. His other productions, such as commentaries on Boethius' collected works, and a hymn in honor of St. Anne which reveals another side of his character, the Hertogenbosch piety, have long been forgotten, and were seldom or never reprinted even in Agricola's own age. His letters, orations, and some of his other works have never been published.

Agricola's works were written during the incunabular period and circulated in manuscript long before the now best known of them found their way into the new printing shops. The publishing of the *Dialectical Invention*[16] occurs in two principal waves. The first originated in the lower Rhineland, where the work was edited in the Low Countries by Alard of Amsterdam and at Cologne by Johann Matthaeus Phrissemius and epitomized by Bartholomew Latomus.[17] This wave reached its crest between about 1515 and 1528, but seems quickly to have spent itself, for Agricolan dialectic was destined to thrive only in the more scholastic Paris atmosphere. Here it was introduced by Johann Sturm when he was teaching at Paris in 1529. Two Paris editions appeared this same year, one published by the house of Wéchel, soon to become the major publisher of Ramus' works. This second, or Parisian, wave of publishing owed much of its force to Latomus, who epitomized Agricola's work and thereupon was named regius professor in 1534. The wave reached its crest between 1538 and 1543, when at least fifteen editions appeared in the French capital.

3. AGRICOLA, SCHOLASTICISM, AND THE GUTENBERG ERA

Ramus' dialectic grows thus out of more than anti-Aristotelianism alone. Its germ is the dialectic of the humanist Agricola, which is activated by contact with the older mental habits of scholasticism (as established particularly at Paris) and nourished by the new typographical culture.

Agricola and his followers demanded of their dialectic that it be congenial to real needs and to the humanists' pupil-oriented teaching as against the universities' teacher-oriented teaching. The truth or scientific soundness of the dialectic was a secondary consideration. Not that Agricola and his followers thought of their dialectic as false or scientifically unsound; they wanted it to be true and scientifically acceptable, but first and foremost they wanted it accommodated to what they felt was real "life" and to the real pedagogical situation. This meant, in effect (although the sense of history in the fifteenth and sixteenth centuries was not developed sufficiently to permit of such flat statement), that the new dialectic was to be adapted to the *Zeitgeist,* fitted expressly into the developments peculiar to this moment of man's cultural development.

Thus it is that the presence of a printing firm, focus of the newly forming typographical civilization, is highly significant in the development of Agricolan dialectic (as later of Ramism). The Agricolan and Ramist dialectic was to prove itself unexpectedly congenial to printing techniques. The complex relations between the mentality encouraged by Agricola and Ramus and the vogue of printing will be discussed in detail later, but one must note here the interplay between Rhineland interest in crafts, a possibly related desire communicated by an artisan and bourgeois culture to the humanists for a "simplified" philosophy whereby any and all reality could be "explained" in terms of simple analogy with mechanical constructs, and the Parisian dialectical engine. All these things seem to have been necessary to make Agricola's dialectic take hold, and this fact hints that the role of the Wéchel printing firm should not be minimized. Like Agricola himself, the Wéchels were of Flemish extraction, and their love of trade and love of culture are not always distinguishable.

It is difficult to believe that these Flemish merchant-printer-humanists, who wrote and signed their own prefaces to Ramus' works and played host to such personages as Sir Philip Sidney, were passive instruments in the process during which Ramist dialectic emerged from the Agricolan *Dialectical Invention,* itself a Rhenish import.[18] Although Agricola's influence had been felt by Hegius, Melanchthon, and others, the Agricolan dialectic had never really flourished in Germany until the Wéchels took it back there from Paris in 1572, reprocessed by Paris scholasticism under the close supervision of themselves and other typographers, and evolved in the tidy, tabular or crypto-tabular form of Ramism. In Italy, Agricola's *Dialectical Invention* had made a fugitive appearance in translation; but it never amounted to much among the Italians. Editions in old Italian libraries today are mostly Paris editions of 1529 and later. Only after its sojourn among the Paris dialecticians did the Agricolan dialectic make its way into other countries,

Spain (in Sanchez de las Brozas' adaptations of Ramus), England, and Holland.

Because it had circulated so long in manuscript form before reaching Paris, there are different textual traditions in the various printings of the *Dialectical Invention*. A later Cologne edition of 1539, which, with the companion volume of Agricola's *Lucubrations* and *Opuscula*, forms the only nearly complete edition of Agricola's works, undertakes to reproduce the complete text from Agricola's autograph manuscript. Some, at least, of the Paris editions of 1529 and after reproduce a somewhat shorter text, with fewer chapters and these differently numbered, but, as far as the general tenor and impact of the work go, the variations seem insignificant. A copy of one of these slightly shorter but probably better-known Paris editions, the Colinaeus edition of 1529, in the Bibliothèque Nationale at Paris was the personal copy of Jean de Bomont, who undertook to defend Ramus in 1544. It has marginal annotations, apparently in Bomont's own hand.[19] Citations here are taken chiefly from this edition (in fact, from this very copy of Bomont's), with occasional supplementary references to other editions doubtless known to Ramus and his entourage.

4. AGRICOLA'S DIALECTICAL INVENTION

Although running counter to the accepted logic more or less derivative from Aristotle, Agricola's dialectic makes no issue of being anti-Aristotelian as Ramus' was to do. On the contrary, Aristotle is one of Agricola's avowed sources, the others including chiefly Cicero, Quintilian, the fourth-century Hellenic philosopher and Aristotelian commentator Themistius, whose work on dialectical invention was known only through Boethius, and Boethius himself.[20]

The *Dialectical Invention* is a diffuse, urbane, and bemused work, divided, as is indicated by its full Latin title, *De inventione dialectica libri tres*, into three books. Book I treats of the dialectical *loci* or places, listing and discussing them. Book II takes up the nature and use of dialectic and the "question" as the "matter" of dialectic. The question is "matter" not in the sense, Agricola explains, that dialectic turns around it (*materia circa quam*), but in the more basic sense that it is like the material of the statue on which the artist works,[21] although elsewhere we are told, with seeming contradiction, that the material is "the thing about which we discourse."[22] The instrument for working on this matter is speech (*oratio*) and the application or use (*tractatus*) of dialectic concerns the preparation of what is going to be said and its application to various subjects.[23] This same book II also treats the division of the oration into four parts. Agricola recommends this highly, for he says that this division of Cicero's mature years is better than the six-part division of the younger Cicero and the two-part division of Aristotle.[24] The *narratio* and *confirmatio*, he adds, are to teach, whereas the *exordium* and *peroratio* are to move (*peroratio* means, as we shall see, no more than to teach in a particular way). In connection with the four parts of the oration Agricola also treats persuasion or *fides*.

Book II also contains Agricola's treatment of argumentation, which consists of judicious, expansive, and, on the whole, random remarks.[25] Of argumentation, there are two perfect kinds, induction and ratiocination, and two imperfect, example and enthymeme. The last is taken in the established Boethian sense, a syllogism which is defective not because it argues from and to probabilities (Aristotle's meaning for enthymeme), but because one of its three members is suppressed or understood. In keeping with this rather quantitative notion of defectiveness, Agricola favors abandoning the term "induction" for that of *enumeratio*.

Agricola's terminology for the parts of the syllogism is midway between that of earlier writers and that of Ramus. The terminology is tallied up and compared with that of others in a table furnished by Phrissemius at the end of book II. Agricola's gracious Latin masks the absence of any particular cogency in his cavalier selection of terms. He calls the major premise the *expositio*, a term which Phrissemius notes is Agricola's own, and for which Ramus will substitute *propositio*. The minor is called the *assumptio*, as it is in Cicero, Quintilian, and Boethius, and as it will be in Ramus. Putting aside Cicero's term *complexio* (which Ramus will adopt) and Quintilian's *connexio*, Agricola calls the conclusion either the *conclusio* (after Aristotle and Boethius) or the *intentio* (Agricola's own term, according to Phrissemius). These terminological shifts give a pretty fair impression of the way in which the traditions exploited and protracted by Agricola all through the *Dialectical Invention* are neither independent nor continuous, but rather overlap one another.

Book III treats: creating "effect" (*de effectibus*), which is close to what would be today styled emotional appeal; expansion (*amplificatio*) and condensation of speech; facility or "copie" of speech, including something like what we should today style imaginative activity; the arrangement of material in poetry, in history, and in the curriculum subjects; the parts of an oration, the order of questions and argumentation, and the application and practice of dialectic (*de usu et exercitatione*). It will be noted that Agricola becomes progressively more and more preoccupied with order or *dispositio*, so that, at its close, the *Dialectical Invention* covers ground strongly suggestive of Ramist "method."

What book III — or, for that matter, book II — had to do with the "invention" which is purportedly the concern of the work as a whole was not entirely clear to Agricola's contemporaries, nor is it clear today. Latomus says that book III has to do with the last two of the orator's three functions of teaching, pleasing, and moving his audience (these are present in the tradition through Cicero's work *On the Best Kind of Orators*, book II).[26] Phrissemius calls the book simply "De effectibus" and undertakes to defend Agricola against charges of introducing it out of pure ostentation. It was commonly asserted, Phrissemius reports, that Agricola had inserted this book "just to be different from Peter of Spain." But this charge is groundless, Phrissemius goes on, because this book really has to do with creating conviction in the audience.[27]

This riposte shows the role which Peter of Spain played as the guardian of tradition and the symbol of scholastic dialectic. It also shows the significance of book III, which changes the whole climate of dialectic as represented by Peter of Spain, and assimilates the art of dialectic to that of rhetoric in many of its aspects. Erasmus' rhetorical interests in the same subject will grow out of Agricola's concern with "copie of words" here in dialectic.

Agricola's work, which never got beyond its first part, invention, to its projected second part, judgment, is calculated to replace the old scholastic dialectic or logic as the third of the trivium subjects, grammar, rhetoric, and dialectic or logic. As we have just seen, dialectic is taken here in a large, loose, and practically undefinable sense to cover the whole field of discourse, in its rational, emotional, and other elements; it is practically everything that has to do with discourse short of grammatical structure and actual delivery. Indeed, today Agricola's book might well be headed, "What Boys Should Know about Discourse," or better, since it is addressed to teachers rather than to pupils, "Thoughts on Discourse and How to Teach It."

Compared with the older dialectic or logic, Agricola's is "humane," in a sense which makes it also amateur, graceful, and as logic scientifically irresponsible. It is concerned more with how to deal with an audience than with strict logical structure. Indeed, Agricola's book setting forth his science is itself a kind of oration, concluding with a *peroratio* expressly labeled such in many editions. It owes its popularity in great part to the happy combination of facile Latin and widely read eclecticism which enables Agricola not only to catch up the loose ends of questions in the minds of schoolteachers in his milieu, but also to approach the classical rhetoricians more or less as an equal, making a concession here, but a stricture there, and giving his readers the impression that Aristotle, Cicero, Quintilian, Themistius, and all the rest had not said the last word, if only because they were to all intents and purposes still living forces, with whom Agricola could converse, and through Agricola, even you and I. In short, the *Dialectical Invention* rang true in the way neo-Latinism at its best could ring true, as a dialogue carried on with a past sensed as still living in the present.

Despite all the affected fine points and digressions of his style (on which Erasmus was to remark),[28] Agricola fails to commit himself outright to any significant theoretical stands, either literary or philosophical. His objections to the views of others terminate chiefly in graceful verbal arabesques and delicate literary innuendos. But the psychological impact of the *Dialectical Invention* was both subtle and profound, particularly with regard to various obscure, but exceedingly real, issues with which the work was covertly involved.

5. DIALECTIC DEFINED: DISCOURSE AND PROBABILITIES

Agricola's definition of dialectic will be echoed in Ramus' early dialectical works. Dialectic, we are told, is the usual term for the "faculty of discoursing" or of "expatiating" (*disserendi facultas*), but popularly refers to the art (*ars*) itself of discoursing.[29] In full, it can be defined as "the art of discoursing with probability on any subject, insofar as the nature of the subject is capable of creating conviction."[30] Aristotle had distinguished the merely probable argumentation of his *Topics* from the scientific demonstration which his *Analytics* treat. Agricola seems by implication to do the same thing here. But actually, his earlier assertion that dialectic is the faculty of discoursing (without any limitation concerning probability or certitude) has the effect of annulling this later and more complete definition, since he lets the terms *ars, facultas, disserendi* and others play loosely through his discussion with no attempt to control their meanings. The definition in terms of probability simply leaks into Agricola's thought, but the leak and the resultant half-conscious blurring of probable argumentation and scientific demonstration is nothing new. It merely follows the central tradition of arts scholasticism as seen in Peter of Spain.[31]

Enlarging on Aristotle and on St. Albert the Great, the theologian St. Thomas Aquinas had discussed the differences between various logics: a logic of scientific demonstration (what would be called simply "logic" today); a logic of probability or of the more probable as used in discussion or debate, styled dialectic in the strict sense; another logic of the probable, rhetoric, where probability had to be sufficient, if not to decide between alternatives intellectually, at least to result in practical decision or action; a logic of poetry, still less probable, being a kind of logic of the "as-if"; and finally a logic of bogus probability, sophistic.[32] But these lucubrations of Aquinas the theologian were hardly viable in the world where scholastic philosophy was taught.[33] It was normal that the medieval philosophical tradition on the whole should perpetuate the impression conveyed by Peter of Spain: namely, there was only one logic, that traditionally called dialectic, "the art of arts and the science of sciences."[34]

6. DISCOURSE AS TEACHING

This implied spread of dialectic to cover all discourse is made fully explicit by Agricola in his assertion that "there are no places of invention proper to rhetoric."[35] Cicero, Quintilian, and Boethius, who treat places in rhetoric, are all wrong on this point we are told. Moreover, no one has ever explained properly the difference between *inventio* and *elocutio*; the latter was the business of the orator, who according to many, with whom Agricola seems to agree, is concerned with ornate speech (*ornate dicere*).[36] Agricola does not attempt to explain what ornamentation is, however, but merely insists that the places or *loci* belong to dialectic alone.

This limitation of loci to dialectic is the critical Renaissance divorce in the chronologically uneasy union of rhetoric and dialectic. Agricola decreed this divorce, which will carry through Ramism. He himself feels his role here is decisive, for he insists that no one before himself had ever properly related invention to ornate or striking expression (*elocutio*). The divorce of rhetoric from dialectic implies at the same time a union of invention and striking expression in any given text — or in "use," as Ramus was to say. In the Aristotelian view, not wholly grasped during the Middle Ages but fairly operative in some quarters,[37] any given piece of discourse was thought to be directed either to scientific, dialectical, or rhetorical ends (the last, in the main tradition, including poetry as a kind of metrical rhetoric). By implication the forces in play in the given piece of discourse were variously organized, and each art — the logic of strict scientific demonstration, dialectical logic, rhetorical logic (and poetic logic, which was almost never in theory effectively separated from rhetoric) — was a completely integrated whole governing monarchically the discourse in question, insofar as this was related to one or the other objective. The logic of science should be so set up as to account for the whole of a scientific performance; for example, geometrical demonstration. Similarly, dialectic should account for everything that enters into a strictly *sic-et-non* dialectical procedure: where the material comes from, how it is organized, its degree of effectiveness, and so on. Rhetoric should be able to do the same for rhetorical discourse. Since rhetorical discourse used places, rhetoric should have its own places, as it does in Aristotle's *Art of Rhetoric* (as against his dialectical *Topics*), and as it does in Quintilian's *Training in Oratory*. The rhetorical places, despite their superficial similarity to the dialectical places, should, in this theoretically implied Aristotelian view have a radically different orientation. As far as possible, the dialectician would want to work through probabilities to truth; the rhetorician, even though by no means indifferent to truth and probability, would work primarily toward an action — or, one might say, a reaction — on the part of his audience.

Agricola's scheme changes this. All discourse is to be directed toward the same objective. The distinction between a dialectic of probabilities and scientific demonstration, uncertain enough in the central medieval tradition, is deliberately eliminated. Either the scholastic disputation striving for scientific certitude (although often falling far short of it) is assimilated to other less scientific forms of discourse (Agricola's sympathies favor this) or all discourse can be assimilated to scientific, and the poem made as "logical" as the mathematical treatise (Ramus' will advance this view explicitly). Rhetoric is kept distinct from dialectic, but only by being given an a-logical assignment, concerned somehow with ornamentation. In his restriction of rhetoric to ornamentation Agricola follows a well-known medieval trend resulting from the decline of public eloquence after antiquity and related to the development of the disputation as discussed in Chapter VII. What in the classical view was rhetorical logic merges with dialectic, the general art of discourse. But the merger leaves definite traces in Agricolan dialectic, for into book III, which treats of effectiveness in speech, Agricola imports much of the quondam rhetorical apparatus.

There is no difficulty in discovering what the ultimate objective is to which all discourse is directed, according to Agricola. Declared repeatedly, the objective is teaching, pure and simple. The other two objectives of speech, traditional at least since Cicero's treatise *On the Best Kind of Orators*,[38] are strictly subordinate to teaching and practically absorbed in it. "Speech seems to have as its proper work to teach something to the listener. . . . Let it suffice to have said that speech can teach without moving or pleasing, but cannot move or please without teaching." [39] This position is unequivocal:

> The aim of speech can never be simply pleasure as distinct from moving and teaching another. For all speech teaches . . . . As far as invention goes, there is no difference between moving and teaching, for to move someone is to teach him as far as this is possible.[40]

As wielded by Agricola, the concept of teaching helps amalgamate the logic of science and the various logics of probability. "Sometimes we teach in order to make a person understand [science], but at other times just to persuade him [rhetoric]." [41] Even discourse which others would consider rhetorical or persuasive, whether a man is being led to persuasion willingly, or forced to it against his will, is seen by Agricola as fundamentally a teaching process.[42] Teaching, and hence producing conviction is "making what is unknown more known." [43] Thus it is the sum and substance of all discourse, and the basic concept from which all consideration of discourse must depart. The stress on teaching or *doctrina* which builds up in the medieval university tradition reaches its apogee here. For dialectic, which swallows up all discourse, is itself engulfed by *doctrina*.

The redistribution of the field of discourse between dialectic and rhetoric is connected not only with the notion of teaching and with the practice of disputation discussed in Chapter VII, but also, from another point of view, is really only an application (quite subconscious on Agricola's part) of his notions of loci to the field of teaching itself, represented, in practice, by the "arts" or curriculum subjects. It is difficult to see how Agricola could have made room for the probable logics in his economy of loci at all. Items conceived with relation to loci are pictured in containers which are insulated from one another and do not overlap. How, then, could two or more arts — dialectic and rhetoric, for example — also couched in this kind of economy, share the same "places," or share the notion of "place" or *locus* at all? The difficulty here will become all too patent with Ramus, and will terminate in his proclamation of "Solon's Law." But the difficulty is already real with Agricola and results in the assignment of a "separate" field of operation to rhetoric, which can apply ornament to what has been drawn out of the loci and turned over to it by dialectic.

7. TOPICS VERSUS CATEGORIES: TOPICAL LOGICS

From the point of view of subsequent intellectual history, the most central operations in Agricola's *Dialectical Invention* are his building up of the old notion of *topoi* (topics) or commonplaces at the expense of the predicaments or categories, and his development of an outlook in which the former rather than the latter control the general logical heritage and teaching.

The nature of the *topoi* — or loci or places or commonplaces — is well-known. They are the headings or key notions to which one turns to find out what is available in one's store of knowledge for discourse on any given subject. The places help thus either to answer questions (which have two members, a subject and predicate, and are often styled "complex themes" in the tradition transmitted via Agricola), or to treat "simple themes" (*themata simplicia*), such as man, animal, body, and so on.[44]

Lists of the topics or places commonly include such things as definition, genus, species, wholes, parts, adjacents (corresponding roughly to what would, in another way, be treated under the various categories of "accidents"), relatives, comparisons, opposites, and (what Agricola's own list omits) witnesses. These are the headings one is to run through when one has to say something on any subject, to pronounce a eulogy or to plead a cause or simply to give a lecture on a question of the day.

The topical tradition is omnivorous in its selection of these headings, and tends to assimilate and adapt any and all sorts of classifications with which its users are likely to be familiar and which thus are likely to be serviceable. Thus, even before Aristotle's *Topics*, and from then on, serviceable bits of the general philosophical apparatus, including the well-known Aristotelian categories or predicaments and the related "predicables" (genus, specific difference, species, property, improper accidents) were more or less incorporated into the classificatory finding-apparatus among the "places."

The manner of conceptualizing is different for the categories and the places: relation (*relatio*) is a category, related items (*relata*) a place: likeness (*similitudo*) falls under the categories, like items or like things (*similia*) are among the places. The topics are thus more concrete conceptualizations than the categories. But, even though this fact will have important psychological and historical consequences, there is little disposition to maintain rigid distinctions between categories and topics, least of all among many of Agricola's followers, including the Ramists.

The items which will soon appear in Ramus' *Dialectic* as "arguments" and will be impaled on the bracketed tables of dichotomies have often been referred to as categories. But since they grow out of the topical tradition and particularly out of Agricola's *Dialectical Invention*, they are not really categories at all. As Ramus himself will make explicitly clear, they are simply these same topics or loci or "places." More explicitly, they are commonplaces, for they are sources of arguments common to all sorts of subjects and available to all as matters of common knowledge. Ramus will call these places "arguments," although it was more common to think of the "arguments" as what was stored "in" the places. However, there was room for latitude; a place, such as genus or species, could itself serve as an argument, and an argument derived from a place could likewise serve as a place for the derivation of further arguments. This telescoped arrangement can be observed in the Ramists' tables or earlier in certain editions of Agricola's *Dialectical Invention*, where, for example, cognates (*cognata*) yield the arguments of cause and consequence, and the latter yield respectively efficient and final cause, and effects and predetermined effects (*destinata*).[45]

Although the topics or places are items of which the orator or the dialectician avails himself to suggest matter for his subject or for proving his case, with Agricola the topical tradition tends to forget its limited objectives and to think of itself as somehow the adequate instrument for dealing with all knowledge whatsoever. With Ramism, it will have absorbed and eliminated the categories and thus interest in predication. But this development is explainable as due in great part to the arts-course curriculum, and to the fact mentioned above that the scholastic philosophy of the arts course, taken as a whole, had proved always quite incapable of maintaining in the curriculum an effective distinction between a dialectic arguing probabilities and a strictly scientific demonstration. A result of this confusion was the persuasion that when one was teaching what was really the topical tradition, oriented toward dialectical discourse (in the sense of probable argumentation), one was also teaching the tradition of scientific logic. The resulting curriculum subject or discipline, in which what has been historically the topical tradition has absorbed the other logical disciplines and proposes to account for more or less the whole of the intellectual processes, I style a topical logic or a place-logic.

Agricola's preoccupation with the topics, and even his bid to improve on their treatment, associates him with a well-known medieval tradition. This was a tradition involving the study of Boethius' *Commentaries on the Topics of Cicero* (derivative from Aristotle's *Topics*) and Boethius' work

On Topical Differences. In these two works Boethius proposed to revamp
the topical classifications of Aristotle and Themistius,[46] each of whom had
himself proposed to improve on the classifications made by his own predecessors. From the Sophists on, the topics had formed a part of the logical apparatus. But the long-term effect of Agricola's work (if not his clear intent), was
that the topics would not only accompany, but would almost crowd out
the rest of the traditional matter.

Hence, the Aristotle whom Agricola exploits is not the Aristotle of the
Categories nor of the *Analytics*, but the Aristotle of the *Topics*, from whom
Agricola's chief other sources, Cicero, Quintilian, Themistius, and Boethius,
are largely derivative. The domination of the topical logical mentality in
Agricola's case is most strikingly evident in his declared objective: to free
his dialectic from the concern with predication which forms a principal axis
of Aristotle's own thought. This concern Agricola says [47] not only obtrudes
in other parts of the *Organon* but beclouds the discussion in the very *Topics*
themselves, for it has no business there. He does not care, he adds, *how* one
thing applies to another, provided only that it apply and that the application
be teachable.[48] He wants a dialectic purged of psychological and epistemological implications, built not out of an account of the nature of human
knowledge, but out of a list of the topics as objects of common knowledge
on which discourse turns.

To a certain extent, Agricola's approach to dialectic is that of a humanist
philologist or "grammarian" dealing with a text and the use of words rather
than that of a thinker interested in constructing an abstract science. This
approach itself favored the exaltation of the places or topics in another way,
by favoring the subordination of dialectic to rhetoric, with which the places
had also been intimately connected. Like Erasmus and other Renaissance
humanists, and like Dante and other medieval Italians, Agricola advocated
a curriculum in which the order was grammar, dialectic, and then rhetoric.[49]
This order, in the event, was never effectively imposed on the European
educational system on any appreciable scale. The older order of grammar,
rhetoric, and dialectic or logic won out. But by featuring the topics, dialectic
or logic became a kind of rhetoric after all.

Although neither Agricola nor his contemporaries seemed aware of the
implications of a logic in which the central classificatory apparatus was something like Aristotle's *Topics* rather than *Categories*, these implications are of
prime importance. The *Categories* or *Predicaments* of Aristotle are not a
classification of things, nor of being-in-general, nor are they a classification of
the whole range of human concepts as such. Neither are they categories in
the modern sense of a system of classes into which items are "put." As their
name indicates and a recent study confirms, they are types of predicates conceived of more or less as "accusations" (or "outcries" in the market place or
assembly, *categoriae*, transformed into Latin as *praedicamenta*, things spoken

out) which can be brought against a subject or "prime substance."[50] They are a generic list of the kind of things one attributes or urges against a subject (of an enunciation) by *saying* something of a subject (κατηγορεῖν καθ' ὑποκειμένου — *Metaphysics* I 2 — 1053b). The categories are therefore concerned with universals in terms of their "attribution" to something; for universals exist not in themselves but by being attributed to a subject. This attribution is effected by a statement, an assertion, a proposition, which expresses a judgment or decision regarding the validity of the attribution, or, the justness of the "accusation" — for example, when "this" is "accused" of being a man in the statement, *This is a man.*

It is a commonplace that, because of the derivative character of our knowledge through the senses, all intellectual cognition must be treated by analogy with sensory cognition, the intellectual "field" by analogy with the sensory fields. All terms by means of which we conceptualize intellectual activity in thinking about it involve some sensory reference, overt or latent. Any treatment of mental activity, logical as well as psychological, from ancient to the most recent times, makes this quite plain. Thus, description of mental activity in terms of "composition" (putting together), or "implication" (folding up, or folding back upon), or "definition" (setting bounds or limits), or "division," or even "description" (drawing a line around or sketching) all exploit, more or less evidently, an analogy between the field of intellectual activity and a field which involves local motion and is sensorily apprehended in terms of sight.[51]

Formal logic is fundamentally an attempt to deal with the activity of the mind in terms of these and related visualist analogies. It is interested in the "structure" of our intellectual activity — a notion which cannot even be conceived except by analogy with some sort of spatial diagram. It does not concern itself with "tone" or other aural-type phenomena. For this reason, formal logic is closely connected with mathematics (from the time of the Greeks to that of Alfred North Whitehead) to the extent that modern formal logic is called, somewhat naively, "mathematical" logic, as though all strictly formal logic were not this sort of thing.[52]

Aristotelian logic admits of formal development,[53] and was so developed by the medieval logicians far beyond where Aristotle had left it. The categories themselves can be treated diagrammatically or spatially, and thus ultimately quantitatively (in terms, for example, of their "comprehension" and, much more, of their "extension") in order to generate various kinds of "class logics." Yet there remains in the notion of the categories a certain residue which cannot be so reduced because it derives not from visual-type but from aural-type analogies.[54]

This residue of the aural or auditory is not explicitly attended to by Aristotle. However, it is inseparable from his thinking because the categories are at root (although not always explicitly) conceived of as parts of enunciations.

Human knowledge for Aristotle exists in the full sense only in the enuncia-tion, either interior or exteriorized in language; the *saying* of something about something, the *uttering* of a statement, the expression of a *judgment* (ultimately a declaring a "yes" or a "no"), or, in what from the point of view of grammar is a sentence, a union of subject and predicate (*praedicatum* = the thing *said*). Simple terms exist in order to be put into enunciations. Syllogisms or other discursive mental processes terminate in enunciations. The enunciation alone makes "complete" sense. But the enunciation cannot be conceived of solely in terms of visual analogies; these must be comple-mented with the aural if we are to form a concept at all adequate to this elemental cognitive process.

As it comes down to us, the enunciation is itself conceived of in a visual-aural tension. The predicate has an auditory orientation, and the "subject" (*sub-iectum*, something thrown under; the Greek equivalent, ὑποκείμενον, means etymologically the same thing) is based on a corresponding visual analogy involving local motion. This is to say that the subject of a proposition is somehow related to the world of "objects" more than the predicate is. It is passive: it is subject, it *undergoes* the predicate. Agricola's scorn of predica-tion in terms of a (visually conceived) logic of "places," and Ramus' corre-sponding failure in his 1545 *Training in Dialectic* to permit any discussion of the enunciation at all, is evidence, therefore, of the general, unconscious veer-ing toward the visual and "objective" which marks the Gutenberg and post-Gutenberg epoch.

There has been no lack of real desire to form a concept of the enunciation based on purely visual analogies. All explanation and all science, metaphysics included, attempts as far as possible, to reduce the sensory analogies it em-ploys to those drawn from vision, and thus tends to traffic in quantity and number. A drift toward the visual is inseparable from any economy of ex-planation. The superiority of vision and of the kind of field in which it works over the other senses has led it to be styled from antiquity the most cognosci-tive (*maxime cognoscitivus*) or most informative of the senses. We are today more than ever witnesses of attempts to reduce everything supplied by the other senses — sounds, smells, tastes, pressures — to charts and tables which can be visually assimilated. Sound is registered by oscillographs. Odors, tastes, and the manifold of sensations which we group together under the term "touch" are tabulated visually in an infinity of ways, in graphs where they can be differentiated (but not experienced) in terms of wave lengths and other spatially apprehensible phenomena. Within the field of sight itself, nonspatial apprehensions (that is, colors), are reduced spatially to wave lengths and the like. Color, of course, is in a special sense the object of vision, but it appears to the sight always in some form of spatial extension, and the maximum of visual perception is represented by a curious absence of color: one sees "as clearly as *black* on *white*." Visually constituted ideals such as clarity do not generally involve color, which assimilates more readily to sound ("tones," "loud" and "quiet" colors, etc.). "Visual education" means education less in terms of colors than in terms of diagrams and charts deployed in space, with color added for purposes which tend to be rather rhetorical, to help fix attention rather than to convey added information.

Reduction of sensory data in the opposite direction — from space vision to color vision, or on to sound, smell, taste, and the various touches — are relatively useless and practically unknown. An exception must be made for certain reductions to the least abstract sense, touch — or, better, the various touches, including kinaesthetic sensation — which, because of their engagement in space through motor activity, can "pinch hit" for sight (as in the Braille alphabet). But touches engage space at a level less advantageous than that of vision insofar as cognition is concerned. Other reductions of visual sensations are seldom even thought of. Arrangements of sounds to represent the shape of the earth's surface, or of smells which would correspond to wave lengths in the diatonic scale would seem to have little to recommend them, even if they may be possible.

The visual is the area most proper to science: if what it registers is not eternal, at least it exhibits the pseudo-eternity of repose. Reduction to spatial form fixes everything, even sound. *Verba volant, scripta manent.* When compared with sight, not only hearing, but all the other senses are curiously fugitive. Smell and taste readily fatigue. Even touch registers space only by moving through it. Vision has a maximum stability in this sublunary world.

For these reasons, qualities will no doubt continue always to be reduced quantitatively and to be studied by the eye in terms of spatial and arithmetical analysis. Even metaphysical analysis will exhibit analogous preferences, for it will find the analogies with sight more *explanatory* than analogies with the other senses. The metaphysician "intuits" or "regards," he does not intellectually "taste" or "feel" or even "hear" his first principles (as the mystic does). Indeed, the more explanation of any sort is the objective of thought or discourse, the more visually based conceptualizations come into play. The very objectives of explanation such as "clarity" and "distinctness" are concepts formed by evident analogy with the realm of vision. This is only another way of saying that all explanation as such moves toward abstraction. For vision is the most "abstract" (analogously) of all the senses, and the sense or senses of touch at the other end of the scale are the most "concrete," so that, although one studies the activity of an object, directly or indirectly, chiefly by vision, one feels assured of an object's *existence* more by touching it than in other ways.

There are difficulties, however, in the tendency to reduce other sensory knowledge to visual terms. An oscillograph of a sound gives everything about the sound — except the sound itself. This is the price of becoming more "abstract," or explanatory. The description of a word (*verbum*, or *vox*) as a sign (*signum*) suffers from the same disability insofar as the notion of sign is based on a visual analogy. A word is more than a sign of some*thing*, even of an intelligible something such as a concept. It is a cry, a voice, something which comes from the interior of a person, who as a *person* can never be "explained," and which somehow manifests this interior. Human cognitive processes and intellectual activity can thus never be adequately grasped for what they are unless they are thought of not only in terms of knowledge-by-sight but also in terms of this knowledge-by-sound and the aspects of this knowledge-by-sound which do not reduce to visual analogies. These aspects are much more evident in the enunciation than anywhere else — which is to be expected, since this is the central act of intellection which has "complete sense." Thus it is that the enunciation is intransigent in the face of all attempts to conceive of it in terms of visual analogies alone. It can be conceived of as a "judgment," a judicial act, a saying yes or no — but there is no adequate visualist equivalent of this act. It can be conceived of as an "enunciation" — a speaking out. It can be conceived of as the coupling of two concepts, but of what kind of concepts, for conjunctions and prepositions couple concepts? It is a coupling of subject and predicate — and this last term conceals an auditory analogy again; *praedicatum* is the thing cried out or *said*.

The categories which give their name to the first of the *Organon* treatises belong not only to the world of explanation and scientific understanding, but also to the realm of the "word." Insofar as they belong to this latter realm, they elude formal logical treatment and also the quantitative implications which such treatment inevitably involves. This irreducibly vocal or audile element in the notion of knowledge which the categories imply was not developed or even clearly adverted to by Aristotle himself, and certainly forgotten by the medieval arts course. Although there are occasional protests against nominalism which show that perhaps its chief objectionable feature was the neglect of the full implications of the enunciation, these protests were ineffectual with regard to the arts course tradition as a whole. This is shown by the way the same protests keep recurring year after year in the pages of the Paris *Chartularium*. It is also clear from the organization of the logic of Peter of Spain. Peter quickly brushes aside the assertion or proposition as such (together with semantics) in the first brief *tractatus* of his *Summulae logicales* in order to devote the remaining eleven treatises to the main business of medieval logic: structure and terms treated in quantified fashion.

The tendency to neglect the oral and auditory, and ultimately existential, repercussions emanating from the concept of the categories and to reduce the latter to a mere classifying apparatus is understandable. It corresponds to a tendency discernible in all formal logic, from medieval logic to that of Boole or Whitehead, to disregard the assertion as a psychological event; and it seems universal. In all the history of logic one can find nowhere a predicational logic — that is, a logic taking as its center of interest the assertion or judgment in its full psychological and metaphysical implications — which develops an analysis of logical structure at all comparable for nicety and finesse with logics which put aside predication and devote themselves explicitly to formal structure. On grounds of purely *formal* logical analysis, St. Thomas Aquinas, insofar as his extant works evince, is an amateur compared to his contemporary Peter of Spain or to Peter's epigoni. Similarly, on grounds of purely *formal* analysis, contemporary neoscholastic logicians (at least those who move only in the orbits commonly taken to be neoscholastic) cannot compete with the tradition of Boole, Whitehead, Carnap, and the rest. One need only compare their books quite summarily to see. The assertion or act of predication is the act which establishes contact between the outer world of reality and the inner world of the person (however one may ultimately explain these two worlds), and the categories or predicaments which enter into this act are denizens of the bridge between the mind and things. This is why, much to Ramus' chagrin,[55] Aristotle discusses predication and the categories not only in his logical treatises but also in his *Metaphysics*.

Because the assertion faces outward to external reality as well as inward to its own logical structure, a logic centered on the act of predication fails — at least as it manifests itself in historical reality — to develop as a formal logic. Formal logic, after a fashion, moves away from the *act* of predication itself. The scientific analysis of logic breaks the statement into its component parts and thus destroys it. As an undivided vital act, it has existential import but is rather unmanageable logically. Human mental activity is circumscribed by these conditions and suffers from a kind of poverty as a result: its principal act, the enunciation, the imputing of a predicate to a subject, really faces outside itself to the extramental and thus, in a way, betrays the conditions of its own (mental) existence. Perhaps this is why any viable *formal* logic has tended to specialize not in statements as such, but in the parts of statements, such as terms, and in combinations of statements.[56]

All these connections of the categories with predication and of predication with existence were seldom if ever adverted to in the logical tradition out of which Agricola and Ramus grow. Certainly, they were never adverted to in precisely the way they are here, for the perspectives just elaborated are unmistakably twentieth century. Nevertheless, the implications were there, caught ineluctably in the terms category or predicament, and discernible to any who had the patience to examine the etymological formation and the full signification of these terms less cursorily than the average logician did. These implications resulted in a curious impasse: the classificatory apparatus which was constantly inviting development in terms of "comprehension" and "extension" — visualist terms — was actually so conceived as to set up a resistance against these terms. For the categories, the ultimate genera of classification, were so conceptualized as to include a latent and irreducible auditory or oral component. They belonged not only to the world of "objects," but to the interior realm of person and word.

The maneuver in which Rudolph Agricola plays such an important part consisted of substituting for the categories as a classificatory apparatus at the center of philosophical studies the topics or loci or "places" (also called commonplaces). These "places" sometimes correspond with the categories in name, for they commonly include references to quantity, quality, relation, and so on, together with a diversity of other items, but what psychologically differentiates a topical classification from a categorical classification (and a topical logic from a categorical class logic) is the fact that the supreme genera or classes themselves are thought of not in a concept which echoes, however faintly, an auditory approach to knowledge, but rather in a concept formed on exclusively visualist, spatial analogies. A "topic," in its Greek ($\tau \acute{o} \pi o s$), Latin (*locus*), English (place, or locus), and other vernacular forms (German, *Ort*, or *Gemeinplatz*; Dutch, *gemeenplaats*; French, *lieu, lieu commun*; Spanish, *lugar, lugar comun*), is conceived of, analogously of course, as a place or location — a formulation connected with the related notion of literary "theme" ($\theta \acute{e} \mu a$, that which is placed or laid down). In this formulation, discourse itself is conceived of as the sort of thing that can be moved into and out of the "places." And the oral-auditory is liquidated in favor of the visual.

8. INVENTION AND JUDGMENT

Agricola's notion of loci is the key to his notion of the parts of dialectic which will be passed on to Ramus. We are told that dialectic has two "parts": invention (*pars inveniendi*), "the part consisting in thinking out the middle term or argument" which will make a conclusion possible; and judgment (*pars iudicandi*) "by which we judge similitudes." [57] This is equivalent to saying that dialectic consists of finding middle terms or arguments in the loci and fitting them into the discourse afterwards. For example, if one wants to answer the question, Is man dialectically inclined? one searches the loci and finds a middle term or "argument" such as "rational." This, one recognizes, is similar to, or "accords" with, "dialectically inclined," whereupon one can argue: Man is rational. But rational beings are dialectically inclined. Therefore man is dialectically inclined.

Directly or indirectly, the two parts of dialectic which Agricola proposes enter the general logical tradition largely through the second book of Cicero's *Topics*, a work rooted in the rhetorical rather than in the logical tradition. Here they are said to be "parts" (*partes*) of all discourse organized by conscious technique. The first part, invention, is identified with the *Topics* themselves; the second part alone is called dialectic. There is another tradition concurrent in the later Renaissance which is represented in the vaguely Agricolan *Witcraft* of Ralph Lever, and in John Seton, Thomas Wilson, and Thomas Blundeville. This tradition reverses the two parts, making judgment or *critica* ($\kappa \rho \iota \tau \iota \kappa \acute{\eta}$) or disposition (*dispositio*) first and invention second. [58] It has been called Aristotelian. But it derives more directly from Boethius than from Aristotle, although it was supported by the fact that the Aristotelian treatises concerned with the three acts of the intellect (simple apprehension, judgment, and ratiocination), which together constitute *critica* in Lever, are commonly placed in the *Organon* before the *Topics*.

The reversibility of these two concepts (Blundeville will not only reverse them but telescope them) reveals that invention and judgment are protean in their applicability to intellectual and linguistic activity. Complex as it is, the field of human knowledge and discourse provides a dazzling variety of phenomena which can be approximated to the invention-judgment allegory. For allegory it is: a man finds something (invention) and pronounces as a judge upon it by comparing it with something else (judgment); a person can "find" an individual sense experience and compare it with another sense experience he has had; he can bring it to bear on an abstract judgment he has already made; he can "find" an abstract judgment and decide something about it; he can find an external object; or he can "find" a word. Since Aristotle's preoccupation with scientific demonstration at least, there has also been the matter of "finding" the items that go into the making of a completely integrated deductive science (regarded as similar to an ideal Euclidean geometry), and of "judging" about the entirety of the ensemble — presumably by comparing it with what it ought to be. This is a kind of central scholastic application of the notion, canonized in the expressions *via inventionis* and *via iudicii* and leading directly to preoccupation with method, for *methodus* is the "way" (*via*) through such a process.

A notion of invention and judgment such as this is transmitted from Aristotle to Hugh of St. Victor [59] and thence through St. Albert into St. Thomas Aquinas, [60] and is accepted by Ramus' adversary Jacques Charpentier. [61] But these same authors have other ways, too, of applying these amoeba-like concepts. Thus, St. Thomas speaks elsewhere of "finding" conclusions by reasoning down to them from first principles, and then of "judging" the results by reasoning in reverse back to the first principles again. [62] And indeed, the text of Hugh of St. Victor just referred to is not free of this last notion of judgment conceived not as an additional process but as a verification of what the inventive act has accomplished.

To try to exhaust all the different ways in which this very elemental invention-judgment apparatus can be applied to human intellection and expression is useless. An excursion into the literature soon leads us to the conclusion that at one time or another all the possible applications, and a good many impossible ones, have been made. Many of these are serviceable, but they often remain awkward. This is true particularly of the suggestion that there are always two clear-cut stages in acquiring or recalling knowledge: one in which isolable items are assembled; and a well marked-off one following in which some sort of judicial decision (like that of a prince-legislator or a judge handing down a sentence) is rendered. [63]

The reason for the difficulties which these two concepts present is that they are not traceable to two such clear-cut steps in cognition, but rather to two different ways of approaching the cognitive process. Invention sees it in terms of an analogy with a high visual and spatial component: one *looks* for things in order to find them; one *comes* upon them (*in-venio*, εὑρίσκω). This notion is allied to the Greek (and Latin) concept of knowledge and understanding, based on some sort of analogy with vision (γιγνώσκω, *intelligere*). Judgment cannot be readily interpreted in terms of such an analogy; it is connected with judicial procedure (and thus with the categories or "accusations"), and suggests the Hebraic concept of knowledge (*yadha'*), which is analogous to hearing. The presence of these two items at the very center of the traditional account of the operations of the mind thus confirms what has been noted above concerning the categories; namely, that any attempt to deal somewhat fully with the intellectual processes must rely on analogies between understanding and hearing as well as between understanding and seeing.

The scientizing impulse, however, favors visual-type concepts and seeks to liquidate the auditory formulations. Consequently, alongside the term *iudicium*, there is observable in the dialectical tradition a marked tendency to think of this second part or its equivalent not as judgment or predication or as anything else so overtly suggestive of the oral and existentially-oriented world of sound, but rather as arrangement (*dispositio* in the Latin tradition, or, in the Greek of book VIII of Aristotle's *Topics*, τάξις), a concept accommodated to the visualist notion of places, so that the operation which follows after drawing the arguments out of the loci is considered to be that of deploying them in a new order adapted to the purpose at hand. In the later editions of his *Dialectic*, Ramus will prefer *dispositio* to *iudicium*, and John Milton, after wrangling with himself and Ramus over the relative suitability of the two terms, will also declare for *dispositio*.[64]

Since the creation of discourse inevitably involves *saying* something, however, and not merely ranging concepts, this second part of dialectic adapts far less well to visualist imagery than the first. This is one of the most profound reasons for a curious impasse at the heart of the topical tradition. Writers in this tradition are rather consistently hard put to develop satisfactorily any part of dialectic other than the topics themselves. Aristotle's treatise on dialectic is called simply the *Topics*; its first seven books treat primarily of the places, and only a part of the eighth and last book deals expressly with the setting up of argumentation or arrangement (τάξις, *dispositio*). Cicero, who, as has been seen, distinguishes the *Topics* from what others call the second half of dialectic or *dispositio* (he calls this second part simply *dialectica*) conveniently forgets to write the second part at all. The same curious procrastination marks the career of Agricola, whose work on dialectic never gets beyond his *Dialectical Invention*. His commentator, Johann Matthaeus Phrissemius, says Agricola would have written *Dialectical Judgment* (or perhaps *Dialectical Disposition?*), too, "if he had only lived longer."[65] This statement would be more credible were it not that others in the Agricolan tradition, such as the English rhetorician Leonard Cox and the Spanish theologian Melchior Cano, likewise fail to live long enough to produce the treatises on judgment or arrangement with which they had promised over and over again they would complement their published treatises on invention.[66] We seem here to be in the presence of some mysterious occupational disease.

The procrastination in getting into the second half of a topical logic or dialectic after having done with the first half will reach its apogee late in the history of Ramism. German secondary school teachers in the Ramist tradition will maintain that they have only to stock the student's head (like an Agricolan locus) with discreet simple apprehensions (corresponding to the arguments), which the student then carries off with him to the university like so many intellectual bricks or stones, where it is the business of this more advanced faculty to teach the young men how to "judge" and assemble the lot of them.[67] Since Ramus had long before supplied the second part of dialectic, missing in Agricola, we have here the Ramist tradition actually reverting to, and attesting the force of the pre-Ramist state of affairs. In this eerie pedagogical recommendation two centuries and a half after Agricola's death, the affinity between the Agricolan and Ramist approach to knowledge through the places and the Cartesian attitudes toward "ideas" as starting places becomes recognizable, and both the Agricolan and the Ramist dialectic appear in some of their larger contexts in the development of thought.

Seen in terms of the parts of dialectic it proposes, the Agricolan-Ramist operation is thus one which substitutes for the more usual three-part dialectic or logic related to the categorical tradition and built around simple terms, propositions, and argumentation, a two-part dialectic rhetorical in orientation in that its two "parts" were the *inventio* and *dispositio* of ancient rhetoric and in that it was shaped radically around the rhetorically oriented topical heritage. Ramus' role in the operation will be to supply the second half of this dialectic which is missing in Agricola and defective in the tradition generally. His performance will yield both a second half of dialectic, reconditioned in a visualist fashion which is not new but is carried to lengths never before realized, and Ramist method itself, which is contained as a "part" in this second half of dialectic but which really to a great extent grows up as Ramus' account of his own procedure in constructing the second half. The whole process through Agricola and Ramus is thus of a piece with the tendencies, discernible somewhat later, to deal with reality in a more visualist, observational, "objective," and, finally, mechanistic way.

Ramus is not exactly a mechanist, and Agricola is one still less. They are Latin stylists, Ramus impassioned, Agricola urbane and mildly Olympian, working in the tradition of Renaissance humanism. This makes it all the

more interesting to discover that beneath their professed humanist interest
in eloquence and the spoken word, they both register and promote a marked-
ly visualist approach to knowledge which actually antedates in great part
the coming visualist emphasis of the physicists in the approach to explaining
the world. Their two-part dialectic reveals some of the curious affinities between the topical tradition which humanism was forcing to the surface and
the use of spatial analogies in describing thought. Its very incoherencies echo
out of the centuries.

9. THE LOCI OR PLACES: WOODS AND BOXES

John of Salisbury reports that Parmenides the Egyptian spent his life on
a rock in order to discover the logical loci, only to have them taken away from
him and exploited by his disciples (of whom he had altogether too many)
because his discovery made him so famous.[68] This report seems to have a
symbolic validity at least. From antiquity, the loci or places were conceived
of as something like Parmenides' rock, notions or ideas to which one betook
oneself when one wanted to find out something about some subject or other
either to answer a question concerning the subject or to prove a point. "Proving" something is taken in a very large sense, for the general logical and
rhetorical tradition tended to regard all assertion as, in one way or another,
a form of teaching or "proving."

Some places provided material or "arguments" only for special classes of
subjects, such as law, physics, or politics, but others were common to all subjects, providing arguments for anything at all, and hence were called commonplaces or *loci communes*, as Aristotle and Cicero had explained.[69] Whether one was looking for something to say about a proposed law, a physical
problem, a political question, or about Plato, honor, or the nature of man, one
could have recourse to the place of *genus*, asking what kind of a thing this
was that was being considered, or to *adiuncta*, asking what sort of things it
was surrounded by or associated with, and so on. By medieval and Renaissance
times, if not earlier, while this distinction between the special or "private"
(*idia topica* in Aristotle) and the "common" places was sometimes honored
in the production of collections of material arranged according to legal places,
theological places, and other places, it generally amounted to little in theory
or practice. Relevant material from the commonplaces could be incorporated
into a collection of specialized places, and the specialized places themselves
could be regarded as refinements of the commonplaces. "Place" and "commonplace" tended to be used quite interchangeably.

The notion of commonplaces or loci, however, was itself certainly commonplace in the more usual modern sense of this word to anyone formed in
the rhetorical-dialectical tradition, as almost everyone who went to school in
Western Europe from antiquity through the Renaissance was formed. At the

height of medieval antirhetorical logicism, Peter of Spain feels it necessary, as has been seen, to include in his *Summulae logicales* a treatise on the places, in which he devotes only a phrase to explaining what a place is. His reason for this short shrift is not hard to guess; the notion of the places is not scientific in any precise logical or psychological sense, since the exact application of the local analogy in play here is very difficult, if not impossible, to determine. It is symptomatic of change that men of the Agricolan age paid more attention to the notion of a place or locus than medieval educators had. And it is symptomatic of Agricola's importance that his definition or description became the dominant one. A dialectic which cites Cicero, Quintilian, Rudolph Agricola, and Aristotle as its sources and which was published at Paris during Ramus' boyhood sums up the common doctrine thus:

A place is some common distinctive mark of a thing by the help of which it is possible to discover readily what can be proven [or what is probable] with regard to any particular thing; or, as Cicero describes it, it is the seat of an argument.[70]

Except for the last phrase, ascribed explicitly to Cicero, this definition is simply a verbatim repetition of Agricola from the *Dialectical Invention*.[71] It will be noted that we are here informed on the one hand what Cicero *says* a place is, and on the other simply what it *is*. What it *is* is what Agricola says it is.

The notion of the "seat" of an argument here is interesting because of its personalist implications (only persons, or at least living beings, properly sit down). But in this Agricolan age, if this suggestion of a personalist mentality lingers, it is yielding to the more diagrammatic concept of place: the seat of an argument is simply its locus, affirms George Valla, who wrote a whole treatise on "seats" of this sort.[72]

The imagery underlying even a carefully controlled scientific conceptualization is crucial. That underlying the far from scientific notion of the places is more crucial still. It is interesting to see Agricola's attempt to build a philosophy of cognition out of this latter notion in his answer to the query regarding why the loci were instituted:

Things are immensely numerous, and their various properties and differences from one another are likewise immensely numerous. Hence it is that all the things which go with each and every individual thing, or which fail to go with it, cannot possibly be embraced by any utterance or by the human mind. However, although everything is distinct from everything else by its own distinctive marks, there is in all these things something common, and all of them tend to a likeness in nature, insofar as all of them have their own proper substances, all of them take their rise from certain causes, and all of them effect something. Thus, greatly gifted men have cut out from this profuse variety of things these common headings (*capita*), such as substance, cause, result, and others which we shall treat of, so that when we set ourselves to thinking about some certain thing, following these headings, we may go immediately through the whole nature and parts of the thing in question, through all the things which agree with it and which disagree with it, and draw out from these headings the arguments adapted to the matters proposed. These things, common in that since they contain within themselves whatever can be said on any matter, they thus contain all arguments, were called by these men places (*loci*), because all the instruments for establishing conviction are located within them as in a receptacle or a treasure chest. A place (*locus*) is thus nothing other than a certain common distinctive note of a thing, by the help of which it is possible to discover what can be proven (or what is probable) with regard to any particular thing. Let that be our definition of a place (*locus*).[73]

The easy and arabesqued flow of Agricola's Latin and the general currency of the notions he deals with masks the philosophical poverty of his explanation, which, from the point of view of formal philosophy, is hardly any explanation at all. Agricola is the informed philosophical amateur writing, like so many humanists, for persons indifferent to science but intensely interested in education-through-literature. With some reason, Jean Riolan castigates Agricola's philosophy, with special reference to his treatment of the loci, as the sort of thing "one might lecture on in God-forsaken country villages to dotards and farm hands."[74] Instead of being given a philosophical treatment, the loci are given a "simplified" treatment. This means, although Agricola does not seem aware of it, that the discussion relies heavily on quantitative and visualist analogies. The point of departure is, "Things are immensely numerous." There is no mystery to occasion wonder here, only superfluous quantity to occasion annoyance. The annoyance is vanquished by the conviction that some sort of spatial imagery — *loci*, *topoi*, receptacles, boxes — can serve as a means of controlling the profusion of concepts and/or things.

This notion of "places," suggesting the pigeonholed formulary rhetoric of the medieval *artes dictaminis*, is weighted heavily toward both mathematicism and the much later associationist philosophies, and it is miles from the categories in the pre-Agricolan Parisian sense. But it is also far from new, as the use of the concept of "places" (*loci*, *topoi*) running back through the Romans to the Greeks makes clear. Pre-Agricolan scholasticism, as has been seen in Peter of Spain's *Summulae logicales*, had also known this sort of conceptualization, in its treatment of Aristotle's *Topics* or *loci* and in what it felt of the all-pervasive influence of Cicero which everywhere filters through the Middle Ages.[75]

In the passage just cited, Agricola's reference to "cutting out" hints at the way in which concepts playing around the Latin term *silva* influence the notion of loci through Renaissance tradition. Like its Greek cognate ὕλη, the Latin *silva* (woods, brush, forest) has as a secondary meaning an abundance or congeries or quantity, as in Cicero, Suetonius, and Quintilian, or in Ramus, who writes of the *silva* of Christian teaching which he feels needs putting in order.[76] The Greek term extends further to mean also felled trees or timber, and finally material in general as the stuff out of which something is made, a notion ordinarily conveyed in Latin by *materia*. The Latin concept of *materia* is associated with the notion of *mater* or mother: *materia* is the mother-stuff out of which something is formed, given outline or molded. The Greek ὕλη can mean this sort of thing too; although because the notion of woods rather than of mother is residual in the Greek concept, this suggests the formlessness of a heterogeneous and confused agglomeration quite as much as the formlessness of a homogeneous mass lacking a certain outline or configuration.

Agricola and other Renaissance rhetoricians show the influence of the Greek concept insofar as they tend to think of the "matter" of discourse in terms of a woods, to be dealt with by a process of "sorting out" or "cutting out" or "arranging." In this tradition Ben Jonson uses the terms *The Forest* and *Under-Woods* (today, *Underbrush*) to designate his two verse miscellanies, which, in his own words "To the Reader" at the opening of his *Under-Woods*, consist of "works of divers nature and matter congested, as Timber-trees . . . promiscuously growing." Even more appositely, Jonson calls his commonplace book *Timber, or Discoveries upon Men and Matter as They Have Flowed Out of His Daily Readings* — the relation of the "woods" to the places of "invention" is patent here. In the same vein, Francis Bacon styles his collection of miscellaneous or random remarks on natural history *Sylva sylvarum*; that is, *A Forest of Forests.*

The protean quality of the notions associated with "place" show clearly that the basis of thinking about the loci was not any settled philosophical outlook but simply an unacknowledged but inexorable disposition to represent thought and communication in terms of spatial models and thus to reduce mental activity to local motion. This local motion can of course be given body in a limitless number of images. One is not surprised to find that the concepts used to represent operations in the topical logics metamorphose and proliferate in countless forms and directions. But always in vain: "sorting," "cutting out," "arranging," "seats," "treasure chests," "woods," and the rest provide at best only the loosest of analogies, hopelessly inadequate as representations of the psychological realities involved in the processes of literary composition and in the mystery of communication between person and person. The limitations of each and every model brought forward to lend plausibility to local motion as an equivalent for mental activity results in a kind of desperate exuberance of constructs within Renaissance dialectical or logical theory. This is nowhere more evident than in a fascinating passage from the first logic book in English, Thomas Wilson's *The Rule of Reason*, in which two notions associated with the places — the notion of invention or discovery and that of "woods" as discussed above — are played against one another in a kaleidoscope of spatial models to produce a marvelous dialectical hunting scene.

A place is, the restyng corner of an argumente, or els a marke whiche geveth warning to our memorie what wee maie speake probably, either in the one parte, or the other, upon al causes that fal in question. Those that bee good harefinders will soone finde the hare by her fourme. For when thei see the ground beaten flatte round about, and faire to the sighte: thei have a narrowe gesse by al like- lihode that the hare was there a litle before. Likewise the Huntesman in huntyng the foxe, wil soone espie when he seeth a hole, whether it be a foxe borough, or not. So he that will take profeicte in this parte of Logique, must bee like a hunter, and learne by labour to knowe the boroughes. For these places bee nothing elles, but covertes or boroughes, wherein if any one searche diligently, he maie finde game at pleasure. And although perhappes one place faile him, yet shal he finde a dousen other places, to accoumplishe his purpose. Therefore if any one will dooe good in this kinde, he must goe from place to place, and by searchyng every borough he shal have his purpose undoubtedly in moste part of them, if not in al.[77]

This passage has been identified as "scholastic logic." But it has very little in common with the central scholastic tradition feeding through Peter of Spain and a great deal in common with the antischolastic humanist logic of Rudolph Agricola, whose definition of a place is echoed, directly or in- directly, at the opening of the passage. The central directive laid down by Wilson (and latterly picked up by Professor Lane Cooper as an integral part of his "expansion" of Aristotle's *Rhetoric*) "knowe the boroughes" in which the foxes are hiding, is nothing more than a telescoped paraphrase of the two rules in which Agricola says he can sum up all his doctrine about the use of the places: know the places (that is, be familiar with the headings as I give them) and draw (*deducere*) out of them the arguments you are after.[78] Wil- son tricks out the arguments as foxes. In this sylvan setting, invention has become hunting, and Agricola's forest primeval, converted by Jonson and others into a wood lot, has now been made over into a game preserve. In each case, under one or another guise, we are presented with a model for mental activity providing a spatial field for local motion of various sorts. Wilson, who was a good teacher, has selected a model designed to appeal to boys. Yet, in the process he has also actually intensified the spatial element, less obvious in Agricola, by suggesting that a place has a kind of shape (the hare's form, the fox's burrow) from which one can predict the shape of the argument which has its "seat" there. Here "shape" (the Latin term in use in exactly this sense was *typus*, an imprint) is doing duty for "nature." This liking for the "shape" metaphor hints that the tradition with which we are here in contact is that which leads directly into our twentieth-century technological era, which finds it so congenial to speak of the "shape" of a speech, or of a program, or of an idea. Through Wilson and others the elements in the tradition trace to Agric- ola and, as legitimate developments of his views, help show of what stuff his dialectical world was fundamentally made.

In their simple, diagrammatic setting Agricola's loci or receptacles were to have an eventful history such as the more complicated categories could hardly have enjoyed. In Ramus the loci will be pictured as individual structures in real-estate developments, separated from one another according to "Solon's Law" by a clear space of so many feet. Jean Bodin will fall back on them in his attempt to "methodize" history. The third chapter of his *Methodus ad facilem historiarum cognitionum* (1566, etc.) echoes verbatim Agricola's description of loci and their function. In conjunction with Euclidean aims, the place-logic tradition will assert itself in Descartes' passion for having things "clear" and "distinct." In German mnemonic systems, the loci will be manifest in a new epiphany as "rooms" with walls and ceiling carefully sectioned off in squares, the better to store their "matter." Ramus will make them appear in a further epiphany as ideas in box-like forms, which are "analyzed" by being "opened." And the Kantian analysis, likewise centered on ideas, is on its way. It will be quite unlike pre-Agricolan analysis, which analyzed or "loosened up" not individual ideas or concepts, but the whole complex of cognitive processes in which the concepts are set, as Aristotle does in his *Analytics*.

Chinese puzzles made of these boxes will turn up in Harvard theses in logic, which assert that "a thing is in place, and time is in the thing."[79] For here time is "in" things as things are "in" space, or species "in" genera, because the mind trained in place logic habitually "locates" things or ideas indifferently one inside the other. We are confronted with our own present-day habits of thought; for we ourselves think of books as "containing" chapters and paragraphs, paragraphs as "containing" sentences, sentences as "containing" words, words as "containing" ideas, and finally ideas as "containing" truth. Here the whole mental world has gone hollow. The pre-Agricolan mind had preferred to think of books as saying something, of sentences as expressing something, and of words and ideas as "containing" nothing at all but rather as signifying or making signs for something. After Agricola the notion of content can serve for and level out all these diversified modes of conceptualization.

10. THE FICKLE PLACES

If judgment, the second part of the art of dialectic which Agricola proposes, is underdeveloped, historically speaking, invention, the first part, is decidedly variable. As the general intellectual tradition changes, the active associative nodes for ideas change, and classification of the loci changes too. Revising the classification had been a common phenomenon in antiquity, when Aristotle differed from the Sophists in the list of topics he proposed, Cicero from Aristotle, Quintilian from Cicero, Themistius from all these, and Boethius from all of them again and from Themistius as well. The revision continues in our day with Professor Mortimer Adler's "Great Ideas" (augmented beyond their original hundred), and with such articles as Père Gardeil's very helpful study of the *lieux communs* in the *Dictionnaire de théo-*

logie catholique, where, after reporting Melchior Cano's description of the loci (which he notes are taken at times verbatim from Agricola) and Cano's organization of theological loci, Gardeil proposes, in true topical tradition, a still better classification of his own.

This tradition of revising the classification was a regular game during the Renaissance. Agricola tallies up seventeen loci in Cicero and twenty-two in Themistius, and thereupon proposes twenty-four better ones of his own, which his editors (such as Johann Matthaeus Phrissemius), will tabulate in their editions of his *Dialectical Invention*: definition, genus, species, property, whole, parts, conjugates, adjacents, act, subjects, efficient agent, end, consequences, intended effects, place, time, connections, contingents, name, pronunciation, compared things, like things, opposites, differences.[80] Unlike Ramus' future list and unlike Aristotle's *Topics,* this list does not include the source of "inartificial arguments," namely, witnesses, but restricts itself to what are sure sources of arguments, because found within the "art" of dialectic itself — which means, in effect, within one's own head, not that of another.

Some authors in post-Agricolan generations preen themselves on abundance of places, others on strict economy. Ramus is soon going to vaunt his own selection over all others, while at the same time revising the selection with nearly every new edition of his dialectical works, as Charpentier complains.[81] Adversaries are going to say that they prefer all sorts of other arrangements to Ramus'. Riolan will say he prefers that of Aristotle because the latter has a grand total of 360 different places which he reduces, moreover, not to Ramus' ten, but all the way down to four.[82] (Modern counts of the places in Aristotle's *Topics* sometimes give 338,[83] not far from Riolan's figure.)

There is, of course, a certain sameness in the variations, for as long as the study of a more or less Aristotelian philosophy remained the core of the curriculum, conceptual formulations from this philosophy were among the items most familiar to all. Around them other items could conveniently be clustered, so that genus, species, and associated terms repeat themselves in all the lists.

Interest in the places, and even more a propensity to reshuffle them and their contents as more or less interchangeable counters, has in any age the tendency to level all the units of knowledge. The different sorts of units in which thought is cast all tend to be assimilated to one another as they come to be viewed as little somethings-or-other which go into and come out of boxes, and which are, on closer inspection, themselves boxes out of which still further units may be "drawn." Such conceptualization had always tended to govern the application of the invention analogy (and ultimately the arrangement analogy). But in Agricola's age it begins to be given *carte blanche,* for the reduction of speech in terms of visual analogy inherent in the topical tradition was encouraged as never before by the humanist determination to make the measure of all speech a fixed *written* tradition. Erasmus' notion of knowledge and communication is complex, but when he maintains that the knowledge of "almost everything" is to be sought in the Greek authors who are the sources or "springs" of all science, there is no mistaking the suggestion that the written works of antiquity have become collectively a kind of commonplace.[84] The notion is not entirely new. There is a parallel in the Hebrew, and particularly the Masoretic, tradition, but Erasmus' age activates it in a special way. This is the age which will be marked by the idea that the Bible — become itself a kind of commonplace — is the sole rule and depository for faith and morals.

Themistius' part in the game of musical chairs played with the topics during the Renaissance deserves brief comment. The works of this Hellenistic philosopher and statesman of the fourth century A.D. are very imperfectly preserved. The Renaissance scholars' acquaintance with what he had to say about the places did not come from his original treatment (which apparently has not survived), but from Boethius, who in book III of his work *On the Different Kinds of Topics* attributes to Themistius the assortment of topics which he gives in book II, and compares this classification with that of Cicero.[85] This work of Boethius' had been put regularly on the medieval arts curriculum. But Themistius had written in Greek, and the humanists would not have missed a chance to cite such a man in preference to one who had been a scholastic favorite. Hence, the places which they knew of only through Boethius' mediation are referred to as those of Themistius, both in Agricola himself, and more specifically in the tables set at the end of book I of the *Dialectical Invention* by Agricola's editor Phrissemius; Boethius is passed over and the places as listed by Themistius, Cicero, and "Rudolph," as Phrissemius calls Agricola, are lined up in comparative tables for a visual summary.

The humanist maneuver in playing up Themistius and playing down the Middle Ages is even more calculated than one might think. In Peter of Spain's *Summulae logicales*, most influential of all medieval textbooks and the horror of all humanists, the selection of places had been determined by Boethius' selection from this same Themistius.[86] The immediate past was closer to them than the humanists liked to own.

II. THE IMPACT OF AGRICOLA'S TOPICAL LOGIC

The weakness of Agricola's *Dialectical Invention* as a formal philosophical treatise (which it hardly pretends to be), is compensated for by the relevance of the work to the unstated and complex psychological needs, pedagogical, linguistic, and literary, created by the maturing humanist outlook. In its relation to these needs, the work is not to be belittled. Indeed, it merits a more exhaustive study to highlight its connection with Ramist methodological developments than the somewhat specialized treatment given here. The presence of Agricola's influence on all sides in the international intellectual milieu at the beginning of the sixteenth century is evident enough. His importance as a prime inspiration for much of Northern European humanism has already been mentioned. But when we look from the general humanist horizons to the specific field of humanist logic, Agricola's place appears even more impressive.

It would seem that almost all attempts to depart from Aristotle's *Organon* after the opening of the sixteenth century have as their direct or indirect inspiration the *Dialectical Invention* of Agricola.[87] Erasmus' work *On the Twofold Abundance* (that is, of "things" to say and words to say them with — *De duplici copia*) endorses a logic of places and follows on Erasmus' avowal, already cited, that Agricola was his leader in dialectic. Melanchthon, who advocates Cicero and Quintilian for rhetoric,[88] favors Agricola's two-part arrangement of dialectic — although he himself will nullify his own declared position here by writing a rhetoric and dialectic himself to replace those he recommends. Others give the same high honors to Agricola's dialectic. Johannes Caesarius, a frank Aristotelian whose ten-book *Dialectic* reflects the composition of the *Organon* itself, as Aristotelian logics generally do, makes Agricola one of his few contemporary sources; the others were mostly classical or near-classical, with, however, Buridan to represent the medieval logicians.[89]

This practice of reserving for Agricola, the only Renaissance savant so chosen, a place of honor among the ancients was a common one. Jean Le Voyer of Le Mans, Sieur de Saint-Pavace, mentions as "first-rate classical authors" Aristotle, Cicero, Quintilian, and Rudolph Agricola — no others by name.[90] In a work dedicated to Jacques Amyot, Pierre Sainct-Fleur of Montpellier mentions the same quartet on his title page as "highly approved authors."[91] Christopher Hegendorf, whose works were published at Antwerp and elsewhere, and much used at Paris, cites Agricola frequently as a source in his *Legal Dialectic in Five Books*,[92] a pre-Ramist forerunner of *The Lawiers Logike* (1588) of the English Ramist Abraham Fraunce. Melanchthon, Caesarius, and Hegendorf are all among those whom Gouveia cites in his attack on Ramus as those from whom Ramus borrows. The other logician (besides himself) whom Gouveia lists as a source for Ramus, Francis Titelmans, like these three foregoing, cites Agricola freely, although he does not often follow him.[93]

Melanchthon, Caesarius, Titelmans, and Hegendorf could be styled Aristotelians in the sense that their dialectics or logics reflect more the approach of the *Organon* than that of Agricola's *Dialectical Invention*. However, they commonly insist on some sort of union between dialectic (or logic) and eloquence,[94] in Agricolan fashion — which means, in effect, that they are against a rigorously scientific formal logic. Titelmans notes that "the whole of dialectic, as Cicero and Boethius bear witness, consists of judgment and invention."[95] Nevertheless, he organizes his own work in six books, treating respectively the predicables (genus, specific difference, species, proper accident, and accident), the predicaments, enunciation, syllogism, the dialectical loci, and sophistic argumentation — an arrangement reminiscent of Aristotle's *Organon* again. Titelmans' concept of what dialectic is, like that of most of his contemporaries, does not admit of clear-cut theoretical statement. He discusses dialectic in a general way, observing that there is no use quibbling about defining it, and concludes finally that, practically speaking, it is what one teaches in the course on dialectic.[96] Dialectic, therefore, rests on concrete, curricular fact, rather than on theory.

Agricola's effect on Titelmans and others in this instance has been to create a general complacency about what can well be styled a residual logic or dialectic. The medieval logical "technicalities" have been set aside in favor of the approach of the enlightened amateur, who was interested in logic in terms of psychology, miscellaneous metaphysical detail, practical pedagogy, and eloquence. The emphasis on practical pedagogy was one of the facets which produced the lawyers' logics of Hegendorf, Everard of Middleburg, Thomas Wilson (i.e., his *Arte of Rhetorique*), Johann Thomas Freige, Abraham Fraunce, and others (the twentieth-century equivalent of this sort of production might be something like *Logic for Business Men*).[97] There are interesting details in these works, both the general and the specialized logics or dialectics, but seldom any important logical insights. By being integrated with "life" ("eloquence" is the sixteenth-century equivalent), formal logic has practically ceased to exist as an autonomous discipline, developed according to its own rigorous and demanding internal economy, with indefinitely expandable horizons, such as it had been in the hands of the medieval scholastic logicians. By being made "practical," all logic has now become a kind of rhetoric.

The Agricolan development, as should by now be apparent, is not an anti-Aristotelian phenomenon in any sense except perhaps in spirit. It coincides with a return to Aristotle's text rather than to the texts of Peter of Spain, Ockham, Buridan, Ralph Strode, Albert of Saxony, Dullaert, and other full-fledged logicians. The return is, in part, due to interest in the Greek tradition as interpreted by Cicero, who remains always the great determinant in so much Renaissance thought. Relying largely on Cicero's reports about Stoicism, the new logic exhibits a certain interest in Stoic logic, together with its other interests. To a certain extent, the Agricolan development participates in the kind of interest in logic evinced by St. Thomas Aquinas in that its focus is primarily metaphysical and psychological rather than formally logical, or, concerned with the labyrinthine detail of logical *structure*. In this, it resembles the logic developed by post-Tridentine Catholic theologians, such as John of St. Thomas, which is, moreover, a kind of rhetorical logic insofar as it specializes in what is taken to be the practical interests of theologians. The other kind of logic taught in late Renaissance Catholic circles, that of the manuals such as Eustachius a Sancto Paulo's *Four-Part Philosophical Summa*, well known to Descartes,[98] is somewhat reminiscent of the Agricolan development, but exact relationships remain to be studied.

All these post-Agricolan works abandon those technicalities, or, as the humanists concertedly style them, those aridities and "prickles" (*spinae*), of medieval logic which are precisely what makes medieval logic interesting to logicians today. The medieval technicalities had not been anti-Aristotelian either, but developments which take Aristotle more or less as a point of departure and venture into areas where Aristotle did not go.[99] Whatever Renaissance humanism or posthumanist scholasticism, Protestant or Catholic, did in other fields, it can hardly be said to have developed any *formal* logic as *intrinsically* interesting and enterprising as that of the medieval scholastics.

Among the humanist dialecticians at the opening of the sixteenth century, there is evidently a desire to bring to completion something that Agricola had only started. But there is no general accord on how the completion is to be achieved. One is left with the impression that the strong attraction exercised by Agricola on the sixteenth-century mind was not very well understood by this mind itself. Agricola's dialectic fitted the age and inspired its users — but why, or to what, was by no means immediately evident. History alone could give the answer.

12. THE COMMENTATORS' AGRICOLA: WORDS AND "THINGS"

Something of the nature of the inspiration which Agricola afforded can perhaps be seen in what his commentators and epitomizers made of him. One of the most important of these is Bartholomew Latomus, whose *Epitome of Commentaries on Rudloph Agricola's Dialectical Invention* was first published, so far as I can find, at Cologne in 1530.[100] This work is, in effect, an epitome of Agricola's text itself in the light of various commentaries on it. It is the immediate prelude to Ramus' first printed dialectical works of 1543; for at Paris, the two or three editions of the *Dialectical Invention* which had been appearing annually are supplemented just before 1543 by the *Epitome*, which had two Paris printings in 1541 and three in 1542, during which latter year, counting these epitomes, *six* separate editions of Agricola's dialectic were published at Paris!

By casting his lot with the *Dialectical Invention*, Latomus abdicates his earlier positions taken in his *Summa* of all discourse,[101] where Agricola's influence had been relatively nugatory. In the *Epitome*, Latomus is in general faithful to Agricola, but via such commentators as Phrissemius and Alard of Amsterdam, so that his emphases and selections and ways of conceiving and presenting his material are representative and significant. He begins by dividing the notion of discourse (*disserendi ratio*) into dialectic and rhetoric, which he equates with teaching (*docendi ratio*) and eloquence (*ratio eloquendi*) respectively.[102] Latomus' two parts of dialectic are, of course, those given by Agricola, invention and disposition, but they are even more rigidly reduced to two ways of "teaching," called *expositio* and *argumentatio*.[103] The *Epitome* is divided into three books just as is Agricola's *Dialectical Invention* itself. The three functions of perfect speech are rehearsed, to teach, to move, and to delight, and a place is defined in Agricola's own words supplemented by examples:

some common distinctive mark of a thing or matter by the help of which it is possible to discover readily what can be proven [or what is probable] with regard to any particular thing or matter. Thus the definition, genus, causes, and consequences are distinctive marks and, in a way, signs by which we are informed that arguments are to be drawn from them in explaining any particular thing.[104]

Immediately after these preliminary explanations, we are introduced to one of the first bracketed outline tables in the Agricolan-Ramist tradition, which Latomus takes from Phrissemius' commentary in the latter's editions of Agricola's *Dialectical Invention*,[105] and which is reproduced here:

TABULA DIVISIONIS LOCORUM

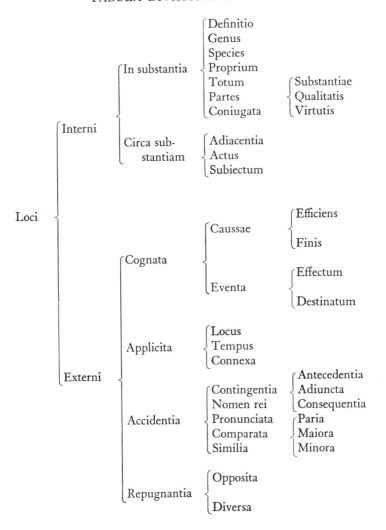

The Ramist proclivity for dichotomies is already present, but the table suggests several other interesting observations. It does not appear in the text by Agricola, who had lived in the infancy of printing when tables were featured occasionally in manuscripts but were hard to reproduce in quantity and with exactitude, and had not yet come into vogue, but rather in the post-incunabular commentary, got up when printing had accustomed man to anchor the word more fixedly in space. Significantly, it is the notion of place or locus itself which the table is pictured as dividing. Place has itself ambitioned becoming one of the places.

The high spatial valence in evidence here shows up again in the curiously modern notion of "structure," which becomes central in Latomus' way of thinking about speech itself:

> The instrument of dialectic is speech, by which the person discoursing attempts to create conviction (*fidem*) concerning the matter which he undertakes to teach. Speech is divided in a dichotomy: according to its structure (*structura*) and according to its effectiveness (*effectu*). In terms of its structure, speech is either continuous, proceeding uninterruptedly . . .; or cut up, interrupted by different speakers in turn, as are the disputations or two-sided contests of scholastics.[106]

It is in this milieu that the notion of "structure" as applied to language will gradually come into its own. Before the Gutenberg era, divisions of speech and, with them, punctuation itself (although this was concerned with reducing language to spatial form) had been thought of in terms not of "structure" but of delivery. The older notions of period, comma, and colon, while spatially formed insofar as they signify some sort of cutting or segmentation, nevertheless preserved an oral point of view which lingered even into the seventeenth century before being finally lost.[107]

The spatial orientation which encourages thinking of linguistic "structure" will also set off the quest of "clear and distinct" ideas. This will become the hallmark of topical logic, the first rule of which, as it is repeated by Latomus, is to get an *exact* knowledge of the places[108] (this despite the fact that seldom did any two authors list them the same way). This rule will echo in Ramus' reiterated statement that the worst possible thing that can happen in discourse is ambiguity. Contrary to the common persuasion, the medieval scholastics, while they practice a certain amount of accuracy and certainly encourage it in their long-term effects, do not make an explicit shibboleth of it. Clear and distinct ideas would become a shibboleth chiefly in the age of topical logic and printing. Many of those who cultivate such ideas with all their might — Johann Thomas Freige, for example — will show what they mean by clarity and distinctness by producing whole folio volumes of dichotomized tables.

The rest of Latomus' *Epitome*, like Agricola's original work, retails much material common to the general rhetorico-logical tradition, gracefully and occasionally with distinctive features. Latomus makes clear Agricola's position, paramount for Ramus too, that rhetoric and dialectic have the same loci and thus that dialectical exposition is common to orators and philosophers.[109] Book II gives a résumé of Agricola's corresponding book, including his summary treatment of induction and syllogism, and adds a bracketed chart which divides the "question" or material of dialectic.

The last section of the *Epitome* is, like that of the *Dialectical Invention* itself, patently concerned with rhetoric — to take this term in its non-Agricolan sense. Effectiveness (*effectus*) involves not only subject matter but personal considerations.[110] Amplification, the old stand-by of medieval rhetoric and poetic, which, with the other stand-by decorum, will disappear from the whole Ramist schema of the arts of discourse, is here still underwritten as indispensable for arousing and sustaining the emotions of the audience.[111] Delighting an audience (*delectatio*) is more the business of the rhetorician than of the dialectician, we are told, insofar as the rhetorician is concerned with words (*verba*) and the dialectician with things (*res*), although, since things are the source of some enjoyment, the first part of dialectic, invention, has something to do with *delectatio*.[112]

Latomus is not clear why or how words are more enjoyable than things, nor why or how things, in such a pass, are enjoyable at all. But the basis of the Ramist distinction between dialectic and rhetoric is evident here. It is the product not only of Agricola or Latomus but of the whole ancient and medieval rhetorico-logical heritage. Rhetorical speech is speech which attracts attention to itself as speech — the showy, the unusual. (Thus poetry is only one kind of rhetoric.) Dialectical or logical speech is speech which attracts no attention to itself as speech, the normal, the plain, the undistinguished, the reporter of "things." The root opposition set up in generating the Agricolan and Ramist notion of "things" (which is also the notion in much of the tradition from which Agricola and Ramus draw) is not that between the mental and the extramental. "Things" are constituted not in opposition to the mind, but in opposition to the word. The word has an obvious vocal and auditory bearing, which tends to make the whole realm of "things" by contrast that which is apprehended visually, and to some extent tactually.

Latomus anticipates Ramus by supplying briefly the second part of dialectic, *dispositio*, which he appends after Agricola's last book. His definition of disposition, although derivative from ancient rhetoric, is nevertheless significant: "Disposition is the distribution of things in speech, and shows what is to be situated in what place."[113] This topical logic thus finishes where it began, in the "places," the whole process of argumentation being conceived of, not as saying something, or as predication, but as a redistribution in other places of the arguments drawn out of the places of invention.

This way of thinking will impart a characteristic reciprocating movement to Agricolan and Ramist logic, making descriptions of argumentation (the putting of what is found in the commonplaces into other places) sound re-

markably like descriptions of invention said backwards. It will be the occasion
for Ramus' own curious gambit, which makes Ramist method what it is and
which consists of trying to impose upon the whole axiomatic tradition of
scholastic philosophy the pattern of a logic of topical invention.

In Latomus' treatment of disposition, there is only a slight suggestion of
this, for axiomatics enters only in a cursory fashion. Disposition is threefold:
natural, "which follows the nature of things, as when animal is treated before
man"; arbitrary, which follows no certain principle; and artificial, "when we
purposely upset the disposition of things and speak last of what is by nature
first."[114] Arbitrary disposition gets most attention from Latomus. It can be
arbitrary in exposition, as in poetry, history, teaching, and oratory. Or it can be
arbitrary in argumentation, which means that there can be arbitrary arrangement of the parts of the oration, or of questions, or of the argumentation
proper or interconnection of syllogisms, or of the parts of the argumentation,
such as when the major and minor are inverted, one or another member of
the syllogism omitted, and so on.[115] In treating of argumentation proper,
where he cites Cicero, Latomus is evidently feeling about in the general area
of Ramist method, but he does not introduce the term *methodus*, and his
discussion is in general vapid and elusive, presenting an essentially indiscrim-
inate assortment of rhetorical debris which has been filtered down through
Agricola and on which order is imposed by another bracketed chart called
Tabula dispositionis at the end of the volume.

CHAPTER VI

THE COMMON BACKGROUND: ARTS SCHOLASTICISM

Newfangled, youngheaded, harebrayne
boyes will needs be Maysters that
never were Schollers.
— "The importunate exclamation of a
raging and fieryfaced Aristotelian,"
in Abraham Fraunce's *Lawiers Logike.*

I. SCHOLASTICISM IN TWENTIETH-CENTURY PERSPECTIVE

THE interaction between the forces of the medieval dialectical tradition which grew out of and around Peter of Spain and the forces in the humanist tradition which were at play around Rudolph Agricola takes place in the huge pedagogical setting of arts scholasticism. This has been the object of much recent study, but must be re-examined here to correct perspectives which have been formed through our neglect of the Petrine-Agricolan sequence and which, once corrected, help explain both that sequence and the Ramism which grows out of it.

The interplay of forces here takes place in a pedagogical tradition in which most of the protagonists will always remain unknown to us. Even had medieval logic included nothing beyond ancient logic, the large-scale, organized teaching of the subject to generation after generation of schoolboys — for that is what university arts students in great part were — throughout some three centuries was a venture destined to give a new framework to man's outlook on the universe. And so with the teaching of other subjects, most notably of physics. There is nothing quite comparable to the scope of this educational venture in the schools of antiquity, the chief reason (or perhaps symptom) being that there were no teachers' guilds quite comparable to those which, since the Middle Ages, have been styled universities.

The forces at work in Ramism cannot be understood without direct reference to the university tradition. And they themselves demand certain refinements of our view of this tradition. Most of the necessary revaluation can be done by asking the right questions about the material in such works as Rashdall's *Medieval Universities,* the *Chartularium* of the University of Paris,

and others which have appeared in recent years. Many characteristics of scholasticism and of the universities — hardly separable from one another —
varied, of course, from year to year in many details. We shall be concerned
mainly, however, with characteristics which did not change, or did not change
much, between the thirteenth and the opening of the sixteenth century, particularly with those effecting Ramus' world at the University of Paris, the
most influential and symptomatic of all universities, with regard to the arts
course. What is said here of Paris applies in general to other universities as
well, especially to Oxford and Cambridge, but less to the Italian and Spanish
universities. It also applies, *mutatis mutandis*, to the grammar schools and
other new humanist schools detached from, but never entirely independent
of the university tradition.

2. SCHOLASTICISM: MORE ARTS THAN THEOLOGY

Although scholastic theology enjoyed a theoretical priority of dignity over
other forms of scholasticism, as soon as one descends from the realm of
theoretical relations into the real university theater where Ramism and other
movements and countermovements took form, theology pales into insignifi-
cance beside the scholasticism of the arts course. The arts faculty prepared
students for the degree of master of arts, that is, for admission to the union
of arts teachers which constituted the faculty itself (the grade of bachelor was
not terminal, but that of an apprentice teacher). After receiving his degree,
the master of arts might rest content, as Ramus was to do, with his teaching
position on the arts faculty. In theory, all masters of arts taught, since all
university degrees constitute, historically speaking, admission to a guild of
teachers, originally a tight, proudly professional, and combative one. Or the
master of arts might go on to the corresponding degrees admitting him to the
higher faculties (again teachers' guilds), medicine, law, or theology. He
might, during his higher studies, teach arts on the side — provided he was
not a member of a religious order, for as a result of a squabble with the guild,
these were disqualified as masters of arts.

The scholasticism of the arts course was thus the scholasticism which
filtered upward into the entire university. No one could escape studying it.
Aristotle had entered theology through arts, and so had Peter of Spain, bringing on the nominalist crises of the fourteenth and fifteenth centuries. Agricola
and Ramus were to follow much the same route.

Arts scholasticism itself was not theology at all. The arts faculty was
periodically warned off theological purlieus, with the result that it tended to
scant, or even to pass over, metaphysics, which neoscholastics today, along
with St. Thomas Aquinas, consider philosophy par excellence, the "first philosophy." Arts scholasticism — that is, most scholasticism — considered it a
marginal subject, not to be entirely passed by and yet dangerously close to
theology for those trained only in arts.[1]

If, however, the theological faculty felt constrained on rare occasions to tell the arts faculty what not to teach, it did not attempt to establish the contents of the arts program. Philosophy programs positively integrated with a theological program come into being with the Renaissance colleges inaugurated by the Reformers or humanists such as Johann Sturm or by Counter-Reformers or humanists such as the Jesuit fathers — all colleges with highly centralized administrations. These colleges were not the chaotically active, oath-infested teachers' guilds such as made up the universities like the University of Paris, nor were they students' guilds such as made up the University of Bologna. They were institutions administered from the top, more often than not by theologians or persons with whom theological preoccupations were foremost. The older university organization was quite the reverse; everything bubbled up from the bottom. At Paris it was the arts faculty who elected the rector — from among themselves — and who ran the entire university, including law, medicine, and theology.

Arts scholasticism was important not only because it framed the mentality of those who governed the university and because it seeped through the whole university, but also because the great majority of arts students and teachers pursued it. In the year 1362, a list of the actual teaching members of each faculty was sent from Paris to Pope Urban V at Avignon. On it we find 25 professors of theology, 11 professors of law, 27 professors of medicine, and 449 professors of arts.[2] At the theological capital of the world, teaching masters of arts thus outnumbered doctors of theology eighteen to one, and all other university teachers together, including these doctors of theology, seven to one.

The proportions between the various faculties changed somewhat from one generation to the next, as they do in universities today. This, however, is the most complete list we have, and similar lists scattered through the *Chartularium* indicate that the proportions here are representative of the medieval university tradition as a whole. The weakness of law is somewhat artificial in this case, since the study of civil law has been suppressed at Paris because it was choking off theology.[3] One might suspect that there were also other reasons — for one, that civil law received short shrift perhaps in part because it was loosely connected with arts scholasticism. To study law the student need not have finished his arts course.[4]

Medicine, on the contrary, was closely allied with scholastic philosophy. Its quondam alliance is still in evidence today in our use of the term "physician" (or in German *Physikus*) to designate a practitioner of medicine. For the physics from which the physician gets his name (the term "physic" is merely a variant of "physics"), as we shall see, was the crowning point of arts-course scholasticism, which is to say of scholastic philosophy. In contrast to medical men, theologians were rather uniformly on record as minimizing physics and as recommending the shortening of the philosophy course.[5]

Although they enjoyed a vague clerical status, medical students, who were seculars and normally laymen, all had to be masters of arts and as such could teach philosophy while studying medicine. On the other hand, large numbers of theological students — namely, all who were members of religious orders — were actually disqualified from teaching on the philosophy, or the arts, faculty even though they had completed the ordinary master of arts studies.

When calculating the influence of the theologians, it must be remembered that the theology course was quite long (the maximum, in the fourteenth century, was sixteen years or more).[6] In a course this lengthy, a given number of teachers turn out a relatively small number of graduates. And the number of teachers of theology, we have seen, was already small. This is not to say that the theological faculty had no influence. Moreover, its primacy was not entirely one of honor, for it could make itself effectively heard if members of the other faculties taught heresy, which meant, in effect, if they encroached on theological grounds. A recent scholar who made a special check of the documents on this score found very much to his surprise that there was very little evidence of heresy hunting on the part of the theologians.[7] The recurrent condemnations of nominalism (which, in its proper context, looks less like an epistemological theory than an inevitable outcome of the arts-course field of interest and state of mind) were prompted by the theologians, it is true, but these condemnations could seldom be made theologically convincing. They lasted commonly for only a few years before they were lifted and banned books put in circulation again.[8]

Generally speaking, professors of philosophy and theology tended to go their separate ways. Individuals often had careers as professors of arts and of theology, but the great theologians — practically the only scholastics read today — seldom taught philosophy. Indeed, if, like Aquinas and Bonaventure, they were members of religious orders, they were not qualified to lecture at all in philosophy at the University of Paris proper (although nothing prevented them from teaching philosophy privately to members of their own orders in their own *studia*). Conversely, the great masters of arts — such as Jean Buridan or Albert of Saxony — were commonly logicians and not theologians. There are some exceptions, but generally those with mixed careers who became outstanding specialized either in scholastic philosophy (sometimes combined with medicine) or in theology, not in both. Peter of Spain dabbled in theology, but his fame was due to his logic and physics and medicine. His contemporaries, St. Bonaventure and St. Thomas, on the other hand, are hardly even amateur formal logicians. Alexander of Hales was a master of arts before he became a Franciscan, but in his later career stuck pretty well to theology. Ockham dragged out his theological training over years, but his interest and competence in logic were such that he never finished theology, remaining to this day the "Venerabilis Inceptor." Surveying the picture as a whole, we find almost no one who was both a major theologian and a major logician; the one noteworthy exception was St. Albert the Great, teacher and inspirer of both Aquinas and Peter of Spain.

If scholastic theologians who were members of religious orders were cut off at Paris from the arts faculty and thereby from philosophy, arts was the stronghold of everybody else, for everybody else passed through it: the masters of arts who remained masters of arts and nothing more (many of the great logicians fall here), and the bachelors and masters of arts who were studying for or had completed further degrees in medicine, law, and theology. The only clergy among bachelors and masters were the secular clergy, most of these probably not priests in major orders but enjoying the vague clerical status of those who had been tonsured, a status lost by marriage (which was forbidden to all those who engaged in actual teaching except, at Paris after 1452, to physicians).

Insofar as its interests were centered on logic, the philosophy of this arts faculty, over the centuries, to a surprising degree was nominalism, or, as it is perhaps better called, terminism. Terminism is a phenomenon inadequately defined by dictionaries as a simple opposition to "realism." Historically, nominalism or terminism was a concomitant of the highly quantified formal logic of medieval scholastic philosophy, and thus contrasts with theology which has closer connections with metaphysics and special commitments to rhetoric.[9]

Thus it is that the resistance to nominalism and sporadic condemnation of it come regularly from the theological faculty. They are also as regularly quieted when a new respect for nominalism is introduced in the theological camp by young men who, fresh from a more or less nominalist philosophy training, move up into theology. This is not to say that some nominalist or terminist propositions were not theologically objectionable, or that there is nothing at all to the nominalist-realist opposition as it is commonly presented in the manuals. But there is an intimate connection between nominalist habits of thought and the formalistic arts-course approach to philosophy through the science of language, *sermocinalis scientia*.[10]

It has sometimes been suggested that the gap between arts and theology is bridged by St. Thomas Aquinas' opinion that theology is a science and thus comparable to the "arts" or "sciences" of the arts course. But St. Thomas' opinion was not the common one.[11] Indeed, the gap between theology and the arts-course subjects is sometimes underlined in surprising perspectives even by early Thomists themselves. To Ramus' contemporary, the Paris-trained Dominican Francisco de Vitoria, for instance, theology recommended itself as the great subject of study because it promised indefinite progress to thought, whereas the arts-course subjects such as logic, physics, or medicine, were dead intellectual weight, already perfect (so Vitoria thought in his innocence), and thus without expanding horizons![12]

Although the race is perishing, it is still possible to encounter today scholars who are persuaded that the chief preoccupation of most medieval scholastics was proof for the existence of God or discussion of the nature of His attributes, or the demonstration of the immortality of the human soul. Such subjects were indeed as interesting to scholars in the Middle Ages as they are now and were occasionally treated by scholastics. But we are oversensitized to them because the grounds of discussion over which they move have remained relatively unchanged to the present day, whereas we are undersensitized to questions — such as those prevailing in old physics or cosmology — the grounds of which have radically altered. But the Aristotelian cosmology was real to medieval man. When theological questions lurked in the back of the minds of philosophy professors, as of course they did, it was often to give power and perspective to an emerging natural science.[13] While scholasticism on the whole did not tear man's mind away from contemplation of the Eternal City, it certainly did orient it toward the observable, physical world more than had been usual before, as research is making increasingly clear.

3. PHILOSOPHY FOR ADOLESCENTS: THE ARTS COURSE

The accent on youth which will characterize Ramism has a long history in the teaching patterns developed by earlier scholasticism. Arts scholasticism over the centuries is in great part philosophy for teen-agers. It was normally not even adolescents (*adolescentes*) but little boys (*pueri*) who studied the logic of Peter of Spain,[14] and they had studied their (Latin) grammar and (Latin) rhetoric before this logic. One of the most important phenomena attendant on scholasticism and the rise of the universities was the fact that the intellectual heritage was constantly being beaten down into simplified form by systematic presentation and re-presentation to the youthful mind, generation after generation.

The rise of para-university institutions, such as the group of regius professors later to be styled the Collège de France, did not change this situation. Ramus complains that of the one thousand or more students who went daily to hear the regius professors, barely two hundred were old enough to profit from the lectures.[15] The rest, he adds, were best sent back to private *gymnasia* or colleges, where little boys properly belonged.

From the thirteenth to the sixteenth century or later, the university arts course, in its general outline, consisted of (Latin) grammar, (Latin) rhetoric, and "philosophy," which began with dialectic and terminated, practically, with "physics." In Ramus' day and earlier, the student might begin all his studies at the university, attaching himself to a master about the age of seven, as Ramus himself explains.[16] The boy studied grammar until the age of ten or twelve, rhetoric from twelve to fourteen, philosophy at about fifteen or earlier. There were occasional students older than the average, and ages varied somewhat from generation to generation and from university to university, but these ages are generally quite representative.[17] The student became a master of arts — which meant, in principle, that he had completed his studies in grammar, rhetoric, and *all* philosophy, for there were only medicine, law, or theology after this — at the age of eighteen except at Paris, where statutes forbade anyone to act as master before twenty.[18]

There were, however, continual tendencies to skimp the age requirements and to abridge the course. We find Ramus bragging that at his Collège de Presles, he was regularly producing the equivalent of masters of arts around the age of fifteen.[19] Pico della Mirandola began canon law at the age of fourteen, which means he had done most of the arts course or its equivalent before. Although Pico was obviously a genius of sorts, contemporary biographers find the fact simply interesting, not astounding, that "yet a child, and berdless, he . . . was in dede both a parfet philosophre and a parfet divine."[20] In later humanist colleges, such as those of the Society of Jesus, philosophy was finished commonly around the age of sixteen or seventeen, at which time the course in medicine, law, and theology (four years) could begin.[21]

The younger students were less integrated in the university than the older students. Once colleges or residence halls began to exist, pupils' names were often not entered on the official college rolls until they began rhetoric or dialectic — their connection with the university before that being apparently a matter of personal arrangement with the master of the college.[22] Although thus loosely incorporated in university life, elementary instruction was nevertheless a real part of university business. For, even when delegated to an apprentice or bachelor, such instruction was at least nominally under the supervision of a university master. It could, of course, be had under other auspices, in nonuniversity schools such as existed even in small villages like Ramus' Cuts. In this case, the boy could enter the university organization at a more advanced age, as Ramus did.

There were, of course, some variations in this arts-course pattern. A notable one was the tendency to lengthen rhetoric in accordance with the humanists' advocacy of a rhetorically centered training. These tendencies reached their maximum outside the universities, but even there no one succeeded in permanently establishing the humanists' program. From the Middle Ages until Latin ceased to be the language of the learned world, rhetoric remained principally the course that inculcated more or less advanced skill in the use of this language, which was native to none who spoke it and was learned by most simply because it was the only language in which logic, physics, medicine, law, and theology could be studied. Although real eloquence in Latin was frequently achieved, rhetoric remained thus, as a curriculum subject and in its textbook form, a small boy's business and a propaedeutic to further studies.

The humanists' ambition to make Greek well known was likewise never realized, though there were individuals who were very learned in Greek. But the ordinary professor, who could without effort roll on in Ciceronian Latin by the hour, could hardly trust himself to utter extempore a single sentence in Greek, although he could perhaps construe a Greek text (in Latin, not in

Greek). As for Hebrew, ordinary university students even at the height of humanist achievement seem seldom to have got much past the alphabet, although there were a few Hebrew specialists.

It should perhaps be added that, like Greek and Hebrew, the complete trivium and quadrivium of the seven liberal arts was an ideal frame of reference, employed alike by scholastics and humanists. The seven liberal arts enter the Western intellectual tradition through the early fifth-century Martianus Capella's *Marriage of Philology and Mercury*, where they appear as allegorical wedding attendants. They did not represent the real organization of the university program, however,[23] even as early as the thirteenth century, nor probably from the beginning of the universities. The trivium of grammar, rhetoric, and logic was, indeed, covered in one way or another, but the quadrivium of arithmetic, geometry, astronomy, and music did not correspond to the rest of the arts course, which, after logic, consisted mostly of "physics" and related subjects, with some moral philosophy.

University professors in Ramus' own day, including Ramus himself,[24] talked glibly about the trivium and the quadrivium and the seven liberal arts. Not only Ramus, as has sometimes been thought, but the whole milieu in which he appears, more or less identified the trivium with the "exoteric" arts (*exoterica*) or arts taught publicly to beginners, and the quadrivium with the "acroamatic" arts (*acroamatica*), or arts taught privately to the initiate. (These were two Greek terms known less because Aristotle used them than because they were explained by the great source of Renaissance erudition, Cicero.) [25] But the seven liberal arts nowhere appeared as the real and complete framework of instruction.

Like everyone else, Ramus mentions other arts which belong to the arts course as it actually existed — notably physics and ethics, and, more tentatively, history and poetry.[26] The great John Major, known as the depository of all medieval learning, thinks nothing of giving a lengthy explanation of the seven liberal arts, as though the whole academic world were supported on them, only to add blandly that, of course, everyone knows there are more than seven.[27] Explanations of the seven liberal arts will be continued resolutely for generations, by Ramists such as Michael Sonleutner, and by hundreds of others[28] who lived when the curriculum was even further from being defined by them than it was in Ramus' day.

The situation which supported the talk about the seven liberal arts was the fact that the university program had always begun with linguistic subjects, the *artes sermocinales*, and proceeded to more specialized subjects. But the university documents register the real structure of the curriculum in other terms — for example, the division between the *grammatici* and the *artistae* which appears in the College of Navarre records. Ramus says that students who were in their first three years of philosophy in the arts course were commonly styled *summulistae* (after Peter of Spain's work), *logici*, and *physici* respectively. And those who were in their final half-year (between the licentiate and the inaugural lecture or *inceptio* as master of arts) were *intrantes* — that is, on the verge of entering upon their teacher's career[29] (these are terms found in university documents). All these philosophy students, Ramus further explains, were lumped together as *philosophi*, while the arts students not yet *philosophi*, that is, those studying grammar and rhetoric, were lumped together as *grammatici*.[30] It will be noted here how far the trivium-quadrivium framework has disintegrated, for dialectic or logic has migrated from the trivium to become associated with "physics" and the rest of "philosophy" which constituted the reality existing where the quadrivium was dutifully imagined to be.

4. LOGIC AND YOUTH

The youthfulness of the pupils and of a great number of the masters of arts could not but make itself felt in the quality of most university courses, not only for the "grammarians" but also for the "philosophers." Lack of maturity is in frequent evidence both among those receiving instruction and among those dispensing it. This was especially true of the lower disciplines, for, although a master of arts was, in principle, able to teach any of the arts-course subjects from grammar to metaphysics, the more elementary subjects tended to be assigned to younger men. Ramus followed the common pattern when he worked up his logic (and perforce his rhetoric) for teaching long before he got around to physics.

Indeed, it was his initial lectures on logic, published almost immediately after their composition, which got Ramus into trouble. His followers were sometimes to be more circumspect. Abraham Fraunce's youthful treatise on the use of dialectic never found its way into print, but exists still in the Bodleian Library[31] in its virginal manuscript form, the precious and taut work of one hardly out of his teens. John Milton waited until he was a distinguished old man before he published, in 1672, the logic which he had got up in his youth. But he was by no means the first to do this. The dean of all the old-time scholastics at Paris in Ramus' day, John Major, published for the first time at the age of fifty-nine his *Questions in Logic*,[32] which, we are told in the dedicatory epistle to John Weddel, represented lectures given at the College of Montaigu many years before, and which have as their warrant for being published not their intrinsic worth certainly, but the fact that their author had later become famous. These questions consist of a brief and somewhat sporadic commentary on Porphyry's *Isagoge* and the "old logic." They are written on a level suitable for an average, intelligent fourteen- or fifteen-year-old — for example when Major explains that a concrete term is distinguished from an abstract term by having fewer syllables: *homo, humanitas*; *album, albedo.*[33]

The influence of youth on teachers' interests is equally evident in Major's earlier work, *Books Got Up While Teaching the Arts Course in the College of Montaigu*.[34] Here, in his dedicatory epistle to his fellow countryman Ninian Hume, he reflects with puckish humor on how he used to be plagued by the little boys Luis Coronel, Luis' cousin Anthony Coronel, Gaspard Lax, Robert Caubra[i]th, David Cra[n]ston, James Almayn, Peter Crockaert of Brussels, and Robert Cenalis of Paris, when they were his pupils — further circumstantial evidence of the youth of University of Paris students.

Even though the great medieval logicians such as Ockham, Buridan, and the rest do not reveal themselves as so obviously influenced by the limitations of young boys, Major's association of logic with youth is nevertheless representative of the main pedagogical tradition of the medieval and early Renaissance universities. For every Buridan, a teacher's logician, there were thousands of unknown lesser masters engaged in purveying the art of logic to youngsters. The disconcerting number of logics which in the Western world are the products of youthful masters producing for still more youthful audiences goes far to explain the status of the logical tradition by the time of the Renaissance. Then, with the weakening of the universities and the strengthening of the extraprofessional control of education, the interest in pupils as future teachers yielded to interest in pupils as pupils, so that a logic which had been unconsciously adapted to a youthful audience became a logic consciously made easy for youth.

It is possible that, earlier, the presentation to youthful students over generations had helped to develop some of the strong points typical of scholastic dialectic or logic in the Middle Ages. If they work hard, bright youngsters can go far in the most advanced mathematics long before they can catch sight of a metaphysical problem. By the same token, the highly quantified formal logic of the old scholastics, "thorny" as it was, was more understandable for youngsters than was Aristotle's logic with its elaboration of the niceties of psychological operations. One learns to think in terms of quantity more readily than to abstract from it entirely. A convincing proof of this is the fact that Peter of Spain was taught before Aristotle, to "simplify" the Stagirite for youngsters. This quasi-mathematical simplification in turn had prepared for the more deliberate simplification sought by Agricola and other humanists.

5. METAPHYSICS, ETHICS, AND THE TEEN-AGERS

If a program focused on the late teens is not likely to produce a serious metaphysics, what would happen to ethics, which Aristotle had suggested could hardly be begun by a man under forty? Both these subjects amount to relatively little in the scholastic curriculum. After being totally proscribed in earlier university documents, the best recommendation that metaphysics gets in the pre-Ramist world is when the 1452 Paris arts-course statutes prescribe that, at his last examination (for the licentiate immediately preceding the M.A.) the candidate need not have already "heard" the *Metaphysics* but should be actually engaged in "hearing" it.[35] In this passage, the "book" (singular) of *Metaphysics* is tucked in after the long list of books on "physics." In the 1255 statutes, it had been a single title among twenty-nine or thirty others, sandwiched between the *Physics* and the treatise on zoology (*De animalibus*).

This casual attitude toward metaphysics can be seen in the philosophy course prepared by Pierre Tartaret, one of the most typical representatives of the old scholastic tradition in Ramus' boyhood. His name is linked by Ramus with that of Buridan, John Dullaert of Ghent, and Peter of Spain,[36] and by Rabelais with Duns Scotus, Ockham, and Raymond Lully.[37] In the Cambridge *Return from Parnassus*, he appears as representative of the whole of scholastic logic.[38] Tartaret's printed lectures on scholastic philosophy were favorites everywhere — were standard, for example, at Wittenberg until dislodged by Melanchthon.[39] His *Commentaries on Aristotle's Books of Natural Philosophy and of Metaphysics* is thus quite representative of the general arts scholastic emphasis. Here one finds that, of the 117 leaves in an edition in use in the early 1500's, six suffice for metaphysics;[40] the rest are concerned with "physics" proper, cosmology, astronomy, and the soul (which means, mostly, metabolism, growth, bodily movement, and sensory perception). When to this work is added the rest of Tartaret's philosophy course, that is, his commentary on the inevitable Peter of Spain and on Aristotle's *Organon*, the six leaves of metaphysics are practically lost in the 297 leaves devoted to the rest of "philosophy."[41]

There can be no doubt that arts professors skimped metaphysics largely for fear of overreaching themselves and tumbling into theological territory. As Ramus, repeating the old medieval condemnations, liked to remind his auditors, Aristotle's metaphysics was seriously out of line with Christian teaching in that it denied the creation of the world and God's providence over creation, and cast doubts on personal immortality.[42] The master of arts, it must be remembered, had never studied Christian doctrine as such in his university arts course and, unless he was also a bachelor or doctor of theology — in this case he was probably no longer teaching arts but theology — he rightly felt himself to be without theological competence. As the rather rare condemnations of arts theses show, what few restrictions there were against a master of arts saying just about whatever came into his mind appeared when he stepped carelessly out of arts into theology.[43] A certain amount of metaphysics, as we shall see, was inherent in the old scholastic physics. But the immaturity of arts students and the diffidence of arts professors makes it no surprise that modern neoscholastics who study philosophy at a somewhat riper age do not find a community of metaphysical interests with

the old scholastic philosophers as much as with the old scholastic theologians
— far fewer in their age and far less known than the arts scholastics.[44]

Moral philosophy, like metaphysics, was generally scanted in the arts
course. Although John Major, somewhat grandiosely, gives his students to
understand that moral philosophy included "monastic, household and political
economy,"[45] such matters were certainly not staples in the university program.
Moral philosophy normally received rather short shrift, perhaps because, insofar as the teacher did not integrate it with Christian theology, it was difficult
to teach at all. It is not mentioned in the 1215 University of Paris statutes,[46]
and in the 1255 statutes it is handled gingerly: the Nichomachean Ethics is
the only moral work mentioned; four books out of its total of ten suffice;
these four are to be done in six weeks.[47] There were occasional courses in the
Politics and in "economics," but the 1272 statutes, distinguishing, without
reference to metaphysics or ethics, between "masters of logical science" and
"masters of natural science,"[48] suggest the real logico-physical polarity of the
philosophy course as such in the high Middle Ages.

Despite the growing attention it received from terminists and from humanists alike [49] at the dawn of the Renaissance, moral philosophy even then
is quite eclipsed. In the 1452 Paris statutes, following a careful title-by-title
inventory of the works on natural philosophy or physics required for the
licentiate, the moral-philosophy requirements are introduced as a kind of
appendage after "some mathematical works" (we know how little this
amounted to). No list of titles is given, but we read only "moral works,"
followed by the qualification, "especially the book on Ethics," which is concluded by the further qualification, "the greater part" of it.[50] Ramus remarks
with relish that the university had always scanted ethics because of its pagan
provenience.[51]

6. SCHOLASTICISM AS PHYSICS

As the popular division of the course into summulistae and logici on one
hand and physici on the other would lead us to believe, scholastic philosophy
(the arts course after grammar and rhetoric) was initiated in logic and
oriented toward "physics" or natural science. Hence, prospective law students
could omit the latter part of the course and proceed to the study of law after
logic, and theologians were commonly in favor of curtailing the philosophy
course as in great part irrelevant to their interests.

It is quite true that there is a liberal sprinkling of metaphysics through
the logical and physical works of Aristotle. But a brief survey of the texts in
use, or of the studies of Duhem, Thorndike, Crombie, Maier, Butterfield, and
others,[52] makes it clear that the metaphysics was seldom there for its own
sake. Curiosity about the intimate working of material phenomena was real,

and Aristotle's treatise *On the Heavens* was studied not to gain metaphysical insight into ultimate causes but to learn the proximate causes which make the universe go. The treatise *On Sleep and the Waking State* sets out to explain what its title indicates, and so with the other treatises which made up physics or natural science, *On the Soul, On Generation and Corruption, On Sensation and Sensible Things, On Memory and Recall, On Length and Shortness of Life.*

The *Metaphysics* itself, insofar as it was studied, fell in the midst of these works on physics, and if it lent its own coloring to them, they in turn lent their coloring to whole fields which we should style metaphysics today. For example, Aristotle's treatise *On the Soul* is now commonly given a metaphysical reading. But it is a curiously unmetaphysical metaphysics which one encounters, for example, in the commentary on this work by Peter of Spain, which mixes explanations of immortality and sensory activity with detailed treatment of cardiac anatomy, of systole and diastole, of cutaneous respiration, and of the localization of memory in the posterior part of the brain.[53]

Perhaps no better illustration of the claims of physics on scholasticism generally could be desired than the letter addressed by the Paris faculty of arts to the Dominican general chapter meeting at Lyons immediately following the death of Thomas Aquinas in 1274. After asking that Frater Thomas' body be sent to Paris, there to be honored together with his writings, these professors of scholastic philosophy go on to beg of the chapter copies of certain "philosophical works" which Frater Thomas had made a special point of promising them and in which they were especially interested. The writings listed are: a commentary on an unidentified work of the Neo-Platonist Simplicius (whose studies of Aristotle's treatise *On the Heavens* and *Physics* were well known and who would give his name to one of the interlocutors in Galileo's famous *Dialogue*); a commentary on Aristotle's work itself, *On the Heavens*; another on Plato's cosmological dialogue the *Timaeus*; and finally a book on *How to Put Up Aqueducts and How to Make Mechanical Devices for Military Operations* (*De aquarum conductibus et ingeniis erigendis*).[54] No other work of the Angelic Doctor is mentioned — certainly not the *Summa theologica*, which was a work still in progress at the time of Thomas' death, but which, because it was theological, was uninteresting to arts scholastics, that is, to *most* scholastics.

To an age which finds Thomas Aquinas appealing as an existentialist metaphysician, these titles are disconcerting, for this letter is no less than a communication in the Golden Age of scholasticism from a faculty which was by far the largest of the faculties at the most scholastic of all universities, registering its concern at the death of the man we know now as the greatest of all scholastics.

A consuming interest in how to construct aqueducts and siege engines burned the brains not only of philosophy professors but of theologians as well.

This had been consistently the case, in the opinion of John Major (a doctor of theology as well as master of arts), who protests loudly and contritely that,

for some two centuries now, theologians have not feared to work into their writings questions which are purely physical, metaphysical, and sometimes purely mathematical. However unwillingly, relying on their example, I have not blushed to follow in their footsteps and to treat similar matters in my disputations, seeing that these days students of theology look down on other rudiments as threadbare, banal, and commonplace. But some ten years ago [i.e., about 1517] a great army of pestilential heretics, having made themselves a covering shed out of the bark of the Scriptures, brought in all sort of abominable ravings — with this good result, however (for the Lord wished by the vices of some to teach proper behavior to all), that professors of theology began really to get to work on the Sacred Scripture and its explanation, and to put aside their other interests.[55]

Metaphysics is here alluded to as part of philosophy, but it is thought of as irrelevant to theology in the way that physics and mathematics are.

The Aristotle with whom Ramus deals is thus far less a metaphysical Aristotle (in the modern sense) than an arts-course Aristotle, supported in a logic-and-physics context much more than in a metaphysics-and-theology one. This is the Aristotle who stood athwart the path of modern astronomy and physics, both marking the way to progress and blocking it, for he, rather than Ptolemy or anyone else, was the great physicist — which made him *the* philosopher.[56] Professor Randall has suggested that in Italy, at least, Thomism and Scotism retreated early to the monastic orders and left the field to a physician's Aristotle.[57] But it might be asked whether we have not attributed an exaggerated role to Thomism and Scotism outside these orders, and whether in the totality of the university consciousness they were ever so central as we sometimes suppose. For scholastic philosophy everywhere, capped as it was by "natural philosophy" or "physics," belonged not so much to the theologians as to the doctors and students of medicine. When Ramus attacks Aristotle, whole battalions of physicians — Jean de Bomont, Jacques Charpentier, Jean Riolan the elder, Nicolas de Nancel, Jakob Schegk, and others — swing into action, together with simple masters of arts and lawyers such as Antonio de Gouveia, the theologians taking a bad fourth place in the fray. Aristotle was the arts-course hero, and that meant that he was the Newton or Einstein or Pasteur rather than the Hegel or John Henry Newman of the age. More than Paris, which was the theological capital of the world, Padua, a center of medicine and physics as well as of law, was the great stronghold of Aristotelianism in the Renaissance.[58]

Because of the university curriculum, a distinctive feature of late medieval civilization was an organized and protracted study of physics which was more intense and widespread than had ever before been the case. Greek or Roman civilizations had seen nothing on this scale. The thousands upon thousands of students studying physics in the universities had also specialized in logic.

But the very juncture of physics and logic becomes understandable with the work of the past decade which makes clear what the old scholastic logic was — an advanced formal logic, highly quantified. The juncture of an advanced formal logic and mathematical physics here is not an isolated phenomenon. Significantly enough, it is repeated in the mathematical logic of our own day, which, like the old scholastic logic in which it is becoming interested, has grown up in close connection with interest in the physical sciences.

7. THE SCHOLASTIC TRAJECTORY OF RAMISM

The constitution of the arts course — the youthfulness of its pupils and teachers, the orientation toward a nonepistemological, mathematical type of logic and a concrete physics rather than toward the more elusive problems of metaphysics or ethics — has been dwelt on because this is the world in which Ramus' dialectic takes form. Ramism emerges when the Agricolan topical logic moves out of the more humanistic Rhineland environment into that of this Paris arts scholasticism.

In many of its apparently revolutionary manifestations, Ramism does not react against arts scholasticism at all. If it does, it reacts against it simply by moving further out along the trajectory originating at the heart of the university arts program. Ramus' hostility to Aristotle, as he himself is at some pains to show, has ample warrant in the thirteenth-century university condemnations of the Greek philosopher because of his incontestable paganism. The gradual establishment of the Stagirite in the medieval university after his condemnation is itself curiously paralleled by his gradual rehabilitation in Ramus' own thought, as revealed in the successive revisions of the *Remarks on Aristotle* and the final *Defense of Aristotle*.

Similarly, Ramus' impression that metaphysics was nothing but theology sieved through logic[59] is a curious reflection of the structure of the arts course, which specialized in logic and remitted metaphysics in great part to theologians. Ramus' persuasion that dialectic is the center and core of all philosophy merely recapitulated the opening words of Peter of Spain's *Summulae logicales* (although this is a work which Ramus repeatedly and wholeheartedly denounces!): "Dialectic is the art of arts, the science of sciences." *Technologia* or *technometria*, the sciences which, in Ames and the later Ramists, will order the various arts and sciences among themselves, are a further protraction of this same medieval tradition.

Ramus' deliberate amalgamation of a logic of scientific demonstration and a dialectic of probabilities is contrary to the philosophico-theological logic of a St. Albert the Great or a St. Thomas Aquinas. But it is in the central tradition of arts scholasticism, as represented by Peter of Spain, for, if some of Peter's commentators work out a distinction between the various logics, the *Summulae logicales* itself perpetuates the amalgam in mixing its highly formalized, quantified supposition theory with a treatise on the commonplaces. With ethics Ramus will have great difficulty, and his disciple William Ames will write a treatise to show that, in the Christian dispensation, ethics is absorbed by theology.[60] But, practically speaking, this was no new position. It had threatened to be an actuality all through the medieval arts course.

Some of the most typical items in the Ramist kit are significant because they are common both to the arts-course terminist logic deriving through Peter of Spain and to the new Agricolan topical logic. Ramus' celebrated conception of "gluing" arguments together, remarked by Perry Miller[61] and others, is an example. With subject-predicate relationships in abeyance, what was there for an Agricolan to do with concepts save "couple" them together with a "copula" or some sort of adhesive? But "glue" is also standard equipment for the pre-Agricolan terminist, since Peter of Spain's suppositional theory had effectively atomized and itemized the contents of the mind, inviting one to pinpoint the pieces on the external universe. Thus it is no surprise to find Ramus' chosen enemy, the terminist Tartaret, speaking what is really Ramus' language when he treats the organization of an axiomatic system as "a collection of several logical statements which stick together."[62]

The suppositional tradition of arts scholasticism likewise lies back of Ramus' attempt to reduce all questions of fate and Providence to matters of logic. Historically, the questions which emerge in the Renaissance disputes over grace and "free futuribles" — God's ability to foresee with certainty the acts of free agents without interfering with freedom — find their most elaborate early treatment not in theology but in terminist logic, where they arise in connection with *ampliatio*, or quantification (supposition) extending terms in time.[63] Thus the *entitatulae* or "little bits of entities" which move through these disputes have affinity both with Peter of Spain's hypostatized terms, which, like real being, have "properties," and with the corpuscle-like "arguments" of Agricolan and Ramist topical logic.

8. RAMISM IN ITS NATURAL HABITAT

One might at this point risk some summary theorems, which, if not taken too absolutely, point up significantly the state of affairs and serve as a useful reference for explaining what Ramism is.

The scholasticism known to most neoscholastics and to the intellectual world in general today is a scholasticism of theologians, who, moreover, are mostly members of religious orders: Aquinas, Albert the Great, Bonaventure, Scotus. In this scholasticism, philosophical problems were often elaborated in perspectives developed in the prolonged theology course and thus in a context derived through Peter Lombard's *Sentences* from classical rhetoric more than from the central scholastic logical tradition.[64]

Arts scholasticism is set against this theological scholasticism. It develops largely outside the religious orders. The only clergy allowed to teach it in the University at Paris were the "secular" clergy, and arts professors were by no means all secular priests or students for the priesthood. They were in great part medical students or, like Chaucer's clerk of Oxenford, scholars not in minor orders, and at Paris they were not necessarily even tonsured — for the scholar's status conferred, if not *de iure*, at least *de facto* status as a clerk, with all the immunities attaching thereto.[65]

There was in addition a close alinement of this arts scholasticism with medicine. Indeed, the name of its major upper-division subject, physics, has to this day clung to medical men — physician, *Physikus*, and the like. Psychologically this scholasticism is ordered largely to the physical, quantitative world, as studies in the history of science are making clearer every day. And, like modern mathematical logic, the logic of this medieval and early Renaissance arts scholasticism is physical in tonality.

This helps explain why it is the permanent seed bed of nominalism: for the nominalist doctrine in its extreme form, that there are no realities corresponding to universal terms, is connected with a habit of conceiving everything in units of the sort imaginable in a quantitative world. Paradoxically, this same mentality can be the seed bed of extreme realism: conceived of by a quantitatively oriented mind, universals themselves are unit pieces, too, like the man and the donkey who inhabit the logicians' syllogisms. The formal logical tradition as such, quite properly, does not attempt to deal with epistemology — it is difficult, if not impossible, to determine where the *Summulae logicales* stands on the question of universals.[66] The nominalist-realist dilemma arises when the habits of mind encouraged by formal logic for its own purposes seek to solve epistemological questions on a formal logical basis.

The great figures of scholastic theology, an Aquinas or a Scotus, are to a certain extent outside the arts-course tradition in that they are neither nominalist nor realist, but are simply theologian-philosophers, solving problems on somewhat different grounds. That nominalism and Thomism existed in different sets of dimensions is suggested by the fact that nominalists by no means always regarded the "conversion" of one of their number to Thomism as a desertion. When Peter Crockaert of Brussels became a Thomist, John Major "continued to consider him one of the best of his followers, and Antonio Coronel was lavish in his praise of this former colleague of his."[67]

Because it tends to picture all issues in more or less quantitative terms (although it is a supple instrument in the hands of the competent), arts scholasticism can also generate a self-confident, *simpliste*, covertly brash approach to the most complex problems. The tonality is detectable in Marsilius of Inghen and John of Jandun, through Ramus and Thomas Hobbes, who was famous for his "constant undaunted resolution of maintaining his own opinions." Such resolution seems to be a property of a mind satisfied that a diagram or its equivalent is adequate to any situation. One thinks of Ramus' dichotomies and of the mass of little men, human atoms, who go to make up the state in the famous frontispiece to Hobbes' *Leviathan*. This is the tradition in which Agricola's and Ramus' topical dialectic or logic finds a home. In this home it is no anomaly at all. But the home itself has long been to modern eyes an unfamiliar structure.[68]

CHAPTER VII

THE PEDAGOGICAL JUGGERNAUT

Formal education brings man
to his natural perfection.
— Caspar Pfaffrad, *De studiis
Rameis* (1597), pp. 18–19.

I. PHILOSOPHY AS PEDAGOGY

Ramism has been commonly regarded as "more a pedagogical than a philosophical reform." The implication is that pedagogy and philosophy are quite separate human activities. This does not hold true in Ramus' world — in a far more profound sense than is commonly realized. In all cultures pedagogical procedure and philosophy have always influenced one another, but in the intellectual milieu from which Ramus emerged, the two activities not only interacted but were effectively fused. The pattern carried over from antiquity had tended to subordinate philosophy to pedagogy by presenting the function of philosophy in terms of teaching. This tradition became most effective in the university structures, from which its influence spread practically everywhere in Europe from the twelfth century on.

The very existence of such a term as "scholastic philosophy" is prima-facie evidence of the cultural and intellectual tradition out of which Ramism emerges. The "schools" with which the term "scholasticism" is obviously related are commonly taken today to mean cliques or sects of philosophers, as when one speaks of disputes between the various schools. It is true that in classical usage *schola* does have this meaning, and together with it the related meaning found in the Theodosian and Justinian codes of a corporation or association. But in medieval times, when *universitas* had gained currency as the word for corporations, what we today would style various philosophical schools were spoken of commonly as "ways" (*viae*): there was the "way" of St. Thomas, the "way" of the "reals" (or realists, as we should say today, for in the earlier, more personalist age, "ists" were rare, and "isms" were not yet thought of), and the "way" of the "nominals" (nominalists).[1]

Although *schola* in the sense of a philosophical sect may occasionally be encountered, the prevalence of this term in medieval and Renaissance Latin derives largely from its use to designate a classroom. This use goes back to

Cicero, who borrows the word *schola* from the Greek and employs it to signify, among other things, the place where lectures are given. Cicero's usage persists throughout the Middle Ages and the Renaissance. Thus the "Old Schools" at Oxford and at Cambridge are old classrooms or lecture halls. Their "new" counterparts, called the New Schools at Oxford, at Cambridge are styled simply the New Lecture Rooms, in accordance with present-day idiom. The names of the individual classes, "Schola Grammaticae et Historiae," "Schola Logicae," "Schola Astronomiae et Rhetoricae," and so on, can still be read over the doors in the Old Schools Quadrangle at Oxford; at Cambridge one still speaks not only of the "Old Schools" but also of the "Law Schools" (in the plural, meaning lecture halls) rather than of a "law school," which in America signifies a corporation or faculty.

The various *scholae* of Ramus and others are to be understood thus to mean lectures which one heard in *scholae* or classrooms. For scholasticism, in its historical context, means classroom-ism or schoolroom-ism, and scholastic philosophy means schoolroom philosophy.

As Abraham Fraunce makes clear, even at the end of the sixteenth century, in the estimation of many, no matter how well a man could weave his syllogisms together, he should not pretend to know scholastic philosophy unless he had actually gone to school. There is something wrong when "every Cobler can cogge a Syllogisme, every Carter crake of Propositions. Herby is Logike . . . made common to all which before was proper to Schoolemen and only consecrated to Philosophers."[2]

The association of scholasticism with teaching is far stronger and more real than its association with deduction. One need only look at random scholastic works to be struck with how little strictly formal deduction, and how much preoccupation with the teaching process is really there. In all St. Thomas Aquinas there is hardly one formally constituted syllogism. But his *Summa theologica* begins with and in its totality is explicitly based on a long discussion of sacred teaching, *sacra doctrina*.[3] Long after Ramus' age, the importance attached to logic in the general consciousness is due less to its association with thinking than with pedagogy. In the first words of Peter of Spain's *Summulae logicales*, dialectic or logic is conceived of not as an art of thought but as "the art of arts and the science of sciences," opening the way to all "methods," that is, to all curriculum subjects. (Whether dialectic or logic actually controlled the setup of curriculum subjects was another question; Ramus answered strongly in the negative.)

Since the new science taking shape in the sixteenth and seventeenth centuries was to be founded so largely on the development of mathematics and on the interpretation of physics in terms of variables mathematically manipulated, it actually involved a more rigorous application of deductive procedures than did the science of preceding ages. This deductive stress has become commonplace knowledge. Thus, while the new science involved a shift in per-

spectives, the shift was not a movement away from deduction. It was a movement away from a concept of knowledge as it had been enveloped in disputation and teaching (both forms of dialogue belonging to a personalist, existentialist world of sound) toward a concept of knowledge which associated it
with a silent object world, conceived in visualist, diagrammatic terms. This
visualist factor in the shift is the basic component; it is the element common
to the otherwise apparently disparate techniques of observation (chiefly visual,
and connected with induction) and mathematics (relying on visualist conceptualization and deduction), which come into their own so curiously and
almost simultaneously.

2. THE TEACHER: MAN BETWEEN TWO WORLDS

Dominating the passage from early discourse-knowledge to observation-
knowledge stands the all-important figure of the teacher. He has grown to
enormous stature in the universities, and straddles both the audile's discourse
world and the visile's object world. Instead of carrying on a dialogue in the
give-and-take Socratic form, the university don had largely reduced the oral
component by converting it into his own classroom monologue, which he
produced not as the spirit moved him but on schedule at fixed places and
hours. At the same time his interest both in logic and in explicitness, in an
"object" (of knowledge) rather than in a "subject" (of discourse), had driven
him further still toward the visile pole with its typical ideals of "clarity,"
"precision," "distinctness," and "explanation" itself — all best conceivable in
terms of some analogy with vision and a spatial field.

The fact that the teacher's auditors (most of them were the arts course
students) were youngsters and the fact that they were compelled to master
standardized material for the examinations which ultimately became a part
of university life,[4] only strengthened the drive toward the visual, in the interests of "clarity" and "simplicity." Under such circumstances, these interests
heavily outweighed profundity as operative ideals. An example of these ideals
fully matured in the Ramist era is Alsted's division of the educational system.
There are two sorts of schools, he explains, the elementary schools and the
more advanced schools. The former are "murky" or "obfuscated" schools
(*scholae obscurae*), whether they are city schools (*civicae*) or rural (*paganae*),
because they achieve the ideals of clarity only imperfectly, while the latter are
more advanced schools because they are "clear schools" (*scholae clarae*).[5] The
advanced knowledge they purvey is not necessarily more profound, but is
clearer and more distinct.

From another point of view, the influence of the university situation upon
the very way of conceiving what knowledge is can be estimated from the fact
that the ancient, pre-university world did not have the concept of an exami-

nation in the medieval or modern sense — a sampling of knowledge through which, by a kind of extrapolation, the whole "content" of a person's mind can be calculated. There is no word for this in the classical tongues because there is no concept or practice for it to designate — *examen* means a swarm of bees, or, at best, such consideration or weighing of matters as might enter into judicial decisions. The examination for certification in a teacher's guild as apprentice (bachelor) or master, or for the related "license" to teach from the papal chancellor, with the peculiar notions of intellectual competence which such examinations and the inaugural ceremony of *inceptio* implied, were products of the teachers' guilds or university situation itself. As purveyed under the supervision of a corporation, knowledge naturally tended to be viewed less as a wisdom transmissible only in a context of personal relationships than as a commodity. It could be measured — indeed, had to be — which meant that it could be manipulated in terms of quantitative analogies. We have not yet arrived, but we are well on the way to report cards, where students can "get" a "70" or an "85" or, given the right questions and some good luck, a "100," cold mathematical evidence of competence in the nonmathematical.

In the university context (and this context determined the tone of much even in nonuniversity schools, which were often taught by university-trained masters), the role of the teacher thus had two aspects. His role was, first of all, still personal. He maintained knowledge in the personalist context in which it had been born in antiquity and from which, of course, it can never be entirely removed. But in the university, the teacher was also part of a corporation which was uncalculatingly but relentlessly reducing the personalist, dialoguing element in knowledge to a minimum in favor of an element which made knowledge something a corporation could traffic in, a-personal and abstract (almost as though it were something which existed outside a mind, as though one could have knowledge without anybody to do the knowing — as Ramists were eventually to maintain one could).[6] This depersonalizing process was the second, although unintentional aspect of the teacher's role.

3. DIALOGUE, DIALECTIC, DISPUTES, AND PEDAGOGY

Early definitions of philosophy do not equate it with teaching so forcefully as the Ramist definitions, sequels of the medieval university experience, were to do. Philosophy, according to Socrates, Plato, and Aristotle, had been the love of wisdom — cultivated by Socrates in real dialogue, reported by Plato in dialogue form but committed to writing, and pursued by Aristotle rather more abstractly and scientifically, but with a residual respect for dialogue evidenced by the notion of predication at the core of his logic. For Isidore of Seville, philosophy was "the knowledge of matters human and divine, joined with an interest in the good life."[7] For Alcuin it was "the investigation of natural things, the knowledge of things human and divine in so far as it is possible for man to evaluate these."[8]

Nevertheless, there was a tendency, even in antiquity, to assimilate philosophy to teaching, which was connected with the fact that all knowledge was generally passed on by a teacher. Thus, the word for any art or science or curriculum subject — grammar, rhetoric, dialectic, physics, and the rest — or even for all arts and sciences together, has, from an incalculably early epoch commonly been a "teaching" (*doctrina*) or, conversely, a "learning" (*disciplina*). This use of these terms was widespread during the patristic age,[9] and it is evident that the incredibly high pedagogical charge built up in logic or dialectic, and through it in all the arts and sciences, owes much to the force developed by the notion of teaching within the economy of Hebraeo-Christian revelation, wherein God personally teaches man and where His teaching is continued through history in the Church. The didactic quality of the "logical" organization in medieval sermons is well known.

But great stress was also placed on teaching in pre-Christian sources. A notable example is Aristotle's statement at the beginning of his *Metaphysics* that the surest sign of a learned and wise man is his ability to teach what he knows. This passage was cited and elaborated on by such scholastics as St. Albert the Great.[10] *Mathēsis*, a word which is often employed by Aristotle, and from which "mathematics" was named by the Greeks, means the receiving of instruction at the hands of a master.[11] Other concepts related to *mathēsis*, such as art, science, and method also tend to be associated with teaching in Aristotle. Thus method ($\mu\acute{\epsilon}\theta o\delta o\varsigma$), which in the opening of the *Nicomachean Ethics* means investigation, tends elsewhere to mean discipline or subject or "branch" of knowledge.[12] Etymologically, method means a "way through" or a "way after," and thus assimilates readily to an art ($\tau\acute{\epsilon}\chi\nu\eta$) or skill, as well as to a doctrine or process of teaching, and to a science or organized body of knowledge held together by first principles.

The initial juncture of philosophy and teaching was to evolve spectacularly in the university. The universities were, in principle, normal schools, not institutions for general education. This was true of all the faculties: arts, medicine, law, and theology; and it was most true at Paris and at universities modeled on Paris (rather than on Bologna), such as Oxford and Cambridge and, later, the German universities. Such universities were, in brief, medieval guilds, or were composed of four teachers' guilds or faculties with their associated pupils. The degree of master or doctor (the terms were equivalents, varying from university to university or from faculty to faculty) was the formal admission to the guild, just as the bachelorship which preceded it was admission to the body of apprentice teachers.

Paris statutes from time to time provided that all those receiving their master's degree must actually teach for two years or more,[13] and, although the provision was equipped with the rider which nullifies so much medieval and ecclesiastical legislation — "unless excused for a reasonable cause" — the strict orientation of the degree toward teaching was unmistakable. Even at Bologna, where the university was a group of associations not of professors but of students hiring their professors, completion of the degree meant in principle admission to the professorial corps (hence a kind of demotion from employer to employee!), and the graduation exercise was, just as at Paris, really an *inceptio* or investiture wherein the new teacher exercised his prerogative of teaching for the first time.[14]

To be sure, many a student who went up to the university did not make a career of teaching, and many certainly never intended to. Some broke off their studies before completion. But for such students, no official provision was made. Officially, the bachelor of arts was an apprentice teacher on the arts faculty; bachelors of theology were apprentice teachers of theology, condemned to a long round of "practice" teaching; and bachelor butchers were apprentice butchers — for all these people were members of their respective trade guilds.

The unbelievable force of this pedagogical tradition, as well as some of its remoteness from actuality is still with us today. In many countries, a physician whom a university faculty certifies as a practitioner of medicine is called a "doctor" of medicine, as though he were going to teach medicine, just as in some countries, one trained to practice the law is also still called "master" or its equivalent. Graduation, too, is still a "commencement" or *inceptio* — in theory, the beginning of a teaching career.

In the university world before and during Ramus' time, dialectic itself, which in its etymological origin was concerned with real dialogue, as both Ramists and their adversaries were well aware,[15] was habitually thought of as implementing not dialogue, but the huge pedagogical apparatus. As the "instrument" of intellectual activity, it became assimilated to the particular intellectual activity being served. Instead of representing an approach to truth through the real dialectic of Socrates' midwifery, or through a series of probabilities as in Aristotle's conception, dialectic or "logic" became the subject a teacher taught to other coming teachers in order to teach them how to teach, in their turn, still other apprentice teachers, and so on ad infinitum.

In this maelstrom, the preservation of some externals of a real dialogue in the give-and-take of scholastic dispute was at best only an equivocal manifestation of concern with real dialogue. The disputations were essentially normal-school exercises, samples of the prowess of aspirant teachers, who had to know their matter so well that no cross-questioning, however clever or persistent, could upset them. As late as Ramus' own day, (as John Standonck's 1503 statutes for the College of Montaigu show), such disputations were the *sole* exercise of all students.[16] Only with the humanists, whose practice Ramus would follow, would written exercises come in. The appearance of written exercises signaled the collapse of the normal-school tradition in the universities and a subtle reorientation of objectives.

The normal-school tradition itself, however, had prepared the way for the humanist assault on the oral disputation. Insofar as knowledge was standardized by being put in the keeping of teachers' guilds, where it inevitably became more and more a commodity, it tended to retreat from the evanescent world of discourse (*verba volant*) to the more stable world of writing (*scripta manent*). Individually, the teacher could afford to be a voice. Corporately, too many voices could result in chaos. If a master was to purvey to his students what as an apprentice he had received from another master, the obvious way of assuring proper continuity or the unity of the total product which was being purveyed by the members of the teachers' guild, was to put the product in writing. The well-known university regulations against teacher's dictating to their pupils and even against pupils' taking pen or ink into the classroom are capital evidence of the persistent tendency of the members of the teachers' guilds to rely slavishly on the written word.[17]

Even where the abuse of dictation was avoided, a teacher who might want to maintain some show of dialogue in the process of relaying his subject matter, but who had to face a class in an assigned subject at routine hours, would find it much more feasible to have a written text than a living person as interlocutor. As we know from class notes and from annotated textbooks, as well as from commonplace present-day experience, control was not easy despite the presence of a written text, and coverage of the whole matter called for was often not completed. Even partial dialogue with the class, in which the pupils volunteered questions or objections, was necessarily severely restricted, or one would never get through the material at all. Hence from the earliest times the commentary on a written text, an attenuated form of dialogue in which one interlocutor (the writer of the text) need not even be alive, competed vigorously with the more completely oral, more strictly dialectical disputation. By the humanists' day the commentary gave definite promise of winning out. Disputations were indeed still prominent features of academic life well into the eighteenth century, but they eventually disappeared except in isolated cases or in equivocal forms — in the seminary course, where disputations helped assure mastery of material for preaching (that is, oral teaching) purposes, or in the thesis examination or *soutenance* for higher degrees, or in papers, followed by discussion (a form of "objections"), read before academic societies. The disputation and with it vestiges of dialectic tend to survive in attenuated form where some normal-school orientation remains.

It becomes apparent that when viewed in these perspectives the notion of teaching or "doctrine" in Western culture is not the inert residue in intellectual developments but a curious catalyst. A recent writer on the development of philosophy, Mrs. Suzanne K. Langer, in an excellent book which has become a minor classic, sees "doctrine" as arriving on the scene when intellectual discoveries, "good answers to appropriate questions," are no longer being made because of the temporary exhaustion of the "motive concepts" of a philosophical epoch.[18] This may be true of doctrine in certain special senses. But in the central intellectual tradition of the universities, the notion of doctrine itself was not a by-product of quarrels between philosophic sectaries but rather one of the most active nodes in the tangle which unravels itself into the modern philosophical and scientific world.

4. THE DIDACTIC ROOTS OF FORMALISM

The pedagogical bent of the universities resulted in a constant agitation of a group of interrelated terms; not only teaching (*doctrina*), learning (*disciplina*), "method" (*methodus*), but also art (*ars*) and science (*scientia*), and, more or less implied as the complement of any and all of these, nature (*natura*). The notion of teaching largely controls the others in this complex — even nature, so that, for Ramus, "natural" dialectic, or, as he will call it, the "nature (*natura*) of dialectic," will be what a little boy knows about dialectic from having used it in discourse unwittingly before he takes up the subject in school.

The other terms, of course, exercised some influence on the notion of teaching, too. This tradition more or less took for granted that teaching is carried on abstractly, since knowledge was generally equated with abstract or scientific knowledge. What is not conveyed abstractly and explicitly, is not taught. *Doctrina* is *scientia*. Teaching something is the same as "proving" it.[19] This can be seen in the common equation of the "demonstrative" (*demonstrativa*) with the "doctrinal" (*doctrinalis*), which the scholastics took over and developed from the Greeks,[20] and, in a coarser and more hectically colored form, in Ramus' notion of method.

The fine psychological distinctions which Aristotle elaborates in the *Nicomachean Ethics* and elsewhere, and which the great scholastics also elaborate, between the notions of *doctrina, disciplina, methodus, ars,* and *scientia* could not be sustained consistently in the rough-and-tumble everyday activity of arts scholasticism. Peter of Spain's *Summulae logicales* is the capital exhibit here. The three terms *ars, scientia,* and *methodus* featured in the opening sentence of this work were, as has been seen, commonly equated by being taken all together to mean curriculum subject. In their lectures on the *Summulae logicales,* Tartaret and others will refine on Peter's expression in their own way. Art refers to a habit or acquired skill of the practical intellect when this latter is concerned with doing or making something; science to speculative knowledge as organized with relation to the general principles, the axioms or *dignitates,* which govern it (presumably as axioms govern geometry); method to something more variable, but generally the order found within a science perfectly and completely organized, or the order of presenting a subject in teaching it. But these are distinctions which some commentators imposed on Peter's text, but which were not found in it, and they were not always understood in the same way. The text itself stood against them, and, as Tartaret is at pains to point out, it does *not* employ *ars* and *scientia* as distinct from one another, but in the "general" sense as synonymous.[21] The text was spokesman for the concrete university situation rather than for doctrinaire dons, and the text prevailed.

The fact that Peter of Spain's text was a general rather than a particular spokesman was true throughout the Middle Ages, for Peter of Spain proved more viable than all his commentators; and it was certainly true among the scholastics at Paris in Ramus' youth. Francis Titelmans, spokesman for a post-Agricolan dialectic which still preserved contact with the pre-Agricolan tradition, as we have seen, cut through the art-science-method-doctrine problem by insisting that it is useless to quibble about defining dialectic theoretically since it is defined practically by the traditional content of the course in dialectic: dialectic *is* what is taught in the curriculum subject.[22] Since the traditional content of the course was precisely what was being contested in Titelmans' day, his position is tantamount to saying, "Dialectic is what *I* am teaching."

In explaining Porphyry, Juan de Celaya took much the same line. He refused to discuss the question whether logic (*logica*) is or is not a science, observing with commendable candor that the question was beyond the capacity of his boyish auditors at this stage of their education.[23] When he did go into the question elsewhere, the weight of the pedagogical tradition made itself felt unmistakably and all the more impressively because it was unconscious. In a mass of refined statement concerning dialectic, Celaya remarked in passing that "as a science it *teaches* to discern the true from the false"[24] — his equation of science with teaching was quite innocent and automatic.

The pedagogical bias was also discernible outside the arts course on the other faculties. Thus, in this climate of opinion, the highest recommendation for the works of the greatest of scholastic theologians, St. Thomas Aquinas, was neither their acumen nor their profundity but simply that they were easy to teach. This was the chief and prosaic reason why he was favored by Francisco de Vitoria, who spearheaded the sixteenth-century movement which finally dislodged Peter Lombard's *Sentences* as the center of the theology course and replaced them with St. Thomas Aquinas. St. Thomas himself, author of a treatise *The Teacher* (*De magistro*), is not free of the pedagogical bias of his disciple and promoter. Not only is his discussion at the opening of the *Summa theologica* whether theology is a science set, as we have seen, within the larger framework of a discussion concerning teaching, but his mortal conflict with the Averroists concerning the nature of the soul has as one of its principal focuses the question whether science in the teacher and the disciple is or is not numerically the same.[25] In this tradition, teaching (and thus dialogue, or at least monologue) enfolds science — not the other way around.

The pedagogical bias at the root of the concept of knowledge shows in the way in which medical lore was preserved before Vesalius and Harvey, and, indeed, even much later.[26] Old illustrations still show the doctor of medicine at his lectern calling out the parts of the human body as his assistant produces them dutifully from the cadaver before him and holds them up to the class, proving that, if you only dissected a body intelligently, you would be able to find what the professor, following Galen, said was in it.[27] This view of research, clearly pedagogical rather than "deductive," seems not to have been embarrassed even by the fact that Galen's original descriptions were in great part based on the dissection of monkeys.

5. RESULTS IN RAMUS' DAY

The pedagogical set of mind was the result less of the explicit doctrine of this or that scholastic than of the ineluctable university situation which bred scholastics. The same situation has unmistakable effects on the early humanists, who sometimes renounced the details of scholasticism without renouncing its substance. For the humanists exhibit the same tendency as the scholastics to shunt discussions of art, science, and method, and even of nature, off onto lines which connect them with teaching.

Thus, in discussing the Greeks' understanding of the term "method" (in Latin, *methodus*), Melanchthon virtually equates every term in the constellation we have been treating with every other, justifying their equation, with true humanist piety, on the basis of ancient Greek usage:

> The Greeks thus define this term: Method (μέθοδος) is an acquired habit establishing a way by means of reason. That is to say, method is a habit, that is, a science (*scientia*) or an art (*ars*), which makes a pathway (*via*) by means of a certain consideration (*certa ratione*); that is, which finds and opens a way through impenetrable and overgrown places (*loca*), through the confusion of things, and pulls out and ranges in order the things (*res*) pertaining to the matter proposed.[28]

Melanchthon is quite obviously giving the Greeks an Agricolan reading. What was for them a "way through" or a "way after" he deftly modulates into a collection of "things" salvaged from the "woods" or from "confusion" or from certain "places" — all echoes from Agricola's description of what a well-kept topical logic should be. But the Agricolan reading does not eliminate any of the established constellation of terms — teaching, art, science, method, and perhaps nature concealed in the "woods."

Melanchthon is only tinkering with the notion of method, which he was one of the first to introduce into dialectic manuals. But his tinkering gets the rest of his inherited apparatus out of line. The result is that the definition of dialectic he proposes sounds curiously like a definition of method itself, which is concerned with a proper sequence of items — indeed, he says that dialectic is, indifferently, an art (*ars*) or a way (*via*). "Dialectic," we are told, "is the art or way of teaching correctly, in order, and lucidly."[29]

Melanchthon further confirms and enlarges on his position here, explaining that the whole efficacy of dialectic consists in teaching, and that the interior organization of a science (and thus deduction itself) — defining, dividing, and reasoning — is nothing but a pure and simple teaching process, since it is the product of dialectic.[30]

Not satisfied with equating dialectic and teaching, Melanchthon also must solve problems external or peripheral to dialectic on a pedagogical basis. Thus, he defends the long-standing distinction between dialectic which controls "plain" speech and rhetoric which controls "ornamental" speech on the grounds that, while not necessarily accurate, the distinction must be held to because it is teachable.[31] He is hewing here to the Agricolan line, for, when Agricola had dismissed a logic of predication in favor of a topical logic, he too had done so because the former is hard to teach and the latter easy.[32] The humanists, who were often hired tutors in wealthy or noble households, thus tend to increase the pedagogical torque given to knowledge by the scholastics, for they add a consideration for pupils' needs greater than the scholastic system had known.

Melanchthon's genteel and not very perceptive stands were popular, and his blunt identification of dialectic with teaching would be stubbornly defended by Abraham Fraunce and many others. Miss Tuve has recently reviewed and developed Fraunce's defense: "Hee teacheth, whosoever maketh any other man know that, whereof he was ignorant."[33] The telling point in Fraunce's defense, however, is that, like Melanchthon, he is concerned about equating teaching with logic, rather than with speech or communication — although he implies the latter equation. Logic does not govern thought, as we should suppose today (man's intellectual processes related to their object), but more specifically does govern communication (the verbalized relationship of man's thought to its object in the presence of another individual), which itself will be resolved into teaching. Furthermore, it must be emphasized that Melanchthon, Fraunce, and the hundreds like them are not writing in terms of their own insights into linguistic or logic; they are writing as teachers, explaining to their boys what is essentially a textbook tradition.

When Melanchthon equates *dicere* (to say) and *docere*, he is quite plainly using this latter term in the sense of "to teach." The secondary meaning of *docere*, to show or to make manifest (a more common Latin term for this would be *monstrare* or *demonstrare*), does not enter into play at all except insofar as it is inevitably associated with teaching. The focus is quite obviously classroom procedure. When the secondary meaning of *docere* is adverted to, the adversion is only to provide an occasion for associating the Greek term *apodeictic*, which does derive from a verb meaning "to show," with *docere*, in order to reduce this Greek term to the same meaning as the Latin and keep it, too, focused on classroom performance. This is Ramus' procedure[34] and, whatever their other differences, also that of his adversary Antonio de Gouveia.[35]

Another of Ramus' adversaries, Jean Riolan the elder, discusses the origins of all philosophy in terms of the office of teaching and the selection of teachers.[36] The common orientation of dialectic, if not of all philosophy, toward teaching would provide the best approach of later irenicists who attempted to reconcile diverse dialectical camps. Conrad Deckher, harmonizing Ramus and Melanchthon, harps on this common cord: "Logic is the art of teaching about anything, correctly, in order, and clearly."[37] The Ramist Alsted would use the same approach in assimilating Aristotle, Ramus, and Raymond Lully: "Logic is the art of knowing . . . . Therefore dialectic [i.e, logic] is the art passing on skill in knowing, and consequently teaching the instrument of knowing."[38]

6. NORMAL-SCHOOL THEOREMS IN RAMISM

The dialectic-and-teaching mixture for which the universities had been the crucible had by Ramus' own day become an amalgam more dense than ever before or since. The amalgam was to give rise to the various searches after method which mark the age — for instance, Francis Bacon's search, which features the division of the faculties of the soul in terms of the curriculum (and vice versa).[39] The source of Ramist method would be this amalgam.

Ramus' colleagues at Paris, Nicolas de Grouchy, Jean Riolan, Jacques Charpentier, and dozens of others, will discuss in detail the relationship of art, science, method, and nature without arriving at any generally acceptable conclusion[40] concerning their relation to teaching. They were touching here on the profound question of the relationship between science and dialogue which would have to undergo incubation through Hegelian and post-Hegelian developments in thought before it could be explicitly stated. The equations of art and science and method with teaching lurk at all the turns of the discussions without ever clearly showing their faces.

Ramus also will present the notions of *ars* and *doctrina* interchangeably: "The *art* of dialectic is the *teaching* of how to discourse."[41] When he becomes nice in his distinctions, he becomes so with regard to the other items, not with regard to the identification of art with teaching: "Logic is not the *teaching* of how to argue about the precepts of logic; . . . logic is the *teaching* of how to discourse well."[42] *Disserendi* was a term which Ramus took over from Cicero and which he neglected to explain fully. In his 1555 *Dialectique*, he transplanted it in French by *disputer*.[43] But his discussion of method through all his works will make clear that the term actually is inseparable in his mind from teaching. This gives to dialectic the curious double-teaching charge characteristic of Ramism: like every other art, it is teaching (*doctrina*) by the very fact that it is an art (*ars*), but it is further the art or teaching *of teaching*. In this view, all wisdom itself (*sapientia*) is nothing if it is not dialectic, which teaches (*docet*) the various causes.[44]

The positions taken here by Ramus were reiterated by his followers. Piscator will be explicit in assigning a didactic role to speech: "to discourse (*disserere*) means "the same as to teach" (*docere*).[45] Indeed, the whole business of expression is to teach (Piscator is in agreement with Fraunce), whereas the business of reason is to learn: dialectic is the art of both these things, of teaching and of learning.[46] Following and epitomizing Agricola, Bartholomew Latomus had made this same equation.[47] Similarly, another Ramist will place "teaching" (*doctrina*) at the head of a list of the various objectives (*proposita materia*) which dialectic sets itself, others being narration, disputation, persuasion, dissuasion, consolation, excuse, and the like.[48]

Having possessed itself thus of dialectic, the instrument of philosophy, teaching inevitably reaches out to include all philosophy. Philosophy becomes what you *learn* when you are *taught* at school. That philosophy may be the love of wisdom is not denied, but the assertion becomes quite nugatory when faced with the unassailable fact that philosophy is in reality defined by the pedagogical situation. Thus, explains the Ramist Severin Slüter, "Philosophy, according to Ramists, is the teaching of the liberal arts"[49] — which, it must not be forgotten, mean the liberal "teachings"! But this is not all; teaching is not only philosophy, but knowledge itself. Slüter adds, "This definition is quite the same as the following: Philosophy is knowledge of the liberal arts."

Teaching will govern the Ramist notion of "method," for the terms in which Ramus tried to discuss the subject are all inextricably involved with the notion of teaching and hence with one another. Thus we find Ramus insisting that in Galen investigation of a subject ($\mu\acute{\epsilon}\theta o\delta o s$) and theoretical speculation ($\theta\epsilon\omega\rho\acute{\iota}a$) both follow the same conceptual order or sequence as didactic arrangement ($\delta\iota\delta\alpha\sigma\kappa\alpha\lambda\acute{\iota}a\ \tau\acute{a}\xi\epsilon\omega s$), and that Simplicius, the sixth-century commentator on Aristotle, only reinforces Galen's equation of these terms.[50] Talon will show no hesitance in equating method and doctrine with one another, and both with curriculum subject; he will translate Aristotle's "method" ($\mu\acute{\epsilon}\theta o\delta o s$) by *doctrina* in a passage where it obviously means the investigation or analysis of a subject or mass of data.[51] Ramus will say the trouble with Aristotle's *Metaphysics* is that it is useless for teaching and learning (*ad docendum et discendum nil utilitatis*), by Aristotle's own admission.[52] When Aristotle is at his worst, it is because he refuses to be dogmatic or magistral, questioning and doubting rather than teaching.[53] The notion of theory (*theoria*), which the anti-Ramist Everard Digby and a few others will play up, will not make half so good a showing in this climate of opinion as the far more frequent *doctrina* which Ramists use for a general descriptive term for knowledge. What is thought of today as medical theory or physical theory or theological theory is still preferably formulated as medical doctrine or physical doctrine or theological doctrine. It is not that sixteenth- and seventeenth-century man wanted to be more dogmatic; it is just that his notion of knowledge enmeshed inextricably with the notion of person-to-person communication.

Certain refinements and distinctions tend only to increase the semantic confusion surrounding science, art, method, and associated terms, and thus ultimately to blur them all in the name of pedagogy. A good example is the common distinction between "teaching dialectic" (*dialectica docens*) and "practical dialectic" (*dialectica utens*), which Nicolas de Grouchy traces to Averroës and Aquinas, and notes is not present in Aristotle.[54] Grouchy adds that *dialectica docens* means "dialectic as posited in its precepts as such," whereas *dialectica utens* is dialectic insofar as it uses its principles to explain other things outside itself. Johann Piscator agrees, and specifies that among the other things which dialectic explains are the other arts besides dialectic.[55] The tendency here to double the teaching tradition back on itself is plain and typical, for the arts which *dialectica utens* explains are themselves also *doctrinae* or teachings. Moreover, the "explaining" which it does is itself teaching. As Piscator remarks: "the use of logic is nothing other than teaching" (*logicae usus nihil aliud est quam docere*). Thus even the logic (or dialectic) which is *not* a teaching logic teaches teachings! "Teaching logic" necessarily does even more: it teaches the teaching of teachings. We can only agree with what Piscator and Grouchy both add here, that the distinction between "teaching logic" and other kinds of logic leads nowhere.

These dizzying equations, which derive ultimately from Peter of Spain and the central scholastic tradition reinforced rather than enfeebled by humanistic ideals, echo far outside the Ramist orbit itself for many a generation. Even those who, if pressed, would take to higher ground and explain an art or science as an intellectual *habitus* rather than as a *doctrina*, when not pressed, often follow the age-old grooves which Ramists trod and deepened. Thus, in the late seventeenth century, Jesuit teachers will note that dialectic "teaches" (*docet*) how to reason, whereas physics only "explains" (*explicat*) its matter.[56] By this time, such distinctions of terms has become more automatic than discerning, and there is little point to them. But the distinction remains, a testimonal to the incredible force of the teaching tradition which had built up the interest in logic and/or dialectic.

Always strong in Germany, since it was connected with Ramus' persistent influence there, the same tradition echoes in Hegel's unconscious distortion of Ramus' reputed master's *inceptio* thesis, which Hegel states as "Alles, was Aristotelis gelehrt habe, sey nicht wahr."[57] The *dicta esse* (said) of Freige's original wording has become *docta esse* (taught, *gelehrt habe*). But Freige could not object to this rewording, for in identifying talking and teaching, it only follows the Ramist line, to which Freige always hewed.

7. DIALECTIC TO DIDACTIC

The didacticism which Ramus inherited from the university tradition completely routes his vaunted humanism when the issue between the two is finally forced. This is apparent in his commentary on the opening passage of Aristotle's *Posterior analytics,* one of the most commented passages in all Aristotle's works:

The Greek text reads διδασκαλία καὶ μάθησις, which is hardly rendered properly by teaching (*doctrina*) or learning (*disciplina*), *because these Latin terms signify integral and complete arts, such as grammar, rhetoric, logic,* whereas the two Greek terms signify anything which is taught and learned, whether it be a whole art or a tiny particle (*particula*) of an art, such as syllogism, enthymeme, induction, example, or a thing defined in the light of its definition, or a whole in terms of its parts, or anything else defined in terms of something else — each of these things is styled διδασκαλία καὶ μάθησις. Therefore the Latin words *doctrina* and *disciplina* are here to be understood [in the Latin rendering of Aristotle's text] as meaning anything that is taught or learned.[58]

This is nonsense from the mouth of a classicist such as Ramus, for in classical usage the terms *doctrina* and *disciplina* do not have the restricted meaning at all which he assigns them here. Ramus' persuasion that by preference they mean an "integral and complete art" such as "grammar, rhetoric, logic" shows the tyranny which the didactic university tradition exercised over his professedly classically trained mind.

Little wonder that as Ramism develops, an art of pure "didactic" will put in its appearance as the direct heir of Ramist dialectic. Didactic will appear chiefly in the German milieu. The *Great Didactic* (*Didactica magna,* 1633) of Jan Amos Komensky or Comenius, the disciple of the German Ramist Alsted, is by far the best-known work in this tradition. Ordering things in "logical" form according to the "method" made current by Ramism, Komensky sets down the way in which curriculum subjects are to be hammered into youthful heads with the greatest possible efficacy.

Komensky's *Great Didactic* has a long, if neglected, history, however. It is foreshadowed by Alsted's *Didactic Scholastic Theology* (*Theologia scholastica didactica*);[59] his mountainous encyclopedias in their various epiphanies might be added. (Alsted never set pen to paper without didactic purpose, and the encyclopedias, certainly the greatest monuments to the definition ever constructed by the mind of man, are as didactic as it is possible to be without bragging about the fact — although they do this, too.[60]) For Alsted, a favorite author at Cambridge University and in New England, didactic is hardly distinguishable from dialectic, for it is "the teaching of the study of philosophy." [61] Alsted had been foreshadowed by Piscator and by all the other Ramists and semi-Ramists who insist that the business of speech is to teach and that of reason to learn. Other contemporaries of Alsted, such as Sophonias Hasenmüller, make didactic a means of expediting teaching and learning in the classroom,[62] without expressly involving extracurricular activity. On Ramist principles, Johann Heinrich Bisterfeld developed a *Sacred Didactic* or "art of reading and learning the Holy Scriptures properly." [63] For Johann Reiskius, rector of the school at Wolfenbüttel, didactic is "the art whereby the teacher or doctor teaches his disciples language, sciences, and good morals and thus furthers the commonweal." [64]

Didactic is evidently almost as protean and all-purpose a concept as the dialectic from which it is descended. Its line of descent makes clear how unrealistic is a separation of the textbook tradition, particularly at this time, from the general intellectual tradition of the Western world, or how unrealistic is any treatment which regards didactic as something incidental and subsidiary to what was going on in extracurricular literature. The "didactic" which rises to the surface of the textbook tradition at this point is the distillation of the scholastic and humanist heritage, which both transmits this heritage and modifies it. For one of the remarkable things about the Western world is that it *has* textbooks and is passionately interested in what we call today "education." All other cultures — which make their own particular and different contributions to mankind and to history — have, since the sixteenth and seventeenth centuries, looked to the West to improve their own techniques of propagating and assimilating knowledge. The West has given to the world not only universities, but the interests and techniques which go with the university state of mind.

Didactic is thus a kind of quintessence of the university. The frank and frantic cultivation of didactic, if regional in some of its aspects, is not simply a freakish by-product of Ramism or of the tradition from which Ramism is descended. It is a normal development which threatens to take place everywhere that arts scholasticism touches.[65] The German universities were relatively new, their accumulation of tradition thinner, so that the didactic drive, indigenous to the whole university movement, appears in Germany unmasked and bare. At Tübingen, so far as we know, for the first time in the history of universities, a university (established in 1477) had been conceived of as a collection of universal knowledge, rather than as a collection of masters and students, in the way common previously.[66] Although such a concept of a university was new, it was not outside the university tradition, for it derived straight from the notion of dialectic and of knowledge itself which the older universities had nourished.

Ramists, of course, when taken at their declared value, were apparently worthwhile acquisitions for a university conceived of as that at Tübingen was since their "method" purportedly gave them mastery of all subjects whatsoever. Unfortunately, their declared value was not always very real, and there are several distressing incidents in Germany in which somewhat wild-eyed and sputtering Ramists are dismissed from university faculties as troublemakers and frauds.[67]

But these incidents did not annihilate didactic nor didactic tendencies. The works of Alsted and other didactic German Ramists were welcomed all over Europe and in the American colonies, for preoccupation with the learning process was everywhere the rule. Boys at Harvard were made to defend a great many theses explaining not what they learned, but what the structure of the curriculum was: "Languages are to be *learned* before the arts," "Languages are more readily *learned* by practice than by rule," "The art of physics is to be *learned* (*discenda*) from things, not fabricated in the mind."[68]

8. PEDAGOGY AND THE INTELLIGIBLE UNIVERSE

Alfred North Whitehead and others[69] long ago made the suggestion that the patience to attack a problem scientifically implies an act of faith in the intelligibility of the universe, and that historically the great impetus to this act of faith has been Chistianity, with its unequivocal belief in a personal God and in a universe created by Him in time and with a determined purpose. Thus explained, the scientific mind dates effectively from the Middle Ages, when the Christian outlook took possession of much that was central in the Western European consciousness.

This explanation is undoubtedly true in the large, and more and more details substantiating it are being filled in as the history of scientific origins is further investigated. Moreover, as has been seen, it explains to some extent the prestige of teaching in the ambit of science, for what the Christian believed in, he believed in as something revealed or taught by God in concrete historical persons — Christ first, and then members of His Church, who dependently on Him continued His teaching.

But Whitehead's explanation is inadequate for understanding the complexity of the framework in which the scientific mentality took shape. It does not explain satisfactorily the phenomena which erupt in Ramism and in the whole question of method, because it does not account for the great faith in a *segmented* explanation of reality which these phenomena reveal, and which are based on a passionate belief in a number of separate sciences each with a tidy economy of its own.

This subordinate act of faith in the division of intelligibility is, it appears, an essential part of the scientific mind. It can readily be seen developing from antiquity on in the Greek's analytic approach to knowledge. However, faith in the segmentation of knowledge never before had reached the intensity it reached in the pre-Ramist scholastic age. As the scholastic passion for distinctions manifests itself here and in Ramus himself, its major concern was to distinguish the arts or sciences within the human mind. This concern was far more central than the preoccupation of scholastic logicians with distinguishing different kinds of beings (*entia*), as it is of course far more real than their legendary preoccupation with calculating the number of angels who can localize themselves on the point of a pin. In order to tidy up the world, the mind must first have sorted out its own possessions.

It will not do to say that this passion for a division of knowledge is a product of the disinterested mind in quest of pure understanding. That is the way the story ought to read. But it is not the way the facts stand. The unit divisions of knowledge in which everyone in the pre-Ramist age so passionately believes are not divisions which function successfully as distinct sciences, and which organize knowledge in terms of intelligibility into real axiomatic systems, although they are often talked of as though they are sciences in this sense, and although they may occasionally in part coincide with sciences so conceived. Historically and psychologically, the unit divisions are effective as units for teaching; they are units in which diverse items are related to one another less by sheer intrinsic cohesion than by the fact that it had proved feasible, for reasons which greatly varied, to throw them together for classroom purposes. This is why Ramus, like his medieval predecessors, while he tends to envision geometry from afar as the perfect science, finds it necessary when he discusses an "art" or "science" in detail, to cite, of all things, grammar.[70] He speaks of and imagines each art, grammar included, as though it were a tightly organized axiomatic system, as all scholastics tend to do. Euclidean geometry certainly is this, in a way in which grammar is not. But grammar was better established as an acknowledged curriculum subject, and being a curriculum subject simply *made* it a science or art *par excellence*, axioms or no axioms.

In terms of the established pattern, humanism forced a crisis by proposing a program which in effect challenged the primacy of dialectic and, in so doing, impugned the whole curricular organization and the teaching profession as such, and thereby threatened the intelligibility of the whole universe. Having lost sight of the close association of teaching with dialectic on the one hand, and with the sense of scientific cosmic order on the other, we often find it difficult today to understand this aspect of the impact of humanism on its age.

While very real, this impact is not altogether easy to discern. With regard to the issues involved in the more or less implicit identification of dialectic and teaching and science, humanism was hardly more clear-cut or articulate than the order which it attacked had been. Although the humanist emphasis on grammar and rhetoric at the expense of abstract logic or dialectic and the humanist assumption that formal education was to be designed for others than prospective teachers struck hard at the half-covered roots of the university organism, the humanists themselves seldom realized the full implication of their position and were commonly agreed in their persuasion that the proper business of logic or dialectic was teaching.

Their policies suggested, it is true, that insofar as formal education was to be organized not just for teachers but for anyone interested in "living," whatever rule dialectic enjoyed should not be defined by the classroom. Dialectic, as Ramus was to insist, should govern all life. This expansion of the purview of dialectic might mean that the art of arts and science of sciences was being pried loose from a close association with pedagogy. But it might also, and often did, mean something rather different, namely, that the purview of pedagogy was itself being expanded so that the world outside the classroom purportedly governed by dialectic was by that fact being assimilated to the classroom itself. Thus, not only did the curriculum expand in the wake of humanism to include such new subjects as geography, history, and many others, all given "methodical" or classroom organization, but also the whole of "life" which was set against classroom activity tended to be interpreted in undisguisedly pedagogical terms. As the Ramist dichotomization of Cicero's life all too plainly makes clear (see Figure I), Cicero's entire career, from birth to death, could be viewed as if it were organized like the "art" of grammar or rhetoric. The pedagogical juggernaut which rolled for so long throughout the Western intellectual world was certainly not to be halted by pointing out to its operators new fields where they should not venture. To believers in dialectic any attempt at limitation was a challenge to themselves, their god, and the entire teaching profession.

Book Three
RAMISM

CHAPTER VIII

THE RAMIST DIALECTIC

In this ile Dialectica, . . .
I began to read Ramus his mapp.
— Madido, in *The Pilgrimage
to Parnassus* (1597), Act II

I. GENERAL SETTING

THE matrix in which Ramism is generated and in which it acquires its proper significance is highly complex. Its constitutents are many: the corpuscular outlook on mental life encouraged by Peter of Spain's highly quantified logic and implemented by the *simpliste* Agricolan logic of places; the mechanistic outlook fostered by an arts scholasticism oriented largely toward physics and taught to young boys, which encouraged, if it did not compel, the neglect of mature moral philosophy and metaphysics; the curious impetus given to the notion of science and dialectic by the didactic, normal-school mentality of the universities; and the unforeseen effects of the pressure exercised by humanism on the university pedagogical machinery. There is no really unified, interior speculative life holding Ramism together — and, indeed, its appearance in this matrix suggests that the speculative aspects of the scholastic, university heritage as a whole have often been exaggerated. Ramism is supported by concrete conditions in which are embedded special mental habits. There are some abstract formulations, but there are also many unformulated assumptions exceedingly difficult to bring to light.

It is true that Ramism functions in this matrix largely in terms of the general cultural patrimony, and that it passed on to succeeding generations the store of concepts, valid and invalid conclusions, hypotheses, literary and rhetorical attitudes, which were also passed on by Aristotelianism or other competing isms. But Ramism has its individualities, too. To identify these, it is best to concentrate attention on Ramist dialectic, and even more critically, on the "method" in which Ramist dialectic terminates, as well as in Ramist rhetoric, which presents in great part simply the obverse of the dialectical design. This dialectic and rhetoric will be discussed in succeeding chapters from the point of view of the background provided in the previous chapters.

2. FIRST FORMULATIONS

In the absence of an inventory of editions, it has hitherto been impossible to view Ramus' writings in any logical pattern of development. The result is that a fixity and inevitability have been attributed to his work which it does not really possess. Ramus' final dialectic was not arrived at by any straightforward route. Its author is the prince of revisionists. André Wéchel complained that Ramus' works all came into the world like bear cubs (which were thought to be born formless and licked into shape by their mother), and that the author kept licking them into new shapes indefinitely.[1] The new shapes are due in part to Ramus' constant reassorting of the commonplaces or *loci* after the fashion of Cicero, Themistius, Boethius, and Rudolph Agricola, in part to the elaborate trappings with which at first he surrounds this game and which he has soon to modify or discard, and in part to the sniping of his enemies, who took toll of his ideas more than Ramus liked to acknowledge.

The new dialectic is first formulated in the *Training in Dialectic* and the *Remarks on Aristotle*. The *Training in Dialectic*, from which the later *Dialectic* emerges, is a curious document and can be described as an attempt to set a vaguely Agricolan dialectic in a Ciceronian psychology, to give it a Platonic surface purportedly in the interests of religion, and to "simplify" the result for reasons of "practice" or pedagogical expediency. The *Remarks on Aristotle* is a whirlwind tour of the Aristotelian *Organon*. It corresponds to an ordinary commentary by a young master on the various books (including Porphyry's *Introduction*) but, in Ramus' case, has as its objective not explanation but annihilation of the text to which it is addressed. This *Remarks on Aristotle* must be read in conjunction with the supplementary *Dialectical Explanations of Porphyry*, published under Talon's name in 1547 during Ramus' forced retirement from philosophy teaching, but, beyond a doubt, written under Ramus' supervision.

3. RAMUS' *Remarks on Aristotle*

Dedicated to Charles de Bourbon, bishop of Nevers, and to Charles de Lorraine, archbishop of Reims, the *Remarks on Aristotle* is written in a high-spirited, occasionally amusing, if not witty, Latin style. The text begins with an interpretation of the Prometheus myth, which Ramus states he derives from Plato and which he resorts to again and again in later works: Prometheus was the first philosopher; the "fire" which he discovered was nothing other than "artificial wisdom" (*artificiosa sapientia*), or, as we might say, wisdom made scientific, by the aid of "certain dialectical principles" (*quaedam circa dialecticam principia*).[2]

All pre-Aristotelian philosophers, such as Prometheus himself, Zeno the

Eleatic, Socrates, Hippocrates, and Plato followed the real dialectic — that of nature, "natural." But among all these, Plato stands out as the philosopher who represents dialectic or philosophy at its zenith. When Aristotle succeeded him, dialectical "truth" and practice became corrupted, although this corruption was due more to Aristotle's followers than to Aristotle, "who himself enriched dialectic by employing it in discursive fashion" in works which have unfortunately been lost.[3] By "discursive fashion," Ramus means informal use, such as one might encounter in a political speech as against a logical or mathematical treatise. But Aristotle tore down with one hand what he built with the other. Despite the value of his practice, his theoretical treatment of logic only succeeded in retarding the real exercise or *usus* of dialectic.[4] The post-Aristotelians who carry forward Aristotle's own corruption of dialectic are Theophrastus, Eudemus, Chrysippus, and other Academicians, Peripatetics and Stoics. Although he avows that he has never read but only heard of these authors, Ramus is perfectly sure that for some six hundred years they did not improve on Aristotle. They based their practice not on Aristotle's practice, but on his written recommendations — which was the worst thing they could have done. Viewed in terms of these written recommendations (Ramus means, of course, the *Organon*), Aristotle's own case and that of the Aristotelians is identical, and he, Ramus, is against the lot of them.[5]

After this initial division of dialecticians or philosophers into the good (those who follow nature) and the bad (those who follow Aristotle's false art), Ramus moves on to consider first the false art and practice of dialectic as manifested in Aristotle's *Organon*. This part of his critique (in *Remarks on Aristotle*) exactly parallels the positive presentation of dialectic in his *Training in Dialectic*, in that it considers successively nature, art, and use or exercise.

Ramus takes up the works in the *Organon* in their traditional order, but treats them as though they were supposed to fit exactly into his own scheme of an art of dialectic which is composed of invention and judgment, followed by practice or exercise. The *Categories* and books I to VII of the *Topics* (together with Porphyry's *Introduction*) have to do with invention, we are told. The books *On Interpretation* and the *Prior Analytics* and *Posterior Analytics* (with which Ramus throws in the *Metaphysics* as well) have to do with judgment. The rest of the *Organon*, that is, book VIII of the *Topics* and the *Sophistical Argumentation*, have to do with the use of dialectic.[6] Ramus' opponents, such as Gouveia, Riolan, Charpentier, and Schegk, violently attack this pressing of a defenseless Aristotle into the service of the Ramist dialectic. But their attacks show no more agreement among themselves regarding the principle underlying the organization of the *Organon* than one meets in the medieval schoolmen. Ramus could always count on a certain amount of dissension among his opponents,[7] who seldom moved into a united battle formation save when he hove in sight.

Ramus' critique of Aristotle labors in a cascade of invective, and is extremely difficult to summarize in a way which does justice to the confusion of his thought. He systematically misrepresents Aristotle's positions and frequently resorts to highly mythical self-dramatization, picturing dialectic as a tree of knowledge with golden apples hanging from the boughs (*rami*) surrounded by screeching and frustrated Aristotelian hobgoblins.[8]

Ramus finds Porphyry in his *Introduction* badly garbling his explanations (which Ramus calculatingly misunderstands), straying from proper usage, particularly with regard to the term *species*, and bringing grammar into dialectic.[9] The *Categories* pretend to contain everything, but they contain things only in confusion and only in potency.[10] The *Topics* set out to provide the "places for finding arguments" (*locis argumentorum inveniendorum*), but are terribly confused and repeat in each of the first seven books the four sophistic questions, What are the accidents? the genus? the properties? the definition?[11] Moreover, in the *Rhetoric*, Aristotle is wrong in assigning three ways of invention, from cause, from universal argument (that is, the places or commonplaces), and from something between the two;[12] he is also wrong in relegating dialectic to the *Topics* alone, for it rules all discourse.[13] The second and third judgment, which Ramus explains at length in his *Training in Dialectic*, are neglected in Aristotle.[14] Everything in the treatise *On Interpretation* and in the *Prior Analytics* and the *Posterior Analytics* really concerns only "first judgment," as Ramus calls it; that is, syllogism. The treatise *On Interpretation* calls for animadversions on grammatical disputes, semantics, psychology, ontology, on knowledge of future contingent events, on the finite and the infinite, on conjoined and disjoined statements, modal propositions, and opposed statements.[15] In treating the *Prior Analytics*, Ramus carps at Aristotle's remarks on universal affirmative and universal negative syllogisms — *dici de omni, dici de nullo* (these terms will later be assimilated in the three rules of method which Ramus will say he derives from Aristotle) — as well as on other Aristotelian syllogistic figures and modes, on conversion of syllogisms, on contingent, necessary, and mixed syllogisms, on induction, example, and enthymeme, and on dilemma and sorites.[16] The *Posterior Analytics* occasions remarks on demonstration *propter quid* and *quia* — the starting point of much medieval and Renaissance axiomatic theory in which Ramus' discussion of method is later entrammeled — on the identification of demonstration and definition, on variables (Ramus is against even Aristotle's tentative use of letters such as "A," "B," as variables for terms), and on propositional logic.[17] Ramus rejects the Stoics' work as faulty.[18] Aristotle is wrong in making no use of examples from the poets and orators in his *Analytics*.[19] The *Sophistical Argumentation* alone of Aristotle's work is well organized in that it states first its end or objective; but it is useless anyhow, for there is no need to study how to avoid error.[20]

At the end of the *Remarks on Aristotle*, Ramus concludes his charges against Aristotle and the Aristotelians in stock humanist terms. Aristotelians are obscurantists. They foster barbarism. They should not be clung to out of mere custom. The Aristotelian logical works must be rejected in favor of the one sole dialectic which rules all.

To whatever limits or areas disputation extends, whether to domestic or public affairs, to matters of moment, to human relations, whether it extends to private persons or to legal procedure, to the people or to the rulers, to few or to many, whether it concerns your own associates or yourself, asking questions or answering them, no matter what the subject or how it is treated, one and the same rhetoric and dialectic work together.[21]

Remarks on Aristotle closes by celebrating the union of philosophy and eloquence, which, we are reminded again, Aristotle himself practiced, despite his ill-conceived rules, as did the other ancient authors, Plato, Theophrastus, Phalereus, Carneades, and Cicero — indeed, all Greece and all Italy.[22] After this outburst of humanist piety, there is a final invocation to God the Father as the source of dialectical light.

Almost all the points touched on in the *Remarks on Aristotle* are also touched on in the *Training in Dialectic*. They will be explained further in connection with this latter treatise or elsewhere as occasion demands.

4. THE NEW PROGRAM: *Training in Dialectic*

For the first time in *The Structure of Dialectic* (*Dialecticae partitiones*, 1543) Ramus expounds positively the one sole dialectic which rules all. In its second edition of the same year, this work was called *Training in Dialectic* (*Dialecticae institutiones*). This edition, which does not differ from the first in any significant way, is the one cited in Francis I's decree condemning Ramus, and since it is therefore better known than the first, it is the point of reference for the discussion here.

The *Training in Dialectic* is the matrix in which Ramus' later and better known *Dialectic* itself, and, to a great extent, his entire thought, is formed. The later *Dialectic* would be essentially an "art" (*ars*) or "teaching" (*doctrina*), consisting of a skeleton of what were commonly referred to as "precepts." In the *Training in Dialectic*, this art appears in an interesting embryonic form, undeveloped and set between two other "parts" of a general power or ability called *dialectica*. The *Training in Dialectic* consists thus of a treatment of these three "parts" of dialectic — nature, art or teaching, and exercise, respectively — sprinkled with frequent attacks on real or imagined opponents, the whole preceded by Ramus' letter to the University of Paris. Particularly in its latter part, the *Training in Dialectic* is larded with excerpts from the (Latin) orators and poets — Cicero, Catullus, Virgil, Martial, and others — in accordance with Ramus' principle that any kind of discourse, provided it was well done, was as good an example of dialectic or logic as any other. This was a key plank in this militantly humanist program for a popularized logic.

i. Dialectic as Nature: Imitation

The text of the *Training in Dialectic* opens with a definition of dialectic as "the ability to discourse" or "the power of discoursing."[23] Discoursing (*disserendi*), the term which will recur in Ramus' definition of the art of dialectic, is equated with "conversing," with "disputing," with "discriminating," and with "using one's reason,"[24] in a way which makes it clear that "reason" is still of a piece with discourse rather than with pure abstract thinking. Ramus stresses the description of dialectic as the discerner, the discriminator, the decision-maker (*disceptatrix, iudex*), dividing the true from the false.[25] This is Cicero's view, he explains, but adds that Quintilian is also right: dialectic is the disputer (*disputratrix*) as well, the party to debate. For Ramus' concept of discerning or distinguishing, like that of the whole antecedent tradition, is again bound up with dialoguing processes.

The statement that dialectic is concerned with resolving questions, with what is doubtful,[26] will occur again and again in Ramus' works. That dialectic, and indeed all science, has somehow to do with what is doubtful, is a position commonly taken since antiquity and one with which even today everyone might agree. The more urgent problem was not whether dialectic aimed at solving what was doubtful but whether the solution it gave was itself certain with the certainty of scientific logic, or only probable — and to that extent still doubtful. This problem, it has been seen, was unresolved in the central medieval arts tradition, which was represented by Peter of Spain. We know from the attacks on Ramus by Jacques Charpentier, Jean Riolan the elder, and others that it was hotly discussed in Ramus' day. Ramus agitates the matter enough to suggest that dialectic secures absolute certainty, but he never really shows that it does.

We are told here as in the *Remarks on Aristotle* that the "power" (*vis* or *virtus*) which is dialectic has three "parts." It has a birth or an origin (*natura*), a teaching or art (*doctrina* or *ars*), and an exercise (*exercitatio*). Ramus thus sets up the "power" of dialectic in terms of the three things which, at least since Plato's *Phaedrus*, the pseudo-Cicero's *Rhetorica ad Herennium*, and Quintilian's *Training in Oratory* (*Institutio oratoria*), had been considered requisite for producing a good speaker or writer, namely, natural ability, knowledge of theory, and practice.[27] Two years later the Talon *Training in Oratory* was to rechristen three similar elements in rhetoric not "parts" but "steps" (*gradus*). These concepts of "parts" or "steps" provide a spatial model to which an "art" can be referred. The sequence natural ability, knowledge of theory, and practice also provides a means of likening an art to one of the youngsters who came up to Paris for his studies: the art is born outside school (*natura*), it receives form or "formation" in school (*doctrina* or *ars*), and finally it matures and leaves school (*exercitatio* — begun in school, but carried out into "life").

Natura, in this context, does not mean specifically essence or principle of operation. This notion is suggested as an overtone or as a possible point toward which its meaning may well shift, but basically it retains its older, more elemental sense of origin or birth. This is why, with some plausibility, Ramus can employ as synonyms in the *Training in Dialectic* the terms *natura dialecticae* (the origin of dialectic) and *naturalis dialectica* (natural dialectic). They signify innate dialectic which all human beings have at their birth and which he styles in Platonic fashion "aptitude, reason, mind, the image of God, the light rivaling the eternal light." [28]

Ramus' discussion of natural dialectic comes to him directly from the pre-Agricolan scholastic logicians. By reason of their greater supply of "natural logic," Tartaret had said, some men are more prone to assent to truth than others.[29] The notion of natural dialectic controls Ramus' notion of what imitation is. "The art of dialectic," he explains in the *Remarks on Aristotle*, "ought to be developed by the imitation and study of natural dialectic," [30] and so with the other arts, too.

In his *Ciceronianus*, Ramus will treat imitation as though it were reproduction of classical models. He does this also in the *Training in Dialectic* when he discusses exercise, saying that the boy should learn by imitating all the good classical writers, especially Cicero.[31] This notion does not entirely accord with his insistence that art is mere reproduction of "natural" preschool speech habits. Ramus never fully resolves the conflict here, although he seems elsewhere to indicate that the speech of the uneducated can be used as a point of departure for "deducing" the art of dialectic rather than for direct imitation.[32] Ramus' own use of examples of logic from the orators and poets stems from the principles that one can readily find dialectic at work anywhere and that all discourse should be continuous and flowing (*perpetua*), that of physics or arithmetic as much as poetry.[33] Since the technique of analyzing discourse, learned or unlearned, is always the same for Ramus, why Cicero and other educated authors are preferred for citation remains a permanent riddle from the point of view of pure Ramist theory.

The didactic tradition asserts itself in another way which brings out the connection in Ramus' mind between an "art" and the process of communication. Others had made works of art copies of nature, or perhaps the artistic process a copy of natural processes. Ramus makes the art of dialectic itself the copy. Nature, he tells us, corresponds to Alexander, art to Apelles' portrait of Alexander.[34] Apelles' role here is clear: he stands for the teacher, who projects the art outside himself into his pupils and without whom Ramus is quite incapable of effectively conceiving an art at all.[35] In Ramus' static, pictorial representation of art, the figure of this inevitable teacher, the *speaker* of the art, will linger long. But only as a relict. For if art is generated in connection with speech, the speech is entirely the monologue of the teacher, not dialogue any more. Apelles' picture communicates, but with no provision for any riposte.

Ramus' opponent, Adrien Turnèbe, an exceptionally discerning classical scholar, was aware of the subtle changes which had come over men's minds at this time. In his *Little Book on Method*, which takes issue with Ramus, he stresses the fact that for the Greeks dialectic was associated with speech rather than with thinking or with reasoning or with invention.[36] By Turnèbe's day, however, in a very profound sense, speech was losing ground in favor of sight in the mind's approach to things, despite the reactivation of the classical ideal of orator. Ramus retains the symbol of the teacher, but it is significant that he disguises him as a painter, and adapts him to less vocal approaches to knowledge.

ii. Dialectic as Art or Doctrine: Its Definition and Description

Ramus defined the art of dialectic, which he sets against natural dialectic, as the doctrine or teaching of discoursing (*doctrina disserendi*).[37] In his mind and that of his contemporaries he equated it with the art of discoursing (*ars disserendi*), the form which will become more common in his later *Dialectic*.[38] This definition has frequently been regarded as peculiar to Ramus, but it comes from the central Western tradition along with most of the other items in this repertory of this "usufructuary,"[39] and is found everywhere throughout the writings of the Middle Ages. It turns up in John of Salisbury's definition of logic "in its widest sense,"[40] and at Paris among the great Victorines.[41] All that Ramus did was to give the Ciceronic definition wider circulation and crystallize its form.

Disserendi is a critical term which controls the whole field of mental activity from classical times through the Middle Ages and into the Renaissance. Its tendency to be assimilated to teaching has already been noted. *Disserendi* could be assimilated to a great many things — that is why it was retained. It does not necessarily mean prove, or argue, or assert, or maintain, or even say, although it may, on occasion, mean any or all of these. John of Salisbury equates it with *loquendi*, or speaking,[42] and the term has explicit oral commitments; it comes close to the English term "expatiate" or to the term "discourse" by which Thomas Granger, an exceptionally urbane and competent Ramist, renders it in his 1620 English adaptation of Ramus' *Dialectic*,[43] and by which it is usually rendered in the present work. "Treat of something" does not fully cover the meaning of the term, for the fact that one treats of a "thing" involves ontological frames of reference which the Latin adroitly bypasses. *Disserendi* has the decided advantage of not even being transitive. Generations of classroom logicians, who had to teach what they did not entirely understand to boys who could understand even less well, found the term highly serviceable. The later attempts, noted by Miller,[44] to account etymologically for the appearance of the term — as meaning "sowing far and wide" — do not give it any clearer meaning.

Ramus' subsequent restoration of the Ciceronian *bene*, to make dialectic mean "the art of discoursing *well*" points up the difference between the "art" of dialectic and "natural" dialectic. A person endowed with natural dialectic can discourse, but not so "well" as he might. There would be no need of formal training in the art otherwise (although Ramus' opportunistic vaunting of the excellence of natural dialectic had brought him to assert paradoxically that natural dialectic *does* function well, in spite of everything). This insistence on superior ability or facility to some extent assimilated the art to the notion of a "habit" (*habitus*) or acquired skill, and might have given the former some kind of theoretical basis in some scholastic "physics" or metaphysics, as that of St. Thomas Aquinas. In point of fact, the insistence more often blurs the discussion further. One was excused from the task of determining the meaning of *disserere*, for regardless of what action it referred to, the point about the "art" as art was that it enabled one to do the action "well" — that is, better than otherwise.[45] The art was the thing.

In preference to *bene*, earlier scholastics had often, although not always, used more geometrically founded qualifications such as "straight" or "correct" (*recte*) — as when Hugh of St. Victor says that dialectic teaches the "rules of correct (or "straight") disputing" and rhetoric the "rules of correct (or "straight") speaking."[46] This correctness suggests technicalities. The humanist insistence on education for life, rather than for the *scholae* or classrooms, often substitutes graciousness or gracefulness or general effectiveness for pure technique, and it is quite clear in Ramus' *Protest to the Privy Council*, as well as in the Talon commentaries on Ramus' text, that Ramus himself, in accord with humanist ideals, understood *bene* to mean "in a practical fashion" or "effectively."

The spread of Ramus' definition of dialectic is also increased by his insistence that an art be governed not only by its object but also by its end, or purpose. One studies geometry "to measure well," not to understand mathematics,[47] and dialectic "to discourse well." This might be thought to effect a distinction between an "art," oriented toward doing or action, and a "science," oriented toward knowledge. Such, however, is not the case. Ramus proceeds as though his art of dialectic and his other arts are oriented toward action and knowledge simultaneously, just as the pedagogical tradition — as witnessed by Peter of Spain — had always tended to do.

Ramus adds here that *disserere* is equivalent to *disputare*. But this stand does not compromise by clarification any of the established ambiguities. *Disserere*, he offhandedly remarks, is *disputare* insofar as it treats of questions.[48]

This is noncommittal, since any utterance whatsoever which is not already in question form can be considered the answer to an implied question, so that "insofar as it treats of questions" means only insofar as it says anything at all. Ramus simply lets the general indecision regarding the relation of *disserere* and *disputare* stand where he found it.

The history of the Ramist definition of dialectic or logic will only point up the indecision in Ramus' use of this cardinal term. In Ramus' 1555 *Dialectique*, he makes dialectic the "art de bien disputer." But the posthumous 1576 French edition alters "disputer" to "raisonner"; M'Kilwein's 1574 English edition renders "dispute," and so does Fage's 1632 translation. Between these dates, in Fenner's 1584 and in Fraunce's 1588 adaptations, one finds "reason." This becomes rather general, especially after the mid-seventeenth century. Beurhaus' 1587 German translation had rendered *disserere* by "die Vernunft . . . zu brauchen," Dietrich's 1655 Latin adaptation by "ratione utendi," Milton's 1672 Latin by "ratiocinandi." In 1609, Alsted had made Ramus' noncommittal terminology more noncommittal than ever by taking dialectic to be the art of knowing (*sciendi*).[49]

To illustrate further what he means by "natural dialectic," Ramus produces in his *Training in Dialectic* a series of analogies. "Natural physics," he tells us, is related to the diagrams of the physicist as "natural mathematics" is to mathematical abstractions (*species*), or as "natural" moral philosophy is to the "virtues" and the properties of the virtues in moral philosophy. Natural dialectic is related to the art of dialectic as "natural purity of speech" is to the rules of grammar, or "natural" ornament to the rules of rhetoric. In general, natural dialectic stands related to the art of dialectic as the "truth of nature" (*veritas naturae*) to the "truth of art" (*veritas artis*). Ramus sums it all up by stating that the art of dialectic (*ars dialectica*) is related to "natural dialectic" as Apelles' picture of Alexander is to Alexander himself.[50]

This series of analogies, coming from nowhere in particular and yet from everywhere, shows much about the furniture which the sixteenth-century mind had accumulated out of several centuries of arts-course scholasticism and a generation or two of humanism. One notes the immediate recourse, before all else, to mathematical — more specifically, to geometrical — analogies. As he fumbles about in the fundamental imaginative constructs on which his notion of an "art" is supported, Ramus' first resort is the diagrams of physics — and a physics, we note to our surprise, which already in this pre-Newtonian era, long before it could be implemented by mathematics in any effective way, is thrown into a geometrical frame! For the theologian-scholastic, such as Aquinas, or for others speculating from on high regarding the nature and interrelation of the sciences, physics might be the science treating of sensible qualities and of change. For Ramus, who represents the larger pedagogical tradition, it is the art or science which features diagrams. Moreover, for this very reason, it appeals to him as an art *par excellence*. The rules of all the arts and the principles of all the sciences are best thought of as, in one way or other, like geometrical figures. The approach which regards the arts and sciences as permanent possessions (*habitus*) or powers (*virtutes*) acquired by the intellect in a process which merits psychological study is here not even refuted. It is not even thought of.

The drift in Ramus' thought is especially evident in the final analogy with which he concludes the passage. An art is indeed a picture of reality — not in any complex or abstruse sense, for there is no *mystique* in this kind of thinking — but in the way in which a map is a picture of a terrain. For arts are tables or charts of things.[51] In the 1543 *Training in Dialectic*, one of these tables had just put in its appearance as "The Summa of the Art of Dialectic." It was the first of the thousands of Ramist dichotomized "outlines" of an art (see Figure XII).

XII. THE FIRST RAMIST DICHOTOMIES

The occurrence of the word *veritas* in the course of Ramus' explanation should not mislead us. The term has almost no explicitly worked out metaphysical or epistemological implications, although it has a multitude of unconscious ones. The "truth of an art" is doing duty for the concept we know as the "content" of an art, for the notion that arts, or books, or the mind have "contents" will come into currency only as Ramus' notion of opening ideas like baskets gains ground. He is already tending to think of a conceptual world which holds reality inside it this way, but there is a lag between the tendency and the formation of the adequate concept and term. *Veritas* is an interim formulation, suggestive of high metaphysics but in fact pointed toward a notion geometrized in form.

If Ramus turns naturally to a geometrized physics and to mathematics to implement his way of conceiving an "art," he makes it clear that among the arts it is not physics or mathematics but dialectic which is theoretically most important. Dialectic, he goes on to say, "seeks to be not only an art, but the queen or indeed the goddess of the arts." [52] It is futile to look for a profound reason for this stand, and, given a knowledge of the tradition, quite unnecessary. Peter of Spain had pounded into the heads of generations of arts-course students that dialectic was "the art of arts, the science of sciences." Ramus is only repeating this lesson in terms which a humanist could stomach; he has added nothing really new.

a. Invention: Questions, Arguments, Places

The art of dialectic consists for Ramus, as it does for Rudolph Agricola, of two "parts," invention and judgment. Ramus does not radically change Agricola's treatment of invention except to order it more closely to the syllogism. Following a Ciceronian and Aristotelian tradition that Agricola follows, Ramus considers dialectic — and, by clear implication, all speech — to be a means of resolving explicitly formulated questions, such as, Is man dialectical? (*An homo sit dialecticus?*). Faced with a question, in order to obtain either an affirmative or a negative answer, one must cast about for a means of joining or dissociating the subject and predicate. Ramus, adopting Agricola's hostility to the notion of predication and to the terminology associated with it, prefers to call these the "minor part" (*pars minor*) and the "major part" (*pars major*) respectively; the terms are associated with syllogistic structure rather than with subject-predicate relationships. Thus, in the example just given, if one can only find or "invent" the middle term "rational" (*particeps rationis*), which links itself both with "man" and with "dialectical," one can arrive at an answer to the question by means of the syllogism: Whatever is rational is dialectical, But every man is rational. Therefore every man is dialectical. [53] It will be observed that in this typical ("A" type) proposition, the subject or "minor part" of the conclusion ("man") occurs in the minor proposition, the predicate or "major part" ("dialectical") in the major.

By what regular technique can these middle terms be found or "invented"? This will be the business of the first part of dialectic. Like Agricola, Ramus now proposes a list of topics or places in which are stored all possible middle terms of "arguments." Here in the *Training in Dialectic* he proposes it as a list of arguments without enlarging on this term. But in the concurrent *Remarks on Aristotle* he makes clear that he wishes to do away with all discussion of categories and of predication in dialectic and all logic in favor of this topical orientation. By the time of his French *Dialectique* in 1555, he has elaborated a full explanation of his rejection of categories and of his own way of designating simply as "arguments" the loci themselves, traditionally conceived rather as the "seats" of arguments.[54] Ramus can designate the loci as arguments because he can think of them as arguments which are generic and of which the other items more commonly styled arguments are species, or, in his way of putting it, "parts." The scholastic preoccupation with genus and with a class logic, to which Ramus was heir at Paris, at this point ingests Agricola's Rhineland topical formulae.

Ramus' generic arguments or places come to fourteen in his initial assortment in the 1543 *Training in Dialectic* — ten less than Agricola's. In their English equivalents which appear in Robert Fage's 1632 translation of Ramus' later *Dialectic*, these fourteen run as follows: causes, effects, subjects, adjuncts, disagreeings; from these five "first arguments" come nine "derived arguments," namely, genus, form, name, notations, conjugates, testimonies, contraries, distributions, and definitions.[55] When one runs through these "arguments," with the terms "man" and "dialectical" from the question just proposed, one comes to "form" or *species*, and recalls that the specific difference of man is "rational," for man is a rational animal. One recognizes, too, that man's rationality is a "cause" of his being dialectical. The hunt for a middle term is thereby ended. The syllogism can be constructed and the answer had.

This 1543 assortment of arguments will undergo an indefinite number of rearrangements as Ramus licks into shape further editions of his *Training in Dialectic* and of the *Dialectic* which succeeds this initial work. The reassortments as such are inconsequential in most of their details, and, had Ramus lived longer, could well have continued indefinitely. They were to be continued by his followers, such as Alsted, in whose hands the first modern encyclopedias take shape as a kind of ultimate elaboration of Ramist arguments or topics.

b. Judgment: First Judgment or Syllogism

How are the answers which are found by invention held together in discourse? Ramist invention threatens to produce only a series of disconnected assertions. The classical device for overcoming this threat, as retailed both by Cicero in his *Topics* and by the scholastics, was the division of discourse into invention and judgment, the *via inventionis* and the *via judicii*.[56] But the difficulty in this division, as has been seen, was that invention involved a notion of knowledge based largely on a visualist, diagrammatic analogy — one "came upon" or "discovered" (uncovered) or, as the result of "looking," "found" the unit arguments. The act of judging on the other hand was seemingly untranslatable in corresponding visualist terms but had to be approached through a view of knowledge wherein cognition was associated with an aural world in which the voice of the judge (*iudex*) could be heard pronouncing sentence.

Ramus accepts judgment (*iudicium*) as the second "part" of his art or doctrine of dialectic. He defines it as "the doctrine of collocating (or assembling) what invention has found, and of judging by this collocation concerning the matter under consideration." He adds, in a pregnant aside which shows the rhetorical cast of his dialectic, that beyond a doubt this teaching of judgment is the same thing as memory training, insofar as this latter can be taught.[57] It will be noted that "collocation" or assembly or arrangement represents an attempt to deal diagrammatically with the second part of the art of dialectic, that is, with utterance itself. The attempt will soon result in the substitution of the term *dispositio* or arrangement for that of judgment — a substitution in which classical usage had acquiesced,[58] but which Ramism would make more urgent than ever before. This substitution has a notable effect on the concept of judgment itself, for, by highlighting the notion of arrangement or assembly, Ramus creates the impression that the auxiliary or complementary "judging of the matter under consideration" is something so simple that it takes care of itself.

By being equated with or subordinated to collocation or arrangement, judgment is also made out to be an act of comparison. What this comparison really is, Ramus never satisfactorily explains, but leaves one with the impression that it is some sort of matching by juxtaposition, as in the case of samples of cloth. Agricola had said that it was the matching of similitudes.[59] The whole Ramist epistemology and psychology will grow from this highly visualist analogy.

Judgment, Ramus says, proceeds by three steps, which he calls first, second, and third judgment,[60] and which he derives respectively from the Stoics, Prometheus, and Plato.[61] The first judgment corresponds roughly to syllogism (with induction, example, and enthymeme thrown in); the second to a lengthier concatenation of arguments, the beginning of Ramist method; and the third to religion.

Undoubtedly the most curious and telling oversight in this threefold division — which is everything in discourse after the invention of individual terms — is Ramus' omission of the enunciation or proposition or "judgment" itself. The formal, quantified logic of the Middle Ages, like modern formal logic, and unlike logic pursued for psychological and metaphysical rather than for purely logical reasons, had given short shrift to the proposition as such. Formal logic is interested in "structure," not in the metaphysical implications of assertion. But the most formal of formal logics has *something* to say about propositions, if only to describe what they are insofar as they affect the interests of formal logic. In Ramus' case, we are treated to the curious spectacle of a man who at first forgets to allow for the proposition at all! The omission represents no calculated policy; it is remedied with the appearance of the *Dialectic*, which introduces a treatment of enunciations that persists in all subsequent editions. It represents simply the cumulative effects of several centuries of formal logic followed by the Agricolan development of a topical logic. The latter, while it was a revolt against formalism and quantification, only succeeded in establishing a quantification of a less sophisticated and more unconscious kind with its key notion of places or loci.

The local-motion analogies associated with places are carried over by Ramus into his treatment of judgment. Since invention dislodges an argument from one or another of the (Agricolan) receptacles, the first judgment is a step (Ramus says a "teaching") in which "one argument is attached firmly and fixedly to a question so that the question itself is thereby recognized as true or false"; this arrangement (*dispositio*) is what is called syllogism.[62] Ramus is thinking of the process whereby the argument which invention has found ("rational" in the foregoing example) is compared with one or the other of the terms in the question ("Is man dialectical?"). Significantly, he does not touch on the psychological or metaphysical aspects of this comparison, which terminates in the mysterious act styled judgment or decision. Instead, he proffers his diagrammatic picture of the process as one whereby the argument is "attached" firmly and fixedly to the question. All accounts are cast up in terms of a psychological mechanics.

Ramus' classification of syllogisms begins in 1543 and proves to be of little interest except as an attempt to treat syllogisms in the same way that the topical tradition had treated arguments: to shuffle them into neat configurations from which they, too, could be marshalled into action as the occasion demanded. His initial division of syllogisms is into simple (*simplex*, categorical) and composite (*coniunctus* — all the rest). In treating categorical syllogisms, Ramus manages to avoid not only the traditional moods (forms and figures) but even the terms subject and predicate. For the latter he substitutes the spatio-temporal surrogates "first" term and "second" term respectively.

Ramus continues subdivision of syllogisms on a quasi-diagrammatic basis. There are three kinds of simple syllogisms, we are told. In the first of these the argument (the middle term of non-Ramists) "precedes the major extreme of the question" (i.e., the middle term is subject in the major premise) while "it follows the minor extreme" (i.e., is predicate in the minor premise).[63] By dint of such schematizing, Ramus manages finally to fit his syllogisms passably onto dichotomized brackets.[64] He uses a terminology adapted from Agricola and Cicero for the members of the syllogism. The first member (major premise) is the *propositio*, the second (minor premise) is the *assumptio*, the conclusion is the *complexio*.

As his terminology shows, Ramus tends to regard noncategorical syllogisms — conditional, conjunctive, and disjunctive — as if they were built up from categorical "simples." He does not regard them as if they were quite different constructs from categorical syllogisms. Moreover, he tends to accord them more attention than they had been commonly allowed. Modern developments in logic since Frege have shown the great progress made in purely formal logic when noncategorical syllogisms are taken as points of departure. Such syllogisms are particularly adaptable to quantification. The question thus immediately suggests itself whether Ramus was on the road which leads to Frege, Russell, Carnap, and their associates. The answer seems to be that he was not — certainly not in any discerning or conscious way. His management of the syllogism is devoid of any valuable and effective insights, and his dialectic is actually less skillfully quantified than that of the medieval arts scholastics such as Peter of Spain or Ockham or Walter Burleigh. The quantifying approach into which he strays is not the technical skill enjoyed by the pre-Agricolan logicians, but rather is the result of loosely organized mental habits acquired in the Parisian milieu and made somewhat more "simple" or crude by the Agricolan influence.

The question whether the calculus of propositions of the old Stoic logic, which has come down through Western civilization only deviously and in fragmentary form,[65] may have exerted some influence on Ramus is intriguing. He pretended to enough indirect knowledge of Stoic syllogistic to damn it as erroneous.[66] The question might merit special study; for, although the influence could hardly be more than indirect and very slight, some kind of similarity of outlook might perhaps be found.

c. Judgment: Induction, Enthymeme, and Example

Since the only kind of organization for discourse which Ramus imagines is the "collocation" of thought-corpuscles or arguments, or of clusters of such corpuscles, the only kind of variation he can imagine is that which arises as the result of the suppression of an argument or argument cluster where it should normally be found. This outlook governs his explanation of induction, enthymeme, and example.

These are all merely syllogisms for Ramus, with one or another part suppressed or understood. Thus, our philosopher glibly explains that for induction one arrives at the principle, "All animals have the power of feeling" by adding to the *propositio* (the major premise), "All men and all brutes have the power of feeling," the suppressed *assumptio* (minor premise), "Every animal is either a man or a brute." [67] Of course, Ramus' pretended induction here is no induction at all. An induction would be necessary to arrive at the principle, "All men and all brutes have the power of feeling," without actually examining every man and every brute animal in existence in the past, present, and future.

Ramus' treatment of induction is due in great part to his own obtuseness. His treatment of enthymeme is more of a piece with the general heritage, and agrees with that of Peter of Spain. In Aristotle and everywhere else, Ramus takes enthymeme to mean a syllogism which is "imperfect" in the crude, *simpliste* sense that one of its premises is suppressed: an enthymeme is a "truncated syllogism." [68] Aristotle never uses the term enthymeme (ἐνθύμημα) in this sense. He always takes it to mean a syllogism defective in the sense that it moves from premises at least one of which is only probable, to a merely probable conclusion.[69] But, in the *simpliste* cadre of the classroom tradition, this view proved one not easily held to. Despite the fact that the *Art of Rhetoric*, where Aristotle explains what he means by enthymeme, was known to him, Boethius had long before given Aristotle the misreading which Ramus gave him, and the Middle Ages had followed where Boethius had led. The Renaissance in general followed, too.[70] And it is the Boethian and Ramist notion of enthymeme which prevails today, when editions of Aristotle still go so far as to interpolate the term enthymeme (in the Ramist sense) where Aristotle is deliberately avoiding the term.[71] The Ramist notion of enthymeme is thus in the main Western scholastic tradition.

In Aristotle "proof" of a general truth by citing an example had been the rhetorical equivalent of induction in science, a movement from a singular to a universal truth. In rhetoric, however, a truth which was universal, unlike a universal truth of science, was probable, not certain. Ramus follows no such line of thought. Consistent with his view that there is only one logic ruling all, example becomes only a truncated induction, one which omits expressing all of its parts.

d. Judgment: Second Judgment, the Beginnings of Method

The second step of judgment, or second judgment, is that which "provides the collocation and arrangement of many and various arguments cohering to one another and linked as by an unbroken chain so as to lead to one determined end." [72] This second step of judgment is to become Ramist method. Already, as Ramus details the subordinate steps which it includes, the difficulties under which his method will labor become evident. "In gluing things together and, after a fashion, forcing their juncture," one should first define and make known the end in view, then bring forward the genera, and finally fill in the "parts" of the genera (which everybody but Ramus would style subordinate species) all the way down to the infinite multitude of individuals.[73] Ramus asserts that this is Socrates' recommendation in his disputation with Protarchus and Philebus, although the passage he quotes here contains nothing about "end" and is concerned with concepts and their division rather than with argumentation. Ramus explains that this second part of judgment proceeds chiefly by definition and division, so that the other things which accompany these two should be used as the little bosses (*thori*) on a crown, as beautifying and ornamenting the definitions and divisions, and which afford a kind of grace that attaches itself to what is already resplendent; among which ornamental bosses, the singular species (which we here style examples) and analogies will be noteworthy.[74]

Since the first step in judgment and indeed the whole syllogistic apparatus has done no more than combine with invention to answer individual, isolated, and abstractly formulated questions, Ramus is still faced with the problem of what this has to do with the continuous discourse which both natural dialectic and his art of dialectic are supposed to govern. Is this discourse a concatenation of concealed syllogisms? He will frequently imply later that it is, but he now implies that in this second part of judgment all discourse is somehow held together by a concatenation rather of definitions and divisions. In the foregoing paragraph, for example, according to these Ramist rules (and, if the paragraph does not correspond to these rules, in Ramus' view so much the worse for it: it makes no sense), the second sentence is thought of as somehow grown out of the first by defining something in the first or by dividing something there.

What has happened here is plain. As a humanist, Ramus wishes to forget about formal logic and to exalt at the expense of formal logic every other type of discourse. He is not, however, the Italianate Rhinelander Agricola, but a Parisian arts professor, heir to the residue of what was once a highly sophisticated tradition of formal logic. Laboring in the wake of this formal logical tradition with a good deal of oratorical vigor but with little or no real insight of his own, he is drawn to think of all discourse as though it consisted of nothing but operations in formal logic. However, what Ramus retains of this formal logic is not real skill as a logician but only a blind drive toward a quantified approach to mental activity. In his case this drive has become a crude mechanistic or diagrammatic view of this activity, warped, moreover, by Agricola's preoccupation with the individual arguments found in the places to the point where it thinks habitually of concepts only as unit-pieces. The proposition as such is not adverted to, and syllogistic is made to serve the purpose of chucking a unit piece or "argument" into a question.

One might suppose that to consider ordinary discourse as subject to formal logic would mean to consider it as somehow reducible to reasoning from axioms, but at this point, there is no axiomatic in Ramism at all, although later on there will be the semblance of one. What holds everything together is solely definition and division. "The principles of the arts are definitions and divisions; outside of these, nothing."[75] Indeed, to demonstrate something is to define it.[76] Syllogism, in geometry or anywhere else, as, for example, in continuous discourse, has an ancillary or therapeutic role: it solves doubts when one encounters them in constructing definitions and dividing. It applies arguments to questions, when these occur. As Ramus' textbook on the subject shows, even geometry will consist not of demonstrations, but of definitions or "rules."

e. Judgment: Third Judgment, Ascent to God

Ramus' "third judgment," or third step in judgment, is the most curious piece in his 1543 plan for dialectic. It is, Ramus says, that by which all men are freed from the shadows of the cave (Plato's cave, clearly) and all things referred to the divine light, that is, to God.[77] The introduction of this "third judgment" is obviously due not so much to its relevance to the rest of his dialectic, but to intellectual politics. It serves to give his dialectic a varnish of Platonism and to rub salt into the wounds of the Aristotelians by enforcing on Aristotle the medieval charge of impiety — for the Aristotelian *Organon* has certainly no such wonderful thing as this.

Ramus' attempts to explain how the third judgment works[78] show once more the pedagogical bias of his philosophical outlook. The mind moves to God by recognizing, first, that of the three parts of philosophy, dialectic, physics, and ethics, it is dialectic which the mind must take as its guide.[79] One moves up through grammar, where many words are contained in relatively few letters (although he says that speech is superior to writing, Ramus habitually thinks of words as reduced to spatial units, not to phonemes). From grammar, one goes to rhetoric, where the variety of tropes, figures, and numbers (poetry is included in rhetoric) reproduces the variety of things. From there one proceeds to dialectic, where all these various tropes, figures, and numbers are contained, as they are contained in the dialectician — how, Ramus does not clearly explain, but apparently because dialectic rules the organization of the art of rhetoric, as it does all the arts or curriculum subjects. In dialectic, one is in contact with all the multitude of things as these are in God's mind.[80] This ascent of the mind to God via dialectic brings one to the spirit which Virgil says feeds the universe from within, to Plato's world soul, and to the Stoic Providence.[81] Ramus launches into a long praise of physics, arithmetic, geometry, astronomy, and music, as these will exist when transmogrified by the real dialectic. Although he does not yet have the term "methodized," the nature of the transformation he looks forward to is evident. It is a tidying up, an elimination of *commentitia* or unstable structures in the curriculum. For it is somehow through a flawless summary or *summa* of all the curriculum subjects that the mind ultimately arrives at God.[82]

A Platonic movement in Ramus' thought is evident here in the ascent he seeks to picture toward pure ideas and thus to the divine. Equally evident is Ramus' inability to give significance by any effective insight to his explanation of this ascent. The peculiar role which "genus" plays in Ramus' thought makes it difficult for him to keep God from being a kind of universal genus for all things, or, even worse, the summary of all the curriculum subjects; and his notion that an art is defined by its end makes the teleology of this whole apparatus at best precarious.[83] But, if Ramus cannot make his Platonism come out even, at least he can make it a fine stick with which to belabor the Aristotelians. Aristotle is only a "bemused theologian," his metaphysics is only theology sieved through dialectic, and his theology itself is so bad and unredeemable that the only thing remaining of value in his metaphysics is simply this "third judgment," which Plato had rightly called the only true dialectic.[84]

This is almost the last we hear of the "third judgment," however. With the appearance of his *Dialectic*, which supersedes the *Training in Dialectic*, this curious Platonist drops this only true dialectic for good, beating a quick retreat from his heady Platonic religiosity. His *Commentary on the Christian Religion* will be more pedestrian Aristotelian Zwinglianism.

iii. Dialectic as Use or Exercise

With the exception of the elementary course in grammar and of the secretarial training developed in the otherwise abbreviated course in rhetoric, the universities of Europe had grown into existence with virtually no exercises for students except the oral disputations. These stemmed in great part, as has been seen, from the normal-school orientation of the universities. Ramus' participation in the humanist movement is plain from his insistence on practical use (*usus*) or exercise (*exercitatio*), which he conceives of as more comprehensive than mere disputation and which he introduces into dialectic as the third part of his discerning or disputing power.

This third "part" is the art or portrait of dialectic come to life, Ramus informs us.[85] He does not advert to the implications of his analogy here, but they are clear and will become increasingly evident in the evolution of Ramism. Art is not a *habitus* of a living being. Significantly, Ramus likes to picture it as a lifeless extended surface rather than as a power or ability or as a "word" or an inspiration — for example, he thinks of it as Apelles' portrait of Alexander,[86] or a "chart of things." [87] Ramus will go on to say that it can be vivified. But life comes to art from without. The art is itself a dead surface, a web of lifeless "precepts," which in the bracketed table printed in this 1543 work already appear in the form of a mat of dichotomized words.[88] It is the business of "use" to "draw out into a work" these "precepts" in a way which will "shape and express in examples the force contained within the precepts." [89]

Use or exercise, Ramus explains, can take any of three forms: interpretation (*interpretatio*), writing (*scriptio*), and speaking (*dictio*). He explains the first in greatest detail.[90] The framework of his explanation is set in the world of reading and writing which emerged at the time of the humanists' concentration on manuscripts and the concomitant development of printing. Interpretation means to Ramus the reading of poets, orators, philosophers, and of all the arts, as well as of outstanding writers, and the hearing and explanation of all of these for purposes of training in the art of dialectic.[91] The procedure in interpretation is simple and invariable: faced with the text, one asks, What is the question? and, the question determined, What is the argument? and so on from start to finish of the discourse in hand.[92] In doing so, one discovers that the great vice of all discourse is ambiguity. One also discovers the real value of the syllogism; in protracted discourse, the thread on which the arguments are strung gets tangled, and the syllogism serves the excellent purpose of enabling one to disentangle or "unweave" (*retexere*) the thread. *Retexere*, as appears earlier,[93] is Ramus' translation for ἀναλύειν, which is generally rendered *resolvere* in Latin and thus is equivalent to "analyze." Properly unwound, any discourse is delightfully simple. Cicero's oration *For Milo* is found to amount to no more than one "dialectical ratiocination": "It is permissible to kill a criminal."[94] We might say today that this is the "meaning" of the oration *For Milo*, for everything beyond such summary statement, according to Ramus, is ornament.

Ramus describes the "unweaving" and the processes incidental to it in detail:

> When you have cut out from the parts of the continuous discourse the many syllogisms therein [after having found them, for they are often concealed], take away all the amplifications, and, after making brief headings to note the arguments used, form into one syllogism the sum total of the discourse, this sum total being ordinarily self-evident, although it may be swelled to undue proportions by accumulation of ornaments.[95]

In connection with Ramus' bland assurance that the sum total of all oratory is usually self-evident, it is to be noted that he is, of course, at a loss to provide any really practicable "precepts" showing systematically how to cut out of a selection of speech or writing the preliminary syllogisms or the final master conclusion ("dialectical ratiocination"). This is the telling critique to be advanced by Jean Riolan the elder and others of Ramus' adversaries.[96]

As Ramus proceeds, we are told in what is really an admission of inability to supply directives, that amphiboly and ambiguity of all sorts can generally be disposed of by "natural dialectic" without the aid of art. The famous amphiboly of the oracle's response, "Aio te Aeacida Romanos vincere posse," can be recognized as unsatisfactory even by the untrained mind. Indeed, its ability to save a man from double-talking oracles is one of the things which shows clearly the superiority of natural over "artificial" dialectic.[97]

The difficulty of ambiguity out of the way, it is again the natural light of sense and reason which roots out the two premises of every syllogism buried in the discourse; art contributes only to drawing the conclusion from the premises, although even here natural dialectic bears a large share of the work.[98] Certainty is achieved in terms of the process, equally natural (so simple, Ramus pretends, that he need not stop even to describe it) by which the premises are disengaged from the text. If the premises are not apparent to the natural light of reason, the "judgment" (that is, the syllogism in terms of its conclusion) will be less than certain, and one can only start again by applying to the text a new question.[99]

Interpretation by examination of the three steps of judgment proceeds in three different ways.[100] In the first step, which sets the arguments firmly in place, interpretation consists in examining the disposition of the argument (that is, the position of the middle term) to test for weaknesses in structure. In the second step, which concerns the collocation of whole chains of arguments, interpretation consists in defining the end and other causes. What end and what causes? The instance which Ramus immediately provides is the defining of the end of grammar and of rhetoric! — although such defining provides a starting point not for an oration at all, but for the construction of these arts or sciences. Such short-circuiting shows why, for a Ramist, a piece of connected discourse and an art or science seen in terms of interior organization are the same thing; they are both aggregates of arguments in which the passage from one argument to the next can be, in principle, only by definition and division.

The didactic procedure, as this was imagined in an ideal or perfect form, has here definitively assimilated to itself all discourse. Like a classroom "art" or curriculum subject, an oration (or a poem), stripped down to its essentials, is a string of definitions and divisions somehow or other operating through syllogisms. Although this seems close to the view of a madman, such a view is nevertheless a real component of the Ramist mentality, always implied and always operative. It has the effective range of Ramism itself, a range which bears witness to the incredible force and tyranny of abstractionist didacticism at this period in European intellectual history.

It has been noted that Ramus' third step in judgment, the ascent of the mind to God through dialectic, is largely an elaborate exercise in mystification, and that it will soon vanish out of the Ramist dialectic. Treating interpretation in terms of the three steps in judgment, Ramus quite openly acknowledges that interpretation in terms of this third step has really not been very much practiced, and that it is hard to find examples of it.[101] The best one can do, he owns, is to say that it exists, but only in a very rudimentary form, in Plato's *Republic* and in Cicero's *De natura deorum*. These two works are singled out by Ramus for the obvious reason that they treat explicitly of the First Cause, but concerning the details of their treatment as a specifically dialectical development, he leaves us in the dark. There is no doubt that Ramus prefers them to something like Aristotle's *Metaphysics* because they are more discursive, that is, because they are in what we might style the non-technical essay form, which means for him the combination of philosophy and eloquence to which he was to dedicate himself.

The other two forms of interpretation, writing and speaking, are given very slight treatment by Ramus. He suggests that the procedure in these activities is subject to the same rules or precepts as interpretation.[102] Later on, interpretation will be called analysis and written or spoken composition genesis (or synthesis, by later followers of Ramus).

Genesis is analysis in reverse: it reassembles, perhaps in a different order, but in a similar structure, the unit pieces into which analysis had broken down discourse. For Ramus and his followers, this process of breaking down and building up constitutes imitation, the basic rule for all use or exercise. In it Cicero is to be followed chiefly, but not slavishly.[103]

a. Classroom and Mnemonics: "Reason" and the Places

At the end of his treatment of the use of dialectic, Ramus returns to the natural dialectic from which his treatise had taken its departure, and to the art of dialectic:

And thus I want art and the exercise of art always joined intimately to nature. Since the whole life of man should be nothing other than the use of reason, that is, nothing other than the exercise of natural dialectic, let us then apply the resources of our whole life to studying and practicing the art of reason and of natural dialectic, however simple and few the precepts by which this is known. Thus, just as in the case of other technicians, so in the case of practitioners of this art which embraces all others, we shall become aware that an art is known not so much by precepts as by exercise. Thus, too, many of the things which as boys in the classroom we found boring and dull, we shall admire as older men thoroughly familiar with actual practice. This familiarity itself, based on habit and experience, will make clear what calm reflection, no matter how discerning, cannot understand.[104]

This passage sounds a keynote in Ramus' program of dialectical and pedagogical reform: the juncture in use of arts which in themselves and in teaching procedure are disparate. It is not very clear what he meant by actually teaching an individual art, since the "use" which forms the major part of his pedagogical practice calls for some sort of mixture of several arts. Apparently, teaching an art meant presenting to students verbatim the contents of a Ramist manual of dialectic, rhetoric, arithmetic, and so through the entire curriculum, although some place had to be allowed for the refutation of adversaries, since Ramus conceives of all his "lectures" or *scholae* as this sort of performance.

It will be noted that Ramus avows that the theory of his natural dialectic is thin ("however few the precepts"), but that he declares his faith in "reason" (*ratio*) all the same. "Reason" is beginning to take on the contours which will characterize it in the next few hundred years and make of it in the age of the Enlightenment a kind of unerring power bearing straight for the truth, with the inevitability of a syllogism but somehow without being encumbered by all the syllogistic formalities after all. As has been seen in a previous chapter, reason (*ratio*) had been given prestige in Peter of Spain's work by association with a rigorously quantified formal logic. But this association had been conveniently loose — *ratio* turned up in the treatise on the *topoi* or loci, the least scientific, most haphazardly organized of all the treatises in the *Summulae logicales*. Reason is still in the topical setting with Ramus' topical dialectic or logic, but it is launched on a yet more promising career by being more closely alined, within this setting, with the all-powerful pedagogical tradition.

Ramus' "natural dialectic," which is the same as the "use of reason," does not have to be scientifically or psychologically explained, but is justified by being practiced. It is first practiced in the classroom. Among the teen-agers to whom the humanist pedagogical tradition looked rather more frankly than the scholastic tradition had, the average pupil could not assimilate a theoretical explanation of dialectic anyhow. The overly curious is cooled with the explanation that he will understand it all when he is "an older man thoroughly familiar with actual practice."

As a matter of fact, the "reason" which this dialectic purportedly expedites is practically identical with memory. The important role of memory in the history of Ramism will need treatment later, but here it can already be clearly seen in the first dialectical analysis worked out in print by Ramus. This is the one which reviews the "reasoning" process in Penelope's complaint as retailed by Ovid.[105] The "practical" value Ramus attaches to this analysis is a salutary lesson to those who have seen in Ramist practicality either a Renaissance Platonism setting a high value on aesthetic experience or some forecast of the pragmatism of the late Professor Dewey. Ramus flaunts his reason for the superiority of this practical analysis with a disconcerting frankness: *it is the best possible method for enabling the schoolboy to memorize the twenty-eight lines of Ovid in question*!

This assertion is as momentous for what it makes of memory as for what it makes of dialectic. The memorization process for Ramus is virtually synonymous with understanding itself, to the extent that the success of the Ramist dialectic as a memory device proves the validity of the dialectic as a true interpretation of reality. Ramus agrees with philosophers and orators in general that order is helpful to memory, but he objects that other teachers use all sorts of arbitrary mnemonic devices, "laying out external and fictitious signs and representations" whereas his dialectic proposes "the order found within things themselves" and thus "the truest possible representations" of reality, suited to memory and recall as Aristotle's *commentitia* are not.[106]

Many mnemonic schemes, such as the old *Barbara, celarent*, and other versified devices, functioned in direct dependence on sound recall. Ramus' own mnemonic scheme, derived from the more or less Ciceronic topical or place-logic tradition and operating by means of diagrams which put things in "places" (as in the tabular "Summary of the Art of Dialectic" which here makes its debut in Ramus' writings [107]), appears "real" to him not by direct reference to the external world but, in fact, by contrast with such sound-recall devices. Because it treats what is already in the mind by analogy with objects in space, it seems to Ramus to be eminently "real."

Ramus' claim that the immediate basis of his mnemonics (and of his dialectic) is the "order found within things themselves" has much of its plausibility in this context. Matters which force themselves constantly on our consciousness can of course be recalled without special aids. Thus, to recall that man is an animal it is easier to resort to our experience of "things" as registered permanently in the mind than it is to remember that the word animal includes the sounds "m," "a," and "n," which are also found in the word man. But it is not so easy to recall the order and structural detail of the internal organs of the human body, or the taxonomy of teleost fishes, although these depend no less on the "order found within things themselves."

Ramus' claim to contact with "things in themselves" is made by resort to instances of the man-animal sort. He conceives of knowledge as though it were supported entirely on a fund of readily available common experience. Full contact with "things themselves" is taken to be the common acquisition of all adults, so that nothing need be sought by means of any special experience or experiments. The position taken here by Ramus reminds us how science in his and an earlier day differed from more modern science largely in that it was based not on mere "deduction" but rather on the data of common experience, more or less critically processed. Ramus' appeal to what is "real" is an appeal to consider the bits of knowledge derived from common experience as though they themselves were items to be observed and manipulated. Thus he tends to think of them not in connection with verbal sounds but in connection with lettered forms ranged in patterns so that they can be "stored" and recalled by "observation" like real things. Ramus' dialectic is certainly what Madido makes it out to be in *The Pilgrimage to Parnassus*, a map of the mind. The Ramist treatment of the loci culminates in diagrams, and Ramus will later ridicule Cicero's treatment of the loci and of imagery for failure to concern itself uniquely with questions of order — "what is first, what second, what third." [108]

Nevertheless, although Ramus does not attack deductive procedure and is not interested in observation in the Baconian, much less in the present-day sense, he is certainly stressing observational attitudes by his cartography of the mind. At the same time that it was an outgrowth of a central logico-pedagogical tradition in Western thought, this stress was something new. Indubitably, it was effective in preparing the human sensibility for a still further stress on observation of the external world. The printing press, the first assembly line, had assembled not tools, but a pattern of words, a pattern for things in the mind. In a parallel maneuver Ramus organizes in an observational field not the external world but the "contents" of consciousness.

CHAPTER IX

THE DIALECTICAL CONTINUUM

Logic is nothing and everything.
— Title-page motto in Alsted's
*Compendium logicae
harmoniae* (1615).

I. RAMUS' TOPICAL LOGIC IN ITS PARISIAN SETTING

THE *Remarks on Aristotle* and the *Training in Dialectic,* written in 1543, show that the rehabilitated topical logic of the Northern European Renaissance has reached a critical stage. The traditional logic of the places or commonplaces, modified by Rudolph Agricola, had been brought by the Strasbourgeois Johann Sturm and the Belgian Bartholomaeus Latomus from Italy to Paris in the incomplete form in which Agricola had left it. The logic has now been completed by Ramus, and judgment, its missing second half, has been added to invention, the first half, which Ramus adapted from Agricola.

In the process of being completed, this dialectic had acclimated itself to the Parisian milieu. Hitherto, topical logic had been only a minor subject at Paris. As in the work of Peter of Spain, it was incidental to a logic in principle centered on predication and developed as a quantified instrument analogous to modern mathematical logic. In Ramus' 1543 works, we encounter for the first time a Parisian logic devoted largely to sorting ideas into convenient groups, that is, a topical logic, emancipated alike from predication theory and from rigorously scientific quantification in the name of pedagogy, and prepared for its debut in the world capital of scholasticism. The logic of the places had been an approach to discourse-in-general; it specialized in "invention" of something to say. After being remodeled in Paris, it felt the full impact of the arts-course heritage: the formidable didacticism of the teachers' guild or university, to which Agricola and his fellow humanists had been relative strangers; the residue of a highly quantified logic or dialectic with which the process of teaching was itself more or less identified; and the tendency, associated with this logic and with the physical-science orientation of scholastic philosophy, to regard the mental world as made up of something like physical corpuscles.

These are the factors which will in great part account for the trajectory which Ramism, legatee of the topic-sorting tradition of the Sophists, Aristotle, Cicero, Quintilian, Themistius, Boethius, and the rest, now begins to describe. In order to clarify certain features of this trajectory, we shall treat several special points in the *Remarks on Aristotle* and the *Training in Dialectic*, which were passed over in the preceding brief of their contents.

2. THE RAMIST ORGANON: THE ARTS AS CATEGORIES

When Ramus descends to detail, his charges against Aristotle (besides that of *commentitia*) such as tautology, bad division and distribution, and even picayunishness, are often little more than the standard objections against faults in discourse which were deprecated by the pre-Agricolan formal logic. Ramus had never mastered this, but it was still active enough in the Parisian milieu to leave distinct traces on his mind.[1] But his thought takes a more significant turn when he charges Aristotle, more basically, with not proceeding in a "natural" fashion, so that there is no real dialectic in his *Organon*.[2] His body of works is thus like the picture of a man without a head and is no full "image of nature" (*imago naturae*) or legitimate "chart of things" (*tabula rerum*) but only *commentitia*, fabrications, and a *monstruosa deformitas*.[3] The "things" which the Greek philosopher fails to chart correctly turn out to be neither external reality, nor the predicaments, nor even the topics, but the arts which make up all philosophy (*tota philosophia*). Ramus assumes that the chief business of all classification is the classification of the arts and sciences themselves; such classification is the starting point of all philosophy.

This curious drift in Ramus' thought is obviously another manifestation of what has just been discussed, his tendency to be "objective" not by turning to the outside world but by treating the contents of the mind as a set of objects. Here this tendency joins the pedagogical tradition, for Ramus assumes that the primary units which the mind "contains" are the subjects in the curriculum. Many of the characteristic developments among Ramus' followers will grow out of this tendency to regard knowledge as a set of objects and to identify these objects with curriculum subjects. This is the source of the coming emphasis on "technology" or *technologia*,[4] originally a systematic treatment of grammar in Cicero. Ramus will extend "technology" to other curriculum subjects and understand it as the art of arranging the contents of the curriculum properly. Ramus' followers, such as Alsted and William Ames, will foster and develop it further into "technometry" or *technometria* (a word which does not occur in classical usage), the science of the exact measurements of the divisions between the arts. It is the source likewise of the odd seventeenth-century Harvard theses: "Languages are to be learned before the arts," "Languages are learned better by use than by formal rules."[5] Instead of talking about what he knows of "things themselves," the student is explaining what curriculum subjects are in his mind and the sequence in which they came to be there.

Aristotle's categories had been predicates uttered or said of things or "first substances." Ramus warps these categories onto the university curriculum. In Aristotle, the categories vary in number, and the ten which occur in the most complete listing were frequently reduced to four by considering the last six — action, passion, situation in place, situation in time, posture, and bodily accoutrements (*habitus*) — as species of the fourth category, relation. Ramus proposes a curricular warrant for the fourfold categorization.[6] Physics, medicine, and theology would study substance; mathematics, quantity; moral philosophy, quality or *dispositio* (Ramus balks at Cicero's neologism *qualitas*), as well as strength and weakness (*potentia et impotentia*), taken as kinds of qualities. Dialectical invention would then take care of relation, together with action and passion, and presumably the other four categories subsumed under relation, although Ramus does not go into these because the whole Aristotelian setting displeases him.

In the fourfold division which Ramus proposes, dialectical philosophy is to explain all other arts (*artes*) and laws (*leges*). Physics attends to nature, corporal substances, and the genera, species, and differences of such substances. Mathematics is to take care of the "genera" of magnitude and of arithmetical number. Ethical philosophy will complete the picture.[7] This is the old Senecan division into logical, natural, and moral sciences abetted by mathematics. Ramus has quietly modulated the classification of the *Categories* into a curricular classification. He has done so in an operation which climaxes one of the central movements in the scholastic tradition, where interest in distinctions focuses typically on distinguishing the arts and sciences among themselves, not on angels and pinpoints as is sometimes popularly believed. This focus is evinced in such diverse works as Hugh of St. Victor's *Didascalicon*, the opening of St. Thomas Aquinas' *Summa theologiae*, or the logical works of any of the "old scholastics" of Ramus' youth, John Major, Juan de Celaya, and the Coronels. The cumulative effect of the preoccupation with classification of the arts is so great here that it leads Ramus to suppose that all "things" are subsumed under the arts. This means under the definitions of the arts, since the first "principle" of any art or science is for him the definition of the art or science, which is constituted by enumerating its parts in order and showing their affections and properties.[8] In other words Ramus finds himself substituting a list of the subjects in the curriculum (which is what the "arts" in reality were) as the supreme genera of "things," for the Aristotelian categories as supreme genera of predicates. This tendency to focus attention ultimately on the arts or sciences will contribute quite a bit to the interest in method which marks the age of Ramus, and will be manifest long afterwards in Francis Bacon, Descartes, and other methodologists.

3. THE DICHOTOMIES: CLASS LOGIC IN SPACE

In *The Massacre of Paris*, Kit Marlowe has the Duke of Guise denounce Ramus as a "flat dichotomist"; Ramus' preoccupation with dichotomies was already well known to Marlowe's audience. Johann Piscator calls Ramus' dichotomies "most beautiful,"[9] and even anti-Ramists would find this beauty seductive and would cut up Aristotelian logic itself into dichotomies to put its beauties back on a competitive basis with the Ramist product.[10]

The use of dichotomies, or division by twos, was not uniquely Ramist, although extreme specialization in them was. Ramus himself is inclined to seek theoretical justification for his dichotomies in Plato, but this seems a pious humanist fiction, assigning a direct source in antiquity to notions assimilated from the Parisian scholastic milieu, where interest in dichotomies stems chiefly from Boethius and Porphyry. The famous John Major, one of Ramus' scorned "Scots and Spaniards" still teaching at Paris during Ramus' youth, cites the other scholastic, George of Brussels, as well as Boethius, to the effect that "every good division ought to be two-membered."[11]

As a matter of fact, the Ramist dichotomies have little, if any real theoretical foundation. There is a bipolarity in being, which echoes everywhere through philosophical history: form and matter, act and potency, Yang and Yin, thesis and antithesis, the one and the many, and so on through an indefinite number of epiphanies. This includes perhaps the Neo-Platonic teaching, well known to Aquinas, that from any given unity only one other unity can be generated, further generation requiring the combination of these two originals. The Ramist dichotomy can be regarded as a reflection or correlative of this bipolarity. But it does not arise from any penetrating insight on Ramus' part into the principles of the bipolarity any more than it does from insight into the principle at stake in Boethius. There is simply no one ground on which we can account for Ramus' dichotomies. The division name-versus-thing has little in common with the division definition-versus-distribution, nor either of these with that of "agreeings"-versus-"disagreeings." It is true that certain marked contrasts tend to repeat themselves, such as that between the mental and the extramental, or the contrast of contradictories (*consentanea, dissentanea; similia, dissimilia*). But these repetitions are sporadic and variable. Ramist theses at Harvard and in the works of Ames and others will later defend the dichotomy as "the most accurate distribution,"[12] but the explanations which go with such things are theoretically thin, and then convey the impression that they are *ex post facto* rationalizations. The urge to, and practice of, dichotomization preceded the theory.

Ramus' preoccupation with dichotomization has its real origin largely in the pedagogical appeal of the tidy bracketed tables of dichotomies which he studied in the printed commentaries and epitomes of Agricola's *Dialectical Invention*. In Ramus' works the first appearance of the bracketed tables is in the *Training in Dialectic*. As in Latomus' edition of Agricola's *Dialectical Invention*, the bracketing is applied to the loci (it has been seen that Ramus thinks of these as "arguments"). The arguments make up only a part of Ramus' dialectic, but the bracketing applied to them is extended even at this early 1543 stage to the whole of dialectic. This art itself becomes thus a kind of commonplace yielding the various parts of itself (and of "things"), which in turn yield more parts through a series of successive openings, like a Chinese puzzle.

Dichotomization is marked in these original bracketed outlines from the start, although it is not universally employed, at first, but is mingled with divisions which are mere clutters of parts, some of them stringing out even to the number of nine. But the evolution toward greater and greater dichotomization gathers momentum immediately and can be seen in the tables which Charpentier reproduces in 1555 to poke fun at Ramus' perpetual change of position.[13] Thus, from the "first edition" (the *Training in Dialectic* of 1543), we have:

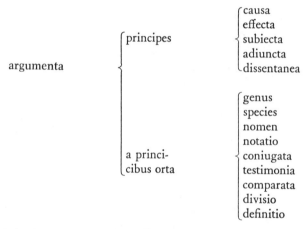

By the "third edition" (the rare *Three Commentaries on Dialectic Published under the Authorship of Omer Talon* of 1546), there is an equivocal shift toward greater simplicity:

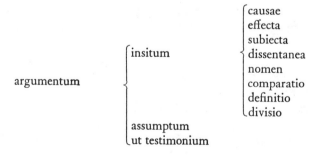

But by the next year, the "fourth edition" of the *Training in Dialectic* is definitely committed to the dichotomy:

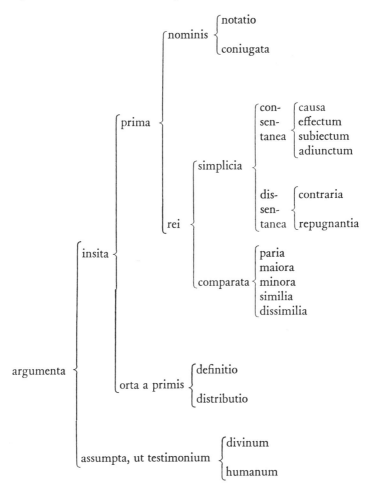

Although some few items escape dichotomization, as in this table, and although variations in the exact arrangement of the dichotomies will continue to appear till Ramus' death, division by dichotomies, established in 1547, remains from now on in effective control of Ramus' arguments through all subsequent editions of *The Training in Dialectic* and all editions of the *Dialectic* (see Figure XIII), whence it spreads to all the other arts and ultimately to all reality.

Ramist dichotomization also takes its origin in part from class logic. A class logic is one which approaches logical structure by considering primarily the way in which certain classes include other classes, each of these latter still further classes, and so on indefinitely. In other words, it is a logic built on the extension of terms, and as such invites quantification and encourages thinking which specializes in quantified analogies, overt or disguised. The great medieval developments in quantification had been in great part class

P. RAMI DIALECTICA.
TABVLA GENERALIS.

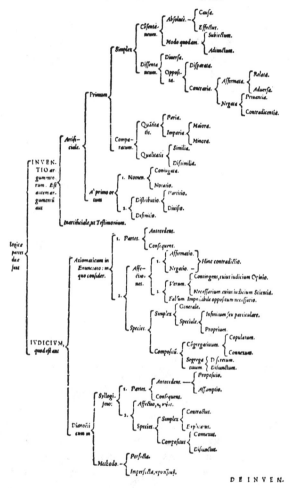

D E I N V E N.

XIII. WHAT LOGIC IS "REALLY" LIKE (RAMUS, ED. FREIGE)

logics, and while it was not new to Ramus the cult of dichotomies which reaches its peak of development with him and his followers, could hardly have taken place independently of this medieval heritage.

4. SPECIES AND GENERA: UNITS AND CLUSTERS

As a popularized or residual class logic, the Ramist dialectic manifests a quantification system which is almost certainly the most recklessly applied one that the world has ever seen. It will never be wholly abandoned by Ramus, but it will be modified and disguised after ugly encounter with brute fact and with adversaries. In 1543, it stands out in all its primitive simplicity.

Under the influence of early arts scholasticism modified in Agricola's *Dialectical Invention*, Ramus had developed the habit of regarding everything, mental and physical, as composed of little corpuscular units or "simples." He never seems expressly aware of this habit, but it dominates all his thinking, subconsciously, yet stubbornly and absolutely. Ramus thus tends to view all intellectual operations as a spatial grouping of a number of these corpuscles into a kind of cluster, or as a breaking down of clusters into their corpuscular units. The clusters, once formed, can be regarded also as corpuscles which in themselves admit of further combination and which form still further clusters of clusters. The apparatus is a familiar one in a class logic, where it effectively serves certain limited purposes in formal logical developments. Ramus allows it to spread everywhere and to solve matters to which it cannot possibly apply.

Thus, having decided to call the groupings or clusters genera, Ramus proceeds adamantly to the conclusion that individuals and species are exactly the same thing.[14] There is a nominalist background for such assertions,[15] but Ramus is not up to following the nominalist niceties. Nor is he saying that in a class logic individuals are treated as the *infima species*,[16] but rather that "man" extends to all individual men in a way parallel in all respects to that in which "animal" extends to various species of animal.[17] The whole problem of individuation is simply wiped off the record by Ramus' insistence, departing from Agricola's usage, that genus refers to what is universal, species to singulars.[18] By a corollary, Ramus insists that man and woman are different species — a corollary which will be sustained by his follower Otto Schwallenberg at Leipzig later in the century and help get Ramism outlawed there.[19] That he did not mean merely logical species is clear, since, when challenged by adversaries, he modified his stand and, as Charpentier notes, owned that the difference was one of "material accidents."[20]

Porphyry, the scholastics,[21] and even Agricola had noted various uses of the term genus, but the Ramist corpuscular epistemology, supposing that knowledge consists of sets of mental items, thereby implied one-for-one correspondence between terms and things. Hence it constitutionally opposes allowing words to mean more than one "thing," and regularly frowns on discussion of divergent meanings (although not necessarily on discussion of etymologies), which Ramus says is the business of grammar, not of dialectic.[22]

Ramus insists that the relation of genus to species cannot even be that of common to proper, but is always the simple relation of whole to part.[23] This view makes it necessary for him to overlook the elemental difference between the comprehension and extension of a term, and to view increase in comprehension by the addition of specifying notes (as when "rational" and "sensitive" are added to "living being") as quite the same thing as the grouping of individuals (or, as he calls them, "species") within a genus.

Of course, this position cannot be put on a coherent theoretical basis and is sustained by a kind of double talk which drove Ramus' opponents frantic. One of Ramus' tactics is to suggest that classes (called by him genera) break down always into individuals (called nevertheless species) and never into subordinate classes: "A species is the thing itself concerning which the genus answers [in replying to the question, What is it?]: thus, the genus man answers concerning Plato, the genus dialectician concerning this particular dialectician."[24] Here Ramus' "man" is no more generic than "dialectician" with reference to the individual. In this vein, the genus "animal" would "answer" not concerning man but only concerning this particular individual animal. Specialization in weighted examples does not suffice, and Ramus resorts frequently to gross misreadings of Porphyry and Aristotle. Thus he distorts Porphyry's meaning when the latter speaks of "predicating a species of many different in number." This means quite evidently no more than "John is a man," "Peter is a man," and so on. Ramus pretends that Porphyry is trying to say, "Man is a species of Plato."[25] In a similar vein, Ramus attacks both Porphyry and Aristotle for attributing difference to genera, since it also, he says, belongs to species.[26] The plain sense of Porphyry and Aristotle is again obvious enough: they are saying that the specific difference "rational" is added to the genus "animal" and not to the already constituted species "rational animal." Other instances of similar misrepresentation in Ramus are too numerous to be catalogued.

5. DEFINITION AND DISTRIBUTION

In the Ramist scheme of things, all intellectual movement takes place with reference to the genus-species apparatus. At the hearings terminating in his condemnation by Francis I, Ramus had tied up the issue for two days by insisting that no subject, particularly dialectic, could be taught until it was first defined. The reason was, of course, that the art itself had to function as a genus or starting point, from which its parts and then their successive parts were to be derived, for all "teaching" is, to Ramus' mind, a movement from the generic to the "specific." Definition itself is subservient to this movement, and so is syllogism, for syllogism operates by definition and distribution or division.

After a term is defined, it is divided or distributed into its parts. But the

principle of this division remains forever a mystery insofar as Ramus' thinking is concerned. Are *coniugata* and *notatio* "parts" of *nomen* in the same way
that *inventio* and *iudicium* are "parts" of dialectic or "animal" and "rational"
parts of man? And having defined dialectic as the art of discoursing well,
how does one thereupon know that its parts are *inventio* and *iudicium*? This
is never explained. Ramus eschews even the elemental distinctions of integral
and essential parts, and rests satisfied with the crude analogy which his
dichotomized tables picture; it is enough that these items can be related to
one another in a spatial diagram. Refinements such as common and proper,
potency and act[27] — terms which elude diagrammatic treatment — are re-
pulsive to this mind.

With all relationships reduced practically to that of genus and species,
conceived of quantitatively or in terms of extension, it was inevitable that the
relationship of dialectic itself to the rest of the arts or sciences become that of
genus to species, as it will be found to be in Harvard commencement theses:
"Dialectic is the most general of all the arts."[28] Even the internal structure of
each art will tend to develop a partition into general and special which complements, or conflicts with, its division into its "parts." This development is
not peculiar to Ramism, for it is found also in Ramus' day in Aristotelians
such as Zabarella,[29] but it is a Ramist specialty. Thus Marcus Rutimeier's
1617 dichotomized edition of Ramus' *Dialectic* is entitled *The Methodical
Idea, or General and Special Logical Analysis* (*Idea methodica, seu analysis
logica generalis et specialis*), and a similar division is found in Alsted's *Harmonic System of Logic* (*Logicae systema harmonicum*, 1614) and *Compendium of Harmonic Logic* (*Compendium logicae harmoniae*, 1623). Sonleutner's 1587 edition of the Ramist *Dialectic* (*Institutionis dialecticae . . .
pars prior*) lists the *artes sermocinales*, grammar, dialectic, and rhetoric as
"general," and all other arts as "particular."

6. THE PLATONIC IDEA AS CONTINUUM

In the fragmented Ramist physico-mental universe, made up of unit corpuscles called species which form parts of wholes called genera, the Platonic
idea functions as a kind of ether which guarantees unity of a transcendental
sort — until it turns out that this idea is only a genus, or supergenus, too.

Ramus' Platonism makes its début in his second step of judgment, and
carries on over from there into the third step or third judgment. The definition and division in which the second step of judgment consists is "the knowledge which Plato's stranger thought should be an attribute of one with a
really great and glowing love of wisdom."[30] Ramus' horror of ambiguity
and his abstractionism, as well as his adulation of mathematics, are doubtless
connected in some indirect way with the ancient Platonic heritage. But, for
all this, Ramus' Platonism is even more tenuous than most Platonism of the

Renaissance, since he played it up largely for its nuisance value in harrying the "Aristotelians." The Ramus-Talon team were industrious commentators of Aristotle, Quintilian, and, most of all, Cicero, but not of Plato. Among their seventy-five-odd works, they produced exactly one very small one devoted to Plato's writings, the edition of the brief *Letters of Plato*, and some of these are not even genuine. Contemporaries who detail the sources which Ramus raids for his dialectic do not mention Plato even as a secondary source.[31]

Despite Ramus' occasional straining for this effect, his works lack entirely the "numinous" or otherworldly quality associated with Plato's thought. The Platonic idea that the sensible world is ephemeral and the world of spiritual or exemplar realities eternal does not appear as a passionate belief in Ramus' thought. Exemplar thinking is missing from the central Ramist tradition in its serious moments, and when William Temple and others introduce it, the appearance indicates only occasional and forced rhetorical growth. Nor does Platonism make itself felt as an exaltation of intuitive knowledge over knowledge arrived at by more pedestrian processes, much less as connected with a Sir Philip Sidney's aesthetic sensibility. It does appear as an exaltation of nonvariants over variants: Ramus exalts the nature of "eternal things," the knowledge of truth, causes, certainty, all human "teaching" (roughly, the curriculum subjects), definitions and distribution, on the one hand, over the nature of perishable things, faith (persuasion in the rhetorical sense — *fides*[32]), effects, probability, judicial and parliamentary disputes and all the other "arguments," on the other.[33] The contrast between these two sorts of things, which Ramus says he finds in the *Timaeus*, admits of any number of developments of course, depending on what analogies are exploited in conceiving of and developing the notions of variant and nonvariant. For Ramus, variant tends to be synonymous with fragmentary, and nonvariant with a kind of fluid continuum, "one idea poured out far and wide through a multitude of separate and distinct ideas, therein to abide permanently."[34]

Ramus is, or will soon become, quite aware of the general tenor and of the complexity of Plato's remarks on ideas. The oppositions just quoted are supplemented by other passages where he explains that Plato means by ideas chiefly the unchangeable species of things, which man lays hold of only as darkened by corporal bodies and which he brightens or illuminates by means of names, definitions, examples, but always with only partial success. Plato's devotion to the divine ideas is such that he denies the possibility of genuine science (*scientia*) for man, whose knowledge of divine things is devious and defective.[35] This is Plato's idea as Ramus finds it represented in the only work of Plato on which he himself comments. Such an idea is too tenuous, however, and has the further disadvantage of laying Plato open to the same charge of weakening the connection between man and God which Ramus is to lodge against Aristotle. The Platonic idea envisioned as a subsistent extramental reality is too tenuous, also, and Ramus waves it aside elsewhere as a poetic metaphor.[36] In preference to such explanations, and to Plato's, Ramus clings to his more diagrammatic notion which in 1543 he imputed to Plato and which he presents unchanged as late as 1569. What Plato says is only "caviling," for the real Platonic idea is not at all what it appears to be in Plato's description of it but rather "is nothing else than genus as this has just been defined by us."[37] The genus, as "just defined," is:

the whole essential to its parts, as the species is the part of a genus; thus genus occurs for animals and for men, because it is a whole essential to parts; thus animal is the genus of singular animals, man is the genus of singular men, because it is a whole essential to parts; thus man is a species of animal, and Socrates a species of man.[38]

In this 1569 revision, Ramus' Platonism is still decked out to function in the unit-cluster apparatus, in which it is assigned the role of presiding as a kind of supreme genus which is at the same time a dialectical or metaphysical ether bathing the parts (species) into a continuum.

This dialectical continuum has many epiphanies. Ramus likes to think of it as what he calls the sphere of the Pythagoreans with "its center every place and its circumference nowhere" — a notion actually derived not from Pythagoras but from an influential anonymous medieval treatise.[39] As something diffuse and too otherworldly to be physically cut up into geometrical diagrams, it associates itself readily with the light stolen for man by Prometheus,[40] a light which pours through all the arts to bind them together and the whole to God.[41] It is a light with a curious preference for a quantified world, burning brightest in mathematics, which "restores man to his ancient heritage and to his home in heaven."[42] Ramus' light is not that which his follower Milton will apostrophize. It furnishes not illumination so much as an ethereal contact among items in a pulverized world. Ramus will later criticize Aristotle for putting together separate ideas (ideae) in geometrical diagrams.[43] This is what one does to arguments, but not to the Platonic idea, genus itself, which must be thought of as ever one and indivisible.

7. ARISTOTLE AND DIVISIVENESS

As Plato is associated with a kind of dialectical continuum guaranteeing the unity of things, so Aristotle is associated by Ramus with divisiveness. Unlike Plato in his *Republic*, Aristotle does not attend to the third step in judgment but fails completely to knit up the raveled fabric of the world by means of dialectic in order to bring it back to God, except perhaps in his *Metaphysics*, where, if he can be said to attempt anything at all, he has the knitting process hopelessly confused.[44] Aristotle and the Aristotelians are charged with failure to put dialectic to practical use, with barbarism, and with sophistry, but, most of all, with the drawing out of endless distinctions[45] — in short, with divisiveness.

Ramus' allegory of the tree, in its unconscious implications, is one of the most telling of his remarks against the Stagirite. Would that the painters Apelles and Timanthes and Protogenes were to paint a tree with golden apples on its branches (rami), surrounded by Aristotle's works pictured as hobgoblins, dragons, and vipers, tearing to pieces Aristotle's followers, themselves pictured as jumping at the golden fruit, but never getting it, only tearing little twigs off the tree itself. In this pageant of disintegration starring Aristotle, the tree, which so masterfully maintains its integrity, functions covertly, but really, as a symbol for the Ramist branching dichotomy (a scion of the Porphyrean tree) as well as, in another way, for Ramus himself, the Branch, soon to be celebrated all over Europe as the new golden bough.[46] The trunk plainly suggests the Platonic idea, or Ramus' genus, pouring its invigorating sap through the whole of knowledge and reality to produce unity. Aristotle is the villain threatening this new world tree which gives knowledge not of good and evil, but of what is better, dialectic.

Highly symbolic projections of this sort are often symptomatic of hidden inquietude and fears. A reason for inquietude on Ramus' part is not far off: his dialectic, as he explains it, actually sides rather with Aristotle and divisiveness than with Plato and unity. His "third judgment" is quite a factitious affair, destined soon to be dropped from the Ramist apparatus for sheer irrelevance. Insisting on the absolute monarchy of definition and division (distribution) in all cognition, Ramus is really equipped to explain nothing but disintegration. Delving more and more into explanation, defining and dividing with greater and greater industry under the pressure of his own dissatisfaction and that of his adversaries, Ramus will only ram harder and harder into the impasse.

8. THE NOMINALIST-REALIST ISSUE

Ramus' pseudo-Platonism poses the question whether he was a nominalist or a realist. As has been seen, the scholastic background out of which Ramism emerges suggests that the distinction between nominalist and realist is a very complicated thing, hardly reducible in terms of dictionary definitions.[47] In its scorn for everything but "things themselves" Ramus' dialectic seems to imply the nominalist doctrine that universal concepts have no basis in reality, while at the same time its way of regarding the "contents" of the mind as equivalent to discrete objects seems to imply the realist doctrine that universals exist as such extramentally.

In Ramus' case one of the reasons for the persistence of bogus dilemmas in the nominalist-realist issue can clearly be seen: the whole question of knowledge was being distorted by simplification for presentation to teenagers. Indeed, from a theoretical point of view Ramus preferred not to go into the matter at all, and blamed Aristotle and all his followers for approaching philosophical problems for what these problems are in themselves, with no eye to the needs of youth.[48] Similar stands had been taken by other humanists, such as Melanchthon in his defense of the common distinction between dialectic and rhetoric.[49]

Thus when questions concerning knowledge are touched on explicitly by Ramus or Talon, they are likely to have as their background some unhappily misleading question such as, Is the universal in the mind or in the world of things? Indeed, this well-known *simpliste* formulation is weighted in the same way as the Ramist dialectic, for it supposes a "universal" as a kind of object which could commute between a real and a mental world, annihilating any meaningful difference between the two worlds by implying that being "in" the mind and being "in" the extramental world is a mere matter of position, so that legitimate epistemological considerations such as, What happens when we know? appear degraded to the order of questions such as, Is the pea under the right-hand or the left-hand walnut shell?

In Ramus' and Talon's works, although epistemological questions tend to rise in this latter form, they are seldom attended to at all in any form, and are never really answered. In Talon's commentary on Porphyry which complements Ramus' two 1543 works and is designed expressly for young boys (*iuventus*),[50] epistemological problems are brushed aside noncommittally. Fainthearted Porphyry, says Talon, bypasses the question of the Platonic ideas, and later commentators such as Ammonius and Boethius only torture themselves with the question. This is a sad state of affairs, indeed, for, Talon goes on:

the whole matter can be settled briefly this way. If you regard the words themselves, genus and species are notions within our souls, and thus are not substances, neither participating in nor lacking body or sensation. On the other hand, if you understand things themselves as genera and species of men, birds, fishes, cattle, colors, magnitude, virtues, vices, then, just as these things themselves are substances and accidents, so genera and species will be substances and accidents.[51]

This is the sum and substance of the Ramist position on universals. It ends where it started, indecisive and neuter, aware of the existence of a problem, but understandably quite unable to state it effectively in terms which both do it justice and are suitable for teen-aged minds.

9. TRUTH AMONG THE CORPUSCLES

Ramus' dialectic makes no allowance for the combination of its arguments into statements. The fact has already been noted that, in its 1543 stage, it forgets to treat of statements or propositions at all. This neglect is due to both the medieval and the Agricolan background. But in Ramus, Agricola's mild allergy to predication develops into a general paroxysm, in which Ramus cries frantically that Aristotle is entirely wrong in restricting truth and falsehood to composition and division — that is, to statements, either affirmative or negative. The true and the false, Ramus protests, in one of his later explanations of his dialectic, are "transcendental, if I may speak inelegantly" (Cicero had never used this vulgar scholastic word), which means that they apply everywhere and to everything.[52] The "simples" of both sensation and terminology (*simplicia sensa, simplicia nomina*) — which Ramists were to have some trouble telling apart[53] — are themselves true or false, just as much as statements are.

Ramus is heading here for a pitfall which most other philosophers, caught willy-nilly in this topical maze, manage somehow to avoid, if only by bringing their thinking to a dead halt and refusing to go further. Ramus plunges ahead. "Man" (*homo*), he proclaims, is true, whereas "non-homo" is false, and in general when opposites are set up, one is true and the other false. If it means anything, Ramus' statement means that when two opposites are applied to something by being predicated each of the same subject, of the two resulting enunciations, one is true and the other false. Thus, in "Ramus is a man" and "Ramus is non-man," "man" is part of a true statement, and "non-man" of a false. But, when the same terms are applied to an ass — "An ass is a man" — just the opposite obtains: "man," Ramus would have to say here, is false, and "non-man" true — a fact which shows that, as terms or concepts, these things are veridically neuter, and that only a proposition can be properly true or false — which, of course, was just what Aristotle had pointed out in the first place. Ramus' refusal to restrict formal truth and falsehood to the proposition or judgment is shared by some other philosophers, but none make the consequences of this refusal clearer than he.

The reason why Ramus hits on *non-homo* rather than *homo* as false is as evident as it is shallow: there is something negative about *non-homo*, and there is something negative about falsehood. One sees here why Nancel reflects with some regret on Ramus' inability to reason "to the point."[54]

However much the second part of the art of dialectic was reduced to "distribution" or argument-shuffling, it proved impossible to avoid all treatment of the enunciation. Thus, in the later *Dialectic*, the enunciation (*enunciatio*), and with it the judgment in something like the now ordinary sense of the psychological act expressed by the enunciation, will appear.[55] But it is only an afterthought, however prolonged. Persisting in his renunciation of predication, Ramus has no adequate way of accounting for this intruder at all.

10. CASUALTIES: THE FOUR PARTS OF THE ORATION, "COPIE OF WORDS," AMPLIFICATION

The structure of the Ramist dialectic is responsible for the liquidation of several items commonly present in other dialectics and/or rhetorics: notably the four parts of the oration, the search after facility in expression or "copie of words" (copia verborum), amplification, and decorum.

It is the second step in judgment, that is, definition and division, which absorbs and thus disposes of the classic four parts of the oration. These had long belonged to rhetoric, and their exact fate when Ramus got his hands on the dialectical and rhetorical machinery has been one of the puzzles of Ramism much discussed since the four parts were first reported missing by Professor Miller in 1939. Miller suggested that somewhere or other they were simply thrown into the waste basket.[56] They were, indeed, done away with summarily, but the process was perhaps less a throwing away than a sublimation or volatilization. The later Dialectic, heretofore the chief object of study, does not reveal too well what happened,[57] but the present Training in Dialectic of 1543 does. The four parts of the oration, exordium, narratio, confirmatio, and peroratio, are simply examples of the second step in judgment,[58] of the "linking of arguments in an unbroken chain" which constitutes an art itself and which will soon be tricked out as full-fledged "method." Here the rhetorical cast of Ramus' dialectic clearly shows itself. However, in Ramus' concentration on mere temporal sequence, the diverse psychological functions of the four parts are lost sight of, and the parts themselves become meaningless. The perorations which occur in Ramus' 1555 Dialectique and some other works are the result of no particular Ramist theory but are simply taken over from Agricola's Dialectical Invention, where they had helped create an oratorical aura around the hitherto "thorny" dialectic.

Among other humanists, the use of the places or commonplaces had been associated with the process of stocking the imagination with "matter" by means of wide and selective reading, and of assuring facility in expression, an abundance or "copie" of words (copia verborum). Here commonplace books and other devices were resorted to, in order to fix in the memory "sentences" or proverbial matter, epigrammatic turns, apothegms, descriptive phrases, allusions, and conceptual and verbal associations of all sorts. In the common medieval and Renaissance tradition, a certain richness is assured by the harum-scarum organization of the "places" in which this material was stored for recall. A mass of abstract truths, hair-raising expressions, detached phrases, comparisons, whole sentences, syllogisms, collections of adjectives — this "copie" could be exploited at all cognitive levels, sensory and intellectual simultaneously. Although it is commonly talked about by rhetoricians and dialecticians and others as operating solely in abstractly logical fashion, as a matter of fact there was no saying whether this whole mass belonged to dialectic or to rhetoric or to poetry. The general tradition wavered and generally assigned it, without much real conviction to all three, or to discourse-in-general. This store is drawn on in the rhetorics for "amplification" of a subject, the process which generates so much medieval and Renaissance abundance or bombast, depending on how well it is brought off. But Rudolph

Agricola and Ramus after him had decided that all commonplaces belonged to dialectic, and that the items in them were always dialectical or logical "arguments." This was the deathblow to profusion of expression as something consciously cultivated. Copie of words and amplification are still residual in Agricola and his commentators,[59] but with Ramus and the Ramists, the corollary has been fully drawn: since the commonplaces belong to dialectic, they form part of a purely abstract economy and are managed not by hoarding a riot of impressions but by the practice of "analysis." Here once again, Ramist dialectic unequivocally takes over, and remakes in its own way, matter to which rhetoric had at least some claim.

This corollary has a plenitude of psychological consequences. The pre-Ramist commonplace tradition could be richly sonorous rather than merely "clear," for it was the echo of a cognitive world experienced as if filled with sound and voices and speaking persons — had not Cicero called even the loci "seats" (*sedes*), as though the very arguments occupying them were living men? With Ramus, the voice goes out of this world. The *loci communes*, Ramus says, repeating Agricola's injunction, are to be worked hard, but the reason, he adds, is that they provide, not richness or vocal abundance, but arguments which can be hooked or "glued" onto questions.[60]

11. DECORUM AND THE "PLAIN" STYLE

The dialectical structure of discourse absorbs, for Ramus, other items properly rhetorical, namely, decorum and the three traditional styles, just as it had absorbed the four parts of the oration. It will be recalled that in the "third judgment" rhetoric functions by reproducing the variety of things in its variety of tropes, figures, and numbers by the observance of decorum,[61] or the accommodation of style to character and subject. This connection of decorum with rhetoric is reaffirmed in the 1545 *Training in Dialectic*. Talon's 1545 *Training in Oratory* treats traditionally of decorum or *decentia* and even of the three styles, applying these latter not only to oratory, but to history, poetry, and letter writing, and explains that decorum or propriety was for Cicero the chief and central concern of the whole art of rhetoric, although it is the one thing which the art cannot teach.[62] Nevertheless, with the appearance of Ramist "method" for the first time the following year in the pseudonymous edition of the *Training in Dialectic*, decorum and the three styles will disappear from the corresponding *Rhetoric* for good.[63] In the revised scheme of things, decorum, we are told, falls principally under dialectic because of its "general" character; its special applications were taken care of automatically in grammar, rhetoric, arithmetic, geometry, physics, ethics, architecture, agriculture, and, in daily affairs where no art rules, by human prudence.[64]

Decorum had always involved a complex notion of adaptation, with a certain personalist valence, since the choice of style depended not merely upon some mechanically conceived adjustment but upon *ethos* or character. It was commonly assumed that low matter was spoken of by those of low degree, high matter by those of high degree, and intermediate matter by those of the middle degree or class. Thus the interlocutors in Virgil's *Eclogues* or in Spenser's *Shepheards Calender*, speak a low style, the characters in Virgil's *Aeneid* high, and those in his *Georgics* middle. Ramus finds this division of styles in Cicero confusing and superfluous,[65] since dialectic again takes care of this sort of thing by disposing arguments in proper order. This order in dialectic is, as has been seen, radically visualist and diagrammatic in conceptualization, so that the transfer of decorum from rhetoric to dialectic and its subsequent volatilization here, together with the volatilization of the three styles, is, in effect, an elimination of the vocal and personalist in favor of the diagrammatic within the concept of accommodation or adaptation itself. Out of this operation, emerges the Ramist plain style. This style is certainly not the high or grand style, nor is it the low or the middle style. It is the phoenix which rises from the holocaust of all three styles, the verbal counterpart of the coming visualist universe of "objects," voiceless and by that very fact depersonalized, which would soon recommend to the Royal Society, as Thomas Sprat records in his history, "a close, naked, natural way of speaking," as near the "mathematical" as possible.

12. AMPLIFICATION, MEMORY, AND METHOD

Amplification (*amplificatio*), which has been mentioned in connection with sententiousness, and which had formed the backbone of medieval rhetoric,[66] was commonly understood to be the building up of, or enlarging on a theme or a case,[67] as by the addition of circumstances, by paraphrasing, by comparisons, and so on. This procedure is obviously congenial to the Ramist operations with arguments — in fact, too congenial, for, like decorum, amplification, which had likewise appertained to rhetoric, disappears from the Ramist scheme of things not by being ruled out, but by being swallowed up by dialectic or logic in the "method" which will grow out of the Ramist topical apparatus.

Along with amplification, memory, which had commonly been a further separate part of rhetoric, is also swallowed up by this same topical apparatus. The topical classifications, as has been seen, are classifications-for-recall, so that working with them is of itself working with a memory device.

CHAPTER X

ATTACKS AND REVISIONS

It is seldom seen that the clunch-fist
of logic (good to knock down a man
at a blow) can so open itself
as to smooth and stroke one with the
palm thereof.
— Thomas Fuller, *Worthies*, of
the Ramist George Downham.

I. RAMUS AND HIS CRITICS

RAMUS has been praised for his self-restraint in not replying —
with two notable exceptions — to the critics[1] of his dialectical works. But the
attacks on his dialectic had their effect, and every one of them occasioned
further revisions. After the first attacks, those of Gouveia and Perion in 1543,
the reaction was somewhat delayed because of Ramus' enforced silence, but
by 1547 there appeared a rewritten *Training in Dialectic in Three Books*
supported by Talon's *Dialectical Explanation of Porphyry*, which tamps down
again much of the ground plowed up by Gouveia. The next year saw a
revision of Ramus' *Remarks on Aristotle*. In 1554, Charpentier attacked Ramus, remarking that, like Aristotle, Ramus should treat the art of dialectic
alone and not nature and exercise as well.[2] The first Ramist art of dialectic
came out immediately with nature and exercise dropped, first in the trial
French edition, the *Dialectique* of 1555, and then in 1556 in the more important Latin edition with Talon's prelections. Schegk and others attacked Ramus on the occasion of his travels through Germany and Switzerland, and,
upon his return to troubled Paris, Ramus worked up a still further revision
of the *Dialectic*, which appeared in 1572 just before his death.

The attacks on Ramus, like the Ramist disputes which raged after his
death, have never fully been studied, and they are too voluminous to be
gone into here. It is worthwhile, however, to go briefly into those by Gouveia and Charpentier, which are two of the earliest of them, in order to relate
better Ramus' thought and its evolution to his contemporary milieu.

There are two attacks, between Ramus' *Remarks on Aristotle* and *Training in Dialectic* of 1543 and the first major shake-up of the latter work in 1546, one by the Benedictine monk Joachim Perion and the other by Antonio de Gouveia. Perion's was oratorical, and Gouveia's more scholarly and lengthier work, *Response for Aristotle against Peter Ramus' Calumnies*, has rightly been regarded as the more significant and influential. It has recently been reprinted in facsimile, and can be summarized briefly.[3]

Antonio de Gouveia (Antonius Goveanus), born in Tunisia about 1505, and thus older than Ramus by some ten years, was a jurist and writer. He was the brother of the more famous Andrea de Gouveia (1497–1548), rector of the College of Sainte-Barbe at Paris. Sainte-Barbe was the important nucleus of the large Spanish and Portuguese student colony at the university and is well known for its connections with Inigo de Loyola and his companions who were to found the Society of Jesus. Antonio was lecturing in philosophy at Paris from 1541 to 1544, and later taught law at Toulouse, Cahors, Valencia, and Grenoble. He died in 1566 at Turin. His works are mostly legal, but include classical commentaries and a Latin translation of Porphyry's *Isagoge*, as well as epigrams and various letters.

Gouveia had been the chief agitator against Ramus' 1543 publications and was to be one of the two hostile members of the 1544 royal commission charged with the hearings which resulted in Ramus' suspension from teaching. In his *Response*, he answers Ramus on behalf of Aristotle out of gratitude for all that he has derived from Aristotle's works, he says.[4] But he also answers because Ramus' cavalier history of philosophy would disqualify all use of ancient Greek commentators and, indeed, of everybody and everything in between Aristotle and Ramus himself for an understanding of Aristotle, and because Ramus is out to upset the whole curriculum.[5] Most of Ramus' stupid distortions of Aristotle could be passed over with no more than a laugh were it not for the fact that he addresses himself to adolescents who have not sufficient background and judgment to see through him.[6]

After rejecting Ramus' pre-history of a "pure" and "uncorrupted" dialectic as sheer uninformed and undocumented fantasy, Gouveia notes that, when Ramus deigns to be circumstantial about the history of philosophy, as in making Prometheus the first and Zeno the second philosopher, his source turns out to be none other than the Aristotle he despises.[7] Although their names are ungraciously suppressed in Ramus' works, Ramus' own sources for his dialectic turn out to be, besides Aristotle, the Rhineland or German manualists Caesarius, Hegendorphinus, Titelmannus, Melanchthon, and Rudolph Agricola, as well as Gouveia himself.[8] Gouveia recognizes the Platonism which Ramus vaunts as a red herring; he does not include Plato at all among Ramus' real sources, and notes that Plato's dialectic is not an art of disputation (*disputatrix*) such as Ramus tries to make it out to be, but rather a kind of prince among the arts and sciences.[9] Cicero's *Orator* is an attempt to present in Latin the Aristotelian dialectic, and when, at the opening of his *Topics*, Cicero divides the whole general process of discoursing (*ratio omnis disserendi*) into invention and judgment, he gives Aristotle the highest marks in both.[10] Gouveia makes no objection to this division of the whole field of discourse, and he uses it without hesitation as a frame of reference himself,[11] but he does not admit that the whole general process of expatiating or discoursing can be made into one "art" such as the Ramist dialectic.

Ramus attacks Aristotle's dialectic without ever condescending to state what Aristotle means by dialectic, namely, "that part of the art of discoursing which provides us with the arguments with which we can dispute either side of a question with a certain probability."[12] In his description of dialectic here, Gouveia does not allow explicit place for the probable proposition and the probable argumentation (these are both given treatment in Aristotle's *Topics*), and thus, like his adversary Ramus, gives evidence of the tendency to view dialectic as though it dealt exclusively with classification of concepts (arguments). But he goes on to imply, contrary to his description, that dialectic includes probable argumentation, for he opposes to dialectical proof the apodeictic proof, certain argumentation of the kind found in mathematics and spoken of by Quintilian and by Cicero in chapter VI of his *De finibus*. Gouveia, however, thinks of this apodeictic proof not precisely in terms of proof but in terms of teaching (*docere*).

Ramus' attack on Aristotle is based on the canard that the Peripatetic followers of Aristotle were diametrically opposed to Plato's Academicians. But, except for the one point concerning their explanation of ideas, where does Ramus find Aristotle or the Peripatetics particularly opposed to Plato? The Peripatetic-Àcademic relationship is not the for-or-against, black-or-white affair dreamed up by Ramus, but the more complex pattern of a development, and one in which, moreover, Cicero's complex role cannot be labeled, as it is labeled by Ramus, anti-Aristotelian.[13]

Dialectic is, of course, related to nature, but it makes no sense to speak of a natural dialectic, since dialectic refers to conscious or cultivated exactitude in discourse (*ratio diligens disserendi*), and there can be no cultivated exactitude without art. Hence the art of dialectic is no image of a hypothetical natural dialectic, but rather the cultivation of the innate aptitude of our minds for reasoning.[14]

The *Organon* of Aristotle's works treats of three things. First comes the art of logic (*ars logica*), in the sense of apodeictic logic which is concerned not with probable opinion but with certain demonstration, and which, first of all, must teach (*docere*) the grounds of such demonstration. Then comes dialectic, concerned with probable opinion, and finally sophistic, concerned with refuting bogus logical procedures.[15] Quite unjustifiably, Ramus would have the *Organon* chopped up in terms of his invention, judgment, and exercise.[16]

Gouveia follows with a careful account of the subject matter of the various *Organon* treatises, which in general would pass muster in any philosophical circles and from which we can only extract what is most relevant to our present purpose. He points out that the question of truth or falsehood is one which arises in the statement or proposition (*pronunciatum*) not in single concepts lifted out of propositions,[17] and that Ramus' assertion that the only species are individuals, such as Plato or Socrates, represents an absolute nadir in the history of logic.[18] Ramus attacks Aristotle's method of teaching, but everyone is agreed that Aristotle's greatest achievement is his unequalled success in erecting teaching into an art (*quod artifex summus esset docendi*).[19] Aristotle's reputation as philosopher, logician, physicist, or metaphysician is not even mentioned in this judgment of Gouveia's, for whom "the Philosopher" has become "the Pedagogue," as he has for Ramus.

Ramus, the self-constituted defender of grammarians who accuses Aristotle of importing grammatical notions into dialectic, only adds confusion to the complex interrelation of these two arts.[20] Under the guise of simplifying, he only complicates the classification of propositions.[21] Castigating the crudity of Ramus' equation of analysis with "unweaving," Gouveia presents a detailed explanation of Aristotle's classification of syllogisms by mood and figure which is at the same time a critique of Ramus' pretended new classification.[22] Induction is not at all reducible to syllogism, as Ramus says it is.[23]

Treating of enthymeme, Gouveia is less true to Aristotle, for he shares with Ramus the mistaken impression, derived from Boethius, that Aristotle takes enthymeme as an imperfect syllogism in the sense that it is truncated by the suppression of one of the premises,[24] whereas, as has been seen, Aristotle without exception always means by enthymeme a syllogism imperfect in the sense that it argues from probability to probability rather than from certainty to certainty.

Ramus had complained that by defining demonstration as a syllogism which brings certain or scientific knowledge (*syllogismus faciens scire*), Aristotle and his followers had in effect made geometry the only science, and thereby impugned, among other subjects, grammar and rhetoric.[25] Gouveia replies that since science in the strict sense is concerned with what is necessarily and inescapably true independently of man's efforts, grammar cannot possibly be a strict science, since it depends on changeable linguistic customs; rhetoric cannot either, since it depends indirectly on these customs, being made up of the rules for ornamenting speech (*quae praeceptis ornandae orationis continetur*).[26] Neither can real scientific demonstration be found in an art of discourse which is not concerned with certainties — this rules out dialectic, which deals with opinion and probabilities. On the other hand, in natural philosophy there are a great many real scientific demonstrations, and in mathematics still more. Ramus had objected that even geometry would not satisfy Aristotle's prescriptions for a science, since Euclid's very first proposition, "To construct an equilateral triangle on a given straight line," would not pass muster as a real demonstration, for it was simply a set of directions.[27] Gouveia replies that just because every single phrase in Euclid is not an instance of what Aristotle means by scientific demonstration, one cannot say, with Ramus, that Aristotle should have kept his mouth shut. Is every single phrase in Cicero or Demosthenes an instance of what Cicero himself says in the *Orator?* Euclid proposes problems of geometrical construction for the beginner in order to make clear the nature of geometrical abstraction.[28]

Ramus condemns as neologisms the expressions introduced by the Aristotelians, *de omni* (universal, or pertaining to each individual) and *per se.*[29] But in dealing with new material, one has to invent new terms, as Cicero himself well knew, for he was the greatest innovator in Latin, and invented terms right and left to express in Latin what he had learned in his studies in Greece.[30] (It is significant that this active linguistic area where the neologisms of the Aristotelians are being contested is that concerned with method: *de omni* and *per se* will soon deploy themselves everywhere through Ramist literature in connection with Ramus' three laws of method, which Ramus has not as yet thought of.)

Ramus had reduced all science to definition and division, but Gouveia finds his notions of definition both primitive and awry. Aristotle had said that definitions were arrived at by studying the various things which can be said about a genus, and thereupon by attempting divisions in terms of differences. Ramus thinks he can pull a definition out of the springs of invention (*a fontibus inventionis hauriri definitionem*). He refers to Cicero, but Cicero does not say that definitions are to be drawn out of the loci, nor indeed how definitions are really got at at all.[31] Ramus obviously cannot follow what Cicero is saying, for he bases his objections to various remarks of the orator's solely on misinterpretations.[32]

Ramist method owes much to Gouveia — perhaps its very existence — for it is Gouveia who first discovers in the confusion of Ramus' remarks on "second judgment" connections with "the order in teaching the arts which the Greeks call method."[33] Gouveia fails to see why this has any place in a treatise on discourse in general, such as Ramus' remarks pretend to be, but, since Ramus has brought it in confusedly under his "second judgment," Gouveia is willing to discuss it and to brief what the best-known writer on method, Galen, has to say.[34] There are reductively, says Galen, three ways to be considered: one by which arts are discovered and two by which they are taught or explained. Arts are discovered by breaking down (*resolutio*) the end into means. This breaking down is effected when men reflect consciously (*diligenter*) on the means available to achieve an end. This is the way medicine, the arts of expatiating and speaking, politics, moral teaching (*moralis disci-*

plina), and indeed the whole of philosophy, as well as the building arts were discovered. Thus men wanted first a roof over their heads; then they found they needed walls to hold up the roof; and finally they needed a foundation on which to set the walls. This order of awareness of their needs (roof, walls, foundation) was reversed in the actual building (foundation, walls, roof). And so it is with discovering an art: one becomes aware first of the end, but builds the art beginning with the means.[35]

While there is only this one way of discovering arts, however, there are two for teaching them. Teaching can be by composition and progression or by defining and dividing. In his *Ars parva*, Galen proceeds by the latter method, and this is the general procedure in compendia. Aristotle teaches the other way, by composition and progression, building up from the ten supreme genera, which he had come upon last of all, through enunciation to syllogism and finally to that obvious and necessary proof which constituted the end of this art. However, in this general assembling process, he defines and divides frequently and illustrates by examples. For in teaching any art there has to be distribution of universals into parts, explanation by definition of what is turned in on itself (*involuta*), the distinguishing of what is complex, a clearing up of what is obscure — all this to eliminate doubt,[36] which (in what is a pre-Cartesian commonplace) is "the mother and parent of all science."[37]

The great controversy has always been over whether an art or "teaching" (*doctrina*) takes its origin from singular abstract forms as from causes, or from the real things it is concerned with. This is a difficult question to solve (Gouveia does not undertake to solve it), and Aristotle cannot be blamed for pointing out how difficult a problem it is.[38]

Gouveia concludes his defense of Aristotle with an explanation of the general nature of metaphysics and of its development by Aristotle. The wisdom (*sapientia*) of which Aristotle speaks in the *Metaphysics* is nothing other than knowledge (*scientia*) in its most perfect form, the knowledge of causes. Arithmetic, geometry, astronomy, and music, and all parts of philosophy concerned with one kind of thing are not considered by Plato worthy of the name of *scientia*, and are hence called by the less honorable title *artes*, because they do not explain their own axioms but merely posit them as true, without going into the reason or cause why they are true.[39] Metaphysics, on the other hand, treats of all first principles of everything, material and immaterial, including the first principles on which the principles of the other parts of philosophy are based. Hence it must treat of things such as genus, of form, which is also called essence or nature, of matter, efficient cause, final cause, and so on. It must also treat of the first principles of demonstration, such as the principle of contradiction (like most scholastics, Gouveia contents himself with instancing this one principle without venturing to go into the question as to whether there are others, or how they may be related to this one).[40] In short, because it cuts back of all the differentiated sciences, metaphysics considers simply being without essence (*ens sine essentia*) — Gouveia seems here to consider being (*ens*) as a kind of genus differentiated by various essences. Metaphysics is thus concerned with the causes common both to natural and to mathematical philosophy.[41] What Plato calls dialectic is not what Ramus says it is, Ramist dialectic; rather, it is really the same as metaphysics.[42] Plato, moreover, himself praises Aristotle, and out of loyalty to a man to whom he obviously owes so much, Ramus would do the same were he not a cheap publicity seeker.[43] With this, Gouveia's book closes.

3. CHARPENTIER'S ATTACK

Like so many of Ramus' friends and enemies, Jacques Charpentier was from northern France; he had been born in Clermont-en-Beauvoisis.[44] Master of arts and doctor of medicine at Paris, he was known as an Aristotelian with a great admiration for Plato, and a thorough knowledge of Hippocrates and Galen. He is a typical example of the strong tradition linking scholastic philosophy with medicine. He seems to have spent his entire career at Paris, teaching philosophy rather than medicine, although he was a married man, as doctors of medicine, alone of all masters engaged in active teaching, were allowed to be. The last eight years of his life, from 1566 to 1574, he was regius professor of mathematics, replacing Dampestre Cosel despite all the pressure Ramus could bring against his appointment. He seems to have been a very popular professor, and, as the "frippelipique" pamphleteering shows,[45] much of Ramus' animus against him was connected with the ascendancy which he seems to have enjoyed in the Picard Nation, to which Ramus also belonged at the university. Charpentier had been elected university rector, and Ramus had not. The rectorship was often conferred on young masters, barely out of their teens, but it had a symbolic importance (from which its real practical importance was derivative) and conferred a sometimes enviable prestige.

When Charpentier published his attack on Ramus in 1554, he had more to go on than Gouveia had. Not only had the interdiction against Ramus' teaching and publishing on philosophy been lifted, but Ramus was Regius Professor of Eloquence and Philosophy with some twenty printed works to his credit, including large masses of Ciceronian commentary and an attack on Quintilian. The Ramist *Rhetoric* was in its twelfth edition. The *Training in Dialectic* had gone through nine editions at Paris and three at Lyons, and had jumped the Rhine, a Cologne edition appearing the same year as Charpentier's attack. The *Remarks on Aristotle* had appeared six times at Paris and three times at Lyons. Even before the interdiction against him had been lifted, Ramus had brought out in 1546, using Talon's name as a pseudonym, the revision of his *Training in Dialectic* which first treats of method, a subject which grows in importance through the subsequent revisions. These revisions were to continue as Ramus repeated his lectures each year, but were already numerous: the nine printings at Paris from 1543 to 1553 include five different revisions of the original text. Charpentier takes particular note of these. His 1554 critique, *Remarks on Peter Ramus' Training in Dialectic in Three Books* (*Animadversiones in Libros tres dialecticarum institutionum Petri Rami*), is directed against the *Training in Dialectic*, as Gouveia's had been against the *Remarks on Aristotle*.

Like Gouveia, Charpentier criticizes Ramus for being unaware of what Aristotle means by dialectic — a logical procedure which is proper to discussion or debate, not to scientific reasoning, and which thus is concerned with what is probable, not what is necessarily so. Not only Aristotle, but Plato gives a special place to this kind of reasoning.[46] Of course Ramus does not find in Aristotle a "general and universal" logic which applies en bloc to everything from mathematics to parliamentary debate. Aristotle's works are based on an acknowledgment that there is no such monolithic logic.[47]

Charpentier criticizes Ramus' definition of rhetoric by analogy with medicine. One must distinguish the end of the art of medicine, which is the explanation (*explicatio*) of what is relevant to curing disease (Charpentier, too, identifies art and teaching), and the use of medicine, which is to secure health by observation of what helps or hinders health.[48] Ramus' division into nature, art, and exercise is common to the "faculty" of every art, but Aristotle is justified in treating the art only, for it is there that you find the precepts. Moreover, Ramus' "little brother" Talon does the same in his *Rhetoric*, where he has omitted nature and exercise.[49]

Method is as burning a question for Charpentier as it was for Gouveia and had become for Ramus, but Charpentier's views do not quite coincide with those of either of the others. Charpentier taunts Ramus that his division of dialectic into invention and disposition leaves him uncertain as to what to do with method, for which Ramus now follows Cicero and Quintilian and now departs from them. Ramus is reminded that even Talon in his work on Cicero's *Topics* notes that the division of the art of discoursing into invention and judgment is faulty because it neglects method.[50] Ramus' insistence that there is only one method of teaching is unacceptable even to Ramus' own sympathizers, such as the doctor of medicine Jean de Bomont, who in 1543 held three methods of teaching.[51]

Having detailed the inconsistencies among the six variants of Ramus' *Training in Dialectic* which had appeared so far, Charpentier treats of the principles (*principia communia*) which Aristotle says in the *Posterior Analytics*, I, i, are common to both arithmetic and geometry because derived by both from a higher science. Ramus simply assumes that this higher science is what he means by his own dialectic or logic, whereas actually the general principles of all knowledge are treated in three different ways respectively by metaphysics, dialectic, and analytic. These are only three aspects which reason can distinguish in one common art (*ars communis ratione diversa*). Analytic is the logic of strict scientific proof and concerned with definition, division, and ratiocination. Dialectic is concerned with opinion and thus considers the more generalized aspects of reality (*commune genus eorum quae sunt*). Metaphysics seeks perfect knowledge "in the universal genus of that which is": (*in universo genere eius quod est*), "and by this fact includes the absolutely first principles of the other sciences, which are concerned with a certain part of that which is, and therefore is called the mistress of the other sciences."[52]

Charpentier's explanation is sprinkled with instances of particular difficulties Ramus has got himself into with his eerie genus-and-species doctrine. His critique of Ramus' ultralogical view of sex has been referred to above.[53] To prove that "man" is the genus for individual men, Ramus had quoted the authority of jurists, whom he elsewhere maintains are worthless as dialecticians.[54] Talon, in his commentary on Ramus' *Training in Dialectic*, says Porphyry *ought* to have employed his terms as Ramus wants; nevertheless, in the third edition of the *Remarks on Aristotle*, Ramus admits that his hero Plato uses the terms genus (γένος) and species (εἶδος) indiscriminately, which gives Porphyry all the warrant he needs, or certainly all that Ramus could reasonably demand.[55]

In the second book of his *Remarks*, Charpentier treats of Ramus' second part of logic in terms of the proposition, argumentation, and method.[56] Method is manifold, not only in the invention of an art but also in the teaching of it; the general principles which in themselves explain most (which are *per se notiora*) may be the hardest things for a student to grasp (may not be *notiora nobis*), so that they are the very last things one comes to in teaching. Ramus had maintained that they should always be first.

The third and shortest book of Charpentier's *Remarks* takes up Ramus' ideas of exercise.[57] Practically, Ramus' tactics destroy the possibility of exercise, which for Charpentier as for Ramus means imitation of an author, for Ramus annihilates one author after another and leaves nobody to imitate (at this point the pedagogical rather than philosophical embarrassment occasioned by Ramus' activities is once again manifest). In passing, Charpentier remarks that Ramus neglects the existential import of the verb "to be," making it a mere copula.[58] Charpentier's remarks are rather cursory here and are aimed against a pure logical formalism which does not concern itself with the metaphysical implications of predication. He gives, at best, only equivocal evidence of thinking in terms of a philosophy of existence such as the twentieth century has discovered in St. Thomas Aquinas. Nevertheless, a pure formalism seemed to Charpentier particularly ill-sorted with professed interest in a real activity such as classroom exercise.

Despite his violent attack on the Ramist dialectic as a whole, Charpentier is seen to agree with Ramus on a good many significant points. An art is not properly a skill, but rather an explanation — in short, art and teaching are identified. Art is founded on nature in the sense that at least some of the results achieved by art can be achieved without art — which does not mean without acquired skill but without *taught* skill. Art, or teaching, is a matter of "precepts." Exercise, of course, follows both art and nature.

With regard to the interrelation of the sciences, Charpentier wants to differ with Ramus without quite seeing how to do so. He is sure that argumentation in terms of probabilities should be treated somehow separately from rigorous scientific proof, and he associates probabilities with "dialectic" and rigorous scientific logic with "analytic," a loosening up or taking apart, or, as Ramus had put it, an "unweaving" or "unwinding." This alinement of dialectic and analytic was not new with Charpentier, but based on Aristotle's own usage. However, Charpentier is unable to establish a meaningful and decisive distinction between these respective arts, a dialectic of probabilities and an "analytic" of science, nor between either of them and metaphysics, although this latter is somehow more "general" than the other two — how, Charpentier cannot effectively say.

Charpentier has often been pictured as an arch-Aristotelian by contrast with Ramus, who is the anti-Aristotelian exploiter of classical authors neglected by Aristotelian scholastics. But Charpentier shows no antagonism to Cicero and Quintilian as opposed to Aristotle; he only points out the difficulty which Ramus has encountered regarding the question which generations of scholasticism had now kindled to white heat, the problem of method, and that specifically as it affects teaching.

4. THE FINAL DIALECTIC

In 1555, Ramus followed Gouveia's and Charpentier's not-too-well-meant advice and dropped the trappings of nature and exercise. In his French *Dialectique*, he produced his first unencumbered art of dialectic. The following year, 1556, this was given its definitive Latin form, and equipped with the Talon commentary which chinked Ramus' text with miscellaneous erudition as well as with material from the *Remarks on Aristotle* and from the parts of the *Training in Dialectic* dropped from the new text itself. In this state, the *Dialectic* was launched on the spectacular career carrying it to some 250 printings in the next one hundred years. The text underwent subsequent alterations, as did the commentary, especially after Talon's death, when Ramus took occasion to foster on his deceased friend lengthy sections on method which Ramus was having trouble making coherent.[59]

In its first part, invention, "the part of dialectic concerned with finding arguments,"[60] this definitive two-part dialectic is not greatly different from what Ramus had proposed in 1543. An argument is "that which is ordered to arguing something," and such arguments consist of "individual species taken separately and in themselves."[61] The arguments are reassorted, but they are radically the same, a more or less rule-of-thumb arrangement of some of the key notions feeding down through the general dialectical and rhetorical tradition, reminiscent of the topics or loci, but treated somewhat like the categories by being ranged in serried classes.

The second part of dialectic, judgment or disposition, is quite different from what it had been in 1543. Gone entirely is the "third judgment," which was supposed to bring all things to their source, God, and which Ramus had piously described as the *only* true dialectic![62] Gone, too, is all talk about definition and division which dominated much of the discussion — this has been relegated to the classificatory apparatus of the first part of dialectic. The other two 1543 divisions of judgment, "first judgment" or syllogism, and "second judgment" or a kind of embryonic method, are not repudiated so much as superseded. Before 1572, they are thrown together in the new second part of judgment called judgment of syllogism and of method, which is paired with an entirely new first part of judgment called judgment of enunciation.[63] In the final 1572 revision, these two parts of judgment are revamped into dianoetic and axiomatic judgment respectively.[64] Ramus describes the second part of his art of dialectic thus:

So far the first part of the art of dialectic has been in invention; the second part follows in judgment. Judgment is the part of logic concerning the arrangement of arguments for judging well; for everything is judged by a certain rule of arrangement, so that this part of logic is indifferently called judgment or arrangement. Judgment is either judgment of enunciation, or judgment of syllogism and method.[65]

The following chapter on method will treat this second part of the art of dialectic.

CHAPTER XI

THE METHOD OF METHOD

Olivia. Where lies your text? . . . .
In what chapter of his bosom?
Viola. To answer by the method, in
the first of his heart.
— *Twelfth Night*, I, v.

I. NOTIONS OF METHOD: MEDICINE AND RHETORIC

R AMUS lived in an age when there was no word in ordinary usage which clearly expressed what we mean today by "method," a series of ordered steps gone through to produce with certain efficacy a desired effect — a routine of *efficiency*. This notion is not entirely missing in early six-teenth-century consciousness, but it has as yet no *independent* existence. It engages consciousness obliquely, as an appendage to other terms such as *ars, clavis, medius* (middle term), *empereia* (experience, sometimes weakly nuanced toward positively controlled experimentation), *scientia, doctrina, via compendiaria, compendium,* or the word *methodus* itself.[1]

Sixteenth-century man, of course, did not deny that what we today call method existed in human activity. But in the university and intellectual milieu especially, theorizing about orderly procedure tended to focus on orderly procedure within the mind, or, more significantly, on orderly procedure in discourse. Even in medicine, a presumably practical discipline, the method or procedure in effecting a cure is curiously tied up with notions of explaining or teaching the procedure. It is only at the term of a long evolutionary proc-ess that general attention focuses on a routine of efficiency itself instead of a routine of thinking or discoursing *about* a routine of efficiency.

We can understand the sixteenth-century use of *methodus* better if we ex-amine its etymology and development from its radical meaning, a "pursuit" or "following after" or "way through." We encounter this notion at the dawn of Western history in a context quite different from that given it today. *Methodia* (μεθοδεία) to the Greeks had meant craft or wiliness in a per-sonalist rather than a technological setting, referring particularly to skill in collecting taxes or debts. The related *methodus* (μέθοδος), a following after or pursuit, had come to mean the pursuit of knowledge or an investigation, or the mode of prosecuting such inquiry, with the emphasis on logical rather than physical procedure — meanings which are common in Aristotle.[2]

In the Socratic tradition, this notion is fused with that of dialogue or dialectical procedure. It is also associated with the process of teaching, although not so strongly as in the opening of Peter of Spain's *Summulae logicales*, where, to the medieval mind, *methodus* means virtually a curriculum subject. The ancient Greeks also used the term in rhetoric to signify a means of recognizing an argument or treating a theme. The high personalist valence of the term in ancient usage is shown by the development of a further sense of a trick or ruse or stratagem — a means of exploiting another individual.

The term *methodus* is particularly associated with medicine. In ancient Greece, medicine had been the only activity set up as a rationalized technique, and its rationalization had been coincident with its emergence as a curricular subject.[3] It is on the grounds of a practical activity forced into a frame and designed to be communicable, not simply intelligible, that we encounter the real beginnings of the notion of "method" in the modern sense. Throughout the Middle Ages and the Renaissance, the standard purveyors of method remain, besides the biologist-philosopher Aristotle, his shadowy predecessor, the physician Hippocrates, and his physician-commentator, Galen. When writing on method, Ramus cites Hippocrates, Plato, Aristotle, Galen, and other "interpreters of Aristotle," but concentrates particularly on Galen's more quarrelsome works, *On the Opinions of Hippocrates and Plato* and *Medical Art* (*Ars medica*, known also as the *Tegni* or *Technē*).[4]

Since the medical tradition had a practical orientation, it tended to generate the notion of a routine of efficiency and to associate this notion with *methodus*. Such notions, however, were never clearly disengaged from others concerned with analytic logical procedure and with discourse, so that the medical tradition remained as much interested in the proper way to approach and to talk about a problem as it was in the proper way to cure a patient. Medicine, such as it was, emerged as a rationalized technique not only by curing its patients but also because of some ability to explain cures. When the patient did get well, it was up to the physician to prove to his students that his method of treatment, not merely nature, had turned the trick.

There were other reasons, too, for the permanent logico-linguistic torque which notions of method retained in the medical setting. Medicine was faced with real logical problems, and was shot through with rhetoric,[5] partly because it was not sure of itself and spent much time justifying its own positions, but more particularly because in the Hippocratic writings and elsewhere medical lore was preserved and studied in aphorisms (Bacon's interest in method and his interest in aphorisms go together). Furthermore, medicine was deeply committed to the use and interpretation of symbols, and to the study of psychological processes such as memory (itself considered a part of traditional rhetoric). It had a tendency to regard patients as psychosomatic wholes and to make much of the physician-patient relationship as one which involved not merely abstract issues but a person-to-person situation of the sort traditionally handled by rhetoric. This is not to say that medicine consciously practiced psychoanalysis or other techniques, but only that it had not yet learned to favor the mechanical elements over the nonmechanical, psychological elements in the physician-patient situation, especially as these latter were involved in the physician's own powers of apprehension and, more darkly, in the symbolism of the different organs and organic processes and in medical aphorisms.[6]

The ancient medical concept of method thus involves, besides the notion of a routine of efficiency in healing, the broader paralogical notion of an intelligent approach (in a social, aphoristic, and more or less pedagogical context) to a complex problem. At this point, the tradition joins that of Aristotle, where this is derivative from that of Plato and, particularly, of Socrates.

Aristotle had concentrated on how to arrange questions in a proper series, and on the most basic of the many questions concerned with method: How can one direct an investigation *toward* knowledge which one wants to secure when one has not yet caught sight of the goal toward which the investigation is supposed to be directed?[7] Method is procedure here — first and foremost, intellectual or logical procedure.

To this one rationalized technique of the Greeks, the Romans added another, that of law,[8] which the Greeks had taught and learned by personal contact and apprenticeship, rather than by formal instruction. But law did not generate an interest in method in the same way medicine did. Law is something of and in the mind. In medicine, the problem of method is concerned with the rational approach to an external world about which certain facts are known and much is unknown. Law has no comparable problem of method. Its terrain is already rationalized: law is rational arrangement. Only through their connection with rhetoric — a very real connection in the Italian universities, where there is no effective break between Cicero and Irnerius, between ancient classical rhetorical tradition and medieval and Renaissance law — have Roman legal developments an appreciable effect on Ramus and other Renaissance methodologists. The effect is indirect, particularly in Ramism, which seldom feels Italian influences immediately. Italian humanist rhetoric, like humanist topical logic, will be operative in Ramism chiefly after it has been processed by Rhineland humanists.

In the course of the Middle Ages notions of method underwent a subtle but profound change. Medieval interest in method grew principally on the common grounds of curriculum organization and pedagogical procedure rather than that of scientific investigation. *Methodus*, which medieval writers encountered in Boethius' translation of Aristotle's *Topics*, came to mean, among other things, a curriculum subject, because it signified, as in John of Salisbury, Lambert of Auxerre, or St. Albert the Great, a short cut to knowledge. It was also called an *ars* (in the Stoic tradition a set of precepts direct-ing some sort of practical activity), or, if it was short enough, a *compendium*.[9] In the university, masters of arts, as well as doctors of medicine, law, and theology, continually sought orderly arrangements for presenting to students on a regular teaching schedule the matter in the curriculum, although, in historical fact, the curriculum had not been set up initially in accord with any fully elaborated theory but, like Topsy, had "just growed."

Thus, long before the sixteenth century, university teachers had been con-cerned with something not unrelated to scientific method — the organization of the matter they were teaching. The dialectical tradition as a whole is di-rected to this end, rather than to establishing an art of abstract thinking or to an order of procedure. And, although it is possible to discern some differ-ence in focus between the "method" on the one hand of the medieval medical men and Averroists, who thought in terms of scientific knowledge, and, on the other hand, of the humanist educators, who were concerned with peda-gogical efficiency, the men engaged in the methodological disputes of Ramus' day were, by and large, unable to establish this difference effectively. The Ramist disputes themselves are ample evidence of this fact. Ramus himself is a classic example of a man who has the humanists' pedagogical preoccupa-tions and who constantly nurtures his interest in method by forays into medi-cal writers without any apparent consciousness that their focus tends to be different from his.

Modern interest in scientific method has its matrix in this mélée, where pedagogical interests give method its first incredible urgency. In the attacks on Ramus just reviewed, neither Gouveia nor Charpentier feels called upon to explain why method was a chief issue. It was simply taken for granted that it was an all-important point, something everybody was willing and anxious to debate. Gouveia held for two methods, Bomont for three. Gouveia and Charpentier have quite different opinions on where method fits into the pro-gram. Gouveia maintains that it does not belong within an art at all; Char-pentier seems to take for granted that it is integral to an art and taunts Ramus with the fact that he cannot properly fit it in.

If neither Gouveia nor Charpentier has any doubt of the urgency of the method question, another adversary of Ramus', the great classical philologist Adrien Turnèbe, was more skeptical about the intrinsic importance of the matter. Nevertheless, he bears outspoken witness to the intensity of the long pre-Cartesian agitation over it:

Method — no word is more popular in our lectures these days, none more often heard, none gives off a more delightful ring than that term. Everything else, if you use it often enough, will end by nauseating your readers. This is the only thing that never makes them sick. If you leave it out, they think the feast you set before them is disgustingly seasoned and poorly prepared. If you use it often, they will believe that anything you give them is the ambrosial and nectared food of the gods.

We ourselves, who have not felt particularly ravished by this food, have almost never bothered with method. If we come across traces of it in authors we are interpreting, we touch it — lightly, since we are convinced that the delights buried in it are not so great that anyone at all cannot be introduced to their utmost mysterious depths in approximately two words.

Unfortunately, Turnèbe leaves us wondering here what the "approximately two words" are, but, continuing, he indicates where to go for fuller explanation:

> I am aware that this subject has been thrashed out to the last grain and meticulously disputed by Peter Ramus, and I do not undertake to turn up anything that he has overlooked. I only propose to satisfy the young men who are anxious to know my views on this matter and whom I don't like to disappoint.[10]

This is two generations before Descartes, and the method agitation has obviously been at a boil for a long time. It is not restricted to Paris by any means, although one of its principal centers is there. Two years before Turnèbe's death, the mathematician Pietro Catena's *Oration for the Idea of Method (Oratio pro idea methodi)* had been published at Padua. In a work which appeared at Basle the following year, and which styled Ramus "the great corruptor of dialectic" and "the Parisian sophist," [11] the Tübingen philosopher and physician, Jacob Schegk, indexes twenty-four different places where, in the body of his work, developed largely out of Aristotle's *Posterior Analytics*, he has something to say about method. The kinds or aspects of method which he treats include analytic method, descending method, ascending method, method of proof, method in a curriculum subject, method of forming definitions prescribed by Hippocrates, method of defining genera, method of teaching the arts, method of teaching and learning, method of dialectical analysis, method of arranging matter in a definition, what a perfect method consists in, Aristotle's notion of method, hypothetical method, nonhypothetical method, ignorance of method as a cause of error, Aristotle's faithfulness to method, method of explaining a problem, the twofold way of method, and the method which Plato calls Prometheus' fire.[12]

Schegk's preoccupations show how the question of method was centered on the logical organization of science rather than on an order of procedure in external activity. They show also how this latter notion of method was intruding on the former one, and they certainly show a frantic interest in the whole question of method which marks the two generations and more preceding Descartes. A few years after Schegk's work, but still well before Descartes' day, William Temple will attest at Cambridge both the same interest in method and the way in which the notion was spreading into new areas despite the Ramist attempt to keep it under control, for he lists no less than one hundred and ten different kinds of *methodi* mentioned by Digby, whom he consequently accuses of tautology. The list takes over three pages and includes method of speculation, method of activity, method of light, method of darkness, descending method, ascending method, popular method, exact method, mental method, sensory method, method of arranging a whole science, and so on.[13]

This tremendous build-up of interest in method in the period just preceding Descartes has never been adequately studied. It is a movement much more extensive even than Ramism, but the phenomena resulting from it in Ramism alone show the utter inadequacy of the view which regards interest in method as stemming from Bacon and Descartes. These late writers on method were great explosive forces indeed, but the reason was less the size of the bombs which they manufactured than the size of the ammunition dumps, stocked by whole centuries of scholasticism, on which the bombs were dropped. In the age of Cicero, or even of Aristotle, method of any sort could certainly never have got anything like the hearing it got in the wake of the scholastic experience.

2. RAMUS' WAY TO METHOD

Method was to become the most famous item in the Ramist repertory, but it was something Ramus backed into unawares. Although the topical logics before Ramus treat of arrangement, *methodus* is hardly present in the tradition which feeds through Agricola into the Ramist dialectic. Gouveia, the first to detect in Ramus' 1543 dialectic a half-conscious concern with method disguised as "second judgment," remarks that he does not understand why this "order in teaching the arts which the Greeks call method" has any place at all in a dialectic conceived of as an art of discourse in general.[14]

In the pre-Agricolan scholastic logic, method had certainly not reached the handbook stage. Peter of Spain has nothing about method as such in his *Summulae logicales*, even though he uses the term at the opening of the work as a loose synonym for *ars* and *scientia* and *doctrina*.[15] Commentators on Peter of Spain among the old scholastic logicians of Ramus' youth will remark on Peter's use of the term, and explain that, in its most general sense, *methodus* means "a short and useful way of attaining something quickly."[16] But the notion of *methodus* does not enter very cogently and explicitly into this scholastic thinking, despite an affinity which such thinking has for the *Posterior Analytics* of Aristotle and derivative scientific works on demonstration and axiomatics. And before 1543, even the post-Agricolan logicians, such as Franciscus Titelmans, provide no section on method in their treatment of logic or dialectic.[17]

Insofar as it gyrates around the term *methodus* itself, the interest in method which marks Ramus' age and which will result a century or more later in Bacon's and Descartes' preoccupations is generated not out of a logical or scientific context, but out of rhetoric. The principal trail seems to lead back

through Johann Sturm to the Hellenic rhetorician Hermogenes (b. *ca.* 161
A.D.), whose elementary book on theme writing, put into Latin by Priscian,
had been a medieval favorite.[18] Hermogenes' interest in method turns up not
in this manual but elsewhere in connection with his seven "great ideas" for
the development of rhetorical prowess, of which the last and culminating
idea is that of adaptable effectiveness or rhetorical irresistibility (δεινότης).

This notion was associated particularly with Demosthenes, and the work
in which Hermogenes treats it features the Greek term "method" in its title
— περὶ μεθόδου δεινότητος. One is tempted to read this "On the method of
securing rhetorical effectiveness." But any current sense of the term "method"
in English fails to convey the signification of the original Greek cognate here,
which means something more like mode of rhetorical organization or
thought structure (*Sinnfiguration* is the literary historian, Wilhelm von
Christ's suggestion), so that the title more properly might be rendered, *On
the Pattern underlying Rhetorical Irresistibility.* The more philosophical or
logical notion of μέθοδος as a systematic investigation — a meaning which
the term conveys commonly in Aristotle — is hardly present in Hermogenes.
For his whole work is dominated by the policy of leaving all explanation to
the "philosophers" and erecting what von Christ calls a "wall of separation"
(*Scheidewand*) between philosophy and his own field, rhetoric. The significance of Hermogenes as a major source of interest in methodology at the
dawn of the modern world lies mainly in the fact that he shows that this interest arises in an area probably as clearly rhetorical and a-logical as rhetoric
can ever be.

Hermogenes' preoccupation with method was beginning to work its way
into humanist rhetoric in the fifteenth century. At this time, as Barroux has
pointed out, the Parisian humanist-printer Guillaume Fichet picked up the
term from the Greek rhetorician and used it in his own 1471 rhetoric.[19] In
1522, a Strasbourg reconditioning of Donatus' Latin grammar was printed
with the title *Methodus grammatica*, and by the 1530's several letter-writing
books were published, also in the Rhineland, featuring the term *methodus*,
as Hermogenes' title had featured it, notably the *Methodus conscribendi
epistolas* by the post-Agricolan rhetorician and dialectician Christoph Hegendorf and the *Methodus conficiendarum epistolarum* by the German Latin
poet and littérateur Conrad Celtis [20] — titles which could both be rendered
The Method of Letter-Writing, or *The Art* or *Science of Letter-Writing*, or
simply *A Course in Letter-Writing*.

These books have nothing explicit to say about *methodus* itself, but at-
tach great importance to *iudicium* as a kind of discernment, good judgment,
or prudence on which effective letter-writing depends. They are interesting
because they associate in their titles the concept of *methodus* with language
rather than with science or abstract thought, and because they attest the
growing currency of the notion. Erasmus' own *Abstract or Compendium of*

True Theology (*Ratio seu compendium verae theologiae*) which, in the
1519 edition introduced itself as "conveying the way (*viam*) and method
(*methodum*) of this heavenly study," was reprinted in Basle the following
year as *Ratio seu methodus compendio perveniendi ad veram theologiam*.
Method seems to have had considerable currency in the Hertogenbosch piety
of Erasmus' circle, where one finds also the *Methodus perveniendi ad summam Christianae religionis perfectionem* of the martyred Bishop of Roches-
ter, St. John Fisher. The later sixteenth- and seventeenth-century spate of
method books has not yet flooded Europe, but evidently something is in the
air. Strangely, it seems to be something humanist rather than scholastic,
rhetorical and devotional rather than dialectical and speculative.

3. STURM: THE TRANSPLANTING OF METHOD FROM RHETORIC TO LOGIC

Of the three early proponents of logical or dialectical method, Melanchthon, Sturm, and Ramus, Sturm, who had brought the Agricolan topical
logic to Paris, was the first to develop a consideration of method in a logical
or dialectical manual. Sturm's interest in method, which marks perhaps the
starting point of the fascination with methodology characteristic of our modern scientific world, is the clear result of a collision between Rhenish humanist rhetoric and Parisian scholasticism.

Fichet's earlier interest in Hermogenes and method had Rhenish overtones, for, while Fichet was a printer in Paris, printing in 1471 was not long
out of its Rhineland cradle. However, with the arrival of Sturm in Paris in
1529 — he was also a printer before he turned schoolmaster — not only Agricola,
but Hermogenes, began to boom. In 1530 and 1531, the Wéchel firm brought
out at least four separate rhetoric manuals of Hermogenes in the original
Greek: the *Ars rhetorica absolutissima*, the *De inventione tomi quatuor*, the
De formis orationum tomi duo, and the *De methodo gravitatis sive virtutis
commode dicendi*. The last was none other than Hermogenes' famous treatise
just discussed on Demosthenes' irresistible "method." The four works give
no indication of the identity of their editor. But, since the Wéchels were
Sturm's (and Ramus') Paris printers, and since Sturm himself was later to
produce translations of, and lengthy commentaries on, these and other treatises of Hermogenes, it is a little difficult to think that he had no interest in
these editions.

Sturm returned from Paris to open his gymnasium at Strasbourg in 1538.
In 1539 his first treatment of method appears, significantly, not in a dialectical
manual but in his dialogues on one of Cicero's rhetorical treatises, *In Partitiones oratorias Ciceronis dialogi quatuor*. Here Sturm makes a distinction
between art and method:

An art is an abundant collection of propositions and general observations looking to some useful end in life. But in this abundance and in setting up the various

arts, a certain, short, and direct way, a kind of short cut, has to be used, which is simple, and clear, and straightforward. This the Greeks call method (*methodus*) and teaching procedure (*didascalia*), such as may be used for teaching and communicating.[21]

Sturm distinguishes three ways of teaching (*rationes docendi*) which would seem to be the same as methods, although he warily avoids too great commitment on this score: (1) that of finding the art by proceeding from simple things (*a minimis simplicissimisque rebus*), called *systasis* or *ratio* συστατική; (2) the reverse procedure, called *analysis* or *ratio* ἀναλυτική; and (3) division of definitions into their parts, called *diaeresis* or *ratio* διαιρετική.[22] Sturm adds that Cicero is probably thinking in terms of this method when he calls his work *Partitiones oratoriae*, and Hermogenes is thinking in the same terms when he gives a division of rhetoric at the opening of his work. This last kind of method, Sturm notes further, is praised by Plato and Socrates and used by medical men in teaching their science.

Although he cites no sources for them, Sturm's three methods are obviously derived from Galen's prologue to his *Medical Art*:[23] resolution (*resolutio, analysis,* ἀνάλυσις), composition (*compositio, synthesis,* σύνθεσις), and division (*partitio, diaeresis,* διαίρησις), or definition (*definitio,* ὁριστική — "horizoning"). These procedures appear in the *Medical Art* not as methods of healing, but as methods of teaching, just as they do in Sturm: "All orderly *teaching* procedures come to these three."[24]

Sturm introduces one interesting variation. He calls Galen's *synthesis* by the term *systasis*, which means much the same thing, except that, first, it opposes the process it designates not to *analysis* but to *diaeresis* (*systasis* and *diaeresis* were paired terms, as were *analysis* and *synthesis*), and, second, it is a term employed by rhetoricians, among them Hermogenes himself, in the sense of probatory or confirmatory. For a rhetorician commonly looks on singular instances as a means of confirming a stand he has taken or an argument he is advancing rather than as something from which to work to a conclusion as a scientist does. Therefore, even though derived from the physician-logician Galen, method at this stage exists distinctly in a rhetorical context.

In the next stage, Sturm will transplant it into dialectic or logic. This he does in his manual of dialectic, but the operation will take time. The manual of dialectic, which is a sequel to his teaching experience at Paris from 1529 to 1536, will appear in installments, beginning with *The Structure of Dialectic in Two Books*. This was published at Paris in 1539, and, in dialogue form, its first book treats of dialectical invention and the second of "dialectical analysis." Dialectical analysis proves to be largely syllogism, since Sturm maintains that all argumentation can be "analyzed" into syllogism. A third book was added in 1543 to this two-book work in an edition appearing at Strasbourg, and a fourth book in 1560, also in a Strasbourg edition. These last two books, also in dialogue form, treat respectively demonstration and sophistic.[25] In the third book, chapter xv entitled "The Threefold Method" (*De triplici methodo*), goes into Galen's three methods again — but with *systasis* now called *synthesis*, in Galen's fashion.

With the whole university and para-university tradition behind him, the educator Sturm steps up Galen's didactic charge unawares: "Thus, as I understand it, this threefold procedure (*ratio*) of teaching the arts (*artes*) and curriculum subjects (*doctrinae*) which the Greeks call method (μέθοδος) is a useful thing." [26] Galen had been, at least in part, concerned with a method which would *set up* medicine as a curriculum subject. In Sturm the curriculum subjects are taken as if they were fully in existence, and Galen's three procedures are applied to them as if they were *already set up*, although on this, as on many points, Sturm's thought is unsteady. He does not refer explicitly to Galen here, but rather to Plato's *Timaeus* and, in a general way to Aristotle. However, not only are his three ways or methods — analysis, synthesis, and definition — Galen's, but also his discussion of them is dominated by medical examples. Analysis, we are told, proceeds according to an order established by the end one has in view. Thus, the end of medicine is health or the healing of the human body, and from this end the means are determined by the reasoning process which considers sucessively: actions, bodily powers (*virtutes*), the members of the body which are the seats of these powers, the (four) bodily humors, and the (four) elements.[27] This is the order of nature, and, Sturm goes on, synthesis proceeds simply by reversing it, working from a consideration of the elements back to the actions. Analysis is used in discovering the arts, synthesis in teaching them. The relationship of definition to this process is not very clear in Sturm, nor, indeed, is the relationship of the whole process to the details of teaching procedure.

In chapter xvi, "The Difference between Method and the Notion of Demonstration," Sturm includes references to Galen, but develops his own explanation in a popular, diagrammatic fashion typical of the Rhineland, home of printing and of the Renaissance topical logics. The explanation focuses on one of the diagrams simple enough to have enjoyed widespread currency even in the primitive geometrization of logic during the pre-Gutenberg ages: the Porphyrian tree. Demonstration, we are told, moves in zigzag fashion from trunk (genus) to branch (specific difference) to trunk again; that is, from substance to sentient body to animal to rational to man to Aristotle. Method, on the other hand, by resolution and division follows three routes (*ordines*): "one, that of the genera which are located in the middle [that is, which form the trunk of the tree]; the other two those of differences and species, which are placed on the sides [that is, the branches to the right and the left]." [28]

Sturm has nothing on the three rules attributed to Aristotle earlier (as rules of demonstration) by Johann Caesarius,[29] and later (as rules of method) by Ramus. But Sturm's delight in climbing up and down the Porphyrian tree betrays an interest (if not a very perceptive one) in the ascent (*ascensus*) and descent (*descensus*) and related processes which figure in the Ramist and other literature having to do with the "structure" of a science and with axiomatics and which are derivative from Aristotle's *Posterior Analytics*.

Sturm's original two-book dialectic of 1539 had treated invention, judgment (as a kind of general power of discernment), and arrangement or *collocatio* (as the structure in discourse resulting from judgment) in a way which makes clear that the author was attempting to complete Agricola's unfinished dialectic, just as Ramus was to do a few years later. Sturm's failure to achieve Ramus' popularity is doubtless due in great part to his inability to reduce things to a savage simplicity comparable to that of Ramism — a fact which may help explain his reserved, if kindly, evaluation of Ramus himself.[30]

Dialectic, which he equates with logic in the accepted fashion, Sturm defines, with wary verbosity, as "the art of examining, judging, and discoursing about what something is and of what sort it is when it is proposed as a matter for investigation and teaching." [31] In this logic or dialectic of discourse-in-general (more or less equated with the inevitable teaching), book II had supplied in some measure the *iudicium* or second half of the art mentioned but never treated by Agricola. Why Sturm felt compelled to add further books on demonstration and sophistic is to some extent a matter of conjecture, but it is quite certain that he did it in part to preserve something like the over-all structure of the *Organon*. Also, his inclusion of method, and to a lesser extent his inclusion of demonstration, in this general art of discourse is due to the tangle of didacticism and axiomatics which at the end of the medieval scholastic experience enveloped all notions of discourse and of cognition. At any rate, when Gouveia spots the suggestion of "method" in Ramus' 1543 *Training in Dialectic* and wonders expressly what such a thing could be doing in an art of discourse-in-general, he has the patience to go into the matter in some detail both because he knew that Sturm had done something like this before Ramus had and because he, too, felt the strong pull of didacticism and mathematics in his own approach to communication and cognition.

The kinship of Sturm's dialectic with that of Ramus is apparent more in the fact that they feed on the same diagrammatic conceptualizations and impulses than in any explicit doctrines. As early as 1551, *The Structure of Dialectic* was to begin to appear in folio volumes made up, from beginning to end, as later editions of Ramus would be, of nothing but bracketed tables, mostly in straight dichotomies, on which Sturm's dissected text was spitted by his enthusiastic editor, Valentinus Erythraeus.[32] This, I believe, is one of the earliest examples of the extreme fascination with deploying words in a kind of abstract space which was to be a characteristic of the Ramist age, and which is still so much a part of us that we can hardly realize it has an origin and a history. Interest in Sturm, and in Sturm's attitude toward method, was keen in Paris right up to the eve of Ramus' first works of 1543. In 1542, a Paris edition of Sturm's first and second dialogues on Cicero's *Partitiones oratoriae* also appeared.

4. MELANCHTHON ON METHOD

Within a few years after the publication of book III of Sturm's dialectic manual, other dialecticians, notably Ramus and Melanchthon, felt obliged to introduce a section on method into their manuals, too. Ramus' first mention of method as such in his pseudonymous 1546 edition of the *Training in Dialectic* preceded Melanchthon's by a year. But since Melanchthon's treatment is apparently quite uninfluenced by Ramus and is in many ways more primitive, it can best be considered first.

Like the manuals of earlier logicians or dialecticians such as George of Trebizond (Trapezuntius), Johann Caesarius, and Francis Titelmans, Melanchthon's early works, *A Brief Notion of Dialectic* (*Compendaria dialectices ratio*) of 1520 and the *Dialectic in Four Books* (*Dialectices . . . libri quatuor*) of 1528 contain no section on method, nor does his brief *Notes on Cicero's Topics* (*In Ciceronis Topica scholia*), but the *Questions in Dialectic* (*Erotemata dialectices*), which first appears in 1547, does. This last work is a development of the *Dialectic in Four Books*, so that once again, as in the case of Sturm and Ramus, method appears as an adventitious, revisionist phenomenon in an already established dialectic.

In the *Dialectic in Four Books*, book I treats of the predicables and predicaments and of definition and division; book II, of propositions; book III, of argumentation and induction; and book IV of the places and of fallacies. This organization perpetuates one of the accepted arrangements growing more or less out of the *Organon*. But Melanchthon was a man who knew how to eat a cake and have it, too. By identifying books I, II, and III with "judicative dialectic" and book IV with "inventive dialectic," he was able to preserve within the Aristotelian framework the Ciceronian and Agricolan division of dialectic into invention and judgment — albeit at the cost of making this latter division work backwards.

The *Erotemata dialectices*, or *Questions in Dialectic*, tacks method onto the end of book I in a separate section entitled "De methodo." This associates method with the judicative part of dialectic, as Ramus was to do, but quite ambiguously, for the predicables and predicaments and definition and division onto which method is tailed correspond to the arguments and hence to invention in Ramus, if they correspond to anything there. The collation of Melanchthon and Ramus need not be pursued further here, since it has been undertaken by large numbers of sixteenth- and seventeenth-century specialists in both the logics, who can still be consulted, and who had infinitely more time for detail than can be spared today.[33]

About method, Melanchthon has this to say:

At the beginning I said that in the first part of dialectic the doctrine concerning the explanation of simple words is presented. Thus the steps and the abodes of the vocables were shown at the beginning. Thereafter the ways of defining and dividing were stated. Now we must explain the use of this last part.

Since elsewhere the noun "method" signifies a straight and economical way or road, so dialecticians transfer this noun to the meaning of the most direct order in an explanation. Here method signifies a straight or direct way or order of investigating and explaining either simple questions or propositions. The Greeks thus define it: Method is an acquired habit establishing a way by means of reason. That is to say, method is a habit, that is, a science or an art, which makes a pathway by means of a certain consideration; that is, which finds and opens a way through impenetrable and overgrown places, through the confusion of things, and pulls out and ranges in order the things pertaining to the matter proposed.[34]

In this capital passage, although Melanchthon is not having an easy time with his own explanation, the connection between his notion of method and Agricola's topical logic is consummately clear, and has already been adverted to in passing above in Chapter VII, Section 5. Agricola had used this same setting for his explanation of the places: the same "abodes" or domiciles or receptacles, the same confusion of things, and the same way or road cut through them as through a woods.[35] There is even the same indecision as in Agricola concerning the connection, if any, between the cutting-out process and the road metaphor: Are the "things" to be thought of as obstacles in a road-building project or as objects of value to be harvested and used?

Agricola's description had been concerned with the places or loci themselves and with the orderly arrangement of items (*argumenta*) within these places. Melanchthon is concerned with the orderly arrangement of items which purportedly belong to the predicaments or categories, for he tacks his treatment of method onto the book devoted to these. But the Aristotelian notion of categories as predicates has here been superseded by the notion of the categories as boxes, all but indistinguishable from Agricola's loci. Melanchthon operates with his "method" in the same way as Agricola with the loci — in terms of local motion. Agricola is concerned with parking the arguments in his receptacles and making them readily available, Melanchthon with mustering them out. This is made clear by his association of method with "use." Method is what you do with the arguments once you have got them out of the Agricolan places. Thus it is that method is tacked on by Melanchthon with the predicables and predicaments rather than with propositions and argumentation, with which it would seem to belong.

As we have seen, Ramus' second half of dialectic is, on the whole, an attempt to deal with judgment or statement in terms of the topics or places which were the concern of the first half of dialectic, invention. In this scheme, dialectic itself, its second as well as its first half, becomes a kind of superplace or supercommonplace which yields up its own parts as arguments. Here with Melanchthon's treatment of method, the same process is observable. Method is taken over by the topical logics only to become subservient to the same imagery which governs the notion of places themselves. Nothing really new has been added. The same situation will be seen to exist when Ramus treats method, too.

In this connection, it is interesting to see in the quotation just given how Melanchthon reroutes the Greek definition of method into his own scheme of things, each "that is to say" edging the meaning over closer to what his own prepossessions require it to be. Thus a "habit" is assimilated to a science or an art — both of these mean for Melanchthon, as for so many other postmedieval men, nothing more abstruse than a curriculum subject — which is in turn assimilated to Agricola's topical apparatus.

The short or economical way (*compendiaria via*) which figures in Melanchthon's description of method here, as it had in Erasmus' *Ratio seu methodus compendio perveniendi ad veram theologiam*, is a common classical Latin expression used by Cicero and others. But in Cicero it does not have the pedagogical or quasi-scientific aura which it acquired in the postmedieval climate.

Melanchthon conceives of method as proceeding by means of questions. "What," he asks, "are the questions of method?" To which he answers that when one is considering a single word (the "simple theme" of logicians as late as John Wesley, and later), one can attack it with ten questions: What does the word mean? Does the thing exist? What is it? What are its parts? What are its various species? What are its causes? Its effects? Its associations? What things are related to it? What contrary to it? [36] Although we are in the book which treats the categories, not the topics, the correspondence of these questions to the topics — Ramus' arguments — can hardly be missed. Melanchthon compares his ten questions with the four questions in Aristotle's *Posterior Analytics*, which had been the object of Ramus' invective, saying that Aristotle's four reduce "chiefly" (*praecipue*) to these four of his own ten: Does the thing exist? What is it? Of what kind is it? Why is it? [37]

Aristotle's questions in the *Posterior Analytics* do not have to do exactly with single terms or "simple themes," as Melanchthon's treatment of method does, but rather with demonstration. This involves questions and proceeds by ratiocination from first principles. Melanchthon never really gets around to presenting this problem, for, although he starts by saying how method works when one is treating a *simplex vox, simplex vocabulum*, or *una res*, he apparently forgets to explain how it works when one is treating something else — such as propositions or syllogisms.

Apart from the general treatment he gives these things in books II and

III, Melanchthon provides no separate discussion of method for them. This fact is commented on later by irenic logicians seeking to reconcile Melanchthon and Ramus, such as Paul Frisius, who notes that Melanchthon treats method very lightly, referring only casually to Galen's three "ways of teaching (*viae doctrinarum*), that is, three methods of the arts (*methodi artium*)," analysis, synthesis, and definition, and that, while Melanchthon uses chiefly synthesis, he does not make an issue of the matter.[38]

5. JOHANN CAESARIUS AND THE THREE REQUIREMENTS

Although his treatment of method had thus been brought to bear on "simple themes" rather than on demonstration, Melanchthon's approach echoes what other humanist manual writers had to say on the subject of demonstration. This can be seen by examining the dialectical manual of Johann Caesarius (1460–1551). He was a Rhinelander who had studied at Deventer and Paris and his career fits the pattern typical of these interim dialecticians flourishing between the Gutenberg inventions and the collapse of the old scholastic logic: a Rhenish humanism overlaid with Parisian scholasticism. Caesarius, who also wrote a seven-book *Rhetoric*, and edited some classical authors, had studied medicine as well as philosophy at Paris, and taught philosophy for several years at Cologne before fleeing the city as suspect of Lutheranism (he died a Catholic). His *Dialectic* was first published at Cologne in 1532, but an edition appeared the following year at Paris, and the work went through numerous reprintings and re-editings. This work is divided into ten treatises, following the common order of the books of the *Organon*, Tractatus VII being concerned with demonstration, and thus with matter in the *Posterior Analytics* referred to briefly by Melanchthon.

Caesarius states Aristotle's famous four questions as "What sort of thing it is, why it is, if it is, and what it is."[39] He confronts the problem which Melanchthon's handling of the questions was later to suggest: Do these questions, which seem to refer to simple terms, not to propositions, bear also on the process of demonstration itself, which proceeds by means of propositions as an axiomatic process? Caesarius answers that the questions do bear on both simple terms and on "questions" (*quaestiones*), but that in the latter case the first question is rather "whether the predicate is in the subject" (*an subiecto praedicatum insit*).[40]

Still without mentioning method as such, Caesarius also treats the first principles of demonstration, demonstration from causes (*propter quod*), and the three requirements for demonstration. These were later to become what Schegk called Ramus' own incessant and nauseating "little song," namely, that the predication be valid *de omni, per se*, and *universaliter*.[41] These three requirements, the first two of which were to figure in the 1543 Gouveia-

Ramus controversy, Caesarius refers here to Aristotle and to Themistius (known to him, of course, only through Boethius).

Among the many other interesting points in Caesarius, one which is relevant to his notion of demonstration occurs in his Peroration. Here he retails from the Preface of Marsilio Ficino's *De voluptate* an account of three kinds of approach to discourse: [42] that of the Peripatetics and Stoics, which regards the elements in a question reducible to certainty; that of the Academics and Socratics, which compares opinions in order to find the more probable; and that of the Sceptics, who refuse to believe even in probability and are thought little of by the more important philosophers.

6. THE PRIORITIES AND AXIOMATICS HERITAGE: ASCENT AND DESCENT

Ramus will develop his own "method" by bringing together various loose ends in the post-Agricolan logical tradition. Sturm's didactic reading of Galen and Melanchthon's topical method will be fused with Caesarius' three requirements for demonstration and various other elements salvaged from Galen and other commentators on Aristotle's demonstration theory. Demonstration and axiomatic systems had come in for a great deal of attention in the great age of scholastic logic. Interest in these matters was fed on the one side by the development of formal logic and on the other by the development of the pedagogical tradition in the universities. For, under the spell of the logical tradition, the subject matter of any "art" or course tended more than ever to be regarded, ideally, as if it were organized like a geometrical treatise around certain first principles or axioms — "dignities" or *dignitates* was the common Latin term, and was a literal translation of the Greek *axiomata* — from which the whole matter of the curriculum subject was purportedly derived.

The central maneuver in Ramus' development of his method will be his attempted extension of this notion of the economy of an "art" to the whole of discourse, conceived of as fundamentally a means of "teaching" and as ruled by a topical logic. In order to see what this comes to, we must examine some aspects of Aristotelian science theory and axiomatics. To Ramus, also, one can certainly apply Randall's verdict that "the more fully the record of late medieval and Renaissance thought is studied, the clearer it becomes that the most daring departures from the Aristotelian science were carried on within the Aristotelian framework." [43]

Insofar as its relevance to Ramus' thought is concerned, Aristotle's discussion of the origins and structure of a science can be summarized briefly as follows.[44] Scientific knowledge is the knowledge of causes, of *why* things are so. Man finds himself faced with facts or data, which are presented to him through his senses and for which at first he cannot assign reasons. From these data, he must proceed by some sort of inductive process to devise principles which will explain the data. Once he has found the principles, he can work from them down to the data again. Thus, given the fact or datum that, unlike stars, the planets do not twinkle, he must somehow or other rise to the principle that what is relatively near in the heavens does not twinkle.[45] Thereupon, he can reason:

> That which is near (in the heavens) does not twinkle.
> The planets are near.
> (Therefore) the planets do not twinkle.

With this *kind* of demonstration — although, of course, not with this one simple instance — the mind can hope to satisfy itself: it sees a cause (at least one cause — there may be others, more profound or "ultimate," which will have to be found, too) of the planets' failure to twinkle. Such a syllogism shows the *why*, or *a* why, of its conclusion. This is called *demonstratio propter quid* (διότι) or demonstration from the cause. The following syllogism is valid, but it is not such a demonstration from the cause:

> The planets do not twinkle.
> That which does not twinkle is near.
> (Therefore) the planets are near.

Such a syllogism shows or proves something: namely, that the planets are near. But it shows this from a result of their nearness, not from a cause. Thus it provides a conclusion, "The planets are near," for which it assigns no *why* —the not-twinkling does not make the planets near, but only makes us *know* they are near. This is a *demonstratio quia* (ὅτι) or demonstration of a fact. It may at times have to suffice, for we cannot always find the causes of things or reasons for things when we want to.

In nature, the effect is the product of its cause; facts or events are dependent on reasons for the fact or event, the not-twinkling on the nearness. This is the *ordo quoad se* or *ordo naturae*, regarding as it does what is more known by nature (*notiora natura* or *notiora simpliciter*). But often the order which we must follow (*ordo quoad nos*, or *ordo inventionis*) does not correspond to this order of nature, for what is more known to us (*notiora nobis*) is likely to be the brute fact demanding explanation, not the explanation of the fact. We often know effects before causes, the not-twinkling before the nearness. Aristotle's rather elemental insights here are amply documented in a modern setting in the Einstein and Infeld account of the discovery of relativity theory in *The Evolution of Physics*, where the basic theorems which give the why for the greatest mass of data are arrived at last of all.

The question of the "priorities" is a difficult one, since the priorities of nature and those of knowledge do not always simply reverse one another, but sometimes coincide. What is more, they sometimes occur in whole cascades of reasoning and induction, through which they partly coincide and partly differ.

Moreover, when the order of knowledge does not follow that of nature, the "effects" from which one must work back to causes are of the most varied sorts, and are related to their causes in the most varied ways. Thus, the search for causes — that is, for the order of nature — involves all sorts of complicated psychological and logical maneuvers, which are discussed by the priority literature in great detail,[46] long before the possibility of equally complicated physical maneuvers (experimentation) have begun to interest the human mind in any effective way.

Ramus, as Nancel had said, found trouble when thinking through complex situations in order to come to the point, and the priorities tangle was just such a situation and one which was to prove particularly disastrous because of a further complexity beyond that of the priorities themselves. The Aristotelian axiomatics involves two series: a series of syllogisms (in which the axioms proper occur), and a series of single terms. It is not always easy to say which Aristotle or the commentators are talking about, and sometimes they were not so sure themselves,[47] especially since the terms tended to be considered not as simple terms but as predicates integrated into enunciations and thereby into syllogisms. The working back from the order of our knowledge to the order of nature is effected, or at least discussed, largely by working on individual terms or concepts themselves. Since these are treated in a terminology of genus and species, the whole of Aristotelian axiomatics is shot through with talk about genus and species. Further complication arises because there is a loose resemblance between an axiom standing at the head of a reasoning process and a genus standing at the head of a number of species — particularly if one is inclined, as were Ramus and many of his contemporaries, to form concepts of the mental processes themselves in terms of simple visual or spatial analogies. Aristotle exploits this resemblance and sometimes confuses the reader with it. Ramus will be completely taken in by it, with significant results.

Before considering these results, it would be well to point out that in the perspectives established by the massive priority literature in which demonstration was commonly set, syllogistic reasoning is less a way of or a substitute for discovery than a sequel of and complement to it. To some extent in Aristotle himself, and to a greater extent in the commentaries, discovery of first principles tends to be assimilated to the *via inventionis* and thus to the topical tradition and to dialogue as represented in dialectic, whereas demonstration is the *via iudicii*, in the sense of a check-up operation verifying the results of invention,[48] or testing by means of syllogism (a notion which Ramus would exploit wildly). Demonstrative ratiocination follows as a further step after the inventive process and is thus an ordering of items discovered in such a way as to produce intelligibility, to illuminate discovery and explain it.

In this tradition, when demonstration is regarded as a way of discovering rather than of illuminating something, it is regularly so regarded *less in a scientific than in a didactic framework.* The conclusion of the syllogism was often nothing new to the investigator — it was rather what he started with. It was new *only to the pupil in the classroom,* who learned without investigating. Thus in Ramus' age and even much earlier, *specialization in syllogisms is regularly evidence less of a scientific mind,* well led or misled, *than of a basically didactic mind and a didactic framework for thought.*

The search for principles which make it possible to construct a demonstration showing the cause or reason for a fact involves, of course, the basic problem of scientific method. For, how can one give conscious direction to a search for something when one does not know what one is looking for, for the good reason that one has never seen or otherwise attained to it? Given the fact that certain celestial bodies do not twinkle, how does one know where to go from there? Must the discovery of the reason be always a haphazard process, or is it possible to give it conscious direction, to work out in advance some sort of consciously directed "way through" (*methodus*) leading to the principles desired? Aristotle thought that it was possible, taking the position that the fact to be explained somehow or other must contain the principles or causes which explained it, so that, in possessing the fact, the mind possessed the principles also, in an obscure or implicit fashion. Thus it could really orient itself toward these principles, although with great difficulty, since they were not disengaged, but hidden in their concrete, factual setting.

Aristotle devotes most of the *Posterior Analytics* and much of other works, such as the *Physics* and the beginning of the *Nicomachean Ethics,* to a consideration of the peculiar difficulties here. His discussion is involved, since the principles he is looking for are both enunciations (formulations similar to what we should today call "laws") and definitions (single terms broken down into their constituent elements). It is often difficult to tell whether he is speaking of one or the other or of both together.[49] In his view, apparently both would be arrived at by some sort of inductive process; that is, by an ascent from experience of singulars to universal principles.[50] At the top of this ascent (*ascensus* in the Latin commentators) are the axioms or "dignities" (*dignitates*) so-called because they are the highest, most unexceptionable, enunciations on which conclusions depend. The complicated question concerning the relationship of the axioms of metaphysics to those of other sciences, not to mention the still more annoying question about just what the axioms of a metaphysics really are, can be skirted here. This last question can be disengaged from the writings of some theologian-philosophers, such as St. Thomas Aquinas, but the role of metaphysics, or "first philosophy" is less well worked out among the mass of scholastic philosophers.

Because these views of Aristotle on demonstration concern the whole field of knowledge and admit of application in all sorts of ways, it is too much to hope that centuries of commentary could have reproduced his original thought undeveloped or undistorted, even had it been less tentative and circumspect than it actually is. In particular, the diagrammatic notions of ascent (*ascensus*) and descent (*descensus*) proved confusing, since they suggest that the deduction, by which one operates with general principles is the exact opposite of the induction by which one "ascends" to them — which, of course, it is not. Moreover, the very same process could be likened under one aspect to an ascent, and under another to a descent, so that these two diametrically opposed terms might be employed to designate exactly the same thing. Thus Digby and Temple will have difficulty in settling whether analysis is *ascensus* or *descensus*, Digby, according to Temple, holding that it was the latter.[51]

There were further confusions. Galen's three *doctrinae*, analysis, synthesis, and dismemberment or definition, had been taken from the prologue of his *Medical Art* and brought to bear on Aristotle's *methodus* after this had been processed in medieval usage and had come to designate a *doctrina* or curriculum subject. Ramus' opponent, Schegk, would have to make a special issue of the fact that for Aristotle *methodus* does not mean a curriculum subject or science (*scientia* — in ordinary usage, roughly equivalent to *ars* and *doctrina*), but rather the way (*via*) or grounds (*ratio*) of science.[52]

In the tenth century, an Arabic commentator on Galen had already identified the first two of Galen's "doctrines" or "methods" respectively with Aristotle's demonstration of a fact and demonstration from cause, and the result had been still further complicated and refined by a threefold distinction advanced by Averroës in his *Prohemium* to his commentary on Aristotle's *Physics*.[53] Averroës here treats of *demonstratio simpliciter* or demonstration of the cause and of being, in which, as in mathematics, the causes are first both for us and for nature; a *demonstratio propter quid* or demonstration from cause, in which we start from what is first in nature but not for us; and demonstration of being or of sign, in which we start from effects to arrive at causes.

The problems of Aristotelian axiomatics were set within Aristotle's still more inclusive view of scientific knowledge as having to do with the universal.[54] The universality which science seeks makes it move away from the singular instances presented by the senses to generalizations which cover many instances. This movement toward the universal can be observed in the search for axioms, but it is conceived of by Aristotle largely in terms of his predicamental theory. "I call universal that which is *said* of all (κατὰ παντός, *de omni*, *du tout*) and of each essentially (καθ' αὐτό, *per se*, *par soi*), and universally (or "catholicly," καθόλου πρῶτον, *de universali*, *universel premièrement*).[55] In keeping with his general orientation, Aristotle is not thinking primarily of universal "ideas" or "things," or even of universal concepts *tout court*, for he is implicitly excluding concepts in one of their possible functions as subjects of enunciations. As has been explained in Chapter V, he is thinking primarily of universal predicates or categories, what is "said of" a subject, and of the condition of universality itself as constituted primarily in predicates and by means of predication or categorizing — not in the sense of classifying, but in the sense of *crying out* against, *accusing* a subject. The basic imagery here is auditory, not visual. With the laws of Ramist method, such orientation will be changed.

7. RAMUS ON METHOD: SCIENCE GOES TOPICAL

Ramus' first treatment of method as such occurs in the exceedingly rare edition of his *Training in Dialectic* which appeared pseudonymously in 1546 as *Three Commentaries on Dialectic Published under the Authorship of Omer Talon (Dialectici commentarii tres authore Audomaro Talaeo editi)*. This revision appeared during the period when Ramus was forbidden to teach or lecture on philosophy and was therefore taking up mathematics and Cicero. The Talon *Training in Oratory*, in which Ramus almost surely had some sort of hand, had appeared the year before. Ramus inserts his remarks on method at the end of book II, which treats the second part of the art of dialectic, disposition. He gives no source for what he has to say, other than a vague reference to Plato among his concluding remarks. The passage on method runs, in translation, as follows:

METHOD: FIRST, METHOD OF TEACHING

Method is the arrangement of many good arguments. It is twofold, method of teaching and method of prudence. Not that both kinds do not make use of prudence, but rather that the latter has almost no training or art in it, depending merely on man's natural judgment and prudence.

The method of teaching, therefore, is the arrangement of various things brought down from universal and general principles to the underlying singular parts, by which arrangement the whole matter can be more easily taught and apprehended. In such method, this alone has to be prescribed: that in teaching the general and universal explanations precede, such as the definition and a kind of general summary; after which follows the special explanation by distribution of the parts; last of all comes the definition of the singular parts and clarification by means of suitable examples.

To say this more simply, I shall use a familiar example. Let us suppose that all the rules, definitions, and divisions of grammar have been ascertained, that all the examples used in grammar have been found, and that all these things have been truly and correctly "judged." Let us suppose that all these prescriptions are written out, each on a separate little ticket, and all of these thoroughly mixed in an urn, as for a game of *blanque*. Now I ask what part of dialectic would teach me how to put together all these mixed-up precepts and to reduce them to order. There is no need here of dialectical invention to discover the precepts, for all have been found and all the parts tested and judged. There is no need here of syllogism, because what is true here is already understood. Therefore method and a sure way of arrangement alone is required, and art (*doctrina*) shows us the one simple method which locates the universal and general things first, then the special and secondary afterwards. Let our dialectician, then, by the light of method first pick out from the urn the definition of grammar, because nothing in all these prescriptions is more general, and set it in the first place. Grammar is the art of speaking well and of writing well. Next let him look for the parts of grammar in the same urn and locate them in the second step, after the universal definition. The parts of grammar are four: orthography, etymology, syntax, and prosody. Then let him separate out the definition of these parts . . . .[56]

Although Ramus' example here is from the art of grammar, he sees this method as operating in all discourse, whether it is concerned with the arts or not. He turns immediately to an example of Cicero's use of such method:

In the disputation cited above [*De natura deorum*], Cicero divides the summary which he has given as follows: "Our friends will divide this entire investigation of ours concerning the immortal gods into four parts in all. First, they will show that the gods exist, then what sort of beings they are, next that the world is administered by them, and finally that they take into account human affairs."[57]

Ramus goes on to explain the second kind of method:

THE METHOD OF PRUDENCE

We must go on to the method of prudence, which advises about disposition according to the condition of persons, things, times, and places. For, although the way and notion of disposition mentioned above is most true and apt, nevertheless one must be cautioned that there is not always place for what is best, and that such clarity of disposition cannot always be maintained, since frequently enough the audience is sluggish, the matter to be explained disagreeable, the time not suitable, the place strange. Hence it is advisable to employ prudence in invention and syllogism when dealing with this difficulty, so as to see what is expedient. For, over and above the foregoing rule of wisdom [apparently the "method of teaching"], no arrangement of this infinite variety of things common to all persons, questions, places, and times can be given. The nature of all persons is not the same: so many different heads, so many different senses, the state of affairs not the same for all, so that persons often completely change in a matter of minutes . . . . Sometimes one has to teach persons who do not want to be taught. Therefore, the summary of the matter, its definition, and the distribution of its parts has to be disguised . . . . Cicero has much to say in praise of this sort of prudence in his *Second Oration on the Farm Laws* . . . . Sometimes, for example, Terence's Thais puts last what, if no emotional consideration stood in the way, should have been put first . . . . Thus Virgil snatches Aeneas out of Sicily, has him talking in the middle of the story about past occurrences, and brings in the conclusion confused by various events.[58]

Concluding his treatment of method with a *peroratio* — a piece of equipment imported from the oration into an "art" in the case of Rudolph Agricola's *Dialectical Invention* which Ramus is here completing — Ramus makes it clear that the "method of teaching" (which he here fathers on Plato) is to be preferred to the "method of prudence" wherever possible:

PERORATION ON METHOD

On this account, it will be advisable for one treating of important and complicated matters to attend to these ways of dialectical method, and especially when there is question of teaching serious matters of some sort of moral import to those willing to learn. It seemed so valuable to Plato that he considered it a discovery not of men but of the gods, and decided that he alone on whose teaching this light had shone could really be said to be eminent as a true philosopher. But if at any time the approach to this route consciously cultivated according to the rules of art (*artificiosi*) be blocked, then one should make another road for native genius and prudence, and make use of every help which nature, custom, practice, and life provide, since one is deprived of art (*doctrina*), and thus, although one be tossed about in the ocean by a storm, since one cannot hold to the right course, one will change sail, and, with the aid of whatever wind is blowing, bring the ship safely to port.[59]

This dialectic which terminates in "method" ends where it began, in an approach to knowledge limited by what is implied originally in the metaphor of the topics. The lottery operation with the little tickets reminds us of Melanchthon's description of method and of Agricola's description of the loci or places. Ramus is occupied with the same "infinite variety of things" and with cutting a road through the confusion in which they exist. Although his metaphor shifts beneath him and he finds himself steering a ship through the storm, Ramus persists here in regarding the order in teaching, and through this, all intellectual order, as reducible by rough analogy to some simple spatial arrangement or rearrangement of intellectual atoms.

This initial incursion into method took place when the Ramus-Talon team was preoccupied with rhetoric. The unsophisticated psychology which Ramus here propounds might do for a time in a nonphilosophical, rhetorical frame of reference. It had sufficed for Melanchthon and for Sturm. But Melanchthon was in far-off Germany, and Sturm, after a stay in Paris long enough to induce him to transplant "method" from rhetoric into dialectic, had retired to the Rhineland once more. Moreover, neither the footloose humanist Reformer nor the Strasbourg printer turned schoolmaster was a university man in the sense that Ramus was. Ramus was sponsoring his method in the very heart of Paris scholasticism, where psychological speculation, if sometimes overly formal and mechanistic, was nevertheless far too sophisticated to be much taken with Agricola's receptacles or Ramus' lottery urn.

The result was inevitable. The attacks on his method draw Ramus into the maelstrom of dispute concerning the internal structure of sciences and the ground of axiomatic reasoning grown out of, around, and back into scholastic logic and, to some extent, physics. In the 1553 edition of Ramus' *Remarks on*

Aristotle, books IX and X, which treat of the *Posterior Analytics* and hence of the structure of science, are radically revised.[60] In the 1555 *Dialectique* and all subsequent revisions of the *Dialectic*, axiomatics is leaving definite traces on Ramus' original nonaxiomatic "method." In 1556, books IX and X of the *Remarks on Aristotle* are reworked once again, and in 1557 the section on method from book IX is separately printed under the title, *The One and Only Method for Setting Forth All Subjects* (*Quod sit unica doctrinae instituendae methodus*).

But Ramus was having trouble in squaring science theory with his original method, and after Talon's death in 1562, he rewrote Talon's commentary on his *Dialectic*, importing into it, in still further revised form, material on method (and much else) from the *Remarks on Aristotle* — material which is thus now fathered on Talon! In the 1569 edition of the *Remarks on Aristotle*, now styled *Lectures on Dialectic* (*Scholae dialecticae*), the section on method is amputated, and the reader referred to "Talon's" commentary on the *Dialectic*, which in the 1569 edition is once again revised, in text and commentary. Schegk's attack on Ramist method followed, and in the 1572 revision of the *Dialectic*, published just before his death, Ramus wipes the slate clean by eliminating all of "Talon's" commentary and revising the section on method in the text of the *Dialectic* itself still more. New commentary would no doubt have followed had Ramus but lived longer, but what it would have said, no one knows.

Because Ramus' career was so tragically cut short, two final versions of method are bequeathed to his followers: 1) the final *explanation* of method, which is basically a section of the 1557 *Remarks on Aristotle* refurbished and finally fitted into the commentaries of "Talon" in the 1569 *Dialectic*; and 2) the final *statement* regarding method, which in the 1572 revision supplanted all earlier explanation, but was itself never explained. Both traditions make their way into English, the former in Roland M'Kilwein's translation of the *Dialectic*, the latter in Robert Fage's, and both are perpetuated in reprintings and adaptations through the massive and more important Latin tradition.

Ramus' shifts in his treatment of method after 1546 show in fascinating detail the vulgarization of science and priority theory as this is fitted to the procrustean bed of a dialectic manual. In 1555, Ramus has reworked his notion of method in terms of priority by nature (*notiora natura, notiora simpliciter*) and priority in knowledge (*notiora nobis*), identifying the order in his method with the former:

> Methode est disposition par laquelle entre plusieurs choses la premiere de notice est disposee au premier lieu, la deuziesme au deuzisme, la troiziesme au troiziesme, et ainsi consequemment.[61]

He adds immediately a remark which shows that in the tradition of which he is the heir and spokesman, *méthode* signifies primarily a curriculum subject and, by extension, any treatise (*dispute*) on any matter, so that, by implication, his prescriptions for method are those that must obtain in the teaching of any discipline: "Ce nom [i.e., méthode] signifie toute discipline & dispute, neantmoins communement est pris pour adresse & abbregement de chemin."[62]

By 1569, in the final edition of the *Dialectic* complete with commentary, Ramus' method has become entirely laid over with science and axiomatics theory:

Method is disposition by which, out of many homogeneous enunciations, each known by means of a judgment proper to itself [i.e., the way an axiom is known, without dependence on syllogisms] or by the judgment of syllogism, that enunciation is placed first which is first in the absolute order of knowledge, that next which is next, and so on: and thus there is an unbroken progression from universals to singulars. By this one and only way one proceeds from antecedents entirely and absolutely known to the declaration of unknown consequents. This is the only method that Aristotle teaches.[63]

In place of the separate "little tickets" containing definitions and divisions, we have now enunciations, for these are the component parts of syllogisms, with which axiomatic systems are concerned. Moreover, instead of mere progression from the definition to its parts, thence to their definitions and the parts of these definitions, down to the ultimate "singulars," we have here a progression from "antecedents" to "consequents." But, interwoven with this, we have also the original progression from general to special, "from universals to singulars." Ramus is attempting, in fact, to amalgamate the two things, his topical approach to classification which deals in terms only of a crude spatial imagery, and the abstruse and highly technical discussion concerning the internal structure and economy of a strict science with which he proves quite incapable of dealing. When he "illustrates" by example what he means by method — it is, primarily, the old business of the arts or curriculum subjects again, with a few expressions from the axiomatic and "priorities" tradition tipped in:

The chief examples of method are in the arts. Here, although all the rules are general and universal, nevertheless there are grades among them, insofar as the more general a rule is, the more it precedes. Those things are most general in position and first in order which are first in luminosity and knowledge; the subalterns follow, because they are next clearest; and thus those things are put down first which are by nature better known (*natura notiora*), the less known are put below, and finally the most special are set up. Thus the most general definition will be first, distribution next and, if this latter is manifold, division into integral parts comes first, then division into species. The parts and species are then treated respectively in this same order in which they are divided. If this means that a long explanation intervenes, then when taking up the next part or species, the whole structure is to be knit back together by means of some transition. This will refresh the auditors and amuse them [!]. However, in order to present things more informally, some familiar example should be used.[64]

Ramus' "familiar example" which follows is none other than that of grammar, cited almost verbatim as it was given originally in 1546 and 1555.

Under the impact of the axiomatic tradition, the "rules" of grammar have become more like rules. Heretofore, they have been definitions and divisions — terms broken down into their essential parts and other parts. Now they are thought of as cast in propositions, from which they can be readily recast into real directives — although this recasting never occurs (except in some isolated instances, such as the second and abortive part of rhetoric, Ramist arts contain few real directives, for these are apparently generated in connection with "use").

Although he is trying to think in terms of enunciations, Ramus is having an obviously hard time making grammar unfold itself as a deductive process starting from the definition of the art as an axiom or first, self-evident premise. Even granted that the definition of the art were such an "axiom," how one knows what the parts of the art are remains here and elsewhere a complete mystery. Indeed, whereas in 1546 Ramus had asserted that the parts of grammar were four, he now asserts with the same aplomb that they are two, etymology, and syntax, each of these, as we learn from consulting the later editions of his *Latin Grammar* being in turn dichotomized to yield the original four, but at one remove.

Unabashed, and relying on the more or less tacit identification of speech with teaching common in the classical and medieval heritage, Ramus goes on to extend this science theory gone topical from the curriculum subjects themselves to any and all discourse:

> But Method is used not only in the matter of arts and curricular subjects (*artium et doctrinarum*), but in every matter which we wish to teach easily and clearly. Thus the poets, orators, and all writers whatsoever, whenever they set out to teach their auditors, follow this way, although they do not always start out this way or follow this way everywhere. In the *Georgics*, Virgil distributes the material he has set down in four parts, as I have said before: in book I, he takes up the things common to all, as astrology and meteorology, and then goes on to grass and grass cultivation . . . ; in book II . . . he writes of trees in general and then of vines in particular. He uses a second and imperfect transition to begin book III about bovines, horses, sheep, goats, and dogs . . . ; at the beginning of book IV, the third transition . . . is again imperfect, with just one proposition [= first antecedent in a syllogism] about bees [the imperfection exists because something general is not treated] . . . .
>
> Orators use this order in the proem, narration, confirmation, and peroration, and call it the order of art, the order of nature, or the order of the thing (*res*) . . . .[65]

"Poor Virgil," mocks Jean Riolan, "who never set out to 'prove' anything at all!"[66]

By the time of the final revision of the *Dialectic* in 1572 (the one never equipped with commentary), the scientific trappings of method have become still more flamboyant:

Method is the intelligible order (*dianoia*) of various homogeneous axioms ranged one before the other according to the clarity of their nature, whereby the agreement of all with one another is judged and the whole committed to memory. As in the axiom one considers truth and falsity, and in the syllogism consequence or lack of consequence, so in method one sees to it that what is of itself clearer (*per se clarius*) precedes, and what is more obscure follows, and that the order and confusion in everything is judged. Thus among homogeneous axioms that is put first which is first in absolute signification (*absoluta notatione*), that second which is second, that third which is third, and so on. Thus method proceeds without interruption from universals to singulars. By this one and only way one proceeds from antecedents entirely and absolutely more known to the clarification (*ad . . . declarandum*) of unknown consequents. And Aristotle teaches this one and only method.[67]

This passage involves Ramus' three laws of method, which will come in for special treatment later and which help to explain what Ramus means by "homogeneous." But it involves several other shifts of focus, the first of which is the substitution of the term *dianoia* for *dispositio*. The substitution is more decorative than functional, but it does attest the fact that the dispute with Schegk and perhaps other events had forced Ramus to think somewhat more of intelligibility as such and less of mere "arrangement."

The new accent on "clarity" is noteworthy in this pre-Cartesian age. The quest for clarity here reveals its rhetorical, rather than logical, inspiration. It is a compromise product, born of the attempt to amalgamate the topical and the scientific traditions under the pressure of practical pedagogy. Science theory had been interested in what was in itself better known (*per se notius*) rather than in what was of itself clearer (*per se clarius*), although the latter expression occurs sporadically in late discussion of the priorities. Ramus is having some difficulty convincing his readers that the definition of grammar, which precedes in his method, is in itself better known than the partition of grammar, which follows, and so with the other items in his elaborate sequences of ideas. It will be easier to settle for something less than "of itself more *known*." Let the definition be "of itself *clearer*." The term is a diplomatic one, skirting the knotty question of knowledge. What is "clearer" for pupils is, in practice, simply what one can make "work" when one is teaching them. Ramus and Ramists, in one way or another, could make their presentation of the arts work. From here one could readily leap to the conclusion that the presentation proceeded from what was "clearer" *of itself* or "in the nature of things" and thereby "more known." To prove this conclusion was a difficult business and best not attempted. One simply supposed that "clarity" (more or less as measured in the classroom) and intelligibility were one. Thus was the ground being prepared for the Cartesian venture.

As he slips into use of the term "clearer," so Ramus in this same final 1572 revision slips also into a new use of the term *axioma*, and employs it to designate any and all enunciations:

An axiom is the arrangement of an argument with another argument, whereby something is judged to be or not to be. In Latin it is called a thing enunciated, an enunciation, a thing pronounced, a pronouncement, or an assertion.[68]

Ramus' shift to *axioma* from *enuntiatio* (his earlier term after 1543, for at first he had simply neglected to treat the matter) sometimes worried his followers. Thus Friedrich Beurhaus wonders why Ramus finally hit on *axioma* when Aristotle does not use the term the way Ramus uses it here and Cicero does not use it at all. Beurhaus' suggested answer is admittedly feeble: other terms would have been too ambiguous or would have been grammatical rather than logical.[69] In his painstaking explanation Beurhaus does not bring in the fact that the Stoic logicians, as well as some of the Renaissance writers such as Melanchthon, had used the term *axioma* in the general sense of enunciation or statement.[70] This fact, indeed, seems of little import in Ramus' case, since, if Ramus picked up the term directly or indirectly from Stoic sources, it plainly occasions no change in the established economy of his thought, any more than his use of *dianoia* does, but is simply a kind of learned décor. With this term inserted inexplicably in the Ramist topical apparatus in the name of method, a curious confusion results: it is suggested that any statement (*axioma* in the Stoic sense) was a starting point for scientific demonstration (*axioma* in the more usual sense). This is part of the story back of that puzzling phenomenon in the Ramist apparatus which has lately been named the "detached axiom."[71]

In the English versions of Ramus' *Dialectic* based on the 1572 text, such as that by Robert Fage, the two terms in question here are rendered by the cognate forms "dianoia" and "axiom" respectively, so that Ramus' usage seems at this point to have invaded the English language.

8. METHOD IN REVERSE: THE PRUDENCE OF POETS, ORATORS, AND HISTORIANS

Ramus' initial treatment of method in 1546 had distinguished a method of teaching and a method of prudence, a distinction which is kept in the 1555 *Dialectique*.[72] By 1569, having wrestled with the axiomatics question and with such opponents as Charpentier, Turnèbe, and Schegk, Ramus shifts his ground. In place of two methods, we find now only one, called simply "method,"[73] but divided into two separate uses: the one in the arts, and the other in the poets, orators, and historians. However, the two "uses" are in reality quite the same as the original two methods, and present the same difficulties. They seem at times to coincide with one another because Ramus is constantly implying that all discourse does, after all, inevitably follow the classroom model. At other times, they seem so far apart that it appears impossible to call the method of prudence, or the "use" to which poets, orators, historians, and such lightfingered gentry are addicted, by the name "method" at all.

Ramus himself senses the difficulty when, by 1569, he begins to treat this latter procedure as "dissimulation in method" (*de crypticis methodi*), styling it also simply dissimulation (*crypsis*), imperfect method, and word-reversal (*hysterologia*):

> Thus when a thing is to be taught perspicuously (*perspicue*), the method will consist in various homogeneous enunciations, each known in itself or by a syllogism. But when the auditor is to be deceived by pleasure or in some other way, some of these homogeneous items have to be put aside, such as the great luminosities of definition, partitions, and transitions, for certain heterogeneous things, such as digressions from the matter and delaying over the matter. But most of all, the order of things from the beginning has to be reversed, and antecedents have to be put after consequents.[74]

He adds further:

> This is what the poet does as a major part of his tactics, when he sets out to sway the people, the many-headed monster. He deceives (*decipit*) in all sorts of ways. He starts in the middle, often proceeding thence to the beginning, and getting on to the end by some equivocal and unexpected dodge (*incerto aliquo et inopinato casu*). Thus, as Horace observes, Homer arranges the *Iliad* . . . .

The uncomplimentary view which Ramus takes of the "people" here is also extended to the poets, orators, and historians, for these all have as their chief objective not teaching, but delighting and moving.[75] This qualifies them as deceivers — a thought which Ramus' Puritan followers would relish — not because they do not teach, for it is impossible for them or anyone to speak without teaching, but because they do so in such a roundabout and underhand way. They "ambush" their audience into drawing conclusions which the audience has no inclination to draw.[76] To this mind, the more flowery delights of poetry, of oratory (other than plain-style or didactic oratory), and of history, were inevitably an insult to the audience, whom Ramus regularly thinks of in this as the enemy (*adversaires*) and as *cault et fin*.[77] One becomes a poet, orator, or historian only as a last resort, when one despairs of teaching in any other way. With this view goes Ramus' persuasion that poetry is something definitely childish because its logic is spread thin, so that it can be taught to those whose tender years make it impossible for them to bear the impact of more "solid" logic.[78]

Theories involving probable logics had allowed for poets, orators, historians and others to work from premises acknowledged as less than certain, and leading to only probable conclusions. Not admitting the existence of anything less than certainty, Ramus has to explain how auditors can be brought to an absolutely certain conclusion unawares. His explanation of the maneuvers necessary is couched almost exclusively in concepts based on local motion: digressions (stepping aside), delaying (not "covering ground"), reversals of the order of things, putting antecedents after consequents. When he states that the poet deceives "in all sorts of ways," the "all sorts of ways" turns out to be simply one way, conceived as another variation in local motion: starting in the middle, going from there back to the beginning, dodging unexpectedly to the end. In fact, it seems to Ramus, musing method-wise over Horace, that the characteristic of poetry is its starting in the middle (*in medias res*).[79] Similarly, the characteristic mark of oratory is its way of lobbing into the audience an irregular succession of fast and slow missiles.[80]

This specialization in geometrical or mechanical imagery throughout his explanation of method hints at perhaps the principal reason why Ramus had eschewed the probable logics. In the simple directional plotting on a plane surface which lies at the base of all his organized thinking, they could not be represented. Here one can picture forward motion and its reversal, but since he has endorsed his picture of forward motion as the only method, Ramus has ultimately to admit that this word-reversal (*hysterologia*), another of his names for *crypsis* or dissimulation in method, is really a perversion of method.[81]

A further difficulty which Ramus encounters is that of differentiating his method of prudence, or dissimulation of method, from rhetoric. Ramus employs a little dissimulation himself in trying to establish this differentiation:

In brief, all the tropes and figures of elocution and all the graces of action, which together make up the whole of true rhetoric, *a separate thing from dialectic*, serve no other purpose than that of pulling along the troublesome and mulish auditor whom we have to deal with, through this method [of prudence], and they are observed for no other reason than his obstinacy and perversity, as Aristotle teaches truly in the third book of his *Rhetoric*. Thus we see how this method of prudence has been taught and practiced by philosophers, poets, and orators.[82]

Here Ramus' insistence that the art of rhetoric is "a separate thing from dialectic" seems to be one more instance of the lady who doth protest too much. For the tropes, figures, elocution, and "action," which together constitute the whole of the Ramist rhetoric, are here totally assimilated by the "method of prudence" which forms a part of Ramus' dialectic, and a part betraying with particular recalcitrancy the rhetorical bent of this dialectic.

9. RAMUS ON THE PRIORITIES

As Ramus' notion of method reproduces vestiges of the axiomatics tradition within its originally topical formulation, it necessarily engages the priorities question deriving chiefly from Aristotle's *Posterior Analytics*. In the famous excerpt which was published in 1557 from book IX of the 1556 revision of his *Remarks on Aristotle*, and in which the quintessence of Ramist teaching on method is distilled, Ramus begins by quoting the passage from Aristotle on which the priorities question turns:

Things are prior and more known in two ways, for to be prior by nature (*prius natura*) is not the same as to be prior with regard to us (*ad nos prius*), and to be more knowable or informative by nature (*notius natura*) is not the same as to be more knowable and informative for us here and now (*nobis notius*). I style prior and more informative with regard to us what is closer to the senses; prior and more informative absolutely speaking, what is further removed from the senses. However, what is most universal is most remote, whereas what is singular is nearest; and these are opposed to one another.[83]

The general bearing of Aristotle's thought here has already been explained. It remains to see what the Ciceronian[84] Ramus makes of it. The present summary of his views expressed in 1556–1557 represents also, in the large, his stand from at least 1553 to 1569.

The opposition, Ramus announces, which Aristotle proposes here between *prius natura* and *ad nos prius*, and between *notius natura* and *nobis notius*, reduces to the simple opposition between genus and species, which itself is nothing more than the opposition between the universal and singular.[85] In the *Categories* Aristotle had mentioned five priorities, explains Ramus, that of time (*tempore*), spatial sequence (*consecutione*), rank (*ordine*), nature (*natura*), and cause (*caussa*), but the last four are really all the same thing, so that all these priorities reduce to priority of time and priority of nature.[86] Ramus comes to this conclusion without really entering at all into the concepts he is dealing with but simply by citing Aristotle, in random passages tendentiously chosen, as an authority in support of his equations (perish all thought of Ramus as a practicing "anti-authoritarian"). The priority of time is, of course, priority *ad nos*, and thus we are back again to the one opposition *prius natura — ad nos prius*.

In terms of this opposition, according to Ramus, the psychological process is always the exact converse of the ontological reality. We start from individuals, moving up one by one through higher and higher species to the genus (Ramus has by this time more or less abandoned his earlier assertion that individuals were "species," although it has left a permanent mark on his thinking). Thus species are always learned earlier in time than genera.[87] But the time involved in mounting from species to genera is short indeed, for children, being exercised in singulars, zoom directly up to genera — Ramus is obviously still half convinced here that there are only individuals and genera — "like eagles to the sun," as Philoponus hints, borrowing from Aristotle.[88] Thanks to this quick ascent, whereas at the beginning singulars are better known to children, now the universals suddenly become better known to them.[89] This conditioning for apprehension in terms of universals or "generals" can be effected permanently and at a tender age, for a child has arrived at this stage when he reacts to a distant object by recognizing it first as some kind of animal (because it is moving), then as a man, then as Plato, proceeding from the more known to the less known — an example which Ramus cites from Aristotle's *Physics*.[90] The ordinary child comes with no difficulty to this point, whereupon *all* universals are more known to him (*notiora nobis*) than are nonuniversals. If he is slow, all one need do is give him a few examples, which will soon clear things up for him.[91] Once the child is confirmed in this outlook, the whole priorities question becomes nugatory, for at this point what are *priora natura* are also *ad nos priora*, what are *notiora natura* are *nobis notiora*.[92]

This sleight-of-hand reduction of all priority to the absolute priority in nature itself will be the foundation of Ramist monomethodology. Here Ramus has effected the reduction by an elaborate, if bogus, description of a child's supposed reactions. As is usual with him, he is carried away by his own eloquence and so convinced by his "explanation" that he elsewhere presents its conclusion supported on even more *simpliste* premises. The order of knowledge will *always* correspond to the order of nature, we are assured, provided only that the mind is really a first-rate one. "As the absolutely good is more known to the good, the absolutely healthy to the healthful, so the absolutely more known (*absolute notiora* [= *natura priora*]) is more known to us if we are mentally well equipped."[93] Having delivered himself of this, Ramus makes haste to attribute the same doctrine to Aristotle. This *simpliste* reduction is capital, because it shows a certain amount of psychology and epistemology being sucked into the quicksand of "method," where Locke was later to find it stogged. Had the architects of the mind been all of the stature of Nicolas of Cusa, Pomponazzi, or Zabarella, the kind of simplifications with which Locke works would hardly have been possible.

Since Ramus blows hot and cold on the priorities issue, he is at times willing to allow that in certain cases it may be impossible to follow the direct route from singulars to what is absolutely prior. In such cases, there is simply no certain method, for, instead of being a solid "body" of knowledge, something continuous (*perpetuus*), our knowledge will be like warts or pockmarks on a body, which never cover the entire surface.[94] Nevertheless, even when things are in this pockmarked state, something can be done to establish the absolute priority necessary. For example, if the definition and division of a genus cannot be arrived at by the direct route, rising to the genus from singulars falling under the genus, it can be reached by a flanking movement, by way of effects, adjuncts, or other arguments which are not causes, and, in this case, the genus, once it is arrived at, has the necessary priority over the things which fall under it. Ramus is here hacking his way through the scholastic discussion concerning demonstration which shows that a thing is so (*demonstratio quia*) and demonstration which shows why a thing is so, also called demonstration from causes (*demonstratio propter quid*). His remarks are so incoherent that any convincing summary will misrepresent them, but their tendency is clear. *Demonstratio propter quid* is, of course, the preferable kind of demonstration, and Ramus is trying to say that, for all practical purposes, *demonstratio quia* can always be reduced to *demonstratio propter quid*, or demonstration from causes — in one way or another. Ramus is at a loss to be very specific about what the ways could be — so much so that when the passage on the priorities from the 1556 and 1557 book IX of the *Remarks on Aristotle* is incorporated into "Talon's" prelections on the 1569 *Dialectic*, much of the passage against which Charpentier and Riolan had directed their attacks simply disappears.

Ramus is at pains to enroll both Plato and Aristotle as sponsors of his notion of method, Plato in *Philebus, Phaedrus,* and *Charmides,* and Aristotle in his *Categories, Topics* (III, vi), *Physics, Metaphysics,* and *Ethics.*[95] At the beginning of the *Nicomachean Ethics,* i — Talon had written a commentary on this, at its opening largely concerned with method — Aristotle seems to advocate a method beginning from *notiora nobis,* but he actually proceeds, Ramus says, quite otherwise in this work, from what is *notiora natura.* This is only to be expected, for there is no other way to organize an art.[96] Galen fares less well than Plato or Aristotle here. Ramus owns that the Greek anatomist is the most important of all commentators on Aristotle's treatment of method — greater than Aspasius and Adrastus, than Alexander of Aphrodisias, than Porphyry, than Ammonius, and the equal of Alexander of Damascus.[97] Nevertheless, he errs in holding sometimes for two methods, as in his interpretation of Hippocrates, and sometimes for three.[98]

10. GALEN AND RAMUS

In developing his notion of method, Ramus refers in a general way to Simplicius and to Galen's work *On the Opinions of Hippocrates and Plato,* but he bases his principal discussion of the problem on the famous opening words of Galen's Prologue to his *Medical Art* which had formed the background of Sturm's observations on method.

Taking up Galen's three "orderly teaching procedures" — *analysis, synthesis* (which, Ramus says, Simplicius calls *genesis*), and the dismemberment of definitions — Ramus pretends that Galen holds that arts are not only "constituted" by analysis, but are also "found" by this process, that is, by reasoning from first principles. He agrees that the arts are "constituted" by this process, if it is identical with what he, Ramus, means by *dispositio* (or arrangement by descent from "genus" to "species" as in a bracketed outline of dichotomies), but he insists that arts are not in the first instance discovered this way, but rather by "ascending" in induction from singulars to the most general.[99]

Galen's *synthesis* is interpreted by Ramus as referring to a movement from the singular to the most general, and thus as coinciding with the induction or ascent by which Ramus insists the arts are found.[100] Galen, says Ramus, believes that this "disposes" the arts, whereas Ramus himself has already made it clear that it is rather analysis which disposes them (provided it be understood in Ramus' way). Moreover, it is fantastic to think that this movement of *synthesis* could be styled *methodus* at all, for it is a movement from the less known to the more known (according to Ramus, the more general is always the more known). Ramus' understanding of what Galen meant by synthesis is badly warped by his own way of reading Galen as though the Hellenic physician were writing a commentary on Ramist dialectic. Other commentators have understood Galen's synthesis as applying to the descent from first principles to a conclusion, and hence as movement quite the opposite of what Ramus takes it to be.[101]

With regard to the third of Galen's so-called methods, the breaking down of definitions, Ramus scorns the idea that such a process could be method, for it is rather the business of method to arrange the definitions and their parts after they have been broken down.[102] The only real method is what Galen (as Ramus understands him) has called analytic, that is, that which disposes the arts (and, by extension, all discourse) in a descent from the most general through the less general to the particular.[103]

Ramus' notion of method is obviously closely connected with the notion of structure. Galen, we are told, is badly confused here and, like Aristotle, erects arts with faulty structure or *commentum*[104] (a cognate of, and synonym for, *commentitium*). What is more, Ramus adds when he incorporates these remarks in revised form into the prelections of his 1569 *Dialectic*, the method by which the arts are discovered is not really method at all (which belongs to the second part of dialectic) since discovery has all been taken care of in the first part of dialectic, invention, for "the art of discovering both the arts and absolutely all other things whatsoever is the first part of logic."[105] In exactly the reverse order from that in which they are found, the arts are taught by descent from the general to singulars,[106] for Ramus belongs to the strictly amateur school of logicians who picture induction and deduction simply as reciprocal movements, not as radically different kinds of psychological performances irreducible to one another.

II. THE THREE LAWS OF METHOD

From Aristotle's *Posterior Analytics*, most likely with the help of Renaissance works on axiomatics and even of schoolboys' manuals such as Caesarius' *Dialectic*, Ramus draws the three laws of method which the scholarly Schegk calls Ramus' "little ditty"[107] about the predicaments and which Bacon says were Ramus' forte.[108] Until Wilbur Samuel Howell's *Logic and Rhetoric in England, 1500–1700*, which notes the presence of the laws in Aristotle and in medieval logicians such as Vincent of Beauvais, recent studies of Ramus have commonly proceeded as though the laws were entirely Ramus' own invention. As they stand in Aristotle,[109] the "laws" are three phrases occurring in a complicated discussion concerning syllogistic demonstration. What Ramus did was to lift the phrases out of their context, fix them in his "little ditty," as Schegk said, and weave them first about the arts or curriculum subjects and then about all discourse indiscriminately. His followers would take the laws seriously and regard their violation as something less than fair play. "It is not quite *kata pantos*," says the Dutchman Rudolph Snel van Roijen, "that multiplication should be multiple addition, for one plus one is two, whereas one times one is only one."[110]

The laws are referred to by Ramus and the Ramists variously. Ranged under the respective laws to which they refer, the terms one encounters[111] are as follows:

FIRST LAW	SECOND LAW	THIRD LAW
Lex de omni or *lex kata pantos* (κατὰ παντός — can be rendered roughly, "law of universal application")	*Lex per se* or *lex kath' hauto* (καθ' αὐτό — can be rendered roughly, "law of essential application")	*Lex de universali* or *lex catholici* or *lex kath' holou* (καθ' ὅλου — can be rendered roughly, "law of total application")
	Lex homogenei (law of homogeneity)	
Lex veritatis (law of truth) or *lex necessariae veritatis* (law of necessary truth)	*Lex iustitiae* (law of justice)	*Lex sapientiae* (law of wisdom)
Lex necessitatis universalis (law of universal necessity)	*Lex necessitatis cognationis* (law of necessary relationship)	*Lex necessitatis proprietatis* (law of necessary association)

The text in Aristotle from which these "laws" are torn concerns the requirements of a middle term in a syllogism which demonstrates not only *that* a thing is so (*demonstratio quia* or ὅτι) but also *why* it is so (*demonstratio propter quid* or διότι, demonstration in terms of causes) in the way explained above.[112] For Aristotle, the first law means that the subject is to be taken in its full extension, the second that the predicate must be referred to the subject essentially, the third that the predicate should not be more extended than the subject is. Involving an insight into predication as a psychological process and being restricted to a limited kind of reasoning, these "laws" require careful handling if they are to make any sense at all. Even in Aristotle's carefully nuanced text, they present a great many difficulties. In Ramus, they serve only for mystification. Following Agricola, Ramus has abandoned, in principle, even the terms of subject and predicate in favor of a view of discourse as an operation with cognitional atoms functioning by analogy with local motion, and, with only this crude mechanism, he sets about applying the "laws" not to demonstrations but to the organization of any and all "arts" or curriculum subjects.

As applied to an art,[113] the first law is said to mean that in any art a statement is to be taken in its full extension, as admitting no restriction or exception. The second law is said to mean that in an art all statements must "join" things necessarily related — cause and effect, subject and proper adjunct, and so on. The third law means that all statements in an art admit of simple logical conversion — a position which equivalently says that all statements in an art are statements of definitions, since universal negative propositions (which also convert this way) are never, or almost never, used by Ramists in an art.

But all statements in a Ramist art are not definitions, for to the statement incorporating the definition of dialectic or grammar, Ramus adds other statements to the effect that the parts of dialectic are invention and judgment, or the parts of grammar etymology and syntax. Ramus cannot make these Aristotelian laws of axiomatics — and a specialized kind of axiomatics at that — apply to something that is really not axiomatics at all, namely his arts. His "explanation" of the laws is thus covered with layers of large and clumsy patches as it appears in the successive revisions of the *Remarks on Aristotle* and the *Dialectic*.

By 1569, his attempt to make the text of his *Dialectic* work like a concatenation of syllogisms has involved him in a specially rigged terminology which protects him from refutation only by total mystification. He speaks of "the proposition of the definition of the thing defined," of "the proposition of the partition of the thing divided," and of "the proposition of the propriety of the subject" — a "proposition" being, in Ramus' own terminology, the first premise of a syllogism. Ramus thus succeeds in talking about the elements of his arts — definition and partition (or division) — as though they were parts of syllogisms, and he further suggests that the partitions of the art flow from its definition as a kind of property. It is a "property" of dialectic to be divided into invention and judgment.

But this rigged terminology remains no more than that. It does not explain the structure of a Ramist art, which is a series of definitions and divisions having as their real, and practically ultimate, base, classroom practicality. Ramist arts explain little or nothing. Division, like definition, is effected in them not by insight, but by ukase, and the ukase is issued in the name of the visual imagination. What goes is what can be readily and convincingly "pictured" in at least semidiagrammatic form (see Figure XIV).

The haphazard Ramist application of the three laws of method is particularly distressing in the case of the "homogeneity" which Ramus demands for his arts (and ultimately for all discourse in its ideal organization). Aris-

P. RAMI PRO-
FESSIO PHILO,
sophica.

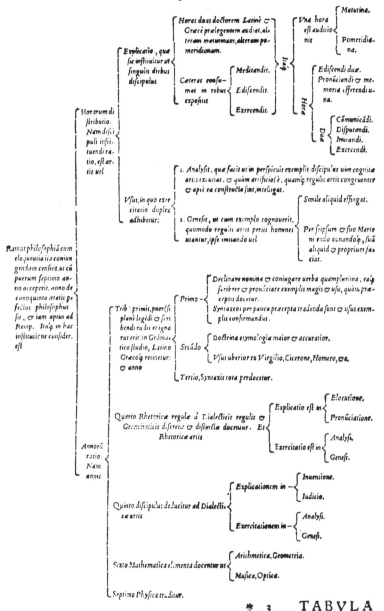

XIV. WHAT IS ART BUT RAMUS METHODIZED? (ED. FREIGE)

totle's "law of homogeneity" had to do with the description of an enunciation.
Ramus transfers it to the description of the whole of an art. Aristotle had
demanded that the predicate be referred to the subject because of *what* the
subject is essentially — as "animal" is referred to man, not as "tall" is referred
to man.[114] Ramus jumps from this meaning of homogeneity to the statement
that the law of homogeneity means that inside any art, "the precepts should
be all of one and the same kind," and that the arts should follow one another
in such a way as to have the more "general" arts first, logic before mathematics, arithmetic before music (i.e., harmonics), and so on.[115] What this being
"of the same kind" comes to can be seen from the fact that Ramus goes on to
insist that in the *Iliad* and the *Aeneid*, no less than in Demosthenes' and
Cicero's orations, all the statements are homogeneous or of the same kind, at
least in looking toward a common end. In fine, the homogeneity which
Ramus demands of an art and of all discourse is nothing more definitive than
what we should call relevance today.

12. HOMOGENEITY AND THE MATTER OF AN ART

Conceived of as "homogeneous bodies" of knowledge which should have
no "warts" or "pockmarks" to mar their "continuous" surfaces,[116] Ramist arts
are constituted of an all but palpable "matter." This matter or material, which
will enter into the development of Ramist and para-Ramist philosophical
"systems" after Ramus' death, is the immediate ground for certain disputes
so intimately connected with Ramus' notions on method just treated that
something must be said about them here.

The disputes break out immediately after Ramus' death and concern the
way in which the elemental theorem of matter and form is to be applied to
a Ramist art. In the most famous of these disputes,[117] Johann Piscator maintains that arguments were the matter of dialectic and disposition the form,[118]
whereas Temple maintained with Ossat that it was the "precepts" (*praecepta*)
which constituted the matter, and method the form.[119] Temple here urges
against Piscator that, since disposition does not apply to invention, it does not
apply to the whole of the art, as it should were it the "form" of the art, whereas
method does apply to invention, as Ramus makes clear. The trouble with
Temple's position is, however, curiously like that which Piscator's creates:
How can method apply to the whole of the art when it, too, is not merely a
part (as disposition also is), but only a part of a part, being a mere subdivision of disposition?

Temple, Piscator, and Ossat — an Englishman, a German, and a Frenchman — together with a great many others, are simply caught in the topical
logic machine which is a Ramist art and Ramist method. In this essentially
spatial economy, "form" is mere grouping of units, all of which are doomed

to be pretty much like one another. Disposition is the grouping of arguments, and method the grouping of groups.

The talk about "rules" is largely irrelevant, for the more one looks for "rules" in the sense of directives — the sense which Ramus and Ramists consistently imply — the less one sees any. Except for the second half of rhetoric and for grammar, Ramist arts consist almost entirely of definitions and divisions of terms. As is apparent in Ramus' wrestling with science theory and axiomatics, the topical economy does not make any effective provision for the difference between terms as units and statements or directives as units. Without regard for what the units are, they are "disposed" on a visual field and visually combined. Grammar is built up from single letters into single syllables (significantly, regarded as *written* items, not as phonemes), thence into single words, and thence into combinations of words, just as geometry is built up from single points into lines, from lines into planes, and from planes into solids.[120] It is difficult, under any circumstances, to formulate meaningfully a question applying the concepts of matter and form to science, but the *simpliste* economy of this mind makes such formulation utterly impossible.

13. ANALYSIS AND GENESIS (SYNTHESIS)

Ramus applies the term analysis not only to his method of disposing the matter of an art, but also to classroom procedure. In this sense, analysis consists of

the examination of our own or others' examples in which invention and composition are to be looked into . . . . In logic, analysis is the marshaling (*examen*) of the argument, enunciation, syllogism, method, in short of the whole art of logic, as is prescribed in the First Book of the *Analytics* [of Aristotle].[121]

The examination here prescribed is conceived in terms of classroom procedure rather than by any obvious connection with Aristotle's *Prior Analytics*. Ramus will describe how it goes forward in the various arts:

Analysis is common to all arts, not proper to one art only, and it is a part of exercise in every art, from the first art to the last . . . .

The grammar teacher . . . sets before his class examples out of Virgil or Cicero, which he unweaves (*retexit*) by analysis and resolves and balances up in terms of the law of the art in question . . . . [Ramus' example which follows here shows that this means simply parsing.]

Rhetorical analysis is the process by which the teacher of rhetoric unweaves the example of ornamented speech which he has presented to his class with the same care into tropes and figures, as he declaims it, bringing out the striking expression in voice and gesture, reminding the pupil of the laws of the art, and asking him whether this gesture or that oral delivery jibes with the rule and decree of the art . . . .

Logical analysis is the process by which a given example of discourse already composed is examined in terms of the laws of the art, the question is extracted, then the invention studied, and the place from which the argument was drawn looked for. This is the analysis of invention. Then the species of propositions used is gone into in the judgment of individual self-evident propositions: whether the simple proposition is common or proper, the composite compound or relative, connective or disjunctive; finally, by what truth whether of science or of opinion it is manifest. Similarly in syllogism and method: in syllogism, how the argument is put together with the parts of the question, in what form or what mode of the form the syllogism is concluded . . . . In method, how the whole universal method, in the case of longer discourse, is arranged: whether definitions, divisions, and illustration by examples proceed downward from what is more general and prior by nature . . . .[122]

Analysis, for Ramus, is thus at root a way of operating didactically upon a text. It belongs not to an art, but to *usus* or exercise,[123] and is complemented by *genesis* or composition, for, once the schoolboy has broken down a sample of discourse — written discourse, for analysis is here growing out of the humanist approach to language through the written word — he can reassemble the parts in configurations of his own, which, according to Ramus, is what one does in composing.

Ramus conceives of genesis, which he also calls *compositio*,[124] as starting with imitation but as moving out from there to greater freedom of expression:

Genesis is not the study of given examples as analysis is, but is rather the making of a new work. This exercise follows the one and the same way of writing and teaching. Now in writing, the first and easiest way is imitation. Hence we must look carefully to whom we imitate . . . But next we must strike out for ourselves, and take our independent arguments from popular daily affairs close to ordinary life; then draw the causes, effects, and other genera of the available arguments from the sources of invention; and finally, make use of all the ways of disposition with equal care, concluding now this way, now that way . . . .[125]

The procedure of which Ramus here speaks is standard Renaissance pedagogy. Of present interest, however, is Ramus' way of representing the practice to himself: genesis is simply the reverse of analysis. Whatever the excellence of the actual practice and of its results, Ramus' abstract description of the process is again little more than a spatial diagram. Composition is not a birth or genesis so much as an assembly-line performance, to which the alternate term synthesis, a "placing together," better applies. Ramus conveys the same outlook to even his earliest followers, such as Francisco Sanchez de las Brozas, who explains that the taking apart of another's work (he is thinking principally of poetry) is simply the opposite of writing a work and is called analysis.[126]

But what did the operation of analysis really produce? By the mid-seventeenth century, Ramists such as Johann Bisterfeld would find that, inspected more closely, Ramist analysis was, in fact, a many-headed monster. It included "real" analysis (*analysis realis*), which works from the single words of a text, resolving them into categories (in the Ramist sense, and thus less categories than topics) and into arts or curriculum subjects, as well as notional or modal analysis (*analysis notionalis seu modalis*). This latter can be either grammatical, rhetorical, or logical. Taking only logical, Bisterfeld finds that it subdivides into thematic, topical, axiomatic, syllogistic, and methodic analysis, which are themselves of various sorts (methodic analysis proceeds by questions: What? Who? How? and so on).[127] Bisterfeld, who in many ways is the Ramist to end all Ramists, finds that "analyzing" means all this in the arts of communication alone, without taking into account the way Ramist analysis can be used in the noncommunicative arts such as arithmetic, geometry, or physics. For to these arts, too, Ramus applies the twin engines of analysis and genesis (or synthesis, his preferred term here), regarding, for example, the "use" of arithmetic as the putting together of numbers which the student had previously shaken loose from some sort of "natural" arithmetical discourse.[128]

Long before Bisterfeld, from Ramus' and others' commentaries and in published classroom performances by students, such as that included in Fraunce's *Lawiers Logike*, it was evident that analysis produced a great variety of things: sometimes an inventory or description of the elements in a given piece of discourse in terms of any or all of the various arts, sometimes a summary or brief, sometimes — quite the contrary — an expansion which details the full syllogistic argumentation which Ramus finds, or believes he finds, compacted and concealed beneath the "ornamentation." Riolan teases Ramus about this "acribological analysis," which sharpens up discourse by supplying the suppressed members of syllogisms, as well as about his analysis by "micrology," which shrinks down inflated discourse, such as Cicero's.[129] Sometimes Ramist analysis produces a commentary which really enriches the text, as Ramus' commentaries on Cicero often do (although there is no real place in the Ramist methodical outlook for such a notion as enrichment). The dichotomized Ramist tables in bracketed outline form, in which the items may be single words or entire sentences and paragraphs, are also the result of analysis, and are often called simply analyses by Ramists, as for example, throughout Marcus Rutimeier's 1617 edition of Ramus' *Dialectic* entitled *The Methodical Idea* (*Idea methodica*). When analysis produces summaries, these summaries are themselves often analyzed, just as analyses are frequently summarized. In a sense, the commentary or explanation or prelection (*explicatio, praelectio, expositio, commentarius, illustratio* are, in Renaissance usage practically synonymous) is itself analysis, or largely so. Applied in another way, analysis can also reduce an oration or any discourse of whatever kind to a simple syllogism, as Ramus does in his edition of Plato's *Letters*, which, its full title tells us, is *Briefly Elucidated with Dialectical Summaries of the Matter:*

The summary of what this [first] letter is about is the following syllogism:
It is dangerous for kings to throw out faithful friends.
King Dionysius threw out his faithful friend Dion.
Therefore it was dangerous for him.[130]

Ramist analysis makes poetry "mean" things of this same sort. If analysis can produce such a syllogism as a summary of any discourse, it can also produce similar syllogisms as partial summaries of bits of the discourse. And so Ramist commentary frequently does. Sometimes, instead of such a summarizing syllogism, we find a kind of inventory styled "dialectical summary":

Dialectical summary (*dialectica summa*) of this letter.
This epistle contains an excuse for the inconsistency which Lentulus and many others had remarked in Cicero because of his return to favor with Caesar, Appius, Vatinius, and Crassus. The leading arguments (*argumenta summa*) of this question are from causes and adjuncts. The causes of the reconciliation are: final, to secure peace, both public, so that discord would not upset the Republic, and private, so that Cicero would be safer and less troubled against Clodius; and efficient, both Pompey, who brought Cicero back into Caesar's favor, and Pompey and Caesar, who reconciled Cicero with Vatinius and Crassus. Adjuncts of persons are much employed: the friendship and dignity of Pompey and Caesar. But to bring out these arguments, almost none of the other arguments are omitted. Achievement, comparisons of all kinds are brought in, as well as factions and divisions, and testimony. Thus there is more than enough abundance (*copia*) of material (*rerum*). Of syllogism and judgment the same cannot be said. For, by his many obscure and captious conclusions, his frivolous digressions and unnecessary repetitions and unrestrained praise of his own work, Cicero shows in his judgment a kind of evil genius which rather dims the brilliant ability of an otherwise great name. His method is of more worth (*laus*). For at the beginning the summary of the matter (*summa rerum*) is proposed, then divided, then the parts explained in order, and finally the peroration finished off with the repetition of the leading headings (*summis capitibus*).[131]

In this welter of end products turned out by the analytical machine, correlation between the kind of a text Ramus is operating on and any particular way of operating on it is rather low. However, some general tendencies can be noted. With regard to Ramus' and Talon's works as a whole, dialectical summaries are generally provided at the beginning of the commentaries for orations and poetry indifferently, but not for philosophical works such as Cicero's *On Fate*, since these would be presumed to have their skeletons, at least their logical skeletons, showing — although Ramus was loath to admit that before his own time anyone, even Euclid, had looked on logic bare. Partial dialectical summaries are common in commentary on orations, and in philosophical commentary, too, but missing from Ramus' commentary on poetry (Virgil), although Talon's pupil Antoine Fouquelin introduced them in his commentaries on Persius.[132] Similarly, dialectical and/or rhetorical summaries are appended to oratorical and other works.

In some measure this is all recognized Renaissance schoolroom practice, undoubtedly effective in getting youngsters "into" a text. It connects, on the one hand with medieval rhetoric and sermon writing and with the medieval practice of summarizing a text before commenting on it, which in turn connects with the late Hellenistic practice of providing "arguments," in the sense of briefs, even for fictional narration.

14. THE ARTS, CONNECTED DISCOURSE, AND STATISTICS

Because all linguistic activity is viewed as a process of taking apart unit pieces by analysis and putting them back together again by genesis or synthesis, there is a permanent ambivalence in the relationship between the arts and connected discourse in Ramism. It has been seen that Ramus regards the setting up of an art in its perfect "methodized" form as a kind of analysis. On the other hand, all discourse is methodized. Does this mean that all discourse is ideally reducible to a curriculum subject? Ramus' pedagogical heritage, which here joins with its collateral descendant, the sermon tradition, implies that it is: both proceed by definition and division. Where, then, do the syllogisms fit which are also the product of analysis? There is no way to answer such questions in the primitive terms in which Ramus has cast up his accounts. Everything is "arrangement." There is no effective provision for differences in kinds of discourse at all.

The weakness of the Ramist notion of analysis and genesis was pointed out by Riolan, who insists that the psychological aspects of discourse and the very notion of judgment itself, as a psychological act, are occluded by this approach.[133] But as a major historical incident, the notion cannot possibly be written off, for, in the huge commentaries and encyclopedias which it leads to, it is a source of whole philosophical systems and a gateway opening into the modern world.

The radically diagrammatic and quantifying drives in Ramus' mind reveal themselves most spectacularly when they work themselves to the surface from time to time in curiously modern tabulations. These appear in his summaries of rhetorical or logical analyses (*analyseos rhetoricae summa* or *analyseos logicae summa*). Thus in Ramus' summary of his rhetorical analysis for Cicero's *Plea for Rabirius:*

Of the tropes, metonymy, irony, and metaphor are most frequent, synecdoche the least used; of the figures of words, *symploce, epanalepsis, anadiplosis, climax, correctio*. Of the figures of sentence, *addubitatio, praeteritio, reticentia, sustentatio* are absent, but the rest are used. Of the figures of words, measure in the sphere of concinnity [i.e., effective prose rhythm] proves the most pleasing. Of the figures of sentence, the deprecation in the exordium is by far the most effective for swaying the audience, the *licentia* in suppressing applause for terrifying the audience, and *communicatio* for moving them to action.[134]

The reference to effects produced in the audience lies rather outside the theoretical economy of Ramist rhetoric, and represents traditional practice which Ramus had been unable to rid himself of, but even it is cast up in quasi-tabular form. At times, this sixteenth-century tabulator can match the most formidably statistical modern *Wissenschaft*:

> In tropes, the elocution is good and rich. Metonymy occurs sixty times, synecdoche about the same number of times, irony not once, metaphor eighty times . . . . Of the figures of sentence . . . *optatio* is not used, *prolepsis* occurs three times; prosopopoeia twice, but concealed as disgression and *dialogismus*; *praeteritio* is used once, other figures of sentence not at all.[135]

The "scientific" approach to literature has arrived.

15. EXPERIMENT AND PROBABILITY

Ramus' writings have been combed by Waddington and Graves for remarks favorable to experimental procedure, but the instances which can be found are no more impressive than those which can be turned up in most intelligent writers from ancient times on, who, in general, do not express themselves against induction, but, on the contrary are extremely interested in it, while remaining largely indifferent to controlled experimental procedure.[136] Waddington makes much of a remark of Ramus' in favor of an astronomy without hypotheses,[137] and of a letter of Ramus' to Joachim Rhaeticus, the man who had prevailed on Copernicus to publish his new system. But, apart from the fact that Waddington is unaware of the rhetorical framework in which the notion of hypothesis was often still set,[138] Ramus' declaration here goes no further than the similar declaration frequently cited from St. Thomas Aquinas and other medieval men.

Indeed, while it gives lip service to induction, because it has a tendency to raise the didactic charge on all sciences and to liquidate all probable logics, Ramism freezes out experimentation and the whole field of predeductive activity. This it does by assimilating to a topical logic, and thereby silencing, the priorities discussion which was a real seed bed of interest in experimental method. Sometimes one feels that Ramus is about to apply his notion of genesis to the abstractive process itself so as to include the steps which lead up to, or can lead up to, scientific knowledge, instead of restricting it to the abstractionist approach of his invention and disposition. But when he thinks of the genesis or origins of knowledge in terms of the concrete situations such as those in which experiment could be arranged, it is to dismiss such a situation as beneath the attention of an educated man:

> As for the genesis involved in deliberation, logic has nothing to do with it, for it is a matter of mechanics and action, that is, of dealing with the thing itself and

effecting it, and is thus managed not by means of arguments but by means of one's hands and feet and other bodily instruments.[139]

Mechanics and action have nothing to do with arguments. Yet even Ramus' notion of practical mechanics is itself curiously nonscientific, for this same passage goes on to explain that when Cicero backed Gaius Manilius in the latter's proposal to confer on Pompey the unlimited command of the war against Mithridates, Cicero's speech provided the "analysis for the deliberation," whereas the genesis for the same deliberation was rather Pompey's military expedition. The practical "mechanics" thus involved is not mechanics in any Newtonian or modern sense but military science — the marshalling of so many thousands of armed men on land and sea.[140]

In its long-term effects, Ramism, with the topical logic which it exploits, is favorable to the emergence of modern science, experiment included, because of the way it loosens up the field of knowledge in encouraging visualist approaches to this field. These effects are quite unintentional, if exceedingly real, but they derive from no penetrating insight on Ramus' part into the need for observation and experiment as a condition of scientific progress.

CHAPTER XII

RAMIST RHETORIC

Hamlet. "Words, words, words . . . .
Polonius. ". . . . Yet there is method in't."
— Hamlet.

I. THE RAMIST RHETORIC AND ITS AUTHOR

I F the Ramist dialectic is the most central item in the complex of cultural phenomena which make up Ramism, Ramist rhetoric is the most symptomatic item in the same complex. Hence it merits close attention. Dialectic and rhetoric have been intertwined at least from the time of the Greek Sophists till our present day, and when Ramus decrees that they must be disengaged from one another once and for all in theory (but always united in practice), he engages some of the most powerful and obscure forces in intellectual history. The divorce between the two disciplines affects rhetoric the most. Ramist dialectic is constructed in the interests of a "simplification" inspired by the topical logic tradition and the vague but powerful premathematicism connected with this tradition; Ramist rhetoric is constructed with the precise objective of making it something different from dialectic. To realize this objective, Ramist rhetoric reserves to itself only two of the more or less traditional five parts of rhetoric: elocution and pronunciation. These had never threatened to overlap with dialectic. Of the other three parts, invention and disposition or judgment, which had threatened to overlap, are surrendered completely to dialectic. The fifth part, memory, is simply liquidated by being identified with judgment.

Ramist rhetoric, however, did not spring full-fledged from the head of its author, any more than did Ramist dialectic. Partly because of this, the identity of its real author is still something of a mystery, which will probably never be solved. In his 1543 *Training in Dialectic*, Ramus had announced that Omer Talon was to provide a complementary treatment of rhetoric.[1] The treatment appeared in 1545 as *Omer Talon's Training in Oratory*.[2] Its title matches exactly that of Ramus' 1543 work, and the author was identified, like Ramus, as "of the Vermandois" (*Veromanduus*).

Omer Talon (Audomarus Taleus) was one of the four sons of Arthur (or Artus) Talon, an Irish colonel under Charles IX permanently settled in

France. He was born around 1510 and according to the biographical dictionaries (there has never been a full study of the man) seems to have been born at Amiens, although Nancel identifies him as "of Beauvais" (*Bellovacus*).[3] Except for a brief time teaching at the College of Beauvais at Paris,[4] Talon was Ramus' man. He lived at the College of Cardinal Le Moine at the time he was sworn in as a teacher at the University of Paris in 1544.[5] Later the same year he joined Ramus and Bartholomew Alexandre in teaching at the little Collège de l'Ave Maria, and remained closely attached to Ramus the rest of his life. Some time before Talon's death, Ramus had him installed as curé of the Church of St. Nicolas du Chardonnet, which was one of the benefices Ramus held and which was very near Ramus' own Collège de Presles. Talon, now ordained a priest late in life,[6] died here in 1562 from some very painful disease.

It is quite likely that Ramus had some hand in *Omer Talon's Training in Oratory*, and even more likely that he had a hand in the *Rhetoric* (*Rhetorica*) which emerged from it in 1548. It is quite certain that the rewriting of the text in the 1567 and 1569 editions after Talon's death is Ramus' own.[7] The Talon *Rhetoric* is the expressly designed complement of Ramus' *Dialectic*, a complement in any and all of its stages as perfect as not only Talon, but Ramus himself, knew how to make it.

2. STAGES OF DEVELOPMENT

The development of the Ramist rhetoric parallels roughly that of the Ramist dialectic. There is a three-phase period represented by the *Training in Oratory* (matching the *Training in Dialectic*), followed by a two-part period represented by the *Rhetoric* of 1548 or *Rhetoric in Two Books* of 1562 (paralleled by the *Dialectic* or *Dialectic in Two Books*).[8] The initial three-phase work treats of a "natural" eloquence, an art or teaching (*doctrina*) of eloquence (this art is what is called precisely *rhetorica*), and the use or exercise of the art. As in the case of dialectic, this initial attempt to include a treatment of "nature" and "practice" with the treatment of the art itself is quickly abandoned; and in 1548 we are presented with the *Rhetorica*, which is the two-part art alone. After Talon's death this is equipped with Ramus' prelections (1567), and still later (1569) it is divided clearly into two books as *Rhetoricae libri duo, Petri Rami praelectionibus illustrati*.

Despite Ramus' coming attacks on Quintilian, the rhetoric of the Ramus and Talon team echoes Quintilian from the start. The *Training in Oratory* opens with an almost verbatim quotation from the Iberian rhetorician: "Eloquentia vis [as against Ramus' 1543 *virtus* for dialectic] est bene dicendi."[9] This may be rendered, "Eloquence is the power of expressing oneself well." *Dicendi* cannot be translated "speaking," since it does not exclude writing to the extent that this English word does.

The three parts — nature, art, and exercise — into which Ramus had divided his dialectic are represented in eloquence not by "parts" but by "steps" (*gradus*). Talon makes the same reduction of the "nature of eloquence" which Ramus has made of the "nature of dialectic." *Natura* is taken in the sense of origin, and the assigning of three "steps" to eloquence is thus the equivalent of saying that eloquence has an origin, an art, and an exercise.

Talon now provides us with a brief description of the origin of eloquence in the individual man.[10] God generates in man "motions" which are rich and abundant (*uberes et copiosi* — with obvious reference to the *copia verborum* or "copie of words" which it was the ambition of every humanist teacher to instill into his pupils). These motions produce successively: thought (*cogitatio mentis*); a discretion which unfolds the instinctive cognition contained in reason; and finally, embellishment. Talon explains that these powers become less dark and more tractable by use and example even without written arts, as in the case of Ulysses, Menelaus, Nestor, and many living persons. Further than this, he does not explain these powers. The reason is evident. It would be quite a task to show how the first and second apply to Ramist rhetoric at all. Thought (*cogitatio mentis*) looks remarkably like Ramus' first part of the art of dialectic, invention, whereas discretion is the image of judgment, the second part of the same art. The third natural activity produced by the primitive rhetorical motion in the soul, "embellishment," is indistinguishable from the art of rhetoric. Thus unveiled, the three "dark" powers of natural rhetoric reveal themselves as the two parts of the dichotomized art of dialectic in not very convincing disguise; they are flanked by the art of rhetoric, not yet dichotomized and also in disguise.

The second step in eloquence is that of the art or teaching, which is rhetoric proper. Talon defines it in a cautious adaptation of Quintilian, and states that rhetoric proper is "the artificial teaching of good expression in any matter."[11] A certain diffidence concerning Ramus' and others' assumption that art is identified with teaching is evident here. Talon circumspectly specifies that rhetoric is both a teaching (*doctrina*) and an art (*artificiosa*). By 1548 this circumspection will be deemed superfluous, Ramus would have his way, and rhetoric would be simply "the doctrine of expressing oneself well" (*doctrina bene dicendi*),[12] which, with *scientia* substituted for *doctrina*, is exactly Quintilian's definition again.[13]

Talon goes on to say that rhetoric, like dialectic, applies to all subjects. The two parts of the teaching or art of rhetoric are said to correspond to the parts of natural eloquence, which turn on the "praise" (*laus*) or — as we might prefer to conceptualize it — the assets of single words, and the "praise" or assets of conjoined words. These two parts are, of course, formed by imposing on rhetoric a division paralleling the unit-cluster partition of dialectic: invention (single arguments) and judgment (conjoined arguments). This partition will be a complete failure in rhetoric. In the 1548 *Rhetoric* and editions derived from it, the parts will be redesigned as *elocutio*; this might be rendered in English "style" or "striking expression," but it was conceived largely as "ornament" or "garnishing," and *pronuntiatio* or delivery. Striking expression is divided into tropes and figures; delivery into voice (*vox*, or, as it was sometimes confusingly called, simply *pronuntiatio*) and gesture (*gestus* or *actio*).[14]

This new division of rhetoric into striking expression and delivery would prove a kind of failure, too. From Talon through Dudley Fenner and his successors, the insufficiency of the new second part of rhetoric will become all too apparent. Delivery is given rather short shrift by ancient rhetoricians such as Cicero and Quintilian. But they did not consider it one complete part of a two-part art. Talon, who later did so consider it, had forgot to mention it at all in 1545, just as Ramus had forgot to mention enunciations and method in dialectic in 1543. In the *Rhetoric* of 1548, the second part amounts to almost nothing, and Talon avers that it comes to the same thing as the first part.[15] In Ramus' revisions done in 1567 and later, it amounts to even less. Fenner would lament that the second part was "not yet perfect,"[16] Piscator's more valid excuse for omitting it would be that it varies from country to country and can be learned only by practice.[17]

All this means, of course, is that the irreducibly vocal and auditory phenomena of actual spoken delivery, which the second part of rhetoric purportedly taught, escape the diagrammatic apparatus somehow intrusive in all explanatory approaches to communication. This apparatus is particularly characteristic of Ramist arts, which were themselves the product of the humanists' outlook, and which, despite real interest and skill in oral delivery, is dominantly and incurably textual (as nothing before the Gutenberg era could be) and controlled by the written rather than the spoken word. Of course, Ramus and Talon and others taught boys to *speak* Latin (Ramus, after all, has been hailed as the greatest orator since Cicero) but how they did so has not come down to us in writing, or has come down very imperfectly. Oral delivery retains an inalienable connection with the spoken tradition — stronger than any connection with written prescriptions. By the same token, it fitted uneasily into a Ramist art. The Ramist "plain style" is a manner of composition, not of voice and gesture.

On the other hand, the first "part" of rhetoric is organized entirely around two well-established, geometrically grounded conceptualizations. These are tropes ("turnings") and figures ("shapes"). Together they constitute all of *elocutio*, and are developed in straightforward Ramist fashion by definition and division; they move toward neater and neater dichotomization from the beginnings in 1545 through the 1548 and later revisions.[18] The Ramist treatment of individual tropes and figures is uneventful and undistinguished by comparison with other rhetorics of the time. It is not insensitive, as when it gives high marks to metaphor. But, like most rhetorics, it maintains the low theoretical level enforced on the subject (in postclassical times) by its place in the lower reaches of the curriculum, and evinces no real understanding of the semantic importance of metaphorical or of any similar processes.

The Ramist distinction between trope and figure is an attempt at tidiness. In the 1545 *Training in Oratory*, the distinction is not in effect, although the various "ornaments" of speech — neologism (*novum ornamentum*), archaism (*vetustum ornamentum*), transfer or metaphor (*ornamentum translatum*), and the rest — are grouped in terms of the unit-cluster division already described. Only in its final form, does the *Rhetoric* mature fairly neat definitions which enable it to divide all the ornaments between trope and figure. A trope consists in changing a word from its "native signification" to another signification — a definition which, in effect, makes all tropes species of metaphor; where a figure varies the "clothing" of speech (*orationis habitus*) from the straightforward and simple.[19]

It is plain that Ramus and/or Talon want to make figure an "ornamentation" of the sound of speech alone. The first examples they give, number or rhythm, repetition of like sounds, and so on, make this clear. To these they apply the old term "figures of diction" (*figurae dictionis*). But they have also to throw in with figures items such as exclamation, apostrophe, personification — which, in traditional fashion, they style "figures of sentence" (*figurae sententiae*) — and thus their notion of figure loses outline. Roughly, although Ramists do not put it quite this way, in the Ramist view trope is always some sort of metaphor, and figure is anything else that strikes one as unusual. The Ramist difficulty here is the difficulty of practically all such rhetoric text books: it may be traced to the attempt to describe and classify the unusual without being able to identify what the usual is.

The last part of the 1545 *Training in Oratory*, concerned with use or exercise,[20] drops out of the later *Rhetoric*. It exactly parallels the section on exercise in the *Training in Dialectic* which dropped out of the later *Dialectic*, and is divided the same way into interpretation, writing, and speaking. Interpretation is rhetorical analysis, or identification of the various ornaments.[21] Writing and speaking are treated solely in terms of imitation, which is explained conventionally and jejunely as the following of classical models. How one or another trope or figure is related to one or another rhetorical effect is not attended to. The ideas on style which Ramus and Talon are expressing are representative of Ramism in general and of the central tradition of post-Renaissance Latin. They are neither rabidly Ciceronian nor rabidly anti-Ciceronian. The "pure and elegant" authors — Terence, Antonius, Crassus, Hortensius, Sulpicius, Cicero, Caesar, Virgil, and Ovid — are to be imitated, and Cato, Ennius, Plautus, Pacuvius, and other *rudes et inculti* to be avoided.[22] Plato, Cicero, and Quintilian are the basic authorities on the subject of rhetoric. The two latter are, of course, among Talon's and Ramus' real sources. Plato, who is not a real, immediate source, is cited for prestige and for what Ramus considered his nuisance value in annoying the Aristotelians.

3. THE FIVE-PART RHETORIC AND RENAISSANCE YOUTH

Talon's and Ramus' redesigning of rhetoric was not a purely whimsical event. It derives from tensions in the educational system which were the product of centuries. The more or less traditional five parts of rhetoric commonly adhered to by non-Ramist Renaissance textbook writers — invention, disposition, memory, striking expression (*elocutio*), and delivery — date from ancient Greek times. They were not five abstract parts of an abstract art then, but five activities in which an aspirant was disciplined so that he might become an orator or public lecturer — the common ideal of all ancient liberal education.[23] In antiquity a boy was given a foundation of general information on all possible subjects (*inventio*). He was taught to use this material in composition (*dispositio*), his mnemonic skill was developed (*memoria*), together with his literary style (*elocutio*) and his oral delivery (*pronuntiatio*). These five activities added up to a rather complete educational program extending over a good number of years. As the training which the normal educated man received, these activities today would be called simply education, or perhaps general education.[24]

The Romans had been able, with little difficulty, to take over these five activities from the Greeks. They, too, had been able to teach "rhetoric," in the sense of a general education framed within native Latin expression. Such is the program which Quintilian proposes. But it was quite different in medieval and Renaissance Europe. Rhetoric, which in ancient times had been general culture purveyed in the vernacular, was now culture set within a foreign tongue; the acquisition of culture became identified with, or subordinate to, acquiring the foreign tongue itself. Rhetoric thus became chiefly a course in Latin — advanced as compared with (Latin) grammar, which was the elementary course (elementary schools today are still "grammar" schools). The pattern, which Ramus himself records, of distinguishing art students into two groups, the grammarians or *grammatici* (studying grammar and rhetoric) and the philosophers or *philosophi* (studying dialectic, physics, and the rest) can be clearly seen in the university practice.[25] Outside the grammar-school and university framework, rhetoric persisted in Ramus' day sometimes in other forms, but nowhere as a course in general culture in the ancient sense. In the Inns of Court, where the subject was of great importance (Thomas Wilson's English *Arte of Rhetorique* [1533] was probably written for young noblemen at the Inns of Court) rhetoric was a still more specialized discipline; it involved not only a tangle of Latin and technicalities but also declamation in still another language foreign to Englishmen (and to everyone else), Law French.[26]

The simplified Ramist rhetoric represents in great part an adjustment to the changed linguistic situation. But the adjustment was far from complete or satisfactory. Ramus' relegation of intention and disposition (this latter including memory) to dialectic and his limitation of rhetoric to style (*elocutio*) and oral delivery suggested still the order which had prevailed in early Greek education. Common sense would dictate that the invention and disposition of matter be taught before its "ornamentation" and delivery, dialectic before rhetoric. Yet Ramus taught rhetoric as a one-year course before dialectic! [27] Indeed, his labored explanation of "natural dialectic," or the ability to discourse which every normal boy supposedly picked up by himself and which saw him through both rhetoric and life until he came to the formal art of dialectic, seems to be a rationalization of Ramus' own procedure and that of almost everyone else. In the school curriculum practice after antiquity, rhetoric was really supplementary to grammar, not to dialectic. Although the Middle Ages witnessed occasional attempts to teach rhetoric after dialectic,[28] such a program proved hardly viable in Northern Europe.[29] If we except the "rhetoric" of various technical secretarial courses (dictamen), which, while highly important in the Middle Ages, was not rhetoric in the classical or ordinary sense, the remark made by Rhabanus Maurus as early as the ninth century remained in force: "It is enough for rhetoric if it be the business of youngsters." [30]

During the Renaissance, especially in England, the Erasmian tradition worked for a while to reverse this medieval pattern. It favored theoretically a curriculum with dialectic or logic placed before rhetoric and subordinated to rhetorical purposes.[31] This theory was at times put into effect, for Ascham writes to Sturm that Cheke was teaching Prince Edward dialectic, ethics, rhetoric, in this order.[32] The *Parnassus* plays as late as 1597–1601 associate rhetoric in the curriculum with poetry and seemingly place it after dialectic — although it is not quite clear that this position represents the curriculum order and not simply the order in which the aspirant to Parnassus' heights considers possible means of ascent.[33] But, insofar as the Erasmian philosophy of education was put into effect, it produced a dialectic or logic so rudimentary that it was little more than an elaboration of rhetoric itself. The precocious dialectic or logic which resulted has well been called rhetoric-logic.[34]

Even in England, however, this rhetoric-logic proved not very viable, and in the curriculum finally fixed on under Edward VI, dialectic or logic followed after rhetoric.[35] This seems to have been the predominant order in most Renaissance universities. Accordingly, the "grammar schools" such as Eton, Winchester, and Westminster, even at a time when they were described as "trivial schools," commonly taught grammar and rhetoric only, and left out the third trivial subject, dialectic or logic, for more advanced work.[36] The alinement was thereby the same as that which Ramus reports for medieval and Renaissance Paris.

Talon is quite representative of the general Renaissance pattern, therefore, when he insists that in rhetoric one must have regard for the "tender" years of the pupils.[37] Rhetoric was practically everywhere a matter for still younger boys than was dialectic, and was comparable to a grade-school or junior-high-school subject in America today. The fact that it was Latin rhetoric taught from Latin textbooks often confuses the twentieth-century mind.

4. ORNAMENTATION THEORY: PRAISES AND HONORS OF WORDS

When Melanchthon accepted the view that dialectic and rhetoric differed in that the former presented things in a naked state, whereas the latter clothed them with ornament, he also was concerned with the age of his pupils. He defends this old and common view of rhetoric on the grounds that, although many persons objected to it, it was one which little boys could understand.[38] Indeed, the idea that rhetoric adds ornament to speech which is originally or natively "plain" would seem to be the common one of the man in the street and quite assimilable by children. Something like it is present in the association of ornamentation with rhetoric which is found in antiquity, particularly in Cicero and Quintilian, and is recurrent through the Middle Ages in the common doctrine concerning the tropes and figures. But in Ramism this ornamentation theory undergoes a significant change — a change which is symptomatic not only of Ramism but of the age, and which reveals much of the significance of Ramist rhetoric.

In its final stage, Ramist rhetoric relies more on ornamentation theory than perhaps any other rhetoric ever has. The basic reason is its restriction of rhetoric to *elocutio*, which meant the use of tropes and figures, commonly considered the "ornaments." As has been seen, the second half of Ramist rhetoric was, practically speaking, nonexistent as a part of the "art" proper. "Just as wisdom treats of the knowledge of all things," Talon states in 1545, "so rhetoric treats of ornamentation and striking expression."[39] These two terms, *exornatio* and *elocutio*, are not complementary opposites but synonyms, as the 1548 *Rhetoric* shows.

Miss Tuve and others have sought to rehabilitate the Renaissance notion of ornament with some success. They have shown that it does not necessarily mean appliqué work in the way the English term ornament suggests today.[40] Indeed, the first meaning of *ornamentum* in Latin — rhetoric as an art existed almost entirely in Latin — is equipment or accoutrements, which the "naked causes" of dialectic, liked naked persons, would need rather more than pretty clothing to get along in this world. Because it conceives of "ornament" as equipment rather than as decoration solely, the fifteenth century can conceive of the hand as "a great help and ornament to the body," and the sixteenth century of tackling as the "ornaments of a ship."[41]

The Renaissance notion of ornament, however, has dimensions of still another sort which seem never to have been explicitly adverted to. The terms *ornamentum* or *ornamentatio* have certain definite synonyms which come from Cicero and Quintilian. An "ornament" of rhetoric is also indifferently styled a "praise" (*laus*) or an "honor" (*honos* or *honor*) or a "light" (*lumen*) of words or of speech.[42] All these concepts, *ornamentum* included, are closely connected with the notion that rhetoric demands a continuous flow of oral sound (*oratio perpetua*), a Ciceronic expression which Ramus makes a shibboleth in his program to re-establish an eloquent and rhetorical, as against a scholastic, philosophy.[43]

It is exceedingly difficult for the twentieth-century mind to form concepts of tropes and figures as "honors" or "praises" of words or of speech in the way in which these concepts are formed by Cicero and, with rather more effort, by Talon, Ramus, and their contemporaries. "Lights" of words or of speech comes perhaps somewhat more naturally to us, although even this formulation has its difficulties. But the concepts honor and praise are too personalistic in their implications to apply convincingly to words; they treat words as if they are the normal objects of honor and praise, persons. Even the notion of light, in this complimentary or honorific sense, is normally applied to a person: we should call a writer, rather than the words he pronounces, a literary "light," or the great "light" of his age.

Nevertheless, the personalist cast of these terms is entirely relevant to their earlier association with *ornamentum*. This is clear from the fact that this latter term and its cognates are also used by Renaissance rhetoricians in certain personalized senses which strike the twentieth-century ear as strange. Thus Ramus refers to the regius professors such as himself as "ornamented" (or "equipped") with an annual grant from the crown.[44] Even had these grants been easier to collect than they were (they often lagged three or four years in arrears) their use to "ornament" persons strikes us as strange, although their use to "honor" persons might not; the latter term exists for us in a context involving persons and personal relations. For the sensibility of the sixteenth century and earlier, the term "ornament" existed in a similar context. The whole field over which *laus, honor, lumen,* and *ornamentum* play is obviously one where the distinctions between persons and objects now made automatically at least by English-speaking persons are more or less blurred.

This is obvious on another score. We think of honor or praise as applied to an object by a person, whereas Ramus and his classical predecessors and Renaissance contemporaries are quite willing to have the object somehow emanate honor and praise, in this way performing a kind of personal role. In the title of the orations by Talon's pupils printed in 1548, *Quinque orationes de laude regiae dignitatis*, it is practically impossible to decide whether this means *Five Orations Giving Praise to the Royal Station* or *Five Orations on the Impressiveness Found in the Royal Station*, since *laus* can either emanate from the orator or from the object he is concerned with. Again — in an

example to which the *New English Dictionary* does not quite do justice —
George Puttenham's *Art of English Poesie* (III, i) says, "The chief prayse
and cunning of our poet is in the discreet using of his figures." Praise, which
in Elizabethan and later texts functions also as the Latin *encomium*, functions
here as the Latin *laus* and is almost exactly the equivalent of "accomplish-
ment," a thing which we should think of not as a "praise" but as *evoking*
praise. A similar use is found in the *Merchant of Venice* (V, v, 108–109),
where the sense might better be rendered as "impressiveness": "How many
things by season season'd are/ To their right praise and true perfection." In
The Praise of Hemp-Seed (1620), the author, John Taylor the Water-Poet,
lists the "praises" of hemp on the title page as "cloathing, food, fishing, ship-
ping, pleasure, profit, justice, and whipping." We should again incline to
think of praise as *applied* freely to hemp because of its value in making these
items possible. For the sixteenth- and seventeenth-century mind, the value in
the object and the praise elicited by the object tend to be viewed as one whole.
This mind does not feel the exterior, objective world and the interior, personal world as distinct from one another quite to the extent that we do. Objects retain a more personal, or at least animistic, glow.

5. THE VISUALIZING OF ORNAMENT

Ramus and Talon, and the rhetorical tradition generally, give no effective
and convincing explanation of what, from a semantic point of view, the
"ornamentation" of language could be. Insofar as their age refrains from regarding this ornamentation, or "garment of style," as appliqué work, it so
refrains because the notion of ornament is tempered in the way just indicated largely through equation with terms such as *laus* and *honor* and
through a close association with a mysterious, interiorized person world
rather than with an object world of surfaces. Nevertheless, at least from its
earliest appearance in the Ramist works, the notion of ornament tends to
dominate the other terms and to reduce the auditory element, the resonance,
of rhetoric, implied in the notions of praise and honor, to something visually
comprehensible, and thereby to the spatial and diagrammatic. In the Ramist
rhetorical tradition as compared with the ancient Ciceronian, *laus* and *honor*
are minimized, and become peripheral notions which occur in the looser discussion of the early *Training in Oratory* and in Ramus' commentary on
rhetoric, but not in the presentation of the art of rhetoric proper. By 1555,
Ramus' offhand references to rhetoric show that he thinks of it in uncomplicated visualist terms as serving "pour orner la parole." [45] Little wonder that
Ramus' followers, such as Bilsten or Alsted, will define rhetoric quite flatly
as "the art of expressing oneself ornately." [46] "Praise" and "honor," and with
them much of the reality of sound itself, are gone.

6. THE CLEAR AND DISTINCT: SOLON'S LAW

The Ramist insistence that the arts be kept distinct from one another further encouraged thinking of rhetoric in terms of models conceived of as existing in space and apprehended by sight, rather than in terms of voice and hearing. To a great extent, in the ancient cultures rhetoric was related to dialectic as sound was to sight. This is not to say that rhetoric was not concerned with the clear and distinct, nor that dialectic, as the art of discourse, was not concerned with sound at all. The difference was a polar difference: rhetoric was concerned with what was resonant and closer to the auditory pole; dialectic with what was relatively silent, abstract, and diagrammatic. In this kind of view, the two arts are not the same, but neither are they sharply "distinct" from one another in any readily definable way.

For Ramus, they had to be distinct. The ultimate reason is that Ramus conceives of them — and of their parts — by analogy with extended, and hence quantified surfaces, and that two extended objects cannot occupy the same space, at least in the ordinary experience of men. From the very beginning of his career, Ramus' ambition was to present the proper "shape" (*conformatio*) of dialectic and of the other arts, which he wants to "plot in unbroken lines" (*perpetuis lineamentis adumbrare*).[47] Out of this preoccupation grows the most striking expression of his extensional or quantifying mental habits, which he himself styles "Solon's Law."

This law is one which determines the distinction between the various arts, and, within each art, the distinction of its various parts. As its name indicates, it derives from Ramus' metaphorical interpretation of Solon's building ordinance at Athens, which he and his followers cite over and over again. Solon had prescribed a clear space of a foot alongside each wall, two feet alongside each house, and so on. Ramus calls on this law when he cries haro at Cicero's and Quintilian's failure to keep dialectic and rhetoric distinct from one another.[48] The quantitative basis of the cult of distinctness is only too evident; Ramus is saying that a "place" is really a "place," and that it cannot be occupied by rhetoric and dialectic jointly.

Within this economy, if rhetoric still has to do with sound more than dialectic does, the way in which one conceives of the art undergoes subtle transformations in spatial terms. Striking expression and delivery are still allotted to rhetoric, but invention and judgment cannot be, since they have been assigned to dialectic. Memory, the fifth part of the traditional rhetoric, is unconvincingly identified by Ramus with judgment on the score that judging properly about things facilitates recall. But the real reason why Ramus can dispense with memory is that his whole scheme of arts, based on a topically conceived logic, is a system of local memory. Memory is everywhere, its "places" or "rooms" being the mental space which Ramus' arts all fill.

Within the two-part rhetoric, the spatial and visual carries the day still further. The second half of rhetoric, *oral* delivery, perishes of neglect, and the first half, *elocutio*, is, by the appearance of the later *Rhetoric*, resolved in terms of tropes ("turnings" — a diagrammatically grounded concept) and figures ("shapes" — another visually based notion). Despite the spatial analogy which they involve, figures have to do largely with the sound of words — among the figures are anaphora and other verbal repetition, rhythmic movement, and the quasi-acoustic effects of exclamation and apostrophe (figures of "sentence"). Hence, shying away instinctively from sound, and thus from figures, Ramist rhetoric will declare in favor of tropes when a choice between tropes and figures has to be made.[49] This is a declaration against sound in favor of (silent) thought; but thought is conceived of in terms of (ornamental) structure, with the aid of a spatial model ("turnings").

Ramus' inclination to explain secret or prudential method or *crypsis* as a kind of reversal of his "one and only method" is due to the fact that in his spatial projection of the notion of method, the only kind of variation possible must be itself spatial. The explanation thus given for method has a further effect in the visualist reduction of rhetoric, for, since *crypsis* is the method resorted to by the specialists in rhetoric — poets, orators, and historians — Ramus exhibits a strong tendency to think of his now soundless rhetoric simply as dialectic in reverse.[50] What this has to do with the hypertrophy of ornament in Ramist rhetoric becomes clear when one recognizes the hypertrophy as part of a shift toward the visual throughout the whole cognitive field.

7. POETRY

Miss Tuve has said that "in so far as they were arts of thought, poetry and rhetoric had not been divided prior to Ramus."[51] This is true of the general scholastic and humanist tradition as the arts of discourse were practiced in the schoolroom, although it is not true, of course, of the upper reaches of the intellectual tradition which were represented by the Italian humanists or even by certain scholastics. Aristotle in his *Poetry* and *Rhetoric* (which were seldom if ever part of the arts course before the sixteenth century) and a few exceptional commentators such as St. Albert the Great or St. Thomas Aquinas differentiated poetry from rhetoric as an art of thought in a way which was relatively decisive, although their differentiation was sketchy and undeveloped (its sponsors were not teaching poetry, and therefore they had not thought painstakingly about it). According to these commentators, poetry, like rhetoric, dealt with the less-than-certain: rhetoric dealt with probabilities and probable conclusions, poetry with feigned conclusions or the semblance of conclusions or of the truth.[52] Because they were abstruse and not without difficulties, if discerning, such views of poetry, like the sometimes even more carefully nuanced views of humanists, were not very viable in a pedagogical tradition. When poetry finally came to be separated from rhetoric, at least within the perimeter defined by Ramism, there was little enough finesse of thought or of poetic sensibility involved at all.

The Ramist notion of poetry is highly quantitative and diagrammatic; it was built up in terms of "number" or counting. Although Ramus elsewhere expresses the opinion that poetry is a separate art, like medicine,[53] from the earliest editions of Talon's *Rhetoric* poetry, in the Ramist tradition, is really treated as a part of rhetoric. The reasons for this are obvious: like rhetorical speech, it is speech which is out of the ordinary in that, as sound, it attracts attention.[54] Poetry is differentiated from the rest of rhetoric in terms of "number" (*numerus*), which of course is the Latin term for rhythm or musical count. By the time of later editions of the *Rhetoric*, poetry has migrated to a somewhat different position within the art, and is given an even more frankly quantitative treatment. It is now a part of tonal "dimension" (*tonorum dimensio*), for which *numerus* is only a second-best synonym.[55] Tonal dimension has become dichotomized into poetic and oratorical dimension, and poetic dimension into rhythm (length of lines) and meter (kind of feet). This is the sum and substance of Ramist view on poetry, which echo the most mechanistic "poetic" of the medieval dictamen. As has been seen Ramus' poet and orator follow the same methodical procedure in their disposition of arguments and method, using the "secrets of method."[56] When these "secrets" are unraveled or exposed the poet's argumentations reduce equally to a sum of definitions and/or syllogisms — one is never sure which. The "garnishing" which New England divines or others in the Ramist tradition might permit themselves to apply to truth in the writing of poetry was thus taken to be the same thing as rhetorical garnishing. Indeed, if all Ramist rhetoric was appliqué work, poetry was appliqué work of the worst mechanical sort, for, as Ramus occasionally hints, the rules which govern it belong perhaps less to rhetoric than to arithmetic.[57]

Thus later Ramists who split off poetry from rhetoric had at least some of Ramus' earlier positions to go on. But even the definitions of those who made the most of poetry did little to refine the Ramist view of what poetry was. "Poetry," they say dryly and uninspiringly, "is the art of versifying well."[58]

Others in the Ramist milieu, of course, often had more adequate views of poetry than the Ramists. Riolan thought of poetry as "philosophy wrapped up in fable."[59] But, apart from the fact that even Riolan's view could be given a Ramist reading by taking the fable as "ornament," Riolan was a physician, not a master of arts teaching poetry to little boys. He did not register so accurately as the Ramists the arts-curriculum pattern. This pattern moved from words and sounds (grammar and rhetoric) to abstractions and silence (logic, physics, and the rest). The inference was inviting; what was taught in the lower reaches of the curriculum was elementary and childish. These pedagogical perspectives are obviously what determine Ramus' view: poetry belongs to words and sounds and thus to elementary classes. Little boys must be accustomed gradually to the strong meat of logic, first in the thin gruel of poets and orators, then in mathematics, where dialectic is more solid (*solidior*), and finally in physics, medicine, jurisprudence, and theology, that is, in all the rest of life (Ramus takes a curricular measure of life itself), where dialectic is fuller and richer (*copiosior et uberior*).[60] This Renaissance view, at least as typical as Erasmus', is noteworthy for the fact that it orders not only poetic, but all linguistic training to strictly practical ends within the upper nonliterary curriculum. Until it disintegrated, virtually the whole linguistic fabric of the Latin world was controlled by this educational pattern. Little wonder that, when Latin poetry finally perishes, we find ranking high among its last major productions such things as the five-thousand-line poem by the Jesuit scientist Boscovich entitled *The Eclipses of the Sun and Moon*, which explained Newtonian physics, or the three-thousand-line paraphrase of Newton's *Opticks* by Paolo Lucini.[61]

In this climate regulated by the classroom tradition, poetry was not commonly distinguished from rhetoric for the practical reason that it really coincided with rhetoric as a means of inculcating a more than elementary knowledge of Latin. When it was finally differentiated as an elementary subject, it was differentiated in elementary terms — by its measure. As Melanchthon had noted about his differentiation of dialectic and rhetoric, the basis of the distinction might be open to objection, but it meant something to young boys.

8. THE PLAIN STYLE

There is little evidence from Ramus' contemporaries that anything very new and distinctive resulted immediately from Ramus' or Talon's prescriptions regarding actual style, in writing or in oral delivery. The plain style, about which so much has been written lately, emerges as ideal and actuality among their followers, particularly the Puritan or other "enthusiastic" or "methodist" preachers whose formal education was controlled by a Ramist dialectic and rhetoric evolved to the limit of its original implications.

Plainness or simplicity of expression had figured as an occasional or possible rhetorical objective from the period of antiquity. The special urgency which plainness ultimately acquired in the Ramist milieu has been described recently in various ways, particularly in connection with the early New Englanders' notion of what a sermon, or composition in general, ought to be.[62] The ideal was "plaine delivery of the Word without painted eloquence" (which is close to saying without "colors"), or, in William Ames' words, expression marked by the "simplicity of the Gospell." The "methodical manner"[63] was to be cultivated, together with "plainness, perspicacity, gravity." Baroque Anglican style, full of sound, was to be put aside for a straightforward technique of "opening" a text by analysis. In place of Donne's way of preaching, "topical" in that it used the topics or places as if they were resonant with sentences or sayings, the advocates of plain style wanted preaching with method and certainty, giving "doctrine" and "reasons" from "axioms."

Axioms are a part of dialectic, of course, whether detached or not, so that what is being recommended is a retreat from rhetoric back into a pure dialectic — in effect, a nonrhetorical style. If this recommendation accords ill with Ramus' injunctions to mingle dialectic and rhetoric, philosophy and eloquence, in practice or use, it accords very well with his view that rhetoric, like prudential method, is, in the last analysis, dissimulation, to be resorted to only when the audience is recalcitrant. Plain style, which is really nonrhetorical style, alone is acceptable to reasonable man. Significantly, one of the earliest Ramist proposals to speak "plainly" occurs in Talon's preface to his *Dialectical Explanations of Porphyry*, a dialectical commentary on a dialectical work, where we are told that Talon will put Porphyry's Greek text into Latin in words which are "proper" (that is, nonrhetorical) and which "signify the matter simply and plainly." [64] Talon's preface is overfull here with talk about the "needs of youth" and "popular use" (*ad usum popularem*). In the name of simplification to serve these ends he rejects not only rhetoric, but the old logical refinements.

Of course, the Puritans, who will bring out the fuller implications of the plain style, use rhetoric, as everyone must. Moreover, their preaching bears a strong sense of kerygma. They preach the "word." And yet their favorite explanations of discourse and communication readily generate such things as William Ames' denunciation of "itching ears" and militate against affection for words as such. Words will languish, finally, in this linguistic climate, suspect of failing to "let through" the meaning of the Scripture intended by God as well as method and diagrams could. It is to be noted that the stylistic recommendations related to plainness, such as "perspicuity" in the sense of translucency, are formulated basically by analogy with visual apprehension and represent an attempt to reduce the process of communication in terms of such apprehension. The medium by which light is transmitted seems to act as though it were not there, whereas the medium of sound is felt rather as though it were acting to sustain and to give resonance to sound.

9. EFFECTS OF RAMIST RHETORIC

Ramist rhetoric and Ramism as a whole are interesting for what they become when the concepts in which Ramism specializes take possession of human sensibilities. There gradually they help to transform man's conceptual life. Ramist rhetoric is perhaps less interesting and less significant when we ask what was its immediate effect on the writing of those who first studied it,

not because it had no effects, but because in the beginning the effects deriving
from its prescriptions were often not appreciably different from those of other
rhetorics. As has been seen, the distinctive plain style emerged later, especially
toward the opening of the seventeenth century, but it was not prescribed by
Ramist rhetoric, although it was made inevitable by the whole mental setting
which constitutes Ramism.

Applied in the individual classroom to the formation of (Latin) style, the
Ramist rhetoric undoubtedly had variable effects depending on the way different teachers exploited it. As an approach to a text, it had most of the ad-
vantages and disadvantages of the other standard rhetorics of the time, such
as Melanchthon's, Susenbrotus', Soarez's, and the rest, for the apocopated
Ramist rhetoric was always to be used with Ramist dialectic, which supplied
all excised parts. But even when supplemented this way by Ramist dialectic,
Ramist rhetoric still had certain lacunae — notably sentence, amplification,
and decorum — and these lacunae would give it from the first a characteristic
torque. Types of discourse like the fourteen taught in Aphthonius' *Progymnasmata* and other elementary rhetoric exercise books or "formulary rhetorics" — retelling of fable, the *chria* or theme on a known person, the *sententia*
or theme on an apothegm or proverb, and so on — were no longer points of
reference for Ramist rhetorical organization. They were not points of reference because all organization or structuring was purportedly dialectical or
logical by its very nature, and where not ruled by syllogism was ruled by
method, which by definition was always one and the same.

Analysis, such as Ramists practiced, was practiced by other rhetoricians,
too, and had been from the time the humanists had focused attention on
literary texts, although the others did not practice it with such ardor as the
Ramists nor make such an issue of it. Although it often meant mere naming
of the "ornaments" of tropes and figures, such rhetorical analysis, particularly
when abetted by dialectical analysis, demanded that the pupil get into the
text, struggle with it, and, in general, involve himself in the linguistic
situation.

The exact relevance of what the pupil *thought* he was doing, and the
adequacy of his tools or definitions to the linguistic richness of the texts he
may have been working on, as well as to the composition or "genesis" with
which he was to follow his analysis, may well be questioned, and, indeed,
have been.[65] Certainly Ramus and most others never explained with any
acumen what the relevance was. Little matter; the boys to whom this and
other rhetorics were directed could not have mastered the explanation anyhow. These rhetorics did give them something to do with a text, made them
beat back and forth over it till the Latin phrases rang in their ears. In the
long run they did this forcefully enough to fertilize their English or other
vernacular imaginations, producing not only Latin stylists but, more important, Marlowes and Shakespeares and Lope de Vegas and Montaignes.

Miss Tuve has devoted a chapter and more to the relationship between Ramism, particularly Ramist logic, and Elizabethan literary imagery.[66] She suggests that the appropriation of all the loci by logic or dialectic strengthens the hold of logic on the poetry and literature of the period in a way which twentieth-century critics have minimized. In particular, Ramism stressed the use of "specials" or individual examples to prove "generals" or universal propositions, and it emphasized the use of disjunction. In these and related ways it seems curiously of a piece with the metaphysical poetry which flowers at the same time Ramism does in the last two decades of the sixteenth century.

These suggestions seem, as a whole, to be well made. At this point, however, some supplementary relationships between Ramism and metaphysical poetry can be indicated. The transfer of all the loci to dialectic or logic and the concomitant development of a logic of places or topical logic, as has been seen, represents a major movement of thought and sensibility. It has at its roots the peculiarly medieval logical developments found in Peter of Spain as well as the pedagogical drives of the humanists; it bears fruit in the mechanism which in Newton's age and later gives the modern mind some of its characteristic outlooks. Within this movement the Ramist interest in "specials" and its emphasis on disjunction come to much the same thing. "Specials" are thought of largely as "generals" cut up into more or less quantitative pieces, and thus as a product of disjunction, effected in concepts more or less openly devised according to visual, spatial analogies.

Therefore, one can, I believe, restate Miss Tuve's contention in even larger perspectives such as these: Ramism assimilated logic to imagery and imagery to logic by reducing intelligence itself, more or less unconsciously, in terms of rather exclusively visual, spatial analogies. The brusque, spatial maneuvers, not to say spastic postures, which conceptualization of the Ramist sort favors (that is, Ramus' ultimate reduction of the "secrets" of method to simple reversal of local motion and his constant invocation of "Solon's Law") obviously have some affinity with the harsh contrasts and grotesquerie of metaphysical poetry as well as of the baroque poetry which grew with or out of the metaphysical.

But Ramists did not write metaphysical poetry, or, indeed, much poetry at all. The lampoons against Ramus on the Paris stage in his own lifetime, the remarks in the *Parnassus* plays at Cambridge, Marlowe's and Jonson's lines, all show Ramus and Ramism as something the poets perennially regarded as fair game. The apparent collusion between Ramist dialectic and rhetoric and the habits of thought and imagination of Elizabethan poets testifies to common background rather than to any conscious sympathy. Indeed, back of the points of agreement there was a divergence extremely profound.

Most of the best Elizabethan and Jacobean poetry is dialogue at root. This is true not only of the stage, but of the lyric as well (although here only one side of the dialogue is commonly set down), and so true as to be a common-place. We may wonder to whom Shakespeare's sonnets are addressed, but there is no mistaking that in them he is talking to someone, real or imaginary. He does not muse, as Wordsworth does at his less than best, or as John Stuart Mill believed all poets should. The overtones of "real" or colloquial speech, that is, of *dialogue* between persons, which sixteenth- and seventeenth-century poetry specializes in, give it its characteristic excellence. Ramist rhetoric, on the other hand, is not a dialogue rhetoric at all, and Ramist dialectic has lost all sense of Socratic dialogue and even most sense of scholastic dispute. The Ramist arts of discourse are monologue arts. They develop the didactic, schoolroom outlook which descends from scholasticism even more than do non-Ramist versions of the same arts, and tend finally even to lose the sense of monologue in pure diagrammatics. This orientation is very profound and of a piece with the orientation of Ramism toward an object world (associated with visual perception) rather than toward a person world (associated with voice and auditory perception). In rhetoric, obviously someone had to speak, but in the characteristic outlook fostered by the Ramist rhetoric, the speaking is directed to a world where even persons respond only as objects — that is, say nothing back.

In this orientation, several phenomena, otherwise apparently isolated from one another, exhibit surprising relationships. Combined with Ramus' own lack of interest in dialogue, as evinced by his silence in company,[67] and his way of lashing out to annihilate his opponents or texts he was commenting on, is his and his followers' marked hostility to drama. His educational "reform" included the abolishing of plays by the students at the Collège de Presles.[68] He decreed this despite his own decidedly florid personal eloquence, for, it must be remembered, such eloquence was, in theory, really an evil, made necessary by a recalcitrant audience. The Calvinists who were to find Ramus congenial — more for the tone of his teaching than for any assignable doctrinal position — exhibit the same combination as Ramus himself: a "methodical" theory of speech, which their performance seldom fits, and a curiously ingrained dislike of drama. These are people somehow deeply distrustful of words, save perhaps in the homiletic monologue. This, of course, is not all such people are, for they exhibit many other tendencies, some of them quite opposed to this, which will develop quite different outlooks and institutions in the course of history. But meanwhile, they do not like metaphysical or other poetry which echoes dialogue, and they do not like the stage, favoring a form of speech which argues from "axioms" with at least a pseudocertainty. Edward Taylor, the one New England Puritan who wrote poetry derivative from the Elizabethan dramatic experience, is the least Puritan and least Ramist of all New England writers.[69] When the Puritan mentality, which is here the Ramist mentality, produces poetry, it is at first blatantly didactic, but shades gradually into reflective poetry which does not talk to anyone in particular but meditates on objects, such as the moon. There is a curious connection here between the plain-style mentality and some later romantic developments.

10. THE MEANING OF RAMIST RHETORIC

The deepest meaning of Ramist rhetoric is to be found in the general framework of man's changing attitudes toward communication, with which rhetoric is so inextricably involved. The history of the arts of discourse is still commonly treated as though, since grammar, rhetoric, and dialectic were and are well-known names, they were transmitted in little packets from generation to generation. Actually, man's approach to speech is too tied up with his attitudes toward himself and toward other persons and toward the universe to admit of such tidy transmission. From the beginning, the arts of communication grow slowly, tortuously, and mysteriously in a curiously strategic position within the human psyche, prolific on the one hand of theories concerning the nature of thought and things, so that they prove to be the seedbed of philosophy itself, and on the other hand deeply involved in action because they are directly concerned with the business of communication, upon which man's other actions so unmistakably depend.

It can be argued that the most distinguishing feature of Western culture is its development of a scientifically managed dialectic and of related formal logics, together with those rhetorics which are the counterparts of such logics. Other civilizations develop no mature formal logic any more than they develop modern science, and the developments in the *artes sermocinales* are more original, more time-consuming, and more fundamental than the scientific developments. Ramist rhetoric belongs to a critical period in the history of these Western *artes sermocinales*, and suggests interrelationships between developments in these arts and the development of letterpress printing, the perfecting of the textbook, the burgeoning of a potentially infinite number of "courses" or "subjects" in the curriculum, and finally the emergence of modern science itself.

Like all rhetoric, Ramist rhetoric is concerned with expression, with communication, with speaking, with not only a subject matter but also an auditor. But it is a rhetoric which has renounced any possibility of invention within this speaker-auditor framework; it protests in principle if not in actuality, that invention is restricted to a dialectical world where there is no voice but only a kind of vision. By its very structure, Ramist rhetoric asserts to all who are able to sense its implications that there is no way to discovery or to understanding through voice, and ultimately seems to deny that the processes of person-to-person communication play any necessary role in intellectual life. It thus throws before us the larger, more generalized perspectives in which exists the Renaissance movement often interpreted as a "revolt against authority." The revolt is not quite against authority, as everyone knows, because, with almost the sole exception of the unfortunate Galileo case, there are few instances of authorities penalizing intellectual enterprise and discovery. What there is, is a deep-felt protest against the obtrusion of voices and persons in scientific issues.

In Ramist rhetoric, dialogue and conversation themselves become by implication mere nuisances. When Ramus first laid hold of the topics (that is, what he styles "arguments"), these were associated with real dialogue or discussion, if only because they existed in both dialectic and rhetoric conjointly and thus kept dialectic in touch with the field of communication and thought-in-a-vocal setting which had been in historical actuality the matrix of logic itself. But by the application of "Solon's Law," which severed rhetoric from dialectic with savage rigor and without any profound understanding of the interrelationship of these two disciplines, the topics, relegated by Ramus to dialectic (or logic) exclusively, were in principle denied any oral or aural connections at all. To the Ramist, Dryden's admission that he was often helped to an idea by a rhyme was an admission of weakness if not of outright intellectual perversion.

Furthermore, Ramist rhetoric is a rhetoric which has not only no invention but also no judgment or arrangement of its own. The field of activity covered by the terms judgment or arrangement (*dispositio*) has likewise been dissociated from voice by being isolated from rhetoric and committed to Ramist dialectic or logic. In the process, judgment — which necessarily bespeaks utterance, an assent or a dissent, a *saying* of yes or no — simply disappears, and with it all rational interest in the psychological activities which such a term covers. Arrangement or "positioning" (*dispositio*) secures exclusive rights as the only other phenomenon besides invention which occurs in intellectual activity, and as the sole principle governing the organization of speech. Unlike judgment, which cannot be conceived of independently of some reference to saying, to utterance, and thus to the oral and aural world of personalities, "arrangement" can be conceived of simply by analogy with visually perceived spatial patterns. With all rhetorical organization governed from outside rhetoric by this "arrangement" (syllogism and method), the role of voice and person-to-person relationships in communication is reduced to a new minimum. When, finally, in this development memory also goes insofar as it is aural, and is replaced — again, at least in theory — by the "natural" order in things, which means, as has been seen, almost any order, however arbitrary, picturable in a dichotomized diagram for the visual imagination, all that is left to this rhetoric is style and delivery. Of these the more vocal, delivery, is regularly underdeveloped or totally neglected, proving in effect uncongenial to Ramist theory, and style itself, as has been seen, is reduced further in terms which can be somehow visually conceived.

To be sure, rhetoric is still called rhetoric and is thought of as committed to a world of voice; it does, as a matter of fact, handle expression. And Ramist dialectic remains, in effect, a rhetorical instrument, since the principles of organization it proposes can in the large be given no really formal logical structure. But in the Ramist account of rhetoric, and of the world of voice in which it reportedly operated, the art has been made over by analogy with the silent world of vision. Ideologically, the world of sound has yielded, unwittingly but quite effectively, to the world of space.

This development which is so typical of Ramism is likewise, however, typical in the large of the whole logical and rhetorical development of the West out of which Ramism emerges, so that in his *Logic and Rhetoric in England, 1500–1700*, Wilbur Samuel Howell, with reason sees Ramism not as something incidental but as a pivotal phenomenon. Professor Howell makes it clear that a distinctive mark of the post-Ramist dialectic or logic is that it is a logic of individual inquiry into issues thought of as existing outside a framework of discourse or dialectic rather than a logic of discourse.[70]

Such a logic of inquiry is implicitly conceived of as operating outside the aural world. But the complexity of the forces here at work can be gauged by the fact that when Ramism moved to make dialectic or logic less aural it did so initially by making it seemingly more rhetorical, so that Prantl and others have described Ramist logic as a rhetoric-logic. Here one must distinguish between actuality and theory. In actuality, Ramist logic was rhetorical by the standards of medieval terminists or of modern formal logicians. That is, in reality it was only loosely or "probably" conclusive. It had sacrificed scientific certainty by basing itself on the dialectico-rhetorical topics. Nevertheless, the absorption of these dialectico-rhetorical topics gave it no rhetorical flair. On the contrary, the topics, rechristened "arguments," themselves were superficially transformed into scientific instruments by their insertion within a structural economy thought of as being even more rigid than that dominated by the categories.

In the post-Ramist developments discussed by Professor Howell one can observe this process actually repeating itself. For the new Port-Royal logic which succeeded Ramism in France, and to some extent in England, moves determinedly away from rhetoric, then ambiguously toward it, only to move finally and still more ambiguously away from it again. That is to say, the Port-Royal logicians begin by discarding not only the categories but the Ramist rhetorically nurtured topics or arguments, too — at least they begin by determining to discard all these, for, after denouncing the topics, they bring them in again by the back door, finding that it is not so easy as one might today suppose to construct an art of pure, solitary thinking.[71] But having determined to discard these rhetorical accoutrements, the Port-Royal logicians took over from the rhetorical field something else, a concern with the passions (in this, like Ramus they go back to Rudolph Agricola and his way of being different from Peter of Spain). But, just as the topics were de-rhetoricized, that is, de-vocalized or mechanized, by the Ramists because they were subjugated in dialectic to a diagrammatic economy, so the passions would be de-rhetoricized or mechanized (processed for diagrammatic or visile thinking) by succeeding generations of post-Ramist associationist philosophers and literary critics.[72]

In this economy where everything having to do with speech tends to be in one way or another metamorphosed in terms of structure and vision, the rhetorical approach to life — the way of Isocrates and Cicero and Quintilian and Erasmus, and of the Old and New Testaments — is sealed off into a cul-de-sac. The attitude toward speech has changed. Speech is no longer a medium in which the human mind and sensibility lives. It is resented, rather, as an accretion to thought, hereupon imagined as ranging noiseless concepts or "ideas" in a silent field of mental space. Here the perfect rhetoric would be to have no rhetoric at all. Thought becomes a private, or even an antisocial enterprise. The sequels of Ramism — method and its epiphenomena, which identify Ramism as an important symptom of man's changing relationship to the universe — connect with Ramist dialectic directly but with rhetoric only negatively or not at all. To be sure, techniques of expression will still be taught (although for a while, at least in Puritan lands, the stage, where speech is at its maximum as speech, will go), but all the while a curious subconscious hostility to speech in all its forms will eat away at the post-Ramist age, bringing Thomas Sprat to fear for the members of the Royal Academy that "the whole spirit and vigour of their *Design* [note this visualist concept], had been soon eaten out, by the luxury and redundance of *speech*" and to denounce roundly all use of tropes and figures.[73] Only after the Hegelian rehabilitation of the notion of dialogue and the later discrediting of the Newtonian universe would this hostility begin effectively to wane.

The effectiveness of the obscure forces at work here can be appreciated only if one remains aware of the obscure and mysterious nature of rhetoric itself. It was never a self-possessed art or science in the way in which Euclidean geometry, or even grammar, might be. As at its beginning, when "rhetoric" constituted the ancient Greek plan of general intellectual education, "rhetoric" in Ramus' day is a complex and somewhat protean product of educational needs and theory, working at its center toward a philosophy of expression, but derivative in fact less from such a philosophy than from a complicated pedagogical situation never entirely under control. Renaissance rhetoric, and Ramist rhetoric in particular, registers the practical pressures of an educational milieu where "rhetoric" is conceived of in actuality as the next language course after grammar, taught only to youngsters, concerned directly with a language foreign to even its most voluble and skilled users, and controlled by silent written and printed documents more than by the spoken word. Within this milieu, Ramist rhetoric registers the further drive toward curriculum simplification and orderliness generated first by the teacher-centered scholasticism of the universities and intensified in other ways by the pupil-centered pedagogy of the humanist schools. These conditions help explain its theoretical deficiencies. Theoretical problems which were involved in the rhetoric-logic dyad or which today would be considered in the general field called communications tended to be concentrated within dialectic, which was more abstract and manageable and which for centuries had commonly existed in a more mature pedagogical context. Ramist rhetorical theory, even abetted by Ramist dialectical theory, is thus understandably thin. But this very fact is meaningful, and, as a gauge of some of the central pressures shaping the evolution of human thought, this rhetoric is one of the most informative there is.

Book Four
SEQUEL

CHAPTER XIII

THE DIFFUSION OF RAMISM

For having now my Method by the end,
Still as I pull'd, it came; and so I penned
It down; until at last it came to be,
For length and breadth the bigness which you see.
— John Bunyan's "Apology"
for *The Pilgrim's Progress*.

I. THE SPREAD OF THE RAMIST MOVEMENT

THE aftereffects of Ramism, which for the past two decades have claimed more attention than its origins and internal development, make an elusive study. For Ramism becomes increasingly difficult to identify when the very forces which it spearheaded gain momentum and finally swallow it up. By the time method and logical analysis have established themselves firmly in the Western European psyche, the paramount role of Ramism in their establishment has been forgotten. Several recent studies point out this gradual loss of identity which marked its seventeenth-century history.[1]

These aftereffects are not only elusive but complicated by their international character, so that except for Waddington's hasty and now long outmoded account,[2] studies on them have all understandably focused on one or another particular country. For this reason, although the full story of post-Ramist developments in the light of the present account of Ramist history would require a separate volume, it is pertinent here to look briefly at some of these developments. The perspectives used will be those suggested in this work and the accompanying documentation provided by the *Ramus and Talon Inventory* (see Figure XV), which records some 800 editions and adaptations of Ramus' and Talon's own works (some 1100 if one numbers separately individual works appearing in collections) and those of nearly 400 Ramist educators and public figures.

Except for sallies into Basle, and into Spain under the aegis of Francisco Sanchez de las Brozas, the Ramist movement as it is represented by printed works is restricted to France up to Ramus' own death in 1572. Its quick disappearance in France after this date, however, should not lead us to conclude too hastily that it was simply transplanted elsewhere after the horrors of the

DISTRIBUTION OF EDITIONS (INCLUDING ADAPTATIONS) OF THE RAMIST DIALECTIC AND RHETORIC (FIGURE XV)[a]

Based on Ong, *Ramus and Talon Inventory*

YEAR	FRANCE (EXCLUSIVE OF ALSACE) Paris Lyons La Rochelle Niort Sedan		SPAIN Salamanca		GERMANY Frankfort/M Cologne Marburg(Lahn) Herborn Hanau Dortmund Nuremberg Speyer Siegen Lemgo Magdeburg Bremen Brunswick Erfurt Giessen Hamburg Hanover Jena Leipzig Lich Lubeck Rostock Stuttgart Coburg Goslar Oppenheim Rinteln Ursel Wittenberg		SWITZERLAND Basle Zurich Bern Geneva		BRITISH ISLES London Cambridge Oxford Edinburgh		ALSACE Strasbourg Mulhouse		LOW COUNTRIES Leyden Amsterdam Utrecht Middelburg (English Puritan colony) The Hague Tiel		ALL ELSE Philadelphia New York		TOTALS	
	Di	Rh	Di	Rh	Di	Rh	Di	Rh	Di	Rh	Di	Rh	Di	Rh	Di	Rh	Di	Rh
1543 –1557	(15 I) (12A)	(4 I)			(1 I)													
1555 –1572	8	20	2	2	2	3	2	1									14	26
1573 –1580	5	6	1	1	14	4 (1 I)(2A)	2	1	3								25	12
1581 –1590		1	1	1	34(2A)	12	7	5	11	1	1		5	3			59	23
1591 –1600		1			49(1A)	15	2	1	1	4				1			52	22
1601 –1610					20	13	2	4						1			22	18
1611 –1620		1			16	8	4	1	1	1	1		1	1			23	12
1621 –1630					9	7	2	3									11	10
1631 –1640		1			2				5	5	1		1				9	4
1641 –1650	1	1				1			1	4	1		6	2			9	8
1651 –1660					2	1			3	6			5	1			10	8
1661 –1700					3	4	2	1	6	5			4	1			15	11
1701 –1800							2	2	2	2			(1 I)(1A)	1			4	6
1801 –1950									7	2					2	2	9	4
TOTAL	14		4		151		23		42		4		22		2		262	
TOTAL		31		4		69		16		33		0		11		2		166

Figures in parentheses, not included in totals, represent editions of the works out of which the Dialectic and Rhetoric grew: (I) *Dialecticae institutiones*, (A) *Aristotelicae animadversiones*, (O) *Inst. oratoriae*.

[a] Under each country, municipalities are arranged according to their publishing activity, the more active preceding the less. 1572 is the year of Ramus' death.

1572 massacre. Prior to 1572, French Ramism had been a phenomenon qualitatively different from the Ramism which was to develop after 1572 in other countries, for unlike this latter, it had not been powered by a dialectic which swept all before it. The tally of editions shows that before 1572 in France Ramist rhetorics are more numerous than Ramist dialectics. The fact is that Ramus' own defense of his dialectic against his critics, Antonio de Gouveia, Charpentier, Riolan, and the rest, who were heirs of the formidably erudite Parisian logical tradition, made a poor showing and left Parisians generally unconvinced.

Ramus' rhetoric was another matter. In the first place, Ramus enjoyed among his compatriots an enviable reputation as an eloquent speaker. Second, rhetoric was not a matter which engaged philosophical theory to the extent that dialectic did, so that it engendered far less dispute. Rhetoric was essentially a subject for small boys, in which not theory but performance in writing and speaking Latin chiefly counted. Here Ramus' reputation as an efficient schoolmaster and dedicated principal of the Collège de Presles served the cause of his rhetoric well. The Talon-Ramus rhetoric was an on-the-spot practical success. And it had a further tactical advantage to recommend it. As the companion piece to a reconstructed dialectic it had the air of something new in rhetoric and thus at least superficially satisfied the humanist concern for reform in this field. At the same time, it did not really disturb the older pattern much. For, by restricting rhetoric to style and delivery (and thereupon regularly minimizing the latter), it left unchallenged the stylistic rhetoric which through the Middle Ages had been the normal curricular counterpart of dialectic. The curious effectiveness of the Ramist "revolution" in reinforcing existing tendencies is nowhere more evident than here.

Nevertheless, by agitating the question of "method" in Paris, the dialectical capital of the world, Ramus left on the scholastic and humanistic traditions a permanent and important mark. By hybridizing rhetorical organization with "logic," Ramist method widened the field in which the passion for at least superficial "methodical" orderliness could play. It released enthusiasms such as that of Jean Bodin, who seeks to "methodize" man's understanding even of history,[3] and prepared the way for the more gargantuan enthusiasms of the German systematic encyclopedists and thus indirectly for the still later French *Encyclopédistes*. Here it served somewhat as a crystal introduced into a supersaturated solution, suddenly precipitating and giving structure to the interest in method with which the scholastic world in Paris was charged. Most notions of method after Ramus' time bear some signs of connection with his thinking, and Professor Howell has recently pointed out in treating the Port-Royalists and Bernard Lamy that the influence of Ramism in France was as real as it was diffuse and vague well through the seventeenth century.[4] The preoccupation with method which haunts the French mind is the legacy of the Ramist experience.

Whether the fortunes of Ramism in France would have been the same had it not been for the horrors of St. Bartholomew's Day is not easy to say. What is certain is that the 1572 massacre led Ramus' most productive publisher, Wéchel, to abandon Paris for Frankfort on the Main. Thereafter for a century Ramism found its real stronghold in Germany, particularly in and near the Rhineland, where the Agricolan dialectic and Sturm's interest in method had been matured before they were exported to Paris to be taken over and developed by Ramus. Here Ramism assumes its classic form, with dialectic in control of everything, even of rhetoric, as well as of innumerable other subjects never dreamt of in Ramus' philosophy. Ramus himself, it will be recalled, exiled from France, unwilling to accept an invitation to Bologna, and sensing the hostility of Geneva, had paid protracted visits to the Rhineland area between Frankfort and Basle. There he found his simplified dialectic and rhetoric welcome not only among the exiled French Huguenots such as the Wéchels, Languet, and Théophile de Banos, but quite as much among the native German-speaking population. As can be seen from Figure XV and in more detail in the *Ramus and Talon Inventory*, the peak of Ramist influence in Germany falls between 1580 and 1620. It was most intense in the sectors of Germany tinged by Calvinism (these correspond roughly to the Rhineland and its environs) and weaker in the more Lutheran parts of the country. The influence of German Ramism also descends the Rhine to the more or less Calvinist sections of the Netherlands.

After Ramus' death, Germany is the real seedbed of Ramism, both as an explicit reform of dialectic and rhetoric and as a *Weltanschauung*. Elsewhere the Ramist reorganization of the curriculum tends to affect chiefly the rhetoric-dialectic dyad, on which Professor Howell has reported for Great Britain. In Germany, however, its diagrammatic approach to knowledge fires the imagination of polyhistors and of codifiers of all the sciences, so that Ramist method moves into the uppermost branches of the curriculum with a drive which cannot be matched in any other country. Nowhere else is the Ramist influence felt on such a monumental scale as in the works of Johann Heinrich Alsted, whose compends of all knowledge mark the confident beginnings of modern encyclopedism; [5] in the analyzer of the Scriptures, Johannes Piscator; in the great systematizer of Calvinist theology, Amandus Polanus von Polansdorf; in Bartholomew Keckermann, who systematized theology, the other sciences, and history as well; or in Johannes Althusius, who methodized politics. To these should be added other slightly less productive, but still prolific, writers: the German-Swiss Johann Thomas Freige; the German physician and chemist Andreas Libau or Libavius; and Jan Amos Komensky (Comenius, 1592–1670), who was a Moravian but received his education and apparently much of the inspiration for his educational reforms from his Ramist teacher Alsted in Germany.

Ramism in Germany did not, of course, go unchallenged. Indeed, in 1592 it had been banned at the University of Leipzig.[6] The theoretical underpinnings of this "philosophy" frankly designed for youngsters in their early teens did not stand up under the inspection of mature university professors. Thus it is that the major figures who register Ramist influence, including the Germans just mentioned, with the exception of Freige, were not pure Ramists. They were known to their contemporaries as "Mixts." "Mixts" were followers in part of Ramus and in part of Aristotle or (in dialectic and rhetoric) of Philip Melanchthon, and in the latter case were often styled more specifically Philippo-Ramists. Some of these Mixts, notably those in the entourage of Keckermann, were also called "Systematics," from the fact that they wrote what they called "systems" of philosophy, metaphysics, physics, logic, and so on. They were apparently the first to be convinced that the notion of "system" could be fruitfully applied on a major scale to philosophical and other knowledge.[7]

The effect of the Ramist experience unmistakably shows through in the work of the great Mixts and Systematics (despite the avowedly hybrid nature of their views), having through these its greatest impact on Western thought. Alsted's huge encyclopedias, which were produced in such a profusion of editions[8] that they earned him the soubriquet of *Sedulitas* or Hard Work (an anagram of the Latin form of his name, Alstedius), undertake to review in semi-Ramist fashion all human knowledge. They organized it topically and "methodically" under an interlocking system of "arts," each of which is set up according to the model of the Ramist dialectic, the art being first defined, then divided into two parts, which are in turn defined and dichotomized, and so on. The Ramist dialectic itself appears as one of the arts in the Alsted encyclopedias, since Alsted is closer to a pure Ramist than Keckermann is.

Among all the Mixts and Systematics, the pursuit of knowledge is sustained by the Ramist's conviction that there is a "natural" or topical approach to anything through some readily available art or science. This approach professes to proceed by "invention," "analysis," and "method," and thus is based on the persuasion that the organization of Ramist dialectic is a satisfactory model for the treatment of any subject whatsoever.

Keckermann and Polanus von Polansdorf and Libavius, together with many others, less purely Ramist than Alsted or Freige or Piscator,[9] all exhibit the same trust in "laying out" material by definition and division after division. Their works often rely on the familiar Ramist dichotomized tables to display convincingly in space the results of their research and thinking, and to satisfy an appetite for "clarity" by a sure-fire diagrammatic recall-mechanism. In like vein, Johannes Piscator sets out to do a "logical analysis" of each and every book of the Old and New Testaments to make it "clear" once for all what the Scriptures really say (they say what Piscator's summaries say they say, all the rest in the Scriptures being "ornament"). Freige (see Figures

XVI and XVII), Keckermann, and others even manage to give pseudo-scientific organization to the Hebrew alphabet, to the bubonic plague, to history, and to other bizarre newcomers among the quondam arts or curriculum subjects particularly resistant to being "methodized."[10] Their achievements are matched by those of Althusius in law and in the new science of politics.[11]

52 DE GRAMMATICA HEBRAEA.

pro omnibus uocalibus: unde Hebraeis matres lectionis dicuntur: prima quippe fuit pro A, secunda pro E & I, tertia pro O & V. At eaedem literae tribus item consonis notandis seruiebant. Quare ut tanta confusio tolleretur, & uocales singulae distinctae nostis explicarentur, punctà à Masuritis inuenta sunt, ut ex Elia intelligitur, annis à Christo quadringentis septuaginta sex. Attamen ex uocalibus breuibus tres ultimae, hiric, camets, & kybuts nunquam plenae scribuntur: sed hiric magnum.

Quottuplex est consona?
. Duplex: Semiuocalis & Muta.

Semiuocalis {
  Acuta {
    Samech ס
    Schin ש quod proprie sonat pinguius, & crassius quà Samech: pro quo interdum sumitur, sed notatur tum sinistro puncto sic ש. Porrò huius tantulae rei ignoratio magnae caedis causam praebuit, cù propterea perierint uno tempore Ephrateorū duo & quadraginta millia, ut est Iud. 12.
    Resch ר
    Lamed ל
  }
  Obtusa {
    Mem מ
    Nun נ
    Vau ו
    Iod י
  }
}

Muta

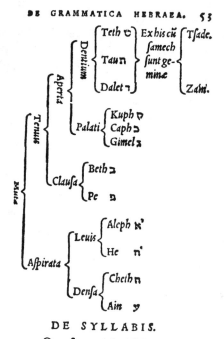

DE GRAMMATICA HEBRAEA. 53

Muta {
  Aperta {
    Densium {
      Teth ט
      Taun ת
      Dalet ד
    }
    Ex his cù samech sunt geminae {
      Tsade צ
      Zain ז
    }
  }
  Tenuis {
    Palati {
      Kuph ק
      Caph כ
      Gimel ג
    }
    Clausa {
      Beth ב
      Pe פ
    }
  }
  Aspirata {
    Leuis {
      Aleph א
      He ה
    }
    Densa {
      Cheth ח
      Ain ע
    }
  }
}

DE SYLLABIS.

Quorsum pertinet Scheua?
Ad syllabas. Nam syllaba è uocali, & consonante mista, plures illa quidem literas, sed binas tantum consonas utrinq; complecti potest: quarum connexionis symbolū uocatur Scheua, & duobus subiectis iectis
d ;

XVI. LANGUAGE IN SPACE (FREIGE)

From this point on, the vexing quest for "first principles" to guarantee the proper scientific foundation for each and every art or science need bother no one. A convincing "methodical" framework was at hand which made first principles in the strict Aristotelian sense superfluous. Insofar as it can be defined, divided, and at least in the visual imagination spitted on a set of dichotomies, any "matter" at all can be given a "scientific" treatment by having its terms "clearly" (that is, diagrammatically) related to one another.

The influence of German Ramism and of the Mixts and Systematics fed back into France itself, where an edition of Alsted's *Encyclopedia* was published in 1649, and where the passion for method and system finally flowered in the work of Diderot and Jean d'Alembert. At the less scholarly, textbook level, Ramism is given some attention by the writers of the Port-Royal *Logique*,[12] but the nature of its presence in the pre-Cartesian French tradition and in the works of writers such as Bayle have still to be more carefully studied.

XVII. MEDICINE IN SPACE (FREIGE)

Ramism in England is the result of two primary infusions. The first was around 1574, when the Ramist *Dialectic* was first printed in two London editions by the Huguenot *émigré* Thomas Vautrollier. One was in Latin and one in English. The latter was prepared by Roland M'Kilwein (Makylmenaeus), a somewhat mysterious character about whom nothing else is known save that he matriculated in 1565 at the University of St. Andrews and there received his B.A. in 1569 and M.A. in 1570.[13] In the same year Andrew Melville, back from the Continent, where he had had personal contact with

Ramus, began his Ramist reform of studies at the University of Glasgow. Melville carried the reform, the extent of which is difficult to assess, on to King's College at the University of Aberdeen in 1575 and to St. Andrews in 1578. Although their relation to one another is not clear, M'Kilwein's editions and Melville's work fit into the pattern of Gallo-Scottish intellectual exchange well-known in the history of literature and of scholasticism and not unknown in the life of Ramus himself, at whose table two natural sons of James V used to dine frequently,[14] and who had come up to Paris to find among the most distinguished recent dialecticians there the Scots John Major, Robert Caubraith, and David Cranston.[15]

The next infusion of Ramism was to come to England from Germany, and particularly from the Huguenot colony of Frankfort on the Main in the wake of the 1572–1575 Continental tour of Sir Philip Sidney. Sidney had lodged in Frankfort at the home of Ramus' printer André Wéchel, where Ramus' quondam traveling companion, Hubert Languet, was also a house guest. The Wéchels, canny Flemings who knew that business grew phenomenally with differences among the dons, promoted much international exchange of scholarly and other neo-Latin writings. Besides 172 or more editions of Ramus' own works,[16] they put out competing works by the Germans Roding and Beurhaus and Piscator, and published Everard Digby's attacks on Ramism, Piscator's and William Temple's attacks on Digby and on one another,[17] and many other works by Englishmen.

Sidney seems to have done much to direct the flood of works pouring from the Wéchel presses into England and ultimately into Ireland as well, for his erstwhile secretary, William Temple, later became provost of Trinity College in Dublin. On April 25, 1576, Wéchel's friend Théophile de Banos writes Sidney that copies of Ramus' posthumous *Commentary on the Christian Religion*, with the prefixed life of Ramus written by Banos and dedicated to Sidney, are being sent to England where, Banos adds brightly, they will "no doubt under your auspices be joyfully welcomed by the English."[18] Banos had reason to count on Sidney's good offices. At the young Englishman's request he had successfully undertaken, "after two thousand copies of the *Commentaries* were already printed," to convince the publisher Wéchel that the reference to Sidney in his dedication should be revised to point up better Sidney's relationship to the house of Warwick and to other lines of English nobility.[19] The incidental revelation here of the size of a Wéchel edition is of considerable value in assessing the impact of Ramist works.

Gabriel Harvey's Ramism appears in the wake of Sidney's visit with the Wéchels and marks the beginning of Ramism in the two English universities, especially among those with Puritan leanings at Cambridge University, and later at Trinity College in Dublin and at Harvard College. In 1574 Harvey was named University Professor of Rhetoric at Cambridge and the following year his *Ode* in memory of Peter Ramus was published by Vautrollier. Although Harvey's role in launching a native British Ramism has been commented on, it has not been sufficiently noted that Ramism makes its first appearance in England under specifically rhetorical auspices — which is to say that it is inserted in the curriculum at a level somewhat below that of logic or philosophy.

Professor Howell has given an excellent account of the further spread of Ramism at Oxford and Cambridge in the late sixteenth and early seventeenth centuries.[20] With the help of this account and of the *Ramus and Talon Inventory*, it can be seen how juvenile was the pattern of Ramism in the English-speaking world. Although there is a great deal of interest in Ramism in England, with very few exceptions almost no one connected permanently with either Oxford or Cambridge writes on Ramism for his colleagues of the university milieu. There is considerable reading of Ramist works by students, with or without direction, and a good deal of shouting for or against Ramism by sophisters or other youthful university disputants, who are echoed and improved by Robert Greene, Thomas Nashe, and the Harveys. Indeed, there are recurrent references to the youthfulness of British Ramists — in Abraham Fraunce,[21] in John Case,[22] and from across the Channel in Johannes Piscator, who patronizingly salutes his British opponent William Temple as "young man."[23]

To complement this ebullient youthful Ramism there is practically no serious and mature scholarship oriented by Ramism in the British Isles. Temple's work hardly qualifies as such scholarship, and Ames' and Downham's Ramism, from which Milton's adaptation of Ramus' *Logic* is derivative, is cradled on the Continent. Oxford's most active Ramist, Charles (or, as he himself would have it, Charls) Butler, was famed not as a seriously scientific logician or philosopher but as an author of preparatory-school textbooks in rhetoric. He did not treat even the logic which came next above rhetoric in the curriculum. Ramism in the British Isles plays out in a spate of such textbooks in rhetoric and in rhetorically oriented logic. Bacon spoke accurately for the learned tradition in England when he judged that Ramism was already over with in his day.

This does not make the Ramist influence in England any the less telling. Quite the contrary. Insofar as it shows that rhetoric and, more significantly, logic were being assimilated independently of a well-worked-out philosophical foundation, the condition of Ramism in the British Isles shows how much Renaissance logic there and elsewhere derived not from an insight into reality but from a state of mind. This logic could effect higher studies or adult activities — such as those of a Richard Mather, who as a young man for a few months read Ramus at Brasenose College, Oxford, with great relish and satisfaction and thereupon quit the University for good to carry his knowledge of "logic" gained so summarily there into his ministerial work and ultimately into New England.[24] The pervasiveness of the Ramist experience can be seen in the circulation of Ramist terms. For example, the term "method" was appropriated from the Ramist coffers and used to form the term "methodists" to designate first enthusiastic preachers who made an issue of their adherence to "logic," and finally the followers of John Wesley, who had been the author of a logic textbook vaguely reminiscent of Ramism.[25] Similarly, the huge market for books proposing various "methods" and "systems" and "analyses," which flood over England as over all Europe from the seventeenth century on, testifies to the abiding reality of the state of mind which Ramism helped establish.[26]

But this state of mind derived apparently from the study of logic as a fairly elementary discipline. Even during the maximum disturbances induced by Ramism from 1581 to 1591 at Cambridge, it is clear that — although a deceptively uncomplicated logic of the Ramist type fitted the actuality of the Renaissance curriculum and the age of the Renaissance students more satisfactorily than did the logics of the *Organon* or the still more highly formalized medieval logics — insofar as logic was maintained at the university level in England, it tended to remain pretty much Aristotle[27] (divested of the genuinely original medieval logical discoveries in supposition theory and quantification). After all, even Ramus' own mature *Lectures on Dialectic* had turned out to be commentaries not on his own work but, despite everything, on the works of Aristotle's *Organon*.

Perhaps the greater age of the English universities gave Aristotle a more secure hold in England and prevented Ramism from producing in the British Isles any comprehensive approach to the higher branches of knowledge comparable to what it produced in Germany. The attempts to bring Ramism to bear, for example, on theology are mostly minor ventures — Fenner's and others' introduction of scriptural examples into editions or translations of Ramus' *Dialectic* and *Rhetoric*, or *A Logicall Analysis of Twentie Select Psalmes* (1605) by William Temple, followed by an only slightly lengthier Latin *Analysis logica triginta Psalmorum* (1611). As examples of the influence of Ramism on mature scholarly minds, these are in no way comparable to the massive works of the Germans Alsted, Polanus, Keckermann, and Piscator, on whose Ramist interpretations of the higher disciplines the English-speaking Ramists depend. Even in the production of textbooks in arithmetic and geometry, English Ramists are outdistanced by the Germans and the Dutch. The one Englishman under Ramist influence who stands out as a possible competitor is William Ames, whose *Philosophemata* (1643, etc.)[28] is a brief compend of various branches of knowledge, methodized in Ramist fashion. But it is noteworthy that Ames, who lived for a long time in the Netherlands, developed his Ramism, like other Ramists such as Richard Mather and William Temple, at a distance from the British centers of learning.

In the Low Countries, Ramism had been known among English emigrants as early as the 1580's, when Dudley Fenner's English translations of the

Ramist *Dialectic* and *Rhetoric* had appeared, and it continued to flourish into the sixteenth century among the English at Franeker, where William Ames taught. The principal Dutch exponent of Ramism was Rudolph Snel van Roijen (Snellius), under whom Ramism showed a tendency to develop along lines explicitly mathematical rather than dialectical or rhetorical.

But Holland also served as a point of dispersion for Ramism of the traditional dialectically centered kind.[29] The partly Hungarian edition of the *Dialectic* appeared in 1658 at Utrecht, where there was a small group of Hungarian Calvinists. In Hungary, there were doubtless German influences on what Ramism existed there,[30] and the same German influences were even more evident in Bohemia and in Moravia. Here the famed Jan Amos Komensky taught after having visited England and Germany, where he studied under the Ramist Alsted and imbibed the spirit of Ramist encyclopedism.[31] As a specifically labeled movement, German Ramism had dropped out of sight in the 1630's, but Komensky's educational reform is one of the myriad ways in which Ramism is perpetuated in disguise. The story of Swiss Ramism is practically assimilable to that of German, for in Switzerland Ramism was almost nonexistent as a special movement outside the German cantons. Ramism in Alsace had been weaker than in Switzerland, possibly because of the dominance of the somewhat similar Sturm tradition. Under Andreas Krag, Ramism made its way into Denmark.

In Spain, the first place to which Ramism had migrated outside France, it had been early nipped in the bud when Ramus became a Protestant and when his disciple Francisco Sanchez de la Brozas got into trouble with the Inquisition. What obtained for Spain, obtained also for the Spanish Netherlands. Ramism never developed in Italy or in other countries or districts which remained Catholic, less because of any real antipathy for what the Ramist development fundamentally meant than because of suspicions attaching to Ramus as a Protestant. In the Catholic countries when the *Dialectic* and *Rhetoric* were actually gone over, as they occasionally were, by Catholic school teachers to see what was in them, they seem to have been regularly marked as harmless to the faith.[32] In preparing their report for the commission charged with drawing up the *Ratio studiorum*, or plan of studies, for Jesuit schools, the German Jesuit fathers take note of Ramism only to warn against Ramus' oversimplifications and exaggeration of the logical element in Cicero.[33]

As has been mentioned earlier, in practically all the countries where Ramism was known, it was at the forefront of the vernacular movements, so that the Ramist *Dialectic* and *Rhetoric* are often the first or among the first such works to appear in any vernacular.[34] Up until about the mid-seventeenth century the *Dialectic* was printed in one or another vernacular (mostly English) about three times as frequently as the *Rhetoric*. The reason for this was not peculiar to Ramism. Dialectic was presumably independent of the linguistic medium. Rhetoric was part of linguistic, and — even though the direct-method approach to Latin which, until it weakened in the eighteenth and nineteenth centuries, took for granted that one's textbooks for a language were written in the language itself — there was no point in having a vernacular rhetoric unless vernacular literature was a school subject. By the later 1600's, the Ramist *Rhetoric*, like other rhetorics, is printed somewhat more frequently in English translation.

2. THE SIGNIFICANCE OF RAMISM: A SUMMARY

The examination which the present book has undertaken reveals Ramism as a development in man's view of his own intellectual activity and of the universe which has its origins in the interaction of humanism and scholasticism. The internal structure and development of the Ramist outlook advertises particularly the mechanistic, quantitative bent in the scholastic mind, and calls attention to the importance of the scholastic arts course (and, indirectly, of the medical course) as against the scholastic theological course in the development of the sensibility of Western man. The structure and evolution of Ramism also points up this same bent in the topical logic tradition encouraged by humanism, and shows the way in which this topical tradition, imported to Paris via the Rhineland — for the contact between Italian humanism and Ramus is in no significant way direct — reacted with the scholastic heritage to produce an even more quantified, diagrammatic approach to reality and to the mind itself.

Furthermore, the history of Ramism, with its tremendous spread, makes clear the fact that while many of the significant reactions in intellectual history were taking place because of new scientific or philosophical insights, they were occurring more inevitably because of the demands of practical pedagogy — even when the pedagogical necessity was given a veneer of quasi-scientific explanation. The order which the mind found in the universe, and which Ramus and Talon, for better or for worse, wanted to revise was, radically, an order existing not in terms of fully developed, "logically" consistent sciences, but one which was sustained largely by a curriculum. This in turn was stabilized by the existence of unions of teachers (universities) who tended collectively to view and to purvey knowledge as a commodity. There was, to be sure, a certain structuring given to knowledge and to reality by a reasoned or scientific framework, but not independently of a structured educational world, which, in the Renaissance as in the Middle Ages, regarded logic or dialectic as an adjunct of teaching rather than of privately undertaken abstract thinking.

The interaction of scholasticism and humanism which Ramus advertises is nowhere more striking than in the evolution of the sixteenth- and seventeenth-century interest in "method." Here at the beginning of the intense preoccupation with this subject, characteristic of the modern world, the notion of "method" in the arts of expression is a somewhat casual scholastic-humanist hybrid. The early sixteenth-century interest in "method" in the field of these arts is clearly an interest in a method of rhetoric or literary composition; it is connected with interest in Hermogenes' account of Demosthenes' "method" of oratorical effectiveness and developed largely in terms of effectiveness in letter writing.

Suddenly, within the five years between 1543 and 1547, Sturm, Ramus, and Melanchthon divert this treatment of method from rhetoric to logic, grafting a section about method into their dialectic or logic books, which had earlier appeared without any such section at all. Here begins the practice of featuring a *tractatus de methodo* in logic textbooks, where Descartes was to find such treatises solidly entrenched. Here, also, begins the impression that, since such a treatise on method is featured as a part of logic, and is called logical method, what is purveyed in the treatise is a bona fide outgrowth of a strictly formal, scientific logic. As a matter of record, however, this "logical" method has no really honest ancestry at all in scientific logic. The order for which it campaigns turns out to be, historically and in reality, the order followed in organizing a literary composition, hybridized, by an afterthought, with certain semilegitimate offspring of logic and medicine. "Method" thus puts in its most decisive appearance in the history of thought not where logic is most strict, but precisely where the line between the residual logic of the humanists and their rhetoric is least distinct. And method puts in its appearance as the product of rule-of-thumb pedagogical adjustments rather than of abstract reason. The original promoters of a purportedly airtight and all-inclusive logical method had no really ascertainable warrant for supposing such a thing existed, or could exist.

3. RAMISM AND PRINTING AS RELATED EPIPHENOMENA

This story of the origin and evolution of Ramism opens the way to certain insights into subsequent developments in the culture of which Ramism is an epiphenomenon. These are most readily discernible in the relationship between Ramism and the invention of letterpress printing.

While the invention of printing has been discussed conventionally in terms of its value for spreading ideas, its even greater contribution is its furthering of the long-developing shift in the relationship between space and discourse. Historically, this shift begins with hieroglyphics or picture writing or with the character writing of the Chinese, whereby sound, which is necessarily fleeting is given a quasi-permanence by reduction to marks fixed in space. *Verba volant, scripta manent.* The shift advances much further when the alphabet is invented, for now words are broken into elements each of which has its own spatial referent. This revolutionary achievement is a tremendous convenience, if a seductive one. In a still unreflective alphabetic culture, a scientific treatment of speech makes possible thinking of it in terms of space rather than of sound, so that the unit of speech is considered as a mark on a surface, rather than as a phone (a speech *sound*). Thus, without even a second thought, Ramus will insist that the elements of words and of all expression are not sound, but such marks; that is, not syllables, but letters [35] — some of which, as mere con-sonants, are considered to have sound not in themselves, but only when they are joined with other "vocal" letters, the vowels. Modern linguists have adverted to the distortions occasioned by this view and are extremely sensitive to the limitations not only of the alphabet in any form and for any language, but of any system for freezing the full complexity of living speech sounds. Pre-Gutenberg man was more awestruck, and less critical, in the presence of the alphabet, which, after all, had been invented only once in the history of the human race.[36]

Block printing, from a solid surface of wood carved in a design, had been an interesting invention. The invention of printing from movable type was momentous; for it was an advance of the same importance as that of the invention of the alphabet itself. Some cultural implications of the switch-over from a manuscript to a typographic culture in the sixteenth and seventeenth centuries have been the subject of recent illuminating studies by H. J. Chaytor, Harold Adams Innis, and others. But why printing in the modern sense was developed when it was and not earlier, since all the necessary elements — punches, molds, lead castings, presses, paper or its equivalent, ink or paint — had been known in Western civilization from antiquity, still remains a mystery. The perspectives developed in the present study of Ramism suggest a new line of attack on this intriguing question. The invention of printing from movable type cast from a mold or matrix made with a punch — for an adequate description of the "invention" of modern printing must include all these terms — had to wait on a profound reorientation within the human spirit which made it possible to think of all the possessions of the mind, that is, of knowledge and of expression, in terms more committed to space than those of earlier times.

The culture of the Middle Ages had been, in an important sense, more of a manuscript culture than that of antiquity. The ideal of the orator played a far smaller role; intellectual activity was largely recovery activity, devoted to writing because it was preoccupied with authors of the past — Augustine, Boethius, and all the rest — less than the humanist age, to be sure, but far more than ancient Greece or Rome had been. The resultant build-up of the association of knowledge with visual apprehension and with space undoubtedly is part of the long-term preparation for the more efficient association implemented by printing — but only a part of the long-term preparation. Associated with it is perhaps the most central development in the medieval preparation for the Gutenberg era: that of the highly quantified logic typified in the *Summulae logicales* of Peter of Spain. This in turn is intimately connected with the appearance of the universities themselves and the curious pedagogical tradition they initiated in the teachers' guilds or unions, which were committed on a truly staggering scale to delivering knowledge at specified times and places within an organized framework which it was to their interest to control. Within this framework, discourse tends to be identified with teaching (and thus with monologue rather than dialogue), teaching with the curriculum subjects, and curriculum subjects with dialectic or logic. In the scholastic tradition logic becomes an instrument far more quantified and amenable to spatial diagramming than it was in Aristotle's time.

Against this background, humanism arises — a phenomenon curiously committed to the written word of antiquity (and hence commonly confused in its own age with another related phenomenon, Bible Protestantism, which committed itself in a similar way, but on religious grounds). In Italy, the roots of humanism are inextricably entangled with a more or less unbroken, or at least indigenous, classical tradition. But they are also coincident with the establishment of humanism in Northern Europe, where the logic of Peter of Spain had had its maximum effect and where a whole cluster of phenomena appear manifesting the new importance of space to human intelligence. Outside, and framing them all is the new cosmology, based on no new discoveries, but on a reorientation within the human spirit itself which led Copernicus (who died the very year Ramus published his first two books) to think of the cosmos in a way more fully abstract, more fully geometrized, than Aristotle or Ptolemy had. Simultaneously (in North-Central Europe) with the development of this new concept of cosmic space, not only printing emerged, but also the topical logic of Agricola. This topical logic liberated the strictly scientific quantification of Peter of Spain and the great scholastic logicians by substituting for suppositional theory the imagery of the "places" where all thought was considered to be "stored" — a substitution as logically unacceptable as it was diagrammatically satisfying.

Agricola died in the incunabular period, but he was certainly a humanist and the progenitor of whole races of humanists. These humanists, his epigoni and proponents of the now ascendant topical logics, are intensely interested in printing. Indeed, not only does the diffusion of manuscripts, which makes humanism, depend on printing for its effectiveness, but there is a close personal identification of humanist and printer everywhere. There are the Aldine circle of humanist-printers in Italy and others down the Rhine valley, where in the Münster at Basle one reads on Erasmus' tomb the names of the great printer-humanists Amerbach, Frobenius, and Episcopius; the Rhineland circle with Sturm, the printer turned humanist-schoolmaster; the Paris circle, where first Fichet and later Oronce Finé, the Wéchels, and countless others mingled interest in erudition and book production; and the English circle where Sir Thomas More's nephew, William Rastell, was to see to the printing of the works of the great humanist and martyr.

The interaction of humanism, the topical logics, and printing is particularly fascinating because it is becoming increasingly apparent that the appearance of printing itself was not something which occurred all at once.[37] Some decades before the Mainz indulgences of 1454 and the Mainz Psalter of 1457, primitive presses were already creaking somewhere in North-Central Europe. Printing from movable type was a kind of disease which Western society was catching, and the Gutenberg-Fust-Schöffer invention, whatever it was, was only one of the crises in its progress, which involved a subtle reorientation of attitudes toward communication and toward what was to be communicated, knowledge itself.

The parallel between the processes involved in printing and what Agricola — and Ramus after him — has to say about the places is little short of fantastic. The printing form itself appears in this setting as a kind of locus, or "common" place from which can be pulled an unlimited number of printed pages, each blanketed with "arguments." And it was so in the very early stages of printing, when designs, or even whole pages of text, were cut on large wood blocks, each producing a full printed page. In this initial stage of printing, individual bits of discourse are frozen into space as sources from which meaning can be dispersed. During the next stage of this development, when movable type began to be used, the Agricolan place or locus is even more strikingly suggested. Now the printer's font where the types are kept comes into being — a real "place," where *elements* of discourse, reduced to a visually apprehensible and spatially maneuverable form, are stored. The font itself is not the only locus-like item turning up with the appearance of movable type, however. The letters in the font are cast from a matrix, which is itself a kind of locus, a place out of which, by suitable operations involving mostly local motion, elements of discourse can be drawn. By bringing little blobs of molten lead into contact with the matrix, an indefinite number of letters can be "drawn" from it. The parallels do not stop here; the matrix is produced, or, in Agricolan-Ramist parlance, "drawn," from another sort of locus, the harder punch or die, which, at a fairly early stage in the history of printing, if not from the very beginning, was used to strike any number of matrices from softer metal.

Thus, if the font, like a dialectical locus, was the storehouse of an indefinite number of books, the matrix was the storehouse of an indefinite quantity of type, and the punch of an indefinite number of matrices. Here, in this entire concept, we have the familiar telescoping arrangement which manifests itself in the Latomus *Epitome* of Agricola, where the notion of locus yields other loci, these still further loci, and so on, into the more elaborate Ramist tables.

This reduction of the elements of intelligibility to the spatial arrangements of printing of the topical logics suggests a further general theorem: the printer's font corresponds to the locus of the topical logics, and the printed page to methodized discourse. This theorem would express no more than a coincidence were it not for the fact that Ramus' notion of method is not only a product of the humanism which sponsors both printing and the topical logics, but also is thought of (by Ramus) as an arrangement of material *in a book*. In this context "method" actually gains definition and final form as the interior of Ramus' own books become better spatially organized during the epoch when printers were freeing themselves from the manuscript tradition and were learning that the format of printing involves a radically different commitment to space than does the format of a manuscript.

Judging from the example of the urn with the lottery tickets bearing the various parts and rules of grammar,[38] which Ramus uses from 1546 to his death, it is evident how he thinks of method as governing book make-up. The methodical arrangement in which he "disposes" the material is simply that of his printed grammars, rather than of his orations. Within these grammars, and within Ramus' books in general, there is a regular progression from early editions (wherein the text is a mass of typographical protoplasm, without running heads, without division into chapters or even into books, with little paragraphing, and almost no sense of spatial display) through later editions (where centered headings, running heads, and the other techniques of typographical display become more and more evident), to the *ne plus ultra* in commitment to space found in the editions in dichotomized outline form featured by Freige and others.[39]

In Ramus' own works, the evolution is complete from the incunabular and near incunabular, quasi-manuscript stage of typography; from the stage at which a book could be assimilated only by being read through (and was thought of as being read aloud), to the definitively typographical stage, when a book could be — at least in part — assimilated by being "looked through" or "skimmed through." In Ramus' case, it is evident that the sense of structure within an art and within discourse itself is developing in connection with the reworking of what has already appeared in *print*.

The diagrammatic tidiness which printing was imparting to the realm of ideas was part of a large-scale operation freeing the book from the world of discourse and making it over into an object, a box with surface and "content" like an Agricolan locus or a Ramist argument or a Cartesian or Lockean idea. This operation can be seen in its sharpest focus in connection with the titles of books, which in Ramus' case, as in the case of other writers of his age, undergo a fascinating and definitive evolution.

The age of the topical logics is the age in which the titles of books become, typically, nouns in the nominative case, and, specifically, nouns which are not merely expressive of the form of discourse but which directly "stand for" the book's "contents." Titles become labels, like those of a pharmacist. Earlier books — those of the manuscript age and of the incunabular or near-incunabular period of printing — had been typically designated by phrases which invite use not as detached labels but as part of some larger utterance.

Cicero's *On Fate* (*De fato*) or Boethius' *De consolatione philosophiae* or Agricola's *De inventione dialectica* are phrases which do not stand on their own feet. With such phrases, an additional noun in the nominative case is, indeed, understood, but it is the noun "book" itself or "books" or an equivalent. One would say that Cicero wrote a book *On Fate* or six books *On the Republic*. Occasionally, it is true, nouns rather than phrases are actually used as direct designations of books. Thus, there occur Cicero's *Orator*, or Isidore of Seville's *Etymologies* (*Etymologiae*), or Aristotle's *Metaphysics* (*Metaphysica* — but also commonly referred to as *Fourteen Books on Metaphysics*).

These nouns, it will be noted, tend to fall into certain special classes. For the most part, they designate either persons (*Orator*) or some sort of art or science or course of instruction, so that in either of these cases a close rapport with the world of discourse is maintained on some special ground. Thus, while Cicero could use as a title *Orator* (he has another work, *De oratore*), it would be somewhat contrary to the genius of the Latin language and of the sensibility formed by it to entitle a book *Fate*, or *The Consolation of Philosophy*, without the "on" (*de*). (One must say somewhat contrary, for such things could, occasionally, be done. Still, the tendency not to do them is marked.) For instance, in Volume V of Erasmus' *Opera omnia*, only nine of the twenty-four titles feature a noun in the nominative case (other than *liber* or *libri*). In eight of these the noun indicates the form of discourse in the book — encomium, panegyric, congratulatory addresses, complaint, prayer, language, a song — and in the ninth it refers to a course of instruction (*institutio*).[40] We are in a world where a book, or a part of a book is less an object, a "thing," than a bit of speech, connected much more closely with an aural world than our present sensibilities would allow.

In keeping with this orientation, book titles are full of real persons. The author normally appears in early Latin titles in the genitive case — *Peter Ramus' Remarks on Aristotle, John Milton the Englishman's Fuller Course in the Art of Logic Arranged according to Peter Ramus' Method*. Only as printing gained ground is the author commonly set off at arm's length by the use of prepositions equivalent to "by" (*per*, *ab*, etc.), as can be seen by examining the evolution of Ramist titles. Not only authors, but dedicatees as well are part of the full title: *Aristotle's Nichomachean Ethics, The Countess of Pembroke's Arcadia, Peter Ramus' Three Books of Arithmetic for the Cardinal of Lorraine*.

Social and economic forces are, of course, at work in this attention to dedicatees, but social and economic forces are here acting in concert with other forces toward depersonalization. If the dedicatee was performing an economic role (supporting writers), he was doing so as a person. When the printing press had come into its own and made large public sales possible, it would take over the work of the dedicatee. But it would do so as an object, and the author's source of income — readers unknown to him — would itself be relatively depersonalized. The earlier situation kept books more surrounded with persons and hence in this sense in a more vocal context.

Before printing matured, in the incunabular period and even later, the reader himself is also more in evidence. One is not yet aware how anonymous he is, or is able to be. Books open with a direct address to the reader without the formality of a title at all: "Here, dear reader, you have a book . . . which was written by . . . about . . . ." From the "about"-phrase (*De amicitia*, etc.), which really designates the book but which does not stand on its own feet in the way a nominative-case noun would do, the whole of this address to the reader is, in a sense, extrapolated. The essentially fractional form of the old-style titles supposed and demanded completion in such fuller utterance. In the sixteenth century when a noun in the nominative case is at long last employed in a title, if it refers neither to persons nor to discourse, it is likely to be introduced with a curiously apologetic or explanatory apparatus, as in Richard Rainolde's work, *A Book Called the Foundation of Rhetoric* (1563). This sort of apparatus sometimes accompanies even a personal noun, as in *The Book Named the Governor* (1531), by Sir Thomas Elyot, or Sir Thomas Hoby's *Book of the Courtier* (1561).

The commitment of discourse to space involved in the printing process changes all this. Titles become a problem, and for a while in some quarters grow nervelessly longer and longer. Complaints by scholars and philosophers are not unknown: Gassendi's, for example, is worth reading, as he berates Robert Fludd, asking why he did not style his treatise simply *Summum bonum* (a noun in the nominative case) instead of equipping it with its "sesquipedalian title" in an effort to "distribute" (a favorite term in Ramist and other dialectic) all the things in the treatise properly and make them "stick together." [41] Books, and their various parts, were becoming objects which should have simple labels or tags.

Furthermore, they were hollow objects or receptacles with "contents" which could be charted in a "table" or ranged, now for the first time, in a "place indicator" (*index locorum*). As such receptacles, they will imperceptibly drift, to some extent, out of the world of discourse, where they had been moments in a dialogue, and become, more than ever before, objects in a world of space approached chiefly in terms of vision. In the post-Gutenberg age where Ramism flourished, the term "content," as applied to what is "in" literary productions, acquires a status which it had never known before. In lieu of merely telling the truth, books would now in common estimation "contain" truth, like boxes.

The habits of organizing thought according to various spatial models which encouraged Ramism and which Ramism encouraged are intimately associated also with the use of letterpress printing in educational circles, where Ramism developed and came into its own. When printed textbooks were introduced to the classroom, it became possible for the schoolmaster or university lecturer to focus the whole pedagogical economy on the spatial arrangement of material before his pupils. "Look at page seven, line three, the fourth word" — this kind of directive became a matter of daily routine in a typographical culture. Millions of schoolboys were inducted into an understanding of language and of the world around them by making their way conjointly through individual texts arranged in identical spatial patterns.

Such directives were impossible before the advent of printing. With some rare exceptions for the Masoretes and a few others, finding a place in a book had been a separate problem for every copy on hand; and books still had been registers of words, aids to the recall of sounds (one ordinarily read aloud even when reading to oneself) rather than places which "contain" well-localized "things." Not only in an oral culture, but even in a manuscript culture, the bright boy is likely to be a word-manipulator, an audile, who excels in aural and oral performance. In a typographical culture the visile can come into his own. The orator is perhaps not extinct, but he is now permanently eclipsed.

4. THE SPATIAL MODEL AS KEY TO THE MENTAL WORLD

The origins of Ramism are tied up with the increased use of spatial models in dealing with the processes of thought and communication. Its later developments, including both those which begin to run riot through the numerous editions of textbooks and terminate in the beginnings of modern encyclopedism, and the stylistic and cultural developments discussed by Miller and others, are also largely interpretable in terms of the further processing of man's understanding of his own mind by means of similar spatial models. Here is to be found the ultimate significance of Ramus' quite justified conviction that his great contribution lay in the reform of dialectic or logic.

At this point we must consider Ramism in relation to the various other phenomena in cultural history which cluster around the invention of printing: for example, the development of Copernican space, so much more truly spatial than Aristotle's less abstract, directional space; the development of the painters' feeling for a similar, abstract space climaxed in the work of Jan van Eyck, which Erwin Panofsky has so masterfully analyzed in his *Early Netherlandish Painting* and elsewhere; the development of interest in philosophical "systems" conceived of in a mental space analogous to that of Copernicus' free-wheeling spheres. In a future book, the author hopes to tell more fully the story of some post-Ramist phenomena connected with these developments; here we will indicate only briefly the general lines which this spatialization follows in the late Ramist age.

These lines of development can be summarized under several headings. The central one is the transformation (discussed in Chapter V), of the Aristotelian categories from predicates or accusations to classifications, which are

subject primarily to the quantification of formal logic, and the further resulting assimilation of these categories to the *topoi* or places, with the eventual
ascendancy of the topical logics best represented by that of Ramus. At the
same time topical theologies emerged — prepared through the Middle Ages
and perfected in the Renaissance. These were got up by Renaissance theologians without number, headed by Melanchthon among the Protestants and
Melchior Cano among the Catholics, both of whom draw directly — and
Cano frequently verbatim — on Rudolph Agricola. Ramus' own *Commentary
on the Christian Religion* opens by setting itself explicitly the task of illus-
trating the theological loci. Just as these "topics" or "places" supplant the
commentaries or remarks on Peter Lombard's *Sentences* (which had been not
"places" but remarks or decisions concerning others' remarks) as a sixteenth-
and seventeenth-century means of organizing theology, so similar loci or
places become more common in the organization of legal material. In the
case of medicine the old collections of "aphorisms" — sayings or utterances —
of the Hippocratic tradition yield to a treatment of various "topics," or what
we should call subjects today. Medicine at this time makes its own special
contribution to the collection of spatial models for thought by encouraging the
fad of thinking of scientific or quasi-scientific treatises as presentations of
"bodies" of knowledge. It also encouraged the related fad of performing intellectual "anatomies," which are analyses or "dissections" of such "bodies" of
knowledge undertaken sometimes in a friendly and sometimes in a polemic
spirit. Lyly's *Anatomy of Wit*, Nashe's *Anatomie of Absurditie*, and Burton's
Anatomy of Melancholy are well-known English examples of the genre, but
this is far more developed in the Latin tradition than the scattered vernacular
production would indicate.

The revision of the notion of analysis which shifts this notion from its
Aristotelian to its Kantian base is accomplished with the help of certain spatial
models for thought processes traceable through Ramism. Ramus had insisted
that analysis opened ideas like boxes, and it is certainly significant that the
post-Ramist age produced so much more than its share of books identified by
their titles as "keys" to one thing or another. In this same age the notion of
"content" as applied to books is extended, so that statements, the words of
which statements consist, and concepts or ideas themselves are habitually
considered as "containing" truth. An epistemology based on the notion of
truth as "content" begins to appear. Out of the twin notions of content and
analysis is bred the vast idea-, system-, and method-literature of the seventeenth and eighteenth centuries. This literature consists of treatises on practically all conceivable forms of knowledge labeled indiscriminately "ideas" or
"systems" or "methods" of the various subjects, and conceived of as box-like
units laid hold of by the mind in such a way that they are fully and adequately
treated by being "opened" in an analysis.

A brief inspection of a book which is as interesting and typical as it is curious will illustrate the new literature. *The Methodical Idea* (*Idea methodica*) was published by the Bernese schoolmaster Marcus Rutimeier in 1617 and again in 1618. Basically, it is nothing other than an edition of Ramus' *Dialectic*. But Rutimeier presents Ramus' work by giving, in connection with each chapter of the text, a display of the material in the chapter arranged in dichotomies on the now common bracketed outlines, which make up the greater part of his edition (see Figure XVIII). Apparently in a brave attempt to counter the inevitable monotony of these outlines, he calls them variously by one or another of the following names: line-up (*lineamenta*), array (*series*), foreshadowing (*adumbratio*), outline (*delineatio*), form or idea (*idea*), table (*tabella*), chart (*tabula*), general view (*synopsis*), arrangement (*dispositio*), schematization (*schematismus*), imprint or outline (*typus*), schema (*schema*), footprint or track (*ichnographia*), method (*methodus*), shape (*figura*), and analysis (*analysis*). To these are to be added system (*systema*), fabric (*fabrica*), and body (*corpus*), used synonymously with these other terms in the dedicatory verses of Rutimeier's book.

Rutimeier's use of the bracketed dichotomized tables is certainly not new and of itself not especially interesting. What is interesting is the names just mentioned which he bestows on his tables, and which, utterly unoriginal, can be not only matched but much further extended by examining the voluminous contemporary literature. Since these tables are all visualized charts, it is inevitable that the names be referable to spatial models of some sort. We are not surprised to find such diagrams called "line-ups" or "arrays" or "schemes." Nor would even pre-Gutenberg man be surprised to find what are obviously pictorial displays called by these names, although he might well be surprised at the ease with which it is assumed that such displays have immediate relevance either to reality or to truth known by the mind (pre-Gutenberg man does not readily think of truth as "content"). But even we are surprised at Rutimeier's willingness to use other terms such as "idea" or "method" to designate these pictures — until we note the common denominator of Rutimeier's terms. All these terms, "idea" and "method" included, have a spatial reference of some sort, evident at least in their etymologies, strong enough to make it possible for them to refer to a visually conceived model or "construct."

Another way of looking at the process culminating here, is that the spatial component present in all of these terms from the beginning has been allowed to exert its maximal force and to assume its most elemental, simple form, and thus to draw them together. Of Rutimeier's tables one can say what Walter Pater once said of the head of "La Gioconda": to this place "all 'the ends of the world are come.' " To here has been brought a trace of Plato, a trace of Aristotle, of Cicero, Themistius, and Boethius, of the medieval scholastics, of Rudolph Agricola, and of many others. And yet this collection is far from a random or freakish one. Our Swiss schoolmaster's outlook is entirely repre-

XVIII. THE METHODICAL IDEA (RUTIMEIER)

sentative not only of the huge international Ramist tradition but of the whole age which fosters Ramism.

Rutimeier's idea charts are indeed the fag end of both antiquity and scholasticism, and of humanism, too, but not entirely the fag end either, for they tie in with something very much alive. The hypertrophy of the visual imagination which we observe here — a hypertrophy extraordinarily striking in the way it crowds spatial models, and nothing but spatial models, into the universe of the mind — is in another way witness to the evolution in human thought processes which is simultaneously producing the Newtonian revolution, with its stress on visually controlled observation and mathematics, and its curiously silent, nonrhetorical universe.

Indeed, as further study of post-Ramist developments clearly shows, it is difficult to say whether the intensification of the use of spatial models which marks this age is initiated first in the approach to the external universe of physics or in the approach to the interior universe of the mind. Parallel to the rise of Newtonian physics is the rise of modern encyclopedism, largely under Johann Heinrich Alsted (Comenius' teacher) and other German polyhistors more or less under Ramist influence. Here the older encyclopedisms organizing knowledge around words (Isidore of Seville's *Etymologies*) or around the various "arts" are replaced by a more widely ranging "systematic" encyclopedism, in which "method" is applied to anything and everything, somewhat in the way in which Copernicus' and Newton's abstract geometrical space is applied to any mechanical "system" in the physical world, and which will be climaxed in the 1750 prospectus for the *Encyclopédie* featuring Diderot's proposal to draw up a "tableau general" of the achievements of mankind.

This parallelism between the physical and the intellectual worlds remains to be developed in a future study. At the stage to which this present book extends, one can hope only to have indicated how the Ramist reworking of dialectic and rhetoric furthered the elimination of sound and voice from man's understanding of the intellectual world and helped create within the human spirit itself the silences of a spatialized universe.

NOTES

NOTES

CHAPTER I

RAMISM IN INTELLECTUAL TRADITION

1. "Rhetorica est affectuum hortus" (1653); "Dialectica est Sol microcosmi, argumenta sunt logici radii" (1653); "Res est in loco, tempus in re" (1647); "Grammatica est perfecta sine Rhetorica non contra" (1653); "Linguae sunt artium gratia" (1653); "Methodus intelligentiae parens est, magistra memoriae" (1653); quoted in Samuel Eliot Morison, *Harvard College in the Seventeenth Century* (Cambridge, Mass., 1936), II, 587–594.

2. Carl von Prantl, "Über Petrus Ramus: ein Vortrag," *Sitzungsberichte der philosophisch-philologischen und historischen Classe der königlich bayerischen Akademie der Wissenschaften zu München*, Band II, Heft II, pp. 157–169. See also his *Geschichte der Logik im Abendlande* (4 vols.; Leipzig, 1855–1870).

3. Charles Waddington, *Ramus: sa vie, ses écrits, et ses opinions* (Paris, 1855), p. 355. The medieval and Renaissance meanings of *thesis* and *hypothesis* were largely controlled by the use of these terms in rhetoric. A nonhypothetical science was not an observational science, as Waddington suggests it was, but precisely a deductive science — see Ramus' adversary Jacob Schegk (Schegkius), *De demonstratione libri quindecim* (Basileae, 1564), p. 124.

4. Abel Lefranc, *Histoire du Collège de France depuis ses origines jusqu'à la fin du premier empire* (Paris, 1893), p. 124.

5. Cousin is the dedicatee of Waddington's work. Waddington had had access to Cousin's excellent collection of works by Ramus, now to be found in the Bibliothèque Victor Cousin in the University of Paris library at the Sorbonne.

6. Frank Pierrepont Graves, *Peter Ramus and the Educational Reformation of the Sixteenth Century* (New York, 1912) p. 57. The term "pragmatist" was new, and Graves apologizes for suggesting such a neologism, but maintains that, except for its newness, "it would render this word [*usuarius*] most aptly." He refers the word to Adrien Turnèbe's *Disputatio ad librum Ciceronis de fato* (Paris, 1556), where we read (fol. 27r–v) a clear confutation of the meaning Graves takes from the term: "You bring out as your last-ditch defence this precious *usus* of yours, which you once brandished in the Parlement to salvage your lost and ruined case, screaming over everybody's roars of laughter, 'Mr. President, I want *usus*, I want *usus!*' The upshot of it was that among our lawyers — for there is no race of men more punctilius or nicer — you began to be called the usufructuary philosopher (*usuarius*). This term was caught up outside your own camp, and you were afraid to look people in the face." The whole passage runs as follows in the original: "Si mihi tecum de natura, arte, et usu disserendum esset, valde id timide dubitanterque facerem. Scio enim hanc causam tibi meditatam millies et declamatam esse. Novi tuos receptus, tua perfugia, tuas latebras. In natura teneris, ad artem elaberis: in ea quoque teneris, praesto est triarius ille tuus aureus usus, quo in Senatu olim causam defendisti tuam iam fractam et profligatam, cum sic clamares ridentibus omnibus, Domine Praeses, usum quaero, usum quaero: ut ex eo iurisconsultis nostris (nullum enim hominum genus elegantius est et venustius) Philosophus usuarius dici coeperis. Hic extra praesidia tua deprehensus est, nec in tam multas facies te convertere

potes." According to Nancel, *Petri Rami vita* (1599), p. 36, the title was also used in an honorific sense, evidently with stress on Ramus' meaning for *usus* and not on his opponent's pun. In Ramus' vocabulary, *usus* is not translated by "use" so well as "practice" or "drill." Its synonym is often *exercitatio* (Ramus, *Dialecticae institutiones*, 1543, fols. 43, 54), and Ramus speaks of the work which tutors do in drilling students in philosophy as *exercere* — Ramus, *Prooemium reformandae Parisiensis Academiae*, in *Scholae in liberales artes* (1569), cols. 1074–1075.

7. Norman E. Nelson, *Peter Ramus and the Confusion of Logic, Rhetoric, and Poetry*, University of Michigan Contributions in Modern Philology, No. 2 (Ann Arbor, Mich., 1947).

8. See especially the *Artes collectae* in Ong, *Ramus and Talon Inventory*.

9. P. Gr. [Paul Greaves? P. Greenwood?] *Grammatica anglicana . . . ad unicam P. Rami methodum concinnata* (Cambridge, 1594; re-edited, Vienna and Leipzig, 1938).

10. Galland, *Contra novam academiam Petri Rami oratio* (Paris, 1551, 4to ed.), fol. 9: "veluti vernaculos ridiculi Pantagruelis libros."

11. In 1729 he began supplementing his Latin compendia with English explanations, and sometime thereafter discarded the compendia. See Norman Kemp Smith, *The Philosophy of David Hume* (London, 1949), p. 23.

12. Stephen d'Irsay, *Histoire des universités* (Paris, 1933–1935), II, 124–125, with the documentation there provided. See William Nelson, "The Teaching of English in Tudor Grammar Schools," *Studies in Philology*, 49:119–143 (1952), in the Bibliography of this present work, and the note there. See also Richard Foster Jones, *The Triumph of the English Language* (Stanford, Calif., 1953).

13. See W. K. Wimsatt, Jr., *Philosophic Words: A Study of Style and Meaning in the Rambler and Dictionary of Samuel Johnson* (New Haven, 1948).

14. James Boswell, *The Life of Samuel Johnson, LL. D.* (London, 1912), II, 159.

15. John Milton, "To the Parlament of England with the Assembly," in *The Doctrine and Discipline of Divorce*, in *The Works of John Milton*, ed. Frank Allen Patterson (New York, 1931–1938), III, Part II, 378–379.

16. Milton, *The Reason of Church Government*, Bk. II, in *Works*, III, 236. The history of Anglo-Latin poetry after 1500 is available in Leicester Bradner's excellent *Musae anglicanae* (New York and London, 1940).

17. See Ong, *Ramus and Talon Inventory*.

18. *The Logike of . . . P. Ramus Martyr*, tr. by Rolandus Makylmenaeus (London, 1574), preface.

19. L. T. Schenkelius (Schenkel), *Brevis tractatus de utilitatibus et effectibus artis memoriae . . .* , in his *Methodus sive declaratio . . . quomodo Latina lingua sex mensium spacio doceri et . . . possit addisci . . .* (1619), pp. [125]–[126].

20. See *Petri Rami et Jacobi Schecii epistolae* in Ong, *Ramus and Talon Inventory*.

21. In the Oxford college libraries and at the Bodleian, there is rather little English-printed Ramist literature, but a great quantity of Continental Ramist material.

22. See Walter J. Ong, "Hobbes and Talon's Ramist Rhetoric in English," *Transactions of the Cambridge [England] Bibliographical Society*, I, Part III (1951), 260–269, and Wilbur Samuel Howell, "Ramus and English Rhetoric: 1547–1681," *Quarterly Journal of Speech*, 37:308–310 (1951). These studies confirm and complement one another.

23. Guilielmus Ursinus (Ursin), *Disputationum philosophicarum pars I . . .* ; accessit disputatio de distinctione reali et rationis (1610), *passim*.

24. The comparison of the use of logic or dialectic to striking with a clenched fist, and of the use of rhetoric to striking with an open palm is cited from Zeno the Stoic and from Cicero's *Orator* by Renaissance writers without number. A few examples are: Ramus, *Scholae rhetoricae* in his *Scholae in lib. art.* (1569), cols. 280–282; Johann Pisca-

tor, *Animadversiones in Dialecticam P. Rami* (1586), p. 125; Gilbert Burnath, *Ethicae dissertationes* (1649); Jacques Charpentier, *Compendium in communem artem disserendi* (1559), fol. 2; Richard Rainolde, *A Book Called the Foundation of Rhetorike* (1563), fol. j; Jean Riolan, *Brevis et facilis isagoge in universam philosophiam* (1562), p. 6; etc. Ramus, in the passage here referred to, perversely exploits the image in his own way so that he can maintain that Zeno is wrong: he says that dialectic should be the palm for it is the "broader" concept, embracing all speech, as rhetoric does not.

CHAPTER II

VECTORS IN RAMUS' CAREER

1. A rather complete list of these sources, up to 1848, and of other sources, mostly derivative from them, is given in C. Waddington-Kastus [i.e., Charles Waddington], *De Petri Rami vita, scriptis, philosophia* (Paris, 1848), pp. 167–168.

2. See "The Ramist Controversies" in Ong, *Ramus and Talon Inventory.*

3. Nancel, *Petri Rami . . . vita* (1599), pp. 47, 16.

4. *Ibid.*, pp. 47, 48, 54.

5. *Ibid.*, p. 62.

6. Ramus' reputation as a marytr, which Nancel notes (*Vita*, p. 63), was mostly of brief duration. He is styled "martyr" on the title page of the English translation of his *Dialectic* or *Logike* by Roland M'Kilwein (1574), but this is quite exceptional, and the title pages of practically all the other hundreds of editions of his works, lavish in allowing him his academic titles, deny him this one. The publication of Nancel's version of Ramus' life, with its spicy anecdotes, undoubtedly discouraged adulation of Ramus' character after 1599. So, too, did Ramus' condemnation by his coreligionists at the 1572 Protestant Synod of Nîmes, three months before his death. Moreover, the precise relation of his death to the horrible St. Bartholomew's Day Massacre remains to this day uncertain. Increase Mather's reference to Ramus as "that Great Scholar and Blessed Martyr" in the Preface to his *Meditations on the Glory of the Heavenly World* (Boston, 1711), is something of an anachronism — matching, in this respect, much of Mather's other intellectual furniture.

7. Howard C. Barnard, *The French Tradition in Education: Ramus to Mme Necker de Saussure* (Cambridge, England, 1922), p. 17, n.1.

8. Waddington's genealogical information can be supplemented from Dr de la Genière de la Ramée, who, in a manuscript entitled "Ramus" in the Bibliothèque du Protestantisme français in Paris (in-4°, Varia 2543.1), gives the genealogy of the La Ramée family, including that of Peter Ramus, together with the family coat of arms in watercolor. The English writer, Mana Louise Ramé, best known under her two *noms de plume* as "Louise de la Ramée" or "Ouida," born at Bury St. Edmunds in 1839, and once styled the George Sand of England, is shown by Dr de la Genière de la Ramée to be a member of the same family as our Peter Ramus.

9. Waddington, *Ramus*, p. 20.

10. Pierre Bayle, *Dictionnaire historique et critique*, 5th ed., rev. by M. des Maizeaux (Amsterdam, 1740–1756), III, 26, and Banosius as there cited.

11. Waddington, *Ramus*, p. 20.

12. *Ibid.*, pp. 20–22, and references there cited.

13. Freige, *Vita*, p. 7, quoting Ramus' epilogue to Schegk.

14. Nancel, *Vita*, p. 13.

15. *Ibid.*, p. 61. Nancel also observes here that Ramus' memory was not remarkable — he measures this, of course, by the high sixteenth-century standards.

16. Ramus, *Ad Papium Bononiensem responsio* in Ramus and Talon, *Collectaneae*

praefationes, epistolae, orationes (1577), p. 197: "Since I began my studies already on in years" (*cum aetas iam grandis* [*me*] *ad literas admisisset*). Taken alone, this is rather ambiguous, since it might conceivably mean that Pierre was admitted to Paris late, for he might consider this his real initiation "ad literas," writing off earlier studies elsewhere. If Pierre had actually been very far behind his class, he made up most of the time, for he received his master's degree, as Waddington points out (*Ramus*, p. 28) at the age of twenty-one, older than most students, but not nearly so old as a few others — for example, his contemporary at Paris, Inigo (later Ignatius) de Loyola.

17. For the details of university teaching and life through the Middle Ages and into the Renaissance, see: Charles Thurot, *De l'organization de l'enseignment dans l'Université de Paris au moyen-âge* (Paris, 1850), an excellent little monograph in many ways still unsurpassed; Hastings Rashdall, *The Universities of Europe in the Middle Ages*, new ed. by F. M. Powicke and A. B. Emden (Oxford, 1936), which treats matters through the fifteenth century and thus practically to Ramus' own day and often cites Ramus; Stephen d'Irsay, *Histoire des universités françaises et étrangères des origines à nos jours* (2 vols.; Paris, 1933–35); and, of course, the *Chartularium Universitatis Parisiensis*, ed. by H. Denifle and E. Chatelain (4 vols.; Paris, 1889–1897), plus the *Auctarium* or additions to the *Chartularium* still appearing, edited by others. These works and others referred to in them are full of voluminous references, but in many details, most of which do not concern us here, our knowledge of actual teaching practice can be much perfected. In earlier days, as now, there was often a great gap between what the statutes or prospectuses said and the pedagogical actuality. Unless otherwise annotated, the present discussion can be documented by consulting the copious indices in Rashdall and M. d'Irsay under the proper heading.

18. Waddington suggests that among Ramus' teachers were Juan Peña, the same professor who threatened to have the over-thirty-year-old Inigo de Loyola thrashed (not to be confused with Ramus' pupil, the younger mathematical prodigy Jean Péna, 1531–1557), and Joannes Hannonius or Jean le Hennuyer, tutor of Henry II and of Charles of Lorraine — Waddington, *Ramus*, pp. 113, 291. Waddington's conclusion that Le Hennuyer was the source of Ramus' anti-Aristotelianism is based entirely on the argument, inconclusive except to Waddington, that since Le Hennuyer courageously refused to promulgate the Edict of St. Bartholomew's Day in his diocese of Lisieux, he was therefore an anti-Aristotelian, the supposition apparently being that a man who resists one thing resists everything. Unfortunately, even the story about Le Hennuyer's resisting the St. Bartholomew's decree has long been known to be inaccurate — see the article on Le Hennuyer in the *Nouvelle biographie universelle*. For Le Hennuyer and Ramus, see also Jacques Charpentier, *Ad Expositionem disputationis . . . responsio* (1564), fol. 3. Abel Lefranc in *Histoire du Collège de France* (Paris, 1893), pp. 141–142, states (on what grounds I do not know) that Ramus followed the lectures of the regius professor Pierre Danès. If so, the youthful La Ramée failed to learn much from Danès, who was professor of Greek, for Nancel assures us (*Vita*, p. 32) that Ramus learned Greek late in life, whereas Danès was professor only from 1530 to 1534. A contemporary, if hostile, source, Jacques Charpentier, *Disputatio de methodo . . .* (1564), fol. 7v, remarks that Ramus tells about his own schooling just those things he wants people to know, thereby creating a calculated impression.

19. *Chartularium Univ. Paris.*, IV, 724–730.

20. Charpentier (Carpentarius), *Disputatio de methodo . . .* (Parisiis, 1564), fol. 17v.

21. Rashdall, *Universities of Europe*, I, 444.

22. "Facile princeps suo saeculo" — Nancel, *Vita*, p. 31.

23. Antonio de Gouveia (Goveanus), Ramus' critic, makes an issue of such matters as Ramus' use of *laboriose* when *diligenter* would have served better. His attack on

Ramus' style in Ramus' first printed works can be taken as evidence that Ramus' style was an item to be reckoned with. See Gouveia, *Pro Aristotele responsio adversus Petri Rami calumnias* (1543), fol. 2.

24. *Scholae dialecticae*, Lib. IV, in *Scholae in liberales artes* (1569), cols. 155–156.

25. See above, Chap. II, n.16. The implications of a philosophy of which a student became a *master* when he was eighteen or twenty are discussed in Chaper VI, for they are not without relevance to the whole Ramist development. Throughout its history, scholastic *philosophy* (not scholastic theology) had normally been such a philosophy — for teen-agers.

26. ' The younger students doing grammar and even all the way up through philosophy (that is, to the M.A.) seem to have been attached to the university chiefly through the person of the master of arts who supervised their instruction and who seems himself to have kept any records that were kept on their achievements. At any rate, college lists, such as that at the College of Navarre, where Pierre had studied, commonly omit, at least by the beginning of the sixteenth century, the names of individual grammar students, and frequently those of the *artistae* (arts students above grammar) although they list the classes *grammatici* and *artistae*. See Jean de Launoy, *Regii Navarrae gymnasii Parisiensis historia* (1677), I, 399 (Pars Ia, Lib. III, cap. ix).

27. See Astrick L. Gabriel, *Student Life in Ave Maria College, Mediaeval Paris* (Notre Dame, Ind., 1955), which includes Ramus' incumbency.

28. Ramus, *Sch. dial.* in *Sch. in lib. art.* (1569), col. 155.

29. Gouveia, *Pro Aristotele responsio* (1543), fol. 2*v*.

30. Galland, *Contra novam academiam Petri Rami oratio* (1551, 4to ed.), fol. 9; Nancel, *Vita*, p. 43.

31. Rashdall, *Universities of Europe*, I, 445; see Ramus, *Oratio initio suae professionis habita* (Paris: M. David, 1551), pp. 16–17, where Ramus describes the 1355 prescriptions for teaching philosophy as "remotis pennis et calamis . . . *perpetua voce* raptim." See also *Chartularium Univ. Paris.*, III, 39–40.

32. "Guillielmo Montuellio Rectore, nescio quo genio malo irrumpente in academiam, ingens facta est studiorum omnium de repente perturbatio, edito recens libello cuius titulus erat Animadversiones Aristotelis [*sic*], composito ad extinguendam in totum doctrinam unius Aristotelis omnium philosophorum facile principis. Cui sane morbo non leviter grassanti et mentibus puerorum ad quidvis quod novum sit et inauditum facile sequacium, paulatim sese insinuanti, mature et consulto est occursum." — *In commentariis Rectoratus Guillelmi Montuellii, ante annos viginti* [i.e., in 1544], as quoted in Charpentier, *Ad Expositionem Disputationis contra Thessalum Ossatum Academiae Parisiensis methodicum responsio* (1564), fols. 4–5. The force of Aristotle's association with *doctrina* in this university context should not be missed: *doctrina* means the curriculum, and Aristotle is the first of philosophers because he implements the curriculum so well. Cf. the "imperitae . . . iuventutis" in Pierre Galland, *Contra novam academiam Petri Rami oratio* (Paris, 1551, 4to ed.), fol. 3.

33. "Studiorum rationem tu praevertere et perturbare voluisti" — Gouveia, *Pro Aristotele responsio adversus Petri Rami calumnias* (1543), fol. 4; cf. *ibid.*, I, 3.

34. Bomont's willingness to string along with Ramus is perhaps to be explained in part by their sharing interest in Agricola's *De inventione dialectica*. I have found a copy of this work (Paris: S. Collinaeus, 1529) bearing Bomont's signature in the Bibliothèque Nationale at Paris (X. 3258).

35. The full text of the decree is printed in Waddington, *Ramus*, pp. 49–52.

36. See Ong, *Ramus and Talon Inventory*, where the individual works are arranged chronologically by first editions.

37. Nancel, *Vita*, p. 27.

38. Waddington, *Ramus*, pp. 62ff.; Nancel, *Vita*, pp. 15–19.

39. Not the Collège de Rheims at Paris — Nancel, *Vita*, p. 15.

40. *Ibid.*, pp. 11–12.

41. See the note with the first edition of *Caesar's Military Science* (*Liber de Caesaris militia*) in Ong, *Ramus and Talon Inventory*.

42. Waddington, *Ramus*, pp. 152–153.

43. Nancel, *Vita*, p. 76.

44. Of the twenty professors before Ramus, all but four had been professors of these languages; Abel Lefranc, *Histoire du Collège de France* (Paris, 1893), p. 381.

45. When other references are not given, the present account can be verified by material in Lefranc, *Histoire du Collège de France*.

46. C. B. du Boulay (Bulaeus), *Historia Universitatis Parisiensis* (1665–1673), VI, 239; cf. Stephen d'Irsay, *Histoire des universités*, I, 271.

47. Lefranc, *Histoire du Collège de France*, p. 162.

48. "In Academia sed non de Academia," the term Academia being affected for the University because *universitas* was a barbarian medieval word — this undated pamphlet was printed in 1600 or later, as appears from its p. 9.

49. *Histoire du Collège de France*, p. 209; cf. *ibid.*, pp. 381–390. Lefranc here cites with approval Waddington, *Ramus*, p. 331, although Waddington does not brush the matter aside quite so lightly as Lefranc does.

50. [Jean Picard?], *In Petri Rami insolentissimum decanatum, gravissimi cujusdam oratoris philippica prima e quatuordecim: The First of Fourteen Philippics by an Important Speaker on the Extraordinary Deanship of Peter Ramus* (Paris, 1567), fol. 8*v*. Cf. Jean Dorat, *Ad Ramum*, quoted in Maurat-Ballange, "Ramus et Dorat," *extrait du Bulletin de la Société archéologique du Limousin*, 63:23 (Limoges, 1913).

51. Turnèbe, *Disputatio ad Lib* [*rum*] *Ciceronis De fato adversus quendam qui non solum logicus esse verum etiam dialecticus haberi vult: A Discussion of Cicero's Book "On Fate" against One Who Wants not only To Be a Logician but also To Be Taken for a Dialectician* (Paris, 1556), fol. 51*v*. See also Turnèbe's declaration in this connection that regarding his own precise title, he is no stickler but leaves the matter "to the decision of others," preferring this to what he may have to announce about himself" — Turnèbe, *Responsio ad Audomari Talaei Admonitionem Leodegari a Quercu nomine edita 1556*, in *Opera* (Strasbourg, 1600), I, 262.

52. To those outside France after his death, Ramus' position as regius professor was not always clear, because of the complicated and shifting relationship of the regius professors to the University, the fact that Ramus was simultaneously regius professor and head of a University college, and the fact that after his death the chair of mathematics which he himself had founded for others was called after his name, together with the fact that he did teach mathematics and write mathematical works. Thus the 1627 Frankfort edition of his *Lectures on Mathematics* (*Scholae mathematicae*) refers to Ramus on its title page as regius professor of eloquence and mathematics. Thomas Hood's 1590 translation of Ramus' *Geometry* refers to the Frenchman as "Professor of the Mathematical Sciences at the University of Paris." It seems that Ramus never referred to himself in this latter fashion, much less in the former fashion as regius professor of eloquence and mathematics, or even as regius professor of mathematics.

Lefranc, in his *Histoire du Collège de France*, makes no mention of any such title of Ramus' and fails to think of him as regius professor of mathematics at all. Still, although he lacked the precise title, regius professor of mathematics, that, it seems, is what he really was. His professorship seems to have evolved as follows. With a brief interruption occasioned by the Wars of Religion, he kept his regius professorship till death, but when he left his originally specified subjects — that is, eloquence and philosophy — for mathematics, he begins to think of himself as a kind of regius professor at large. In the parlance of the time, mathematics could be taken loosely as part of the "philosophy" of which he had been professor, but among the regius professors those who were to lecture on mathematics, such as Pierre Forcadel or Ramus' brilliant young pupil Jean Péna, were known specifically as regius professors of mathematics. Ramus' preempting to himself this field in great part prompted the anonymous attacks on him by the Charpentier faction as "roving about at large through the whole curriculum, following no particular route but merely barking at theoretical odds and ends" — *In Petri Rami . . . philippica prima* (1567), fol. 8. However, of the two chairs of which Jean Dorat complains in the verses *Ad Ramum*, the second is not mathematics but, apparently, the deanship of the regius professors — see A. Maurat-Ballange, "Ramus et Dorat," *extrait du Bulletin de la Société archéologique du Limousin*, 63:22–23 (Limoges, 1913).

53. See "The Ramist Controversies," in Ong, *Ramus and Talon Inventory*.

54. Nancel, *Vita*, pp. 58–59, where Nancel reports that Ramus sometimes talked of marriage. Here he also reports the story that Ramus had an illegitimate son, but says he himself was never able to identify any such son, try as he might.

55. Rashdall, *Universities of Europe*, III, 396, etc.

56. Moréri, *Grand dictionnaire historique* (1759), article, "Talaeus, A."; Nancel, *Vita*, p. 40.

57. Ramus, *Oratio de professione lib. art.* (1563).

58. Nancel, *Vita*, pp. 70–71.

59. The letter is quoted in French translation in Waddington, *Ramus*, p. 135.

60. Nancel, *Vita*, p. 72; Waddington, *Ramus*, p. 137.

61. Nancel, *Vita*, p. 71.

62. Banosius, *Vita*, in Ramus, *Comm. de rel. chr.* (1576), fol. ir.

63. Waddington, *Ramus*, pp. 212–214.

64. *Ibid.*, p. 217; cf. Ramus' preface in *Dialecticae libri duo A. Talaei praelectiones illustrati* (Parisiis, 1566), fol. a3. See also the articles by Moreau-Reibel and Kot in the Bibliography of this present work.

65. Waddington, *Ramus*, pp. 243ff.

66. Nancel, *Vita*, p. 77.

67. Jean-Papire Masson, *Vita Iacobi Carpentarii* (1574), fol. A3.

68. Nancel, *Vita*, pp. 74–75. Waddington, who was a Protestant, goes curiously out of his way to disqualify Ramus as a Protestant martyr by "proving," without benefit of real evidence, that Ramus was killed out of personal enmity by his chief rival among the university professors, Jacques Charpentier, whom Waddington makes out to be an Aristotelian first and everything else afterwards (an interpretation which Charpentier's writings hardly support). See J. Bertrand's little-known exposé of Waddington's treatment of Charpentier, "Jacques Charpentier est-il l'assassin de Ramus?" *Revue des deux mondes*, 44:286–322 (1881), with Waddington's feeble reply, *ibid.*, 44:719–720 (1881), where Waddington says his omission of evidence contrary to his thesis was just an oversight, and Bertrand's curt rejoinder, *ibid.* Another of Waddington's remarkable resorts to oversight is his curious reference on p. 323 in his *Ramus* to Nancel's life of Ramus, where the pages referred to recount stories directly compromising Ramus' character, which Waddington is engaged in presenting as irreproachable. Elsewhere Waddington studiously bypasses Nancel's often amusing and sometimes acrid comments on Ramus' character and behavior, but it is curious that he should refer the reader to a passage of the sort he had been systematically bypassing, especially when the passage actually disproves what Waddington intends it to prove. For a seventeenth-century attempt to interpret Ramus' murder in order to prove that he was not a Protestant, but a Catholic, see Walter J. Ong, "Père Cossart, Du Monstier, and Ramus' Protestantism in the Light of a New Manuscript," *Archivum historicum Societatis Iesu*, XXIV, Fasc. 47 (Ian.–Iun., 1955), pp. 140–164. This deals with documents unknown to Waddington or to Bertrand.

69. British Museum Add. MS 18675, f.6.

70. See Ramus' *Will* (*Testamentum*) in Ong, *Ramus and Talon Inventory*. Nancel, *Vita*, pp. 56–57 and 79, notes that Ramus was rather wealthy (*opes mediocres*), with a fortune of some 10,000 gold crowns or 33,333 pounds, yielding an annual income at six percent, to which was added about 100 pounds annually for lecturing at the Collège de Presles, something less than 500 pounds as regius professor, income from rooms he rented at the Collège de Presles, 100 pounds from a priory which he had at Rennes in the diocese of Quercy, an unspecified sum from the Paris church of St. Nicolas du Chardonnet (which he eventually made over to Talon), and further income from investments with Paris merchants. These latter were doubtless Ramus' Huguenot friends with connections at Frankfort and elsewhere in the Rhine valley, where money was being made off Ramus' many books. Ramus had turned down an abbey offered him by Charles of Lorraine, perhaps, Nancel adds in this same place, because it was not a very rich one and he thought he deserved a "fatter prelacy."

71. Ramus' *Scholae* were all outside the art (*extra artem*), explains Nancel, *Vita*, p. 38.

72. *Ibid.*, p. 21.

73. See Chapter XI, section 7; also the notes with the various Ramist arts in Ong, *Ramus and Talon Inventory*.

74. In the edition of Ramus' arts entitled *Professio regia*, Freige styles the *Bucolics* and *Georgics* commentaries simply *Physica*.

75. See Ferdinand Brunot, *Histoire de la langue française*, II, *Le seizième siècle* (Paris, 1906), pp. 116ff.

76. Nancel, *Vita*, p. 27.

77. *Ibid.*, pp. 33–34.

78. *Ibid.*, p. 27. A contemporary pamphleteer taunts Ramus with one of these occasions, when he had to "crawl off the platform, mute as a fish" [Jean Picard? or another of Charpentier's friends], *In Petri Rami . . . philippica secunda* (Paris, 1567), fol. 9r.

79. Nancel, *Vita*, p. 28.

80. *Ibid.*

81. Waddington's account in his *Ramus*, pp. 168–180, should be read with close attention to the documents and awareness of his anti-Charpentier bias.

82. See Péna's tribute to Ramus at the end of his Preface in his *Euclidis Optica et Catoptrica* (1557).

83. Nancel, *Vita*, p. 34. Here we are told, with what conscious irony it is hard to say, that Ramus learned from Galen to exploit "in methodis ἀμέθοδον" — "nonmethodical," or perhaps nonsyllogistic, method.

84. Nancel, *Vita*, p. 34.

85. *Ibid.*

86. *Ibid.*, pp. 22–23, 32.

87. *Ibid.*, p. 21.

88. *Ibid.*, p. 32.

89. "In hoc tamen laudandus"; Nancel, *Vita*, pp. 60, 62, 48.

90. Ramus, Preface in his *Dialecticae libri duo* (1572).

CHAPTER III

THE STRUCTURE OF REFORM

1. "En vain tous les peripatétiens de la faculté des arts réunirent leurs efforts pour accabler Ramus . . . . A la fin de la scéance il fut proclamé maître ès arts avec applaudissement." — Waddington, *Ramus*, p. 29.

2. For details, see Hastings Rashdall, *Universities of Europe* new ed. (Oxford, 1936), I, 283–286.

3. *Ibid.*, I, 477.

4. An informative selection of sophismata from Albert of Saxony, together with a succinct explanation of the nature of sophisms, is given by Father Philotheus Boehner, O.F.M., in his *Medieval Logic* (1952), pp. 8–9, 97–101. See also Joseph P. Mullally, *The Summulae logicales of Peter of Spain* (Notre Dame, Indiana, 1945), pp. xcixff., and references given there.

5. Ralph Strode, *Incipiunt obligationes Strodi*, fol. iiijra, in David Cranston, *Tractatus insolubilium et obligationum . . . cum obligationibus Strodi . . . .* (Paris: [ca. 1512]).

6. Almost all editions of logicians such as Strode, Buridan, Walter Burleigh, Ockham, and the like seem to cease abruptly about 1540. See the Appendix in Mullally, *Summulae logicales of Peter of Spain* (1945), pp. 132ff., and the Bibliothèque Nationale, British Museum, and other large library catalogues.

7. Freige, *Petri Rami Vita*, in Ramus, *Praelectiones in Ciceronis orationes* (Basileae, 1575), here cited from the 1580 edition of this latter collection, where the thesis occurs on p. 10: "Problema igitur sumpsit [Ramus]: Quaecumque ab Aristotele dicta essent, commentitia esse."

8. *Allgemeine deutsche Biographie* and Moréri, *Grand dictionnaire historique*, articles "Freigius"; Waddington, *Ramus*, pp. 193ff.

9. Banosius, *Petri Rami vita*, in Ramus, *Commentariorum de religione Christiana libri quatuor* (1576), fols. e6–e8. Following Nancel's error, Waddington, *Ramus*, p. 190, says that Banosius accompanied Ramus on the latter's trip through Germany, but Banosius says otherwise, and his association with Ramus was of much shorter duration — see Moritz Guggenheim, "Beiträge zur Biographie des Petrus Ramus," *Zeitschrift für Philosophie und philosophische Kritik* (Leipzig), 121:145 (1903); also E. Droz, "Des autographs," *Bibliothèque d'Humanisme et Rennaissance*, 19:502–503 (1957).

10. Nancel, *Vita*, p. 57.

11. *Ibid.*, p. 12.

12. See "The Ramist Controversies" in Ong, *Ramus and Talon Inventory*.

13. The text cited for reference here is that printed under the revised title of *Lectures on Dialectic* or *Scholae dialecticae*, in *Scholae in liberales artes* (1569), cols. 155–156 (Lib. IV).

14. Waddington, *Ramus*, pp. 24–27; following Freige and Banosius, Waddington makes the reference to Ramus' *Lectures on Dialectic* read book IV instead of book V.

15. Galland, *Contra novam academiam Petri Rami oratio* (1551, 4to ed.), fol. 8.

16. As when Ramus says in *Aristotelicae animadversiones*, (1543), fols. 74–75, that the only way to save Aristotle's reputation is to show that the writings attributed to him are not his, at least in the form in which we have them.

17. *Sch. dial.*, Lib. IV, in *Sch. in lib. art.* (1569), cols. 155–156.

18. The Ramist Friedrich Beurhaus (Beurhusius) proposes these three definitions out of Cicero (his references are erroneously crisscrossed and are corrected and completed here): "Dialectica est ars bene disserendi," *De oratore* ii. 138; "dialectica est diligens disserendi ratio," *Topica* ii. 6; "logicam rationem disserendi voco," *De fato* i. See Beurhaus, *M. T. Ciceronis Dialecticae libri duo* (1593), p. 1. Cf. John of Salisbury, *Metalogicon*, II, iv, in *PL* CXCIX, col. 860 B–C: "Dialectica, ut Augustino placet, bene disputandi scientia." Ramus' explanations of his own terms stem out of the Augustinian tradition for which John of Salisbury speaks, and keep him in substantial agreement with this tradition, for he equates his own *disserendi* with *disputandi*, and *ars* with *scientia* (in this he simply accepts the general arts course tradition).

19. With the foregoing passages, from *Sch. dial.*, Lib. IV, in *Sch. in lib. art.* (1569), cols. 155–156.

20. Georg Wilhelm Friedrich Hegel, *Vorlesungen über die Geschichte der Philo-*

sophie, III, in *Sämtliche Werke* (Stuttgart, 1928), XIX, 252. Hegel relies on Buhle's *Geschichte der neueren Philosophie.*

21. "Tout ce qu'a dit Aristote est mensonge" — M.–M. Dassonville, "La genèse et les principes de la dialectique de Pierre de la Ramée," *Revue de l'Université d'Ottawa,* 23:323 (1953).

22. Graves, *Peter Ramus,* p. 26. See also Henri Lebesgue, *Les professeurs de mathématiques du Collège de France* [1922], p. 44.

23. J.–P. Niceron, *Mémoires* (1729–1741), XIII, 262: "Tout ce qu'Aristote avoit dit étoit faux."

24. "Quaecumque ab Aristotele dicta sint falsa esse et commentitia," *Encyclopédie* (1751), Supplément, IV, 364a. This variant is translated "wrong and false" by Astrik L. Gabriel, *Student Life in Ave Maria College* (Notre Dame, Indiana, 1955), p. 234.

25. Morison, *Harvard in the Seventeenth Century* (Cambridge, Mass., 1936), I, 189. Miller, *New England Mind: The Seventeenth Century* (New York, 1939), p. 123: "All that has been said from Aristotle is forged."

26. Ramus, *Arist. anim.* (1543), fols. 74–75. See also the quotation from Galland in section 2 of this Chapter.

27. Nancel, *Vita,* p. 32.

28. Duhamel, "Milton's Alleged Ramism," *Publications of the Modern Language Association,* 67:1036 (1952).

29. "Mi Cicero . . . interponis res alienas et commentitias" — Ramus, *Sch. rhet.* in *Sch. in lib. art.* (1569), col. 252.

30. "His commentitiis somniis . . . respondebo" — *Scholae rhetoricae* in *Sch. in lib. art.* (1569), col. 241. "Commentitium somnium" — Ramus, *Ciceronis de legibus* in *In Ciceronis orat. . . . prael.* (1582), p. 668.

31. "Ego contra respondebo in praeceptis artium catholicis ac methodice collocatis . . . quaeri . . . ex antecedentibus caussis effecta, subiectis adiuncta: non Aristotelis commentitia illa quidem, sed certa naturali et aperta demonstratione singulariter et eximie demonstrari" — Ramus, Preface to *Arithmeticae libri tres,* in Ramus and Talon, *Collectaneae praefationes, epistolae, orationes* (1599), p. 126.

32. Ramus, *Ciceronis pro Rabirio* in *In Ciceronis orationes . . . praelectiones* (1582), pp. 2–3.

33. "Scholasticam et commentitiam [i.e., *illusory*] opinionem" — *Sch. rhet.* in *Sch. in lib. art.* (1569), col. 281. "[Cicero mi,] aut Rhetoris tui praecepta commentitia esse, aut exempla tua non ferenda fateare" — *ibid.,* col. 314. What Quintilian says about figures' changing frequently is true only "de . . . commentis, . . . nam verae figurae perpetuae [i.e., *stable*] sunt" — *ibid.,* col. 380. "Nos confictis et commentitiis criminibus accusat . . . . Haec crimina ficta et falsa esse respondemus" — *Pro philosophica Parisiensis Academiae disciplina oratio* in *Sch. in lib. art.* (1569), col. 999. "Hanc legem neque nova lex ulla neque contrarius centum annorum mos, ut quidam improbi commenti sunt, abrogavit" — *Oratio initio suae professionis habita* (1551), p. 26; this last example suggests the connections between *commentitia* and *commentarius* or commentary.

34. "Philosophi et oratores . . . aiunt . . . ordinem prodesse memoriae: sed externis et commentitiis eam signis et simulachris instruunt: nos ordinis rebus ipsis insiti doctrinam certissimam, rerumque verissimas imagines adhibemus" — Ramus, *Dialecticae institutiones* (1543), fol. 57.

35. Ramus, *Sch. dial.* in *Sch. in lib. art.* (1569), col. 156.

36. See "The Ramist Controversies," in Ong, *Ramus and Talon Inventory.*

37. Ramus, *Dialectique* (1555), Preface.

38. "Respondi dialecticam esse filiam illam, quae Heidelbergae incredibili non Germanarum modo, sed Gallorum et Italorum admiratione ab Agricola restituta esset. Quid vis amplius? Addidi Agricolae cinera et epitaphium illud ab Hermolao Barbaro tam

nobile in cella lignaria iacere, nec ideo alienum doctoribus istis videri, ut eodem oblivionis sepulchro Agricolae filia contegeretur." — Letter to Theodor Zwinger, professor of Greek at Basle, January 23, 1570, printed in Waddington, *Ramus*, pp. 424–435.

39. Stephen d'Irsay, *Histoire des universités françaises et étrangères des origines à nos jours* (Paris, 1933), I, 263; cf. A. Renaudet, *Préréforme et humanisme à Paris*, 2d ed. (Paris: Librairie d'Argences, 1953), pp. 121ff.

40. See Chapter II, section 2, and Chapter IV, section 1.

41. Cf. Franco Burgersdijk (Burgersdicius), *Institutionum logicarum libri duo . . .*, ed. nova (Lugduni Batavorum: Abrahamus Commelinus, 1645), *Praefatio*, where Valla, Agricola, and Vives are said to have turned logic from Aristotle to Cicero and the Stoics (these latter apparently as known through Cicero's writings).

42. Ramus, *Oratio de studiis philosophiae et eloquentie coniugendis* in Ramus and Talon, *Collectaneae praef., ep., or.* (1599), p. 252: France, Germany, Italy, Britain, in that order.

43. Ramus, *Pro philosophica disc.*, in *Sch. in lib. art.* (1569), cols. 1034–1035.

44. *Ibid.*, col. 1010.

45. See "The Ramist Disputes" in Ong, *Ramus and Talon Inventory*.

46. Nancel, *Vita*, p. 52.

CHAPTER IV

THE DISTANT BACKGROUND: SCHOLASTICISM AND
THE QUANTIFICATION OF THOUGHT

1. Medieval logic has been admirably described in general outline, axiomatics apart, in Philotheus Boehner, *Medieval Logic* (Manchester, England, and Chicago, 1952). See also Ernest A. Moody, *Truth and Consequence in Medieval Logic* (Amsterdam, 1953); Joseph T. Clark, *Conventional Logic and Modern Logic* (Washington, D.C., 1952); Joseph Dopp, *Leçons de logique formelle* (Louvain, 1949); and I. M. Bochenski's edition of Peter of Spain, *Summulae logicales* (Turin, 1947), as well as his *Formale Logik* (Freiburg, Switzerland, and Munich, 1956). Moody's historical survey in his introduction, pp. 1–12, is an invaluable synthesis.

2. See Ramus, *Aristotelicae animadversiones* (1543), fols. 4, 79, etc. Cf. *ibid.*, fol. 61r: "Tota haec ars [i.e., Ramus' own dialectic] nihil habet non ad communem, et quotidianum sermonem formandum et instituendum."

3. Moody, *Truth and Consequence in Medieval Logic*, p. 4.

4. See Jacques Maritain, *Petite logique* (Paris, 1933), pp. 73–94, esp. pp. 93–94, where the limitations of suppositional theory, together with the limitations of the symbolic systems of modern logic, are criticized in terms of "la transcendance de la pensée à l'égard de ses symboles *matériels*" (my italics).

5. Quoted from a 1947 neoscholastic textbook in Boehner, *Medieval Logic*, p. 115.

6. See Boehner, *Medieval Logic*, pp. 19ff.

7. The biographical material here is taken from Joseph P. Mullally, *The Summulae Logicales of Peter of Spain* (Notre Dame, Indiana, 1945) and from *Petri Hispani Summulae logicales*, ed. by I. M. Bochenski, O.P. (Turin, 1947). Mullally's work includes a (noncritical) text and English translation of the part of the *Summulae logicales* known as the *Parva logicalia*, and is referred to hereafter as Mullally, *Summ. log.* Bochenski's is a complete text of the *Summulae logicales*, and is referred to hereafter as simply *Summ. log.* (1947). The English translations of passages here are based often on Mullally but include modifications of my own.

8. See *Chartularium Univ. Paris.*, II, 505–507.

9. Maurice de Wulf, *Histoire de la philosophie médiévale*, II (Paris, 1936), 85–86.

10. "Dialectica est ars artium et scientia scientiarum ad omnium methodorum principia viam habens." — *Summ. log.* (1947), Tr. 1, 1.01, p. 1.

11. I follow the order in the Bochenski edition of 1947.

12. Ramus, *Pro philosophica Parisiensis academiae disciplina oratio*, in *Scholae in liberales artes* (1569), col. 1049.

13. Mullally, *Summ. log.*, p. xlvii.

14. See Boehner, *Medieval Logic*, p. 77.

15. Erasmus, *Ratio seu methodus* . . . (Basileae, 1520), p. 23. See also the Index under "Thomas de Aquino" in Erasmus, *Opera omnia* (1703–1705), vol. X.

16. M.–D. Chenu, "L'humanisme et la Réforme," *Archives d'histoire dominicaine*, 1:147 (1946).

17. "Summularum liber, totius logices ianua" — John Major, *Introductorium in Aristotelicam dialecticen totamque logicen* . . . . (Paris, 1521), fol. IIII (Libellus I, Tr. i).

18. *Chartularium Univ. Paris.*, IV, 728 (Statutes of the year 1452).

19. See the editions listed in Mullally, *Summ. log.*, and cf. Mullally's Introduction; see also the catalogues of the larger European libraries. Cf. Ricardo G. Villoslada, *La Universidad de Paris durante los estudios de Francisco de Vitoria, O.P., 1507–1522* (Rome, 1938).

20. Maurice de Wulf, *Histoire de la philosophie médiévale*, II, 85.

21. *Ibid.*, III, 42–43.

22. P. Ramus, *Pro phil. disc.* in *Sch. in lib. art.* (1569), col. 1049.

23. "Artistas, maxime Summulistas, et Logicos . . . ." — Decree of Louis XI in 1464 for the government of the College of Navarre at Paris, in J. de Launoy, *Regii Navarrae gymn. Paris. hist.* (1677), I, 170 (Pars Ia, Lib. II, cap. ix).

24. See *Chartularium Univ. Paris.*, II, 505–507. A number of recent studies treat Ockham's supposition theory. See, for example, Boehner, "Ockham's Theory of Signification, Supposition, and the Notion of Truth," *Franciscan Studies*, 6:163–170, 261–292 (1946).

25. See the editions in Mullally, *Summ. log.*, pp. 132–158, and note the commentators.

26. Boehner, *Medieval Logic*, p. 77.

27. More, letter to Martin Dorp, from Bruges, October 21, 1515, in *The Correspondence of Sir Thomas More*, ed. Elizabeth Frances Rogers (Princeton, New Jersey, 1947), pp. 38–39; my translation from the Latin original.

28. Act II, sc. i, 1. 528, in *The Pilgrimage to Parnassus with the Two parts of the Return from Parnassus*, p. 42; cf. *ibid.*, pp. 18, 19.

29. Caesarius, *Dialectica* (Coloniae Agrippinae, 1567), *Praefatio* to Tract. VII, "De demonstratione," fol. R2v.

30. Riolan, *Disputationes duae* (1565), fol. 12.

31. Phrissemius, "Argumentum operis," in Agricola, *De inv. dial.* (Parisiis: S. Colinaeus, 1529), fol. a6.

32. Ramus, *Pro phil. disc.* in *Sch. in lib. art.* (1569), col. 1049.

33. *P. Rami . . . Dialecticae . . . libri duo . . . quaestionibus illustrati . . . auctore Frederico Beurhusio* (Tremoniae, 1581). This partial appearance of the *Summulae logicales* is not listed in Mullally, *Summ. log.* Beurhaus also compares Ramus with Francis Titelmans (Titelmannus), the post-Agricolan logician and philosopher to whom Gouveia says Ramus owes a debt.

34. Mullally, *Summ. log.*, p. xxix.

35. "Dialectica est ars artium et scientia scientiarum ad omnium methodorum principia viam habens. Sola enim dialectica probabiliter disputat de principiis omnium aliarum artium et ideo in acquisitione scientiarum dialectica debet esse prior." — *Summ. log.* (1947), Tr. I, 1.01, p. 1. Cf. Cicero *Brutus* xli–xlii, "His enim attulit hanc artem

omnium artem maximam, quasi lucem, ad ea, quae confuse ab aliis aut respondebantur aut agebantur"; and Mullally, *Summ. log.*, p. lxxiv. Cf. Emerson, "Plato," *Complete Works* (Boston, 1903), IV, 62: "There is a science of sciences, — I call it Dialectic."

36. "Id unde ad propositam quaestionem conveniens trahitur argumentum." — *Summ. log.* (1947), Tr. V, 5.06, pp. 45–46.

37. *Summ. log.* (1947), Tr. V, 5.02, p. 44. Cicero *Topica* ii.8.

38. *Summ. log.* (1947), Tr. V, 5.02, p. 44.

39. *Ibid.*, p. 45.

40. See Otto Bird, "How to Read an Article of the *Summa*," *New Scholasticism*, 27:129–159 (1953); and M.–D. Chenu, "La théologie comme science au XIII⁰ siècle," *Archives d'histoire doctrinale et littéraire du moyen âge*, 2:31–71 (1927).

41. University statutes at Paris forbade a master of arts actually to teach until he was twenty years old, thus making the Paris faculty of arts rather more venerable than, for example, faculties in Italy, where a seventeen-year-old M. A. could function without trouble. Other university statutes, at least until 1452, obliged all those receiving degrees to teach for a certain number of years, for a degree was admission to a teachers' guild, although these statutes — like all university statutes — were often indifferently enforced. See Hastings Rashdall, *Universities of Europe*, new ed. (1936), I, 125, 363, 464–465.

42. Rashdall, *Universities of Europe*, I, 445, with Ramus' remarks there cited.

43. See Mullally, *Summ. log.*, pp. xxx–xxxii, lix.

44. *Summ. log.* (1947), Tr. V, 5.03, p. 45.

45. See Mullally, *Summ. log.*, p. xxxvi.

46. "Locus maxima idem est quod ipsa maxima. Maxima autem est propositio, qua non est altera prior vel notior, ut 'omne totum est majus sua parte.'" — *Summ. log.* (1947), Tr. V, 5.07, p. 46.

47. *Ibid.*

48. "Posita causa formali, ponitur eius effectus," "Cuius finis bonus est, ipsum quoque bonum est," "Posito toto integrali, ponitur quaelibet eius pars." — *Summ. log.* (1947), Tr. V, 5.26, 5.27, 5.18, pp. 49–52.

49. *Ibid.*, Tr. V, 5.01, p. 44. Cicero *Topica* ii.8.

50. *Ibid.*, Tr. VI, 6.01, p. 57.

51. *Ibid.*, Tr. VI, 6.02, p. 57.

52. *Ibid.*, Tr. VI, 6.03, pp. 57–58.

53. Boehner, *Medieval Logic*, p. 28.

54. *Ibid.*

55. Thus, Jean Buridan's *Sumulae*, which parallel but vary from Peter of Spain's, insist that a term can have supposition only in a proposition which is verified (Buridan treats verification itself as a kind of supposition for the whole of the proposition) — see in the edition in use in Ramus' day at Paris, Jean Buridan, *Textus summularum magistri Iohannis Buridani* (Parisiis, 1487), fol. [A8b]. John Major, with many others, modifies Peter of Spain's definition of supposition to specify that the terms with supposition must be in a proposition: "Suppositio est terminus in propositione existens verificabilis . . . ." — John Major, *Parva logicalia* in his *Libri quos in artibus . . . compilavit* ([1506]), fol. lxxxvi, a.

56. Mullally, *Summ. log.*, p. lxxxi.

57. *Ibid.*

58. The denominative-connotative distinction is not explicitly developed in Peter of Spain, although the rudiments of the development are present in what he says (borrowing from Aristotle's *Categories*) about denominative terms (*denominativa*) — *Summ. log.* (1947), Tr. II, 2.22, p. 22. Ockham and others develop the theory, which is propounded by Paris logicians of Ramus' early youth, for example, Celaya, *Expositio . . . in librum Predicabilium Porphyrii . . .* (Parisiis, 1516), fol. vii, a; Tartaret, [*Com-*

mentarii in Summulas logicales Petri Hispani . . . (Parisiis, *ca.* 1514)], fol. lix, F [i.e., fol. H3]. English logicians treat denominative terms with some modification of the denominative-connotative apparatus as late as the close of the sixteenth century. See Thomas Blundeville, *The Art of Logick* (1599), Book VII, 4.

59. *Summ. log.* (1947), Tr. VI, 6.04–6.13, pp. 58–60ff.

60. *Ibid.*, Tr. IX, 9.2, p. 100.

61. *Ibid.*, Tr. X, 10.01, p. 102.

62. *Ibid.*

63. Boehner, *Medieval Logic*, pp. 4, 20.

64. Ramus, *Arist. anim.* (1543), fol. 60r. For Aristotle's role in initiating this use of variables, see Jan Lukasiewicz, *Aristotle's Syllogistic from the Standpoint of Modern Formal Logic* (Oxford, 1951), pp. 7–8.

65. Tartaret, *Physic.*, Lib. II, in his *Commentarii . . . in libros philosophie naturalis et metaphysice Aristotelis* . . . ([1514]), fol. xviii, F.

66. *Ibid.*, Lib. III, fol. xxvii, A.

67. A modern exponent of a residual suppositional theory, far more interested in cultivating metaphysics as such than were medieval scholastic philosophers, has pointed out the limited serviceability of supposition, in treating of propositions "concerned with pure essences" or "eternal truths" disengaged from time, such as "The triangle has such-and-such a property," for in this kind of proposition, the supposition is always simply universal — Jacques Maritain, *Petite logique* (1933), p. 77. Still, the formal logic of modern times which is related to and a protraction of supposition theory (perhaps in a larger sense than is intended by M. Maritain) is so much at home with such propositions that it is known as "mathematical" logic!

68. For example, Robert Caubraith, *Quadrupertitum in oppositiones, conversiones, hypotheticas, et modales* . . . (1516), fols. CXXXIX–CXLI. Cf. Philotheus Boehner, *The Tractatus de Praedestinatione et de Praescientia Dei et de Futuris Contingentibus of William of Ockham* (St. Bonaventure, New York, 1945).

69. Quantification is explained in Willard Van Orman Quine, *Mathematical Logic* (Cambridge, Mass., 1951), and in Clark, *Conventional Logic and Modern Logic.*

70. Bochenski regards this as a separate work — Peter of Spain, *Summ. log.* (1947), Introduction, p. xiv. But it appears in manuscript and print often as a part of, or appendix to, the *Summulae logicales* and, as Bochenski points out, in any case is by Peter of Spain.

71. With regard to Peter of Spain, this is explained in Mullally, *Summ. log.*, pp. lxviii–lxxiii, in some detail but without reference to the great advances in quantification made in modern logic. See Boehner, *Medieval Logic, passim,* for the perspectives which these advances provide.

72. Ramus, *Arist. anim.* (1543), fols. 61, 73.

73. See Julien Peghaire, *Intellectus et ratio selon St. Thomas d'Aquin* (Paris, 1936), for an exhaustive treatment of this whole matter.

74. See the full title of Fenner, *The Artes of Logike and Rethorike* . . . (1584; 1588), listed in Ong, *Ramus and Talon Inventory.*

75. "Secunda regula est quod propositio de infinito, syncategorematice capto, exponitur per unam copulativam, cuius prima pars affirmat praedicatum de subiecto sumpto sub aliqua quantitate, continua vel discreta, et secunda negat praedicatum inesse tali subiecto secundum determinatam quantitatem: ut ista: 'Infiniti homines currunt,' quae sic exponitur: 'Aliqui homines currunt et non tot quin plures duobus vel tribus,' vel sic: 'Homines aliqui currunt et quotlibet plures.'" — *Summulae logicales*, "Treatise on Exponibles" (*Tractatus exponibilium*), in Mullally, *Summ. log.*, p. 121. I have emended Mullally's translation slightly. Bochenski, in his edition of the *Summulae logicales* (1947), p. xiv, assigns this "Treatise on Exponibles" to another work but one which he

considers also by Peter of Spain, the *Syncathegoremata*. The distinction between the two works is irrelevant here, since they occur so frequently together.

76. Ramus, *Scholae grammaticae*, II, in *Scholae in tres primas liberales artes* (1595), p. 29: "Incredibile prope dictu est, sed tamen verum, et editis libris proditum, in hac eruditissima Academia doctores exstitisse, qui mordicus tuerentur ac defenderent, *Ego amat* tam commodam orationem esse, quam *Ego amo*: ad eamque pertinaciam comprimendam, consilio publico opus fuisse." For a similar case in 1227 at Oxford, see Charles Homer Haskins, *The Rise of the Universities* (New York, 1923), pp. 74–75.

77. For information regarding this interest, I am indebted to Father Joseph T. Clark, S.J., for it seems that nothing on this matter has appeared in print at the time of the present writing, although papers on the subject of the indexical use of "I" have been delivered by Professor R. Carnap and perhaps by others.

78. Not to be confused with the relatively new term "connotation" — see section 6 above in this present chapter.

79. Thus the decree of Louis XI from Senlis March 1, 1474, condemns Ockham, Jean de Mirecourt (*Monachus Cisterciensis*), Gregory of Rimini, Buridan, Pierre d'Ailly, Marsilius of Inghen, Adam Wodeham, John Dorp, Albert of Saxony, "and the others like them who are called Nominalists (*nominales*) or Terminists (*terministae*). — E. Amman, article "Occam," in *Dictionnaire de théologie catholique*; Rashdall, *Universities of Europe*, I, 564.

80. M.–D. Chenu, "Grammaire et théologie au XIIᵉ et XIIIᵉ siècles," *Archives d'histoire doctrinale et littéraire du moyen âge*, 10:1–28 (1935–1936).

81. See Karl Heinrich Graf, "Iacobus Faber Stapulensis, ein Beitrag zur Geschichte der Reformation in Frankreich," *Zeitschrift für die historische Theologie*, 1852, pp. 1–86, 165–237; P. Imbart de la Tour, *Les origines de la Réforme* (Paris, 1905–1935) II, 382–395, etc.; Ricardo G. Villoslada, *La Universidad de Paris durante los estudios de Francisco de Vitoria, O.P., 1507–1522* (Rome, 1938), pp. 220ff., etc., and references there; Augustin Renaudet, *Préréforme et humanisme à Paris* (Paris, 1916), *passim*.

82. Lefèvre d'Etaples, *Ars suppositionum* . . . (Parisiis, 1500).

83. *Ibid.*, fols. [fviii], [evi], [bvi].

84. *Ibid.*, fol. bi.

85. See Villoslada, *Universidad de Paris*, pp. 223ff.

86. Jacques Lefèvre d'Etaples, *Grammatographia ad prompte citoque discendam grammaticen tabulas tum speciales continens* . . . (1529).

87. George of Trebizond, *De dialectica commentarius* . . . ; *huc accessit Iacobi Fabri de hoc libello censura* (Lugduni, 1543), *passim*.

88. "Audierat [aetate priore] Alexandros de Villa Dei, Facetos, Graecismos; in philosophia, Scotos et Hispanos; in medicina, Arabas; in theologia, nescio unde ortos: audiet [hac aetate nova] Terentium, Caesarem, Virgilium, Ciceronem, Aristotelem, Platonem, Galenum, Hippocratem, Mosen et Prophetas, Apostolos ac reliquos Evangelii veros germanosque nuntios, et quidem omnibus linguis loquentes." — *Oratio de studiis philosophiae et eloquentiae coniugendis*, in *Praelectiones in Ciceronis orationes* (1575), p. 6.

89. B. L. Ullman, *Studies in the Italian Renaissance* (Rome, 1955), pp. 28–29.

90. Villoslada, *Universidad de Paris*, pp. 197–199. My translation from the Spanish.

91. Aristotle seems to have been the first so to employ letters of the alphabet. See Lukasiewicz, *Aristotle's Syllogistic*, pp. 7–8.

92. Ramus, *Arist. anim.* (1543), fol. 6*or*.

93. Murner, *Logica memorativa: Chartiludium logice sive Totius dialectice memoria; et nonus [i.e., novus] Petri Hyspani textus emendatus, cum iucundopictasmatis exercitio* . . . (Argentinae [Strasbourg], 1509). Unless otherwise noted, all references here are to this edition.

94. Several of Murner's more important works, but not the *Mnemonic Logic*, are available in critical editions. Bibliographies can be found in recent encyclopedia articles under his name.

95. "Dialectica est ars artium, ad omnium scientiarum principia viam habens" — Murner, *Log. mem.*, fol. Bir.

96. See "The Ramist Disputes" in Ong, *Ramus and Talon Inventory*.

CHAPTER V

THE IMMEDIATE BACKGROUND: AGRICOLA'S PLACE-LOGIC

1. See Philotheus Boehner, *Medieval Logic* (Manchester, England, and Chicago, 1952); Joseph T. Clark, *Conventional Logic and Modern Logic* (Washington, D.C., 1952).

2. Gouveia, *Pro Aristotele responsio* (1543), fol. 2v.

3. Letter to Theodor Zwinger, 10 cal. feb. (January 23), 1570, published in Waddington, *Ramus*, p. 424.

4. Burgersdijk (Franco Burgersdicius), *Institutionum logicorum libri duo* (Lugduni Batavorum, 1645), Preface.

5. Erasmus' and other humanists' estimates of Agricola cited here are conveniently collected in Woodward, *Studies in Education during the Age of the Renaissance* (Cambridge, England, 1904), pp. 79–80.

6. Unsigned preface in Ramus, *Scholae in liberales artes* (1569), fol. a2v. This preface is apparently not by Ramus, as it has often been made out mistakenly to be, but probably by Eusebius Episcopius, the publisher, a humanist in his own right. It refers to Ramus in the third person.

7. Ramus, *Sch. in lib. art.* (1569), fol. a2v.

8. *Ibid.*

9. Charles Henry Cooper, *Annals of Cambridge* (Cambridge, 1842–1853), I, 375.

10. Joseph P. Mullally, *The Summulae Logicales of Peter of Spain* (Notre Dame, Indiana, 1945).

11. *Pro Aristotele responsio* (1543), fol. 9r.

12. C. A. du Boulay (Bulaeus), *Historia Universitatis Parisiensis* (1665–1673); Boehner, *Medieval Logic*, pp. 8, 97–101.

13. Du Boulay, *Hist. Univ. Paris.*, VI, 227.

14. The best and most complete study of Agricola to date is H. E. J. M. van der Velden, *Rodolphus Agricola* (Leiden, 1911). Since this work there has been no full treatment of Agricola. Theodor E. Mommsen in his "Rudolph Agricola's Life of Petrarch," *Traditio*, VIII (1952), 367–386, notes some incidental recent literature on Agricola, but nothing lengthy and nothing on the *De inventione dialectica*. Dr. van der Velden's bibliography is full, but his account in chapter v of Agricola's *De inventione dialectica* is summary and incidental to his larger, more biographical aims. The best general account of Agricola in English is a single chapter devoted to Agricola in William Harrison Woodward, *Studies in Education during the Age of the Renaissance* (Cambridge, England, 1906), pp. 79–103. T. P. Tressling, *Vita et merita Rudolphi Agricolae* (Groningen, 1830), Adolphe Bossert, *De Rudolpho Agricola Frisio* (Paris, 1865), and Georg Ihm, *Der Humanist Rudolph Agricola, sein Leben und seine Schriften* (Paderborn, 1893), are all three quite slim monographs.

15. See Donald L. Clark, "The Rise and Fall of Progymnasmata in Sixteenth and Seventeenth Century Grammar Schools," *Speech Monographs*, 29:259–263 (1952).

16. Van der Velden gives no list of editions, and Tressling's is scant. See "Agricola Check List" in Ong, *Ramus and Talon Inventory* for a fuller account of editions.

17. Bartholomäus Steinmetz or Barthélemy Le Masson in the vernacular (*ca.* 1485–1570). Waddington, *Ramus*, p. 384, finding in Nancel's *Petri Rami vita* the name Latomus, mistakenly identifies him as Jean Le Masson. The "Agricola Check List" in Ong, *Ramus and Talon Inventory*, includes Latomus' *Epitome*. Latomus has a pre-Agricolan stage, when he publishes a quite different dialectic in his *Summa totius rationis disserendi* (Coloniae, 1527).

18. The Wéchels maintained all sorts of contacts with travelers, especially from the Rhine Valley and Germany. M. Emile Coornaert, professor at the Collège de France, has, for example, come across a 1561 record stating that André Wéchel that year received in Paris the baggage of Thomas Redinger, a German nobleman from Breslau, and has been kind enough to communicate this information to me from his personal notes.

19. See the "Agricola Check List," No. xiii, with the accompanying illustration, in Ong, *Ramus and Talon Inventory*.

20. Agricola, *De inv. dial.* (Parisiis: S. Colinaeus, 1529), Lib. I, cap. iii, p. 10; cf. Lib. II, cap. xvii.

21. *Ibid.*, Lib. II, cap. v, p. 240.

22. *Ibid.*, Lib. II, cap. ii, p. 56.

23. *Ibid.*, Lib. II, cap. ii, p. 206.

24. *Ibid.*, Lib. II, cap. xvii, p. 299.

25. *Ibid.*, Lib. II, cap. xii–xiv, pp. 240–258.

26. Latomus, *Epitome commentariorum dialecticae inventionis Rudolphi Agricolae* (Parisiis: S. Colinaeus et F. Stephanus, 1542), fol. 4, and title given to Liber III.

27. Phrissemius, "Argumentum operis," in Agricola, *De inv. dial.* (Parisiis: S. Colinaeus, 1529), fol. [a6].

28. "Immortali gloria dignus, Rudolphus Agricola scripsit autem exactissima cura, phrasi vero qua nihil esse potest expolitius; sed acumina quaedam affectata, velut de prima materia, ac digressiones, quibus nunc a Boetio, nunc ab Aristotele, nunc ab aliis magna quidem subtilitate dissentit, satis declarent, illum hoc opus non cudisse pueris ediscendum, sed eruditis viris admirandum." — Erasmus, *Ecclesiastes, sive De ratione concionandi*, Lib. II, in *Opera omnia* (1703–1706), V, cols. 920–921.

29. Agricola, *De inv. dial.*, Lib. II, cap. ii, p. 156.

30. "Dialectice [est] ars probabiliter de qualibet re proposita disserendi, prout cuiusque natura capax esse fidei poterit." — Agricola, *De inv. dial.*, Lib. II, cap. ii, p. 156.

31. See the opening of the *Summulae logicales* and the treatment of Peter of Spain in Chapter IV above.

32. St. Thomas Aquinas, *In I Post. anal.*, lect. 1. Cf. Walter J. Ong, "The Province of Rhetoric and Poetic," *Modern Schoolman*, 19:24–27 (1942).

33. Hastings Rashdall, *Universities of Europe*, new ed. (Oxford, 1936), I, 247, 303, etc.

34. Peter of Spain, *Summulae logicales*, ed. Bochenski (Turin, 1947), 1.01, p. 1.

35. Agricola, *De inventione dialectica libri omnes integri et recogniti iuxta autographi, nuper D[omini] Alardi Æmstelredami opera in lucem educti fidem, atque . . . scholiis illustrati Iohannis Phrissemii, Alardi Æmstelredami, Reinardi Hadamari, quorum scholia . . . contulit . . . Ioannes Noviomagus* (Coloniae: Hero Alopecius, 1518), Lib. II, cap. xxiv, p. 375. This is one of the chapters missing in the 1529 Paris Colinaeus edition (and other editions derivative from the same manuscript sources), but equivalent positions are taken in Lib. II, cap. iii, pp. 215–220, of this latter edition.

36. Agricola, *De inv. dial.* (Coloniae: Hero Alopecius, 1518), Lib. II, cap. xxiv, p. 375.

37. See Walter J. Ong, "The Province of Rhetoric and Poetic," *Modern Schoolman*, 19:24–27 (1942); Richard McKeon, "Rhetoric in the Middle Ages," *Speculum*, 17:1–32 (1942).

38. Cicero *De optimo genere oratorum* ii.

39. "Oratio . . . proprium habere videtur officium ut doceat aliquid eum qui audit . . . . Dixisse sufficiat posse docere orationem ut non moveat, non delectat; movere aut delectare ut non doceat, non posse." — Agricola, *De inv. dial.*, Lib. I. cap. i, p. 1; cf. *ibid.*, Lib. II, cap. xii, p. 240, where *oratio* is said to be the instrument of dialectic.

40. "Delectare . . . ut sit a movendi docendique officio seiunctum finis esse nulli orationi potest. Omnis enim oratio docet . . . . Motus [i.e., officium movendi] a docendo nullam habet quod inventionis est differentiam. Docet autem quantum in ipsa [sic] est." — Agricola, *De inv. dial.*, Lib. II, cap. iv, p. 167.

41. "Docemus autem nonnunquam hoc tantum pacto, ut intelligat auditor, quandoque ut fiat illi fides." — Agricola, *De inv. dial.*, Lib. I, cap. i, p. 2.

42. *Ibid.*

43. *Ibid.*, Lib. II, cap. iii, p. 163.

44. The notion of "theme," which survives today where students speak of "doing a theme," is transmitted to the Renaissance largely through Rudolph Agricola's Latin translation of the Greek *Progymnasmata* of Aphthonius, a fourth-century Greek. See T. W. Baldwin, *William Shakspere's Small Latine and Lesse Greeke* (Urbana, Illinois, 1944), II, 62. In the Ramist tradition, much about themes is to be found in Friedrich Beurhaus (Beurhusius), *De Petri Rami Dialecticae capitibus disputationes scholasticae . . .* (Coloniae, 1588), pp. 220, etc.

45. Agricola, *Epitome primi libri De inventione dialectica . . . per Alardum Æmstelredamum* (Parisiis: C. Wechel, 1539), fol. 7.

46. See Richard McKeon, "Rhetoric in the Middle Ages," *Speculum*, 17:10 (1942).

47. Agricola, *De inv. dial.*, Lib. I, cap. iii, pp. 10, 13.

48. *Ibid.*, Lib. I, cap. iii, p. 13.

49. See Ihm, *Der Humanist R. Agricola*, p. 42; Bossert, *De Rudolpho Agricola*, pp. 44ff.

50. See Aristotle *Posterior Analytics* I, 1–7 (71a–74b) and *Categories, passim.* In its general bearing, what is here said about the *Categories* and the *Topics* is the common property of Aristotelian scholarship. See H. W. B. Joseph, *An Introduction to Logic*, 2d ed., rev. (1916), pp. 48–65, etc. Many distorted interpretations imposed on Aristotle, particularly those which reduce the categories to mere classes are explicitly corrected in Richard Joseph Blackwell, "Aristotle's Theory of Predication" (Unpublished Ph.D. dissertation, Department of Philosophy, St. Louis University, 1954). Recent works covering the matter include also J.-M. Le Blond, *Logique et méthode chez Aristote* (Paris, 1939), pp. 52ff., etc.; Léon Robin, *Aristote* (Paris, 1944), pp. 99–102, etc. For a modern account of Aristotelian logic, see J. W. Miller, *The Structure of Aristotelian Logic* (London, 1938). The categories are variously given in Aristotle, but the most complete list makes them ten: substance, quantity, quality, relation, action, passion, location, situation in time, position (as sitting, standing), and *habitus* or the condition of being clothed or equipped.

51. Local motion and thus spatial patterns can also be apprehended in terms of touch, but this sense is not directly in play here.

52. See Clark, *Conventional Logic and Modern Logic*. The term "mathematical" applies to modern formal logic or "logistics" not, of course, because this can be reduced to mathematics, but because mathematics can be reduced to it.

53. See Jan Lukasiewicz, *Aristotle's Syllogistic from the Standpoint of Modern Formal Logic* (Oxford, 1951).

54. For a discerning and profound treatment of the visual-aural opposition on which the present discussion turns, the reader is referred to the works of Louis Lavelle, especially *La parole et l'écriture* (Paris, 1942), and Jean Nogué, *Esquisse d'un système des qualités sensibles* (Paris, 1943).

55. Ramus, *Scholae metaphysicae, Praefatio*, in *Sch. in lib. art.* (1569), before col. 829.

56. In his *Mathematical Logic*, rev. ed. (Cambridge, Mass., 1951), p. 32–33, Willard Van Orman Quine has some interesting observations on what would happen "if we were willing to reconstrue statements as names of some sort of entities." He concludes that "it . . . seems well to adhere to the common-sense view that statements are not names at all, though they contain names along with verbs and adverbs and the rest." This conclusion is, it seems, related to the gravitation of logical interest toward either breaking statements down into their parts or combining them among themselves. The "state of affairs" to which the judgment expressed in a statement refers is represented by the whole judgment and the whole statement precisely as *not* broken down. The question which logicians have raised and which Quine considers here is tantamount to asking whether the "state of affairs" referred to by this non-broken-down item can be profitably considered as though it were like one of the parts into which the judgment or statement is broken down.

57. Agricola, *De inv. dial.*, p. 7.

58. Ralph Lever, *The Arte of Reason, Rightly Termed Witcraft* (1573); John Seton, *Dialectica* (1572); Thomas Wilson, *Reason* (1551); Thomas Blundeville, *The Arte of Logicke* (1619). See Baldwin, *William Shakspere's Small Latine and Lesse Greeke*, II, 1–4; also Richard McKeon, "Rhetoric in the Middle Ages," *Speculum*, 17:9 (1942).

59. Hugh of St. Victor, *Didascalicon*, Lib. II, cap. xxx, ed. Buttimer (Washington, D.C., 1939), p. 46.

60. St. Thomas Aquinas, *Summa theologiae*, I–II, q. 57, a. 6 ad 3 (the *inquisitiva* of this text is synonymous with *inventiva* — see *Summa theologiae*, I, q. 79, a. 8 c.). See also J. Isaac, "La notion de dialectique chez Saint Thomas," *Revue des sciences philosophiques et théologiques*, 34:481–506 (1950).

61. Charpentier, *Ad expositionem disputationis . . . responsio* (1564), fol. 27.

62. St. Thomas Aquinas, *Summa theologiae*, I, q. 79, a. 8 c. Cf. Isaac, "La notion de dialectique . . . ," *Rev. des sci. phil. et théol.*, 34:491–493 (1950).

63. See Isaac, "La notion de dialectique . . . ," *Rev. des sci. phil. et théol.*, 34:486–487, 493 (1950).

64. Milton, *Artis logicae plenior institutio ad Petri Rami methodum concinnata* (1672), Lib. I, cap. i, in *Works*, XI, pp. 294–297.

65. Phrissemius, "Argumentum operis," in Agricola, *De inv. dial.*, fol. a6r.

66. Cano turned the topical tradition into Catholic theology with his *Theological Places* (*De locis theologicis*), and the article on him in the *Dictionnaire de théologie catholique*, Vol. II, Part 2, col. 1539, states explicitly that (like Agricola) he would have written the second part (on theological judgment or disposition) if only he had lived longer. The case of Leonard Cox, reported by Wilbur Samuel Howell in his *Logic and Rhetoric in England, 1500–1700* (Princeton, New Jersey, 1956), pp. 92–94, is particularly interesting. Having taken over from Melanchthon a notion of rhetoric which has obvious affinities with Agricolan dialectic, he puts out a work on rhetorical invention, *The Art or Crafte of Rhetorike* (*ca.* 1530), and, after repeated promises to go on to the next parts (which Melanchthon had made out to be judgment *and* arrangement, separately conceived), he, too, passes off the scene with nothing but invention to his credit.

67. This curious and revealing position is taken explicitly in Heinrich Carl Schütze in a brochure inviting — at some length — attendance at the commencement exercises in his school at Wernigerode in Germany. The full title of the work is: *A[d?] D[isputationem?] de prima mentis operatione in scholis inferioribus potissimum emendanda et excolenda strictim disserit et ad exercitium oratorium de usu et abusu imaginum, a novem florentissimis iuvenibus quorum sex ex academia abibunt, die XVI aprilis, anno MDCCXXXXII in Lyceo Wernigerodano instituendum invitat Henricus Carolus Schütze, Rector* (Wernigerodae, [1742]). See pp. VI and VII. The Ramist tone of Schütze's thought is discernible in his insistence that students learn the structure (*constitutio*) of

each subject (p. X), in his interest in outlining ideas (*in adumbrandis ideis* — p. XI), and his insistence in building up knowledge from something like psychological atoms (commonly called in his day "simples"). Thus (p. XIV), Schütze believes that in geometry the student should be drilled first in mathematical points and how to lay hold of them (*animo comprehendi*).

68. John of Salisbury, *Metalogicon*, Lib. II, cap. i, in *PL*, CXCIX, 858–859.

69. Aristotle *Rhetoric* i.2(1358a), ii.18(1391b); Cicero *De inventione* ii.14. sec. 47ff.

70. "Locus est communis quaedam rei nota cuius admonitu quid in quaque re probabile sit invenire facillime potest, vel, ut Cicero describit, est argumenti sedes." — Jean Le Voyer (Visorius), *Ingeniosa nec minus elegans ad dialectices candidatos methodus* (1534). This same work was also published with an epitome of Agricola's *De inventione dialectica* at Basle in 1535 — see the "Agricola Check List" in Ong, *Ramus and Talon Inventory*.

71. Agricola, *De inv. dial.*, Lib. I, cap. ii, p. 8: "Non ergo aliud est locus, quam communis quaedam rei nota, cuius admonitu quid in quaque re probabile sit, potest inveniri. Sit ergo nobis locus hoc pacto definitus." Agricola's remarks on the loci are very briefly summarized and treated in Van der Velden, *Rudolphus Agricola*, pp. 171–176.

72. Georgius Valla (1430–1499), *De sedibus argumentorum pariterque argumentis*, in *Dialecticae Philippi Melanchthonis libri quatuor* . . . (Lugduni, 1539).

73. "Res autem numero sunt immensae, et proinde immensa quoque proprietas atque diversitas earum. Quo fit, ut omnia quae singulis conveniant aut discrepent, singillatim nulla oratio, nulla vis mentis humanae possit complecti. Inest tamen omnibus, tametsi suis quaeque discreta sunt notis, communis quaedam habitudo, et cuncta ad naturae tendunt similitudinem, ut quod est omnibus substantia quaedam sua, omnia ex aliquibus oriuntur causis, et omnia aliquid efficiunt. Ingeniosissimi itaque virorum, ex effusa illa rerum varietate, communia ista capita, ut substantiam, causam, eventum, quaeque reliqua mox dicemus, excerpsere, ut cum ad considerandam rem quampiam animum advertissemus, sequentes ista, statim per omnem rei naturam et partes, perque omnia consentanea et dissidentia iremus, et duceremus inde argumentum propositis rebus accommodatum. Haec igitur communia quia perinde ut quicquid dici ulla de re potest, ita argumenta omnia intra se continent, idcirco locos vocaverunt, quod in eis velut receptu et thesauro quodam omnia faciendae fidei instrumenta sint reposita. Non ergo aliud est locus quam communis quaedam rei nota, cuius admonitu, quid in quaque re probabile sit, potest inveniri. Sit ergo nobis locus hoc pacto definitus." — Agricola, *De inv. dial.*, Lib. I, cap. ii, p. 8.

74. Jean Riolan the elder, *Ad Dialecticam P. Rami* . . . (1568), fol. 4.

75. See Richard McKeon, "Rhetoric in the Middle Ages," *Speculum*, 17:1–32 (1942).

76. "Omnis ubertas et quasi silva dicendi [*congeries of material for discourse*] ducta ab illis [Academicis] est" — Cicero *Orator* iii. 12. "Primum silva rerum comparanda est," i.e., "First one must amass a supply of rhetorical material" — Cicero, *De oratore* iii. 26. 103. See also Suetonius *De grammaticis* 24, *ad fin. poet.*; Aulus Gellius, *Noctes Atticae*, praef., 6; Quintilian *Inst. orat.* x. 3. 67. In the last two instances, *silva* designates a book, such as a miscellany. See Ramus, *Comm. de doct. Christ.* (1577), p. 5.

77. *The Rule of Reason* appeared first at London in 1551 and again in 1552 and 1553. This quotation is from the 1553 edition, fol. 37r.

78. Agricola, *De inv. dial.*, pp. 321, 331; Lane Cooper (trans. and ed.), *The Rhetoric of Aristotle: An Expanded Translation* (New York: D. Appleton and Co., 1932), pp. xiv and 155.

79. "Res est in loco, tempus in re" — *Theses logicae*, 1647, in Morison, *Harvard College in the Seventeenth Century*, II, 588.

80. "Definitio, genus, species, proprium, totum, partes, coniugata, adiacentia, actus,

subiecta, efficiens, finis, effecta, destinata, locus, tempus, connexa, contingentia, nomen, pronunciata, comparata, similia, opposita, differentia" — Agricola *De inv. dial.*, Lib. I, cap. xxxviii, p. 139.

81. Charpentier, *Animadversiones in . . . Dial. inst. P. Rami* (1554), fols. 19–20. See the notes with the early editions of Ramus' *Dialecticae partitiones* in Ong, *Ramus and Talon Inventory.*

82. Jean Riolan the elder, *Ad Dial. P. Rami* (1560), fol. 4. The "four" are really not arguments but procedures or "instruments": securing propositions, distinguishing word meanings, discovering differences, and investigating likenesses — Aristotle *Topics* i.13 (105a21–25).

83. Thus Otto Bird, "How to Read an Article of the *Summa*," *New Scholasticism*, 27:141 (1952–1953).

84. Erasmus, *De ratione studii* (Argentorati, 1512), fol. aiiv. The same passage appears in a somewhat revised form, but with its tenor unaltered, in Erasmus, *Omnia opera* (Basileae, 1540–1542), I, 445. Cf. Woodward, *Desiderius Erasmus concerning the Aim and Method of Education*, p. 164, where the passage is translated, if rather freely.

85. Boethius, *De differentiis topicis*, Lib. II, in his *Opera omnia*, II, in *PL*, ed. J. P. Migne, LXIV (Paris, 1860), cols. 1195–1206. Migne's text reproduces tables suggestive of the tabular component in the notion of *topica* itself, as well as of Ramist tables.

86. Joseph P. Mullally, *The Summulae Logicales of Peter of Spain* (Notre Dame, Indiana, 1945), p. xxxvi.

87. Many of the Renaissance logicians and humanists referred to here are discussed and the relevant passages from their works cited in Baldwin, *William Shakspere's Small Latine and Lesse Greeke*, II, 21–34.

88. See Baldwin, *William Shakspere's Small Latine and Lesse Greeke*, II, 9.

89. Caesarius, *Dialectica* (Parisiis: M. Vascosanus, 1533), title page, verso.

90. Le Voyer, *Ingeniosa . . . ad dial. cand. methodus* (1534), fol. 3.

91. Pierre Sainct-Fleur (Petrus Sainct-Fleur), *Institutionum rhetoricarum libellus, ad Aristotelis, Ciceronis, Quintiliani, Rodolphi Agricolae, et aliorum probatissimorum auctorum praeceptiones de arte dicendi interpretandas et intelligendas necessarius; ad . . . D[ominum] Iacobum Amyotum . . . .* (Parisiis, 1577).

92. Hegendorf (Hegendorphinus), *Dialecticae legalis libri quinque* (1534), pp. 8, etc.; *Dialecticae legalis libri quinque recogniti* (Antverpiae, 1534).

93. Titelmans (Titelmann, Titelmannus), *De consideratione dialectica . . . libri sex* (Parisiis, 1544), fols. 12, 15, etc.

94. See, for example, Titelmans, *De cons. dial.* (Parisiis, 1544), fols. 12r, 15v. Cf. Titelmans, *Compendium dialecticae . . . ad libros logicorum Arist[otelis] admodum utile et necessarium* (Parisiis, 1539).

95. Titelmans, *De cons. dial.*, fol. 166.

96. *Ibid.*, fols. 4–16, esp. fol. 4.

97. The influence of dialectic and rhetoric on law, and of law on dialectic and rhetoric in the Renaissance would be a fascinating study. An excellent start has been made by Richard J. Schoeck, "Rhetoric and Law in Sixteenth-Century England," *Studies in Philology*, 50:110–127 (1953).

98. See Etienne Gilson, *Index Scolastico-Cartesianum* (Paris, 1912), p. V. Gilson cites the 1609 Paris edition of Eustachius, whose work was also published in England: *Summa philosophiae quadripartita, de rebus dialecticis, ethicis, physicis, et metaphysicis . . . infinitis mendis repurgata* (Cantabrigiae, 1648).

99. See Boehner, *Medieval Logic*, Introduction and *passim*; Clark, *Conventional Logic and Modern Logic, passim*, and the exceedingly useful references there.

100. See the "Agricola Check List" in Ong, *Ramus and Talon Inventory*, where the Latomus *Epitome* is listed among the editions of the *Dialectical Invention*.

101. Latomus (*ca.* 1485–1570), *Summa totius rationis disserendi, uno eodemque corpore et dialectices et rhetorices partes complectens* (Coloniae: Petrus Quentell, 1527).

102. Latomus, *Epitome commentariorum Dialecticae inventionis Rudolphi Agricolae* (Parisiis: S. Colinaeus et F. Stephanus, 1542), fols. 2–3. Unless otherwise noted, citations hereafter are from this edition.

103. Latomus, *Epitome,* fol. 4.

104. "Locus est communis rei nota cuius admonitu quid in re quaque probabile sit facillime inveniri potest: ut definitio, genus, caussae, eventa, notae sunt *et* veluti signa, quibus admonemur in re quaque explicanda ab eis ducenda esse argumenta." — Latomus, *Epitome,* fol. 5. See Agricola, *De inv. dial.,* Lib. I, cap. ii, p. 8.

105. Latomus, *Epitome,* fol. 6. For the Phrissemius editions, see the "Agricola Check List" in Ong, *Ramus and Talon Inventory.* Latomus alters Phrissemius' original table only slightly and insignificantly.

106. "Instrumentum dialecticae est oratio per quam qui disserit fidem facere conatur de eo quod docendum suscepit. Ea bifariam dividitur: a structura, et ab effectu. A structura oratio alia continens est . . . quae perpetuo ductu progreditur; . . . [alia] concisa, quae per vices dicendi interrumpitur, ut disputationes et alternantia scholasticorum certamina." — Latomus, *Epitime,* fol. 42. The distinction between rhetoric and dialectic based on the continuity of rhetorical as against dialectical delivery is traced to Zeno the Stoic by Iohannes Caesarius in his *Rhetorica in septem libros sive tractatus digesta* (Parisiis: Christianus Wechelus, 1536), p. 14.

107. See Walter J. Ong, "Historical Backgrounds of Elizabethan and Jacobean Punctuation Theory," *Publications of the Modern Language Association of America,* 49:349–360 (1944).

108. Latomus, *Epitome,* fol. 62.

109. *Ibid.,* fols. 53, 56.

110. *Ibid.,* fol. 63.

111. *Ibid.,* fol. 64.

112. *Ibid.,* fol. 66.

113. "Dispositio igitur est rerum distributio in oratione quae demonstrat quid quoque loco collocandum sit" — Latomus, *Epitome,* fol. 71.

114. *Ibid.,* fols. 71–72.

115. *Ibid.,* fols. 77–79.

CHAPTER VI

THE COMMON BACKGROUND: ARTS SCHOLASTICISM

1. See Hastings Rashdall, *Universities of Europe,* new ed. (Oxford, 1936), I, 422–445, and section 5 in the present Chapter.

2. *Chartularium Universitatis Parisiensis,* III, 78–92.

3. Rashdall, *Universities of Europe,* I, 322.

4. *Ibid.,* I, 437–439. The lists in the *Chartularium* are full of law students marked as simple bachelors of arts, not masters; see, for example, *Chartularium Univ. Paris.,* I, 120–121, etc.

5. Thus, at the same time that the university philosophy course was normally three and one-half years, at the Dominican house of Saint-Jacques, the course was only two and one-half years. — Ricardo G. Villoslada, *Universidad de Paris* (Rome, 1938), pp. 22–23.

6. Rashdall, *Universities of Europe,* I, 472.

7. Charles Homer Haskins, *The Rise of the Universities* (New York, 1923), pp. 74–75.

8. Rashdall, *Universities of Europe,* I, 561–565, etc., with Powicke's and Emden's

emendatory notes there; Charles Thurot, *De l'organization de l'enseignement* (Paris, 1850), p. 107.

9. The work of Pierre Duhem in the last century, and of Anneliese Maier, Lynn Thorndike, and others today has underlined the importance of nominalism or terminism in the growth of the natural sciences, and the great value of the formal aspects of the terminist logic is now being stressed by modern "mathematical" logicians. For the persistence of nominalism and its dominant role in late scholastic philosophy (as such, in the arts course), see Rashdall, *Universities of Europe*, I, 561–565, etc.; Thurot, *De l'organization de l'enseignement*, p. 107; Villoslada, *Universidad de Paris*, pp. 89–90, 419, etc.

10. See Ernest A. Moody, *Truth and Consequence in Medieval Logic* (Amsterdam, 1953), p. 1. In this otherwise excellent account, Moody's statement that what the arts faculty taught besides the trivium was the quadrivium of "mathematical sciences" perpetuates the common misapprehension that the much talked of quadrivium (arithmetic, geometry, music, and astronomy) was a reality, whereas, although these subjects were not unknown, their neat quadrivial organization was little more than an ideal point of reference. See Louis John Paetow, *The Arts Course at Medieval Universities* (Urbana, Illinois, 1910); Rashdall, *Universities of Europe*, I, 439ff.

11. See M.–D. Chenu, "La théologie comme science au XIII⁰ siècle," *Archives d'histoire doctrinale et littéraire du Moyen Age*, 2:31–71 (1927), and, by the same author, "Un essai de méthode théologique au XII⁰ siècle," *Revue des sciences philosophiques et théologiques*, 24:258–267 (1935).

12. Villoslada, *Universidad de Paris*, p. 24.

13. Some scientific implications of theological speculation are ably discussed in A. C. Crombie, *Augustine to Galileo: The History of Science, A.D. 400–1650* (London, 1953).

14. Sir Thomas More, Letter to Martin Dorp from Bruges, Oct. 21 (1515), in *Correspondence*, ed. Elizabeth Frances Rogers (Princeton, 1947), p. 38.

15. Ramus, *Prooëmium reformandae Parisiensis Academiae* in *Scholae in liberales artes* (1569), cols. 1075–1076.

16. Ramus, *Pro philosophica Parisiensis Academiae disciplinae oratio* (1551) in *Sch. in lib. art.* (1569), cols. 1044–1046, and *Oratio de studiis philosophiae et eloquentiae coniugendis*, in Ramus and Talon, *Collectaneae praefationes, epistolae, orationes* (1599), pp. 248–250. In defending his own reforms against his fellow professors, Ramus discusses the old university program and statutes in detail and is frequently cited by Rashdall as a source even for the Middle Ages.

17. Rashdall, *Universities of Europe*, I, 125, 247, 303, 462, 472, 474; II, 89.

18. *Ibid.*, I, 462–464.

19. Ramus, *Pro philosophica . . . disc.* (1551) in *Sch. in lib. art.* (1569), col. 1020; cf. cols. 1011ff.

20. *The Life of John Picus della Mirandola* (by Pico's nephew Giovanni Francesco), translated by More in *The Works of Sir Thomas More Knyght* (1557), p. 3.

21. See George E. Ganss, S.J., *St. Ignatius' Idea of a Jesuit University* (Milwaukee, 1954), pp. 44–51.

22. Thus Ramus' name as a youngster is missing from the lists at the College of Navarre, where, for some curious reason, not only the *grammatici* but the rest of the *artistae* are also in part missing. See Jean de Launoy (Launouis), *Regii Navarrae gymnasii Parisiensis historia* (1677), I, 399 (Pars I, Lib. III, cap. ix).

23. Louis John Paetow (ed.), in Henri d'Andeli, *The Battle of the Seven Arts* (Berkeley, California, 1914), p. 42, note. See also Rashdall, *Universities of Europe*, I, 34–36.

24. Ramus, letter to Charles de Guise, Cardinal of Lorraine, written probably around

October 1570 (see Waddington, *Ramus*, pp. 223–224), in Ramus and Talon, *Collectaneae praef., ep., or.* (1577), pp. 254–255: "At quinque liberales artes primae adhuc a nobis elaboratae et excultae, et par vel etiam maior alacritas, ad reliquas elaborandum et excolendum, longe alia praemia sibi proposuerant."

25. Cicero *De finibus* v. The terms are traced to this place in Cicero by Charpentier, *Disputatio de methodo* (1564), fol. 13r — see "The Ramist Disputes" in Ong, *Ramus and Talon Inventory.*

26. Ramus, *Quod sit unica doctrinae instituendae methodus* (1557), fol. 18v; *Scholae rhetoricae* in *Sch. in lib. art.* (1569), cols. 234–235, 246.

27. Major, *Quaestiones logicales . . . iam primo in lucem misse, cum . . . literali expositione in veterem Aristotelis Dialecticen, Ioanne Argyropilo interpraete* (Paris, 1528), fol. iir.

28. See Sonleutner's adaptation of Ramus' *Dialectic,* entitled *Institutionis dialecticae . . . pars prior* (1587), fol. i. Among the countless earlier logicians who mention the seven liberal arts are Pierre Tartaret (Tartaretus or Tataretus), [*Commentarii in Summulas logicales Petri Hispani . . .* (ca. 1514)], fol. ii, E; Thomas Wilson, *The Rule of Reason* (1551), fol. Biir.

29. Ramus, *Prooëmium ref.,* in *Sch. in lib. art.* (1569), col. 1075. Cf. note 22 above for the *grammatici* and *artistae* in the Navarre records, and Ramus, *Pro philosophica disc.* in *Sch. in lib. art.* (1569), cols. 1044–1045. These terms long antedate Ramus' time. See, for example, the decree of Louis XI in 1464 for the government of the College of Navarre in Launoy, *Regii Navarrae Gymn. Paris. hist.* (Paris, 1677), I, 170 (Pars I, Lib. II, cap. ix): ". . . artistas, maxime summulistas, & Logicos"; *Chartularium Univ. Paris.,* I, 499: "Magistri logicalis scientie seu etiam naturalis."

30. Ramus, *Pro philosophica disc.* in *Sch. in lib. art.* (1569), col. 1022.

31. Rawlinson MS D. 345, fols. 1–16.

32. John Major, *Quaestiones logicales . . . iam primo in lucem misse, cum . . . literali expositione succincta in veterem Aristotelis Dialecticen Ioanne Argyropilo interpraete* (Parisiis, 1528).

33. Fol. xxv.

34. Major, *Libri quos in artibus . . . compilavit* [1506].

35. *Chartularium Univ. Paris.,* IV, 729. Cf. Rashdall, *Universities of Europe,* I, 442–445.

36. "Buridanus, Dulardus, Tartaretus, Petrus Hispanus . . ." — Ramus, *Pro philosophica disc.* in *Sch. in lib. art.* (1569), col. 1049.

37. "Formicarium Artium; Tartaretus, *De modo cacandi; Barbouilamenta* Scoti, *Les Marmitons* de Olcam à simple tonsure. R. Lullius, *De batisfolagiis principium*" — books among those found by Pantagruel at the library of St. Victor at Paris. Rabelais, *Pantagruel,* Chapter VII, in *Oeuvres,* ed. Abel Lefranc and others (1912–1931), III.

38. *Return from Parnassus* (second part), Act II, sc. i, 1. 528, in *The Pilgrimage to Parnassus with the Two Parts of the Return from Parnassus,* ed. W. D. Macray (1886), p. 528; cf. pp. 18, 19.

39. Villoslada, *Universidad de Paris,* pp. 218–222.

40. Tartaret, *Commentarii . . . in libros philosophie naturalis et metaphysice Aristotelis* (Parisiis, [1514]).

41. Tartaret, [*Commentarii in Summulas logicales Petri Hispani* (Parisiis, ca. 1514)].

42. Ramus, *Commentariorum de religione Christiana libri quatuor* (1577), pp. 26–27, and, in the same volume, Banosius, *P. Rami Vita,* fol. [a5r]. Ramus says the *Metaphysics* is nothing but a work on logic with some few remarks on theology and a coating of "mathematical ideas" — *Sch. met.* in *Sch. in lib. art.* (1569), Preface, between cols. 828–829.

43. See Haskins, *The Rise of the Universities,* pp. 72–76.

44. In a lecture delivered a few years ago, *Thomas Aquinas and Our Colleagues* (1953), Professor Etienne Gilson has made many points concerning philosophy and youth similar to those I make here. One hesitates even to offer corroborative material to a scholar who is so distinguished and with whose conclusions one so largely and heartily agrees. However, I may be permitted one remark. In stressing the incompatibility between youth and serious philosophizing (not, of course, between youth and serious activity with philosophical import), Professor Gilson remarks that "Thomas never foresaw a time when teen-agers would be taught metaphysics and ethics" (p. 12). Thomas did not have to foresee a time when it was *prescribed* that teen-agers *be* taught metaphysics and ethics: the 1255 statutes for the arts faculty at the University of Paris prescribe both subjects, and evidently for students who were teen-agers — with what effectiveness, I have attempted to discuss. Of such a program in the modern world Professor Gilson takes a rather dim view, which the medieval picture well bears out.

45. Major, *Quaestiones logicales* (Paris, 1528), fol. iir.

46. *Chartularium Univ. Paris.*, I, 78–80.

47. Or twelve weeks if read conjointly with another work — *ibid.*, I, 278.

48. *Ibid.*, I, 499.

49. Villoslada, *Universidad de Paris*, pp. 88, 104.

50. "Et quod aliquos libros mathematicales audiverat; quodque audiverat libros Morales, specialiter librum Ethicorum quantum ad maiorem partem" — *Chartularium Univ. Paris.*, IV, 729.

51. Ramus, *Pro philosophica disc.* in *Sch. in lib. art.* (1569), cols. 1010–1020.

52. For example, George de Lagarde, *La naissance de l'esprit laique au déclin du moyen âge* (Paris, 1934–1946), esp. Vol. III, *Secteur social de la scholastique*.

53. See Diamantino Martins, "O 'De anima' de Pedro Hispano," *Revista portuguesa de filosofia*, VIII (1952), fasc. 3, "Pedro Hispano" (anniversary number), pp. 260–294.

54. *Chartularium Univ. Paris.*, I, 504–505. The only one of these works known today is the commentary on Aristotle, and that in unfinished form. Perhaps the others were never written, although the masters of arts aver that St. Thomas had promised them that he would both write them and send them copies.

55. John Major, *In Secundum Sententiarum disputationes theologiae . . . denuo recognitae . . .* (1528), Major's preface to Noël Béda and Pierre Tempête, dated 5 kal. sept. 1528.

56. Herbert Butterfield, *The Origins of Modern Science* (London, 1949), p. 73.

57. John Herman Randall, Jr., "The Development of Scientific Method in the School of Padua," *Journal of the History of Ideas*, 1:177–206 (1940).

58. *Ibid.*

59. Ramus, *Scholae metaphysicae*, in *Sch. in lib. art.* (1569), Preface, between cols. 828–829.

60. See Ames' *Adversus ethicam disputatio theologica* in his *Philosophemata* (1643), pp. 119–142. Cf. in the same work, pp. 101–118, his *Adversus metaphysicam disputatio theologica*.

61. Miller, *The New England Mind: The Seventeenth Century* (New York, 1939), p. 131.

62. "Collectio plurium noticiarum adhesivarum logicalium" — Tartaret, *Expositio . . . super textu log. Arist.* (Parisiis, 1514), fol. iir.

63. See Antonio Coronel, *Prima pars rosarii . . . in qua de propositione multa notanda, de materiis propositionum, de contradictoriis in obliquis, de conditionatis et conversionibus ex libro co[nseque]nt[iarum] eiusdem assumptis, de modalibus, de propositionibus de futuro contingenti, et de modo arguendi ab affirmativa ad negativa, omnia de novo ab erratis multis castigata . . .* (Parisiis, [ca. 1512]).

64. See Richard McKeon, "Rhetoric in the Middle Ages," *Speculum*, 17:21 (1942), where the point is made that scholastic method itself in theology grew, via Lombard, out of rhetoric rather than out of dialectic or logic.

65. Rashdall, *Universities of Europe*, I, 290–292; cf. *ibid.*, 91, 181–182.

66. See Mullally, *Summ. log.*, pp. xxx–xxxii, lix.

67. Villoslada, *Universidad de Paris*, p. 94.

68. For later scholastic developments, often relevant to Ramism, see William T. Costello, S.J., "The Scholastic Curriculum at Early Seventeenth Century Cambridge" (Cambridge, Mass., 1958).

CHAPTER VII

THE PEDAGOGICAL JUGGERNAUT

1. This usage of *via* is current in Ramus' day. See, for example, the titles of Celaya's printed works in the British Museum and Bibliothèque Nationale catalogues.

2. Fraunce, *The Lawiers Logike* (1588), Preface, fol. 992.

3. See Gerald F. Van Ackeren, S.J., *Sacra Doctrina: The Subject of the First Question of the Summa Theologica of St. Thomas Aquinas* (Rome, 1952).

4. See Emile Durkheim, *L'évolution pédagogique en France* (Paris, 1938), I, 165–168.

5. Johann Heinrich Alsted, *Syntagma mnemonicum duplex* (Francofurti, 1610), [II], 2–3.

6. Thus at the opening of the seventeenth century, Nicodemus Frischlin was maintaining in a dispute against Karl Bumann that it was unthinkable that an art such as dialectic be inexistent, even under the condition that there were no teachers or other men existing — Frischlin and Bumann, *Disputatio logica de partibus dialectices . . .* (Marburgi, 1605), fol. A2. This might be taken to mean that the principles of dialectic exist anyhow in the divine mind (which says very little, for they are here indistinguishable in reality from the Divinity itself, being simply the Divinity considered as imitable in such principles when these are found in the human mind). But Frischlin means more than this. He goes on to say that an art is much more than a mere intellectual or moral "habit" (*habitus*). He is under the compulsion to make the art somehow self-subsistent. He has got rid of the teacher, even if the price has been to make the art itself into a kind of supposit. Frischlin was an anti-Ramist, but like many anti-Ramists, hardly differed at all from Ramists in his mental habits, conceptualizing as Ramists did, setting up the questions as they did, only saying yes where they said no and no where they said yes. See his *Dialogus logicus . . . contra P. Rami . . . sophisticam* (Francofurti, 1590).

7. "Philosophia est rerum humanarum divinarumque cognitio cum studio bene vivendi coniuncta" — Isidore of Seville, *Etymologiae*, II, 24, in *Opera omnia*, ed. J. P. Migne, in *PL*, LXXXII, col. 141.

8. "Philosophia est naturarum inquisitio, rerum humanarum divinarumque cognitio quantum homini possibile est aestimare" — Alcuin, *De dialectica*, cap. i, in *Opera omnia*, ed. J. P. Migne, in *PL*, CI, col. 952.

9. See H.-I. Marrou, " 'Doctrina' et 'disciplina' dans la langue des Pères de l'Eglise," *Bulletin du Cange*, 9:1–23 (1934).

10. Albertus Magnus, *Lib. I Post. anal.*, Tract. I, cap. iii, in *Opera omnia* (Paris, 1890), II, 11.

11. See Marrou, " 'Doctrina' et 'disciplina' . . . ," *Bulletin du Cange*, 9:1–23 (1934).

12. J.-M. Le Blond, *Logique et méthode chez Aristote* (Paris, 1939), p. 219, citing the preamble to Aristotle's *Meteors* I.1 (338a20–26).

13. *Chartularium Univ. Paris*, I, 78. Hastings Rashdall, *Universities of Europe*, new ed. (Oxford, 1936), I, 409, etc.

14. Rashdall, *Universities of Europe*, I, 224–231.

15. See the Talon prelections to the opening words of Ramus' *Dialectic* in any edition; Antonio de Gouveia, *Pro Aristotele responsio* (1543), fols. 4*v*–5*r*.

16. Charles Thurot, *De l'organization de l'enseignement dans l'Université de Paris au moyen-âge* (Paris, 1850), pp. 99–100.

17. See Ramus, *Pro philosophica Parisiensis Academiae disciplina oratio*, in *Scholae in liberales artes* (1569), col. 1005; Rashdall, *Universities of Europe*, I, 445.

18. Suzanne K. Langer, *Philosophy in a New Key* (London, 1951), pp. 9–10.

19. Ramus, *Scholae rhetoricae* in *Sch. in lib. art.* (1569), cols. 275–279, discussing Cicero: "docere seu probare."

20. See, for example, Albert the Great, *Lib. I Post. an.*, Tract. III, cap. v, in *Opera omnia* (1890), II, 80.

21. See, for example, Tartaret, [*Commentarii in Summulas logicales Petri Hispani* . . . (Parisiis, *ca.* 1514)], fol. ii, F, H. Tartaret was a Scotist.

22. Titelmans, *De consideratione dialectica . . . libri sex* (Parisiis, 1544), fols. 4–16. The first edition of this work had appeared in 1533.

23. Celaya, *Expositio . . . in librum Predicabilium Porphyri . . .* (Parisiis, 1516), fol. iir–v*v*.

24. Celaya, *Expositio in primum tractatum Summularum magistri Petri Hispani* . . . (Parisiis, 1525), fol. Aiii, a.

25. St. Thomas Aquinas, *Summa contra gentes*, II, 75. See also Van Ackeren, *Sacra Doctrina*.

26. Herbert Butterfield, *The Origins of Modern Science* (London, 1949), pp. 30ff.

27. See Butterfield, *The Origins of Modern Science*, p. 33.

28. "Graeci definiunt: μέθοδος ἐστὶν ἔξις ὁδοποιητικὴ μετὰ λόγου, id est, Methodus est habitus, videlicet, scientia, seu ars, viam faciens certa ratione, id est, quae quasi per loca invia et obsita sentibus, per rerum confusionem viam invenit et aperit, ac res ad propositum pertinentes, eruit et ordine promit." — Philip Melanchthon, *Erotemata dialectices* . . . , Lib. I, *a fine*, in *Opera* (1834–1860), XIII, col. 573.

29. "Dialectica est ars, seu via recte, ordine, et perspicue docendi . . ." — *Erotemata dialectices* . . . , Lib. I (opening words), in *Opera*, XIII, col. 513.

30. *Ibid.*

31. Melanchthon, *Elementa rhetorica*, Lib. I, in *Opera*, XIII, col. 420.

32. Agricola, *De inventione dialectica*, I, iii (Parisiis: S. Colinaeus, 1529), p. 13.

33. Fraunce, *Lawiers Logike* (1588), fol. 3*r*. Rosemond Tuve, *Elizabethan and Metaphysical Imagery* (Chicago, 1947), p. 384.

34. Ramus, *Sch. rhet.* in *Sch. in lib. art.* (1569), cols. 275–279: "docere seu probare, delectare, movere seu flectere." Here Ramus castigates Cicero's confused notions of these things, making it quite clear that, in his own mind, *docere* — the business of dialectic — swallows up *probare*.

35. Gouveia, *Pro Aristotele responsio* (1543), fol. 5.

36. Riolan, *Disputationes duae* (1565), fol. 1ff.

37. "Logica est ars recte, ordine, et perspicue de quavis re proposita docendi." — Deckher, *Logica Philippo-Ramea* (1620), p. 1.

38. "Logica est ars sciendi . . . . Ergo dialectica est ars tradens modum sciendi et per consequens docens instrumentum sciendi." — Johann Heinrich Alsted, *Clavis artis Lullianae* (1609), p. 164.

39. See Maurice B. McNamee, "Literary Decorum in Francis Bacon," *Saint Louis University Studies*, Series A, vol. I, no. 3 (March, 1950), pp. 1–52.

40. See Grouchy (Gruchius), "De nomine dialectices et logices," in his *Aristotelis logica* (1576), pp. 687–692.

41. "Ars dialectica doctrina est disserendi" — Ramus, *Dialecticae partitiones* (1543),

fol. 5; "ars dialectica est doctrina disserendi" — Ramus, *Dialecticae institutiones* (1543), fol. 8. Cf. the following variants: "Dialectique est art de bien disputer" — Ramus, *Dialectique* (1555), p. 1. "Dialectica est ars bene disserendi, eodemque sensus logica dicta est" — Ramus, *Dialecticae libri duo A. Talaei praelectionibus illustrati* (1573), p. 1. The definition "Dialectique est l'art de bien raisonner" occurs in the 1576 adaptation of Ramus, *Dialectique*, fol. 1, where it is due to his adapter.

42. "Logica non est doctrina de logicis praeceptis altercandi: . . . logica . . . est doctrina bene disserendi." — Ramus, *Scholae dialecticae*, Lib. IV, in *Sch. in lib. art.* (1569), col. 148.

43. For fuller treatment of this term, see Chap. VII, section 14.

44. Ramus, *Scholae metaphysicae*, Lib. I, cap. ii, in *Sch. in lib. art.* (1569), col. 833.

45. Johann Piscator, *In P. Rami Dialecticam* (1580), p. 12.

46. "Sermonis docere est: rationis, discere. Quare Dialectica et docendi et discendi ars est." — *Ibid.*, p. 13.

47. Latomus, *Epitome* (Parisiis: S. Colinaeus et F. Stephanus, 1542), fols. 2–3.

48. Johann Bilsten (Bilstenius), *Dialectica in qua Petri Rami et Philippi Melanchthoni praecepta logica coniuguntur* . . . (1594), p. 1–2.

49. "Philosophia iuxta Rameos est liberalium artium doctrina: a qua definitione non dissentit haec: philosophia est liberalium artium cognitio." — Severin Slüter (Sluterus), *Syncresis . . . de philosophiae definitione ac distributione* . . . (1608), pp. 17–18.

50. Ramus, *Quod sit unica doctrinae instituendae methodus* (1557), fol. 10.

51. Translation of the opening lines of Aristotle's *Nicomachean Ethics* in Talon, *In primum Aristotelis Ethicum librum expositio* (1550), p. 5.

52. Ramus, preface to *Sch. metaph.*, in *Sch. in lib. art.* (1569), cols. 828–829.

53. *Ibid.*, col. 872: "Aristoteles . . . dubitator est hoc libro, non affirmator aut doctor."

54. Grouchy, "De nom. dial. et log." in his *Arist. logica* (1576), pp. 701–702.

55. Piscator, *Responsio ad G. Tempelli Epistolam*, in William Temple (Tempellus), . . . *Epistola de Dialectica Petri Rami* . . . (1582), p. 25.

56. See, for example, François Pomey, S.J., *Indiculus universalis* (Lyon, 1672), under these terms, "dialectica" and "physica." This work was often reprinted.

57. Hegel, *Vorlesungen über die Geschichte der Philosophie*, III, in *Sämtliche Werke*, XIX, 252. Hegel is following Buhle, *Geschichte der neueren Philosophie*.

58. Ramus, *Scholae dialecticae*, Lib. IV, cap. i, in *Sch. in lib. art.* (1569), col. 317. My italics.

59. Alsted, *Theologia scholastica didactica* (Hanau, 1618).

60. Since they inevitably include an adaptation of the Ramist *Dialectic* and *Rhetoric*, these encyclopedias of Alsted and other similar encyclopedic works are listed in Ong, *Ramus and Talon Inventory* under Collected Arts.

61. Alsted, "Encyclopaediae liber quartus, exhibens didacticam, id est, doctrinam de studio philosophiae," pp. 102–146 in his *Cursus philosophici encyclopaediae* (1620).

62. Hasenmüller, *Didactica; hoc est, Ratio minus molesta, minus laboriosa in scholis docendi et discendi* (1615); also his *De faciliore docendi et vel unius anni spatio perdiscendi linguam Latinam, ratione didactica speciali* ([*ca.* 1615]).

63. *Didactica sacra*, in *Bisterfeldus redivivus* (1661), II, Part II, pp. 50ff.

64. Reiskius, *Dissertatio qua dialecticam . . . delineare . . . voluit* ([*ca.* 1690]), p. 4.

65. Cf. Chenu, "La théologie comme science . . . ," *Archives d'hist. doct. et litt.*, 2:31–71 (1927), where the role of dialectic in developing the idea that theology was a science (or *doctrina*) is treated.

66. Stephen d'Irsay, *Histoire des universités* (Paris, 1933–1935), I, 292–293.

67. See Georg Voigt, "Über den Ramismus an der Universität Leipzig," *Berichte*

über die Verhandlungen der königlich sächsischen Gesellschaft der Wissenschaften, Philologisch-historische Classe (Leipzig) XL (1888), 31–61. Voigt reviews the cases of the late sixteenth-century Johann Cramer, Franz Tidicäus, and Otto Schwallenberg. Cramer held, among other things, that man is a genus, that male and female are different species, that besides substance and accident there are little intermediate "physical predicable principles," that there is only one method in all knowledge (as against the three held by the opposition on the faculty), and that the sense of sight is a substance, not an accident. In 1592, Ramism was outlawed altogether at Leipzig.

68. 1643 and 1646 theses in Samuel Eliot Morison, *Harvard in the Seventeenth Century* (Cambridge, Mass., 1936), II, 583, 586.

69. Whitehead, *Science and the Modern World* (Cambridge, England, 1926), p. 17.

70. [Ramus,] *Dialectici commentarii tres authore Audomaro Talaeo editi* (1546), pp. 83–84; Ramus, *Dialectique* (1555), pp. 122–123; Ramus repeats this instance till his death through all the revisions of 1556, 1566, 1569, and 1572.

CHAPTER VIII

THE RAMIST DIALECTIC

1. Wéchel's Preface in Talon, *Rhetorica P. Rami praelectionibus illustrata* (Parisiis, 1657).

2. *Aristotelicae animadversiones* (1543), fol. 2.

3. "[Qui dialecticae] utilitatem proposita perpetuae disputationis exercitatione uberiorem reddidit" — *Arist. anim.* (1543), fol. 2.

4. *Ibid.*

5. *Ibid.*, fol. 3.

6. *Ibid.*, fol. 8. Ramus later specifies that the *Prior Analytics* has to do with syllogism and the *Posterior Analytics* with "method" (*methodus*) — *Dialecticae libri duo A. Talaei praelectionibus illustrati* (Parisiis, 1566), p. 423. In 1543, Ramist method was not yet.

7. See the works in "The Ramist Controversies" in Ong, *Ramus and Talon Inventory*, especially Jacques Charpentier, *Ad expositionem disputationis . . . responsio . . .* (Parisiis, 1564), fol. 27r, and Jacob Schegk, *Hyperaspistes responsi . . .* (Tübingen, 1570), pp. 14–51.

8. *Arist. anim.* (1543), fols. 64–65.

9. *Ibid.*, fols. 9–15.

10. *Ibid.*, fols. 16–19.

11. *Ibid.*, fols. 20–24. Cf. Ramus, *Scholae dialecticae*, Lib. X, cap. i–ii, in *Scholae in liberales artes*, (1569), cols. 445–446.

12. *Arist. anim.* (1543), fol. 26.

13. *Ibid.*, fol. 22.

14. *Ibid.*, fols. 62–63.

15. *Ibid.*, fols. 26ff.

16. *Ibid.*, fols. 32–50.

17. *Ibid.*, fols. 50–61.

18. *Ibid.*, fol. 61.

19. *Ibid.*, fol. 60.

20. *Ibid.*, fol. 70.

21. *Ibid.*, fol. 78.

22. *Ibid.*, fols. 79–81.

23. "Dialectica virtus est disserendi" — *Dialecticae institutiones* (1543), fol. 5.

24. "Διαλέγεσθαι (unde Dialectica nominatur) et disserere unum, idemque valent, idque est disputare, disceptare, atque omnino ratione uti." — *Dial. inst.* (1543), fol. 5.

25. *Ibid.*
26. *Ibid.*, fol. 8.
27. *Ibid.*, fol. 5, where *doctrina* is the second part; cf. fol. 17: "partes . . . dialecticae tres: natura, ars, exercitatio." The equation of *doctrina* and *ars* is, as earlier explained, common from antiquity through the Renaissance, as is the equation of both with *scientia* and with *disciplina.* For the roots of these three parts in classical antiquity see Francis R. Johnson's Introduction to his edition of Richard Rainolde, *The Foundacion of Rhetorike* (New York, 1945), p. xi, and references there given.
28. "Ingenium, ratio, mens, imago . . . dei, lux . . . aeternae lucis aemula" — *Dial. inst.* (1543), fol. 6.
29. Pierre Tartaret (Tartaretus), *Expositio . . . super textu logices Aristotelis* (Parisiis, 1514), fol. ii, a.
30. "Ars enim dialectica debet ab imitatione et observatione naturalis dialecticae profiscici." — *Arist. anim.* (1543), fol. 3.
31. *Dial. inst.* (1543), fols. 52–53.
32. Ramus, *Pro philosophica Parisiensis Academiae oratio* (1551), in *Scholae in liberales artes* (1569), col. 1018.
33. Ramus, *Oratio initio suae professionis habita* (1551), pp. 16, 21–22, 25–30.
34. Ramus, *Dial. inst.* (1543), fols. 7–8; cf. *ibid.*, fols. 5, 17.
35. Ramus, *Pro phil. disc.* (1551), in *Sch. in lib. art.* (1569), col. 1018, where he insists that the philosophy curriculum (i.e., the arts of dialectic, physics, etc.), should include not whatever is useful but whatever demands the services of another person, the teacher. See the discussions of *doctrina*, etc., above.
36. Adrien Turnèbe, *De methodo libellus* (Parisiis, 1600), in his *Libelli de vino, calore, et methodo nunc primum editi* (Parisiis, 1600), fol. 22.
37. Ramus, *Dial. inst.* (1543), fol. 8.
38. "Dialectica est ars bene disserendi" — Ramus, *Dial. lib. duo A. Talaei pr. ill.* (1560), p. 9.
39. Cicero *De oratore* ii. 38: "[Dialectica est] ars bene disserendi et vera ac falsa diiudicandi."
40. John of Salisbury, *Metalogicus*, Lib. I, cap. x, in *PL*, CXCIX, 837 B–C: "Est itaque logica (ut nominis significatio latissime pateat), loquendi vel disserendi ratio."
41. "Ratio disserendi integrales partes habet inventionem et iudicium, divisivas vero demonstrationem, probabilem, sophisticam." — Hugh of St. Victor, *Didascalicon*, Lib. II, cap. xxx, ed. Buttimer, p. 40.
42. "Est itaque logica . . . loquendi vel disserendi ratio." — *Metalogicus*, Lib. I, cap. x, in *PL*, CXCIX, 837 B–C.
43. Thomas Granger, *Syntagma logicum, or The Divine Logic* (1620), fol. a2.
44. Perry Miller, *The New England Mind* (1939), p. 125–127.
45. There are lengthy disputes, of course, in Ramist literature as to whether the *bene* belongs in the definition or not, Ramus himself being quotable by both sides: see Chapter VII, n.41, above. The same disputes extend to the other arts, in the definitions of which *bene* also figures: *Geometria est ars bene metiendi*, etc. See especially the works of William Temple and of Piscator in Miller, *The New England Mind*, pp. 125ff.
46. *Didascalicon*, Lib. I, cap. xi, ed. Buttimer (1939), p. 21.
47. "Geometria est ars bene metiendi" — Ramus, *Geometria*, Lib. I, in *Arithmeticae libri duo, geometriae septem et viginti* (Basileae, 1569), p. 1. Cf. the definitions of Ramus' other arts at the opening of each of his various textbooks.
48. Ramus, *Dial. inst.* (1543), fols. 7ff.
49. Alsted, *Clavis artis Lullianae et verae logices* (1609), p. 164.
50. *Arist. anim.* (1543), fols. 3–4.
51. "Artes . . . rerum tanquam tabulae" — *ibid.* (1543), fol. 4.

52. "Dialectica . . . non modo ars esse, sed artium regina, deaque vult" — *ibid.* (1543), fol. 4.

53. Ramus, *Dial. inst.* (1543), fols. 8, 20–21.

54. Ramus, *Arist. anim.* (1543), fol. 19r-v; *Dialectique* (1555), p. 5.

55. *Dial. inst.* (1543), fols. 9, 13–14: *caussae, effectus, subiecta, adiuncta, dissentanea; genus, species, nomen, notatio, coniugata, testimonia, comparata, divisio, definitio.*

56. St. Thomas Aquinas seems ordinarily not to use the term *iudicium* in the way "judgment" is often used today as referring to the psychological process which produced the statement or enunciation, joining predicate to subject, but rather as referring somehow to the verification of a demonstrative process. In this sense, *iudicium* complements *inventio*, concerned with the finding of means of demonstration, but the manner in which these paired processes work together is described in a quite different fashion from Ramus'. See J. Isaac, "La notion de dialectique chez Saint Thomas," *Revue des sciences philisophiques et théologiques*, 24:486–487 (1950). The terms *via inventionis* and *via iudicii* are similar but not exactly the same in the main tradition of scholastic philosophy (arts scholasticism) and in St. Thomas. In the latter's works, these terms occur frequently, for example, in *Summa theologiae* I. 79. 8c; I–II. 57. 6 ad 3; II–II. 51. 2 ad 2, 2 ad 3, 4 ad 2; II–II. 53. 4c; *In 1 Metaph.*, lect. 5; *In IV Metaph.*, lect. 4; *In 1 Post. Anal.*, lect. 1, *ante medium* (this last is not too clear). Various other studies treat these notions which St. Thomas inherits from the past and, with hundreds of other scholastics, passes on to the Renaissance; for example, Louis Lachance, "S. Thomas dans l'histoire de la logique," *Etudes d'histoire littéraire et doctrinale du XIIIᵉ siècle* (1932), pp. 61–103; Louis-Marie Régis, "Analyse et synthèse dans l'oeuvre de saint Thomas," *Studia Mediaevalia* (Bruges, 1948), pp. 301–330.

57. "Iudicium . . . definiamus, doctrinam res inventas collocandi, et ea collatione de re proposita iudicandi: quae certe doctrina itidem memoriae (si tamen eius esse disciplina ulla potest) verissima, certissimaque doctrina est: ut una eademque sit institutio duarum maximarum animi virtutum, iudicii et memoriae. Itaque cum de iudicio dixero, de memoria (quae in iudicii arte est) etiam dixero." — *Dial. inst.* (1543), fols. 19–20.

58. Ramus, *Dial. A. Talaei prael. ill.*, Lib. II, cap. i (Basle, 1569), p. 273.

59. Agricola, *De inventione dialectica*, Lib. I, cap. ii (Paris: S. Colinaeus, 1529), p. 7.

60. Ramus, *Dial. inst.* (1543), fol. 20.

61. Ramus, *Arist. anim.* (1543), fol. 73.

62. "Primum itaque iudicium est doctrina, unius argumenti firme, constanterque cum quaestione collocandi: unde quaestio ipsa vera falsave cognoscitur. Dispositio autem ipsa, collocatioque syllogismus appellatur. Syllogismus igitur (ut dispositio definiatur) est argumenti cum quaestione firma, necessariaque collocatio, unde quaestio ipsa concluditur, atque aestimatur: latine ratiocinatio a Cicerone nominatur." — Ramus, *Dial. inst.* (1543), fol. 20.

63. *Ibid.*, fols. 20ff; cf. his *Dial. A. Talaei prael. ill.* Lib. II, cap. ii (Basileae, 1569), pp. 401–402.

64. Ramus, *Professio regia*, ed. Freige (1576), fol. 95.

65. See Benson Mates, *Stoic Logic* (Berkeley and Los Angeles, 1953).

66. *Arist. anim.* (1543), fols. 61, 73.

67. *Ibid.*, fol. 51.

68. *Ibid.*

69. It occurs throughout the *Rhetoric*; also in *Topics* viii, 14 (164a6), in the verbal form and with the qualification "in rhetorical matters"; in *Problemata* xvi, 3 (916b27–30), with a similar qualification.

70. Johann Sturm is one of the relatively few authors to note Aristotle's use of the term enthymeme for a probable syllogism, but he misses the force of Aristotle's position and, in effect, succeeds in explaining it away. — Sturm, *Partitionum dialecticarum libri*

IIII (Argentorati, 1571), fols. 139–140. Cf. Titelmans, *De consideratione dialectica* (Parisiis, 1544), fol. 163r, where an enthymeme is a syllogisme *manqué*, one that "works fast," and Marescotius' much later revision of Titelmans, where an enthymeme is redefined in the Aristotelian sense as an "imperfect ratiocination from probabilities and mere signs" — Titelmans, *Dialectica, puriori sermone donata opera Michaelis Marescotii Lexoviensis* . . . (1621), p. 30.

71. For example in the *Prior Analytics* II. 27. 2, in *Aristotelis Opera omnia Graece et Latine* (Paris: Firmin-Didot, 1927), I, 119, where Aristotle is speaking of the truncated syllogism, the Greek words σημεῖον . . . μόνον are rendered by *signum tantum et enthymema*, the *enthymema* being a purely gratuitous addition, with nothing in the Greek to correspond. See also James H. McBurney, "Some Recent Interpretations of the Aristotelian Enthymeme," *Papers of the Michigan Academy of Science, Arts, and Letters*, XXI (1936), pp. 489–500.

72. "Collocationem tradit, et ordinem multorum et variorum argumentorum cohaerentium inter se et perpetua velut catena vinctorum, ad unumque certum finem relatorum" — *Dial. inst.* (1543), fol. 27.

73. "In rebus conglutinandis, et certa ratione . . . constringendis, ut finis primum definiatur, demonstreturque: deinde genera proponantur: generum partes subiciantur: nec prius illa progressio conquiescat, quam ad infinitam individuarum partium multitudinem pervenerit." — *Ibid.*, fols. 27–28.

74. *Ibid.*, fol. 29.

75. "Principia igitur artium definitiones, divisiones sunt: praeterea nulla" — *Arist. anim.* (1543), fol. 58.

76. *Ibid.*, fol. 60: "Idem . . . demonstrare rem et definire."

77. *Dial. inst.* (1543), fols. 35ff.

78. *Ibid.*, fols. 35, 58, etc.

79. *Ibid.*, fol. 36.

80. *Ibid.*, fols. 38–39.

81. *Ibid.*, fol. 38.

82. "Hanc artium summam dialectica [facit]" — *ibid.*, fol. 35.

83. For Ramus' troubles, see *ibid.*, fols. 35, 58, etc.

84. *Arist. anim.* (1543), fols. 63–64; cf. *Dial. inst.* (1543), fol. 20.

85. *Dial. inst.* (1543), fol. 43.

86. *Ibid.*, fols. 5, 7–8, 17.

87. *Arist. anim.* (1543), fol. 4.

88. *Dial. inst.* (1543), fol. 57.

89. "Exercitatio . . . artis praecepta in opus educat, et vim praeceptis inclusam exemplis effingat et exprimat" — *ibid.*, fol. 43.

90. *Ibid.*, fols. 44ff.

91. "Interpretationem voco poetarum, oratorum, philosophorum, omniumque artium et excellentium scriptorum lectionem, auditionem, et ad instituta dialecticae artis explicationem" — *ibid.*, fol. 44.

92. *Dial. inst.* (1543), fols. 44–45.

93. *Ibid.*, fol. 36.

94. "Vis autem praecipua commoditasque syllogismi est in longioribus disputationibus resolvendis retexendisque: . . . sic Miloniana Cic[eronis] in unum dialecticae ratiocinationis vinculum est inclusa, Sceleratum hominem licet interficere" — *ibid.*, fol. 48.

95. "Cum in perpetuae orationis partibus syllogismos multos distinxeris: uno summam totam (ut plerumque ex sese, sed multis ornamentis amplificata comprehensa est) omnibus detractis amplificationibus, notatis tamen capitibus argumentorum succincte complectare" — *ibid.*, fol. 48.

96. Riolan, *Ad Dialecticam P. Rami una ex praelectionibus* (1568), fol. 2.

97. *Dial. inst.* (1543), fol. 50.
98. *Ibid.*
99. *Ibid.*
100. *Ibid.*, fols. 50–52.
101. *Ibid.*, fol. 52.
102. *Ibid.*
103. *Ibid.*, fols. 52–53.
104. "Volo enim naturae coniunctam esse artem, artisque exercitationem: et quoniam tota hominis vita, nihil aliud esse quam rationis usus, id est, dialecticae naturalis exercitatio debet: sic rationis, et dialecticae naturalis artem, quanquam breviter, et paucis praeceptis cognitam, tota vita tamen in rebus omnibus meditemur et exerceamus, tum certe ut in caeteris artificibus omnibus, sic in hoc universo et omnia alia complectente verissimum illud esse percipiemus, artem non tam praeceptis quam exercitatione cognosci, multaque quae otiosis in scholis pueri ieiuna, atque arida putabamus, senes in hoc usu diligentissime versati mirabimur; atque ipse sensus consuetudine et exemplis informatus aliquid ostendet, quod quieta cogitatio, quamvis acutissima non poterat intelligere." — *Ibid.*, fol. 54.
105. *Ibid.*, fols. 54–56.
106. "Philosophi et oratores . . . aiunt . . . ordinem prodesse memoriae: sed externis et commentitiis eam signis, et simulachris instruunt: nos ordinis rebus ipsis insiti doctrinam certissimam, rerumque verissimas imagines: illi verborum memoriam infinitate formarum conturbant, dum propter singula verba ad singulas species est respiciendum: nos hanc partem rerum compositione et collocatione (quantum natura fert) adiuvamus." — *Ibid.*, fols. 57–58. Cf. Ramus, *Scholae rhetoricae*, Lib. XIX, in *Sch. in lib. art.* (1569), col. 392. Ramus is obviously referring to such mnemonic schemes as the *Barbara, celarent* . . . of the pre-Agricolan logicians.
107. *Dial. inst.* (1543), fol. 57r.
108. *Sch. rhet.*, in *Sch. in lib. art.* (1569), col. 268.

CHAPTER IX

THE DIALECTICAL CONTINUUM

1. See, for example, Pierre Tartaret, [*Commentarii in Summulas logicales Petri Hispani*], [(Parisiis, *ca.* 1514)], fols. ii–iii. Here the question of definition is thrashed out in every conceivable aspect, the third objection against Peter's definition being that it is *nugatoria*.
2. "In commentariis autem Aristotelis nihil est ad naturae monitionem propositum; . . . ars igitur dialectica in commentariis Aristotelis nulla est" — *Aristotelicae animadversiones* (1543), fol. 4.
3. *Arist. anim.* (1543), fols. 7–8.
4. The term *technologia*, which Cicero had imported into Latin from Greek in its Greek sense of systematic treatment of grammar, occurs early and frequently in Ramus' own works. "Deinde ordinis nostri τεχνολογίαν tanto gratiorem iuventuti et aptiorem esse, quanti pluribus artibus breviorem facilioremque disciplinae viam doceat" — Preface to *Oratio de studiis philosophiae et eloquentiae coniugendis* (1547), in Ramus and Talon, *Collectaneae praefationes, epistolae, orationes* (1577), p. 90. Cf. *ibid.*, p. 2, in Ramus' Preface to his Latin *Grammatica*: "τεχνολογίαν primum populo exhibuimus"; etc. Ramus extends the term to other arts, referring for example to "rhetorical technology" (*rhetorica technologia*) — *Oratio de sua professione* (1563), in *Scholae in liberales artes* (1578), col. 1139.
5. 1643 theses, in Samuel Eliot Morison, *Harvard College in the Seventeenth Century* (Cambridge, Mass., 1936), II, 583.

6. *Arist. anim.* (1543), fol. 19.

7. *Ibid.*

8. *Ibid.*, fol. 57.

9. "Author [i.e., Ramus] singulari studio διχοτομίαν consectatus est, pulcherrimam certe et fortassis unicam legitimam dividendi rationem" — Piscator, *Animadversiones in Dialecticam P. Rami* (1586), p. 24.

10. Jacobus Martinus, *Logicae Peripateticae per dichotomias in gratiam Ramistarum resolutae libri duo*, 4th ed. (Wittenberg, 1614).

11. John Major, "Primus tractatus Summularum" in his *Libri quos in artibus in Collegio Montis Acuti Parisius regentando compilavit* (Parisiis: [1506]), fols. xxvi, xxviiff. Cf. Boethius, *In Isagogen Porphyrii commentarii*, Lib. I, cap. ix, ed. Brandt (1906), p. 22.

12. Harvard thesis for 1678, in Morison, *Harvard College in the Seventeenth Century*, II, 608. Cf. William Ames, "Theses logicae," in his *Philosophemata* (Cantabrigiae, 1646), p. 35 of the section, "Disputatio adversus ethicam": "Accuratissima distributio est dichotomia quia ibi est summa consensio et summa dissensio."

13. Jacques Charpentier, *Animadversiones in . . . Dialecticae institutiones P. Rami* (1555), fols. 19–20.

14. Ramus, *Dialecticae institutiones* (1543), fol. 14.

15. Cf. Celaya, *Expositio . . . in lib. Pred. Porph.* (Parisiis, 1516), fol. viir, a–b: "In quolibet homine est una humanitas quae est species et una animalitas quae est genus, ergo tot sunt species et genera quot sunt individua . . . intelligendo de speciebus habentibus eundem respectum rationis sicut non inconvenit secundum viam nominalium quod sint tot species sinonime quot sunt individua."

16. Talon will inveigh against Porphyry's distinction between the lowest species (*infima species*) and intermediate species (*alterna species*) in his *Praelectiones in Porphyrium* (1547), in *Opera Socraticae methodicaeque philosophiae studiosis pernecessaria* (1584), p. 491, although both Talon and Ramus have finally to avail themselves of this same distinction, as Charpentier gleefully points out — *Animadversiones in libros tres Dialecticarum institutionum P. Rami* (Parisiis, 1555), fol. 27. The Ramist usage here represents utter chaos, for Talon actually employs *genus* and *species* interchangeably on occasion — *Institutiones oratoriae* (1545), pp. 54–55.

17. See Talon, *Prael. in Porph.*, in *Opera Socrat.* (1584), pp. 489–491. Here Talon insists that Socrates and Plato are species in precisely the sense in which Porphyry says they are not.

18. "Est igitur nomen generis universum, speciei singulare" — *Arist. anim.* (1543), fol. 11. Cf. *Dial. inst.* (1543), fol. 14; Talon, *Prael. in Porph.*, in *Opera Socrat.* (1584), pp. 489–491. Rudolph Agricola, *De inventione dialectica* (Coloniae: E. Cervicornus, 1538), p. 61, says: "Genus . . . de pluribus speciebus; species . . . de pluribus numero differentibus; individuum . . . de solo uno dicatur."

19. See Georg Voigt, "Über den Ramismus an der Universität Leipzig," *Berichte über die Verhandlungen der königlich sächsischen Gesellschaft der Wissenschaften, Philologisch-historische Classe*, 40:31–61 (Leipzig, 1888).

20. Jacques Charpentier, *Animadversiones in libros tres Dialecticarum institutionum Petri Rami* (Parisiis, 1555), fol. 27, citing Ramus' "sixth edition" of the *Dial. inst.*, i.e., that of 1552ff., for Ramus' original stand.

21. Peter of Spain distinguishes three meanings of genus: 1) a collection of those descended from a common ancestor, as the Romans from Romulus; 2) the principle of any generative process, as a father or a fatherland; 3) the genus which species is "put under" (*genus cui supponitur species*) — *Summ. log.* (1947), 2.02, p. 15.

22. *Arist. anim.* (1543), fol. 14; Talon, *Prael. in Porph.*, in his *Opera Socrat.* (1584), pp. 483–491.

23. *Dial. inst.* (1543), fol. 14; Talon, *Prael. in Porph.*, in his *Opera Socrat.* (1584), p. 491. Cf. Ramus, *Dialectica*, cap. xxvii (Basileae, 1569), p. 201, where the drive of Ramus' thought has been obscured, but can still be detected without great difficulty; also *Scholae dialecticae*, Lib. III, cap. v, in *Sch. in lib. art.* (1569), col. 88.

24. "Species est res ea de qua genus ita respondetur: ut hominis, Plato: dialectici, hic dialecticus" — *Dial. inst.* (1543), fol. 14.

25. Ramus, *Arist. anim.* (1543), fols. 10–11. See also Talon, *Prael. in Porph.*, in *Opera Socrat.* (1584), pp. 489–491.

26. Ramus, *Arist. anim.* (1543), fol. 11.

27. Ramus objects to Aristotle's categories because they contain things only in potency, being supreme genera by means of which things *can* be classified — *Arist. anim.* (1543), fol. 19. For the Ramist, things *existed* classified.

28. "Dialectica est omnium artium generalissima" — "Theses rhetoricae" for 1643, in Morison, *Harvard in the Seventeenth Century*, II, 584.

29. See Richard McKeon, "Rhetoric in the Middle Ages," *Speculum*, 17:30 (1942).

30. "Ista est scientia cuius laudem platonicus hospes magnifice et splendide philosophanti tribuendam arbitratur" — *Dial. inst.* (1543), fol. 34.

31. See Antonio de Gouveia, *Responsio* (1543), fols. 2, 14, 17.

32. In Ramus, as in many other Renaissance writers, *fides* — which was the theologian's term for Christian faith — even when used in the theological sense, is strongly influenced by rhetorical usage, in which it meant the persuasion or conviction produced by a moving oration. This rhetorical sense will be recognized as kindred to the Protestant notion of faith and to the whole Protestant economy of preaching. It provides one of the many points of contact which make Protestant theology — particularly Calvinist theology — look very much like a direct development of arts course scholasticism, cut free from a formal theological tradition. Calvin had, of course, followed university courses in arts (and law) but not in theology. Emphasis on arts course training, including scholastic philosophy, was the hallmark of the Calvinist or dissenting minister, of Anabaptists, Brownists, and other "enthusiasts." The permanent monument to this fact is the name of Methodist, which is a kind of summary of the whole medieval arts scholastic development and which so surprisingly attaches itself to a sect known for "enthusiasm" but whose founder wrote a logic in which he included a detailed treatment of method. See Walter J. Ong, "Peter Ramus and the Naming of Methodism," *Journal of the History of Ideas*, 14:235–248 (1953).

33. *Dial. inst.* (1543), fol. 31.

34. "Unam ideam per multas singulasque seorsum positas longe, lateque fusam et manentem" — Ramus, *Dial. inst.* (1543), fol. 34.

35. "Significat [Plato] ideas, id est viva et sempiterna rerum exempla in divina mente: item formulas idearum animis nostris insitas, quae velut emicantes oculorum radii, ideis velut stellarum radiis illustrantur. Plato autem duo genera animalium ratione praeditorum statuebat, Deum et hominem, magna rationis et mentis similitudine coniuncta. Itaque cum videret ab hominibus nil percipi nisi per imagines et species rerum, iudicavit in Deo simile quoddam esse, sed species illas et notitias divinas (quas ideas dicebat) quoniam Deus aeternus et immutabilis esset, aeternas quoque et immutabiles esse. Tum vero statuit, cum animus hominis ex illo divinitatis fonte delibatus esset, divinarum idearum formulas illinc haustas esse, sed corporis tenebris obscuratas, tandem illustrari nominibus, definitionibus, exemplis, sed tenuiter et infirme: cum et nomina et definitiones et exempla caduca sunt et commutabilia: plenissime vero illuminari, cum formula humana divinae ideae splendore collustraretur.

"Quae ratio Socratem et Platonem induxit, ut aestimarent res divinas intelligi non posse. [The text of the letter here being commented on states that 1) the name, 2) the definition, and 3) the example or concrete instance, such as a circle actually drawn, lead to 4) *scientia*, and this to 5) the thing itself.] Quod uno syllogismo hic concluditur. Cum et nomen et definitio et exemplum et scientia rei non conveniunt, scientia vera non est. At illorum quatuor nihil plane convenit essentiae divinae: eius igitur nulla est vera scientia." — Ramus, *Platonis epistolae latinae factae et expositae*, Epist. 7 (1549), pp. 60–61. The *formulae* in Ramus' explanation here suggests a trace of Ficino's Platonism. See P. O. Kristeller, *Philosophy of Marsilio Ficino* (New York, 1943), pp. 236 ff. Ficino receives passing mention as a translator of Plato in Ramus, *Scipionis somnium* . . . , *P. Rami praelectionibus explicatum* (1546), p. 54.

36. Ramus, *Scholae metaphysicae*, Lib. XIII, cap. x, in *Sch. in lib. art.* (1569), col. 985.

37. "Platonis idea nil est aliud quam genus hactenus a nobis definitum . . . licet multis locis Platonem hac de re cavillari videatur" — Ramus, *Sch. dial.*, Lib. III, cap. vii, in *Sch. in lib. art.* col. 96.

38. "Genus est totum partibus essentiale. Species, pars generis: sic animalium, sic hominum genus, quia totum partibus essentiale: sic animal genus animalium singulorum, sic homo genus singulorum hominum, quia totum partibus essentiale: sic homo species animalis, sic Socrates species hominis." — Ramus, *Sch. dial.*, Lib. III, cap. v, in *Sch. in lib. art.* (1569), col. 88.

39. *Dial. inst.* (1543), fol. 41. See Gilson, *History of Christian Philosophy in the Middle Ages* (New York, 1955), pp. 175–176.

40. *Arist. anim.* (1543), fol. 2.

41. *Dial. inst.* (1543), fols. 37, 39, 40–41.

42. *Ibid.*, fols. 40–41.

43. Ramus, *Sch. met.*, Lib. IX, cap. ix, in *Sch. in lib. art.* (1569), col. 943.

44. *Arist. anim.* (1543), fol. 63.

45. *Ibid.*, fols. 67, 71–73.

46. See, for example, Jodelle's French poem in the 1576 French edition of Ramus' *Dialectique*, fol. [ajv], or the Greek poem at the beginning of Ramus' *Commentariorum de religione Christiana libri quatuor* (1576, and all later editions). The notion is repeated *ad nauseam* in countless prefatory verses in Ramist works.

47. See Chapter VI above.

48. *Arist. anim.* (1543), fol. 19; cf. *ibid.*, fol. 26: "an non est longe, multoque facilius puero paucis monitis artium discere?"

49. "Dialectica res nudas proponit: Rhetorica vero addit elocutionem quasi vestitum. Hoc discrimen etsi nonnulli reprehendunt, ego tamen non repudio, quia et ad captum adolescentium facit, et ostendit, quid rhetorica maxime proprium habeat, videlicet elocutionem, a qua ipsum rhetorices nomen factum est." — Melanchthon, *Elementa rhetorica*, Lib. I, in *Opera* (Halle, 1834–1860), XIII, col. 420.

50. Talon, *Prael. in Porph.*, Preface, in *Opera Socrat.* (1584), p. 476.

51. *Ibid.*, 483: "De quibus sic breviter statui potest: genera et species, si verborum ipsorum rationes attenderis, notiones esse animis nostris comprehensas: quare non esse substancias, nec corporis aut sensus participes aut expertes. Si vero res ipsas ut hominum, avium, piscium, pecudum, colorum, magnitudinum, virtutum, vitiorum genera et species intelligas, quemadmodum res ipsae, sic genera et species et substantiae et accidentia erunt."

52. *Sch. dial.*, Lib. V, cap. ii, in *Sch. in lib. art.* (1569), fol. 161. Cf. Ramus, *Sch. met.*, Lib. V, cap. xxix–xxx, in *Sch. in lib. art.* (1560), cols. 914–915, where Ramus quarrels again with both Aristotle and Aristotle's opponent Antisthenes, and shunts the question of truth and falsity partly off into grammar, where he had also lodged epistemology but where he treats none of these questions.

53. See James Martin of Dunkeld, *De prima simplicium et concretorum generatione* . . . *disputatio* . . . (Cambridge, 1584), with a preface by William Temple.

54. Nancel, *Vita* (1599), p. 61.

55. Ramus, *Dialectica A. Talaei praelectionibus illustrata* (Basileae, 1569), pp. 309ff.

56. Miller, *The New England Mind* (New York, 1939), p. 315.

57. Still, see Ramus, *Dial. A. Talaei prael. ill.*, Lib. II, cap. xviii (Basileae, 1569), pp. 565–566, where the four parts still appear, each as an example of the one and only Ramist method. Elsewhere Ramus says that Quintilian's five parts of the oration are proper only to judicial questions and hence worthless in the general art of rhetoric — *Scholae rhetoricae*, Lib. XI, in *Sch. in lib. art.* (1569), col. 349.

58. Ramus, *Dial. inst.* (1543), fol. 30.

59. See Bartholomaeus Latomus, *Epitome commentariorum dialecticae inventionis Rudolphi Agricolae* (Parisiis: S. Colinaeus et F. Stephanus, 1542), fols. 56, 64.

60. *Dial. inst.* (1543), fols. 52–53.

61. *Ibid.*, fol. 37.

62. Talon, *Inst. orat.* (1545), pp. 69–72.

63. It will be remembered that Ramus' *Dialectic* had likewise eliminated the "third judgment" which earlier, in his *Training in Dialectic*, Ramus had said, quoting Plato, was the only true dialectic. Reversals of stands such as these, which Ramus never explained, understandably demoralized his opponents, who simply could not keep up with him, and called forth comment even from his followers, who occasionally remark on the exclusion of decorum from rhetoric. See, for example, Rudolph Snel van Roijen (Snellius), *In A. Talaei Rhet. comment.* (1596), pp. 96–101.

64. Ramus, *Sch. rhet.* in *Sch. in lib. art.* (1569), cols. 390–392. The passage suggests vaguely that Ramus thought of decorum as falling under "causes" in dialectic. Ramus' views are compared with those of others in Rudolph Snel van Roijen's edition of the Talon *Rhetoric*, entitled *In A. Talaei Rhetoricam commentationes* (1596), pp. 96–101.

65. *Sch. rhet.* in *Sch. in lib. art.* (1569), cols. 275ff.

66. Edmond Faral, *Les arts poétiques du XIIᵉ et du XIIIᵉ siècles* (Paris, 1924), pp. 61–85.

67. Quintilian, *Institutiones oratoriae*, viii, 4.

CHAPTER X

ATTACKS AND REVISIONS

1. See "The Ramist Disputes" in Ong, *Ramus and Talon Inventory*.

2. Charpentier, *Animadversiones in libros tres Dialecticarum institutiones Petri Rami* (1554), fol. 8.

3. Page references are to the 1543 Paris edition, *Pro Aristotele responsio adversus Petri Rami calumnias*, reprinted in facsimile with Portuguese translation by Aquilino Ribeiro under the title, Antonio de Gouveia, *Em prol de Aristoteles* (Lisbon: Livraria Bertrand, 1940).

4. *Responsio* (1543), fol. 1.

5. *Ibid.*, fols. 4, 9.

6. *Ibid.*, fol. 27.

7. *Ibid.*, fols. 2–3.

8. *Ibid.*, fols. 2, 14, 17. On Ramus' connection with Italian humanism, see Chapter III.

9. *Ibid.*, fol. 3.

10. *Ibid.*, fol. 4.

11. *Ibid.*, fol. 12.

12. "Dialectica ea artis disserendi pars Aristoteli est, quae nobis argumenta subministrat quibus de proposita quaestione possimus in partem utranque probabiliter disputare" — Gouveia, *Responsio* (1543), fol. 5.

13. *Ibid.*, fols. 5–6.

14. *Ibid.*, fol. 7.
15. *Ibid.*, fols. 7–8.
16. *Ibid.*, fol. 10.
17. *Ibid.*, fol. 11.
18. *Ibid.*, fols. 14–15.
19. *Ibid.*, fol. 17.
20. *Ibid.*, fols. 17–21.
21. *Ibid.*, fols. 22–26. This was a common charge against Ramus, repeated, for example, in Jean Riolan the elder, *Ad Dialecticam P. Rami una ex praelectionibus* (1568), fol. 4.
22. *Responsio* (1543), fols. 27–37.
23. *Ibid.*, fol. 37.
24. *Ibid.*, fol. 39.
25. Ramus, *Aristotelicae animadversiones* (1543), fol. 56.
26. Gouveia, *Responsio* (1543), fol. 40.
27. Ramus, *Arist. anim.* (1543), fol. 56.
28. Gouveia, *Responsio* (1543), fol. 40.
29. Ramus, *Arist. anim.* (1543), fols. 31ff., 42.
30. Gouveia, *Responsio* (1543), fol. 42.
31. *Ibid.*, fols. 44–45.
32. *Ibid.*, fols. 45–48.
33. "Secundum iudicium credo vocas rationem artium tradendarum, quam graeci μέθοδον appellant." — *Responsio* (1543), fol. 48.
34. *Ibid.*, fol. 49.
35. *Ibid.*
36. *Ibid.*, fols. 49–50.
37. *Ibid.*, fol. 52.
38. *Ibid.*, fol. 50.
39. *Ibid.*, fols. 51–52.
40. *Ibid.*, fols. 52–53.
41. *Ibid.*, fols. 54–55.
42. *Ibid.*, fol. 56.
43. *Ibid.*, fols. 57–58.
44. See the contemporary life of Charpentier, *Vita Iacobi Carpentarii* (Parisiis, 1574), by Jean-Papire Masson, author of other lives of Calvin, Lorenzo de Medici, Claude and François Guise, etc.
45. See "The Ramist Controversies" in Ong, *Ramus and Talon Inventory.*
46. Charpentier, *Animadv.* (1554), fol. 6.
47. *Ibid.*, fol. 7.
48. *Ibid.*, fol. 8.
49. *Ibid.*, fol. 9.
50. *Ibid.*, fol. 14.
51. *Ibid.*, fol. 11.
52. *Ibid.*, fols. 25–26.
53. Chapter IX, section 4; Charpentier, *Animadv.* (1554), fol. 27.
54. *Animadv.* (1554), fol. 27.
55. *Ibid.*, fol. 27.
56. *Ibid.*, fols. 28–37.
57. *Ibid.*, fols. 37–42.
58. *Ibid.*, fol. 40.
59. See the *Dialectic* in Ong, *Ramus and Talon Inventory.*
60. "Inventio est pars dialecticae de inveniendis argumentis" — Ramus, *Dialectica*

A. Talaei praelectionibus illustrata (Basileae, 1569), p. 21; the definition is unchanged in the 1572 edition.

61. "Argumentum est quod ad aliquid arguendum affectum est: quales sunt singulae rationes solae et per se consideratae." — Ramus, *Dial. A. Talaei pr. ill.* (Basileae, 1569), p. 21; the 1572 edition is identically worded. Later Ramists would hedge the definition around in various ways as the result of disputes or syncretizing tendencies. Thus Johann Bilsten in his *Syntagma Philippo-Ramaeum artium liberalium* (1588), p. 279: "Argumentum est omne ens vel verum vel fictum, quod ad aliquid arguendum affectum est."

62. *Arist. anim.* (1543), fol. 64.

63. Ramus, *Dial. A. Talaei pr. ill.* (Basileae, 1569), p. 273.

64. This significant shift is discussed in the following chapter on method.

65. "Adhuc prima dialecticae artis pars fuit in Inventione; pars altera sequitur in iudicio. Iudicium est pars Logicae de disponendis argumentis ad bene iudicandum: Certa enim dispositionis regula unumquodque iudicatur: unde haec pars Logicae et iudicium et dispositio pro eodem dicitur. Iudicium est enunciati aut syllogismi et methodi." — Ramus, *Dial. A. Talaei pr. ill.*, Lib. II, cap. i (Basileae, 1569), p. 273.

CHAPTER XI

THE METHOD OF METHOD

1. The general evolution of the Renaissance notion of method is studied with great competence by Neal Ward Gilbert in *Concepts of Method in the Renaissance and Their Ancient and Medieval Antecedents* (Ph.D. dissertation, Faculty of Philosophy, Columbia University, 1956; "Doctoral Dissertation Series," Publication No. 16,809; Ann Arbor, Mich.: University Microfilms, 1956). The present chapter and book were completed before this dissertation was available. Nevertheless, in making minor revisions I have incorporated occasional references to Dr. Gilbert's work where his findings help corroborate or further explain my own. Martin Grabmann's two-volume work, *Die Geschichte der scholastischen Methode* (Freiburg-im-Breisgau, 1909–1911), treats chiefly what we should style method or procedure today, not what the scholastics or their predecessors commonly called method.

2. Aristotle *Posterior Analytics* I; see also the opening of the *Nicomachean Ethics*. The question of method in Aristotle is given excellent treatment in J.–M. Le Blond, *Logique et méthode chez Aristote* (Paris, 1939).

3. H.–I. Marrou, *Histoire de l'éducation dans l'antiquité*, 2d ed. rev. (Paris, 1950), pp. 262–265.

4. Ramus, *Dialectique* (1555), pp. 121–122; *Quod sit unica doctrinae instituendae methodus* (1557), fol. 16. Lib. I, cap. viii of Ramus' *Scholae dialecticae* in his *Scholae in liberales artes* (1569), cols. 26–30, is largely a list of Galen's works on Aristotle's and others' logical treatises (a list which Ramus borrows from Galen's own *De libris propriis*), concluding with the moral that Galen obviously did not think that Aristotle had said the last word on logic. Other places where Ramus cites Galen include: *Scipionis somnium . . . praelectionibus explicatum* (1546), fols. 14, 20ff. (on dreams); *M. T. Ciceronis De fato liber . . . praelectionibus explicatus* (1550) in *In Ciceronis orationes et scripta . . . praelectiones* (1582), p. 432; *Oratio initio suae professionis habita* (1551), p. 17; Preface to *P. Virgilii Maronis Georgica . . . praelectionibus illustrata* (1564), p. 13.

5. See Richard McKeon, "Rhetoric in the Middle Ages," *Speculum*, 17:11–12 (1942).

6. Ramus' secretary and biographer, Nicolas de Nancel, is a key figure in the tradition of medical symbolism with his posthumous *Analogy of the Microcosm to the Macrocosm — Analogia microcosmi ad macrocosmon* (1611).

7. *Posterior Analytics* I; see the opening also of the *Nicomachean Ethics*.

8. Marrou, *Histoire de l'éducation dans l'antiquité*, pp. 263–265.

9. See Gilbert, *Concepts of Method*, pp. 92–94.

10. Turnèbe (1512–1565), *De methodo libellus* (Parisiis, 1600) in his *Libelli de vino, calore, et methodo nunc primum editi* (Parisiis, 1600), fol. 2; my translation. This little treatise of Turnèbe's on method has been translated into English by Frederick E. Brenk in an unpublished master of arts dissertation, St. Louis University, 1956.

11. Schegk, *De demonstratione libri XV* (Basileae, 1564), pp. 8, 142 (see under Ramus' name in Schegk's Index).

12. Schegk, *De demonstr. libri XV* (Basileae, 1564), Index — (since this index is descriptive, the entries seem worth quoting): "Methodus analytica via regia ad virtutem; methodus ἀπ' ἀρχῆς quae sit, et quae ἐπ' ἀρχήν [the former is from principles in things, the latter from principles in ourselves]; methodus argumentorum, quibus problemata demonstrantur; methodus artium qualis esse debeat; methodus conficiendi definitiones praescripta ab Hippocrate; methodus definiendi genera; methodus definiendi maxime in tribus cernitur; methodus docendi disciplinas artium [in the arts or curriculum subjects, many things are highly particularized or individualized, and in these conjecture or opinion must be followed]; methodus docendi et discendi qualis esse debeat [the speculative arts demand reason and talent; the practical, experience]; methodus dialecticae analyticae ducit ad veritatem; methodus exquisita non ubique locum invenit, sed ad subiectam materiam accommodari debet; methodus ordinis collocandi partes in definitione; methodus perfecta quae sit [the perfect method is a syllogism of the first figure, a universal affirmative proposition, as in mathematics]; methodus quid sit Aristoteli interdum [for Aristotle, method is not the science itself, but the way (*via*) and grounds (*ratio*) of science]; methodus quid sit, eiusdemque elogium; methodus scientiarum ὑπόθετος et ἀνυπόθετος [the former goes back to the simplest principles, the latter involves some uncertainty, or some unknown aspect]; methodi gnarus artem efficere potest; methodi ignorantia causa errorum; methodi nemo observantior Aristotele; methodi ope et constituit et correxit Aristoteles omnes philosophiae disciplinas; methodi problemata explicandi praecepta; methodi tractandorum problematum exempla; methodi via duplex; methodum quam Plato ignem Promethei dixerit."

13. Temple, *Admonitio Francisci Mildapetti* (Francofurti, 1589), pp. 97–100.

14. Gouveia, *Responsio* (1543), fol. 48.

15. A good idea of the bearing of much scholastic discussion can be had from A. C. Crombie, *Robert Grosseteste and the Origins of Experimental Science, 1100–1700* (London, 1953), esp. pp. 1–90. Crombie's extensive bibliography should also be consulted. For the Stoic equation of *ars* (τέχνη) and *methodus*, see Gilbert, *Concepts of Method*, pp. 72–74.

16. Celaya, *Expositio . . . in Primum tractatum Summularum* (1525), fol. A3, b: "Methodus . . . est via brevis vel utilis ad cito attingendum aliquid."

17. See Titelmans, *De consideratione dialectica* (1st ed., Antwerp, 1533; also Paris, 1544, etc.); and the same author's *Compendium dialecticae* (Parisiis, 1539).

18. Unless otherwise noted, the information here on Hermogenes is taken from Wilhelm von Christ, *Geschichte der griechischen Litteratur*, 6th ed., ed. by Otto Stählin and Wilhelm Schmid, II, Part 2 (1924), 929–936 (No. 780). See also Francis R. Johnson's Introduction in his edition of Richard Rainolde, *The Foundacion of Rhetorike* (New York, 1945), for the displacement of Hermogenes' elementary exercise book in the sixteenth century by Latin versions of Aphthonius' *Progymnasmata* (Rudolph Agricola's version was a favorite).

19. Robert Barroux, "Pierre de la Ramée et son influence philosophique," *Ecole nationale des Chartes: Positions des thèses* (Paris, 1922), pp. 13–20. Barroux seems to suggest that the term thereupon became established in Latin; however, as has been seen, it was already very well established in medieval Latin in a different but related context in Peter of Spain. The listing of a 1516 edition of Nicolaus Vigelius' *Methodus universi*

iuris pontificii absolutissima in Neal Ward Gilbert, *Concepts of Method*, p. 169, seems certainly an error, for Vigelius' dates are 1529–1600. I have not been able to trace this title of Vigelius' but do know his *Methodus universi iuris civilis*, first printed in 1561 at Basle.

20. See Lewis W. Spitz, *Conrad Celtis, the German Arch-Humanist*, (Cambridge, Mass.: Harvard University Press, 1957).

21. "Est enim Ars propositionum et comprehensionum perpetuarum, et ad exitum vitae utilem spectantium, copiosa perceptio. Sed in hac copia et in artibus instituendis viam certam, brevem, rectam, et quasi compendiariam ingredi oportet, quae simplex sit, et aperta, et directa: hanc Graeci Methodum vocant, et didascaliam, quae ad docendum tradendumque adhibeatur." — *In part. orat. Cic.* (Argentorati, 1549, preface dated 1539), Dialogue I, p. 2. Unless otherwise noted, subsequent citations are from this edition.

22. *Ibid.*, Dial. I, p. 3.

23. Galen, *Ars medica*, in *Opera*, ed. Kühn, I, 305–306; cf. *De locis affectis* i. 6, *ibid.*, VIII, 60ff.; *De sophismatibus, ibid.*, XIV, 583; *De febrium differentiis* i. 2, *ibid.*, VII, 273, 275–276, 352.

24. Galen, *Ars medica*, in *Opera*, ed. Kühn, I, 305–306: "τρεῖς εἰσὶν αἱ πᾶσαι διδασκαλίαι τάξεως ἐχόμεναι."

25. Johann Sturm, *Partitionum dialecticarum libri duo* (Parisiis: C. Wechelus, 1539). This is the first edition so far as I know, and the first edition according to Charles Schmidt, *La vie et les travaux de Jean Sturm*, where a chronological list of the editions of Sturm's works is given, pp. 314–331. I rely on Schmidt also for the statement that books III and IV first appeared at Strasbourg in 1543 and 1560 respectively. I have never seen a copy of either the 1543 or the 1560 edition in question, which I here assume are substantially the same as the corresponding parts in the *Partitionum dialecticarum libri IIII emendati et aucti* (Argentorati: J. Rihelius, 1571), from which citations from books III and IV are here made. The two-book dialectic is here cited from the first edition, *Partitionum dialecticarum libri duo* (Parisiis: C. Wechelus, 1539). Sturm's works do not appear in the *Corpus Reformatorum* or elsewhere in modern editions and were not at all so widely reprinted as Ramus' works were.

26. Sturm, *Part. dial. lib. IIII* (1571), fol. 167.

27. *Ibid.*, fols. 168–169.

28. "Unum generum, quae in medio collocantur, alteros duos differentiarum atque formarum quae ponuntur in lateribus" — *Ibid.*, fols. 170–171.

29. Caesarius, *Dialectica* . . . (Parisiis, 1533; preface dated from Cologne, *id. iun.* 1532), Tract. VII, "De demonstratione."

30. "If you ask, as you do ask, what I think about Peter Ramus, I consider him a good man, and a well educated man, with a cultivated judgment" (*De P. Ramo, si petis, ut petis, quid sentiam: Virum bonum illum esse iudico; et hominem bene literatum, et iudicio expolito praeditum*). Sturm adds that, in judging freely of Aristotle's precepts, Ramus did no more than Aristotle had done with his own predecessors or than the Aristotelians themselves had done — for those who defend Aristotle against Ramus change Aristotle's order and otherwise diverge from his treatment — or than Rudolph Agricola had done. Although we must be equable and humane in judging others, "if the same thing has to be thought and said all the time, nothing new can ever be discovered." — Sturm, "Clariss[imi] Viri Ioan[nis] Sturmii de Petro Ramo iudicium," as quoted in Piscator's edition of Ramus' *Dialectic* entitled *Animadversiones . . . in Dialecticam P. Rami* (1586), p. 3, and in Frisius' adaptation of the same work entitled *Comparationum dialecticarum libri tres* (1590). Ramus and Sturm had earlier fallen out over scholarly matters and over Ramus' hesitancy in embracing Protestantism — see Moritz Guggenheim, "Petrus Ramus als Reformator der Wissenschaft," *Humanistisches Gymnasium*, 18:2 (1904).

31. "Ars perspiciendi, diiudicandi, disserendi quid sit et quale sit id quod ad disquirendum docendumque est propositum" — Sturm, *Part. dial. libri duo* (1539), p. 11.

32. See Sturm's works in the Bibliography.

33. See the list of editions of Ramus' *Dialectic* in Ong, *Ramus and Talon Inventory*, where the collations of Melanchthon and Ramus which contain the latter's text, even in modified form, are included.

34. "Dixi initio in prima parte Dialectices tradi doctrinam de explicatione simplicium vocum. Ideo gradus et domicilia vocabulorum initio monstrata sunt. Postea dictum est de modis definitionum et divisionum: nunc usum huius partis ostendamus. Ut autem alias nomen μέθοδος significat rectam et compendiariam viam [*text reads erroneously* vitam], ita Dialectici ad ordinem explicationis rectissimum transtulerunt [*the ordinary Latin term for metaphor was* translatio, *formed from this same verb*] hoc nomen: ac significat hoc loco μέθοδος rectam viam seu ordinem investigationis et explicationis sive simplicium quaestionum sive propositionum. Et sic Graeci definiunt: μέθοδός ἐστιν ἕξις ὁδοποιητικὴ μετὰ λόγου, id est: Methodus est habitus, videlicet scientia, seu ars, viam faciens certa ratione, id est, quae quasi per loca invia et obsita sentibus, per rerum confusionem, viam invenit et aperit, ac res ad propositum pertinentes eruit ac ordine promit." — *Erotemata dialectices*, Lib. I, in *Opera*, XIII, col. 573. For possible Stoic echoes here, see Gilbert, *Concepts of Method*, pp. 72–74.

35. See above, Chapter V, section 5.

36. "Cum de una voce dicendum est, viam monstrant hae decem questiones: Prima, quid vocabulum significet. Secunda, an sit res. Tertia, quid sit res. Quarta, quae sint rei partes. Quinta, quae sint species. Sexta, quae causae. Septima, qui effectus. Octava, quae adiacentia. Nona, quae cognata. Decima, quae pugnantia." — *Erotemata dial.*, Lib. I, in *Opera*, XIII, cols. 573–574.

37. "Aristotelis in libro 2 Resolutionum posteriorum quaestiones recenset quatuor, quae sunt in nostro catalogo praecipue: An sit, Quid sit, Quod sit, et Quare sit." — *Erotemata dial.*, Lib. I, in *Opera*, XIII, col. 574. Cf. Ramus, *Aristotelicae animadversiones* (1543), fols. 24, 26, and *Sch. dial.*, Lib. X, cap. i–ii, in *Sch. in lib. art.* (1569), cols. 445–446.

38. Paul Friese, *Comparationum dialecticarum libri tres* (1590), Comparatio XIX, "De methodo," pp. 98–101.

39. "De quatuor quaestionibus scibilibus . . . : quod est, propter quid est, si est, quid est" — Caesarius, *Dialectica* (Parisiis, 1533), p. 157.

40. *Ibid.*, pp. 157ff.

41. *Ibid.*, pp. 147–149.

42. "De tribus apud philosophos disserendi generibus ex praefatione Marsilii Ficini in librum de voluptate" — Caesarius, *Dialectica* (Parisiis, 1533), pp. 244–245.

43. John Herman Randall, Jr., "The Development of Scientific Method," *Journal of the History of Ideas*, 1:203 (1940).

44. See Ramus' *Quod sit unica* (1557), and the excellent explanation of Aristotle in Le Blond, *Logique et méthode chez Aristote*, pp. 73ff., with the texts of Aristotle cited there.

45. See Le Blond, *Logique et méthode*, p. 103.

46. A sample of the early discussion might be St. Albert the Great, *Topica*, Lib. IV, Tract. ii, cap. iff., in *Opera omnia*, II, 439ff. A sample from a perhaps more influential author of Ramus' own day might be Pierre Tartaret, *In Post. anal.*, I, in his *Expositio . . . super textu logices Aristotelis* (Parisiis, 1514), fols. LXXIIIIff.

47. See J.-M. Le Blond, "La définition chez Aristote," *Gregorianum*, XX (1939), 351ff.; Le Blond, *Logique et méthode*, pp. 147ff.

48. See above, Chapter VIII, section 4, ii, b.

49. Le Blond, *Logique et méthode*, pp. 147ff.; Le Blond, "La définition chez Aristote," *Gregorianum*, XX (1939), 351ff.

50. See Edmund H. Ziegelmeier, "The Discovery of First Principles according to Aristotle," *Modern Schoolman*, 23:132–143 (1945). St. Thomas Aquinas and many Renaissance *theologians* or *theologian*-philosophers whose metaphysics is investigated by Father Peter Hoenen (who does not investigate medieval arts scholasticism) hold that first principles, including those of metaphysics, have their origin in some sort of inductive process. It is only later that scholastics adopt the Kantian and Ramist view that the principles are got by a process which is seldom if ever described psychologically, or otherwise established as a reality, but which is simply styled "analysis." Father Hoenen reports that (in 1933) he found growing interest among exponents of scholasticism in the earlier inductive theory, but that the whole question was (by 1933) hardly adverted to by modern neoscholasticis — indeed that most of them seem quite unaware that the inductive theory was ever even held. — P. Hoenen, "De origine primorum principiorum scientiae," *Gregorianum*, XIV (1933), 153–184, esp. 153, 157, 160.

51. See the quotation from Digby's *De duplici methodo* (1589), in Temple, *Admonitio Francisci Mildapetti* (1589), cap. x, pp. 70–71. *Ascensus* and *descensus* appear, among many other places, in Porphyry and in Peter of Spain's *Summulae logicales*, and proliferate through the late scholastic logic of John Major and others at Paris directly into Ramus' world. See Peter of Spain, *Summ. log.* (1947), Tr. VI, 6:11, p. 60, and Tr. XII, 12:26, p. 119. Ramus, *Quod sit unica* (1557), traces the two ways of ascent and descent not to Aristotle but to Porphyry, Ammonius, Philoponus, Simplicius, and other commentators. See also in the present chapter, sections 9 and 10 below.

52. Schegk, *De demonstr. libri XV* (Basileae, 1564), p. 437.

53. See Randall, "The Development of Scientific Method," *Journal of the History of Ideas*, 1:186–188 (1940).

54. Aristotle *Post. Anal.* I.xxxi (87b38); Le Blond, *Logique et méthode*, pp. 75ff.

55. Aristotle *Post. Anal.* I.iv (73b25).

56. "METHODUS AC PRIMUM DOCTRINAE. — Methodus est multorum et bonorum argumentorum dispositio: ea duplex est, altera doctrinae, altera prudentiae, non quod utraque prudentis non sit, sed quod altera doctrinae et artis nil fere habeat, sed ex hominis naturali iudicio prudentiaque pendeat.

"Methodus igitur doctrinae est dispositio rerum variarum ab universis et generalibus principiis ad subiectas et singulares partes deductarum, per quam tota res facilius doceri, percipique possit. In qua tantum illud est praecipiendum, ut in docendo generalis et universa declaratio praecedat, qualis est definitio et summa quaedam comprehensio, tum sequatur specialis per distributionem partium explicatio: postremo partium singularium definitio, et ex idoneis exemplis illustratio. Quod ut facilius dicatur, familiari utar exemplo. Grammaticae sint omnes regulae, definitiones, divisiones repertæ, sint exempla grammaticae inventa, omniaque vere et recte iudicata ac aestimata; sint omnes illae praeceptiones tabellis varie dissectis inscriptae, et mille modis in urna aliqua ut in olla ludo fit, circunvolutae. Hic quaero quae pars dialecticae me doceat confusa illa praecepta componere et in ordinem redigere. Inventionis dialecticae praeceptis nihil hic opus est, inventa enim sunt omnia, sunt omnes partes vere probatæ, atque iudicatæ. Syllogismo nihil opus hic erit, quia quid hic verum sit, intellectum iam est. Methodus igitur et certa dispositionis via sola requiritur, quam unam simplicem doctrina nobis ostendit universa primum generaliaque, deinde specialia et secondaria collocantem. Dialecticus igitur hic noster methodi lumine seliget in illa urna grammaticæ primum definitionem, quia nihil est in omnibus illis praeceptis generalius, et primo loco constituet. Grammatica est doctrina bene loquendi, beneque scribendi. Tum partes grammaticae in eodem vase requiret, et secundo post universam definitionem gradu locabit. Grammaticae sunt quattuor partes,

Orthographia, Etimologia, Syntaxis, Prosodia. Tum partium definitionem in illo eodem vase separabit . . . ." — [Ramus,] *Dialectici comm. tres* (1546), pp. 83–84.

57. "Cicero breviter positam superioris disputationis summam sic partitur. 'Omnino divident nostri totam istam de diis immortalibus quaestionem in partes quatuor.' Primum docent esse deos, deinde quales sint. Tum mundum ab hic administrari, postremo consulere eos rebus humanis." — [Ramus,] *Dialectici comm. tres* (1546), p. 84: marginal reference to Cicero *De natura deorum* ii.

58. "METHODUS PRUDENTIAE. — . . . . ad methodum prudentiae transeundum nobis est, quae pro conditione personarum, rerum, temporum, locorum, consilium disponendi dabit; quamvis enim superior illa via et ratio dispositionis verissima commodissimaque sit, admonendum tamen illud est optimis locum non semper esse, nec eam dispositionis lucem perpetuo retineri posse, cum frequenter impediant morosus auditor, res quae docetur odiosa, tempus inimicum, locus alienus; commodum vero advocabitur in consilium difficultatis huius inventionis syllogismique prudentia, ut videamus quid expediat; nam praeter illam antecedentem sapientiae regulam, infinitae huiusce varietatis dispositio, communis omnium personarum, caussarum, locorum, temporum tradi nulla potest; nec enim personarum omnium natura una est, tot capita, tot sensus, non una rerum conditio, qua minimis saepe momentis commutantur . . . . Aliquando docendae personae quae doceri tamen nolunt. Itaque dissimulanda summa rei propositio, definitioque, distributio partium reticenda . . . . Multae sunt prudentiae huius laudes in uno Cicerone, secunda Agraria . . . . Tum scilicet extremum posuit [Terentiana Thais], quod si nullus affectus obstitisset, initio proponendum fuerat . . . . Sic Virgilius Aeneam a Sicilia excepit, in medio narrantem praeterita finxit, postrema variis perturbata casibus induxit . . . ." — [Ramus,] *Dialectici comm. tres* (1546), pp. 87–90.

59. "PERORATIO METHODI. — Quamobrem has dialecticae methodi vias diligenter animadvertere atque intueri res magnas et varias tractantem decebit, atque illam imprimis cum docere discendi cupidos res graves et honestas deliberabit. Quae tanti Platoni visa est, ut non hominum sed deorum inventam esse duceret, eumque solum, cui lux ista docenti affulsisset, vere splendideque philosophari iudicaret. Tum vero si fuerit artificiosi illius itineris obstructus aditus, aliam viam ut ingenii, prudentiaeque sibi faciet, omniaque naturae, consuetudinis, usus, vitae exemplorum auxilia undique comparabit, quoniam doctrinae praesidiis destituitur; et tamquam in Oceano tempestate iactetur, (quoniam rectum cursum tenere non potest), velificationem mutabit, et quibus ventis poterit, incolumem navem ad portum deducet." — [Ramus,] *Dialectici comm. tres* (1546), pp. 90–91.

60. For the revisions and other developments here discussed, see Ong, *Ramus and Talon Inventory*, including "The Ramist Controversies" there.

61. Ramus, *Dialectique* (1555), p. 119.

62. *Ibid.* For the broad meaning of *dispute*, cf. [Ramus,] *Dialectici comm. tres* (1546), p. 84, cited above, where Ramus designates by this term (*disputatio*) even Cicero's treatise *The Nature of the Gods*. Practically, the term means treatise, or even a discourse of any sort.

63. "Methodus est dispositio, qua de multis enunciatis homogeneis, suoque vel syllogismi iudicio notis, disponitur primo loco absoluta notatione primum, secundo secundum, tertio tertium, et ita deinceps: ideoque ab universalibus ad singularia perpetuo progreditur. Hac enim sola et unica via procedit ab antecedentibus omnino et absolute notioribus ad consequentia ignota declarandum eamque solam Methodum Aristoteles docuit." — Ramus, *Dialectica A. Talaei praelectionibus illustrata* (Basileae, 1569), pp. 465–466.

64. *Ibid.*, Lib. II, cap. xvii, pp. 542–543.

65. *Ibid.*, Lib. II, cap. xviii, pp. 563–564. Snatches of Virgil thrown into the text are here omitted.

66. Riolan, *Ad Dialecticam P. Rami una ex praelectionibus* (1568), fol. 5.

67. "Methodus est dianoia variorum axiomatum homogeneorum pro naturae suae claritate praepositorum, unde omnium inter se convenientia iudicatur, memoriaque comprehenditur. Atqui ut spectatur in axiomate veritas et falsitas, in syllogismo consequentia et inconsequentia, ita in methodo consideratur ut per se clarius praecedat, obscurius sequatur, omniumque ordo et confusio iudicatur. Sic disponetur ex homogeneis axiomatis primo loco absoluta notione primum, secundo secundum, tertio tertium, et ita deinceps; ideoque methodus ab universalibus ad singularia perpetuo progreditur. Hac enim sola et unica via proceditur ab antecedentibus omnino et absolute notioribus ad consequentia ignota declarandum, eamque solam methodum Aristoteles docuit." — Ramus, *Dialecticae libri duo* (Lutetiae, 1574 [text identical with the edition of 1572, Lutetiae]), Lib. II, cap. xvii, pp. 72–73.

68. "Axioma est dispositio argumenti cum argumento, qua esse aliquid aut non esse iudicatur. Latine enunciatum, enuntiatio, pronuntiatum, pronuntiatio, effatum dicitur." — Ramus, *Dial. lib. duo* (Lutetiae, 1574), Lib. II, cap. i, p. 51.

69. Beurhaus' commentary in Ramus, *Dial. lib. duo* [1572 text], ed. Beurhusius (Coloniae, 1587), p. 302.

70. See Benson Mates, *Stoic Logic* (Berkeley and Los Angeles, 1953), pp. 132–133.

71. See T. S. K. Scott-Craig, "The Craftsmanship and Theological Significance of Milton's Art of Logic," *Huntington Library Quarterly*, 17:15 (1953).

72. P. 120.

73. Ramus, *Dial. A. Talaei pr. ill.* (Basileae, 1569), Lib. II, cap. xvi–xix, pp. 465ff., 542ff., 563ff., 576ff. In the final revision of the *Dialectic*, this single method is retained. See Ramus, *Dial. lib. duo* (Lutetiae, 1574), Lib. II, cap. xvii–xx, pp. 72–79.

74. Ramus, *Dial. A. Talaei pr. ill.* (Basileae, 1569), Lib. II, cap. xix, p. 576.

75. *Ibid.*, pp. 577–578.

76. Ramus, *Dialectique* (1555), pp. 128–129: "executer l'embusche."

77. Ramus, *Dialectique* (1555), pp. 128–129.

78. Ramus, *Scholae rhetoricae* in *Sch. in lib. art.* (1569), col. 246.

79. Ramus, *Dial. A. Talaei pr. ill.* (Basileae, 1569), Lib. II, cap. xix, p. 582 ("Talon's" commentary): "Propria autem poeticae κρύψεως illud videatur, a medio incipere, tum per occasionem aliquam praeterita narrare, denique notabili aliquo casu concludere."

80. *Ibid.*, p. 579.

81. *Ibid.*, p. 578 ("Talon's" commentary).

82. "Et bref, tous les tropes et figures d'elocution, toutes les graces d'action, qui est la Rhetorique entiere, vraye et separée de la Dialectique, ne servent d'autre chose sinon pour conduire ce fascheux et retif auditeur, qui nous est proposé en ceste methode: et n'ont este pour autre fin observees que pour la contumace et preversité d'icelluy, comme Aristote vrayement enseigne au troiziesme de la Rhetorique. Ainsi doncques nous voyons comme ceste methode de prudence a este enseignée et practiquée par les philosophes, poetes, et orateurs." — Ramus, *Dialectique* (1555), p. 134; italics mine.

83. "Priora autem sunt et notiora dupliciter: non autem idem est prius natura et ad nos prius: neque notius natura et nobis notius. Dico vero ad nos quidem priora et notiora, quae ad sensum propius accedunt: absolute autem priora et notiora, quae longius a sensu remota sunt: remotissima vero sunt quae maxime sunt universalia: proxima vero quae sunt singularia: atque haec inter se opponuntur." — Aristotle *Post. Anal.* I.ii.sec. 10 (71a33 to 72a5), as quoted in Ramus, *Quod sit unica* (1557), fol. 1, and often elsewhere (see *Quod sit unica* in Ong, *Ramus and Talon Inventory*).

84. Cf. Turnèbe, *De methodo libellus* (1600), fols. 8–9, where Turnèbe says "some" [i.e., Ramus] assert that Cicero denies Aristotle's distinction between *notiora naturae* [*sic*] and *notiora nobis*, saying that there is only one *via* and *ratio* of teaching.

85. Ramus, *Quod sit unica* (1557), fol. 2.

86. *Ibid.*, fols. 2–3. Ramus, *Dial. A. Talaei pr. ill.* (Basileae, 1569), 509ff.
87. Ramus, *Quod sit unica* (1557), fol. 3.
88. *Ibid.*
89. "Eruditioribus autem factis contra, universalia sunt notiora" — *Ibid.*
90. *Ibid.*, fols. 3–4.
91. *Ibid.*, fol. 4.
92. *Ibid.*
93. "Ut absolute bona bonis, absolute sana sanis, sic absolute notiora nobis mente bene affectis notiora sunt. Hae similes Aristotelis collationes, sensum habent apertum. Idem notiora esse nobis et natura." — Ramus, *Dial. lib. duo A. Talaei pr. ill.* (Parisiis, 1566), p. 372.
94. Ramus, *Quod sit unica* (1557), fol. 4.
95. *Ibid.*, fols. 4–5.
96. *Ibid.*, fol. 7.
97. *Ibid.*, fol. 10. Ramus here also compares Galen's doctrine with that of Simplicius.
98. *Ibid.*, fols. 10–16.
99. *Ibid.*, fol. 17*v*. When Ramus says elsewhere, "The arts are found by analysis, just as they must be passed on and taught by genesis" — *Dialecticae libri duo A. Talaei praelectionibus illustrati* (Parisiis, 1560), p. 211 — he seems to be speaking of classroom analysis of texts and of composition (mostly written) respectively. See also in this present Chapter section 6 above.
100. Ramus, *Quod sit unica* (1557), fol. 18*r*.
101. Crombie, *Robert Grosseteste*, pp. 77–78; cf. R. I. Markus, "Method and Metaphysics," *Dominican Studies*, 2:356–384 (1949).
102. Ramus, *Quod sit unica* (1557), fol. 18*r*.
103. *Ibid.*, fol. 18*r-v*.
104. *Ibid.*, fol. 16.
105. "Ars enim inveniendi (ut praedictum est) et artes et reliquas omnino res omnes prima pars fuit logicae artis, talisque methodus prima artis libri fuit." — Ramus, *Dial. A. Talaei pr. ill.* (Basileae, 1569), Lib. II, cap. xvi, p. 532.
106. Ramus, *Quod sit unica* (1557), fols. 16–22; *Dial. A. Talaei pr. ill.* (Basileae, 1569), p. 534.
107. "Cantilena" — Schegk, *Hyperaspistes responsi ad quatuor epistolas Petri Rami* (1570), p. 11.
108. Francis Bacon, *De augmentis scientiarum*, Lib. IV, cap. ii, in *Works*, ed. J. Spedding, R. L. Ellis, and D. D. Heath (London, 1861–1874), I, 668.
109. Aristotle *Post. Anal.* I. iv (73b): "Τὸ κατὰ παντὸς καὶ τί τὸ καθ' αὐτὸ καὶ τί τὸ καθόλου." For an excellent technical discussion of the whole problem here, see Le Blond, *Logique et méthode*, pp. 73–106.
110. Rudolph Snel van Roijen (Snellius), *In P. Rami Arithmeticam* (1596), p. 34.
111. From Ramus, *Sch. dial.*, Lib. IX, cap. iv, in *Sch. in lib. art.* (1569), cols. 354–366; Ramus, preface to *Scholae physicae*, in *Sch. in lib. art.* (1569), after col. 616; also *passim* in Ramus' other works, especially those written after 1555; William Temple's notes and Ramus' text in Ramus, *Dial. lib. duo, scholiis G. Tempelli illustrati* (1591), pp. 57, 61, 62; Abraham Fraunce, *The Lawiers Logike* (1588); Guilielmus Ursinus (Ursin), *Commentarius in P. Rami Dialecticam* (Francofurti, 1615), pp. 458–461.
112. See above, Chap. xi, section 6.
113. Ramus, *Sch. dial.*, IX, iv, in *Sch. in lib. art.* (1569), cols. 354–366.
114. See Le Blond, *Logique et méthode*, pp. 76–78.
115. "Ars omnis constat ex homogeneis, ut antea iam dictum est . . . ; ut essent praecepta uno et eodem genere comprehensa, ut etiam e generalibus et antecedentibus rationes ad subalternas artes deduci possent, ut a logica in mathematicas omnes, ab arith-

metica in musicam et reliquas: et a geometria in omnes artes geometricis figuris innexas."
—Ramus, *Dial. A. Talaei pr. ill.* (Basileae, 1569), Lib. II, cap. xvi, p. 468 ("Talon's" commentary).

116. Ramus, *Quod sit unica* (1557), fol. 4, and Ramus' three laws of method as just explained.

117. See "The Ramist Disputes," in Ong, *Ramus and Talon Inventory.*

118. Piscator, *In P. Rami Dialecticam animadversiones* (1580), p. 14.

119. Temple, *Epistola de Dialectica P. Rami* (Francofurti, 1590), pp. 6–7; Arnaud d'Ossat, *Additio ad Expositionem de methodo,* in his *Expositio in disputationem de methodo* (Francofurti, 1589), p. 38.

120. Ramus, *Dial. A. Talaei pr. ill.* (Basileae, 1569), Lib. II, cap. xvii, p. 553 ("Talon's" commentary). Gouveia, no mathematician, had nevertheless balked at Ramus' attempt to manufacture lines out of points.

121. "Analysis est examinatio in propositis exemplis nostris vel alienis, quorum et inventio et compositio exploranda sit . . . . Analysis in logica est examen argumenti, enuntiati, syllogismi, methodi, id est logicae artis universae: ut Primo Analytico percipitur." — Ramus, *Sch. dial.*, Lib. II, cap. viii, in *Sch. in lib. art.* (1569), col. 54.

122. Ramus, *Sch. dial.*, Lib. VIII, cap. i, in *Sch. in lib. art.* (1569), cols. 191–193.

123. *Ibid.*

124. Ramus, *Dialectici comm. tres* (1546), p. 52.

125. "Genesis non est inspectio propositi exempli ut analysis, sed effectio novi operis; quae meditatio unam et eandem viam scribendi docendique sequitur. In scribendo vero prima facillimaque via est imitatio; in qua providendum diligenter erit quem imitemur . . . . Deinde vero nobiscum ipsi certabimus, et argumentum liberum sumemus de quotidianis et popularibus negotiis, et ad communem vitam dumtaxat attingentibus, tum caussas, effecta, ceteraque argumentorum (quae licebit) genera e fontibus inventionis hauriemus, postremo omnes dispositionis modos simili diligentia exercebimus, modo hac, modo illa specie concludendum . . . ." — [Ramus,] *Dialectici comm. tres* (1546), p. 110. Genesis is further treated, with analysis, in book III of the subsequent three-book editions of the *Institutiones dialecticae.* See also Ramus, *Ciceronianus, passim.*

126. Francisco Sanchez de las Brozas (Sanctius Brocensis), *De autoribus interpretandis sive de exercitatione* (Antwerpiae, 1581), p. 3.

127. Johann Heinrich Bisterfeld (Bisterfeldus), "Usus lexici," V–X, in *Bisterfeldus redivivus* (1661), Vol. II, Pars II, pp. 57–64.

128. Ramus, *Algebrae liber primus a Lazaro Schonero emendatus,* cap. i, in Ramus, *Arithmeticae libri decem, geometriae septem et viginti* (1599), p. 190. Cf. Ramus, *Dialecticae institutiones* (1543), fol. 3*v*; *Sch. dial.*, Lib. VIII, cap. i, in *Sch. in lib. art.* (1569), cols. 191–193. Cf. also Sir Isaac Newton's *Arithmetica universalis, sive De compositione et resolutione arithmetica* (1707).

129. Riolan, *Ad Dial. P. Rami una ex prael.* (1586), fol. 5*v.* Riolan's terms are ἀκριβολογία and μικρολογία, which are established Greek rhetorical terms, of course. See Aristotle *Rhet.* 1361b34, *Metaph.* 995a15. It might be suggested that the term "acribology" may well have influenced the formation of the schoolboy's term "crib," which the *New England Dictionary* derives, without great conviction, from crib — meaning a fodder rack.

130. Ramus, *Platonis Epistolae Latine factae et expositae* (Parisiis, 1549), p. 5.

131. Ramus, *M. T. Ciceronis Epistola nona ad P. Lentulum . . . praelectionibus illustrata,* in *In Cic. orat.* (1582), p. 394.

132. Fouquelin, *In Auli Persii Flacci Satyras commentarius . . .* (Parisiis, 1555), p. 145, and *passim.*

133. Riolan, *Ad dial. P. Rami una ex prael.* (1568), fol. 7*r*: "Est autem analysis non retextio aut partitio (male siquidem Strebaeus analyticos libros Dialecticas partitiones

vocat), sed κρίσις potius ut visum est Boetio, nec enim ex analytico dicit artifex suae artis materiam invenire, sed eandam inventam aestimare et ordinare, quare soleo analysim definire μέθοδον διδασκαλίας."

134. Ramus, "Analysis rhetoricae summa," M. T. Ciceronis pro C. Rabirio . . . oratio . . . praelectionibus illustrata, in In Cic. orat. (1582), p. 39.

135. Ramus, "Summary of Rhetorical and Logical Analysis of the Third Catilinarian," M. T. Ciceronis in L. Catilinam orationes . . . praelectionibus illustratae, in In Cic. orat. (1582), pp. 329–330.

136. See A. C. Crombie, "Scholastic Logic and Experimental Method," Archives internat. d'hist. des sciences, 1:280–285 (1947).

137. Waddington, Ramus, pp. 354–355, citing Ramus' Scholae mathematicae, Lib. II (1569), p. 47.

138. In rhetoric, a thesis or propositum was a general proposition, such as, "Human societies need a ruler." An hypothesis or causa was a limited proposition concerned with a particular case, such as, "The present King of the Two Sicilies is a bad ruler." See McKeon, "Rhetoric in the Middle Ages," Speculum, 17:4, 15ff. (1942); and, for a good example in scientific context, see in the Hippocratic writings the opening passage of the treatise On Ancient Medicine, in Great Books of the Western World, Vol. X, Hippocrates, Galen, p. 1. In this tradition, limitation is secured not by a supposition or conditional arrangement (if . . . then . . .) in the way in which we think of hypothetical proceedings today, but rather by specification of a generality. The two modes of achieving limitation are related, but are not quite the same. Moreover, the rhetorical concept of hypothesis was likely to color the other concept, giving an "if" proposition the appearance of a special case as against a categorical proposition, which was "general."

139. "Genesis autem deliberationis omnino nullum est logicum opus, sed ipsa μηχανικὴ καὶ πρᾶξις, id est administratio et effectio rei, quae non argumentis, sed manibus et pedibus caeterisque corporum instrumentis peragitur." — Ramus, Dial. A. Talaei pr. ill. (Basileae, 1569), Lib. II, cap. xvi, p. 520 ("Talon's" commentary).

140. Ramus, Dial. A. Talaei pr. ill. (Basileae, 1569), Lib. II, cap. xvi, p. 520 ("Talon's" commentary).

CHAPTER XII

RAMIST RHETORIC

1. Ramus, Dialecticae institutiones (1543), fols. 50–52.

2. Audomari Talaei Veromandui Institutiones oratoriae, ad celeberrimam et illustrissimam Lutetiae Parisiorum Academiam (Parisiis: Iacobus Bogardus, 1545).

3. Nancel, Vita (1599), p. 12.

4. Ibid., p. 15.

5. "Talaeus," Grand dictionnaire historique, ed. Louis Moréri, Goujet, and Drouet (1759).

6. Nancel, Vita (1599), p. 40.

7. See the introductory note with the editions of the Rhetorica listed in Ong, Ramus and Talon Inventory.

8. For the detailed relationships, consult Ong, Ramus and Talon Inventory.

9. Talon, Institutiones oratoriae (1545), p. 5. Cf. Quintilian Institutiones oratoriae ii. 1. 5: "Rhetorice, cui nomen vis eloquentiae dedit."

10. Talon, Inst. orat. (1545), pp. 6–7.

11. "Rhetorica est . . . artificiosa de qualibet re bene dicendi doctrina" — ibid., p. 8.

12. Talon, Rhetorica (1548), p. 1.

13. Quintilian Institutiones oratoriae v. 10. 54: "Rhetorice est bene dicendi scientia."

14. Talon, Rhetorica (1550), p. 63.

15. "Nec alia pronuntiationis est doctrina quam elocutionis" — *ibid.*

16. Dudley Fenner (adapting Talon), *Art of Rhetorick*, in *The Artes of Logike and Rethorike* (1584), fol. E1*v.*

17. Piscator's preface to his edition of Talon, *Rhetorica* (1590).

18. See the descriptions of the various editions in Ong, *Ramus and Talon Inventory.*

19. "Elocutio est exornatio orationis . . . . Elocutio est tropus aut figura. Tropus est elocutio qua verbum a nativa significatione in aliam immutatur." — Talon, *Rhetorica e P. Rami praelectionibus observata* (Lutetiae: A. Wechelus, 1574), p. 6. "Figura est elocutio, qua orationis habitus a recta et simplici consuetudine mutatur" — *ibid.*, p. 24.

20. Talon, *Inst. orat.* (1545), p. 73–83.

21. *Ibid.*, pp. 73–75.

22. *Ibid.*, pp. 82–83.

23. See H.–I. Marrou, *Hist. de l'éducation dans l'antiquité*, 2d ed. rev. (Paris, 1950), pp. 272–276. As Marrou makes evident, the objectives of Socrates, Plato, Aristotle, and other "wisdom lovers" or philosophers were exceptional — a fact to which we have been more or less blinded because they have subsequently proved the most valuable. The typical product of Greek education was the sophist, a rhetorician, and the typical Greek regarded the "philosopher" as a sectarian and crank. Socrates' execution was consistent with a large pattern of attitudes.

24. In one place, Ramus himself says that these five parts of rhetoric, as given by Quintilian, are wrong because they are against the third law of method, that general matters be taught first in a general way (*generale generaliter doceatur*), and that they divide "things," not the art itself. — Ramus, *Sch. rhet.* in *Sch. in lib. art.* (1569), col. 344.

25. Ramus, *Pro philosophica Parisiensis Academiae disciplina oratio*, in *Scholae in liberales artes* (1569), col. 1022.

26. See R. J. Schoeck, "Rhetoric and Law in Sixteenth-Century England," *Studies in Philology*, 50:120 (1953), and *passim.*

27. Ramus, *Pro phil. disc.* in *Sch. in lib. art.* (1569), cols. 1010–1020.

28. See Richard McKeon, "Rhetoric in the Middle Ages," *Speculum*, 17:1–32 (1942).

29. See Louis John Paetow, *The Arts Course in Medieval Universities* (Urbana, Illinois, 1910); Hastings Rashdall, *The Universities of Europe*, new ed. (Oxford, 1936); etc.

30. "Satis est ut adolescentulorum cura sit," quoted in Emile Durkheim, *L'évolution pédagogique en France* (Paris, 1938), [I], *Des origines à la Renaissance*, 69.

31. T. W. Baldwin, *William Shakspere's Small Latine and Lesse Greeke* (Urbana, Illinois, 1944), I, 76, 94, etc.; cf. Sir Thomas Wilson as cited by Baldwin, *ibid.*, I, 81.

32. *Ibid.*, I, 237.

33. *The Pilgrimage to Parnassus*, Acts I, II, and III in *The Pilgrimage to Parnassus with the Two Parts of the Return from Parnassus*, ed. W. D. Macray (Oxford, 1886), pp. 5, 9, 11.

34. Baldwin, *William Shakspere's Small Latine*, I, 82 and *passim.*

35. *Ibid.*, I, 289.

36. *Ibid.*, I, 76, quoting F. Watson, *The Beginnings of the Teaching of Modern Subjects in England*, p. xxii.

37. Talon, *Inst. orat.* (1545), pp. 3–4: "teneros adolescentium animos."

38. Melanchthon, *Elementa rhetorica*, Lib. I, in *Opera* (Halle, 1834–1860), XIII, col. 420. Cf. Melanchthon, *Erotemata dialectices*, I (opening words), in *Opera*, XIII, col. 513.

39. "Ut sapientia rerum omnium cognitionem, ita Rhetorica exornationem praestaret atque elocutionem." — Talon, *Inst. orat.* (1545), p. 8.

40. Rosemond Tuve, *Elizabethan and Metaphysical Imagery* (Chicago, 1947), pp. 61ff.

41. John Trevisa, *Bart. de P. R.*, V, xxviii (1495), 137, and Cooper, *Thesaurus amphistre* (ca. 1565–1573), both as cited in the *New English Dictionary.*

42. *Inst. orat.* (1545), pp. 8–9, 21–22, 28. The two parts of the art of rhetoric turn on the *laus* of single words and of conjoined words — p. 8. "Singula per se et separatim quam laudem quodve lumen adferant . . . ." — pp. 8–9. "Quamobrem honos verborum singulorum quatuor maxime existit . . . ." — p. 21. "Verba continuata . . . in quorum laudibus et ornamentis quatuor has res animadvertere oportebit . . . ." — pp. 21–22. The passages which follow these explain that these four terms are all referring to tropes and figures. For instances of Cicero's and Quintilian's similar use of these terms, see any large Latin dictionary. Cf. Cicero, *Orator* xxxixff., where the *lumina singulorum verborum* and the *lumina collocatorum verborum*, which together are grammatical schemes or "figures of language," are opposed to the *sententiarum ornamenta* (figures of sentence, which become by the eighteenth century figures of "sentiment"). It is difficult to draw any consistent or telling theoretical distinction between Cicero's *lumina verborum* (in which he hesitatingly includes metaphor) and his *sententiarum ornamenta*, although the latter tend to be rather large-scale operations, such as rhetorical questions, repetitions, the use of dialect and impersonation, and the like. Miss Tuve has remarked on Renaissance attempts to straighten things out and the resulting further entanglements in her *Elizabethan and Metaphysical Imagery*, pp. 105–106, and Sister Miriam Joseph, in her *Shakespeare's Use of the Arts of Language* (New York, 1947), pp. 31ff., juxtaposes some of the manifold classifications and discusses others in detail. Miss Tuve here makes the statement that insofar as the classifications "reflect the purposes of various figures, I have not observed damaging misunderstandings" as between one Elizabethan author and another. This statement I should regard as quite tenable, charitable, but in that it perhaps implies a deep grasp by Renaissance rhetoricians (often teen-agers) of the inherent nature of one or another figure, certainly optimistic.

43. Ramus, *Oratio initio suae professionis habita* (1551), pp. 16–17, where Ramus ties his program up with the earlier statutes of the University of Paris which called for philosophy to be taught to students "without quill or pen, in continuous and flowing discourse" (*remotis pennis et calamis . . . perpetua voce raptim*) — such statutes being, of course, attempts to do away with the vicious practice of dictation, whereby young masters simply read to their pupils notes which, in turn, had been read to them.

44. "Regiis etiam stipendiis ornatos" — Ramus, *Oratio init. suae prof.* (1551), p. 5; cf. *ibid.*, "liberas, . . . alis, . . . ornas."

45. Ramus, *Dialectique* (1555), Preface. Earlier, he had explained ornamentation as like the bosses or little raised decorations (*thori*) on a crown, although here he is thinking of examples or analogies in dialectic as "ornamenting" definitions and divisions — *Dial. inst.* (1543), fol. 29.

46. "Rhetorica est ars ornate dicendi" — Johann Bilsten (Bilstenius), *Syntagma Philippo-Rameum* (1588), p. 261; Johann Heinrich Alsted (Alstedius), *Compendium rhetoricum* (an adaptation of Talon) in his *Compendium philosophicum* (1626), p. 1600.

47. Ramus, *Dialecticae partitiones* (1543), fol. C2.

48. Ramus, *Scholae rhetoricae*, in *Sch. in lib. art.* (1569), fols. 255–256, again in cols. 237–238, 292, etc.

49. Miller notes the fact that the Puritans favored tropes over figures, but does not assign the reason — *The New England Mind: The Seventeenth Century* (1939), p. 356.

50. Ramus, *Dialectica A. Talaei praelectionibus illustrata* (Basileae, 1569), Lib. II, cap. xix, pp. 577–578.

51. Tuve, *Elizabethan and Metaphysical Imagery*, p. 339.

52. Albertus Magnus, *In Lib. l Post. anal.*, Tract. I, cap. ii, in *Opera omnia* (Paris, 1890–1899), II, 7; Thomas Aquinas, *In Post. anal.* I, i; etc.

53. Ramus, *Sch. rhet.*, in *Sch. in lib. art.* (1569), col. 246.

54. Talon, *Rhetorica*, 4th ed. (1550), pp. 55–63.

55. Talon, *Rhetorica e P. Rami praelectionibus observata, postrema editio* (Lutetiae: A. Wechelus, 1574), pp. 25–36.

56. Ramus, *Dialectique* (1555), pp. 129–135; etc.

57. Ramus, *Sch. rhet.*, in *Sch. in lib. art.* (1569), col. 251.

58. "Quid est poetica? Est facultas bene scribendi versus." — Johann Thomas Freigius (Freige), *Paedagogus* (1582), p. 131. "Poetica est ars bene versificandi" — Bilsten, *Syntagma Philippo-Ramaeum* (1596), p. 271.

59. Jean Riolan the elder, "Disputatio altera," in *Disputationes duae* (1569), fol. 9*v*.

60. Ramus, *Oratio init. suae prof.* (1551), p. 31. Cf.: "Poetica, inquam, sunt ista miracula [quae fingis tibi proponendo hunc oratorem perfectum — qui fieri non potest] plena quidem puerilis admirationis, prudentiae vero ac veritatis inania" — Ramus, *Sch. rhet.*, in *Sch. in lib. art.* (1569), col. 246.

61. See James R. Naiden, "Newton Demands the Latin Muse," *Symposium*, 6:111–120 (1952).

62. The quotations immediately following here are from Perry Miller, *The New England Mind: The Seventeenth Century* (New York, 1939), Chapter XI, esp. pp. 331ff. and 349ff.

63. Cf. Ong, "Peter Ramus and the Naming of Methodism," *Journal of the History of Ideas*, 14:235–248 (1953).

64. ". . . verba pene verbis, propriis tamen, et rem pure planeque significantibus redderem" — Talon, *Praelectiones in Porphyrium* (1547), Preface, in *Opera Socraticae methodicaeque philosophiae studiosis pernecessaria* (1584), pp. 476–477.

65. I. A. Richards, "The Places and the Figures," *Kenyon Review*, 11:17–30 (1949), where he discusses Baldwin's *William Shakspere's Small Latine and Lesse Greeke*, Sister Miriam Joseph's *Shakespeare's Use of the Arts of Language*, and Donald Lemen Clark's *John Milton at St. Paul's School* (New York, 1948).

66. Rosemond Tuve, *Elizabethan and Metaphysical Imagery*, Chapter XII, "Ramist Logic: Certain General Conceptions Affecting Imagery," pp. 331–353, and *passim*.

67. Nancel, *Vita*, p. 62.

68. *Ibid.*, p. 15.

69. See Kenneth B. Murdock, *Literature and Theology in Colonial New England* (Cambridge, Mass., 1949).

70. Wilbur Samuel Howell, *Logic and Rhetoric in England, 1500–1700* (Princeton, New Jersey, 1956), pp. 361, 350–360.

71. Howell, *Logic and Rhetoric*, pp. 350–361.

72. Walter J. Ong, "Psyche and the Geometers: Aspects of Associationist Critical Theory," *Modern Philology*, 49:16–27 (1951).

73. Howell, *Logic and Rhetoric*, p. 389.

CHAPTER XIII

THE DIFFUSION OF RAMISM

1. Paul Dibon, "L'influence de Ramus aux universités néerlandaises du 17ᵉ siècle," *Proceedings of the XIth International Congress of Philosophy, Brussels, August 20–26, 1953*, XIV (Amsterdam, 1953), 307–311; see also the same author's *La philosophie néerlandaise au siècle d'or*, Tome I, *L'enseignement philosophique dans les universités à l'époque précartésienne, 1575–1650* (Paris, New York, etc., 1954); Wilbur Samuel Howell, *Logic and Rhetoric in England, 1500–1700* (Princeton, New Jersey, 1956), pp. 282ff.; Ray Nadeau, "Talaeus versus Farnaby on Style," *Speech Monographs*, 21:59–63 (1954).

2. Waddington, *Ramus* (Paris, 1855), pp. 386–397. For some of Waddington's in-

adequacies see M. Guggenheim, "Beiträge zur Biographie des Petrus Ramus," *Zeitschrift für Philosophie und philosophische Kritik* (Leipzig), 121:140–153 (1903).

3. See Kenneth D. McRae, "Ramist Tendencies in the Thought of Bodin," *Journal of the History of Ideas*, 16:306–323 (1955).

4. Howell, *Logic and Rhetoric in England, 1500–1700*, pp. 354–363, 378–382.

5. See the article "Encyclopaedia" in the *Encyclopaedia Britannica*, 14th ed. (1929).

6. See Georg Voigt, "Über den Ramismus an der Universität Leipzig," *Berichte über die Verhandlungen der königlichen sächsischen Gesellschaft der Wissenschaften, Philologisch-historische Classe*, 40:31–61 (Leipzig, 1888).

7. See Walter J. Ong, "System, Space, and Intellect in Renaissance Symbolism," *Bibliothèque d'Humanisme et Renaissance*, 18:222–239 (1956).

8. Since they contain adaptations of Ramus' *Dialectic* and of the Ramist *Rhetoric*, the various editions of Alsted's encyclopedias can be found listed in Ong, *Ramus and Talon Inventory*, under "Collected Arts."

9. See the list of Ramists, semi-Ramists, etc., in Ong, *Ramus and Talon Inventory*.

10. See the works listed under "Collected Arts" in Ong, *Ramus and Talon Inventory*. For Keckermann, see his *Opera omnia* (1614).

11. See Pierre Mesnard, *L'essor de la philosophie politique au XVIᵉ siècle* (Paris, 1936); Carl Joachim Friedrich, Introduction in his edition of Johannes Althusius, *Politica methodice digesta of Johannes Althusius* (Cambridge, 1932).

12. Howell, *Logic and Rhetoric in England, 1500–1700*, pp. 354–363.

13. James Maitland Anderson (ed.), *Early Records of the University of St. Andrews* (Edinburgh, 1926), pp. 164, 165, 273.

14. Nancel, *Petri Rami vita* (1599), p. 51: "Stuarto Scoti regis filio utrique." Ramus' guests were apparently two of the three best known illegitimate children of James V: James Stewart, Earl of Murray (later the regent Murray), Lord John Stewart (1531–1563), later prior of Goldingham, and Lord Robert Stewart, Earl of Orkney.

15. See Ricardo G. Villoslada, *La Universidad de Paris* (Rome, 1938), pp. 127ff.

16. This tally is based on the works in Ong, *Ramus and Talon Inventory*, and represents Wéchel editions between 1555, when André Wéchel first took up the publishing of Ramist works by bringing out Ramus' *Dialectique* and its companion piece, Fouquelin's Ramist *Rhetorique*, and 1603, after which year the Wéchel firm seems to have passed out of the Wéchel family's hands. Apart from the *Rhetoric*, here included among the 172 works of Ramus for reasons given in Chapter XII above, the Wéchel firm brought out only one of Talon's works, *Praelectiones in Ciceronem, Porphyrii Isagogen, et Aristotelis primum librum Ethicum* (1583), a fact perhaps connected with Wechel's Protestantism and Talon's ordination as a priest toward the end of his life, but more likely with the fact that, apart from the *Rhetoric*, the works published under Talon's name did not sell. Even Ramus, as published by the Wéchels, runs little to classical authors, mostly to "arts," and no art other than the *Rhetoric* had ever appeared under Talon's name.

17. See "The Ramist Controversies," in Ong, *Ramus and Talon Inventory*.

18. British Museum MS Add. 15914, fol. 28r; my translation from the Latin of the original.

19. Letter of Théophile de Banos to Philip Sidney dated March 19, 1576, British Museum MS Add. 15914, fol. 27r; my translation from the Latin of the original.

20. Howell, *Logic and Rhetoric in England, 1500–1700*, pp. 354–363.

21. "Newfangled, yougheaded, harebrayne boyes will needs be Maysters that never were Schollers" — this is "the importunate exclamation" assigned to "a raging and fiery-faced Aristotelian" in Abraham Fraunce, *Lawiers Logike* (London, 1588), Preface.

22. See Howell, *Logic and Rhetoric in England, 1500–1700*, p. 191.

23. Johannes Piscator, *Responsio*, in *Guilielmi Tempelli . . . Epistola de Dialectica*

P. Rami . . . una cum Ioan. Piscatoris ad illam epist[olam] responsione (Francofurti, 1582), p. 19.

24. Howell, *Logic and Rhetoric in England, 1500–1700*, pp. 192–193.

25. See Walter J. Ong, "Peter Ramus and the Naming of Methodism," *Journal of the History of Ideas*, 14:235–248 (1953).

26. See Walter J. Ong, "System, Space and Intellect in Renaissance Symbolism," *Bibliothèque d'Humanisme et Renaissance*, 18:222–239 (1956).

27. See William T. Costello, *The Scholastic Curriculum at Early Seventeenth-Century Cambridge* (Cambridge, Mass., 1958).

28. Since it includes an adaptation of Ramus' *Dialectic*, Ames' *Philosophemata* is listed under this work in Ong, *Ramus and Talon Inventory*.

29. See Dibon, "L'influence de Ramus . . . ," *Proc. XIth Int. Cong. of Philos.*, 14:307–311 (1953), and *La philosophie néerlandaise*, Tome I.

30. See Lajos Racz, "L'inspiration française dans le protestantisme hongrois," *Revue des études hongroises* (1925), pp. 261–263.

31. See in Ong, *Ramus and Talon Inventory*, the 1602 Prague edition of Ramus' *Grammatica graeca*.

32. See in Ong, *Ramus and Talon Inventory*, the entries: *Inst. dial.* (Basileae, 1554), *Arist. anim.* (Lugduni: Antonius Vincentius, 1545), and *Rhet.* (Lugduni, 1557).

33. Allan P. Farrell, *The Jesuit Code of Liberal Education* (Milwaukee, 1938), p. 269.

34. See Ong, *Ramus and Talon Inventory*, introductory remarks under *Dialectic*.

35. *Dialecticae institutiones* (1543), fol. 37.

36. See A. C. Moorhouse, *The Triumph of the Alphabet: A History of Writing* (New York: Henry Schuman, 1953).

37. See Pierce Butler, *The Origin of Printing in Europe* (Chicago, 1940), and the bibliographical notes therein, pp. 144–150.

38. See above, Chapter XI, section 7.

39. For examples of this evolutionary process, see the early editions of Ramus' *Training in Dialectic, Dialectic*, etc., in Ong, *Ramus and Talon Inventory*.

40. Erasmus, *Opera omnia* (1703–1706), Vol. IV, Table of Contents.

41. Pierre Gassendi, *Examen philosophiae Roberti Fluddi, Medici*, Pars III, in *Opera omnia* (1727), III, 228–229; "sesquipedalus . . . titulus . . . ut distribuatur apposite, ut omnia in ipso cohaereant."

BIBLIOGRAPHY

BIBLIOGRAPHY

This annotated bibliography is intended to supplement the present author's *Ramus and Talon Inventory*, which appears concurrently with the present book, and to be used jointly with that work, to furnish the apparatus for a complete bibliography of Ramism. The *Ramus and Talon Inventory* lists, besides all known editions and adaptations of Ramus' and Talon's own works (some 800 in all, or some 1100 if individual works appearing in collections are counted separately), the publications by all parties figuring in the major Ramist disputes, together with nearly 400 Ramist, anti-Ramist, and semi-Ramist writers (as well as all known editions of Rudolph Agricola's *Dialectical Invention* or *De inventione dialectica*).

The present bibliography includes, first, titles and location of copies for all early editions (before 1800) of all works actually cited in the text of the present book, whether concerned directly with Ramism or not, which are not to be found in the widely accessible published catalogues of printed books in the British Museum and the Bibliothèque Nationale or in one or the other *Short-Title Catalogue* of books printed in the British Isles or in English abroad (to 1640, and 1641 to 1700).

The hundreds of other early works concerned with Ramism or showing Ramist influence but not mentioned by name in the text of the present book or in the *Ramus and Talon Inventory* — for example, works such as Johann Althusius' Ramist methodization of Roman law, *Iuris Romani libri duo, ad leges methodi Rameae conformati et tabula illustrati* (Basileae, 1586) or Jean Bodin's Ramist-oriented *Methodus ad facilem historiarum cognitionem* (1566, 1572, etc.) — can be found by checking the list of Ramist, anti-Ramist, and semi-Ramist or syncretist writers in the *Ramus and Talon Inventory* against the authors in the catalogues mentioned above and other major library catalogues.

Secondly, this bibliography lists all known later works treating Ramus or Ramism significantly or at some length (not, however, completely derivative treatments such as those in most encyclopedias, histories of philosophy, and histories of literature). Third, it lists the few manuscripts relevant to Ramism referred to in the text of the present book.

Finally, this bibliography includes a few other incidental or rare works for various special reasons — for example, some of Johann Sturm's works, displayed here in an important sequence which would otherwise remain unnoticed, since it had to be reconstructed by collating the holdings of several libraries.

Copies of editions anterior to 1800 are located here if they do not appear in any of the four catalogues just mentioned above. Ordinarily, only one edition of any work (the earliest known) is given a listing here.

An asterisk (*) indicates titles of works not treating directly of Ramus or Ramism.

Arthus, Gothardus. *Ramo-Philippus, hoc est, In Petri Rami et Philippi Melanchthonis . . . de dialectica libros commentarius . . . .* Francofurti: Vincentius Steinmeyerus, 1604. 8vo. [16]+653+[2] pp. Copy in the Universitätsbibliothek, Basle.

Austin, Warren B. "Gabriel Harvey's 'Lost Ode' on Ramus," *Modern Language Notes,* LXI (1946), 242–247. This article refers to the Cambridge University copy of the edition of Harvey's *Ode* as "apparently unique." There are, however, at least two other copies, one in Jesus College, Cambridge, and the other in Trinity College, Dublin.

Bacon, Francis, Baron Verulam, Viscount St. Albans. *The Works of Francis Bacon,* edited by James Spedding, Robert Leslie Ellis, and Douglas Denon Heath. 7 vols. London: Longmans and Co., etc., 1861–1874. Bacon comments *passim* on Ramus.

Baldwin, Charles Sears, and Clark, Donald Lemen. *Renaissance Literary Theory and Practice.* New York: Columbia University Press, 1939.

Baldwin, T. W. *William Shakspere's Small Latine and Lesse Greeke.* 2 vols. Urbana, Ill.: University of Illinois Press, 1944.

Banosius (de Banos), Theophilus (Théophile). *Petri Rami vita.* This work, dated cal. ian. 1576, first appeared in Ramus, *Commentariorum de religione Christiana libri quatuor* (Francofurti: A. Wechelus, 1576), and was reprinted in the subsequent editions of it; all were published by the same publishing firm at the same place, in 1577, 1583, and 1594. See all these editions in Ong, *Ramus and Talon Inventory.*

—— Unpublished letters to Sir Philip Sidney, four in Latin and four in French, dated from January 30, 1575, to May 8, 1576. British Museum Add. MSS 15914, ff. 21, 27, 28; 17520, f. 8; 18675, ff. 4, 6, 7, 8. These letters contain material on Ramus and on his *Commentariorum de religione Christiana libri quatuor*, which Banosius edited.

Barnard, Howard C. *The French Tradition in Education: Ramus to Mme Necker de Saussure.* Cambridge: Cambridge University Press, 1922.

Barroux, Robert. See *Dictionnaire des lettres françaises* . . . .

—— "Pierre de la Ramée et son influence philosophique: essai sur l'histoire de l'idée de la méthode à l'époque de la Renaissance," *Ecole nationale des Chartes, Positions des thèses,* 1922 (Paris: Librarie Alphonse Picard, 1922), pp. 13–20.

—— "Rapport [sur le Ramisme en Ecosse]," *Ecole pratique des Hautes Etudes, Section des sciences religieuses et philosophiques: Annuaire, 1921–22* (Paris, 1921), pp. 67–71.

Bayle, Pierre. *Dictionnaire historique et critique.* 5ᵉ édition revue . . . par M. des Maizeaux. 8 vols. (including 4 vols. of Supplément). Amsterdam: P. Brunel, etc., 1740–56.

Bement, Newton S. "Petrus Ramus and the Beginnings of Formal French Grammar," *Romanic Review,* XIX (1928), 309–323.

Bernus, Augustin. "Pierre Ramus à Bâle," *Société de l'histoire du Protestantisme français, Bulletin historique et littéraire,* XXXIX (1890), 508–523.

Bertrand, Joseph (of the Académie des Sciences, geometrician). See Waddington, Charles.

—— "Jacques Charpentier est-il l'assassin de Ramus?" *Revue des deux mondes,* XLIV (1881), 286–322. Shows the insufficiency in the grounds advanced by Waddington in his *Ramus* (1855) as evidence that Charpentier was the one responsible for Ramus' murder, and charges Waddington with bad faith in presenting his evidence.

—— [Letter of fifty or sixty words, undated, in reply to Waddington's of March 2, 1881.] *Revue des deux mondes,* XLIV (1881), 720. "La lettre de M. Waddington ne contient aucun argument qui ne soit développé déjà dans le livre très savant dont j'ai discuté les assertions."

Beurhaus (Beurhusius), Friedrich. *De Petri Rami Dialecticae capitibus disputationes scholasticae* . . . . Coloniae: Maternus Cholinus, 1588. Copy in the Bodleian Library.

——— M[arci] T[ullii] Ciceronis Dialecticae libri duo, ex ipsius Topicis aliisque libris collecti, ex Aristotele vero Boetioque uspiam completi, et propriis ipsius exemplis illustrati, additis . . . notis, studio et opera Frederici Beurheusii . . . . Coloniae: Gosvinus Cholinus, 1593. 8vo. Copy in the Staatsbibliothek, Munich.

Beuzard, P. "La Famille de la Ramée," *Société de l'histoire du Protestantisme français, Bulletin historique et littéraire,* LXXXVIII (1939), 88.

Blount, Sir Thomas Pope. *Censura celebriorum authorum* . . . . Londini: impensis Richardi Chiswell, 1690.

Brunot, Ferdinand, and Bruneau, Charles. *Histoire de la langue française des origines à 1900.* 12 vols. Tome II. *Le seizième siècle.* 2ᵉ édition revue et corrigée. Paris: Armand Colin, 1922.

Buisson, Ferdinand. See *Répértoire* . . . .

Buxton, John. *Sir Philip Sidney and the English Renaissance*. London: Macmillan and Co., Ltd.; New York: St. Martin's Press, 1954.

Camerarius. See Languet, Hubert.

Carrière, Victor. "Pierre de la Ramée et la principalité du Collège de Presles," *Revue d'histoire de l'Eglise de France*, XXVI (1940), 238–242. Ramus was, at least in fact, principal of the Collège de Presles in 1543, or perhaps 1544 (Waddington, *Ramus*, p. 62, had said 1545). Discusses Ramus' troubles in retaining his place as principal. Based chiefly on the *Archives nationales*.

Case, John. *Summa veterum interpretum in universam dialecticam Aristotelis, quam vere falsove Ramus in Aristotelem invehatur, ostendens*. Oxonii: T. Vautrollerius, 1584. Other editions 1592, 1598, Oxford; 1593, 1606, Frankfort.

Chagnard, Benjamin. *Ramus et ses opinions religieuses*. Doctorate thesis. Strasbourg: J.-H.-E. Heitz, 1869. 36 pp.

—— *Rhetoric and Poetry in the Renaissance*. New York: Columbia University Press, 1922.

Clément, Louis. *De Adriani Turnebi regii professoris praefationibus et poematis thesim Facultati litterarum in Universitate Parisiensi proponebat L. Clément*. Paris, 1899.

Cocus, Ioannes (of Wittenberg). *Speculum philosophicum, in quo universae philosophiae et artium imagines ac simulacra ad vivum relucent* . . . . Lichae: e typographia Kezeliana, 1604. Copy in Saint Louis University Library.

Coring, Gustav. *Das Gymnasium zu Dortmund und die Pädagogik des Petrus Ramus*. Inaugural dissertation, Cologne. Emsdetten (Westfalen): H. und J. Lechte, 1933.

Cossart (Cossartius), Père Gabriel, S.J. *Orationes duae: I. Adversus novitatem doctrinae; II. Extemporalis defensio adversus satiram Francisci Dumonstier*. 2 parts in 1 vol. Paris: S. et G. Cramoisy, 1651. 4to. The first of these orations treats briefly of Ramus; the second at length.

—— *Orationes et carmina*. Edited by Carolus Ruaeus. Paris: S. Mabre-Cramoisy, 1675. 12mo. Contains Cossart's *Orationes duae* . . . (1651).

—— *Orationes et carmina*. Nova editio auctior et emendatior. Parisiis: Fratres Barbou, 1723. 8vo. Contains Cossart's *Orationes duae* . . . (1651).

Costello, William T., S.J. *The Scholastic Curriculum at Early Seventeenth-Century Cambridge*. Cambridge, Mass.: Harvard University Press, 1958.

Cragius, Andreas. See Krag, Anders.

Craig, Hardin. *The Enchanted Glass: The Elizabethan Mind in Literature*. New York: Oxford University Press, 1936.

Curio, C. J. "C. J. Curio Petro Ramo suo S. D." [a letter to Ramus from Basle, prid. cal. Dec. 1555, here edited for the first time by M. Grunwald], *Archiv für Geschichte der Philosophie* (Berlin), IX, neue Folge II (1896), 335. This letter introduces to Ramus a Pole, Andreas Sienicius, who wished to study with Ramus.

[Cuts (Oise), France.] See "Inauguration . . . ."

Cyprianus, Iohannes. *De philosophiae Rameae fatis*. This work is listed in Struve, *Bibliothecae philosophicae Struvianae emendatae* . . . (1740), I, 117, but I know of no copy.

Dassonville, Michel-M. "La 'Dialecticque' de Pierre de la Ramée: Première ouvrage philosophique originale en langue francaise," *Revue de l'Université de Laval*, VII (1953), 608–616.

—— "La genèse et les principes de la dialectique de Pierre de la Ramée," *Revue de l'Université d'Ottawa*, XXIII (1953), 322–359.

Delcourt, M. "Ramus et l'Alsace," *Alsace française*, 27 déc. 1931.

Desmaze, Charles. "Notice biographique sur Pierre Ramus," *Bulletin de la Société académique de Laon*, II (1853), 190.

—— *P. Ramus, professeur au Collège de France, sa vie, ses écrits, sa mort (1515–1572)*.

Paris: J. Cherbuliez, 1864. Lists documents having to do with Ramus still unpublished. Bibliographies.

—————— *L'Université de Paris, 1200–1875: La Nation de Picardie, les Collèges de Laon et de Presles, la loi sur l'enseignement supérieur.* Paris: Charpentier et Cie, 1876.

Dibon, Paul. "L'influence de Ramus aux universités néerlandaises du 17ᵉ siècle," *Proceedings of the XIth International Congress of Philosophy* (Brussels, August 20–26, 1953), XIV (Amsterdam: North-Holland Publishing Co., 1953), 307–311.

—————— *La philosophie néerlandaise au siècle d'or.* Tome I. *L'enseignement philosophique dans les universités à l'époque précartésienne, 1575–1650.* Paris, New York, etc.: Elsevier Publishing Co., 1954.

Dictionnaire des lettres françaises: Le seizième siècle. Edited by Mgr George Grente, Albert Pauphilet, Mgr Louis Pichard, and Robert Barroux. Paris: Arthème Fayard, 1951. The articles on Ramus and related matters are done by Robert Barroux.

Dodd, Mary C. "The Rhetorics in Molesworth's Edition of Hobbes," *Modern Philology,* L (1952), 36–42.

Dorat, Jean. See Maurat-Ballange, A.

Du Chesne (à Quercu), Léger (Leodegarius, Ludovicus). *De internecione Gasparis Collignii et Petri Rami sylva; ad Carolum IX regem Christianissimum.* Paris: G. Buon, 1572. 4to. 4 ll. Latin verse hostile to Ramus and Colligny, but with nothing at all on Ramus' murderers themselves.

Duhamel, Pierre Albert. "The Logic and Rhetoric of Peter Ramus," *Modern Philology,* XLVI (1949), 163–171.

—————— "Milton's Alleged Ramism," *PMLA,* LXVII (1953), 1035–1053.

Du Monstier, François. ["Oraisons pour Ramus accusé de Calvinisme."] Archives Nationales, Paris, MS M 827. No. 3. Attributed in this MS itself to [Godefroi] Herman[t], 1617–90. See Ong, "Père Cossart . . . ," below, where the facts that these orations are by Du Monstier and the MS an autograph of his are established.

Du Monstier (Du Moustier), François. Fl. 1646–1661. See also Cossart, Gabriel.

"En l'honneur de Pierre Ramus," *Société de l'histoire du Protestantisme français, Bulletin historique et littéraire,* LXXXVIII (1939), 367–368.

Erasmus, Desiderius. Brevissima maximeque compendiaria conficiendarum epistolarum formula. See Juan Luis Vives, *De conscr. ep.* . . . (Basileae, 1536; and Coloniae, 1537). This is one of the earlier redactions of Erasmus' *De ratione conscribendi epistolas,* the later revision of which appears in his *Opera omnia* (1703–06), where the earlier redactions are not printed.

————— De ratione studii . . . . Argentorati: ex aedibus Schürerianis mense iulio, 1512. 4to. Copy in the Harvard University Library.

—————— *Ratio seu compendium verae theologiae.* Basileae: Ioannes Frobenius, 1519. 4to. Copy in the British Museum. The first edition under any title or in any form in [F. van der Haeghen,] *Bibliotheca Erasmiana* (1893), p. 167.

—————— *Ratio seu methodus compendio perveniendi ad veram theologiam.* Ex accurata auctoris recognitione. Basileae: J. Frobenius, 1520. 219 pp. Copy in the British Museum. The earliest edition by this title in [F. van der Haeghen,] *Bibliotheca Erasmiana* (1893), is that dated Moguntiae: Io. Schoeffer, 1521; 8vo. Often reprinted under this title.

—————— *Ratio seu methodus compendio perveniendi ad veram theologiam, ab ipso authore castigata et locupletata; Paracelsis, id est, Exhortatio ad studium evangelicae philosophiae per eundem.* [s.l.,] 1523. 214 pp. Copy in the Harvard University Library.

Erythraeus, Valentinus. See Sturm, Johann, Διαγράμματα and Σχηματισμοί.

Feugère, Léon Jacques. *Les femmes poëtes au 16e siècle: étude suivie de Mlle de Gournay; Honoré d'Urfé; le Maréchal de Montluc; Guillaume Budé; Pierre Ramus.* Nouvelle édition, Paris, 1860. The little essay on Ramus is based entirely on Waddington.

Forbes, Robert. *Theses philosophicae pro veterana veritate et antiqua philosophandi methodo tuenda adversus petulantis huius saeculi subdolam novitatem et heterodoxiam Cartesianam.* Aberdoniae: Ioannes Forbes, Universitatis typographus, 1680.

Fouquelin (Foquelin, Foclin, Foquelinus), Antoine. *In Auli Persii Flacci Satyras commentarius ad Petrum Ramum* . . . . Parisiis: Andreas Wechelus, 1555. 4to.

Freige (Freig, Frey, Freigius), Johann Thomas. *Petri Rami vita.* This work first appears in Ramus, *Praelectiones in Ciceronis orationes octo consulares una cum ipsius* [*P. Rami*] *Vita per Ioannem Thomam Freigium collecta* . . . (Basileae: Petrus Perna, 1575), pp. 1–60. It is reprinted in the 1580 edition of the same; also in Ramus and Talon, *Collectaneae praefationes, epistolae, orationes; quibus adiunctae sunt P. Rami Vita* . . . (Marpurgi, 1599); also, in John Milton's own abbreviated redaction, in his adaptation of Ramus' *Dialectica,* the *Artis logicae plenior institutio* . . . (1672, 1673, and 1935; in this last printing, with parallel English translation by Allan H. Gilbert). See these works in Ong, *Ramus and Talon Inventory.* The printing of Freige's *Vita* listed in the British Museum catalogue as [Basle, 1585?] is no more than the 1575 printing excised from the *Prael. in Cic. orat. octo cons.*

French, J. Milton. "Milton, Ramus, and Edward Phillips," *Modern Philology,* XLVII (1949), 82–87.

Friedrich, Carl Joachim. Introduction in his edition of Johannes Althusius, *Politica methodice digesta of Johannes Althusius.* Cambridge: Harvard University Press, 1932. This Introduction discusses Althusius' reliance on Ramist dialectic.

Frischlin (Frischlinus), Nicodemus. *Dialogus logicus* . . . *contra P. Rami* . . . *Sophisticam pro Aristotele, addita eiusdem refutatione, scripta a C. Neubecker.* Francofurti: I. Wechelus impensis N. Bassaei, 1590. 8vo.

———— Disputatio logica de partibus dialectices: Brunsvvigae inter Nicodemum Frischlinum et Carolum Bumannum instituta, iam vero publici iuris facta, et praefatione ornata, a M[agistro] Ioachimo Nisaeo, Gymnasii Berolinensis collega. Marburgi: Iohan[nes] Francus, 1605. 8vo. Copy in the Stadtbibliothek, Mainz.

Frissell, Harry Lee. *Milton's Art of Logic and Ramist Logic in the Major Poems.* Microfilmed Ph.D. dissertation, Department of English, Vanderbilt University. "Doctoral Dissertation Series," Publication No. 4394. Ann Arbor, Mich.: University Microfilms, 1952.

Gabriel, Astrick L. *Student Life in Ave Maria College, Mediaeval Paris: History and Chartulary of the College.* "Publications in Mediaeval Studies, The University of Notre Dame," XIV. Notre Dame, Indiana, 1955.

Gassendi, Pierre. *Opera Omnia.* 6 vols. Florentiae: typis Regiae Celsitudinis apud Ioannem Caietanum et Sanctem Franchi, 1727. Quite a lot on Ramus *passim.*

Genebrard, Gilbert. *Oraison funèbre sur le trespas de reverend pere en Dieu Messire Pierre Danes, Evesque de la Vaurs, premier lecteur du Roy és lettres Grecques, prononcee à sainct Germain des prez, le samedy 27 iour d'Avril 1577* . . . . Paris: Martin le Ieune, 1577. 8vo in 4's. 71 pp.

Gilbert, Allan H. "Some Critical Opinions on Milton," *Studies in Philology,* XXXIII (1936), 523–533.

Gilbert, Neal Ward. *Concepts of Method in the Renaissance and Their Ancient and Medieval Antecedents.* Microfilmed Ph.D. dissertation, Faculty of Philosophy, Columbia University. "Doctoral Dissertation Series," Publication No. 16,809. Ann Arbor, Mich.: University Microfilms, 1956.

Graves, Frank Pierrepont. *Peter Ramus and the Educational Reformation of the Sixteenth Century.* New York: The Macmillan Co., 1912.

Gr[eaves?], P[aul?] or Gr[eenwood?], P. *Grammatica anglicana, praecipue quatenus a Latina differt, ad unicam P. Rami methodum concinnata* . . . . Authore P. Gr. Cantabrigiae: Iohannes Legatt, 1594. Includes a Chaucer vocabulary with a separate title page, *Vocabula Chauceriana quaedam selectiora* . . . , which explains the meaning of Chaucerian words in Latin equivalents. Re-edited by Otto Funke. Vienna and Leipzig: W. Braumüller, 1938.

Greenwood, P. See Greaves, Paul.

Grunwald, M. See Curio, C. J.

Guggenheim, M. "Beiträge zur Biographie des Petrus Ramus," *Zeitschrift für Philosophie und philosophische Kritik* (Leipzig), CXXI (1903), 140–153. A very careful study of Ramus' dealings with Sturm, Beza, Gwalter, Bullinger, etc. It notes that the current impression that Sturm was a follower of Ramus is wrong, and that Sturm was rather a forerunner of Ramus in opposing Aristotelianism, but that his slavish Ciceronianism and total neglect of the vernacular was anti-Ramist.

—— "Petrus Ramus als Reformator des Wissenschaft," Sonderabdruck, *Humanistisches Gymnasium*, XVIII (1904).

[Hart, John, D. D.] *A Godly Sermon of Peter's Repentance, after he had denyed his Lord and Master Jesus Christ, as it is in his Repentance, he wept bitterly for his sins.* 2d edition, corrected and enlarged . . . . London: for Eliz. Andrews, 1663. sig.: A8, B4. Copy in the Yale University Library; not in the *Dictionary of National Biography* nor in Wing. On fol. A1*v* is a portrait of Ramus, with the heading, "Petrus Ramus aet. LVII." There is no reference at all to Ramus in the text of this noncontroversial sermon. Perhaps the name "Peter" on a cut already in his possession gave the chapbook printer the idea of including the portrait for its decorative value. But perhaps there is more to the story than this.

Harvey (Harveius), Gabriel. Autograph marginalia in Christ Church, Oxford, copy of *M. T. Cic.* . . . *Topica A. Talaei prael. exp.* (1550). See this work in Ong, *Ramus and Talon Inventory.*

—— Autograph notes in the Harvard University Library copy of: William Fulke, OYRANOMAXIA, *hoc est, Astrologorum ludus.* London, 1572.

—— *Gabriel Harvey's Ciceronianus.* Edited by Harold S. Wilson, with translation by Clarence A. Forbes. Lincoln: University of Nebraska, [1945]. vii + 149 pp. Introduction discusses Harvey's indebtedness to Ramus' *Ciceronianus.*

—— *Gabriel Harvey's Marginalia.* Collected and edited by G. C. Moore Smith. Stratford-upon-Avon: Shakespeare Head Press, 1913. Filled with references to Ramus and the whole Ramist entourage.

—— *Ode natalitia, vel opus eius feriae quae S[ancti] Stephani protomartyris nomine celebrata est anno 1574: in memoriam P[etri] Rami, optimi, et clarissimi viri.* Londini: Thomas Vautrollerius, 1575. Copies in the Cambridge University Library; Jesus College, Cambridge; Trinity College, Dublin.

—— *Rhetor.* Londinii: H. Binneman, 1577.

Hasenmüller (Hasenmullerus), Sophonias. *De faciliore docendi et vel unius anni spatio perdiscendi linguam Latinam ratione didactica specialis.* Noribergae: Simon Halbmayer [ca. 1615]. 8vo. Copy in the Universitätsbibliothek, Basle.

—— *Didactica: hoc est, Ratio minus molesta, minus laboriosa, in scholis docendi et discendi* . . . ; *seorsim adiecta est Schola poetica et ethica* . . . . Noribergae: Simon Halbmayerus, 1615. 8vo. Copy in the Universitätsbibliothek, Basle.

Hermant, Godefroi. See Du Monstier, François.

Hermogenes, the rhetorician. Τέχνη ῥητορικὴ τελειότατη. Ars rhetorica absolutissima. Parisiis: C. Wechelus, 1530. 4to. Copy in the Harvard University Library.

—— Περὶ ἰδέων τόμοι δύο. De formis orationum tomi duo. Parisiis: Christianus Wechelus, 1531. 8vo. Copy in the Harvard University Library.

—— Περὶ εὑρέσεων τόμοι τέσσαρες. De inventione tomi quatuor. Parisiis: C. Wechel, 1530. 4to. Copy in the Harvard University Library.

—— Περὶ μεθόδου δεινότητος. De methodo gravitatis sive virtutis commode dicendi.

Parisiis: Christianus Wechelus, 1531. 8vo. Copy in the Harvard University Library.
*——— *Opera.* Edited by H. Rabe. Leipzig, 1913.
*——— See also Sturm, Johann.
Howard, Leon. "The Invention of Milton's 'Great Argument': A Study in the Logic of 'God's Ways to Men,'" *Huntington Library Quarterly,* IX (1945), 149–173. Treats Milton's debt to Ramist logic.
Howell, Wilbur Samuel. *Logic and Rhetoric in England, 1500–1700.* Princeton, New Jersey: Princeton University Press, 1956. An invaluable study, long needed, this work focuses chiefly on the rhetorical tradition and on logic or dialectic as connected with rhetoric. It shows Ramism as the central phenomenon signalizing a shift in rhetorical and logical orientation in these two hundred years.
——— "Ramus and English Rhetoric: 1547–1681," *Quarterly Journal of Speech,* XXXVII (1951), 299–310.
"Inauguration du médaillon érigé à Cuts en mémoire de Pierre Ramus le 9 juillet 1939," *Société archéologique et historique de Noyon: Comptes rendus et mémoires,* XXIX (Chauny: Imprimerie-Librairie A. Baticle, 1941), pp. LXVII–LXXXVII, and pp. 1–6 in the section following entitled "Mémoires."
In Petri Rami insolentissimum decanatum, gravissimi cuiusdam oratoris philippica prima e quatuordecim. [By one of the Charpentier faction, perhaps Jean Picard.] Parisiis: Thomas Brumennius, 1567. 4to.
Irwin, Franklin. "Ramistic Logic in Milton's Prose Works." Unpublished Ph.D. dissertation, Princeton University, 1941.
Jöcher, Christian Gottlieb. *Allgemeines Gelehrten-Lexicon.* 4 vols. Leipzig: Johann Friedrich Gleditschens, 1750–51. Copies in the Harvard University Library and the Bibliothèque Nationale. With its *Fortsetzung,* the most helpful of all biographical dictionaries, old or new, for the Ramist milieu.
[Jöcher, Christian Gottlieb]; Adelung, Johann Christoph; and Rotermund, Heinrich Wilhelm. *Fortsetzung und Ergänzungen zu Christian Gottlieb Jöchers allgemeinen Gelehrten-Lexico.* 7 vols. Vols. I–VI, Leipzig and Bremen, 1784–1819. Vol. VII, Leipzig, 1897. Copy in the Harvard University Library. See Jöcher, Christian Gottlieb, *Allgemeinen Gelehrten-Lexicon.*
Johnson, Francis R. *Astronomical Thought in Renaissance England.* Baltimore: Johns Hopkins Press, 1937.
Jourdain, Charles. *Histoire de l'Université de Paris, au XVIIe et au XVIIIe siècle.* Paris: Firmin-Didot, 1888.
Kahlius, Lud[ovicus] Mart[inus]. See Struve, Burchard Gotthelff.
Kocher, Paul H. "Contemporary Pamphlet Backgrounds for Marlowe's *The Massacre at Paris,*" *Modern Language Quarterly,* VIII (1947), 151–173, 309–318.
——— "François Hotman and Marlowe's *The Massacre at Paris,*" *PMLA,* LVI (1941), 349–368.
Koller, Kathrine. "Abraham Fraunce and Edmund Spenser," *ELH,* VII (1940), 108–120.
Kot, S. "Polish Protestants and the Huguenots," *Proceedings of the Huguenot Society of London,* XVII, No. 4 (London, 1945).
Krag (Kragius, Cragius), Anders. *Q[uinti] Horatii Flacci Ars poetica ad P. Rami dialecticam et rhetoricam resoluta.* Basileae: Sebastianus Henricpetri [1583]. 4to.
La Genière de la Ramée, Docteur de. "Ramus (La Ramée): Notice sur cette famille communiquée par le Dr de la Genière de la Ramée, 1939." Bibliothèque du Protestantisme français, MS in 4to. Varia. 2543. I. Typescript, illustrated in water colors, giving armorial bearings and history of the La Ramée family, beginning from the thirteenth century at Liége, and including Peter Ramus and "Louise de la Ramée" (pen name of Mana Louise Ramé, also known as "Ouida," 1839–1908).
Languet (Languetus), Hubert. *Ad Ioachim Camerarium patrem et Ioachim Camerarium*

filium, medicum, scriptae epistolae . . . , *nunc primum editae a Ludovico* . . . *Camerario.* Groningae: I. Nicolaus, 1646. 12mo.

La Ramée, Docteur de La Genière de. See La Genière de la Ramée.

La Ramée, Louise de. See Ramé, Mana Louise.

La Ramée, Pierre de. See Ramus, Petrus.

Łasicki, John. See Moreau-Reibel, Jean.

Launoy (Launoius), Jean de. *De varia Aristotelis in Academia Parisiensi fortuna, extraneis hinc inde adornata praesidiis liber.* 3a editio, auctior et correctior. Lutetiae Parisiorum: Edmundus Martinus, 1662. 8vo.

———— *Opera omnia.* 10 vols. Coloniae Allobrogum: Faber et Barrillot, socii, et Marc-Michel Bousquet et socii, 1731.

———— *Regii Navarrae gymnasii Parisiensis historia.* 2 vols. Parisiis: vidua E. Martini, 1677.

Lebesgue, Henri. *Les professeurs de mathématiques du Collège de France: Humbert et Jordan, Roberval et Ramus.* Leçon d'ouverture du Cours de mathématiques pures du Collège de France. Paris: Editions de la Revue politique et littéraire et de la Revue scientifique [1922]. 8vo. 48 pp.

Lefranc, Abel–Jules–M. *Histoire du Collège de France depuis ses origines jusqu'à la fin du Premier Empire.* Paris: Hachette, 1893. Lefranc's account of Ramus is completely derivative from Waddington, *Ramus.*

———— "Ramus," *Société de l'histoire du Protestantisme français, Bulletin historique et littéraire,* LXXXVIII (1939), 63–65.

Lenz, Christian Friedrich. *Disputatio historico-literaria, qua historiam Petri Rami* . . . *anno MDCCXV, die VI febr., pro loco inter magistros Lipsienses obtinendo* . . . *examine eruditorum placido submittit Christianus Fridericus Lenz* . . . *respondente Christiano Gottlieb Roegnero.* Lipsiae: Joh. Andr. Zchau [1715]. 4to.

———— *Historiam Petri Rami* . . . *disputationibus duabus edissuerunt publice praeses M[agister] Christ[ianus] Fridericus Lenz et respondens Johann Daniel Weisiger* . . . *prid. id. april. et XVII kal. mai MDCCXIII.* Vitembergae: Christianus Gerdesius [1713]. 4to. A rather eulogistic treatment of Ramus' life and works which notes that Ramus was midway between Aristotle and Raymond Lully, but that his philosophy has now fallen into a certain oblivion. The scholia or *epimetra* are very interesting: e.g., "Cum copula EST neque sit pars subiecti neque pars praedicati, neque singularis totius enunciationis pars proprie dicta, ideo virtus ipsi nulla concedenda, qua possit singularis quid significare: sed modo, qua praedicati habitudinem ad subiectum copulando demonstret."

Lobstein, P[aul]. *Petrus Ramus als Theologe: Ein Beitrag zur Geschichte der protestantischen Theologie.* Strassburg: C. F. Schmidt's Universitäts-Buchhandlung [Friedr. Bull], 1878. 86+[2] pp. An excellent summary study of Ramus' *Commentariorum de doctrina Christiana libri quator.*

Marlowe, Christopher. *The Massacre at Paris,* edited by H. S. Bennett. Vol. III of *The Works and Life of Christopher Marlowe.* Edited by R. H. Case. London: Methuen and Co., 1931. Includes a treatment of Ramus' murder.

Marolles, Michel de. *Paris, ou Déscription de cette ville* (first edition, 1677). Edited by l'Abbé Valentin Dufour. Paris: A. Quintin, 1879. Verse on Ramus, pp. 50–51.

Martin (Martinus, Martin of Dunkeld), James. *Logica peripatetica per dichotomias in gratiam Ramistarum resoluta.* Editio 4a. Wittebergae, 1614. Copy in the Universitäts-bibliothek, Basle. Draud, *Bibliotheca classica* (1625), p. 1408, refers to a 5th ed., Wittebergae, Zacharias Schurer, 1622.

Martini (Martinus, Martinus of Antwerp), Cornelius. See Nothold, Anton.

———— *Commentariorum logicorum adversus Ramistas libri quinque.* Helmaestadii, 1623. 8vo. Copy in the Bodleian Library.

Maurat-Ballange, A. "Ramus et Dorat," *Extrait du Bulletin de la Société archéologique du Limousin*, LXIII (Limoges, 1913), pp. 5–27 (in *extrait*, pp. 3–25). The attacks on Ramus by Dorat, a fierce *ligueur* and quite as famous a man as Ramus himself, were not pleasant, as Waddington makes out, but savage. With regard to the Bertrand-Waddington dispute concerning Ramus' death, Maurat-Ballange believes that Waddington has failed to prove his case that Charpentier had Ramus killed, but that Bertrand has also failed to prove all his charges against Waddington himself (suppression of evidence, etc.). Perhaps Charpentier somehow contributed "morally" to Ramus' death by his general hostility to him.

McLuhan, Herbert Marshall. "Tradition and the Academic Talent," [an article review of Rosemond Tuve, *Elizabethan and Metaphysical Imagery*], *Hudson Review*, I, 270–273.

McRae, Kenneth D. "Ramist Tendencies in the Thought of Bodin," *Journal of the History of Ideas*, XVI (1955), 306–323.

Mesnard, Pierre. *L'essor de la philosophie politique au XVIᵉ siècle*. Paris: Boivin et Cie, 1936. Treats Ramism in connection with Johann Althusen (Althusius).

Miller, Perry. *The New England Mind: From Colony to Province*. Cambridge, Mass.: Harvard University Prass, 1953. (Always referred to by its complete title. A continuation of *The New England Mind: The Seventeenth Century*.)

——— *The New England Mind: The Seventeenth Century*. New York: Macmillan Co., 1939. Re-issued at Cambridge, Mass., by Harvard University Press, 1954. (Referred to as *The New England Mind*.)

Miriam Joseph, Sister, C.S.C. *Shakespeare's Use of the Arts of Language*. New York: Columbia University Press, 1949.

Monin, Louis-Henri. *Theses philosophicae de H. Corn[elio] Agrippa et P. Ramo, Cartesii prenuntiis*. Doctoral thesis. Paris: F. Locquin, 1833. 8vo. 21+8 pp.

Moreau–Reibel, Jean. "Sto lat podrózy róznowierców polskich do Francji od polowy XVIᵉ wieku [One Hundred Years of Travel by Polish Heretics in France, Beginning with the Mid-Sixteenth Century]," *Reformacja w Polsce*, IX–X, 1–27. Discusses John Łasicki and his friendship with Ramus.

Morgan, Alexander. *Scottish University Studies*. Oxford: Oxford University Press, 1933. Treats Andrew Melville's Ramist reforms of Scottish universities, pp. 65–73, 136, etc.

Morison, Samuel Eliot. *The Founding of Harvard College*. Cambridge, Mass.: Harvard University Press, 1935.

——— *Harvard College in the Seventeenth Century*. 2 vols. Cambridge, Mass.: Harvard University Press, 1936.

Mullinger, James B. *The University of Cambridge*. 3 vols. Cambridge: The University Press, 1873–1911. Fairly extensive treatment of Ramism at Cambridge.

Nadeau, Ray. "Talaeus versus Farnaby on Style," *Speech Monographs*, XXI (1954), 59–63.

Nancel (Nancelius), Nicolas de. *Petri Rami Veromandui, eloquentiae et philosophiae apud Parisios professoris regii, vita, a Nic[olao] Nancelio Trachyeno Noviodunensi Rami discipula et populari descripta*. Parisiis: Claudius Morellus, 1599. 8vo. With this foregoing title page and its own separation pagination, in: Nancel, *Declamationum liber, eas complectens orationes quas vel ipse iuvenis habuit ad populum vel per discipulos recitavit . . . ; addita est P. Rami, summi oratoris, vita, ab eodem Nancelio eius discipulo conscripta . . .* . Parisiis: Claudius Morellus, 1600.

Nelson, Norman E. *Peter Ramus and the Confusion of Logic, Rhetoric, and Poetry*. University of Michigan Contributions in Modern Philology, No. 2. Ann Arbor: University of Michigan Press, April, 1947. Warns against making too much of the inner consistency of Ramus' thought.

Nelson, William. "The Teaching of English in Tudor Grammar Schools," *Studies in*

Philology, XLIX (1952), 119–143. This competent article makes as strong a case as can well be made for the existence of a desire on the part of grammar-school masters to teach the English language in school. But the common ineffectiveness of such velleities remains all too evident in terms of the real academic machinery, adjusted to a world where learned and professional works as well as textbooks were uniformly in Latin. Fraunce's *Arcadian Rhetorike* is one of the documents here cited. What such a once-issued and, so far as the two extant copies show, relatively unused vernacular rhetoric amounts to among the mass of well-thumbed Latin rhetorics in the Ramist tradition can be seen by examining the entries and notes in Ong, *Ramus and Talon Inventory*. One thinks of the statements which could be culled from some teachers today favoring the teaching of Latin to most high-school students, and of how little such recommendations represent actuality or real trends.

Neubecker, Conrad. See Frischlin, Nicodemus.

Niceron, Père Jean-Pierre. *Mémoires pour servir à l'histoire des hommes illustres dans la république des lettres, avec un catalogue raisonné de leurs ouvrages.* 42 vols. Paris: Brison, 1729–41. 8vo. "Ramus," XIII (1730), 259–304; "Ramus," addenda, XX (1732), 64.

Nothold (Notholdus), Anton. *Diatribe philosophica qua doctrina de definitione et divisione dialecticae, de notionibus primis et secundis, de argumentis inventionis et praedicabilibus, de analysi logica Rameorum, de metaphysica et praedicamentis ad Philippi et Rami documenta revocatur ac iudicatur, et simul fundamenta eorum quae M[agistrum] Cornelius Martinus secunda disputatione sua his nuper opposuit discutiuntur . . . edita per M[agistrum] Antonium Notholdum.* Lemgoviae: Magnus Holstenius, 1598. 8vo. Copy in the Stadtbibliothek, Mainz.

Ong, Walter J., S.J. "Fouquelin's French Rhetoric and the Ramist Vernacular Tradition," *Studies in Philology*, LI (1954), 127–142.

———— "Hobbes and Talon's Ramist Rhetoric in English," *Transactions of the Cambridge [England] Bibliographical Society*, I, Part III (1951), 260–269.

———— "Johannes Piscator: One Man or a Ramist Dichotomy?" *Harvard Library Bulletin*, VIII (1954), 151–162.

———— "Père Cossart, Du Monstier, and Ramus' Protestantism in the Light of a New Manuscript," *Archivum Historicum Societatis Iesu* (Rome), XXIV (1955), 140–164.

———— "Peter Ramus and the Naming of Methodism," *Journal of the History of Ideas*, XIV (1953), 235–248.

———— *Ramus and Talon Inventory.* Published conjointly with the present work.

———— "Ramus and the Transit to the Modern Mind," *Modern Schoolman*, XXXII (1955), 301–311. English version of "Ramus et le monde anglo-saxon d'aujourd'hui."

———— "Ramus et le monde anglo-saxon d'aujourd'hui," *Revue de littérature comparée*, XXVIII (1954), 57–66.

———— "Ramus: Rhetoric and the Pre-Newtonian Mind," *English Institute Essays 1952*, pp. 138–170. Edited by Alan S. Downer. New York: Columbia University Press, 1954.

———— "Space and Intellect in Renaissance Symbolism," *Explorations: Studies in Culture and Communication* (University of Toronto, Canada), [No.] 4 (1954), 95–100. A brief of "System, Space, and Intellect . . . ."

———— "System, Space, and Intellect in Renaissance Symbolism," *Bibliothèque d'Humanisme et Renaissance*, XVIII (1956), 222–239.

———— "Voice as Summons for Belief: Literature, Faith, and the Divided Self," *Thought*, XXXIII (1958), 43–61.

Ouida. See Ramé, Mana Louise.

Owen, John. *The Skeptics of the French Renaissance.* New York: Macmillan and Co., 1893.

Pasquier, Etienne. *Les recherches de la France . . . revuës . . . .* Paris: G. de Luyne, 1660 [first edition, 1596].

Péna, Jean (editor). *Euclidis Optica et Catoptrica, nunquam antehac Graece edita, eadem Latine reddita per Ioannem Penam . . . ; his praeposita est eiusdem Ioannis Penae De usu opticis praefatio . . . .* Parisiis: Andreas Wechelus, 1557. 4to. Ramus is mentioned in his pupil Péna's preface.

Perrin, Porter Gale. "The Teaching of Rhetoric in the American Colleges before 1750." Unpublished Ph.D. dissertation, University of Chicago, 1936.

────── *Text and Reference Books on Rhetoric before 1750.* Extract from a University of Chicago dissertation. [Chicago:] University of Chicago Libraries, 1940.

Pfaffrad (Pfaffradius), Caspar. *De studiis Rameis et optime institutionis legibus commentatio: qua Ramea institutio, longe alia quam quae a multis deformata pingitur, atque adeo non improbanda, sed maxime excolenda ostenditur.* Francofurti [ad Moenum]: Ioannes Saurius impensis Petri Kopfii, 1597. 8vo. Copy in Trinity College Library, Dublin.

Pontanus (Spanmüller), Iacobus, S.J. *Tyrocinium poeticum.* Ingolstadii: David Sartorius, 1594. 8vo. Contains a Latin epitaph on Ramus.

Pour l'Université de Paris, contre les professeurs du Roy. Imprimé par le mandement de M. le Recteur. [Paris?: 1600 or later, see p. 9.] 8vo. 21 pp.

Prantl, Carl (von). *Geschichte der Logik in Abendlande.* 4 vols. Leipzig: S. Hirzel, 1855–70.

────── "Über Petrus Ramus: Ein Vortrag," *Sitzungberichte der philosophisch-philologischen und historischen Classe der königlichen bayerischen Akademie der Wissenschaften zu München,* Band II, Heft II (1878), pp. 157–169). Ramus' fame as a reformer of logic has, from the point of view of the science as a science, no real basis. Once a loud and ineffectual critic of Aristotle, he became one convinced that he and he alone understood Aristotle correctly.

Quercu, Leodegarius (Ludovicus) à. See Du Chesne, Léger.

Racz, Lajos. "L'inspiration française dans le protestantisme hongrois," *Revue des études hongroises et finno-ougriennes,* III (1925), 11–20, 255–268. Treats Ramus and Ramists (Alsted, Bisterfeld, Piscator) briefly, pp. 261–263.

Radouant, René. "L'union de l'éloquence et de la philosophie au temps de Ramus," *Revue d'histoire littéraire de la France,* XXXI (1924), 161–162.

Ramé, Mana Louise. See La Genière de la Ramée, Docteur de.

[Ramus (La Ramée), Petrus (Pierre de). History of the chair of mathematics founded by Ramus.] Bibliothèque Nationale, MS nouv. acq. fr. 5853.

Répertoire des ouvrages pédagogiques au XVIᵉ siècle: bibliothèque de Paris et de Départements. [Edited by Ferdinand Buisson.] Paris: Imprimerie Nationale, 1886. Inaccurate, but invaluable. Locates copies.

Richardson, Alexander. *The Logician's Schoolmaster, or a Comment upon Ramus' Logicke.* London: [M. Flesher] for J. Ballamie, 1629. 4to. Contains no text of Ramus.

────── *The Logician's Schoolmaster, or, A Comment upon Ramus' Logick . . . , whereunto are added . . . Prelections on Ramus His Grammar, Talaeus His Rhetorick, also His Notes on Physicks, Ethicks, Astronomy, Medicine, and Opticks.* London: Gertrude Dawson to be sold by Sam Thomson, 1657.

Richer (Richerus), Edmond. *Obstetrix animorum, hoc est, Brevis et expedita ratio docendi, studenti, conversandi.* Parisiis: A. Drovart, 1600. 8vo.

Rögner (Roegnerus), Christian Gottlieb. See Lenz, Christian Friedrich.

Rommel, Christoph. *Geschichte von Hessen.* 10 vols. Cassel and Marburg, 1820–52. Contains short biographical notices on various Ramists or anti-Ramists.

Ryner, Han. *Dans le mortier.* Paris: Albert Messein, 1932. 8vo. Pp. 113–125. A wild eulogy of Ramus preparing for death "en se reprochant ses rares fautes," all details of which are circumstantially imagined.

Saisset, Emile-Edmond. *Précurseurs et disciples de Descartes.* 2ᵉ édition. Paris: Didier et Cie, 1862.

Sandford, William Phillips. *English Theories of Public Address, 1530–1828.* Columbus, Ohio: H. L. Hedrick, 1931.

Sandys, John Edwin. *A History of Classical Scholarship.* 3 vols. Cambridge: The University Press, 1903–08.

*Schegk (Schegkius, Schecius; original name, Jacob Degen), Jacob. *De demonstratione libri XV; novum opus, Galeni librorum eiusdem argumenti iacturam resarciens* . . . . Basileae: Ioannes Oporinus et Episcopii fratres, 1564. fol. Copy in the Bodleian Library. The title page explains that this is a commentary on the two books of Aristotle's *Posterior Analytics.*

Scheurlius, Heinrich Julius. *De Petri Rami libris, Francisci Regis Galliae decretum, deque iisdem iudicium a iudicibus quos tum Rex tum partes elegerant anno 1544, denuo post centum annos editum, ex bibliotheca H. J. S.* Helmstadii, 1644. 4to. 1 l. only. I have never seen a copy of this broadside, which is mentioned in Niceron, *Mémoires,* XIII (1730), 304.

——— *De Petro Ramo iudicia aliquot clarissimorum virorum.* [Helmstadii?:] 1620. 4to. 1 l. only. I have never seen a copy of this broadside, which is also mentioned in Niceron, *Mémoires,* XIII (1730), 304.

Schmitz, Wilhelm. "Über P. Ramus als Schulmann," Anhang, F. *Fabricius Marcoduranus, 1527–1573: Ein Beitrag zur Geschichte des Humanismus* (Köln: M. Dumont-Schauberg, 1871), pp. 58–68. A laudatory account of Ramus' procedure, giving full approval to his "logical analysis" and remarking that many of Ramus' points of view are today self-evident matters.

Schreider, S. (translator). ראמום. In his חולדות אנשי חשם. Wilna, 1873. 12mo. Copy in the New York Public Library.

Schweizer, H. "Die Entwickelung des Moralsystems in der reformirten Kirche," Iᵉʳ Artikel, 10, "Die Philosophie des Petrus Ramus: Untersuchung ihres Einflusses auf die reformirten Ethik," *Theologische Studien und Kritiken,* I (1850), 69–78.

[Serres, Jean de.] *The Fourth Parte of Commentaries of the Civill Warres in Fraunce, and of the Louue Countrie of Flaunders.* Translated out of Latine into English by Thomas Tymme . . . . London: Henry Binneman for Humfrey Toy, 1576. 4to. Copy in the Harvard University Library.

——— *The Three Partes of Commentaries . . . of the Civill Warres of Fraunce . . . .* Translated out of Latine into English by Thomas Timme . . . . 3 parts in 1 vol. London: F. Coldocke, 1574. Sometimes erroneously attributed to Ramus himself. See in Ong, *Ramus and Talon Inventory,* under Spurious Works.

Slüter (Sluterus), Severin. *Syncresis controversiarum ad disputationem, quae a Rameis et Peripateticis motae sunt, de philosophiae definitione ac distributione . . . in Schola Stadensi ad disputandum proposita a M[agistro] Severino Slutero eiusdem Scholae rectore, respondente Hermanno Hallervordio Westphalo.* Darmbstadii: Balt[hassar] Hofmannus sumptibus Zachariae Palthenii, 1608. 8vo.

Smith, A. J. "An Examination of Some Claims for Ramism," *Review of English Studies,* VII (1956), 349–359.

Smith, G. C. Moore. "A Note on Milton's Art of Logic," *Review of English Studies,* XIII (1937), 335–340.

Société de l'histoire du Protestantisme français, Bulletin historique et littéraire. Paris: Bibliothèque du Protestantisme français, 1931. The "Table alphabétique, analytique, et chronologique," p. 450, lists all references to Ramus throughout the *Bull. hist. et litt.*

Spannmüller, Jacob. See Pontanus, Iacobus.

Struve, Burchard Gotthelff. *Bibliothecae philosophicae Struvianae emendatae . . . atque auctae a Lud[ovico] Mart[ino] Kahlio.* 2 vols. Gottingae: Vandenhoeck et Cuno, 1740.

*Sturm (Sturmius), Johann. *De literarum ludis recte aperiendis.* Argentorati: V. Rihelius, 1538. Copy in the Harvard University Library.

*———— *De universa ratione elocutionis rhetoricae libri IIII.* Nunc primum in lucem editi opera et studio C. Thretii Poloni. [Strasbourg, 1576.] 8vo. Copy in the British Museum.

*———— Διαγράμματα, *hoc est, Tabulae tertii et quarti libri Partitionum dialecticarum Ioannis Sturmii . . . autore Valentino Erythraeo . . . .* Argentinae: C. Mylius, 1555. fol. Copies in the Bibliothèque Nationale, Paris. An edition with Sturm's text strung out on bracketed outlines, mostly in dichotomies, which fill this huge tome uninterruptedly from start to finish. See also the two Σχηματισμοί volumes of Sturm below.

*———— *Hermogenis Tarsensis rhetoris acutissimi De dicendi generibus sive formis orationum libri ii Latinitate donati, et scholis explicati atque illustrati, a Ioan[ne] Sturmio.* [Argentorati: I. Rihelius], 1571. 8vo. Copy in the Harvard University Library.

*———— *In Partitiones oratorias Ciceronis dialogi duo.* [Argentorati], 1539. 8vo. Copy in the British Museum.

*———— *In Partitiones oratorias Ciceronis dialogi duo.* Parisiis: M. Vascosanus, 1542. 4to. Copy in the Bibliothèque Nationale.

*———— *In Partitiones oratorias Ciceronis dialogi quatuor, ab ipso authore emendati et aucti.* Argentorati: [colophon, B. Fabricius; printer's mark on title page, that of Crafft Müller (Crato Mylius)] 1549 [preface dated idus martias 1539, the year of the first edition of the first two dialogues]. 8vo. Copy in the Harvard University Library.

*———— *In Partitiones oratorias Ciceronis dialogi quatuor, ab ipso authore emendati et aucti . . . ; adiunximus . . . eiusdem authoris libros duos De amissa dicendi ratione et quomodo recuperanda sit.* Argentorati: T. Rihelius [s.d.]. 8vo. 2 parts in 1 vol. Copy in the Bibliothèque Nationale.

*———— *Partitionum dialecticarum libri duo.* Parisiis: C. Wechelus, 1539. 8vo. Copy in the Bibliothèque Nationale.

*———— *Partitionum dialecticarum libri IIII, emendati et aucti.* Argentorati: I. Rihelius, 1571. 8vo. Copy in the Bibliothèque Nationale, and in the Biblioteca del Seminario, Padua.

*———— Σχηματισμοὶ διαλεκτικοί, *Tabulae duorum librorum Partitionum dialecticarum Ioannis Sturmii, una cum praecipuorum locorum explicatione addita, cum ex ipsius authoris annotationibus tum ex ipso Aristotele aliisque eius artis melioribus scriptoribus confectae a Valentino Erythraeo . . . cum epistola Ioannis Sturmii.* Argentinae: C. Mylius, 1551. fol. Copy in the Bibliothèque Nationale, Paris — an edition in bracketed outlines like Sturm's Διαγράμματα.

*———— Σχηματισμοὶ τῆς διαλεκτικῆς, *hoc est, Tabulae Valentini Erythraei . . . in quatuor libros Dialecticarum Ioannis Sturmii . . . quibus addita est praecipuorum illius artis locorum explicatio, cum ex Sturmii annotationibus, tum ex Aristotele, caeterisque disserendi rationis peritis scriptoribus.* Argentinae: C. Mylius, 1561. fol. Copy in the Bibliothèque Nationale, Paris. An edition in bracketed outlines like Sturm's Διαγράμματα.

*———— *Scholae in librum Hermogenis De ratione tractandae gravitatis occultae* [i.e, Hermogenes' Περὶ μεθόδου δεινότητος]. Argentorati: I. Rihelius, 1571. 8vo. Copy in the Bibliothèque Nationale.

*———— *Scholae in libros duos Hermogenis De formis orationum seu dicendi generibus.* Argentorati: I. Rihelius, 1571. 8vo. Copy in the Bibliothèque Nationale.

*———— *Scholae in libros IIII Hermogenis De inventione.* Argentorati: I. Rihelius, 1570. 8vo. Copies in the Bibliothèque Nationale.

*———— *Scholae in Partitiones rhetoricas Hermogenis.* Argentorati: I. Rihelius, 1570. 8vo. Copy in the Bibliothèque Nationale.

Talon (Talaeus), Omer (Audomarus) — *ca.* 1510–62. For all Talon's works here cited, including adaptations by other authors (who often omit Talon's name), see Ong, *Ramus and Talon Inventory,* where copies are also located.

Tartaret (Tataret, Tartaretus, Tataretus), Pierre. [*Commentarii in Summulas logicales Petri Hispani, addito tractatu obligationum Martini Molenfelt.*] [Parisiis: François Renault, *ca.* 1514.] 4to. 73+[3]ll. Copy in the Bibliothèque Nationale (shelf number: Rés. m. R. 68). The title page of the copy is missing. Fol. 2 begins: "Incipiunt Summulae domini Petri Tartareti, una cum textu magistri Petri Hispani iuxta mentem Scoti . . . ." The conjectural title here is based on the colophon, fol. [76]: "Commentariorum Petri Tateriti [sic] in textum Petri Hispani, insertis tractatibus consequentiarum, sophismatum, insolubilium et descensus, addito etiam tractatu obligationum magistri Martini Molenfelt, finis."

Taylor, Henry Osborn. *Thought and Expression in the Sixteenth Century.* 2 vols. New York: Macmillan Co., 1920.

Théry, A. *Mémoire sur l'enseignement publique en France au XVIe siècle et spécialement sur les écrits et la personne de Ramus, lu à la Société des sciences morales et politiques de Seine-et-Oise.* Versailles: Montaland-Bougleux, 1837.

Thorne, J. P. "A Ramistical Commentary on Sidney's *An Apologie for Poetry*," *Modern Philology,* LIV (1957), 158–164.

Timme, Thomas. See Serres, Jean de.

Tuve, Rosemond. *Elizabethan and Metaphysical Imagery: Renaissance Poetic Imagery and Twentieth-Century Critics.* Chicago: University of Chicago Press, 1947.

———— "Imagery and Logic: Ramus and Metaphysical Poetics," *Journal of the History of Ideas,* III (1942), 365–400.

Tymme, Thomas. See Serres, Jean de.

Vaassen, Jakob van. "Dissertatio de vita et scriptis Antonii Goveani," in Antonii Goveani *Opera iuridica, philologica, philosophica,* edited by Iacobus van Vaassen (Roterodami: Henricus Beman, 1766), p. III–LX. Copy in the Bibliothèque Nationale and the St. Louis University Library. Includes a full and thoroughly documented account of the Ramus-Gouveia debates.

Vasoli, Cesare. "Retorica et dialettica in Pietro Ramo," pp. 95–134 in *Testi umanistici su la retorica* . . . a cura di Eugenio Garin, Paolo Rossi, Cesare Vasoli. "Archivio di filosofia." Roma, Milano: Fratelli Bocca Editori, 1953.

Voigt, Georg. "Über den Ramismus an der Universität Leipzig," *Berichte über die Verhandlungen der königlichen sächsischen Gesellschaft der Wissenschaften, Philologisch-historische Classe,* XL (Leipzig, 1888), 31–61.

Waddington (Waddington-Kastus on the title page of his *De Petri Rami vita* . . .), Charles [Tzaunt]. See Bertrand, Joseph.

———— *De Petri Rami vita, scriptis, philosophia, scripsit C. Waddington-Kastus, philosophiae professor, in Parisiensi literarum facultate ad doctoris gradum promovendus.* Parisiis: apud Joubert, 1848. Dedicated to Victor Cousin. Bibliographies.

———— [Letter dated March 21, 1881, in reply to Joseph Bertrand's "Jacques Charpentier . . . ."], *Revue des deux mondes,* XLIV (1881), 719–720. Waddington admits that he omitted part of Monantheuil's remarks, as Bertrand had charged, but says it was not prejudice or partiality, but an oversight. He urges first, that Charpentier approved the Massacre of St. Bartholomew's Day and second, that Ramus, as a victim, deserves sympathy, but he adds nothing to his arguments for Charpentier's guilt in his book *Ramus* (1855), which had been attacked by Bertrand. In justice to Bertrand, it should be noted that other curious "oversights" can be found in Waddington's handling of evidence. See Chap. iii, sec. 2, n. 14, etc., in the present work.

—— *Ramus: sa vie, ses écrits et ses opinions.* Paris: Ch. Meyrueis et Cie, 1855.

Waddington-Kastus, Carolus. See Waddington, Charles.

Walker, D. P. "The *Prisca Theologia* in France," *Journal of the Warburg and Courtauld Institutes*, XVII, Nos. 3–4 (1954), 204–259.

Watson, George. "Hobbes and the Metaphysical Conceit," *Journal of the History of Ideas*, XVI (1955), 558–562.

—— "Ramus, Miss Tuve, and the New Petromachia," *Modern Philology*, LV (1958), 259–262.

Werenfels, Samuel. *Dissertatio de logomachiis eruditorum; accedit diatribe de meteoris orationis.* Amstelaedami, 1702. 8vo. Copy in the British Museum. There are several later editions of this work, including an English translation (London, 1711), where Ramus is treated, pp. 34–37.

Wilson, Harold S. See Harvey, Gabriel, *Gabriel Harvey's Ciceronianus.*

Wundt, Max. *Die deutsche Schulmetaphysik des 17. Jahrhunderts.* Tübingen: J. C. B. Mohr (Paul Siebeck), 1939.

Würkert, [Johannes] Georg. *Die Encyclopädie des Petrus Ramus, ein Reformversuch der Gelehrtenschule des 16. Jahrhunderts* .... Inaugural dissertation, Leipzig. Leipzig: O. Schmidt, 1898. 4to. 56 pp.

Zedler, Johann Heinrich. *Grosses vollständiges universal Lexikon aller Wissenschaften und Kunste.* 64 vols. Halle: Zedler, 1732–1750. *Nöthige Supplemente.* 4 vols; no more published. Leipzig: 1751–54. Copy in the British Museum. Referred to as Zedler, *Universal Lexikon.* After Jöcher, the best encyclopedia on Ramists and Ramism.

INDEX

INDEX

404 INDEX